Contents

Programme Committee

General Conference Chair
Quasim Mehdi
School of Computing & Information Technology
University of Wolverhampton, UK

General Programme Chair
Fred Mtenzi
School of Computing
Dublin Institute of Technology
Dublin, Ireland

Local Chair Conference Organisers

Bryan Duggan

Co-Local Chair Conference Organisers

Hugh McAtamney

International Programme Committee

Don Anderson
Intellas Group LLC, Quantum Int.Corp., USA

Professor David Al-Dabbass
Nottingham-Trent University, UK

Professor Marc Cavazza
University of Teesside, UK

Dr Darryl Charles
University of Ulster, UK

Professor Ratan Kumar Guha
Central Florida University, USA

Dr Johannes Fuernkranz
Technical University of Darmstadt, FRG

Dr John Funge (iKuni Inc, Palo Alto, USA)

Dr Julian Gold, Microsoft Research Centre, Cambridge, UK

Dr. Kamal Bechkoum, University of Wolverhampton, UK

Dr.Carlos Cotta, Malaga University
Spain

Dr. Pieter Spronck
University of Maastricht, The Netherlands

Professor David Kaufman, Simon Fraser University, Canada

Dr Daniel Livingstone
University of Paisley, UK

Professor Ian Marshall
University of Coventry, UK

Dr Stephen McGlinchy
University of Paisley, UK

Professor Stephane Natkin
CNAM Paris, France

Professor Yoshihiro Okada
Kyushu University, Fukuoka, Japan

Professor Mark Overmars, Utrecht University, The Netherlands

Professor Leon Rothkrantz
University of Delft, Netherlands

Dr Ian Wright
iKuni Inc, Palo Alto, USA

Prof. Pascal ESTRAILLIER, University of La Rochelle, France

Jocelyne Kiss, University Marne-la-Vallée, LISAA, France

. roceedings of CGAMES'2006

9th International Conference on Computer Games: Artificial Intelligence and Mobile Systems

22-24 November 2006

Hosted by

Dublin Institute of Technology
Dublin, Ireland

Organised by

University of Wolverhampton

in association with

Dublin Institute of Technology

and

IEEE Computer Society
Society for Modelling and Simulation (SCS-Europe)
Institution of Electrical Engineers (IEE)
British Computer Society (BCS)
Digital Games Research Association (DiGRA)
International Journal of Intelligent Games and Simulation (IJIGS)

Edited by:

Quasim Mehdi
Fred Mtenzi
Bryan Duggan
Hugh McAtamney

Published by The University of Wolverhampton
School of Computing and Information Technology
Printed in Wolverhampton, UK

Proceedings of CGAMES' 2006
Designed by Lindsey Taylor
School of Computing and Information Technology
University of Wolverhampton

Published by The University of Wolverhampton, School of Computing and Information Technology

ISBN 0-9549016-2-2

Preface

We are delighted to welcome you to Dublin to participate in the 9th International Conference on Computer Games: AI, Animation, Mobile, Educational & Serious Games. CGAMES is part of Game-On® International Conference of Wolverhampton University, UK. We have the privilege this year to bring the conference to Dublin, Ireland. The 7th event was held in CNBDI-Angouleme, France which was a huge success and well supported. Our 10th International conference will be hosted by the University of Louisville, Kentucky, USA, 25th-27th July 2007 and the 11th International event of CGAMES will be hosted by the University of Malaga, Spain.

The conference aims to bring together researchers, scientists, and games developers from around the world to discuss advances in design methods, tools, programming techniques, games concepts and their applications. The theme has been chosen to reflect the major changes in the way in which digital games are developed and played.

We are very proud to announce that the conference has successfully maintained its links with its sponsors and this year gained some new ones: *IEEE Computer Society, British Computer Society, Digital Games Research Association (DiGRA), Society for Modelling and Simulation (SCS), Irish Computer Society, Microsoft Ireland, Enterprise Ireland, DIT School of Computing, DIT Faculty of Science and DIT Oifig na Gaeilge.*

The conference endeavours to help new researchers and MSc/MPhil/PhD research students to present their work to their peers and experts in the field in order to improve the quality of their work in this exciting subject area. The quality of submitted papers has been maintained at a high standard by having them reviewed by our reviewers who have been delighted with the work produced by the authors. Our special thanks go to the reviewers who have been most diligent in their task by providing detailed and useful feedback to authors. The best papers will be reviewed for possible inclusion in the *International Journal of Intelligent Games & Simulation* (IJIGS).

This conference has flourished as a result of the hard work put in by our colleagues in Dublin. Our big thanks and appreciation go to them for their generosity, time and effort in helping to organise this conference and provide invaluable support. We particularly wish to thank the General Programme Chair, Dr Fred Mtenzi, Local Chair Conference Organiser, Bryan Duggan, and Co-Local Chair Conference Organiser, Hugh McAtamney. We would also like to thank the School of Computing, Dublin Institute of Technology and the School of Computing & Information Technology, University of Wolverhampton, UK, especially Dr. Brendan O'Shea, Professor Matt Hussey and Professor Rob Moreton for their generous support and enthusiasm.

We trust that you will all enjoy your stay in the vibrant and historic city of Dublin and benefit from this conference by making new contacts for future mutual collaboration.

Quasim Mehdi, On Behalf of CGAMES Organising Committee
University of Wolverhampton, November 2006

CGAMES 06

Proceedings

Tools and Systems for Games and Virtual Reality (1)

Fuzzy User Satisfaction in Games

Jeff Craighead
Institute for Safety, Security and Rescue Technology
University of South Florida
4202 E. Fowler Ave.
Tampa, FL, USA
craighea@cse.usf.edu

***Abstract*— This paper presents a fuzzy logic based method to track user satisfaction without the need for devices to monitor users physiological conditions. User satisfaction is the key to any product's acceptance; computer applications and video games provide a unique opportunity to provide a tailored environment for each user to better suit their needs. We have implemented a non-adaptive fuzzy logic model of emotion, based on the emotional component of the Fuzzy Logic Adaptive Model of Emotion (FLAME) proposed by El-Nasr, to estimate player emotion in UnrealTournament 2004. In this paper we describe the implementation of this system and present the results of one of several play tests. Our research contradicts the current literature that suggests physiological measurements are needed. We show that it is possible to use a software only method to estimate user emotion.**

***Index Terms*— Fuzzy Logic, User Satisfaction, Adaptation**

I Introduction

User satisfaction is the key to any product's acceptance; computer applications and video games provide a unique opportunity to provide a tailored environment for each user to better suit their needs. The question is how to judge user satisfaction in an non-intrusive manner.

Typical methods, such as those proposed by Rani[1] use external devices that can monitor heart rate, stress level, brain activity, and other physiological conditions. The devices required to measure physiological conditions are intrusive, requiring the user to be attached to a machine with several wires, wearing the device, or by using a special controller. This approach is cumbersome to set up and would detract from the user experience in a commercial application.

Online, affective tuning of an application using fuzzy logic to approximate a user's emotional state will allow the application to provide the user with a better experience, without the need for cumbersome wires or special controllers. This paper presents a proof of concept fuzzy logic based method for tracking user satisfaction via estimated emotional state. Our test case measures user satisfaction of players of the UnrealTournament 2004 game. Section II presents a review of recent work in the area of user satisfaction and fuzzy logic based affective user models. Section III explains the approach taken for developing the fuzzy satisfaction tracker. Section IV details the implementation of this system. Section V presents the results from one test run of the application. Finally in Section VI we conclude with a discussion of fuzzy logic as a viable tool for judging user satisfaction.

II Related Work

This section contains a review of recent work in the area of determining user satisfaction. Popular methods in the literature are to attach to the user a device that measures some physiological condition such as heart rate, brain activity, or skin conductivity. Several of the works reviewed use fuzzy logic to fuse physiological measurements in order to gauge a user's stress level. While these methods can successfully measure user satisfaction, they require the use of an external sensor. This makes them impractical for use in commercial products.

Rani[1], [2] uses a fuzzy logic based measurement of a user's heart rate in order to facilitate human robot interaction. Rani states that a device measuring a user's physiological state could be built into a small wearable device, however this is not demonstrated in the paper. Instead the experiment was conducted using a MATLAB based system on a desktop PC. The system is able to successfully capture the user's anxiety level and send this to a robot using an architecture based on Brooks' subsumption architecture[3]. The user is not directly controlling the robot, but issuing commands to a semi-autonomous system; when the user is under stress the robot activates a certain behavior. However, in the case of a typical computer application, the need for yet another input device is cumbersome. Rani's work shows that the idea of fuzzy logic based affect measurement is sound, but a nonintrusive implementation is needed.

Other work such as that presented by Conati[4] and Zhou[5] attempt to ascertain the emotional state of a student playing an educational game. Conati examined several physiological conditions, deciding on EMG and skin-conduction as the means of determining the players emotional state. One thing noted is that these metrics use a series of thresholds to determine the user's state, and these thresholds change with each user. This requires a calibration routine to be performed for each user. Zhou attempts to assess user goals based on personality traits and game interaction style using the OCC cognitive theory of emotions[6]. Personality traits were identified in a written test given before the study. In order to evaluate the success of the real-time assessment, the students were given a survey after playing the game with questions about their goals. Zhou shows that it is possible to assess user emotion based on game interaction and non-physiological metrics such as personality traits. Our method attempts to improve on these works by assessing user emotion using only interaction and performance data obtained during game play.

III Approach

The work presented in this paper uses a scaled down version of the Fuzzy Logic Adaptive Model of Emotion (FLAME) developed by El-Nasr, et al.[7]. El-Nasr states that FLAME is a "computational model of emotions that can be incorporated into intelligent agents and other complex, interactive programs". FLAME allows an agent to learn about its environment via emotional attachment to objects and interactions with other agents and users. In this article we use a similar but less complex, non-adaptive fuzzy model of emotions to gain some insight into a human player's emotional state.

FLAME consists of three components that allow an agent to learn and make decisions based on emotions: a learning component, an emotional component, and a decision making component. We focus on the emotional component. It should be noted that unlike this work which adapts the emotional portion of FLAME to a commercial video game, El-Nasr constructed an environment in which an agent using FLAME could interact with and learn about every facet of its environment. FLAME's emotional component is based on an agents goals and events that impact those goals. Events occur as the agent interacts with the environment and the emotional component assesses those events' desirability with respect to the agents goals. In our case we assume the agent, a player in an FPS deathmatch game, has two goals:

1) Stay alive (prevent others from scoring)
2) Kill others (score as much as possible)

These goals are affected by a set of six game play statistics. Each statistic represents the number of times a particular event has occurred over a given period of time. This is necessary as our implementation does not have direct access to the game engine's event system. Each statistic is evaluated similarly to events in FLAME. Fuzzy logic is used to determine the magnitude of each statistic[1]. The set of statistics used is as follows: Kills, Kills Per Minute, Kills Last Minute, Deaths, Deaths Per Minute, and Deaths Last Minute. After the statistics are fuzzified they have a value that ranges from VeryLow to VeryHigh. These values are then passed to the fuzzy emotion evaluation system, which determines the player's emotional state.

The player's final emotion is based on two component emotions, Fear and Joy. Fear and Joy are evaluated by a set of fuzzy rules to determine which emotional state the player is in. The six emotional states are: Gloating, Excited, Complacent, Anxious, Angry, and Frustrated. The emotion Fear is affected positively by statistics involving Deaths. The emotion Joy is positively affected by statistics involving Kills. Just as FLAME uses a decay rate for emotions, the statistics in our system decay over time. Our statistics are based on kills or deaths per unit of time, thus the emotional system naturally decays if the player's performance worsens.

Once the emotional state of the player has been determined it is recorded in a log for analysis, we also display it on screen for testing purposes (see Figure 1). While this information could be used to change game rules or bot behavior, that is outside the scope of this paper. Section VI discusses future work in which a full implementation of FLAME may be used.

IV Implementation

Our system builds on the emotional component of El-Nasr's FLAME. The emotional model was implemented and tested in UnrealTournament 2004[8]. The system was implemented as a game mutator so that it could be used in any game type[2]. Development and testing took place using deathmatch type games.

The fuzzy emotional system is based on the set of statistics listed in Section III. In addition to those listed, Average Health and Most Kills Before Death were also considered as potential mood altering statistics. While these two extra data items could potentially increase the

[1]The magnitude of a statistic is relative to some game parameter.

[2]An UnrealTournament game type defines the set of rules for the game. Default game types include deathmatch, capture-the-flag, bombing run, etc.

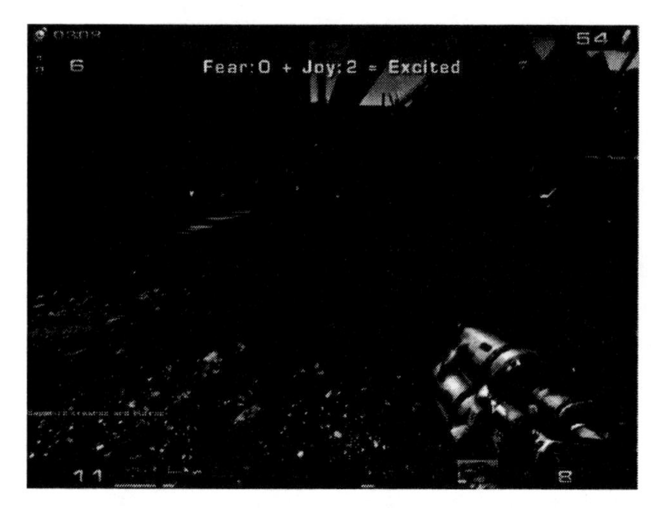

Fig. 1. Screen shot showing the emotional state of the player.

accuracy of the fuzzy system, the additional complexity of the rule set is undesirable. As we will show in Section V the system performs adequately without them.

Each of the statistics are fuzzified using a similar function. The result of the function is a fuzzy value representing the desirability of the statistic. The statistics are given one of five values: VeryHigh, High, Medium, Low, and VeryLow. A VeryHigh fuzzy value is most desirable for Kill statistics and least desirable for Death statistics. Conversely, VeryLow is most desirable for Deaths statistics and least desirable for Kills statistics.

Kills - Kills represents the total number of kills the player has, this is the score within the game. Kills is directly accessible to the mutator as an integer value indicating the players score. Kills is fuzzified based on either the goal score for the game or the game time limit if no goal score is defined. To fuzzify Kills, we first normalize the value with 0 being the minimum and the maximum based on goal score or time limit. The maximum for normalization is either 80% of the goal score, 3 times the time limit[3], or 15 kills. This value is the baseline for the emotion Joy and is used as such because it is the indicator of player performance over the entire game. Kills is combined with Kills Last Minute and Kills Per Minute in a fuzzy rule set to determine Joy.

Kills Last Minute - Kills Last Minute represents the number of kills made within the last 60 seconds of game play. It is a measure of instantaneous performance identifying periods of play where a player is performing extremely well. Kills Last Minute is not provided by the engine, it is derived by monitoring the number of kills each second and comparing that to the previous value to get the number of kills in the last second. These are saved in a 60 entry array and summed to get Kills Last Minute. Kills Last Minute has the most effect on Joy which causes the amount of Joy to quickly change to match the players current state. Kills Last Minute is fuzzified using either 20% of the goal score or 5 as the maximum.

Kills Per Minute - Kills Per Minute is the average number of kills per minute the player has made during the game. This serves as a short term memory of past kills. Kills Per Minute has a slower decay rate than Kills Last Minute. As the game progresses, the player must keep killing other players for Kills Per Minute to remain high. If the player is unable to maintain a certain kill rate, Kills Per Minute begins to decay. Conversely, if a player begins to kill more (has a high Kills Last Minute) Kills Per Minute will increase. Kills Per Minute affects Fear less than Kills Last Minute, but more than Kills. Kills Per Minute is fuzzified using either 20% of the goal score or 5 as the maximum.

Deaths - As Kills is to Joy, Deaths is to Fear. Deaths is the total number of time a player has died during a game. Deaths sets the baseline value for Fear and has the least effect over the course of a game. The maximum for normalization is 80% of the maximum number of lives a player can have if this value is present. If max lives is not set, 5 times the time limit is used allowing a player to die up to 5 times per minute before reaching VeryHigh Deaths. If neither a maximum lives or time limit is set, we set 25 deaths to be our maximum.

Deaths Last Minute - Deaths Last Minute is tracked exactly like Kills Last Minute. The number of Deaths are compared each second, and any difference is entered into a 60 entry array. The values in the array are summed giving the total number of player deaths occurring in the last 60 seconds. Fear is most influenced by Deaths Last Minute as it is a good indicator of brief periods of poor performance. If a maximum number of lives is specified in the game rules, we use 10% of this value as a VeryHigh Deaths Last Minute. Otherwise, we choose 5 deaths as a VeryHigh number of Deaths Last Minute.

Deaths Per Minute - Deaths Per Minute is the average number of times the player has dies over the course of a game. Deaths Per Minute has less of an effect on Fear than Deaths Last Minute, but more of an effect than Deaths. Deaths Per Minute is a good indicator of past periods of high Fear levels. If the player has a period of high Deaths Last Minute, Deaths Per Minute will increase. In a period of fewer deaths, Deaths Per Minute will decay. A Medium level of Deaths Per Minute

[3]The time limit is in minutes.

indicates that the player has at several points in the game had a high death rate, or has had a constant rate of deaths throughout the game. If a maximum number of lives is specified in the game rules, we use 10% of this value as a VeryHigh Deaths Per Minute. Otherwise, we choose 5 deaths as a VeryHigh number of Deaths Per Minute.

To fuzzify the game statistics it was necessary to implement a function within the UnrealTournament mutator that would normalize an integer value and return the fuzzy set to which the value corresponds. A function $fuzzify()$ was created for this purpose. $fuzzify()$ takes three arguments: *min*, *max*, and *value*. It normalizes *value* based on *min* and *max*, then uses the normalized value in a set of if...then statements and a maximization function to determine fuzzy set membership. Note that the numbers chosen for normalization limits are subjective. They were chosen empirically based on testing with several players. This is one parameter of the fuzzy system that could be adjusted based on player skill or game rules. Figure 2 shows the membership functions used in $fuzzify()$. These membership functions were chosen arbitrarily to provide some overlap between sets. Tuning the membership functions could provide a more accurate estimation of player emotion.

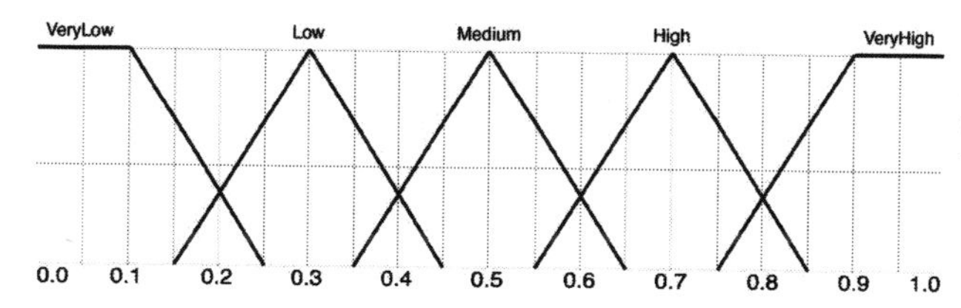

Fig. 2. Fuzzy Membership Functions for Event Fuzzification

V RESULTS

This section will show that it is possible to design a fuzzy system to estimate a user's emotional state using in-game statistics. We present the results of a five minute deathmatch game played with our fuzzy emotion estimator active. The game was played with ten players, we show results from one of these players.

The player's statistics are shown using data from the game log file to present the transitions of Joy, Fear, and Emotion over the course of the game. This data is recorded for all players, however this player was chosen because they reach every emotional state possible. Figure 3 shows a graph of Joy, Figure 4 shows a graph of Fear, and Figure 5 shows a graph of Emotion. The transition points in the graphs have been numbered so that changes in Joy and Fear can be identified with corresponding changes in Emotion.

In Figure 5 we can see that the player begins in the Complacent state. At roughly 15 seconds into the game Transition 1. occurs; the player becomes Angry. Transition 1. is caused by an increase in Fear as seen in Figure 4. Transition 2. occurs around 30 seconds into the game. Fear transitions from VeryLow to Medium, most likely because they have just been killed. Joy and Fear are at equal levels and the player becomes Complacent. Figure 3 shows Transition 2. Transition 3. occurs at 45 seconds. The player becomes angry again because its Fear has reached VeryHigh. Transitions 4. and 5. demonstrate the natural decay of emotions over time. The player becomes Frustrated as Joy transitions from Medium to Low and then to VeryLow. This is because the player has not scored recently. In addition, Fear remains at VeryHigh indicating that the player is repeatedly dying. Transitions 6. and 7. show a short spike in emotion from Frustrated to Angry as the player's Joy increases to Medium because of one or more kills in a short period of time. This Joy quickly wears off and the player becomes Frustrated again. Transitions 8., 9., and 10. show a particularly high point in the game for the player. Joy quickly rises to VeryHigh because of many successive kills and Fear decays naturally. Transitions 11. through 18. show that while Joy is VeryHigh emotion is still dependent on Fear. When Fear spikes because the player dies, the player's overall emotion dips until the Fear of death decays.

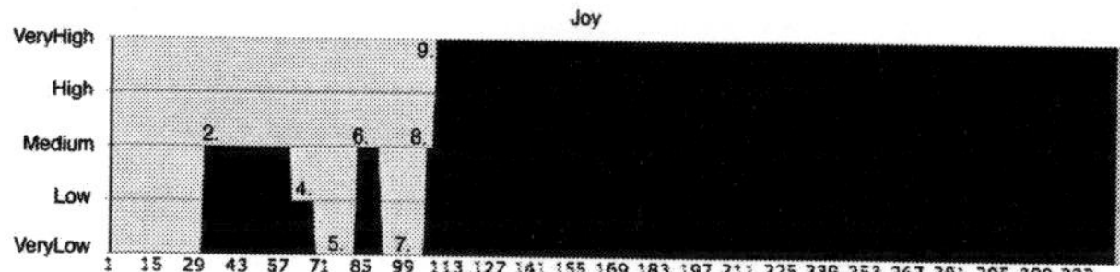

Fig. 3. Transitions of Joy during game play.

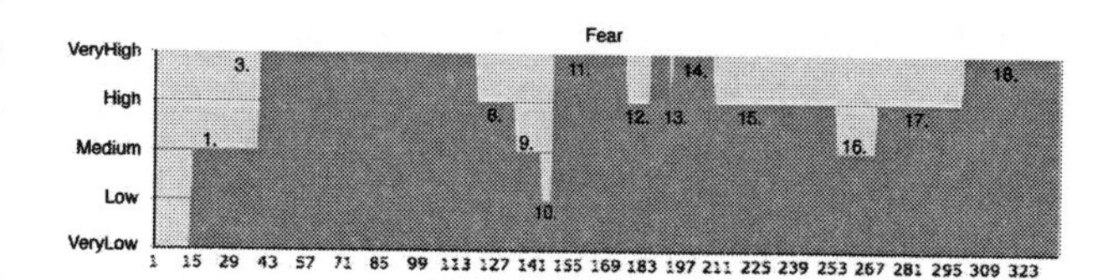

Fig. 4. Transitions of Fear during game play.

VI CONCLUSION

We have shown that it is possible to estimate player emotional state without monitoring physiological conditions. We assume that a user in a positive emotional state is satisfied with their gaming experience. As with

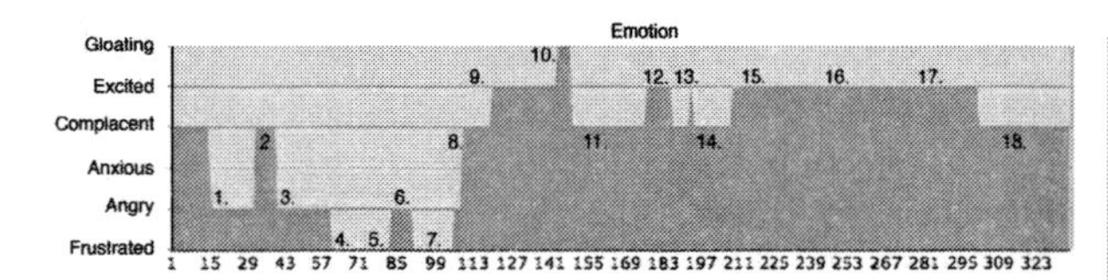

Fig. 5. Transitions of Emotion during game play.

all fuzzy logic applications, the fuzzy conversion is subjective based on the opinion of a subject expert. In this case the subject expert was an experience player of video games. Our experiment used a video game, UnrealTournament 2004, to test the fuzzy system proposed. Video games present the user with a limited number of goals, thus making it easier to define a fuzzy system to estimate the user's emotional state based on interaction and performance.

The system proposed uses a simplified version of the Fuzzy Logic Adaptive Model of Emotion (FLAME) demonstrated by El-Nasr. The current implementation of our system uses a non-adaptive fuzzy logic model of emotions. Due to the limited amount of data available from the game engine, our model consists of only 2 motivational states, Fear and Joy, which combine to determine one of five emotional states the game player is in. Those emotional states are Frustrated, Angry, Complacent, Excited, and Gloating. The player begins each game in the Complacent state, and then based on interaction with other players, reaches different levels of Fear and Joy, thus varying emotional states.

We believe a full implementation of FLAME within a video game or other application would eliminate some of the subjectiveness surrounding the definition of goals and motivations. The version of FLAME presented by El-Nasr is able to learn about the environment to determine which interactions benefit or hurt an agent as well as determine the goals of an agent by monitoring its actions. While this type of system could be implemented in any application, video games present the best case because of the limited number of goals and interaction types a user may have.

The benefits of a system such as the one presented in this article are clear. The literature shows that an application that can dynamically adapt to users goals and interaction style is desired. However, existing work suggests that physiological measurements are needed to determine a users emotional state. Our research contradicts this notion by estimating user emotion in software only.

Jeff Craighead Jeff Craighead is a Doctoral Candidate at the University of South Florida. He received a B.S.C.S. from the University of South Florida in 2004. Since that time he has worked with Dr. Robin Murphy's Center for Robot Assisted Search and Rescue and Institute for Safety Security Rescue Technologies. His research interests include robotic systems, human robot interaction, machine learning, and serious games. Current research involves the use of serious games for training robot operators to successfully conduct urban search and rescue operations.

REFERENCES

[1] P. Rani, J. Sims, R. Brackin, and N. Sarkar, "Online stress detection using psychophysiological signals for implicit human-robot cooperation," *Robotica*, vol. 20, pp. 673–685, 2002.

[2] P. Rani, N. Sarkar, C. A. Smith, and L. D. Kirby, "Anxiety detecting robotic system – towards implicit human-robot collaboration," *Robotica*, vol. 22, pp. 85–95, 2004.

[3] R. A. Brooks, "A robust layered control system for a mobile robot," *IEEE Journal of Robotics And Automation*, vol. RA-2, no. 1, March 1986.

[4] C. Conati, R. Chabbal, and H. Maclaren, "A study on using biometric sensors for detecting user emotions in educational games," in *Proceedings of the Workshop "Assessing and Adapting to User Attitude and Affects: Why, When and How? ". In conjunction with the 9th International Conference on User Modeling*, 2003.

[5] X. Zhou and C. Conati, "Inferring user goals from personality and behavior in a causal model of user affect," in *Proceedings of the International Conference on Intelligent User Interfaces*, 2003, pp. 211–218.

[6] A. Ortony, G. L. Clore, and A. Collins, *The Cognitive Structure of Emotions*. Cambridge University Press, 1988.

[7] M. S. El-Nasr, J. Yen, and T. R. Ioerger, "Flame-fuzzy logic adaptive model of emotions," *Autonomous Agents and Multi-Agent Systems*, vol. 3, no. 3, pp. 219–257, September 2000.

[8] "Unrealtournament 2004." [Online]. Available: http://www.unrealtournament.com/

An Evaluation of the Effectiveness of Recorded Game Footage in Increasing Player Skill Levels

Thomas JJ. Welsh
David Moffat
Glasgow Caledonian University
E-mail: T.Welsh@gcal.ac.uk

Abstract

By studying video of professional games players competing in international tournaments, the ability levels of those who watch the videos is increased. This paper sets out a simple experiment which shows conclusively that the performance of a group of novice players will significantly and measurably increase after watching video footage of more skilled players. After setting out the difference in ability before and after the video, some discussion is made regarding the reasons for the increase in skill level. The intention of this paper is to show the success of this technique in improving human playing ability. As this paper considers human skill levels and learning in gaming environments, the results will be of interest to educational games researchers and games designers.

Keywords

Unreal Tournament 2004, Games Design, Bots, Games, E-Sports, E-Athletes

1 Introduction

The purpose of opponents in commercial computer games is to provide an entertaining playing experience. [Touzour, 2002]. If a computer opponent behaves in a less than human fashion then the gaming experience is less convincing, less immersive and ultimately less enjoyable [McGlinchey, 2002]. Recently however computer game developers are starting to recognize the need for human-level AI [Laird, 2001]. Cutting edge work is underway to replicate human like play behaviour; for example the application of BDI architecture for computer controlled enemies [Davies et al, 2004]. It is proposed that these more convincing opponents will be correspondingly more entertaining.

Last year, six of the top ten best selling games claimed to have "cutting edge AI" [Elspa, 2006]. Whether the general level of Artificial Intelligence in games truly is cutting edge however remains debatable. It could be argued that to date every successful computer game is an existence proof that you can create good games without human-level AI. [Magerko et al, 2004]. There is evidence to suggest that human players are less inclined to play against AI opponents when given the choice. This evidence is that in the First Person Perspective Shooting (FPS) genre, multiplayer titles such as *Battlefield 2* and *Unreal Tournament* generally sell more than their single player competitors [Elspa, 2006]. All of these titles are primarily focused on on line human versus human conflict, rather than human versus computer. This suggests that on line FPS's are one area where human-level AI would be of benefit.

Previous work has suggested that to better understand how we can create truly convincing computer controlled opponents, we must first study human play behaviour [Welsh, 2005]. One of the ways that we can do this is by considering how human players improve and develop their skills in FPS games and what the differences are between good and bad players. By considering how humans learn and play games and how they progress through different levels of ability, we can begin to map this knowledge to the opponents we create. To fully understand human play behaviour Spronk comments that we should first consider the most skillful players [et al, 2004]. It is proposed that the best way to find the most able players is to look towards international tournaments and professional gamers.

The rise of video game tournaments or "Esports" has created demand for video footage of these competitions. From videos of individual preparation and team rituals, to direct recordings of the events of individual games, the tournament organisers are trying to popularise their business by producing slick, entertaining short films and replays of matches between increasingly famous players, many of whom endorse events and use their name to sell games products [Richards, 2004].

The footage of games tournaments fall into two distinct camps. The first is documentary style movies, providing insight into the rituals, motivation and even the private life of the tournament champions. These videos serve as promotional tools for games tournaments and often focus on the amazing prizes available and the high specification hardware that the players are using. PC component vendors are increasingly realising the potential of these competitions and sponsorship comes with banners, media footage and branded prizes [Richards, 2004].

The second of these forms of footage is game engine based replays. Most modern FPS games and many RTS (real time strategy) games offer a method to record a game as it is played. These replays are not recorded as a movie file. Rather they are stored as a series of instructions for the game engine to recreate the game. This means that the replay can be observed from any camera angle the viewer chooses including the points of view of the players during the game. Clearly the viewer must own the game that they want to observe, but the recording offers a wealth of information to those prepared to look through all of the available data.

This paper argues that the data that can be extracted from game engine replays represent a mine of information that can be exploited to study human play behavior in FPS games. It has been argued that only by observing, studying and understanding human play behavior can we begin to create computer controlled bots which will replicate this behavior [Laird and van Lent, 2001]. Other work in this area has included the use of bayesian learning to directly influence the believability of game bots and represents a slightly different but successful application of observing game footage [Thurau et al, 2005]. Furthermore, work has also been done on the effect of videos on training darts players and in this case, the training proved very successful [Joseph et al, 2004] This video footage can be used to instruct less skilled players how they can improve.

The process of learning from video footage is effectively an example of learning from an advanced peer. The success of such a method often depends more on the individuals interest in the subject than the delivery medium, but video footage is recognised as one of the best ways to deliver simple information [Cennamo, 93]. Observation of a peer confers a number of advantages and is an established and effective method of teaching and learning [Lin, 92]. This paper aims to begin that process of study, and identifies tournament game engine replays and the observation of professional players as the first step in that process.

2 Methodology

To test the assumption that the observation of game footage will increase skill levels in beginner to intermediate players, a simple experiment was devised. This involved showing a group of player's game footage with the intention of improving their game playing abilities. The first step was to take a base measure of the skill level of a group of players. To do this the players faced a single bot of a high skill level in the FPS Deathmatch title "Unreal Tournament 2004". The game rules followed standard FPS Deathmatch conventions.

In a normal FPS Deathmatch game, the players compete in a closed virtual environment and score a point each time they kill another player. In an FPS game, a kill is often called a "Frag". Players can frag other players by shooting them with weapons which they can pick up from around the arena or sometimes using a hand held weapon such as a knife. Each time they themselves die, they are instantly reborn (spawned) but they lose any of the weapons they may have picked up. The game continues until a certain score-limit is reached by one player or until the time runs out, in which case the player with the highest score wins the game [Laird, 2000].

The mean of the players performance over a series of ten games was to give an accurate measure of their ability in the game. Once the ten games had been completed, half the players were then shown some footage captured from an international tournament featuring Esports professionals in one specific evenly matched game. This footage was captured in a Deathmatch game which used the same game environments, rules and format as the players has been practicing in and was shown from the point of view of the winning player. After the footage was complete, these players took part in a further set of ten games and once again the scores and data was obtained and analysed to identify differences in scores, accuracy and playing style. The second half of the group acted as a control group and played the same number of games, but did not watch the video footage. The assumption is that the process of watching the professional level competitors would improve the skill level of the subjects.

The twenty subjects for this experiment were described as being of an "intermediate" skill level. This categorisation was determined by the Unreal tournament ranking system, *"UTstats"*. This is a web based application which provides a rating for Unreal Tournament players which is updated each time they play a game. The rating it generates is based on a number of factors such as accuracy and weapon choice but is most greatly influenced by performance against opponents based on their own UTstats rating. For example, to defeat someone ranked highly by UTstats would confer a large increase to your own rating, while defeating a lower ranked opponent would make little difference to your rating. The skill level for the players was termed as "intermediate" as according to UTstats there were approximately the same number of players rated higher than them than there were rated lower.

The subjects, although all of comparable skill levels, were split evenly between both genders and were of an age range between twenty and thirty. In the pre-experiment questionnaire all subjects stated that they enjoyed the game, but played other similar titles more often. These similar titles included Doom 3, Counter Strike and Battlefield 2. All of the subjects were unfamiliar with Unreal Tournament video footage and had never considered video footage as a means to improve their own game performance.

As well as the pre-experiment questionnaire, the subjects were all interviewed after the game and their thoughts were recorded. The interviews gave them a chance to reflect on what effect the observation of the footage had on their performance and how it influenced the playing style they adopted.

The games that they played were also recorded and part of the interview involved the subjects watching themselves and reflecting on their own performance and the decision making process they went through at key moments in their matches.

3 Findings

The results clearly verify the assumption that observation of professional play leads to an improvement in the performance of intermediate players. Almost all of the players improved to a measurable degree. The qualitative data is clear, the improvements ranged from a few extra frags (kills) each game to a complete turnaround in fortune with the most improved player developing from mostly losing against their opponent to mostly winning.

The most important results were the average number of times the player killed their enemy (frags) and the number of times that they themselves were killed. The abridged data in figure 1 highlights the difference in overall performance as measured by final games scores.

	Average Frags per game (game 1 to 5)	Average Deaths per game (game 1 to 5)	Average Frags per game (game 1 to 5)	Average Deaths per game post video (game 6 to 10)
Subject 1	18	4	19	4
Subject 2	9	10	10	8
Subject 3	15	6	14	6
Subject 4	10	7	15	3
Subject 5	9	9	13	11
Subject 6	5	12	9	6
Subject 7	10	6	11	5
Subject 8	8	11	12	10
Subject 9	9	8	12	7
Subject 10	7	9	10	9
Subject 11	6	10	6	8
Subject 12	4	9	4	8
Subject 13	7	9	8	8
Subject 14	8	5	9	6
Subject 15	8	6	8	2
Subject 16	8	8	6	6
Subject 17	5	10	4	11
Subject 18	6	10	7	6
Subject 19	11	9	12	5
Subject 20	13	2	13	4

Figure 1: Results

In the above table, the first ten play players watched the video footage in games six to ten and the second ten acted as the control and did not. The sample group is large enough to show that the increase in scores are substantial.

Statistical analysis of the data shows that the increase in scores are far beyond what might be expected by random chance. Using a t-test on the average frags per game for the sample group and comparing with the same data from the control group, a significance level of just 0.002 allows us to dismiss the null hypothesis.

Also of note is the increase in performance experienced by the players immediately preceding and following their observation of the video. We can compare this to the mean increase in performance between each of the initial ten games played prior to the video. By comparing both of these values we can measure the potential benefits for the individual of watching the footage compared to the benefits of simply practicing by playing the game (figure 2).

	Mean increase in score per game pre video	Increase in score immediately before and after video
Subject 1	2	4
Subject 2	1	1
Subject 3	1	0
Subject 4	0	2
Subject 5	0	3
Subject 6	-1	4
Subject 7	1	1
Subject 8	1	3
Subject 9	2	3
Subject 10	1	2

Figure 2: Game performance improvements of sample

As can be see the benefits of watching the video are greater than the benefits of practicing by playing one more game. As both the game and the video both take ten minutes to complete, players interested in developing their skills would be advised to watch the video.

4 Exposition

With a clear understanding that watching the video footage was beneficial to most players, we must consider what this implies and how this knowledge can be used. The results above tell us that the video footage helps the players to develop their own abilities, but the results themselves give us no indication why this is the case. To determine this we must look at the recorded games and consider the feedback provided by the subjects in interviews.

What seems clear from the interviews with the players is that they are developing several of the parameters of human FPS play identified in previous work[Welsh, 2005] The subjects are developing game environment knowledge, game mechanics knowledge and what has been previously termed "tricks". In this context, a trick refers to a special technique individual to a particular game which is non-obvious to beginner and intermediate players.

Tricks are often exploits of bugs in a game, secret moves activated by a complex sequence of commands or environment specific peculiarities which can weigh a game in the favor of the player who knows of their existence. Two examples in Unreal tournament include the ability to dodge quickly sideways avoiding incoming fire by using a quick combination of key presses or to perform a "platform rocket jump" which uses a moving platform as a catapult to reach difficult areas or to fire downwards on a hapless opponent. Often these tricks require a degree of reflexes, timing or manual dexterity to achieve but once learned they offer a permanent and noticeable advantage to the player who masters them. These techniques were all in evidence in the video the subjects watched.

Game environment knowledge is simply the player's familiarity with the topographical layout of the virtual environment that they are in and the features of that environment. To exploit the terrain, the player must know how to navigate through that terrain. In Unreal Tournament, the higher ground confers an advantage and without knowledge of how to reach the high ground the player will be at a disadvantage. Additionally, the knowledge of unique features of the environment such as where the best weapons are located can greatly aid a player as they can quickly find the best weapons before their opponents.

Game mechanics refers to the player's knowledge of the rules of the virtual world in which they play. The world of unreal tournament is not like our own; players are able to jump tens of feet in the air and survive huge falls. The laws of physics and the way that a real life weapon is fired do not apply to the game and therefore the player must become accustomed to these idiosyncrasies before they can develop their abilities in the game.

From the interviews with the subjects and the videos that were recorded of their playing experience, it is clear that they all developed their game mechanics knowledge and game environment knowledge and learned to use some tricks that they observed from the video. Five of the eight subjects said they learned the game environment layout better when watching the game rather than playing and seven of the eight players said that they had identified tricks which they would use themselves in future games. On watching their own performance, the subjects were quick to point out the mistakes they were making early in the series of games. Most of these related to misconceptions on how the game mechanics operated. Often the subjects would comment that they took a few games to understand what was possible in the game. For example, three of the players commented that they didn't realize that falling from a high distance was something that they avoided until they saw the professional players do just that. As observation of this feature helped them understand how to exploit the game, they amended their own play style and correspondingly increased their game performance.

This initial effort at identifying how the footage aided the subjects has shown that they improved by both observing a better players practices and also by learning more about the world in which the game takes place. The players showed distinct, measurable improvement following their observation of the video and seventeen of the twenty subjects vocalized their appreciation of observation as a means to improve their skills. As a final point of interest, the players who gained no benefit from the video commented that their interest in the game had declined. Clearly the player's engagement with the game that they play will affect the effort that they put into playing the game. Whether the game was not sufficiently engaging for these subjects or whether they were discouraged by their poor performance is difficult to ascertain.

5 Conclusions and Further Work

As professional gaming attracts more sponsorship and the number of professional games players or E-Athletes increases, the techniques which can be used to improve games playing ability will be of interest to those hoping to develop their own abilities for financial motives. The techniques which are effective in improving the abilities of E-Athletes will also be of interest to games researchers as they help us understand how we play and how we develop as games players. It remains to be seen if the study of video footage has limits on the benefits it can confer to those games players.

The viability of video footage in the development of the abilities of intermediate players has been conclusively demonstrated in this test case. Our understanding of what makes a good games player is as far from clear as what makes a good athlete or what makes one person more intelligent, creative or organised than another. We can be sure however that for some groups of players, simply watching another gamer, particularly one who has high levels of ability, is beneficial.

The data that has been gathered here will be of interest to games designers, educators and those with an interest in games AI. The benefit of this data to games designers is subtle but considerable. Developer Ubisoft used a technique in the Prince of Persia games whereby each level of the game was preceded by a brief movie showing what the player was to do next. This was a step intended to ease the player into the game slowly and serve as a continuous tutorial. This is a clear concession by the Developer that the player can be aided by watching footage of the game to guide them and manager the difficulty level of the game. If the player learns best through observation of a more skilled player, then the difficulty of the game can be balanced by the inclusion of such a skilled player. In the genre of FPS games, the player could have AI team mates who play the game very well. Through observation of these AI team mates tactics when playing the game, the player should develop some of these skills themselves.

Furthermore, this work represents an initial step in determining how humans learn while playing games. While the players are learning through practice, they are also learning through the observation of others playing. This could be of interest to educators who for logistical reasons may not be able to use educational software for all members of a class. The suggestion is that perhaps the observation of games playing confers almost as much benefit as games playing itself. AI researchers will also be interested in how humans develop their skills and how they can represent challenging enemies that will surprise the player and encourage them to develop their own skills.

The success of the approach taken shows that some fundamental advantage is gained from the observation of professional players. The nature of how this advantage is conferred must now be considered. While there is some initial supposition here, more careful and considered work must be done to identify which aspects of the individuals play style is affected by the video footage.

If we are to evaluate the value of player observation as a training technique for E-Athletes, we must compare it to other training routines available. The most obvious comparison would be with simple practice. Is one hour of video observation more or less beneficial than one hour's worth of practice? Does this confer a different form of benefit to play style; for example will it aid anticipation but make no difference to aim? A more complete parameterisation of the constituents of FPS playing ability will be key in evaluating the impact of various training regimes for E-Athletes. Only when we have some parameters to measure and the means to measure them will we be able to determine how player's abilities in games develop.

This work is the first step in developing a fuller understanding of how humans learn to play games better. As games designers continue to realise that gameplay and not graphics is the fundamental core of a great game, they will be required to develop a fuller understanding of how humans play games, how they learn about the game world and how they get better at playing. Increasingly interactive game worlds in both single and multiplayer games are correspondingly becoming more complex to play in. Games players learn by watching experts play. The abilities of professional gamers may represent vital data that designers will seek in the future to market, sell and even integrate into their games.

REFERENCES

CENNAMO, KATHERINE. 1993, Learning From Video: Factors Influencing Learners' Preconceptions and Invested Mental Effort, Vol 41, No 3, p33-45

DAVIES, N P. MEHDI, Q H. and GOUGH, N. 2005. Creating and Visualising an Intelligent NPC using Game Engines and AI Tools, *19th European Conference on Modeling And Simulation conference proceedings*, game-06.

ELSPA, Elspa UK Interactive Entertainment Industry Yearbook, 2006 p 29, p40,

JOSEPH, TODD ALLEN. 2004, "The Effect of Mental Practice On Dart Throwing Performance, *Masters thesis at the University of South Florida,* http://etd.fcla.edu/SF/SFE0000509/FinalSubmission.pdf (online)

LAIRD, J. van Lent, MICHAEL. 2001, Human-Level AI's Killer Application: Interactive Computer Games, *Proceedings of AAAI 2000, Austin, Texas*

LAIRD, A. 2000, It knows what Your Going to do: Adding anticipation to a Quake Bot Papers from the *AAAI Spring Symposium on Artificial Intelligence and Interactive Entertainment*, Technical Report SS-00-02, AAAI Press.

MAGERKO, BRIAN. LAIRD, JOHN E. ASSANIE, MAZIN. KERFOOT, ALEX. STOKES, DEVVAN. 2004, *Proceedings of the 2004 Innovative Applications of Artificial Intelligence Conference, San Jose, CA*, AAAI Press

MCGLINCHEY, STEPHEN. 2002, Learning of ai players from game observation data, *Proceedings of CGAIDE 2004, University of Wolverhampton, UK*

RICHARDS, MATT. 2004, Multiplayer Games: A Spectator's View, *PhD thesis at Parsons School of design, New York City s*

LIN, LONG_JI. 1992, Self-Improving Reactive Agents Based on Reinforcement Learning, Planning and Teaching, Machine Learning, Vol 8 No 3-4, p293-321

SPRONK, PIETER. SPRINKHUIZEN-KUYPER, IDA. POSTMA, ERIC. On line Adaption of Game Opponent AI with Dynamic Scripting, *International Journal of Intelligent Games and Simulation,* Vol 3 No 1, p45-53

THURAU, C. PACZIAN, T. BAUCKHAGE, C. 2005, Is Bayesian Learning the Route to Believable Gamebots, *Game-On North America proceedings page 3-9*

TOUZOUR, P. 2002, The Evolution of Game AI, *AI Game Programming Wisdom*, (Ed S Rabin), ISBN 1584502894 p3-15

WELSH, THOMAS. 2005, Parameterisation of human fps strategies, *CGAIMS 2005 conference proceedings*, *Louisville, Kentucky*

The E-Motion System: Motion Capture and Movement-based Biofeedback Game

D.Kelly*, D.Fitzgerald**, J.Foody*, D.Kumar**, T. Ward***, B.Caulfield** and C.Markham**

*Department of Computer Science, N.U.I Maynooth, Ireland.

**School of Physiotherapy & Performance Science, University College Dublin, Dublin, Ireland.

***Department of Engineering, N.U.I. Maynooth, Ireland

dan_kelly_ie@hotmail.com

Abstract:

This paper describes the development of a movement based training game aimed at teaching users an exercise program. This is achieved through analysing body posture as the player performs the exercise routine while concurrently receiving real-time feedback from the game. An in-depth post game feedback system also features, giving the player a detailed account of their performance after completing the exercise routine. Analysis of the player's posture is achieved by placing orientation sensors on appropriate parts of the players' body. The game can then read and interpret data from these sensors reconstructing a live 3D model of the players' posture. The game has the kinematic data of an expert performing the current exercise routine stored in memory, which is compared to the kinematic data of the current player and appropriate feedback is given to aid the player in performing the exercise. The theme of the prototype game currently developed is that of a yoga training game (E-Yoga).

Keywords: Motion Capture, Real time motion rendering, Biofeedback, Exercise Training, Kinematics, Performance feedback, Orientation Sensors,

I Background and Introduction

With the increasingly sedentary lifestyles of modern living, more and more people are suffering from various musculoskeletal pathologies such as back pain and neck pain. In addition obesity particularly amongst children is emerging as the most serious health challenge of our times. Ironically in the light of the contribution of this paper, computer and video games have been identified as one of the main culprits in contributing to the low level of exercise engaged in by children in the developed world. Therapeutic exercise programmes are advocated both to prevent and treat these physical conditions but adherence levels to such programmes are poor. Motivating people to participate in such exercise programmes is a challenge. We feel creating a computer game to increase the enjoyment during the exercise and give feedback and encouragement during the programme; players' motivations to participate in therapeutic exercise programs can be enhanced.

Current movement based games (i.e. EyeToy games) are based on 2 dimensional movements and allow the player to deviate from the desired exercise sequence without direct warning or feedback. This can be solved by tracking body movements using orientation sensors and analyze all 3 dimensions of the players' movement. We utilized commercial orientation sensors [1] to develop a prototype game with the view of integrating our own low cost sensors [2] at a later date.

The theme of the currently developed game is that of a yoga training game. Kinematic data of a yoga expert performing the sun salutation yoga exercise sequence was recorded by equipping a trained yoga teacher (i.e. the expert) with the orientation sensors and recording the kinematic data of the sequence (see Figure 1). The experts' data is stored in the system and a players' performance of the routine is calculated using a comparison system between the players' and experts' kinematic data.

Figure 1 Expert training poses for Sun Salutation sequence.

The graphics and 3D environment of E-Yoga were designed with the aim giving the game a relaxing feel. The game was developed using the DirectX 9 API within a managed environment using C# as the development language. The main contribution of this paper is the design and building of a real time kinematic feedback application capable of live motion rendering and feedback.

II Development

The development of the game can be divided into two components. (1) Motion capture development using orientation sensors and (2) development of the game framework, engine and graphics. Each of these two components will now be described:

Motion Capture Engine:

Ten orientation sensors are used as the basis of the kinematic sensor system for the development of the game. The Xsens Mtx sensor, seen in Figure 1, is the sensor used for the current version of the system. Each Xsens sensor is a small lightweight sensor which detects 3 dimensional orientation using 2 accelerometers, a magnetometer and a gyroscope [3].

Figure 2 MTx orientation tracker

Each of the ten sensors is connected to a small wearable base unit which sends data to the motion capture engine via Bluetooth. If each of the sensors is placed on appropriate parts of the body, the orientation of each part can be tracked dynamically. Using this data it is then possible to animate a 3D character model mimicking the movements of the player wearing the orientation sensors.

When modelling a 3D character for animation, the model is set up such that the bones of the character are in a hierarchical tree structure with the hips being the root of the tree [4]. This data structure means that a bones' position is described relative to its parent bone. However, each of the orientation devices detects its orientation relative to the global world meaning that some computation must be applied to the raw output of each sensor before the corresponding bone in the 3D model can be repositioned to a new orientation. The motion capture engine developed here does all orientation calculations using quaternion algebra [5]. To calculate the orientation of a bone relative to its parent bone the following equations are used:

$$q_{relative} = q_{raw} \times q_{parentRaw}^{-1} \qquad (1)$$

Where:

$$q^{-1} = \frac{q_0 - iq_1 - jq_2 - kq_3}{q_0^2 + q_1^2 + q_2^2 + q_3^2} \qquad (2)$$

Where q_{raw} is the quaternion representing the global orientation of the current sensor and $q_{parentRaw}$ is the quaternion representing the global orientation of the parent sensor of the current sensor.

Using these equations we can now calculate a quaternion for each bone to describe its orientation relative its parent, and in the case of the root bone its orientation is defined by the corresponding sensors' raw output only as it has no parent. The game is developed using the DirectX 9 API, therefore all movements of objects within the environment must be defined as a rotation and translation using homogenous matrices [6]. To convert the quaternion calculated in (1) to a rotation matrix that can be used to rotate a particular bone within the game environment, (3) is used [5]:

$$M = \begin{pmatrix} 2q_0^2 \square 2q_1^2 \square 1 & 2q_1q_2 \square 2q_0q_3 & 2q_1q_3 \square 2q_0q_2 \\ 2q_1q_2 \square 2q_0q_3 & 2q_0^2 \square 2q_2^2 \square 1 & 2q_2q_3 \square 2q_0q_1 \\ 2q_1q_3 \square 2q_0q_2 & 2q_2q_3 \square 2q_0q_1 & 2q_0^2 \square 2q_3^2 \square 1 \end{pmatrix} \quad (3)$$

In order for the 3D character model to accurately mimic the players' movements, the game must perform some calibration. The calibration consists of getting the player to stand upright with legs straight, arms parallel to the ground and looking straight. Then to calibrate, the sensors are reset having the effect of setting the current orientation of all sensors to zero degrees rotation about all axes, setting the origin pose for the player. All orientation changes made to the sensors, and thus the corresponding bone on the 3D model, will be made relative to the same origin pose. Therefore the 3D model now mimics the players' movement.

This motion capture engine is utilized within a game architecture to playback live and recorded motion, to record motion and to analyze and give feedback on motion. An overview of this game architecture is provided in the next section. Figure 4 shows the motion capture engine in operation within the game system.

Figure 3 Real Time Motion Capture and Rendering

Game Engine / System Design

A game was developed to utilize the motion capture engine. The aim of the game is to teach players, wearing the motion sensors, an exercise routine by analyzing players movement and giving feedback. A screenshot of the game can be seen in Figure 3.

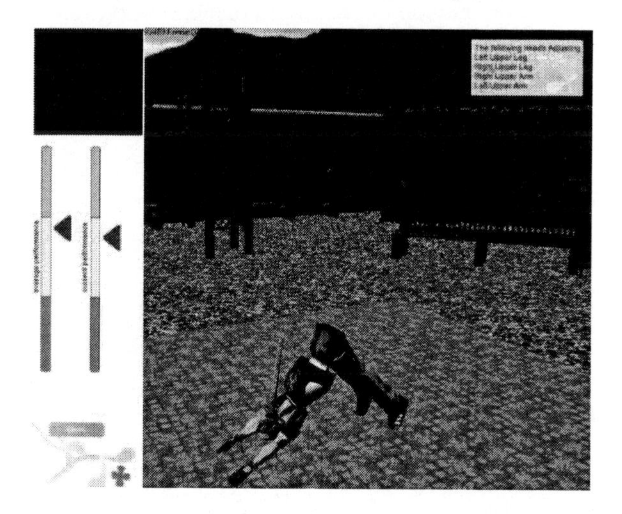

Figure 4 In game display; Expert in a Yoga pose (Pose 8: Downward facing dog pose)

The game system consists of the following main components:

1. Game Engine

This module manages creation of game modules, communication between game modules, input via mouse and keyboard, timing and rendering to the screen.

2. User Interface Modules

Modules which render user interface graphics and manage user input via buttons and text boxes.

3. In-game Controller

When in game mode the game can be in one of four different states at any given time:

i. Calibrate Mode

The character model is animated using live Xsens data. A button is provided so users can invoke sensor calibration. After a successful calibration the 3D character model will mimic player movement.

ii. Expert Playback Mode

The character model is animated using pre-recorded expert kinematic data and an audio description of each milestone pose is played at the beginning of each milestone sequence.

iii. Live Mode

The character model is animated using pre-recorded expert kinematic data, while kinematic data for live player is being retrieved and stored in background. The experts exercise sequence contains a number of milestone poses which the player must perform before progressing (see Figure 1 for the 12 milestone poses for the sun salutation sequence). On completing each milestone pose, an audio playback encourages the player to the next pose. After completing the motion sequence, offline analysis is performed on the players' kinematic data. This is achieved by comparing data to that of the expert. Feedback on performance is then given and a detailed breakdown of the players' performance is displayed.

iv. Player Playback Mode

The character model is animated using pre-recorded data recorded during the live mode i.e. playback of users motion.

4. Character Renderer

Creates a character 3D model from a specified .X file and animates the character given data from a specific instance of a Motion interface module (see below for Motion interface module description).

5. Motion Interface Module

This module provides kinematic data to the character renderer object from live Xsens sensors or pre-recorded Xsens data. A choice of 2 constructor overloads determines the source of the kinematic data. These two calls reflect the two possible modes of operation for the motion interface module. The first mode sets up the object so that data is retrieved from the set of live Xsens sensors and relative orientation calculations are performed on the data. The second mode sets up the object so that data is retrieved from a specified pre-recorded motion file. Regardless of the mode, data is retrieved by the calling object in the same manner, that is, a method is called with the input being an instance of a bone enumerator. The enumerator specifies which bone s' kinematic data is to be returned. As a result, different instances of motion interface modules can be easily interchanged within the character render module, therefore changing between live animation and pre-recorded animation can be done in a transparent way.

6. Motion storage and control module

This module manages the loading and saving of kinematic data to and from file. When parsing from a file, kinematic data is stored in a 2D array with each row of the array corresponding to a single frame of animation. Associated with each frame of animation is a time, indicating when that frame should be used to animate the 3D character model, and a marker. Each motion sequence contains milestone postures which players must perform before progressing. The marker is used to indicate if the corresponding frame is or is not a milestone pose.

The motion object also controls frame timing. This is achieved by monitoring the amount of time elapsed since the last frame was returned to the motion interface module. Using this value it can calculate which frame to play next using the timing data associated with each frame. When in live mode and retrieving data from an expert sequence, the *get_frame* method requires an extra Boolean parameter specifying whether or not the player is in the same pose as the expert. If the expert is currently in a milestone pose then the time will not be advanced until such time as the player performs the same pose.

7. Environment Renderer

Manages loading and rendering of the 3D environment, lighting and camera position.

8. Player Info storage and control module

Manages storing, loading and creating player accounts.

9. Offline Feedback

After completing a motion sequence, the players' motion data is saved and loaded in a motion object. The offline feedback takes as input both the players and the experts motion object and calculates performance values for each of the sequences between milestones (4). Currently this figure is calculated using a distance metric in Euler space.

$$PoseSequenceRating \; \sum_{i \; Milestone_X}^{MileStone_{X\square 1}} \left(\frac{\sum_{j \; 0}^{NumBones} |PT_{i,j} \square ET_{i,j}| \square |PI_{i,j} \square EI_{i,j}| \square |P\therefore_{i,j} \square E\therefore_{i,j}|}{NumBones \upsilon \square MileStone_{X\square 1} \square MileStone_X \square} \right) \quad (4)$$

Where E represents Expert, P represents Player, θ represents yaw, φ represents pitch and ψ represents roll

In addition a timing rating and a smoothness score is calculated for the sequence. The smoothness score is determined through differentiation and comparative analysis of the respective movement loci.

III Conclusion

In this paper we have demonstrated the possibility of a movement based biofeedback system allowing a player to learn, and get feedback on, an exercise routine such as a yoga routine. It has been shown that the posture of a person wearing orientation sensors, positioned at different parts of the body, can be modelled and analysed by the system. Modelling and analyzing a sequence of postures performed by an expert and an amateur (i.e. the player) and comparing the results can be used as the basis for a feedback system.

IV References

[1] www.xsens.com, Xsens Technologies B.V.

[2] J Foody, D Kelly, D Kumar, D Fitzgerald, B Caulfield, C Markham, T Ward, *A real time motion capture system, using usb based tri-axis magnetic and inertial sensors, for movement based relaxation,* Irish Systems and Signals Conference 2006

[3] MT Software Development Kit Documentation, Document MT0200P

[4] M. Meredith and S.Maddock, *Motion capture file formats explained,* Department of Computer Science, University of Sheffield.

[5] Jack B. Kuipers, *Quaternions and Rotation Sequences – A primer with applications to orbits aerospace and virtual reality,* Princeton University Press, ISBN 0-691-05872-5

[6] Tom Miller, *Managed Direct X 9, Graphics and Game Programming,* ISBN 0-672-32596-9, Sams Publishing

V Author Biography

Dan Kelly is a 23 year old Computer Scientist/ Software Engineer and has just graduated with a first class honours degree in Computer Science from N.U.I. Maynooth. Dan also has over 15 months experience working in the software industry working for Microsoft.

Integration of kinematic Analysis into Computer Games for Exercise

D.Fitzgerald*, J. Foody**, D. Kumar*, D.Kelly**, T.Ward***, C.Markham and B.Caulfield *

**School of Physiotherapy and Performance Science, University College Dublin, Dublin, Ireland.*

****Department of Computer Science, N.U.I Maynooth, Ireland.*

******Department of Electronic Engineering, N.U.I Maynooth, Ireland.*

diarmaid.m.fitzgerald@ucd.ie

Abstract

This paper incorporates a review of current methods for integrating body movement or physical activity into computer games and a rationale for a new approach in this genre. Computer games are frequently implicated in the increasing sedentary nature of modern lifestyles and associated problems such as childhood obesity. Any measures that help to incorporate physical exercise into computer games will help to advance the notion that they can be used to promote rather than hinder health. Current approaches to integrating physical exercise into games can be divided into 2 categories: (1) camera based tracking of gross 2-D body movement and, (2) sensor based tracking of 2 or 3-D kinematics of regional body segments. These approaches are appropriate for their means yet they do not permit integration of whole body 3-dimensional kinematics into a computer game. Such a system should have the capability to monitor 3-D kinematics from all body segments and reconstruct the body's movement in real-time on screen. Integration of physiological sensors could augment the kinematic data to add features to the game. This approach to gaming could be used to guide and analyse a user while performing a series of exercises such as Yoga or Pilates and give feedback both during and after the exercise regime to help improve future performance.

Key Words

Computer Game, Serious Games, Exercise, Motion Capture, Biofeedback

1. Introduction and Background

Regular physical activity is associated with enhanced health and reduced mortality [1-4]. Along with the impact on preventing mortality, physical activity has many disease prevention benefits, including reduced risk of cardiovascular disease [5-6] and stroke [7-9]. Despite these benefits of regular physical activity many people still fail to engage in the recommended amounts of physical activity (30 minutes of moderate-intensity activity on 5 or more days per week, 20 minutes of vigorous-intensity activity on 3 or more days per week) [10].

Playing computer games has been associated with many health problems particularly among children and adolescents. The sedentary nature of using only the movement of fingers and thumbs to manipulate hand held controllers or keyboards while playing computer games results in hours of inactivity usually spent sitting. Studies outlining some of the problems associated with playing computer games in the past include wrist pain [11], hand arm vibration syndrome [12], neck pain [13], and repetitive strain injuries [14]. However, computer games for exercise where the players' own body actually takes the place of the mouse or joystick are now being developed and can instead lead to many health benefits.

These exercise games such as the EyeToy: Kinetic or Dance Mat Revolution for the Sony Playstation®2 (PS2) console encourage players to perform physical exercise in an enjoyable fashion. These games capture the players' body movements and use it as input control during virtual exercise games and classes. Virtual reality-type games are typically employed where the player can see themselves or an animated avatar mimicking their movements on-screen in a computer-generated environment. Engaging with a game in this fashion makes the exercise experience more enjoyable therefore increasing their motivation to participate [15]. Inadequate knowledge of how to perform exercise may often limit people from taking part but these games demonstrate how to perform the exercise so the player can copy the movements. O'Connor [15] in a study involving wheelchair users using a purpose built roller system interface (GAME^{Wheels}) to play Need for Speed II (Electronic Arts, Inc) showed a significantly higher level of exercise intensity was achieved during the computer game compared to the control condition of exercising without any game. There was also a self-reported increased motivation to partake in wheelchair propulsion exercise shown in participants. This suggests that such systems can provide a very engaging and motivating form of physical exercise training.

Section 2 will give an exposition of current technologies in use for such integration while Section 3 proposes a more advanced method of motion capture in that could be implemented in gaming.

2. Existing Approaches to Integrate Exercise and Computer Games

There are many movement based human computer interfaces on the market. These include camera-based systems and position sensor systems. Position sensor systems include systems with a single sensor worn on the body at a key reference point (usually worn on a belt around the waist) or dance mats. All approaches work well in achieving instantaneous feedback and interaction with onscreen objects.

In camera based computer games the player can view themselves in a virtual environment as they interact with on-screen objects in real-time. Games are quite simple and usually involve the tracking or evasion of on-screen objects. For example the Sony EyeToy for the PS2 employs a single USB camera to place the player in an on screen environment. Games such as EyeToy: Kinetic feature a host of fitness exercises ranging from combat games where players must use their limbs to hit specific moving targets to exercise programmes where the player must copy the on screen virtual personal trainer. Performance rating scores can be recorded for games where on screen targets have to be hit.

GestureTek Inc™ have produced many camera-enabled computer control systems. The Gesxtreme system is a virtual reality-type game where the player can also see their virtual body on-screen and interact with objects to play the games. The IREX exercise system, by the same company, is used as a tool in physical rehabilitation and is also a camera-based system. While these sorts of camera-based systems are very engaging from an interaction point of view the problem is that they can only track gross body movements in a single 2-dimensional (2-D plane (up-down and left-right). It lacks a sense of 3-dimensional (3-D) immersion. The addition of this depth dimension would allow far more realistic and challenging physical interaction with the gaming experience.

The Cybex Trazer® (Cybex International, Inc.) employs a single infrared beacon mounted on a belt worn around the waist of the player. The position of this sensor is monitored by the tracker bar of the system to capture motion of the player which can move an on-screen avatar as one rigid block to play various drills and games. Heart rate is also monitored through sensors located in the belt in this system and information relayed to the computer.

Dance mats are used in games have a number of sensors located at specific sections. These are used sense pressure and therefore identify when the foot is placed over them. During these games such as, Dance Factory for the PS2 or Dancing Stage Unleashed™ for the XBOX Live, the player must step on an arrow on the mat to match the on-screen directional arrow while listening to music and press the feet on the correct area of the dance mat controller at the correct time. Speed and timing are important and increase through the difficulty levels.

Although these systems meet the goals of each game successfully they lack the capability to capture detailed human movement and administer accurate biofeedback on individual body segment. All human motion is 3-D therefore requiring some form of discreet motion tracking. These systems are only useful for cardiovascular type exercise as they have no discreet movement analysis capability and therefore they cannot be used in games where accurate measurement of body alignment and posture is required in order to judge player performance. This means that games based on movement therapies or martial arts cannot have an accurate scoring system based on full body movements with current approaches. For this to be achieved a method of quantitatively tracking the different limb segments must be employed.

3. A More Expansive Approach: Whole Body Kinematics

Advanced motion capture technologies that analyse discreet body movements have been continuously developed and improved in recent years. These are utilised to study the biomechanics of the human body and investigate clinical problems, as well as to provide realistic animation for the entertainment industry. This has usually taken place in a laboratory setting but technologies are increasingly being employed in peoples' natural environments at home, at work and during sporting participation.

The most commonly used method for accurate capture of 3-D movement require attachment of markers or fixtures on the skin's surface of the segment being analysed [16] (Figure 3.1). These are used to derive data on position and orientation of joints. Physiological sensors could also be utilised to monitor heart rate or breathing rate during the exercise.

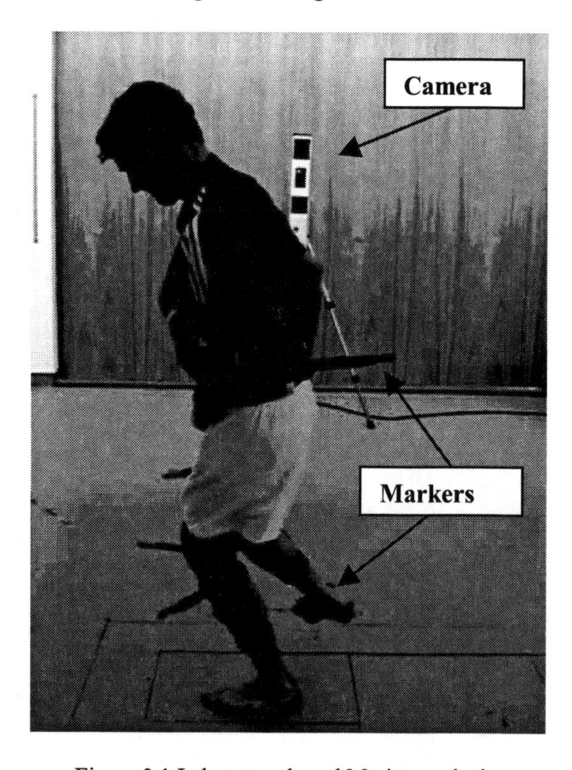

Figure 3.1 Laboratory based Motion analysis.

Integrating kinematic analysis technology into computer games for physical activity would bring this type of gaming to a higher level. Detailed analysis of joint movement would allow a virtual personal trainer to give more effective instantaneous feedback on the postures and movements achieved during the gameplay. Users can be guided through a series of exercises and receive immediate and accurate feedback regarding the quality of their performance based on a combination of their movement and physiological indicators. The system could then serve as an educational tool for learning movement based exercise techniques. Objective measures of performance over successive sessions with the game could be recorded and progression of performance0 mapped over time. It could be argued that such a system is preferable to a personal instructor as it offers a greater level of accuracy in judging the quality of movement and physiological control than would be visible to the naked eye. It also allows the user to be less self-conscious in their engagement with the exercise as they can play the game in the privacy of their own home.

All human motion is 3-D therefore requiring some form of discreet motion tracking. This means that games based on movement therapies or martial arts are not possible with current approaches. Obviously, extending the scope of the computer gaming spectrum to include this type of exercise would be beneficial to encourage greater levels of participation in exercise designed to improve mind and body function as well as the cardiovascular aspects of fitness that are catered for in existing gaming technology.

4. Design Features

From the afore-described discussion it is apparent that whole body tracking is perhaps the next step forward for physical movement controllers. To this end then we tentatively suggest some basic components and specifications for such systems and how the game will be designed.

4.1. Motion and Physiological Sensors

For robust 3-D motion tracking, an orientation sensor is preferable as it can easily be applied to a body segment and will produce continuous movement data without the need to be 'in-view' of a camera at all times as some marker systems require. In selecting a sensor it is important to mention the difficulties that may be encountered such as tolerance, fidelity or noise with the data. From work others and ourselves have done previously we would suggest the use of 3-D accelerometers for this purpose [17]. A body sensor network of one sensor on each of the shin, thigh, forearm and upper arm along with one on the back and head is the minimum requirement. Physiological sensors to monitor heart and breathing rate may also be included in the system.

The sensors can be embedded in a lycra garment which will be worn by the player during the gameplay. The continuous development of smart fabrics, which are have sensing materials either coated on or woven in the textile structure, may eventually lead to the possibility of using textile-based sensors.

4.2. Wireless Interface

A tetherless controller would in our opinion be more suitable for such a device that current wired systems such as GameTrak have not achieved. This would allow freedom to perform exercises without the restrictive wires or cables. Indeed controllers for all the next generation games consoles (Xbox 360, PS3, Revolution) are all wireless. Clearly this is what we want to see then in any sensor based kinematic controller.

4.3. Software

Software will process sensor data in real-time to administer audio and visual biofeedback to the users along with recording data for post game analysis. This will be based on their performance in the game (i.e. how close the player is to the correct postures throughout the exercise programme) against pre defined expert level of performance. Modifiable programmes to meet the goals and capabilities of all ages can be included. Games designers can incorporate this into the games using their own creativity.

4.4. Playing the game

Playing the game will require wearing the sensor-based garment as the human computer interface. Initial calibration of the sensors will be required before the game begins and screen display will instruct the player to calibration position. Progression mapping of performance over time will be used to generate short-term goals for players. Applications for such a game include training to improve cardiovascular fitness and endurance, reaction time, spatial awareness, physical rehabilitation and injury prevention programmes.

4.5. Obstacles and Limitations

With the large amount of input data from sensors a large amount of real-time processing will be required by the system. Cost effective hardware must be producible so an affordable system can be reproduced. Also, performance data must be generated from analysing experts performing the exercises for the games to be designed.

5. Conclusion

Detailed motion capture and physiological monitoring technologies employed to give real-time visual and audio feedback could be employed to design the next generation of computer games for exercise. Such a system could accurately progress a player through increasing difficulty levels and eventually be used as a training device during movement rehabilitation.

References

[1] Lee IM, Hsieh CC, Paffenbarger RS Jr. *Exercise intensity and longevity in men.* The Harvard Alumni Health study. JAMA 1995;273:1179-84.

[2] Paffenbarger RS Jr, Hyde RT, Wing AL. Lee IM, Jung D, Kampert JB. *The association of changes in physical-activity level and other lifestyle characteristics with mortality among men.* N Engl J Med 1993;328:538-45.

[3] Paffenbarger RS Jr, Kampert JB, Lee IM, Hyde RT, Leung RW, Wing AL. *Changes in physical activity and other lifeway patterns influencing longevity.* Med Sci Sports Exerc1994;26:857-65.

[4] Blair SN, Kohl HW III, Barlow CE, Paffenbarger RS Jr, Gibbons LW, Macera CA. *Changes in physical fitness and all-cause mortality.* A prospective study of healthy and unhealthy men. JAMA 1995;273:1093-8.

[5] Wannamethee SG, Shaper AG. *Physical activity in the prevention of cardiovascular disease: an epidemiological perspective.* Sports Med 2001; 31:101-14.

[6] Sesso DH, Paffenbarger RS Jar, Lee IM. *Physical activity and coronary heart disease in menthe Harvard alumni Health Study.* Circulation 2000; 102:975-80.

[7] Hun FB, Stumper MJ, Cowlitz GA, et al. *Physical activity and risk of stroke in women.* JAMA 2000; 283:2961-7.

[8] Gore licks PB, Sacco RL, Smith DB, et al. *Prevention of a first stroke: a review of guidelines and a multidisciplinary consensus statement from the National Stroke Association.* JAMA 1999; 281:1112-20.

[9] Wannamethee SG, Sharper AG, *Physical activity and the prevention of stroke.* J Cardiovasc Risk 1999;6:213-6.

[10] U.S. Department of Health and Human Services. *Healthy people 2010: conference edition.* Washington, DC: U.S. Department of Health and Human Services, 2000.

[11] McCowan T.C. *Space Invaders Wrist.* New England Journal of Medicine 1981;304:1368.

[12] Cleary AG, McKendrick H, Sills JA. *Hand-arm vibration Syndrome may be associated with prolonged use of vibrating computer games.* British Medical Journal 2002;324:301

[13] Miller DLG. *Nintendo Neck.* Canadian Medical Association Journal 1991;145:1202.

[14] Mirman MJ , Bonian VG. *A new repetitive stress injury. Journal of the American Osteopath Association.* 1992;92 6, pp. 701

[15] O'Connor TJ, Fitzgerald SG, Cooper RA, Thornman TA, Boninger ML. *Does computer game play aid in motivation of exercise and increase*

metabolic activity during wheelchair ergometry? Med Eng & Physisc 2001; 23:267-273.
[16] Benedetti M, Cappozzo A. *Anatomical landmark definition and identification of computer aided movement analysis in a rehabilitation context.* In Internal Report Universita Degli Studi La Sapienza 1994
[17] Foody J, Kelly D, Kumar D, Fitzgerald D, Ward T, Caulfield B, Markham C. *A Prototype Sourceless Kinematic-Feedback Based Video Game for Movement Based Exercise 2006.* 28th Annual International Conference of the IEEE Engineering in Medicine and Biology Society: Engineering Revolution In BioMedicine Marriott Marquis at Times Square, New York City, New York, USA, August 31-Sept 3, 2006

Author Biography

Mr. Diarmaid Fitzgerald is a postgraduate researcher at the School of Physiotherapy and Performance Science at University College Dublin. Mr. Fitzgerald is currently involved in a research project aimed at producing a virtual reality-based computer game to teach a player an exercise programme. This involves using motion and physiological sensors to analyse the player and give instantaneous feedback on the players' performance. Mr. Fitzgerald holds a BSc in Physiotherapy from University College Dublin.

Tools and systems for Games and Virtual Reality (2)

REDUCING SENSOR DENSITY REQUIREMENTS FOR KINEMATIC CONTROLLERS IN A FULL POSTURE YOGA GAMING APPLICATION

D.Kumar*, J. Foody**, D. Fitzgerald*, D.Kelly**, T.Ward***, C.Markham** and B.Caulfield*

*School of Physiotherapy & Performance Science, University College Dublin, Dublin, Ireland.
**Department of Computer Science, N.U.I Maynooth, Ireland.
***Department of Electronic Engineering, N.U.I Maynooth, Ireland.

damini.kumar@gmail.com

Abstract:
Integration of whole body movements with virtual reality environments and computer games has many benefits for exercise training and rehabilitation. Such applications can serve as a virtual personal trainer for different exercise therapies. Current examples of this are based on provision of visual feedback to the user via a webcam yet these allow the player to deviate from the desired exercise sequence without direct warning or feedback. This can be solved by tracking body movements using orientation sensors. However, tracking and providing real time feedback for whole body movements for exercise therapies such as Yoga can prove very complex and require the use of a large number of sensors on body segments. In this paper we describe a methodological approach that can facilitate the development of a body movement driven Yoga exercise computer game that can discriminate player performance level with the use of minimum instrumentation.

Key Words: computer game, therapeutic exercise, kinematics, performance level, joint angular displacement, wearable feedback system, yoga, sensors, minimum instrumentation, 3D motion capture.

I. Background & Purpose

Therapies such as yoga have been shown to have many therapeutic benefits in rehabilitation including enhancing postural awareness and reducing chronic pain & stress. This paper reports on studies and analyses on movement based relaxation activities such as Yoga with the aim of determining biomechanical correlates of action fidelity that can be harnessed to automate some aspects of the instruction cycle in the form of a gaming system. This work feeds into a technical project discussed elsewhere, which is 'The E-motion System' (a movement-based biofeedback application), to develop a computer game in which the player's performance is determined by their ability to master one of these physical arts and in doing so bring about a state of mental relaxation. A wireless, unobtrusive garment -based physiological and kinematic measurement system provides our primary method of communication with the game. This lightweight garment will ultimately monitor heart and breathing rate, muscle activity and alignment of body segments using embedded invented miniature sensors.

A typical scenario of the final game could be that the player wears the suit fitted with motion tracking sensors. On the screen will be an animation of a yoga expert guiding the player through the different yoga poses. This guidance will be given visually on the screen and also instructions will be given through audio. The player will then follow the instructions from the computer game to correctly perform the yoga poses. The sensors embedded in the suit worn by the player will continuously give feedback to the game as to the player's position and where each part of the body is in real time. As the feedback is monitored from the sensors within the suit the game will know if for example the player's knees are flexed in a particular yoga pose when they should be mid-range. Verbal instructions will then be given to the player to reduce the flexion of their knee. This artificial intelligence will characterise and monitor the player's performance in the game and be able to give them a score. Also a players skill and level of performance will be remembered so that when the player goes back to play the game, the game will know how to instruct them further to perform the correct yoga pose so the game will act as a virtual trainer for yoga.

In the game, success is determined by the player reproducing the physical postures displayed by a animated model on the screen whilst still maintaining a relaxed and controlled breathing pattern. Feedback is provided by means of reproduction of the player's body image on screen. Quality of movement and posture, and degree of mental relaxation will determine the player's performance. This system could be used by patients suffering from many conditions including stress, anxiety disorder and chronic pain. The envisaged complete system could also eventually lead to the development of wearable feedback training systems for other exercise therapies such as core stability training.

Clearly one of the most significant challenges in such a project is the development of an expert system capable of rating and classifying user input with respect to varying levels of performance. In addition graded progression from novice to expert practitioner has to be incorporated for playability purposes. Later stages of the project will involve design of methods for processing of user input to affect changes in the game state of the virtual reality application to facilitate an effort free feedback process. The final part of this whole project will be the design of a suitable virtual reality game, e.g. 'The E-motion System', which would enhance and augment the experience of

Yoga or other therapies for a user through the facilitation of incremental improvement recognition and appropriate game progression strategies. The primary contribution of this paper however is the development of a knowledge base from which heuristics regarding biomechanical correlates of effective yogic positions can be ascertained for the purposes of game developments in this area. In particular we show how the required numbers of sensors for adequate assessment of Yoga postures for such a game can be significantly reduced through thorough biomechanical analysis.

The rest of the paper is composed as follows: Section II Method overview, Section III Methods, Section IV Results, Section V Conclusion, Section VI Discussion, Section VII References ending with Section VIII Author's Biography.

II Method Overview

A 6 camera 3D motion capture system was used to collect kinematic data from upper and lower extremity joint angular displacement (including extremity joints, trunk and head) during performance of the Sun Salutation yoga exercise sequence in 11 healthy adults, divided into expert (n=5) and novice (n=6) groups. Kinematic data relating to all joints were analysed and compared between expert and novice groups for each of the 8 separate poses included in the exercise sequence and the critical body joints were identified.

III. Methods

The CODA motion capture system (Charnwood Dynamics, UK) was used to track motion and movement of the joints. The CODA system contained three cameras mounted on a rigid frame. The kinematic data was recorded using the 2 sets of CODA cameras, 6 cameras in total, placed at a 30 degree angle to each other on the right side of the subject to give maximum detection of the markers from the right side of the body.

These cameras were the detectors and high-accuracy tracking sensors which were pre-calibrated for 3-D measurement. Two sets of these units were used to give an 'extra set of eyes' and maximum redundancy of viewpoint. The cameras at each end of the CODA system unit measured horizontal movement and the middle sensor measured vertical movement. This design allowed each CODA unit to be calibrated to give 3D coordinates. The cameras had flat windows instead of lenses which sensed the position of the small infrared Light Emitting Diode (L.E.D) markers. In this system the LED markers were placed on the subject at the joints of interest and their location in image frames tracked to yield a measure of the motion enacted with very high resolution. Through using the six cameras varying degrees of fidelity could be obtained. The LED markers were powered by small rechargeable battery packs called marker driver boxes. The LED markers were plugged into the battery packs and each marker driver box had a unique identity so the CODA system always knew which marker was which.

To record the kinematic data a protocol was first designed for the study. Approximately 40 pilot studies were conducted using CODA sensors and placing them at various points on the body to be able to measure joint kinematics. In total 16 markers and 8 driver boxes were used. Due to the number of markers and battery packs available it was then decided that only the right side of the subject's body would be analysed, thus giving kinematic data for the right side of the body only. This also meant that the markers had maximum visibility for the cameras which were positioned to the right hand side of the subject as shown in Figure 1.

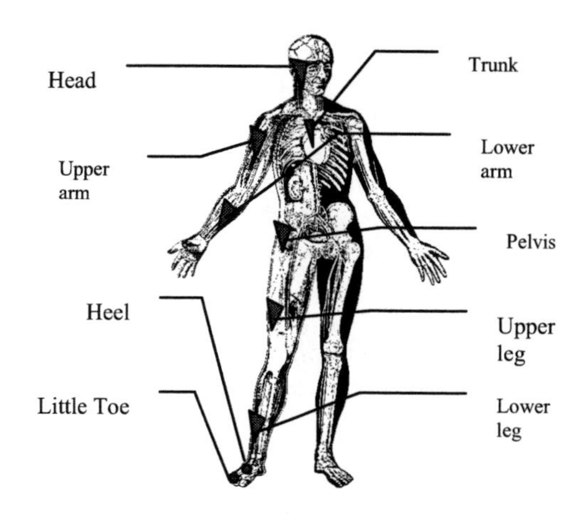

Figure 1: Placement of sensors

Each subject was required to complete the 12 set of yoga postures in the classical sun salutation sequence, which includes 8 different poses as shown in Figure 2.

Pose Number in Sun Salutation Sequence	Name of Pose (Asana)	Picture Showing Pose
Pose 1	Mountain Pose Tadasana	
Pose 2	Hands Up Pose Urdhva Hastasana	
Pose 3	Head to knees Pose Uttanasana	
Pose 4	Lunge Pose Ashwa Sanchalanasana	
Pose 5:	Plank Pose Plank Asana	
Pose 6:	Four Limbed Staff Pose Chaturanga Dandasana	
Pose 7:	Upward Facing Dog Pose Urdhva Mukha Svanasana	
Pose 8:	Downward Facing Dog Pose Adho Mukha Svanasana	

Figure 2: The eight different poses in the Sun Salutation Sequence

The subjects were 11 healthy adults, divided into expert (n=5) and novice (n=6) groups. Each subject performed all the yoga poses in a slow controlled manner under the direction of the investigator, who was also a qualified yoga instructor.
The sequences were also recorded on video. The sequence was repeated and recorded 5 times for each subject and saved separately for each sequence. Each subject attended one testing session which lasted approximately one hour.

Kinematic data relating to all joints were analysed and compared between expert and novice groups for each of the 8 different poses included in the exercise sequence as shown in Figure 2. Both group's kinematic profiles were compared to identify the critical body joints that discriminated between groups..

The kinematic variables associated with the chosen yoga poses were quantified. This entailed carrying out a cross sectional study of yoga kinematic patterns in a motion analysis laboratory. Upper and lower extremity joint angular displacement including spinal alignment of markers were measured and recorded in both groups, expert and novice. This was carried out using a LED (Light Emitting Diodes) detection using a CODA motion capture system (Charndyn Electronics, UK). Averaged kinematic profiles were calculated and kinematic 'key points' were identified for each exercise and analysed.

The data was analysed for the full sun salutation sequence in CODA Motion's software programme for each subject and the three sequences with the greatest marker visibility were chosen for each subject out of the five sequences recorded. A different setup was created in CODA Motion's software for each subject's individual sequence with the necessary offsets, a total of 33 setups (3 sequences X 11 subjects in total). Graphs showing change in movement of individual markers were analysed so as to see when the subject was static i.e. in a particular pose. A stick figure diagram was also created in each setup for each subject so as to replay some of the movements of the subject. This stick figure diagram and the analysis of the graphs showing static marker movement together with video capture of the performed sun salutation sequence in CODA, enabled timelines to be created for each pose for each subject for each sequence so as to know when each pose was performed in the whole sequence. To enable the CODA software to give joint angular displacement for the elbow, knee, head, ankle, shoulder, trunk and hip, for each of the poses, vectors were input so as to create vector lines between the 4 markers in question so joint angles could be analysed. An example of a vector created for the knee joint is detailed below in Figure 3.

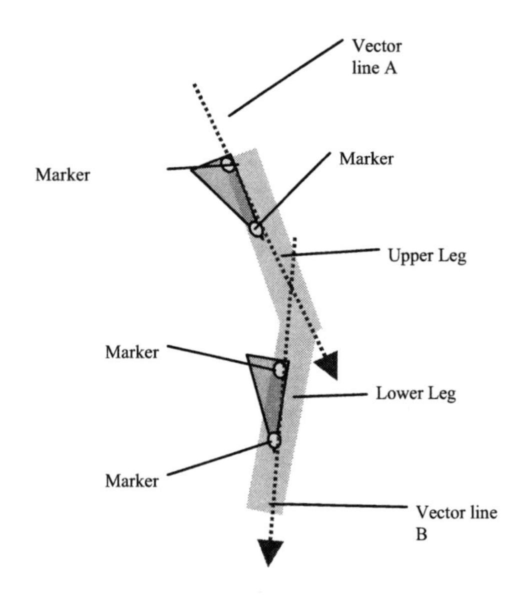

Figure 3: Vectors for knee joint

IV. Results

Joint angular displacements for the elbow, knee, head, ankle, shoulder, trunk and hip, for each of the poses were analysed. Our results indicated that knee joint angular displacement in the sagittal plane could be used to discriminate between groups in 6 out of the 8 key poses in the Sun Salutation. The graph below, Figure 4, shows the range for each group for the knee joint angular displacement for each of the eight poses in the sun salutation sequence. The dots on the end of each line are the range of standard deviation for each group, i.e. expert and novice. The green line is for the novice group and the blue line for the expert group.

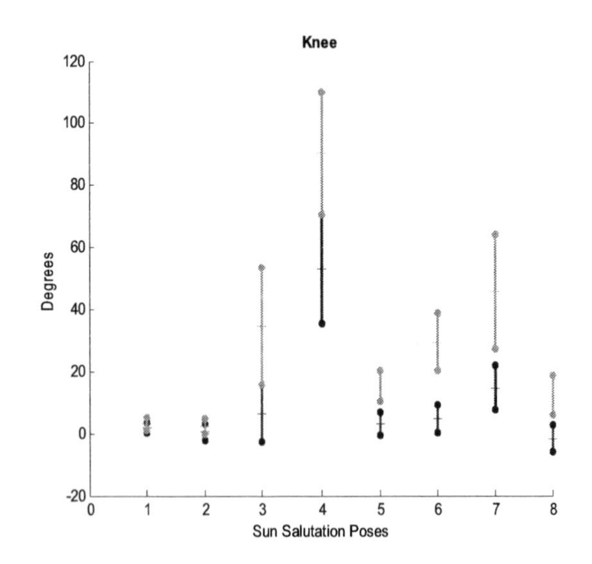

Figure 4: Graph showing joint angular displacement (degrees) for the Knee for each of the eight poses in the sun salutation sequence.

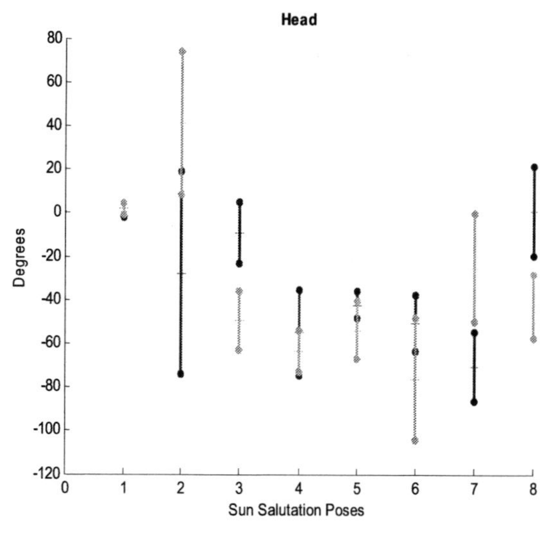

Figure 5: Graph showing joint angular displacement (degrees) for the Head for each of the eight poses in the sun salutation sequence.

Figure 4 shows that the joint angular displacement (in degrees) for the knee is different for the two groups. For each pose the knee can be measured with sensors and from this it can be easy to determine whether a person is a novice or an expert for 6 out of the 8 poses.
Whereas if the Elbow joint angular displacement is measured, as shown in Figure 6, it can be seen that you are not able to discriminate between both groups for any of the poses, as the novice group's range of standard deviation is greater than the experts and also overlaps the expert group range in most poses.

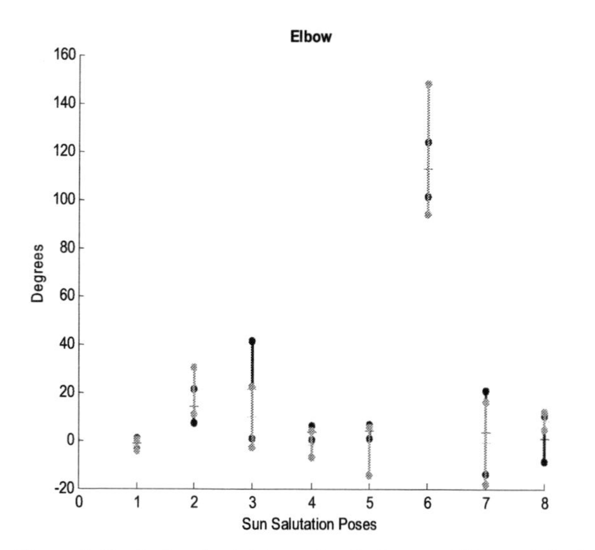

Figure 6: Graph showing joint angular displacement (degrees) for the Elbow for each of the eight poses in the sun salutation sequence.

From the graphs you can also see that the just from the head and knee sensor, Figures 4 &5, you can discriminate between the two different levels for 7 out of the 8 poses in the sun salutation exercise sequence. For the knee sensors, poses 1 and 2, both of which involve standing upright, indicate that both groups have similar knee joint angular displacement and therefore you can not discriminate between the groups. However, the graph showing the head movement indicates again that for 4 out of the 8 poses you can determine the performance level of the subject, and one of these poses is pose 2 which could not be distinguished by the knee sensor alone. The only pose left, out of the 8 poses, to discriminate performance when using the knee and head sensors is pose 1. However pose 1 in the sun salutation sequence is standing upright and is the pose where all the necessary offsets were input in CODA motion's software for each person. If it was absolutely required to distinguish between the groups for pose 1, the standing upright pose, a third set of sensors could be introduced which discriminates pose 1. The ankle joint angular displacement can therefore be added as this distinguishes pose 1 better, Figure 7, and then this gives you the performance level for all 8 poses separately.

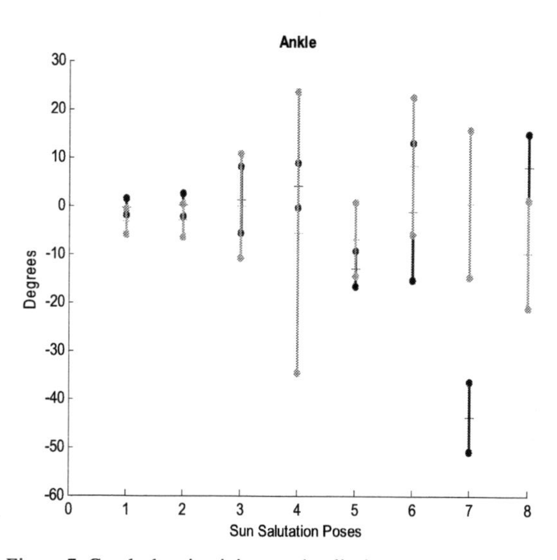

Figure 7: Graph showing joint angular displacement (degrees) for the Ankle for each of the eight poses in the sun salutation sequence.

V. Conclusion

These results suggest that a game based on the yoga sun salutation exercise sequence could be developed using a limited amount of sensors. For example one set of sensors, monitoring the knee joint position can discriminate between different levels of skill performance for 6 out of the 8 poses. When the knee sensor is combined with the head sensor it allows you to distinguish between the groups for all the poses apart from pose 1, which is standing upright pose. If it was required to discriminate performance levels for all 8 poses, including pose 1, then the ankle sensor could be introduced to the head and knee sensors. Therefore using three sets of sensors, monitoring knee, ankle & head joint position can be used to discriminate between different levels of skill performance rather than using 8 sets of sensors. Combining data from these three sensors with visual feedback from a webcam would afford a low cost method of providing a virtual personal trainer that can objectively measure performance. This methodological approach could be of value in development of games based on exercise sequences.

VI. Discussion

Analysis shows that from this method the knee, which showed significant differences for 6 out of the 8 poses, was the critical body joint that discriminated between groups and was therefore the most significant source of differences between the groups. The joint angular displacements for the other sensors showed that any significant difference in performance level could only be seen for a maximum of 4 out of 8 poses, which can be seen in the head sensor. The joint angular displacement for the elbow on the other hand, shown in Figure 6, doesn't show any significant differences for any of the poses and therefore is not a critical body joint for discriminating between levels.

So by using limited instrumentation, i.e. 3 sets of sensors on the head, knee and ankle, you are able to discriminate the different performance levels of the sun salutation sequence for all 8 poses and there is no need to use 8 or more sets of sensors which is very complex and requires the use of a large number of sensors on body segments, which also makes it difficult to perform the poses comfortably and correctly. The number of sensors can be further reduced if pose 1, standing upright is not included in the analysis and then only two sets of sensors are required for the head and knee to discriminate between performance level.

VII. References

(Books)

[1] STILES, M. (2000): 'Structural Yoga Therapy' (1st ed. York Beach, ME: Samuel Weiser)

[2] GERMAIN-CALAIS, B. (1993): 'Anatomy of Movement'. (19th ed. Seattle, WA: Eastland Press.)

[3] COULTER, D. H. (2001): 'Anatomy of Hatha Yoga' (1st ed. Honesdale, PA: Body and Breath)

[4] SCHIFFMANN, E. (1996): 'Yoga: The Spirit and Practice of Moving Into Stillness' (1st ed. New York, NY: Pocket Books.)

(Journal publications)

[5] RAY US ET AL. 'Effect of yogic exercises on physical and mental health of young fellowship course trainees.' *Indian J Physiol Pharmacol 2001; 45: 37-53*

[6] TRAN MD, HOLLY RG, LASHBROOK J, AMSTERDAM EA. 'Effects of hatha yoga practice on the health related aspects of physical fitness'. *Prev Cardiology 2001; 4: 165-70*

[7] SCHULTHEIS M.T. AND A. RIZZO (2001): The application of virtual reality technology for rehabilitation. *Rehabilitation Psychology, vol. 46, no. 3, pp. 296-311.*

[8] GURA ST. 'Yoga for stress reduction and injury prevention at work'. *Work 2002; 19: 3-7*

[9] WILLIAMS ET AL. 'Effect of Iyengar yoga therapy for chronic low back pain.' *Pain. 2005;115:107-17*

(Conference Proceedings)

[10] DAVID FONTANE., DOMINIQUE DAVID, YANIS CARITU. (2003): 'Sourceless Human Motion Capture', -Grenoble 2003.-www.grenoble-soc.com/proceedings03/Pdf/30 fontaine.pdf.

[11] ALBERT KROHN, MICHAEL BEIGL, CHRISTIAN DECKER, UWE KOCHENDORFER, PHILIP ROBINSON AND TOBIAS ZIMMER. (2004) 'In expensive and Automatic Calibration for Acceleration Sensors', -Krohn 2004. *http://www.es.cs.utwente.nl/smartsurroundings /publications/Krohn04.pdf.*

VIII. Author Biography

Damini Kumar is a Product Design Engineer with over 7 years experience in engineering. She has worked in many fields including in design, engineering, innovation and medicine and is also a part time lecturer at Dublin Institute of Technology. Damini holds a BEng (Hons) in Mechanical Engineering from Imperial College London, an MSc in Engineering Product Design from London South Bank University, an MSc (1st Class Hons) from the School of Physiotherapy from University College Dublin, Ireland and also is a qualified yoga teacher.

A DUAL-CHANNEL OPTICAL BRAIN-COMPUTER INTERFACE IN A GAMING ENVIRONMENT

Christopher Soraghan[1] *Fiachra Matthews*[23] *Dan Kelly*[3]
Tomas Ward[4] *Charles Markham*[3] *Barak A. Pearlmutter*[23] *Ray O'Neill*[1]

[1]Physics [2]Hamilton Institute [3]Computer Science [4]Electronic Engineering
National University of Ireland Maynooth, Co. Kildare, Ireland

ABSTRACT

This paper explores the viability of using a novel optical Brain-Computer Interface within a gaming environment. We describe a system that incorporates a 3D gaming engine and an optical BCI. This made it possible to classify activation in the motor cortex within a synchronous experimental paradigm. Detected activations were used to control the arm movement of a human model in the graphical engine.

1. INTRODUCTION

We demonstrate the use of an Optical Brain-Computer Interface (OBCI) within a gaming environment. A possible application for this new technology, outside the usual biomedical realm, is investigated in this paper. To date no practical application has been developed for the novel OBCI used in these experiments.

BCIs have been developed using a number of different physiological signal measurement techniques such as functional Magnetic Resonance Imaging (fMRI) [1] and electroencephalography (EEG) [2]. The BCI we will discuss is based on Near-Infrared Spectroscopy (NIRS). This system uses near-infrared light to measure the subtle and correlated changes in oxy-haemoglobin and deoxy-haemoglobin due to activation of parts of the cerebral cortex.

Potential applications of NIRS including neuroprosthesis and Human Computer Interaction (HCI) have been proposed, predominantly for the severely disabled [3]. However, applications of brain imaging BCIs for gaming have been developed using EEG [4], and fMRI [5]. In these previous studies the objective was to navigate a virtual cave or maze using thought processes alone. The subject evokes a haemodynamic response simply by carrying out a predetermined mental task such as mental arithmetic (Frontal Cortex) or mental visualization of limb movement (motor imagery in the Primary Motor Cortex / Supplementary Motor Area) [6]. The elicited signals are quite reproducible, and highly localized within specific regions of the cerebral cortex.

A single channel NIRS-BCI [3] was used for the initial experiments. The responses were passed into a graphical 3D front-end and experiments were conducted to test whether responses elicited from the system were sufficient to control a human avatar. Dual-channel motor imagery trials have been conducted, and preliminary results are presented below.

2. BACKGROUND

2.1. Near-Infrared Spectroscopy

With the advent of optical measurement of tissue oxygenation by Jobsis [7] came the possibility of cerebral haemodynamic monitoring through non-invasive means, namely Near-Infrared Spectroscopy (NIRS). A simple description of spectroscopy is that it is the study of matter using electromagnetic (EM) radiation. In the Near-Infrared region of the EM spectrum there is an optical window (600–950 nm) for light to penetrate the skull and brain tissue. Within this EM region water is largely transparent, and haemoglobin's absorption properties vary slightly depending on its oxygenation level. Light in this EM region can penetrate 2–4 cm below the scalp. Due to the similar refractive index of skull and brain tissue in the NIR region, a portion of the light not absorbed is reflected, exits the skull, and is collected by a detector.

The two main chromophores in brain tissue that are not constant absorbers and that indicate tissue oxygenation are oxy-haemoglobin (HbO) and deoxy-haemoglobin (Hb). These chromophores have different absorption coefficients depending on the wavelength of light used. Based on the analysis of the light detected after absorption and scattering in brain tissue, HbO and Hb concentrations can be determined. These concentrations are then used to assess tissue oxygenation in the region of the cerebral cortex directly below the source and detector.

With an elicited activation, e.g., movement or visualization of movement of a limb, a neurovascular process ensues resulting in changes in Cerebral Blood Flow (CBF), Cerebral Blood Volume (CBV) and Metabolic Rate of Oxygen Consumption ($CMRO_2$). The collective result is an increase in oxy-haemoglobin and decrease in deoxy-haemoglobin within the activated period. When activation ceases these levels the baseline. By monitoring these concentrations the detected activations can then be translated into commands to a device or a prosthetic limb.

2.2. Brain-Computer Interfacing.

A Brain-Computer Interface is a device which can give the user an output channel other that the normal output pathways of the brain. Physiological signals are detected from the brain and translated into commands to control an external device. A BCI can be utilized to write letters as a word processor, control a cursor or move a prosthetic limb. Implanted electrodes or surface EEG have been used within a BCI [8]. Physiological signals include visual evoked potentials, differential modulation of the α-rhythms, P300 evoked potentials (oddball response used in brain fingerprinting of convicts [9]), μ- and β-rhythms, and slow cortical potentials.

Some of these systems require a extensive user training to obtain a reasonable success rates. This can lead to frustration and even abandonment of the device. Other systems use motor imagery as the control signal [4]. However, an Optical Brain-Computer Interface [10] is less invasive, less cumbersome, and more user friendly than other functional brain imaging modalities. To date, insofar as the authors are aware, no application of an OBCI has been previously developed.

2.3. NIRS-BCI

The feasibility of the exploitation of NIRS for a BCI was explored recently with a novel OBCI [10]. This was implemented by visualization of hand movement as the control signal. As well as being non-invasive, advantages of an OBCI include high temporal resolution (100 ms), portability, no ionizing or otherwise potentially dangerous radiation, and suitability for long-term use rendering it safe even for chronic use in a neonatal monitoring [11]. In addition, it requires little or no training (first person kinesthetic imagery has been mooted to require training) [12]. The system also has the potential for use with neuroprosthesis [3] and it has been suggested in literature that a non-invasive BCI may be a more prudent approach for subjects with disabilities such as cortical atrophy [13].

Disadvantages include a lengthy time constant due to the inherent slow haemodynamic response, which limits the baud rate of the device to about 5–6 bits/minute/channel.

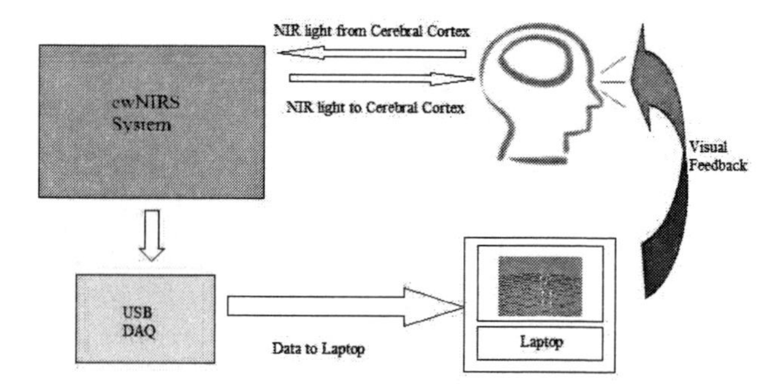

Fig. 1. Hardware Flow Diagram

Development of a multi-channel OBCI device, along with more advanced signal processing and source-detector configurations should all help to increase the system bandwidth. Altering the source detector geometry has been shown to improve spatial resolution [14]. A direct neural correlate, or Fast Event-Related Optical Response (EROS), with a temporal resolution comparable to EEG, has been discussed in the literature; however although its origins and even its existence are still highly contested [15].

3. METHODS

3.1. Hardware

The Continuous Wave NIRS (cwNIRS) system (see Figure 1) is composed of two lock-in amplifiers (Ametec 5210), an LED driver, two Avalanche Photodiodes (APD) (Hamamatsu C5460-01), function generators, and LEDs at 760 nm and 880 nm for determination of Hb and HbO, respectively. A dual-channel system was used to monitor the cerebral cortex at C3 and C4 on the primary motor cortex of the International 10-20 electrode placement system. Light from the two sources (each with a 760 nm and 880 nm LED) are driven with carrier waves ranging from 3.4–12 kHz. Infrared light penetrating the subject's head is collected by the highly sensitive APDs after being modulated by the brain, and sent to the lock-in amplifiers for demodulation, filtering, etc.

A new data collection system was introduced for these experiments. The system required more robust data acquisition as well as a simpler interface that would function under the Microsoft .NET Framework. A National Instruments USB-6009 Multi-function DAQ was used to digitize the output of the analogue filters. Commands generated by analysis of detected signals described below control the avatar. Realtime feedback is displayed for the subject. Such feedback has been shown to increase the performance of the response as the user learns to control the asymmetry of their cerebral hemispheres [16].

Initially, simple moving-average filters were used as an

online low-pass filter with a cutoff of 1 Hz. During offline experiments the data was preprocessed with different algorithms to attempt to derive the best system to implement online. (Further methods designed specifically for NIRS like the pulse regression algorithm [17] and those developed by Coyle et al. [18] will be implemented in later iterations of the software.)

3.2. Subjects and Experiments

Three subjects (all healthy, two right-handed and one left-handed, two male and one female, all 23–24 years old) participated in the experiments after giving informed consent. All subjects had normal or corrected-to-normal vision, and no pertinent medical history. Two of the subjects had no previous experience with NIRS experiments.

Each subject was placed in a supine position in a dimly lit room. The supine position is known to reduce the effect of the Mayer Wave: inherent slow oscillation thought to be due to blood pressure fluctuations and usually with a period of 10–15 sec [19]. These phenomena are a significant cause of frustration in the NIRS field, as they are the main source of physiological noise within the bandwidth of the haemodynamic response. Each subject remained still with eyes fixed on the laptop screen for commands and avatar feedback. Monitoring cortical regions C3 and C4 on the homunculus measured responses to overt motor movement or motor imagery. (Electrode positions C3 and C4 are widely accepted as being related to right and left hand movement, respectively.) Each subject was instructed to observe commands from the screen to perform or visualize performing a non-sequential finger opposition task of either the left or right hand, at a rate of 2 Hz (thumb opposing each finger in a random fashion). The user then observed the reactions of the avatar on the screen.

3.3. Gaming Engine

This system used a graphics engine originally designed for a motion tracking system [20], which presents an upright human model. This subsystem is written in C#, and allows easy real-time control of a simple human skeleton, or other geometric model. These models are laid out in a Biovision BVH file which deals with the recording and playback of motion tracking. The skeleton is drawn using the DirectX 9c libraries. Using this engine, it was straightforward to use both off- and online data to test the system.

Offline data was fed into the system initially to classify and analyze activation periods and set response intensities. In this way, it was possible to model the effect of real-time data on the system. Using different data sets that varied in quality, the system's response to both poorly- and well-defined activations could be measured and understood.

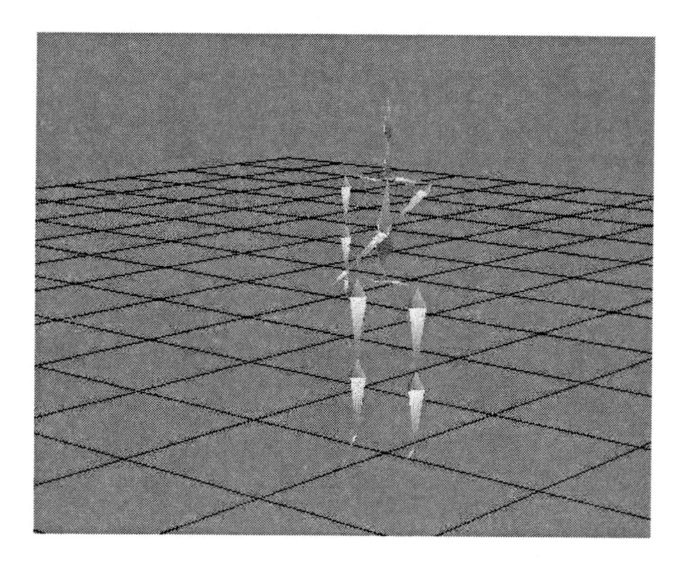

Fig. 2. Graphics Engine in Action

The first implementation of the interface within this engine induced arm movement that followed the trends of the Hb and HbO data. The left arm followed the Hb, while the right followed HbO. During online experiments the subject was encouraged to attempt to move the arms of the avatar to given positions using an overt or visualized stimulus. The software gave commands to the subject to begin activation. The model's arms would then begin to move up and down according to the haemodynamic response. During these experiments the software calculated, in real time, the concentrations of Hb and HbO from the raw light intensities using the modified Beer-Lambert law. The high frequencies were then filtered out, and the resulting trends were stored for processing within the graphical engine, and used to control the direction and intensity of the arm movement.

In a further implementation, classification of true activation was demonstrated by comparing Hb and HbO trends. The inverted correlation between these concentrations properly defined brain activation. A single-channel system would cause an arm to rise as long as a genuine activation was detected.

To implement a second channel, an optode was placed over the C4 region of the user's primary motor cortex. The data from this channel was analyzed to control the avatar's second arm in a similar fashion.

4. RESULTS

4.1. Data

The protocol for these experiments were 15 seconds rest followed by 25 seconds of stimulus, repeated 5 times. The initial 10 seconds of data was discarded. All experiments presented here are single-trial results, with no multi-trial av-

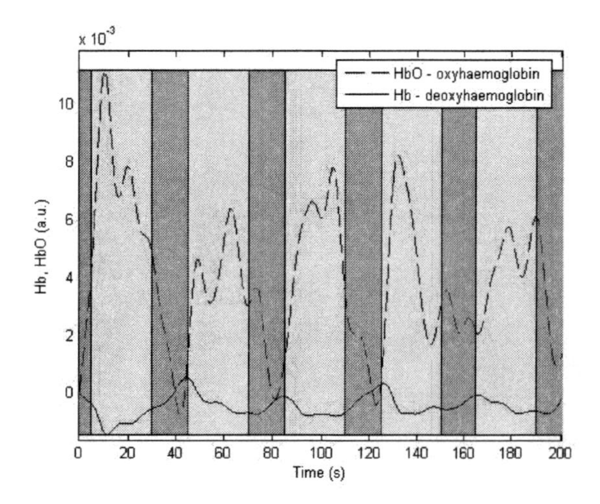

Fig. 3. Motor stimulus data from activations detected in the area under C4 during Overt Tasks

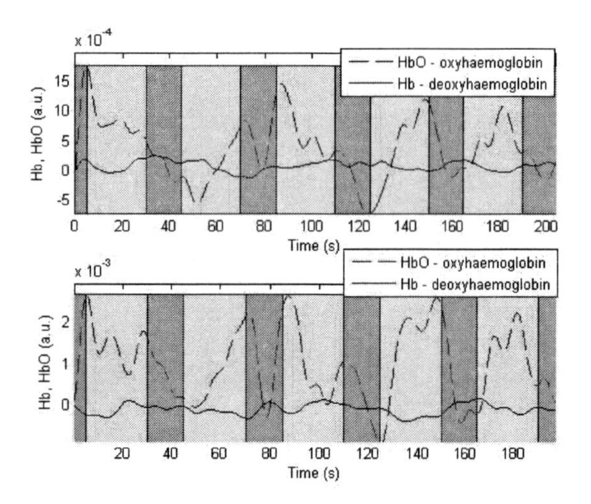

Fig. 4. Stimulus data from a dual-channel motor imagery experiment

eraging.

This system was able to classify activation in the motor cortex in a synchronous paradigm. Figure 3 shows the results from a single experiment in which data was recorded from the C4 area while the subject performed a finger opposition task. Activations can be seen as the inverse correlation of the Hb and HbO trends during stimulus periods.

Figure 4 is the result of data recorded from a dual-channel motor imagery experiment. In both channels it is apparent that the user failed to successfully visualize the task during two of the trials. This may possibly be improved by more user training and increased visual feedback.

4.2. Gameplay

The final system challenges the user to raise the arms of the avatar to a particular point. Using the dual channel setup to detect separate lateralized activation has yet to be investigated. Better classification of the response will maximize the potential for independent activation detection in an asynchronous paradigm.

The gaming system represents a significant advance in the application of OBCIs. Insofar as the authors are aware, it is the first time an OBCI has been used outside of the biomedical area. It would be possible to use the system, as it stands, in other gaming environments. The next stage of our plan is to implement the avatar negotiating a maze using motor imagery alone. At each intersection the user will be given a choice of direction. These choices will be highlighted in sequence, and the user will be instructed to visualize movement while the direction they wish to turn or proceed in is highlighted.

5. CONCLUSION

This above data would seem to indicate that an Optical Brain-Computer Interface based on near-infrared spectroscopy shows promise for simple gaming. A single-channel system can exert control in the gaming environment with similar accuracy to that of previous testing applications [3]. The limitations of a single-channel implementation, such as the low bit rate, restricts the possible complexity of the applications. We have demonstrated that imagined arm movement on the part of the subject can be translated into arm movement of a model in a game. Although the dual-channel experiments are still in their infancy, results have shown that with better signal processing and classification techniques it should be possible to integrate the system into a gaming experience.

Acknowledgments

Support for this work was provided by grants from Science Foundation Ireland (SFI), grants from the Higher Education Authority of Ireland (HEA), and fellowships from IRCSET. Special thanks to Ger Barrett and Aoife Cuddihy for their assistance and council.

6. REFERENCES

[1] N. Weiskopf, K. Mathiak, S. W. Bock, F. Scharnowski, R. Veit, W. Grodd, R. Goebel, and N. Birbaumer, "Principles of a brain-computer interface (BCI) based on real-time functional magnetic resonance imaging (fMRI)," *IEEE Transactions on Biomedical Engineering*, vol. 51, no. 6, pp. 966–70, June 2004.

[2] C. Guger, A. Schlögl, C. Neuper, D. Walterspacher, T. Strein, and G. Pfurtscheller, "Rapid prototyping of an EEG-based brain-computer interface (BCI)," *IEEE Transations On Neural Systems And Rehabilitation Engineering*, vol. 9, no. 1, pp. 49–58, 2001.

[3] S. Coyle, "Near-infrared spectroscopy for brain computer interfacing," Ph.D. dissertation, National University of Ireland, Maynooth, 2005.

[4] G. Pfurtscheller, R. Leeb, C. Keinrath, D. Friedman, C. Neuper, C. Guger, and M. Slater, "Walking from thought," *Brain Research*, vol. 1071, no. 1, pp. 145–52, 2006.

[5] S.-S. Yoo, T. Fairneny, N.-K. Chen, S.-E. Choo, L. P. Panych, H. Park, S.-Y. Lee, and F. A. Jolesz, "Brain-computer interface using fMRI: Spatial navigation by thoughts," *Neuroreport*, vol. 15, no. 10, pp. 1591–5, 2004.

[6] R. Beisteiner, P. Höllinger, G. Lindinger, W. Lang, and A. Berthoz, "Mental representations of movements. brain potentials associated with imagination of hand movements," *Electroencephalogr. Clin. Neurophysiol.*, vol. 96, no. 2, pp. 183–93, Mar. 1995.

[7] F. F. Jobsis, "Noninvasive infrared monitoring of cerebral and myocardial oxygen sufficiency and circulatory parameters," *Science*, vol. 198, no. 4323, pp. 1264–7, 1977.

[8] J. R. Wolpaw, D. J. McFarland, and T. N. Vaughan, "Brain-computer interface research at the Wadsworth Center," *IEEE Trans Rehabil Eng*, vol. 8, no. 2, pp. 222–6, June 2000.

[9] L. A. Farwell and S. S. Smith, "Using brain MERMER testing to detect concealed knowledge despite efforts to conceal," *Journal of Forensic Sciences*, vol. 46, no. 1, pp. 1–9, Jan. 2001.

[10] S. Coyle, T. Ward, C. Markham, and G. McDarby, "On the suitability of near-infrared (NIR) systems for next-generation brain-computer interfaces," *Physiol. Meas.*, vol. 25, no. 4, pp. 815–22, July 2004.

[11] A. Bozkurt and B. Onaral, "Safety assessment of near infrared light emitting diodes for diffuse optical measurements," *Biomed Eng Online*, vol. 3, no. 1, p. 9, 2004.

[12] C. Neuper, R. Scherer, M. Reiner, and G. Pfurtscheller, "Imagery of motor actions: differential effects of kinesthetic and visual-motor mode of imagery in single-trial EEG," *Brain Res Cogn Brain Res*, vol. 25, no. 3, pp. 668–77, Dec. 2005.

[13] R. A. Bakay, "Limits of brain-computer interface. case report," *Neurosurg. Focus.*, vol. 20, no. 5, p. E6, 2006.

[14] D. A. Boas, K. Chen, D. Grebert, and M. A. Franceschini, "Improving the diffuse optical imaging spatial resolution of the cerebral hemodynamic response to brain activation in humans," *Opt Lett*, vol. 29, no. 13, pp. 1506–8, 2004.

[15] J. Steinbrink, F. C. D. Kempf, A. Villringer, and H. Obrig, "The fast optical signal—robust or elusive when non-invasively measured in the human adult?" *Neuroimage*, vol. 26, no. 4, pp. 996–1008, 2005.

[16] C. Guger, A. Schlögl, C. Neuper, D. Walterspacher, T. Strein, and G. Pfurtscheller, "Rapid prototyping of an EEG-based brain-computer interface (BCI)," *IEEE Trans Neural Syst Rehabil Eng*, vol. 9, no. 1, pp. 49–58, 2001.

[17] G. Gratton and P. M. Corballis, "Removing the heart from the brain: Compensation for the pulse artifact in the photon migration signal," *Psychophysiology*, vol. 32, no. 3, pp. 292–9, May 1995.

[18] S. Coyle, T. Ward, and C. Markham, "Physiological noise in near-infrared spectroscopy: Implications for optical brain computer interfacing," in *The 26th Annual International Conference of the IEEE Engineering in Medicine and Biology Society*, San Francisco, CA, Sept. 2004.

[19] C. E. Elwell, R. Springett, E. Hillman, and D. T. Delpy, "Oscillations in cerebral haemodynamics: Implications for functional activation studies," *Adv Exp Med Biol*, vol. 471, pp. 57–65, 1999.

[20] J. Foody, D. Kelly, D. Fitzgeralg, B. Caulfield, and C. Markham, "A real time motion capture system, using USB based tri-axis magnetic and inertial sensors," in *The IET Irish Signals and Systems Conference 2006*, Dublin, Ireland, June 2006.

SINBA – A new approach for Modeling Social Behaviors in Interactive NPCs

Roberto Cezar Bianchini* and Romero Tori†
Interactive Technologies Lab,
Politechnic School, University of São Paulo

Keywords
Agents Architecture, BDI, Human-Interaction, Emotions, Social Agents

Abstract

This paper presents SINBA, an architecture to Non-Player Characters (NPCs) based on the BDI model with the inclusion of emotions and social rules in the inference process. The architecture also includes *Anytime Algorithm* to improve the efficiency in the response in the very dynamical environments of Computer Games. SINBA is proposed to handle very interactive and cooperative situations between human players and NPCs.

1 Introduction

The increase in the processing capacity of computers has led the visual quality of computer games to a very realistic level [1]. The expansion of high speed networks has also allowed that the activities in games could be shared by dozens, hundreds and even thousands of players at the same time. These improvements in the technology have changed games from solitary interaction with simple shining patterns on the monochromatic screens to a multiplayer interaction with realistic graphics, spacial sound, hundreds of entertaining tasks to do, and many others.

Games are also populated by characters controlled by human players or algorithms. When they are controlled by algorithms, these characters receive the name of Game Agents or Non-Player Characters (NPCs). The improvement in the other areas and the possibility to interact with other human players, with unexpected behaviors, tend to generate expectations in human players that NPCs should also have behaviors as good as the quality of the images they see [2].

Some proposals had appeared to make the behavior of the NPCs more complex. Laird et al uses the SOAR architecture to control NPCs in commercial games, and to make them as skillful as a human player [3]. Kaminga et all use techniques of Multiagent Systems to turn commercial games into an educative experience [4]. Nareyek et all use planning models to develop NPCs with directed behaviors the objectives [5].

This paper presents an agent architec-

*robertob@emailaccount.com
†romero.tori@usp.br

ture based on the Belief-Desire-Intention (BDI) model [6] to control NPCs in non physical simulated fighting situations, for example like in first person shooter games [7]. These situations are very often found when the NPCs have to support the player finish some task. The architecture is called Social and Interactive Npcs based on a BDI Architecture (SINBA).

2 SINBA Architecture

SINBA is a hybrid architecture, with deliberative and reactive processing. The reactive processing is used to handle simple situations that do not require great amount of processing, or when the response needed must be available very fast. Any fast technique or algorith, Finite State Machines for example, can be used in the reactive process. The deliberative one is done by a modified BDI model. SINBA architecture will be explained in two parts: Structural and Logical Components.

2.1 Structural Components

Figure 1 shows the structural components of SINBA.

The *Sensor* component perceives the changes in the environment and receives the messages from other players and NPCs. *Actuator* acts in the environment in order to fulfill the desires of a SINBA NPC. *Level of Detail* (LOD) uses the informations contained in *Sensor* to decide between the *Reactive System* or the deliberative system to handle the stimulus perceived. The decision is based on the nature of the stimulus and on the internal state of the NPC stored in the *Personality Component*. If the *Reactive System* is chosen, it selects one *Behavior* object from *Behavior Lib* and send it to *Actuator* without any sort of modification.

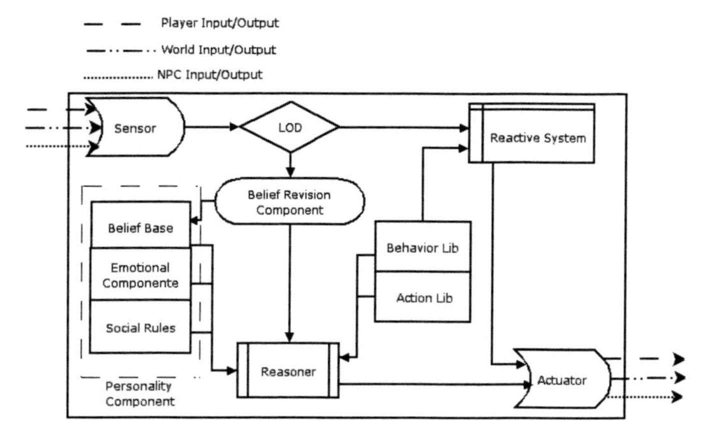

Figure 1: Structural Components of the SINBA architecture.

In the case that the deliberative system is chosen, LOD sends the informations received by *Sensor* to *Belief Revision Component*. This component analysis the current beliefs stored in the *Belief Base* component in order to remove the inconsistencies between the previous believes and the new information gathered. Besides *Belief Base*, *Personality Component* is also composed by the emotions the NPC may have, stored in the *Emotional Component*, and the *Social Rules* the NPC respects.

Reasoner is the component with the inferential algorithm BDI that generates the desires and intentions (the *Behaviors* in the SINBA architecture). The intentions may be chosen by previously *Behaviors* stored in the *Behavior Lib* or may be generated on the fly by *Reasoner*. After the *Behavior* is chosen, *Reasoner* modifies its components, and adapt it to the beliefs, desires, emotions and social rules of the NPC.

2.2 Logical Components

Logical components are the objects which allow the structural ones to exchange informations with each other. SINBA has three logical components: *Context, Action* e *Behavior*. These objects are predicates of first order logic and are used by *Reasoner* in the inference process. They are defined as:

Context = (PreconditionList, PosConditionList, InternalState).

Action = (Name, Target, MovementState, Feature).

MovementState = (Type, Velocity, Orientation).

Feature = (Animation, Sound, Message).

Behavior = List(Actions).

PreConditonList e *PosConditionList* are lists with informations that the NPC believes are true before the *Behavior* becomes active and the informations that the NPC desires to be true after the execution of the *Behavior*, respectively. *InternalState* is used by *Reasoner* to infer the believes, objectives, emotions are valid to the *Context* perceived.

Actions represent what the NPC can carry out in the environment, and they are stored in the *Action Lib*. Each *Action* has a *Name*, a *Target*, the object which will receive the effects of this *Action*, and a *MovimentState*, which states the type of the movement the NPC – walking, flying, running – and its features – velocity, orientation –. *Features* are related to the parameters that customize the *Action*: the visual representation of the *MovimentaState*, *Animation*, the *Sound*, some message that should be sent to some other player in the game.

Behavior is a list of *Actions*, that might be created by the designers previously or may be generated on the fly by *Reasoner*, selecting *Actions* from *Action Lib*, and defines how the global behavior of the NPC is in some context. The *Behaviors* created on the fly can be stored in the *Behavior Lib*.

2.3 Execution of SINBA

Figure 2.3 shows the functioning of the SINBA architecture.

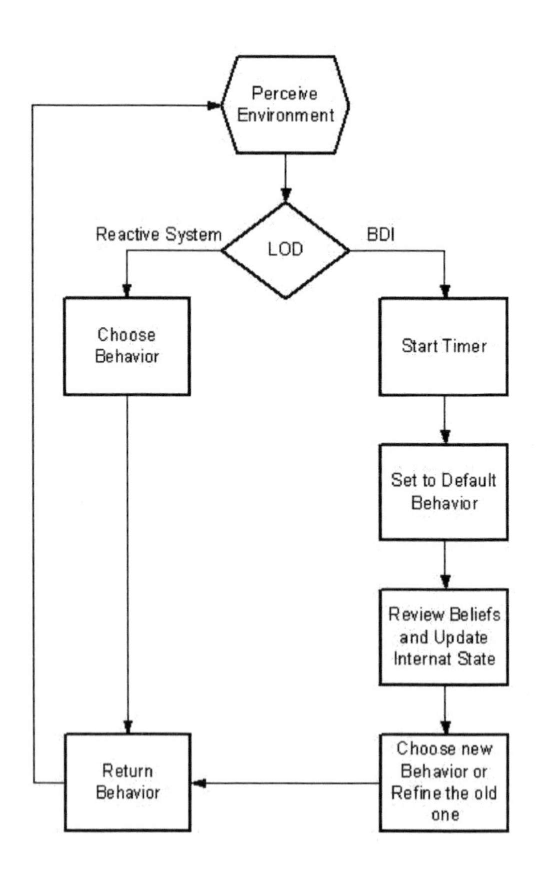

Figure 2: Algorithm of SINBA.

Sensor perceives the environment, parses these perceptions and sends them to *LOD*, which defines whether the *ReactiveSystem* or the deliberative system should be used to choose the best *Behavior* to handle what the NPC perceived. When *ReactiveSystem* is chosen, it uses simple rules to select one *Behavior* from *Behavior Lib* and then sends it without any modification to *Actuator*.

If *Reasoner* is chosen, *LOD* starts a timer. SINBA uses the concept of anytime algorithms [8] in order to always have a plane to handle the very dynamical environment of computer games. When the time is over, timer tells *Reasoner* to stop the inference process and sends the *Behavior* in its current state to *Actuator*. When *Reasoner* receives back the control of the CPU, it can improve the last plane, *Behavior*, or it can selects another one.

After the timer starts, *LOD* sets the *Behavior* to be returned by *Reasoner* to a default one, which may be the *Behavior* from the last inference cycle or another one defined by the designers. Timer can stop the inference process anytime from now on. After the default behavior is set, *Belief Revision Component* updates the *Belief Base* with informations *Sensor* received and remove inconsistences from the base.

Reasoner then updates the *InternalState*, the objectives and desires of the NPC, and uses these informations to refine the last *Behavior*, or selects a new one from *Behavior Lib*, or generates a new *Behavior* with *Actions* stored in *Action Lib*. The *Behavior* determined is then send to *Actuator* and the cycle may restart again.

3 Discussion

BDI is a model of agency proposed to infer, moment to moment, which action an agent/NPC should carry out to reach its objectives. In most of the cases, situations evolving human interaction do not result from a process of problem solution, and a pure BDI approach to the problem would limit its application in games.

Emotions influence people's decision process [9]. Using emotions in the inference process brings a bigger range of reactions NPCs can show when interacting with human beings, enriching the gameplay. Also, Suleiman et al [10] argue that the social aspect is an important factor when humans interact with each other. People tend to regard the social context in their process of deciding what to do, not only their desires.

Emotions and social rules can be viewed as additional desires the agent can use to reason which new intention should be selected. When a SINBA agent is reasoning which intention it should be commit to, it considers not only its believes and desires, but also its emotions and social rules. They modify the weight of the rules in the BDI reasoning process, suppressing or emphasizing the tendency to select specific intentions.

With emotions and social rules, the NPCs have more parameters besides rational ones to decide what actions it should do to achieve their desires. Although it is possible to achieve these results with traditional Game AI techniques, say Finite State Machines, using BDI model with emtions and social rules favours formalizing more human-like behaviors.

4 Conclusion

This paper presented SINBA, an hybrid agent architecture for NPCs, with deliberative and reactive inference processing. The deliberative processing is made with the BDI model with emotions and social rules influencing the decisions of the NPC. SINBA is proposed to more interactive and non-combative situations between human players and NPCs, but its hybrid nature, together with anytime algorithms, makes it useful in other types of interactions. Next steps include an implementation of SINBA in a computer game and tests with typical aspects of human-NPC interaction.

5 Biography

Figure 3: Roberto Cezar Bianchini.

Roberto Cezar Bianchini. Graduated in Physics, whit Masters Degree in Applied Physics and PhD in Computer Engineering. Research in the college involves numerical simulation and scientific visualization of Proteins and his Masters Degree was in Computation Fluid Dynaminc, simulation and visualization of reactive flow. In the PhD thesis, he proposed a new architecture for Game Agents using BDI model of inference, which included Affective Computing in the deliberative process. Topics of interest include Artificial Intelligence applied to Computer Games, Emergent Systems, Affective Computing and Real Time Rendering.

Dr. Romero Tori is Associate Professor at University of Sao Paulo (USP), a Full Professor at SENAC University, and general manager of Interlab (Interactive Technologies Laboratory) at USP. Research areas of interest: game technology, virtual and augmented reality, technology in education.

Figure 4: Romero Tori.

References

[1] Theresa-Marie Rhyne. Computer Games and Scientific Visualization. *Communicatins of the ACM*, 45(7):40–44, 2002.

[2] R. Zubek. Towards Implementation of Social Interaction. In *Proceedings of the 2000 AAAI Spring Symposium on Artificial Intelligence and Intercative Entertainment.* AAAI Press, 2000.

[3] John E. Laird. It knows what you're going to do: adding anticipation to

a Quakebot. In Jörg P. Müller, Elisabeth Andre, Sandip Sen, and Claude Frasson, editors, *Proceedings of the Fifth International Conference on Autonomous Agents*, pages 385–392, Montreal, Canada, 2001. ACM Press.

[4] R. Adobbati, A. N. Marshall, A. Scholer, S. Tejada, G. A. Kaminka, S. Schagger, and S. Sollito. Gamebots: A 3d virtual world test bed for multiagent research. In *Proceedings of the Second International WorkShop on Infrastructure for Agents, MAS and Scalable MAS*, Montreal, Canada, 2001.

[5] Alexander Nareyek. Intelligent Agents for Computer Games. In *Computer and Games, Second International Conference*, pages 414–422, 2002.

[6] Georgeff, Barney Pell, Martha Pollack, Milind Tambe and Mike Wooldridge. The Belief-Desire-Intention Model of Agency. In *Proceedings of the 5th International Workshop on Intelligent Agents V: Agent Theories, Architectures, and Languages (ATAL-98*, volume 1555, pages 1–10, Heidelberg, Germany, 1998. Spring-Verlag.

[7] Bianchini, R. C. *A BDI Architecture of Interactive Behaviors of Agents in Computer Games.* PhD thesis, Escola Politécnica, Universidade de São Paulo, 2005. In portuguese.

[8] Alexander Nareyek. Intelligent Agents for Computer Games. In *Computer and Games, Second International Conference*, pages 414–422, 2002.

[9] Sloman, A., R. Chrisley and M. Scheutz. *Who Needs Emotions?: The Brain Meets the Machine*, chapter The Architectural Basis of Affective States and Process. Oxford University Press, 2005.

[10] Ramzi Suleiman, Klaus G. Troitzsch, and G. Nigel Gilbert, editors. *Tools and Techniques for Social Science Simulation [Dagstuhl Seminar, May 5-9, 1997].* Physica-Verlag, 2000.

MULTIMEDIA APPLICATIONS FOR WIRELESS ENVIRONMENTS

Moira J. McAlister and Wei Li
School of Computing & Information Engineering, University of Ulster
Coleraine, Co. Londonderry, N. Ireland, UK
E-mail: ***m.mcalister@ulster.ac.uk***
E-mail: ***Li-W@ulster.ac.uk***

KEYWORDS
Data Streaming, Mobile Devices, Wireless Networks.

ABSTRACT

With the availability of interface cards, mobile users are no longer required to be confined within static network premises in order to get network access. Mobile users may move from one place to another and yet maintain transparent access through wireless links. Information exchanged between users can include voice, data, image, audio, video or any combination although the restrictions of any mobile device to transmit such rich data are limited by its scope and range. This paper uses the results of initial simulation experiments to analyse what types of mobile devices users are limited to, the approach which can be used to design the multimedia applications and the data representations most suited to multimedia applications for current mobile devices. The paper will then discuss what developments in wireless technology are needed to enhance future dynamic multimedia applications for mobile technology.

INTRODUCTION

A subject that has been gaining interest is that of handling multimedia data on mobile devices. The issue is a recurring theme which requires regular evaluation since continuous evolutions in hardware and software technology dictate that the perception of what can be achieved rapidly becomes outdated. A previous survey highlighted the fact that current mobile devices do not provide a suitable platform for activities such as online gaming but developments expected in 2006 would cause this to be re-evaluated (McAlister and Wilson, 2005). The constant changing position has a subsequent impact on the type of software applications which are developed for mobile platforms such as educational environments which want to utilize mobile technology by exploiting developments that significantly address the needs of others such as gamers.

The authors therefore decided to use simulation experiments to analyse the extent to which current mobile technology addressed the perceived limitations of range, bandwidth, encoding and network availability to provide an end-to-end quality of service that will allow multimedia data to be streamed effectively across current wireless networks. The results are summarized to address a number of key questions including: What types of devices provide a stable hardware platform for multimedia data? What are the Quality of Service (QoS) requirements for wireless networks? What types of data are suited to particular mobile devices? How can the quality of communication be improved? What level of interaction is possible between the devices? The answers to the questions describe an interesting picture which illustrated how multimedia applications such as learning environments could be best represented on current and future wireless technology.

WIRELESS TRENDS

As mobile devices gain popularity communication options for these devices have matured allowing wireless networking technologies to gain widespread use. A number of standards have been defined including Bluetooth and 802.11a, b and g. Bluetooth works in 2.4GHz spectrums and operate within a small range of low bandwidth. Thus it is not applicable for multimedia applications with large data volume. 802.11b and g operate at 2.4GHz while 802.11a operates at 5GHz regions with a smaller range. 802.11b has a bandwidth of 11Mbps while the other two standards have a higher bandwidth of 54Mbps. Thus 802.11a and g can support more simultaneous users with higher data rates than 802.11b. 802.11a and g also operate in hybrid modes allowing 802.11a channels to be used to deliver video data packets and 802.11g channels for text providing a bandwidth which is sufficient for interactive access of multimedia databases. In this way current advances in communications technology are creating an environment where common handheld devices can run basic applications. However, multimedia applications create new dimensions which place more demands on the devices and the network technologies. Future mobile networks have to address the transmission of multimedia traffic as a mandatory requirement among heterogeneous networks.

The implications for the Internet which will be expected to provide a wide range of services to a user means that it must be able to allow seamless transition from a geographically fixed environment into a mobile environment. The wireless mobile Internet is not just an extension of Internet services into the mobile environment giving users access to the Internet services while they are on the move. It is about integrating the Internet and telecommunications technologies into a single system that covers all communication needs. The transition from the traditional wired Internet to the wireless Internet will require network protocols and network architecture to change dramatically.

The main motivations for the changes needed in next generation network technologies are:

1. Demand for better availability of services and applications.
2. Global connectivity.
3. Rapid increase in the number of subscribers who want to use the same handheld terminal while roaming.
4. Support for bandwidth intensive applications such as real-time multimedia, online games and videoconferencing as well as traditional voice services (VoIP).

The scalable and distributed 4G network architecture consequently required must offer any-type services over a diverse set of places such as indoor, outdoor, pedestrian and vehicular. These services will be offered over a large range of overlapping access networks including WLAN, 2G, 3G, xDSL, DVB, DAB, DVB and so on that offer different rates, coverage, bandwidth, delay and packet loss (Frodigh, 2001 and (Kellerer, 2002). The key features necessary to achieve these expectations include (Jamalipour, 2005):

1. Mobile terminals which auto-configure to the specific access technology at the location
2. Subscribers who will have access to the various services offered yet enjoy wired LAN QoS, cost and security.
3. The development of QoS management schemes which offer ubiquitous and seamless connectivity.
4. Limits in the changes required for multi-access mobile terminals in terms of hardware and software which reduce the investments made by the subscriber.

In the area of mobile information usage these requirements help to define the term mobility from the user's perspective. The user can simply be in motion or work in a non-office environment with mobile digital equipment. In either case the quality of the information which can be handled by mobile devices enables the user's attention to be maintained while working on several tasks in parallel. The information system would no longer restrict a user to rather specific information that was needed in a certain situation. Instead focus could be placed on context management and the concept of the situation (Grimm, 2002).

Provision of such flexibility therefore enhance the capabilities of the network from the user's perspective and enable it to handle affects such as delay, jitter, bandwidth, availability and packet loss rate more effectively. For critical applications such as multimedia this can include video rate, video smoothness, picture detail, picture colour accuracy audio quality; cost and security. However, multimedia applications impose a great burden to the underlying network in terms of bandwidth resources and non-elastic traffic. E-learning applications, for example, generate non-elastic traffic that must be protected from the Internet's best effort traffic. Thus, the allocation of resources must be dynamic and more adaptable to the changes of the state of the network.

THE INVESTIGATION

Multimedia is a combining and pervasive technology which comprises communication, broadcast and computer data. The features of the data include its size, type, format, level of interaction and distribution. To ensure that mobile devices can handle multimedia files the equipment must satisfy two requirements; first, sending and receiving data and second, sufficient memory to store media files. One of the main challenges in mobile multimedia data streaming is the requirement that the link must be continuously available for a period of time to enable uninterrupted data transmission and a smooth media performance. The authors therefore conducted an investigation which focused on simulation experiments that could be used to evaluate the effectiveness of current mobile devices to handle multimedia data. The authors chose a range of mobile devices including PDAs, standard mobile phones and smart-phones which represented the most commonly used mobile devices and provided a basis from which to extrapolate the results of the simulation experiments to predict future usage. The experiments were lab based and the authors defined a basic network environment of the mobile devices, traffic types and applications which best modelled real world usage of the platforms.

Study Material Design Approaches

Two approaches were used to design the simulation experiments: Non-Interactive and Interactive. Each approach addresses a particular type of application such as a website for non-interactive or a game for interactive. Prior to the investigation the authors speculated that most mobile devices would handle non-interactive application well but that interactive applications would illustrate some differences.

The non-interactive approach required the client terminal to send a control signal when it wanted to access multimedia data. The server validated the signal and sent the requested data. See Figure 1.

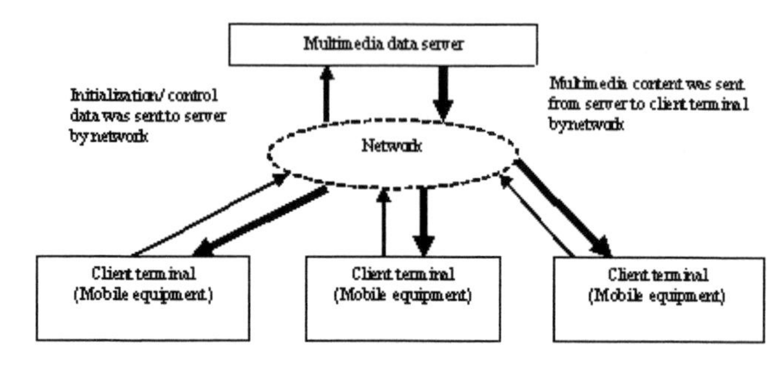

Figure 1: Non-Interactive Approach

The interactive approach required real-time data which was less tolerant of errors. The client sent a signal to have the information renewed to the server. The server validated the signal and ensured that the client could see the renewed information. See Figure 2.

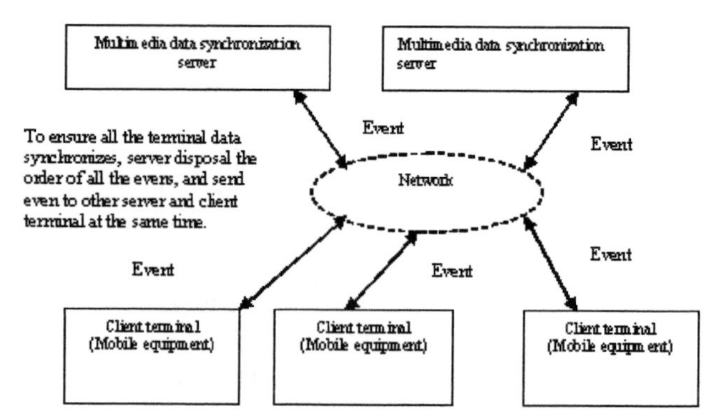

Figure 2: Interactive Approach

The running system had to satisfy a number of criteria:

1. Interfacing with other servers or applications.
2. Shielding terminals since each terminal could use a different processor or protocol.
3. Dynamic bandwidth configuration which reflects the user's current network state.
4. Management of the media streaming operation.

Platform

The Sun Microsystems application Java 2 Micro Edition (J2ME) is designed for use within mobile devices and is a suitable choice for the domain. It provided an application developing environment that was transplantable, secure, managed limited memory capability for a device and provided connection ability within the network. The storage restriction of the majority of wireless devices was handled by the Record Management System (RMS). The RMS provided an input database storage system that allowed transfer of permanent memory storage data.

EVALUATION

The results of the initial simulation experiments were designed to evaluate one of the standard issues related to multimedia data streaming, namely media content delivery. The function of streaming data requires considerable resources which can cause problems including net block, server overloading and error acceptance. Highly compressed streams of data are sensitive to transmission errors which seriously affect the data transmission rate. The simulation experiments therefore evaluated how effectively currently commonly used mobile devices handled rich data.

The experiments focused on four types of transmission including text, graphics/images, web connections and applications software which reflect the main data types.

Text

When operating, the page is as shown in Figure 1. The message theme is input, destination address and content added. Since the sent message would be counted on the Internet, a security alert page would appear which would require permitting access to the internet link. In order to know if the message had been sent successfully, the receiving program would then check the received message.

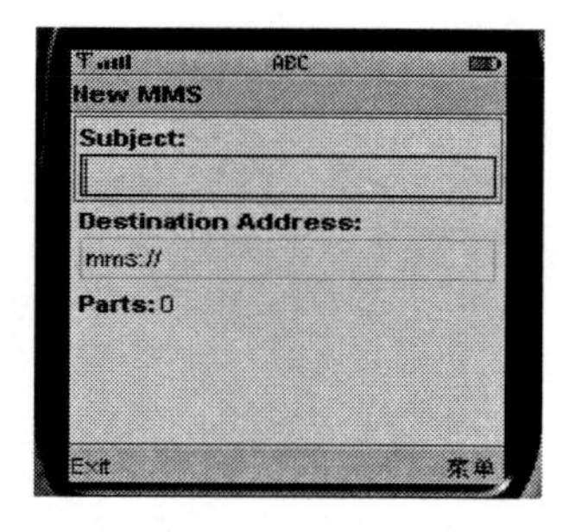

Figure 1: Sending & Receiving SMS

The reason for experimenting with such a simple task was to allow the mobile devices to be assessed across a range of data types. For example, a short message with 160 bytes created on a Samsung D608 by the sender cannot be successfully transmitted to a receiver using a Nokia 8250 since packet loss occurs when a message is being transmitted or received as the Nokia 8250 only allows 70 bytes input per SMS message. Messages therefore have to be divided into several sequential smaller messages.

Graphics/Images

The test with graphics/images produced a similar result as shown in Figure 2.

Figure 2: Sending & Receiving Images

HTTP Connection

The purpose of the test was to confirm the status of the server. To make use of the HTTP end user agreement communication and TCP agreement communication, the Tomcat agreement with the HTTP agent was used to create a communication bridge between the user and server. In this way the agent takes use of the HTTP agreement to communicate with the end user but takes use of the TCP agreement to communicate with the server.

Applications Software

As mobile equipment and wireless networks limit the setup of wireless applications systems compared to most desktops J2ME designs the user end to operate at the lowest request of the Mobile Information Device Profile which is part of the J2ME application development environment. The profile defines the hardware and software framework and then provides the associated basic function and interface standard. The MIDP therefore applies itself to neatly add its environment into the layer of existing software. The result of downloading application software through the J2ME Wireless Toolkit is shown in Figure 3.

Figure 3: Downloading Applications Software

FUTURE OF WIRELESS DATA STREAMING

The initial experiments illustrated that although a variety of data can be downloaded across a range of selected mobile devices a number of research areas still need to be investigated in order to define standards for wireless transmission. The research areas include:

1. Integration of all existing and future communication access systems through a common IPv6 protocol.
2. Development of a modular and scalable architecture with well defined distributed network functionalities.

3. Development of effective mobility, resource and QoS management schemes to offer seamless connectivity and end-to-end QoS peer end terminals.
4. Development of physical architecture of a QoS enabled mobile terminal capable of accessing the Internet and real-time services over a multitude of access technologies.
5. Offering similar services (subject to network capacity and service policy) in both home visited networks based on preferences and service agreements in the subscription.

The implications of using these devices for multimedia applications to deliver non-trivial software means that the type of material, interaction level, profiling or feedback which could now be provided is not limited to the platform on which the information is available since the generic nature of the developments for wireless media are reducing the gap between hardware and software.

CONCLUSIONS

Clearly there has been a significant improvement in terms of handling rich data including multimedia messages and video services. However, there are limitations such as communication channels with limited bandwidth, the need for efficient architectures, better transcoding and improved compression of multimedia data under changing conditions especially when a very large number of clients are present. This aspect is further exasperated when users are moving around causing increased stress on already stretched networks. Limitations between devices has become significantly reduced and provided a solid base on which software developers can construct non-trivial software which addresses goal setting, pace, distributed environments and presentation/assessment. The complete simulation results should enable the authors to predict how effectively future mobile devices will be able to handle rich multimedia data.

References

[1] Frodigh, M 2001 "Future Generation Wireless Networks" IEEE Personal Communications 8(5) 10-17.

[2] Grimm, M et. al. 2002 "Towards a Framework for Mobile Knowledge Management" Proceedings of Practical Aspects of Knowledge Management 326-338.

[3] Jamalipour, A and Lorenz, P 2005 "End-toEnd QoS Support for IP and Multimedia Traffic in Heterogeneous Mobile Networks", Computer Communications 1-12.

[4] Kellerer, W 2002 "A Communication Gateway for Infrastructure-Independent 4G Wireless Access" IEEE Communications Magazine 40(3) 126-131.

[5] McAlister, M. J. & Wilson, P., "Has a Wireless Online Gaming Environment a Future?", CGAMES2005-7th International Conference on Computer Games: AI, Animation, Mobile, Educational & Serious Games, France, November 2005, Proceedings CGAMES2005, pp314-317.

BIOGRAPHY

Moira McAlister joined the University of Ulster, Coleraine, as a lecturer in Computer Science in 2003. Before that she worked in Germany at Trend Micro (2000-2003) as the Global Training Services Manager developing the company's online and offline training programme. She was also employed as a contractor to the Business Systems section at Philips (2000) in The Netherlands. From 1992-2000 she was a senior lecturer at the University of Sunderland responsible for teaching and developing a range of modules including project management, Operations Research and programming for undergraduate and postgraduate courses, research on specialized applications software in conjunction with local industry, research on educational applications at the university and as a consultant/trainer for the business wing of the School of Computing and Engineering, University of Sunderland. At Ulster, she is responsible for teaching modules on networks, developing e-Learning modules and projects at undergraduate and postgraduate level. Her current research interests are focused on using digital games to build interactive learning environments. She is a founder member of the Games Research Group at the University of Ulster.

AI Tools

A SET OF GUIDELINES FOR THE EVALUATION OF REAL-TIME MACHINE LEARNING TECHNIQUES FOR USE IN DIGITAL GAMES

Leo Galway, Darryl Charles, Michaela Black
School of Computing & Information Engineering
University of Ulster, Coleraine Campus
BT52 1SA, N. Ireland
Email: {galway-l1, dk.charles, mm.black}@ulster.ac.uk

KEYWORDS
machine learning, real-time, evaluation criteria

ABSTRACT

Digital games use a variety of Artificial Intelligence (AI) techniques within dynamic, real-time environments. However, the majority of AI approaches used lead to predefined and predictable computer controlled character behaviours, with no capability to learn from the behaviour or playing style of the player. The incorporation of real-time machine learning techniques is vital to the digital games industry in order to improve the reactive behaviours of computer controlled characters and to tailor game-play to the individual player. Nonetheless, the use of real-time learning raises a number of issues and concerns for game design and development. In this paper we outline a set of guidelines that may be applied during the evaluation of machine learning techniques to be used for real-time learning within digital games.

INTRODUCTION

Representing a departure from traditional board and card games, digital games make use of increasingly complex and detailed virtual environments, often incorporating many computer controlled characters or opponents (*game agents*) which require an ever more realistic and believable set of behaviours for a game engine's AI sub-system (*game AI*) to generate (Schaeffer and Van den Herik 2002). By utilizing a percentage of the overall computational resources used within a game, typically dictated by genre specific computational requirements, game AI facilitates the autonomous selection of actions for game agents through game specific perception, navigation and decision making sub-systems (Woodcock 2002). Both traditional and modern AI techniques have been adopted by game developers and incorporated into game AI, including the use of rule-based systems for goal planning, finite state machines and neural networks for behavioural control, evolutionary algorithms for game engine parameter tuning and the A* algorithm for path-planning (Van Lent and Laird 1999; Charles and McGlinchey 2004; Schwab 2004). However, the majority of existing game AI implementations are primarily constrained to the production of predefined decision making and control systems, often leading to predictable and static game agent responses (Charles 2003). Attempts to incorporate machine learning into game AI have been restricted to the use of learning and optimisation techniques during game development (*offline learning*), with only a handful of commercial digital games, including "Creatures", "Black & White" and "Virtua Fighter 4" (Grand et al. 1996; Evans 2001; Graepel et al. 2004), providing the ability to perform in-game learning (*online learning*). Through the use of online learning, game AI may be enhanced with a capability to dynamically learn from mistakes, player strategies and game-play behaviours in real-time, thus providing a more engaging and entertaining game-play experience. However, the use of online learning raises a number of issues and concerns regarding the choice of a learning algorithm suitable for online use, and the effects the integration of online learning will have on both game design and development (Manslow 2002).

While the overriding goal of utilising machine learning techniques is to enhance the entertainment value of digital games, this paper does not aim to address game specific uses of machine learning. Rather, the objective of this paper is to provide a set of guidelines to aid in the evaluation of machine learning techniques for potential online use within digital game environments and to present a preliminary evaluation of the most commonly discussed machine learning techniques found in the digital game research literature.

ONLINE LEARNING APPROACHES AND ASSOCIATED ISSUES AND CONSTRAINTS

Although problems for which learning may be applied are both game and genre specific, two main approaches to the use of online learning exist: learning information from the player (*player-centric learning*) and learning information from the game environment and game agents (*environment-centric learning*). In the player-centric approach, information about the behaviour and playing style of the player may be implicitly or explicitly learned in order to allow game agents to improve their responses for future interactions with the player. Similarly, player-centric learning may be used to perform statistical analysis of the player for the purpose of player profiling in order that game-play can be tailored to the individual (Charles 2003).

In the environment-centric approach, both information about the state of the game environment and information pertaining to game agent behaviours may be implicitly or explicitly learned in order for game agents to improve or select more appropriate behaviours for future interactions with the player or other game agents.

Issues and Constraints for the Use of Online Learning

In order to determine a set of criteria for the evaluation of machine learning techniques, the constraints and concerns inherent in the use of online learning within digital games must first be considered. Research has shown that a player's interest in a game can be partially considered as the product of interactions with game agents within a game environment (Yannakakis and Hallam 2004), where the game environment is characteristically nondeterministic and dynamic (Spronck 2005), containing multiple game agents with potentially discontinuous inputs and partial communication (Duan et al. 2002; Kirby 2004). In addition, the state-action space manipulated by a game AI is typically high dimensional, therefore the use of exhaustive search during learning may not be possible (Stanley et al. 2005).

One of the primary concerns regarding the use of machine learning within digital games is the requirement for computational efficiency. Any chosen learning technique should be capable of performing all necessary operations, in order that the learning algorithm may work effectively, within a specific time frame using a limited set of resources as defined by the amount of game specific AI resources available (Spronck 2005; Baekkelund 2006). The choice of a suitable knowledge representation scheme places a constraint on the capabilities of a learning technique as it implicitly defines the space of all possible functions the learning algorithm is able to represent and subsequently learn. By making use of a high-level, symbolic knowledge representation scheme, the manipulation of knowledge by the game AI will be straightforward and visible to game developers, however a high-level scheme should only be used when the computational expense incurred in obtaining and manipulating the knowledge is low enough to allow for its efficient and effective use. As such, the choice of representation scheme often requires a trade-off between expressiveness and the number of training examples required in order to perform effective learning (Mitchell 1997; Kirby 2004). By incorporating domain specific knowledge into the representation scheme or initial state of the learning algorithm, performance improvements may be gained (Manslow 2002; Baekkelund 2006).

An issue that arises as a consequence of learning is the problem of over-fitting. Within the context of digital games, over-fitting occurs when a game agent has learned to adapt its performance according to a very specific set of states from the game environment and remains unable to generalise across these states, resulting in poor performance when new states are encountered (Manslow 2002). Although the use of a set of validation examples is a common approach to alleviating over-fitting (Mitchell 1997), this approach is not necessarily suitable within a game environment. This is primarily due to the additional time and resources required for learning the validation set, alongside the problems that may arise with the selection and acquisition of the validation set, particularly if a useful example may involve a sequence of actions with delayed or compound results (Kirby 2004).

One of the major game design and development concerns is the unpredictable nature of learning, giving rise to increased costs in development time and resources associated with bug reproduction, resolution and game testing (Woodcock 2002). Subsequently, there exists a requirement for a set of game-specific, developer defined constraints over the learning process in order to ensure that features or behaviours learned do not cause deterioration in the game-play or degradation of the overall game experience for the player (Charles and McGlinchey 2004). Game agents should behave believably and within the context of the game environment, learning behaviours that are neither mechanistic nor predictable and remain consistent throughout the duration of the game (Maes 1995; Van Lent and Laird 1999; Spronck 2005).

The degree of visibility that the learning process provides to game designers and developers should also be taken into consideration. In order for designers and developers to effectively tune the game AI, they must be capable of following and understanding the learning process, therefore the use of a meaningful knowledge representation scheme is desirable. Subsequently, it is preferable that any chosen learning technique can be developed, implemented and maintained in a straightforward manner without any undue complexity (Van Lent and Laird 1999; Baekkelund 2006). The outcome of the learning process should also be explicitly visible to the player.

EVALUATION CRITERIA

Within both the academic and industry digital games research literature, requirements for the implementation of reliable and effective game agents, game AI and game related machine learning have been proposed (Van Lent and Laird 1999; Maes 1995; Manslow 2002; Spronck 2005; Baekkelund 2006). These requirements specify the need for computational and resource efficiency; consistent, reactive and robust operation; and the desire for a highly visible and easy to develop implementation strategy. Within this paper, such requirements have been collected together and incorporated into a set of criteria to be used for the evaluation and selection of potential online machine learning techniques, where individual criterion have been grouped according to three classes of requirement. Criteria within these classes may overlap and potentially conflict as the individual classes and individual criterion are not mutually exclusive (Spronck 2005). In the choice of a suitable online learning algorithm, a trade-off between conflicting criteria will most certainly need to be resolved. Priority should be given to those requirements that satisfy game specific design objectives and fulfil the overriding goal for the utilisation of the learning technique. The criteria, defined according to class, are as follows:

Class A: Performance Requirements:

- **Speed** – The amount of CPU time taken for all aspects of the learning algorithm's operation must be restricted to predefined game specific limits (Maes 1995; Spronck 2005; Baekkelund 2006).

- **Efficiency** – System resource usage should be kept to a minimum during all aspects of a learning algorithm's operation (Spronck 2005; Baekkelund 2006). Efficiency must be considered in terms of the number of trials and system resources required in order to achieve effective learning and recollection of learned knowledge. A trade-off may exist between the efficiency of the learning algorithm and its expandability and visibility.

Class B: Functional Requirements:

- **Reactivity** – As the game environment and behaviours of game agents change, subsequent changes to the input conditions of the learning algorithms require that appropriate new behaviours are obtained efficiently and in real-time (Maes 1995; Van Lent and Laird 1999).

- **Robustness** – The learning algorithm should perform in accordance with changing system resources and when noisy or missing data is presented to the algorithm (Maes 1995; Spronck 2005).

- **Expandability** – The operative capabilities of the learning algorithm should be preferably scalable to an arbitrary number of game agents. The extent to which a chosen learning algorithm can be expanded will be restricted by the underlying efficiency of the learning technique.

- **Consistency** – Game agent behaviours generated by the learning algorithm should be consistent throughout the lifetime of the game (Van Lent and Laird 1999; Spronck 2005).

- **Prior Knowledge** – Where possible, prior knowledge of the learning task should be incorporated into the learning algorithm's knowledge representation and initialisation in order to improve the efficiency of learning (Manslow 2002; Baekkelund 2006).

Class C: Design Requirements:

- **Believability** – Game agent behaviours generated by the learning algorithms should be appropriate and within the context of the underlying game (Maes 1995; Van Lent and Laird 1999).

- **Simplicity** – The design and implementation of the learning algorithm should be no more complex than necessary for sufficient and effective implementation (Van Lent and Laird 1999; Baekkelund 2006).

- **Visibility** – The knowledge representation scheme and the learning process should preferably be visible to game designers and developers in order to permit effective testing and debugging. Results from the learning process should be visible to the game player (Spronck 2005; Baekkelund 2006).

DISCUSSION AND EVALUATION OF MACHINE LEARNING TECHNIQUES COMMONLY USED WITHIN DIGITAL GAMES

The following section aims to provide an overview of the most commonly utilised and discussed machine learning techniques, from existing academic and game industry literature, together with a brief preliminary analysis of the techniques according to the evaluation criteria. Although a large number of learning algorithms exist, together with variations, optimisations and extensions, than those discussed herein, the techniques under consideration are those most frequently found in both academic and industry digital game research literature.

Neural networks provide a possible alternative to the use of finite state machines and scripting systems for the specification of game agent behaviours. By making use of predictive capabilities, they may be used to determine a player's game-play patterns and behaviours (Charles and McGlinchey 2004; Schwab 2004). Feed-forward neural networks, in particular, have been notably used in order to control the motion of game agents and provide a foundation for the generation of adaptive agent behaviours (Yannakakis and Hallam 2004; Stanley et al. 2005). The most well known examples of the use of neural networks within commercial games include the use of Perceptrons as part of a flexible representation scheme in "Black & White" (Evans 2001), the use of multi-layer networks for the offline training of game agents in "Colin McRae Rally 2" (Manslow 2002) and the use of a hybridisation of neural networks and evolutionary computation techniques in order to evolve game agent behaviours in "Creatures" (Grand et al. 1996). Unsupervised neural networks, such as the self-organising map, have been successfully used within academic game research to provide game agent control after being trained offline on player control data (McGlinchey 2003) and game agent state space reduction as a pre-processing step for the use of other learning techniques (Thurau et al. 2003).

The pattern recognition and classification capabilities of neural networks make them suitable for both player-centric and environment-centric learning however, handling missing inputs is problematic and the speed and efficiency of convergence during training is typically slow for traditional learning algorithms (Mitchell 1997; Baekkelund 2006). Although highly suitable as a method for integrating learning into digital games, the issues of obtaining an appropriate network topology and set of training examples present further obstacles that have prevented their widespread use within commercial games (Le Hy et al. 2004; Baekkelund 2006). Academic digital game research has shown that optimisations which make use of a hybrid of neural network and evolutionary computation techniques are effective in determining the network architecture and optimal set of connection weights, thereby circumventing the use of traditional neural network learning algorithms (Yannakakis and Hallam 2004; Stanley et al. 2005).

The inability of neural networks to make use of prior knowledge beyond network initialisation, coupled with the lack of a visible target function representation, prevents them from fully satisfying the prior knowledge and visibility criteria (Baekkelund 2006). Although unsupervised neural networks, such as self-organising maps, exhibit high computational efficiency during learning, they remain largely unused by the games industry (McGlinchey 2003; Charles and McGlinchey 2004). Alternative neural network approaches, such as the use radial basis functions may also be used to provide an efficient learning mechanism, however their use has not yet been reported in the literature.

Another supervised learning technique that has been successfully used within a commercial game is decision tree learning. A variation of the ID3 algorithm has been used within the game "Black & White" to dynamically model a game agent's beliefs and opinions about objects in the game environment as part of the game agent's hybrid decision making architecture (Evans 2001).

Decision tree learning, in particular the ID4 and C4.5 algorithms, potentially satisfy the majority of the evaluation criteria therefore initially appear highly suitable for application to online learning. Although the computational resources required for learning a decision tree increase in relation to the number of possible values for instance attributes, decision tree learning generally provides a computationally efficient, robust learning mechanism which can make use of prior knowledge during initialisation. Providing sufficient training data exists for the learning task, containing a large number of relevant attributes with a finite number of unique values, decision tree learning is suitable for both player-centric and environment-centric learning approaches (Baekkelund 2006).

Bayesian learning methods have been used within the "Gamebots" control framework for the "Unreal Tournament" game as part of academic digital game research. Such methods have been used to reliably and efficiently determine the real-time selection of behaviours for a game agent from the game agent's current state and perception system (Le Hy et al. 2004). In general, Bayesian learning methods make use of prior knowledge during classification and allow probability distributions for variables to be incrementally altered by learning individual training examples (Mitchell 1997). Although Bayesian learning techniques are suitable for learning based on reasoning in the presence of unobserved variables (Tozour 2002), depending on the type of Bayesian learning technique used, the need to calculate posterior probabilities may prevent Bayesian learning from satisfying the speed and efficiency criteria. Given a set of training examples with a sufficient number of discrete inputs, containing a finite number of unique values, the Naïve Bayes Classifier is efficient and accurate for both learning and classification (Baekkelund 2006), suitable for both player-centric and environment-centric learning approaches.

Reinforcement learning has been attempted for the generation of a variety of game agent behaviours and strategies within academic digital game research. The uses of reinforcement learning have varied between the successful adaptation of reinforcement learning for the generation of game agent behaviours within a fighting game (Graepel et al. 2004), improvement of agent communication and coordination in an N-Person Iterated Prisoners Dilemma test-bed (Duan et al. 2002), and as part of a hybrid learning algorithm for offline learning within a strategy game (Pfeiffer 2004).

Although reinforcement learning may provide a powerful set of learning algorithms, without constraints imposed on the number of actions and states permitted a number of issues preventing its use within digital games may arise including slow convergence rates, erratic behaviour during exploration of the state-action space and convergence to undesired behaviour if the magnitude and frequency of feedback is not correctly balanced (Duan et al. 2002; Baekkelund 2006). Reinforcement learning also suffers from exponential growth in terms of the computational resources required for the number of states and actions used (Duan et al. 2002). However, by making use of a small number of inputs, containing a small range of actions for each possible state, coupled with the use of a look-up table for its internal model, convergence during learning may be improved in order to be sufficient for online use. Subsequently, the use of a look-up table also provides a degree of visibility and may permit the use of prior knowledge during learning (Baekkelund 2006).

With the notable exceptions of "Creatures" and "Black & White" (Evans 2001; Grand et al. 1996), evolutionary algorithms have not, to date, gained widespread use in online learning within commercial games. Instead, they have mainly been used as an offline method for automated parameter tuning (Schwab 2004; Baekkelund 2006), such as the use of genetic algorithms during game development to determine an optimal set of handling characteristics for game agents in the commercial game "Re-Volt" (Kirby 2004). However, academic digital game research has shown that evolutionary algorithms provide the capability for incorporating adaptation in game agents within a variety of game environments. Predominantly used for the generation of game agent behaviours and strategies (Demasi and Cruz 2002; Stanley et al. 2005), genetic algorithms adopting canonical (Yannakakis and Hallam 2004), co-evolutionary, (Demasi and Cruz 2002; Pfeiffer 2004; Yannakakis and Hallam 2004) and speciation techniques (Stanley et al. 2005), have been used for both offline and online learning.

As evolutionary algorithms, such as the canonical genetic algorithm, have typically high resource requirements and slow convergence rates (Mitchell 1997; Baekkelund 2006), they fail to satisfy the speed and efficiency criteria during learning however, such requirements may be overcome using a suitable extension to the canonical genetic algorithm, such as population-based incremental learning or the structured genetic algorithm (Fyfe 1999). Genetic algorithm variations, such as the use of the steady-state or structured genetic algorithm do not yet appear to have been attempted in a learning system for commercial digital games. Similarly, the use of alternative evolutionary algorithms such as evolutionary strategies has not yet been reported in the literature.

CONCLUSION

From the literature it can be seen that the desire to use learning in games is gaining momentum within the games industry, however only basic implementations of the key learning techniques have been used thus far. In particular there exist very few examples of the use of online learning within commercial digital games however, the use of such a mechanism is very important for the implementation of effective adaptive digital games. The focus of this paper has been to provide an initial set of guidelines to be used during the selection of machine learning algorithms for online use within digital games, independent of the learning task or game genre. We have presented evaluation criteria for the selection of potentially suitable algorithms and have discussed the most commonly used techniques with respect to these criteria. In future work we expect to explore further optimisations and variations of these commonly implemented techniques and use our criteria to investigate other techniques from mainstream AI research that have not yet been applied to commercial digital games.

REFERENCES

Baekkelund, C. 2006. "A Brief Comparison of Machine Learning Methods." In *AI Game Programming Wisdom 3*, Rabin, S. ed. Charles River Media, Hingham, MA, 617-631.

Charles, D. 2003. "Enhancing Gameplay: Challenges for Artificial Intelligence in Digital Games." In *Proceedings of Digital Games Research Conference*. University of Utrecht

Charles, D. & McGlinchey, S. 2004. "The Past Present and Future of Artificial Neural Networks in Digital Games." In *Computer Games: Artificial Intelligence, Design and Education*, Mehdi, Q., Gough, N.E., Natkin, S., Al-Dabass, D. eds. University of Wolverhampton, UK, 163-169.

Demasi, P. & Cruz, A., J. de O. (2002). "Online Coevolution for Action Games." *International Journal of Intelligent Games and Simulation*, 2, 2: 80-88.

Duan, J., Gough, N.E. & Mehdi, Q.H. 2002 "Multi-Agent Reinforcement Learning for Computer Game Agents." In *Intelligent Games and Simulation*, Mehdi, Q., Gough, N.E. & Cavazza, M. eds. University of Wolverhampton, UK, 104-109.

Evans, R. 2001. "The Future of AI in Games: A Personal View." *Game Developer*, 8: 46-49.

Fyfe, C. 1999. "Structured Population-Based Incremental Learning." *Soft Computing*, 2: 191-198.

Graepel, T., Herbrich, R. & Gold, J. 2004. "Learning To Fight." In: *Computer Games: Artificial Intelligence, Design and Education*, Mehdi, Q., Gough, N.E., Natkin, S. & Al-Dabass, D. eds. University of Wolverhampton, UK, 193-200.

Grand, S., Cliff, D. & Malhotra, A. 1996. "Creatures: Artificial Life Autonomous Software Agents for Home Entertainment." Technical Report CSRP434, University of Sussex.

Kirby, N. 2004. "Getting Around the Limits of Machine Learning." In *AI Game Programming Wisdom 2*, Rabin, S. ed. Charles River Media, Hingham, MA, 603-611.

Le Hy, R., Arrigoni, A., Bessiere, P. & Lebeltel, O. 2004. "Teaching Bayesian Behaviours to Video Game Characters." *Robotics and Autonomous Systems*, 47: 177-185.

Maes, P. 1995. "Artificial Life Meets Entertainment: Lifelike Autonomous Agents." *Communications of the ACM*, 38, 11: 108-114.

Manslow, J. 2002. "Learning and Adaptation." In *AI Game Programming Wisdom*, Rabin, S. ed. Charles River Media, Hingham, MA, 557-566.

McGlinchey, S. 2003. "Learning of AI Players From Game Observation Data." In *Intelligent Games and Simulation*, Mehdi, Q., Gough, N.E. & Natkins, S. eds. University of Wolverhampton, UK, 106-110.

Mitchell, T.M. 1997. *Machine Learning*. McGraw-Hill Book Co, Singapore.

Pfeiffer, M. 2004. "Reinforcement Learning of Strategies for Settlers of Catan." In Computer Games: Artificial Intelligence, Design and Education, Mehdi, Q., Gough, N.E., Natkin, S. & Al-Dabass, D. eds. University of Wolverhampton, UK, 384-388.

Schaeffer, J. & Van den Herik, H.J. 2002. "Games, Computers, and Artificial Intelligence." *Artificial Intelligence*, 134, 1-2: 1-7.

Schwab, B. 2004. *AI Game Engine Programming*. Charles River Media, Hingham, MA.

Stanley, K.O., Bryant, B.D. & Miikkulainen, R. 2005. "Evolving Neural Network Agents in the NERO Video Game." *Proc. IEEE Symp. Computational Intelligence and Games*.

Spronck, P. 2005. "A Model for Reliable Adaptive Game Intelligence." In *05 Workshop on Reasoning, Representation, and Learning in Computer Games IJCAI NCARAI*, Aha, D.W., Munoz-Avila, H. &Van Lent, M. eds.Washington.

Thurau, C., Bauckhage, C. & Sagerer, G. 2003. "Combining Self Organizing Maps and Multilayer Perceptrons to Learn Bot-Behaviour for a Commercial Game." In *Intelligent Games and Simulation*, Mehdi, Q., Gough, N.E. & Natkin, S. eds. University of Wolverhampton, UK, 119-123.

Tozour, P. 2002. "Introduction to Bayesian Networks and Reasoning Under Uncertainty." *In AI Game Programming Wisdom*, Rabin, S. ed. Charles River Media, Hingham, MA, 345-357.

Van Lent, M. & Laird, J. 1999. "Developing an Artificial Intelligence Engine." *Proc. of the 1999 Game Developer Conference*, San Jose: 577-588

Woodcock, S. 2002. "Game AI: The State of the Industry." *Game Developer*, **7:** 26-31.

Yannakakis, G.N. & Hallam, J. 2004. "Interactive Opponents Generate Interesting Games." In *Computer Games: Artificial Intelligence, Design and Education*, Mehdi, Q., Gough, N.E., Natkin, S., & Al-Dabass, D. eds. University of Wolverhampton, UK, 240-247.

BIOGRAPHY

Leo Galway was awarded a Masters with Distinction in Computing & Intelligent Systems from the University of Ulster in 2005. He is currently pursuing a PhD degree at the School of Computing & Information Engineering from the University of Ulster with an emphasis on applied intelligent techniques for digital games. His research interests include evolutionary computing, artificial intelligence and machine learning.

LEARNABLE BUDDY: LEARNABLE SUPPORTIVE AI IN COMMERCIAL MMORPG

Theppatorn Rhujittawiwat and Vishnu Kotrajaras
Department of Computer Engineering
Chulalongkorn University, Bangkok, Thailand
E-mail: g49trh@cp.eng.chula.ac.th, vishnu@cp.eng.chula.ac.th

KEYWORDS

Artificial Intelligence, Genetic Algorithm, Massively-Multiplayer Online Game.

ABSTRACT

In commercial massively-multiplayer online role-playing games (MMORPG), players usually play in a populated environments with simple non-player game characters. These non-player characters have fix behaviour. They cannot learn from what they experience in the game. However, MMORPG environments are believed to be greatly suitable for training AI, with plenty of players to provide tremendous amount of feedback, and persistent worlds to provide learning environments. This paper presents an experiment to find out the potential of MMORPG environments for fast learning evolutionary AI. The genetic algorithm is chosen as our learning method to train a non-player character to assist real players. We use a game server emulator and custom game clients to simulate and run a commercial MMORPG. Clients are divided into two groups, real players and "helpers". The results show that helpers can learn to assist real players effectively in small amount of time. This confirms that evolutionary learning can be used to provide efficient learning in commercial MMORPG. It also verifies that MMORPG provide great platforms for research in evolutionary learning.

INTRODUCTION

Recent game AI research and developments in online games are mostly focused on player opponent AI. Seu simulated and tested the system for evolving distribution, physical parameters, and behavior of monsters in game (Seu et al 2004). They found that monsters special qualities could be evolved according to their environments by using GA technique. Group movement was expressed by the flocking algorithm. However, actual learning was restricted to animal behaviour such as looking for food. Also, the length of time spent before monsters displayed satisfactory intelligent behaviour was not discussed. Spronck proposed a novel technique called "Dynamic Scripting" (Spronck et al 2004). Dynamic scripting used an adaptive rulebase for the generation of intelligent opponent AIs on the fly. In his experiment, a module for the commercial game NEVERWINTER NIGHTS (NWN; 2002) was created. A group of agents using dynamic script were pitted against various groups of pre-coded opponents. The results showed that dynamic scripting succeeds in providing clever AI in an acceptable period of time (around 50 battles needed for fighting with well coded opponents). However, a predefined rulebase was needed in this technique, meaning the actual time when learning from scratch was longer. Furthermore, although an agent learned using information from other agents in its team, one agent could only learn for itself at one time. A genetic algorithm was later used to create a rulebase for dynamic scripting (Spronck et al 2005). However, the work was carried out as an offline learning and learning time from scratch was not discussed. Stanley introduced the real-time NeuroEvolution of Augmenting Topologies (rtNEAT) (Stanley et al 2002). This is a learning method that was extended from NeuroEvolution of Augmenting Topologies for evolving increasingly complex artificial neural networks in real time, as a game is being played. The rtNEAT method allows agents to improve play style during the game. He demonstrated a new genre of games in which a player trains an agent team to compete with another player's team in NeuroEvoling Robotic Operatives (NERO) game (Stanley et al 2005). However, the nature of NERO implies that only one player can be training agents at one time.

MMORPG provides a very different environment and gameplay compared to other kinds of games.

With a massive number of players, these players can act as trainers for an evolving agent. Also, players spend more time playing MMORPG than other genres of games, and persistent world is used as a setting. This means MMORPG is likely to be a great environment for fast learning, even though we may use a slow learning method such as a GA. This paper presents the result of an experiment that evolves a player's helper in a commercial MMORPG game using a genetic algorithm. We call our player assistant a "Learnable Buddy".

Our learnable buddy technique has been tested by using the MMORPG server emulator of eAthena and custom client of OpenKore. eAthena is an open-source project, emulating a Ragnarok Online Server. It is written in C. Using its server emulator, a game server can be simulated and studied. OpenKore is an advanced bot for Ragnarok Online. It is free, open-source and cross-platform. In real MMORPG, many human players play in the same game server. We simulate human players by using OpenKore. Learnable buddy also makes good use of OpenKore. By modifying OpenKore code, we build AI-control units that are able to learn to improve their behavior.

Learnable Buddy

Learnable Buddy uses a genetic algorithm to set its configuration, which is a bot script. By evolving the chromosome of our population bots, our bots are able to perform various behaviors. The system consists of the following components.

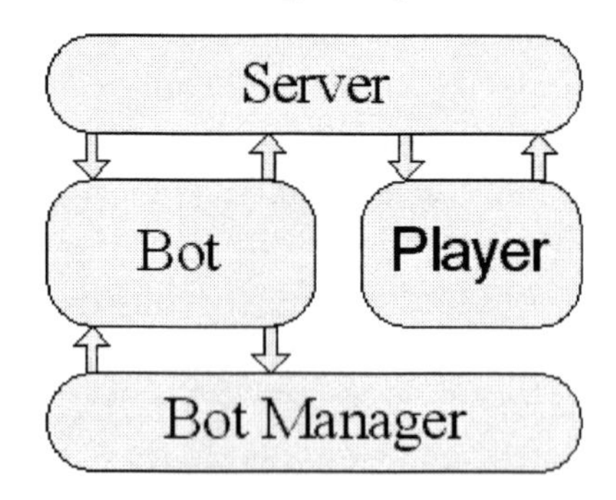

Figure 1: Learnable Buddy system overview.

1. Server: The game server sends game state information to every client and receives commands from clients. It keeps updating game state.
2. Player: All players are online, each can give us feedback.
3. Bot: Our bot is a supportive AI that travels along with a player. That player is a master and the bot is a slave. Bot systems have already been in use in various commercial games, such as the homunculus system in Ragnarok Online (RO; 2006). In Raknarok Online, players who play the alchemist or the biochemist can get a homunculus. The homunculus system surpasses other commercial MMORPG bots such as Guildwars's pet (Guildwars; 2006) because players are able to manually rewrite the bot's AI script. In this study, instead of using monsters as bots, we used player's character class as our supportive AI because a player character can perform more varying kinds of behavior. OpenKore was used to control each supportive AI. OpenKore was modified to send information and receive commands from the bot manager.
4. Bot manager: A module was written in Java. This module receives information from each bot, then determines their fitness and replaces low fitness bots with new ones. The detail is described below.

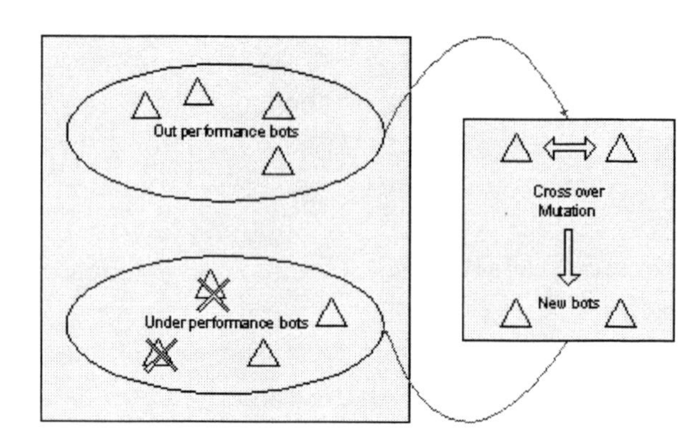

Figure 2: The replacement cycle

A bot plays using the first script it receives from the bot manager for a fixed period of time. Then, the bot manager will determine the fitness of each script. For this study, we use a fixed fitness equation. The fitness is calculated based on experience points a bot receives and the number of times that bot dies during the period. The value of fitness F, for bot b, is formally defined as:

$$F(b) = \frac{botEXPperHour(b)}{botDeadCount(b)^2}$$

The experience points that a master or its slave bot gain from any action will be divided in half. The bot receives the same amount of experience points as its master. New chromosome generation is similar to regular GA techniques. First, good parents are chosen. Half of the bot population, whose with high fitness, are selected to produce offsprings that replace the half with lower fitness result. Each couple will perform a crossover, obtaining two new chromosomes. After that, new chromosomes will go through mutation. After a new chromosome is generated, the bot manager will read its attributes, transforming the attributes into a script, and replace a poorly performed bot with the new script.

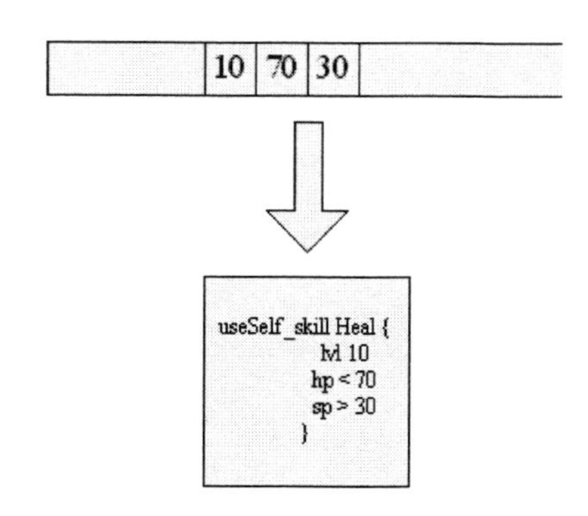

Figure 3: Example of chromosome to script translation

The openKore main script consists of 2 formats. The first format is of the form:

<configuration key> <value>

This format is used for a simple task. For example, in order to specify whether our OpenKore bot automatically attacks monsters, we use the following script:

```
attackAuto 1
```

where the proper value for this configuration is 0 (false) or 1 (true).

The second format is of the form:

```
<configuration key> <value> {
        <attribute1> <value1>
        <attribute2> <value2>
}
```

This format is called "block" format. It is used for a complicated task. In figure 3, OpenKore will use level 10 Heal skill on itself when its hp is less than 70% and its sp is greater than 30%. With this configuration structure, it is quite straightforward to translate between a script and its corresponding chromosome.

After new scripts are generated from the chromosomes of offsprings, half of the learnable buddies that used to have lower fitness results will reload new scripts and continue playing the game for another fixed period of time before repeating this cycle. The cycle can be done fast enough not disrupt the game play.

THE EXPERIMENTS

We assessed the performance of parties of two characters. We set up a private server using eAthena server emulator. Each party had the same members consisting of the following character.

1. Knight: The knights are bots that represent the real players who play a game. In this study, we used controlled experimental environments such that every player shared the same play style. All knights were implemented with the same script. This allowed learnable buddies to share their knowledge and learn together in a consistent way. The knights always attack the nearest monster that no one attacks. If a knight's health is reduced to half, it will rest until its health is fully recovered.
2. Priest: All priests are controlled by our learnable buddy technique. They will try to learn and adapt themselves to best serve their master. The priests support the knights with healing and buffing. Their behavior follows the script that they receive from the bot manager.

Testing was initiated using 16 pairs of knights and priests. Every party played in the same map that has only one kind of monster. The time cycle that we used for our fixed period was 30 minutes. Having a shorter cycle would affect the accuracy of the fitness result because the number of enemies faced might be too small and the fitness function might not show its effect because of that. On the other hand, our test platform could not run more than 30 minutes without a bot failing due to too much load the system had to handle. Therefore, the cycle of 30 minutes was our best choice.

To quantify the performance of each learnable buddy, after each time cycle, we calculated the fitness for each learnable buddy by the function from our previous section and replaced poorly performed bots with new ones. We ran 3 tests, each test ran for 50 generations of learnable buddy. The results of these experiments are presented in the next section.

RESULT

Figure 4 shows fitness mean of bots. A solid line represents fitness mean of each generation. It can be observed that, from the beginning until around the fifteenth generation our bots' fitness mean rapidly increases. The fitness does not vary much after that. Figure 5 shows the result of figure 4 after smoothness adjustment, using polynomial degree 5 trend line.

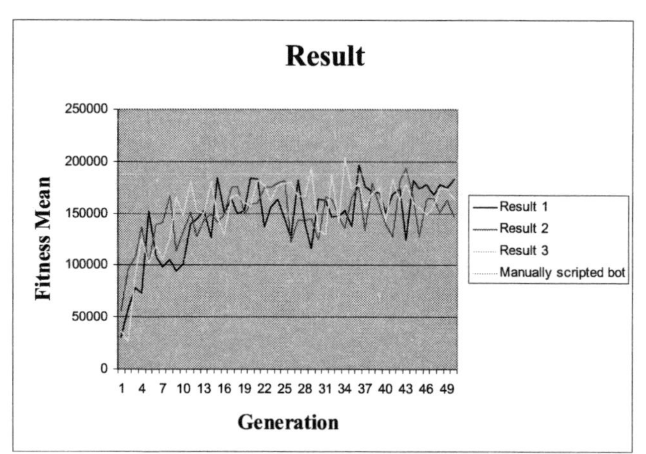

Figure 4: Resulting graph of learnable buddy, using three test runs.

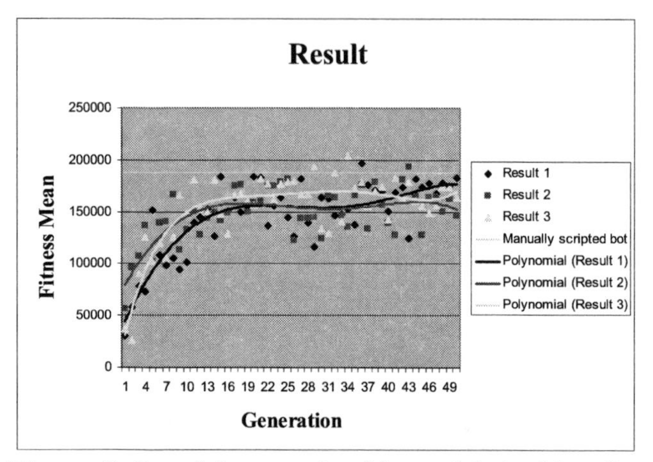

Figure 5: Resulting graph of learnable buddy after smoothness adjustment using polynomial degree 5 trend line.

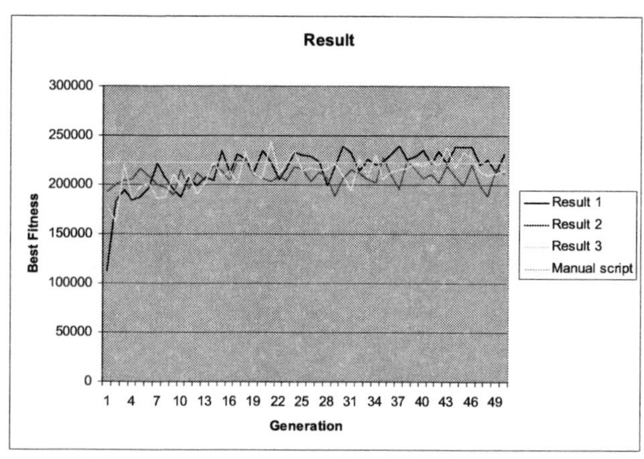

Figure 6: Resulting graph of best fitness in each generation competing against best fitness of our manully scripted bot.

We observed and compared the 15th generation of learnable buddies with manually scripted supportive characters configured by an experienced game player. The mean fitness of our bots came close to the mean fitness of the manually scripted bot. Not all of our best bots in the 15th generation could beat the manually scripted bot's best score. But observing the results for their future generations suggested that our best bots could compete well with the manually scripted bot (see figure 6). From the result, we believe that, in order to help one master with a task, our learnable buddies can improve themselves to their proper performance in around fifteen generations or 7.5 hours of playing. The survey from America Online shows that teenage players spend 7.4 hours per week on average playing online games (AOL 2004). Therefore our 7.5 hours figure is significant. It means one task can be learned in just a week for the same group of real players. Most MMORPGs plan to let players play for several months or maybe a year, therefore one week is considered to be very efficient. It can even be improved further. A bot can be kept running for 24 hours by assigning it to another player. Therefore, fast learning for a task can be achieved.

CONCLUSION AND FUTURE WORK

In this paper we investigated whether evolutionary-learning can provide fast online adaptation of player supportive AI in commercial MMORPG. From our experimental results, we conclude that genetic algorithm is fast and effective enough for commercial MMORPG. The original game does not need to be adjusted in any way. Different genes can be used for different tasks and players can switch between tasks to allow more suitable behaviour at each situation.

Currently, our bot manager only supports fixed fitness function given by game developers. That means, only common tasks can be learned. To allow supporting AI to be able to learn more tasks or even improve upon old tasks, especially ones specific to events or groups of players, players must be able to craft their own fitness function through an intuitive interface. We also plan to experiment with genetic programming, which allows builds-up of complex behaviour. One of our research goals is to be able to categorize player behavior while playing. This will permit learnable buddies to automatically switch to the script that best fits the situation, thus adding more sense of realism.

ACKNOWLEDGMENT

This research is sponsored by Ratchadaphiseksomphot Endowment Fund, Chulalongkorn University.

REFERENCES

Kenneth O. Stanley, Bobby D. Bryant and Risto Miikkulainen. 2005. "Evoling Neural Network Agents in the NERO Video Game." In Proceeding of IEEE 2005 Symposium on Computational Intelligence and Games (CIG'05).

Kenneth O. Stanley and Risto Miikkulainen. 2002. "Efficient Reinforcemant Learning through Evoling Neural Network Topologies." In Proceedings of Genetic and Evolutionary Computation Conference (GECCO-2002).

Kenneth O. Stanley and Risto Miikkulainen. 2002. "Evolving Neural Networks through Augmenting Topologies." The Massachusetts Institute of Technology Press Journals, Evolutionary Computation 10(2). 99-127

Jai Hyun Seu, Byung-Keum Song and Heung Shik Kim. 2004. "Simulation of Artificial Life Model in Game Space." Artificial Intelligence and Simulation, 13th International Conference on AI, Simulation, and Planning in High Autonomy Systems. 179-187

Marc J.V. Ponsen, Héctor Muñoz-Avila, Pieter Spronck, and David W. Aha. 2005. "Automatically Acquiring Adaptive Real-Time Strategy Game Opponents Using Evolutionary Learning." Proceedings, The Twentieth National Conference on Artificial Intelligence and the Seventeenth Innovative Applications of Artificial Intelligence Conference, pp. 1535-1540. AAAI Press, Menlo Park, CA.

Pieter Spronck, Ida Sprinkhuizen-Kuyper and Eric Postma. 2004. "Online Adaptation of Game Opponent AI with Dynamic Scripting." International Journal of Intelligent Games and Simulation, Vol 3 No 1, 45-53

America Online (2004)
http://www.aol.com

eAthena (2006). Ragnarok Online Server Emulator
http://www.eathena.deltaanime.net

GuildWars (2006)
http://www.guildwars.com

Neuro-Evolving Robotic Operatives (2006)
http://nerogame.org

NEVERWINTER NIGHTS (2002)
http://nwn.bioware.com

OpenKore (2006). Ragnarok Online Bot
http://www.openkore.com

Ragnarok Online (2006)
http://www.ragnarokonline.com

Galvanic skin conductance in games AI evaluation (Work in progress)

Thomas JJ. Welsh
David Moffat
Glasgow Caledonian University
E-mail: T.Welsh@gcal.ac.uk

Abstract
Modern FPS games represent the cutting edge of games development. With the latest game engines and graphics rendering methods becoming more complex, it is proposed that current AI techniques may not be sufficient to portray human-like behaviour. This paper considers the current state of Bot AI in First person perspective shooting (FPS) games. It represents preliminary work intended to determine if current AI technologies used in games are capable of portraying human or human-like behaviour. To do this a a piece of hardware which reads galvanic skin conductance and heart rate will be used together with software which has been developed to accurately measure changes in the subjects base line physiological responses. The intention is to determine if there is a physiological difference in how players interact with computer opponents and humans. The hypothesis is that the players will be able to accurately differentiate a Bot from a human and their physiological responses will clearly show the difference as well. The difference in what is termed as physiological awareness and conscious awareness of the nature of the opponent will also be investigated.

Background
Computers games are becoming ubiquitous in our society. From a quick game of solitaire during quiet moments in the office to multiplayer robot battles on long distance flights or Quake on our mobile phone, you are always just a few seconds away from playing a computer game. The game industry is now huge, with more disposable income going towards games than dvd sales or movie tickets (Laird, 2001). With such a huge industry the highest quality games are very lucrative for developers and publishers alike. To achieve this quality games are becoming visually more realistic. Despite this the inhabitants of these virtual worlds are not human-like. The purpose of opponents in commercial computer games is to provide an entertaining playing experience. (Touzour, 2002). Recently however computer game developers are starting to recognize the need for human-level AI to make these opponents sufficiently convincing (Laird, 2000). It is proposed that more convincing opponents will be correspondingly more entertaining.

In early games like Space Invaders, there was no need for sophisticated AI techniques, as the enemies simply scrolled down the screen in a line, ready to be dispatched by the player. In such a game, the AI would not react to the player's movements or actions. To play the most difficult games well a program must contend with fundamental issues in AI: knowledge representation, search, learning, and planning (Epstein, 2001).

Modern games expose the player to human-like enemies and allies. To make these human-like characters behave in a convincing manner they must be responsive to the player's movements and actions; hence the programming that controls them must be more sophisticated. To create these responsive, learning, intelligent opponents we look to academic AI, and how it has dealt with the creation of human-like agents and the solutions to real-world problems. To apply these techniques however, we have to fully understand what we need that technology to achieve.

It is proposed that to understand how to advance games AI and Bot behaviour in FPS games, we must first study and consider human play. Only by examining how humans play, and understanding the decisions that they make, will we understand how to replicate this behaviour.

This paper is initial work which considers the use of a piece of hardware called a galvanometer in the measurement of player engagement. If it is possible to use this hardware to produce meaningful results indicating a players engagement with a game, then we can use this as a tool to measure which aspects of bot behaviour affect that players engagement. By determining the viability of this method of measuring engagement, it should be possible to determine if this will be a useful way of evaluating believability in current and future implementations of Bots.

The use of the galvanometer in games is not new. Some games make use of biofeedback devices as peripherals to control the game (Johnson, 2003), or even make control of the individuals bio-responses a game in itself (Sakurazawa, 2004). Further work has used galvanic skin response in a game environment to help overcome depression or trauma (Hermida, 2002). Despite this, the ability to identify exactly which aspects of bot behaviour are not believable is a key step in the development of more convincing game AI. If the game events which cause an increase or decrease in engagement can be identified using a galvanometer, we can determine what these events are and how to bring them about or avoid them. It is commonly accepted that computer controlled bots are not believable enough (Laird, 2000), but to understand why it is necessary to examine what behaviours bots exhibit which decrease engagement for the human player.

Methodology

The hardware used, a galvanometer, takes readings of skin conductance and also measures heart rate. A measure of electrical resistance is interpreted as a reflection of changes in emotional arousal. This measurement is taken by attaching the electrodes of the galvanometer to any part of the skin and acquiring a base measure then recording changes in moment-to-moment perspiration and related activity of the autonomic nervous system.

Galvanic skin response (GSR), also known as electro dermal response (EDR), psychogalvanic reflex (PGR), or skin conductance response (SCR), is a method of measuring the electrical resistance of the skin. There is a relationship between sympathetic activity and emotional arousal, although one cannot identify the specific emotion being elicited. The GSR is highly sensitive to emotions in some people. Fear, anger, startle response, orienting response and sexual feelings are all among the emotions which may produce similar GSR responses. (Bersaket al, 2001).

There are two ways to perform a GSR - in active GSR, current is passed through the body, with the resistance measured. In passive GSR, current generated by the body itself is measured. GSR originated in the early 1900s. It was used for a variety of types of research in the 1960s through the late 1970s, with a decline in use as more sophisticated techniques (such as EEG and MRI) replaced it in many areas of psychological research. GSR is still used today, as it is appropriate for use with low levels of technology. (Mika et al, 2001)

In marketing research the clinical measurement of a subject's response to stimuli, such as an advertisement, can be measured in terms of the change in skin resistance to electrical current; also called psychogalvanic skin response or sweaty palms. Theoretically, the greater the change in resistance, the more positive the subject's reaction to the stimuli. Its proponents argue that it is more objective than research that relies on voluntary responses like interviews or surveys. (Barrett, 2005)

For the purposes of this experiment a group of games players engagement will be measured using GSR while playing an FPS game. In this case, passive GSR will be used with three electrodes connected to the three middle fingers of the players right hand. Heart rate is also monitored through connected sensors on the fingers. The data is processed by software which produces graphs and tables and also outputs a log file. The software which has been developed goes some way to overcoming the shortcomings of GSR which are discussed later.

The game used for this experiment will most be Halo 2 on the Microsoft XBox. The game is played with a control pad which is easier to use than a keyboard and mouse when wearing the electrodes. They will be asked to keep their hands resting on a stationary surface such as a table to ensure that their GSR readings are not overly influenced by movement. Data will be transferred during their ten minute playing session to a PC which is connected to the galvanometer.

Ten participants will play a ten minute game of Halo in two five minute segments with a one minute break between each. The game will be a one vs one deathmatch game; in the first five minutes the participants will play against a human opponent who is located in another room and in the second segment they will face a computer controlled opponent. They will be given no clues as to the nature of their opponents. Their opponents will look the same and their on-screen name will also stay the same. The only difference will be that the opponent will have changed from human to computer controlled. The participant will simply know that they will be playing a death match game of Halo on the XBox console.

Base line GSR will be measured for each of the participants before the game begins. This process will take four minutes and is intended to gather an average GSR reading for each individual. During the calibration period, the individual will be asked to sit and relax but perform no activity which would affect their GSR reading. The base line measure of GSR varies from person to person and therefore the percentage variance is the vital measure for gauging arousal.

Many of the criticisms of GSR as a measure of engagement revolve around its fluctuating readings caused by occasional movements and contractions of muscles on the part of the participants (Sykes and Brown, 03). The software that has been developed for this experiment takes base line readings and averages out results while disregarding sudden spikes resulting from participant muscle contractions. By taking this into consideration, initial results show promise in gathering meaningful results in measuring engagement.

The test group will consist of ten male and ten female gamers. All of the test subjects should enjoy playing FPS games, and all will have a chance to play Halo before the experiment. Despite their comfort with the game itself, none of the players will be experts and the skill level of the players should be approximately equal. The data gathered will consist of the galvanic skin response and heart rate over the course of the two five minute games. The galvanic skin response takes ten readings per second and the results are compiled into a graph with the y axis corresponding to the time of the reading. By comparing recorded video footage of the games with the corresponding galvanic skin response data, it should be possible to identify which actions performed by the computer controlled opponent elicit which responses in the player. For example, if during the game the bot performs a difficult manoeuvre, the time of the manoeuvre can be compared with the players galvanic response at that time to determine if that particular action increases or decreases the players perceived engagement.

The players will be briefly interviewed after their play session on how they felt about the whole experience. They will also be asked whether they believed that they have been playing against a human or a bot in each of the two sessions.

Exposition and Conclusions

The primary purpose of the experiment is to determine the physiological difference exhibited by the player when facing both the Bot and human opponents while playing an FPS game. The difference in heart rate and GSR rating should tell us which of the two opponents is the more stimulating to play against. It is postulated that the participants will have greater measure of arousal when facing the human opponent and this will be represented by a corresponding change in heart rate and GSR.

If this technique is successful, the data gathered could be invaluable to games designers and AI programmers. AI programmers will have an evaluative tool to measure the believability of the bots they create. With this feedback, the AI programmer should be able to determine how far they still have to progress to achieve genuine believability. Games designers meanwhile can use the same technique to identify less stimulating aspects of their games as well as populating their game worlds with believable characters.

For this particular experiment using the galvonometer, the hypothesis of this paper is that the participants will reach a point where their initial high level of arousal from their first session with the human opponents will start to drop during the second session when facing the computer controlled opponent. By correlating the time of the drop in GSR and heart rate to the game time, it should be possible to identify which aspect of the bot opponents behaviour was responsible for the drop in engagement. It is possible that the individual behaviours that induce the disbelief and corresponding drop in engagement could be eliminated, however it is more likely that the play behaviour of the bot not only includes individual give-aways, but also lacks some of the higher level planning, anticipation and learning that is a feature of human play (Welsh, 05). Nonetheless, any method of judging the success of an AI technique will be invaluable in achieving the goal of believability in bots and computer controlled npc's in games of all genres.

The difference in what is termed as physiological awareness and conscious awareness of the nature of the opponent is a further area of interest. Rather than playing two separate games against both humans and bots, it could be possible to switch between them mid-game without revealing the switch to the participant. The participant could then be asked to verbalize when they believe their computer opponent has become a human opponent. The GSR rating could then be examined and the time when it drops to indicate lower levels of engagement could be compared to the time when the participant verbalizes their belief that they are facing a human opponent. This variation of the basic experiment could show that physiological and conscious awareness of the nature of the opponent could be divorced or one could lag behind the other.

The primary aim of this paper has been to discuss a piece of work in progress concerning the measurement of player engagement in the context of measuring and evaluating the believability of agents or bots in FPS games. The paper also explores the difficulties of GSR the potential outcome of the experiment and some variations of that experiment. Only once the work has been completed will the viability and usefulness of the technique become more clear. If successful, it will create a powerful tool to help us determine how far we have to go before we create genuinely believable game characters who can pass the GSR test.

References

BARRET, S. MD, Quak "Electrodiagnostic" Devices, 2005, *Article onuqckwatch.org, http://www.quackwatch.org/01QuackeryRelatedTopics/electro.html*

BERSAK, D. MCDARBY, G. AUGENBLICK, N. MCDARBY, P. MCDONNELL, D. MCDONALD, B. KARKUN, R., 2001, Intelligent Biofeedback using an Immersive Competitive Environment, *Online Proceedings for the Designing Ubiquitous Computing Games Workshop*, Atlanta GA, www.viktoria.se/play/workshops/ubigame.ubicomp

EPSTEIN, SUSAN L. 2001, Game Playing: The Next Moves, Hunter college of the City of New York, www.aaai.org/Resources/Papers/AAAI99-193.pdf

LAIRD, A. 2000, It knows what Your Going to do: Adding anticipation to a Quake Bot Papers, *AAAI Spring Symposium on Artificial Intelligence and Interactive Entertainment*, Technical Report SS-00-02, AAAI Press.

LAIRD, J. van Lent, MICHAEL. 2001, Human-Level AI's Killer Application: Interactive Computer Games, *Proceedings of AAAI 2000*, Austin, Texas

MIKA P. TARVAINEN, ANU S. KOISTINEN, MINNA VALKONEN-KORHONEN, JUHANI PARTANEN, PASI A. KARJALAINEN, 2001, Analysis of Galvanic Skin Responses with Principal Components and Clustering Techniques, *IEEE Trans Biomed Eng,*

SHIGERU SAKURAZAWA et al, 2003, A computer game using galvanic skin response, *Proc 2nd international conference on Entertainment,* Pittsburgh.

STEVEN JOHNSON, 2003, The Anti-Video Game - A revolutionary idea that could convert critics of these virtual worlds, *Emerging Technology, Vol. 24 No. 12*

SYKES, J. BROWN, S. 2003, Affective Gaming: Measuring Emotion Through the Gamepad, *Published at CHI New Horizons 2003,* Fort Lauterdale, Florida

TOUZOUR, P. 2002, The Evolution of Game AI, AI Game Programming Wisdom, (Ed S Rabin), ISBN 1584502894 p3-15

WELSH, THOMAS. 2005, Parameterisation of human fps strategies, *CGAIMS 2005 conference proceedings*, Louisville, Kentucky

CONTENT ADAPTATION AND SHARED STATE DISTRIBUTION FOR MULTIPLAYER MOBILE GAMES

Qasim Mehdi, Pawan Kumar, Aly Salim and Kamal Bechkoum
School of Computing and Information Technology
University of Wolverhampton
Wolverhampton, UK WV1 1SB
{Q.H.Mehdi, Pawan.Kumar, A.Salim2, K.Bechkoum}@wlv.ac.uk

Abstract:

Typically games on mobile devices are limited to standalone single player games that are not only simple but also are limited by the device capabilities on which they are being played. With the advancement of networking technology, mobile multiplayer games have started to evolve. Nevertheless, these games are played on homogenous devices that have limited functionality and performance. For performance, scalability and heterogeneity, it is important that mobile multiplayer games be played on heterogeneous devices and able to support large number of players for an immersive experience. This demands that players not only receive the content as quickly as possible but also the content be adapted to the device capabilities. Further as different devices have different computing capabilities; it seems reasonable to distribute resources dynamically among the mobile players' devices so that the overall shared state is maintained in a consistent state. In this paper we highlight the issues related to multiplayer gaming on mobile devices and provide a proposal for content adaptation and shared state distribution for multiplayer games on mobile devices based on dynamic scripting approach

Key words:

Content Adaptation, mobile games, WIMAX, WIFI, Bluetooth 2.0, QOS, interest management, dynamic scripting

1. Introduction

As more and more mobile devices grace the earth there is a need to use them in different scenarios and situations to the best of their abilities. Thus in gaming terms utilising them on multiplayer mobile gaming should maximise their potential. Mobile devices as we know them are different i.e. there are PDA's, smart phones, tablets etc. The ability to play multiplayer games over heterogeneous devices seamlessly and without the device user's knowledge (while distributing processing loads to different mobile devices as per resource availability) would not be possible. This raises issues such as content adaptation and distributed processing on mobile devices as well as networking issues that crop up within these situations especially when wireless communication is involved. These are challenging issues that need attending to. Some concepts of content adaptation are covered in some depth in the Olga report where UMA (Universal Media Access) is looked at. This is a concept that encompasses the ability of different constrained mobile devices to access rich media resources [1].

Some work has been accomplished in this area while some research is still in progress, which will be looked at later in the paper. Limitations arising from using wireless networking over mobile devices include limited battery power, constant change in device location, network traffic due to bandwidth being used by other types of communication (including Bluetooth and infra-red). As far as these limitations are concerned there has been some work carried out to optimise the use of network resources. This includes work done in areas of distribution concepts, which involves the choices of architectures and protocols suitable for mobile device multiplayer gaming for example peer to peer, client server and server network [3]. An area that does focus on some aspects of reducing these network issues includes compensatory techniques whereby messages compressed and aggregated reducing bandwidth and transmission frequencies. Another technique is Interest management which will be detailed later on in this paper [3]. Work has been carried out using peer-to-peer overlay architecture for interest management in multiplayer games especially in addressing scalability issues. In this case P2P is used with an interest management mechanism to reduce some of the side effects such as limited visibility that comes with P2P architecture [4]. There are a few limitations as far as grid computing on mobile devices is concerned. These are similar to the networking limitations and include unreliable wireless connectivity, power consumption sensitivity, and software interoperability between different devices [6]. There are some main research projects that have been undertaken thus yielding some interesting results including mobile OGSI.NET which looks at creating a mobile specification for mobile grid computing using pocket PC's running Microsoft operating system [2]. The research on mobile ad-hoc grid networks is still quite a new field. A fair bit of work in this area does not deal with gaming as a beneficiary but rather looks at distributing processes among mobile devices to reduce computing power, increase energy saving, and build efficiency in running more powerful applications on mobile devices. The seamless integration of networking protocols with grid computing principles and interest management in-order to develop a middleware that can actually provide multiplayer gaming regardless of devices hardware and software capabilities is what researchers are moving towards. This paper deals with content adaptation in multiplayer games with regards to different devices being used as such. It raises questions on how multiplayer gaming is conducted on mobile devices which are detailed in the next section. The primary aim of this paper is to try and dissect these questions raising probable solutions to be explored during the investigation. In order to do that, and in addition to these introductory notes, this paper is organised as follows. Section 2 is dedicated to giving a detailed description of the questions related to multiplayer gaming on mobile devices. Section 2.1 deals with the associated networking issues. Software architectures for online games are briefly reviewed in Section 2.2. Section 2.3 deals with scalable-shared state distribution and section 2.4 elaborates on content representation in games. Section 3 deals with content adaptation and shared state distribution on multiplayer games with a twist on how we propose to tackle the issues while Section 4 concludes the paper.

2. Multiplayer gaming on mobile devices

For a game to be successful on mobile devices, several issues need to be addressed upfront. Depending on the genre, these may include the issues of latencies, bandwidth, scalability, real-timelines, etc. For instance, a first person shooter would demand a low latency, real-time responses whereas a role-playing game can get away with a higher latency but may require supporting several hundreds of simultaneous users. In addition, the device capabilities and networking infrastructure add constraints that need to be dealt with appropriately for a successful gaming application. Device capabilities include its operating environment such as resources available in form of processing, memory, connectivity and battery usage. Networking support in these devices may range from wireless LAN, WIMAX, GPRS and Bluetooth. Given the heterogeneity in the devices available in the market, mobile multiplayer games have been limited to homogeneous devices over fixed settings and thus are not truly mobile. For performance, scalability and heterogeneity, it is important that mobile multiplayer games are played on heterogeneous devices in a truly mobile environment and are able to support large number of players for an immersive experience. This demands addressing several key questions. Firstly, how the game content comprising representations of geometry, texture, animations, audio and video to be stored and distributed in order to provide a consistent view of the virtual world? Secondly, how to support large number of players having different devices and interacting with the virtual world without degrading the performance? Thirdly, how to distribute the shared state and the processing intensive tasks across multiple mobile devices? Fourthly, how to adapt the content and the shared state in these purely mobile and distributed games with respect to changes in device connectivity and usage?

In the following sections we briefly provide an investigation of networking issues in mobile games, software architectures for supporting online games, approaches for scalable shared state distribution and content representation in games.

2.1 Networking issues in mobile games

Multiplayer mobile gaming involves networking. It does have a big bearing on how the game performs in terms of seamless distribution of game states and messages. This may include getting round limitations like latency, bandwidth, scalability etc. These however can be minimized to an extent depending on network communication chosen (e.g. WIBREE, ZIGBEE, Bluetooth 1.0, Bluetooth 2.0 EDR, WIFI, WIMAX, and WIBRO. These are currently available standards that can be found on different mobile devices, some being more widespread than others. Mobile devices have different capabilities as far as communication with other devices is concerned. These include WIFI, Bluetooth1.2 and 2.0, WIMAX, ZIGBEE, and WIBREE etc. Mobile devices pose a few challenges in terms of seamless uninterrupted communication. Challenges faced include mobility where some devices can go out of range resulting in a reduction in the number of devices connected to the network [5]. This has its pitfalls with regards to state of the application (game state) at the time of departure from the network. ZIGBEE, WIBREE are not suitable for real-time multiplayer gaming communication and data exchange over wirelessly due to their limitations in data transfer rates as well as availability on devices too [7, 8]. Bluetooth 1.2 and WIFI have been used so far in multiplayer gaming but mostly on handheld gaming devices like Nintendo DS and PSP. However their operating range and support for mesh topology can be a problem [9, 10 & 13]. There are other issues that are related to content distribution for gaming applications over the wireless network such as different standards and limitations. Therefore the main issues that concern network aspects for multiplayer games include: scalability which allow the games to adapt to resource changes as seen fit; distribution concepts which encompass architectures for communication (client/server etc); networking resources which include the latency; bandwidth; and computational power available)[3].
However with the advent of Bluetooth 2.0 EDR and WIMAX the range, scalability and QOS (Quality of Service) have been improved. Therefore it can be argued that the best way to induce better communication and data exchange between devices during game playing is by looking at better distribution concepts and compensatory techniques including interest management and process redistribution using grid concepts [3]. The communication protocol being trialled for this investigation and prototyping is a contraption of WIMAX and Bluetooth 2.0 EDR. Bluetooth 2.0 is used as a communication protocol between different devices within range of each other forming Pico-nets that communicate through a nominated server points. The nomination process of these points would depend upon a few set rules taking into account necessary factors including power levels and computational resource. This would be a good way to tackle some issues with regards to range and strength of signal between mobile devices.

2.2 Software architectures for online games

Network architectures namely client/server, P2P and hybrid [4] do play an important role in multiplayer games. They form the backbone of how the game is distributed around the network of players. The manner in which data is relayed across the multiple player devices with respect to their

capabilities dictates how well the game is executed on the whole.
There are numerous architecture models used in networking including client server, peer to peer and hybrid. Client server being the more popular architecture with gaming companies due to a number of reasons such as:

- Easy to implement.
- Easy to maintain state consistency due to having a centralized server.
- Hard to cheat and hack into the game.

The client-server inherently suffers from single point failure if triggered would result in server failure and the loss of game content. High bandwidth requirement at the server would present a challenge especially with wireless networks due to their limited bandwidth capabilities [15].
The peer to peer architecture does tend to be used for some games but not as much due to a few factors that include inability to harness control over game administration due to each device having to run its own game software thus messaging other devices to relay game states and update its own too. This may prove detrimental towards mobile devices due to them having limited storage and processing power [14, 15]. It does however pose a few advantages that could be of good use for multiplayer gaming which include the elimination of one point of failure, reduction of bottleneck and reduced message latencies. However it is harder to implement the P2P architecture. One reason being its difficulty in scaling with proportion to users engaged. State consistency among players would then become an issue [15]. This may not be suitable to content adaptation due to the fact that while playing multiplayer games with different devices of different capabilities the ability to adapt content to suit each device format is crucial. It does show strain in coping with increased amount of users due to its increased messaging thus containment of users is not easily achievable. There is also the issue of computational power and battery life, which are all constrained factors on mobile devices. P2P does rely on these two factors due to the fact that there is no central repository to work with. This thus brings about some issues with regards to computing resource management and battery life management [14].
The hybrid/mirrored server architecture takes into account the advantages from both architectures and presents a sound case for deployment of multiplayer games on it. There is a more structured coupling with the hybrid system though it still has to cope with message bottleneck that does trigger network traffic. This in-turn affects other aspects of mobile device limitations.
The bandwidth requirement for P2P and client/server is nearly the same. Thus for this particular investigation the client/server architecture seems to be a more reliable approach to start with. It would suit mobile devices due to their limited capabilities and thus it can take up a lot of the processing away from them ensuring a sound gaming experience on the client side. It would be also be a lot easier to implement and work with. This will be intertwined with the use of interest management that will be detailed later in the paper.

2.3 Scalable shared state distribution

Performance and scalability in multiplayer games requires efficient distribution of the shared state. Typically, a player's node will contain some subset of the shared virtual world whose state is influenced and maintained by the player. In order to have a mutual consistent view of the virtual world, events or messages are exchanged between player nodes (either directly or indirectly through a server). However, an update occurring at one node is likely to have an immediate significance for only a subset of other nodes in the system. The techniques that exploit this *interest* of each node to minimise the number of messages sent are referred as *interest management* (IM) schemes [16].

Interest management systems have been incorporated in several large-scale distributed simulators [17,18], collaborative virtual environments [19,20,21] and multiplayer online games [22,23,24]. These have been incorporated mainly to allow systems to scale seamlessly and efficiently. The scalability in these systems is primarily related to the number of nodes that can participate and the computational complexity of the model that is being simulated e.g. in a game it could be the number of entities the game has. Without the IM system, every update or state changes at one node would need to be communicated to all the other nodes. This could significantly increase the bandwidth usage, message sent per second and computational requirements at processing these messages. However, incorporating IM systems would try to minimise the above at the expense of computational costs for its processing and thus affecting the real-time requirements of these systems and potentially reducing performance. Thus, performance and scalability of these systems mainly depend on the effectiveness of the deployed IM scheme in these systems. In our previous work [25] we presented a scalable algorithm for interest management in online games and highlighted some of the related works in the area. These would be highly appropriate for addressing the second and third questions of scalable-shared state distribution in multiplayer games on mobile devices.

2.4 Content representation in games

Game content mainly comprises representation of geometry (for characters, entities, levels, etc), textures, animation sequences, audio and video. All these are used to create a virtual world that the user can interact with. Several techniques have been developed for efficient representation of these elements. For geometry, these include polygonal approaches and triangulation to form 3D meshes. *Triangle soups* can be used to represent entities and geometries from semantically unrelated parts. However, these approaches require prior knowledge about device rendering capabilities and make a compromise between the number of triangles and the quality of the model. Several scalable approaches for geometry representation have also been used that adapt to fast rendering with decreased visual quality and slow rendering with high detailed model. One of these approaches is the *Level of Detailed* (LOD) [26] modelling where a model is represented with several planer meshes having different levels of granularity. Apart from rendering benefits, this approach is highly appropriate for sending entities from content servers to client devices depending on the communication infrastructure supported by the device and the available bandwidth. Further, if procedural approaches are used for moving from one detailed representation to another, this approach can further be exploited where coarser LOD is transferred first to the client device while the remaining ones are sent gradually and incorporated within the rendered mesh. This approach clearly compliments rendering and transfer of content in the wake of variable device capabilities and connectivity.

Another approach that is used in scalable geometry is based on mesh reduction algorithms and techniques. Mesh reduction algorithms reduce the polygon count of highly detailed meshes and optimise them for rendering. This can be achieved by an offline tool or can be done more dynamically at runtime based on the constraints such as distance from the viewer, frame rate, etc. These reduction approaches can be very fast and yield good approximations to the original model that can be appropriate on mobile devices that have variable degree of constraints associated with them. Other approaches to scalable geometry include representations based on curved surfaces (Bezier, splines, etc) that are more efficient and require less storage than polygonal techniques discussed above. These have been well adopted in multimedia standards such as MPEG [27]. In addition, MPEG standard incorporates special encoding and compression techniques that would be highly appropriate for their usage on mobile devices. For textures, audio and video content, several standards exist [27,28,29,30] that use state of the art encoding and compression techniques that can be used appropriately depending on the constraints associated with the devices and the quality of service requirements.

Once we have geometry representation and textures for an entity, it needs to be placed and moved in the virtual world with respect to others and/or have deformations applied on it. Animating an entity thus requires applying and updating geometric transformations such as translation, rotation and scale by either applying dynamics or key framing (based on interpolation of some function of time). Further, in case of deformations, the animation continuously changes the shape of the entity. This typically requires deformation controllers attached to the entity that influences its shape. These controllers are typically defined by a means of geometric support (such as points, lines, curves, surfaces, and volumes) and any changes made to these are reflected on to the entities to which they are attached. There exist several representation techniques for representing the actual animation data. These can be in human readable XML-based coding or have advanced compression based compact binary formats [27]. Furthermore, compact representation of animation parameters can consist of decomposing transformations into elementary motion and using quaternion or Euler angles for rotations. Other such optimisations and compression-based representation schemes have been well researched and used in games for animation that would be incorporated for content representation and their adaptation for mobile multiplayer games. In the following section we present a new approach for content adaptation in mobile multiplayer games

3 Content adaptation and shared state distribution for multiplayer mobile games

Adaptation for mobile devices has been an active research area and several projects have been developed that address one aspect or the other [31,32,33,34,35]. However, previous research work is mainly limited to generic and web based applications rather than content rich multimedia applications and games. Some provide a manual [36] and user feedback [37] mechanism for adaptation whereas other uses automatic adaptation techniques based on rule-based [38,40] and constraint based [39] approaches. For scalable multiplayer games on mobile devices we are mainly interested in adaptation of the content that is received by the client devices. At the same time we are also interested in the dynamic adaptation and distribution of computing tasks among those devices. A successful implementation of online adaptation in games demands several computational and functional requirements as suggested by Spronck [41]. These include four computational requirements of speed, robustness, effectiveness and efficiency and four functional requirements of clarity, variety, consistency and scalability. To meet these requirements, Spronck suggested '*dynamic scripting*' technique that we plan to use for content adaptation and task distribution on mobile devices. According to Spronck, dynamic scripting is an online machine –learning technique that is characterised by a stochastic optimisation technique. It maintains several rule bases one for each agent and every time an agent is generated, the rule bases are used to create a new script that controls agent's behaviour. Each rule is associated with a weight value and adaptation of the rule base proceeds by changing the weight values to reflect the success or failure of the rules in the script. The learning mechanism in this technique is inspired from reinforcement learning techniques where the weights of the rules are adapted depending on their contribution to the outcome of the script. Rules that lead to success are rewarded with weight increase whereas the rules that lead to failure are punished with weight decrease. The key to successful implementation of this approach is design of rule base from domain specific knowledge, knowledge of successful scripts and evaluation function for evaluating the success of the script.

For our work, we draw an analogy for implementing dynamic scripting for content adaptation and shared state distribution. The key here is that the devices are considered as agents where we specify rules based on device capabilities, its usage environment and networking constraints (Figure 1). These domain specific characteristics will be evaluated to select the desired quality of service and content representation most suitable for the device that gets adapted as its usage is changed (e.g. variation in connectivity, battery status, variable load, etc). Specifying and updating these constraints would update the weights associated with rules and would therefore augment the adaptation procedure by generating appropriate

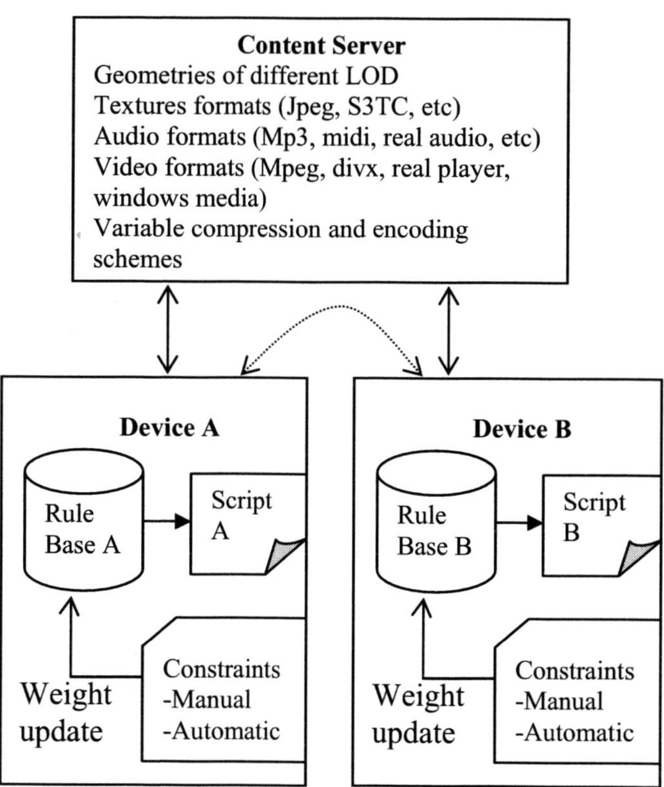

Figure 1 Dynamic scripting for content adaptation and shared state distribution on mobile devices

scripts. For truly mobile games, clients would be moving around in the real world as well as in the virtual world. This movement would clearly affect the underlying network topology. Given such a dynamic networking topology (this may comprise mirror content servers based on client-server approach and sending game update based on P2P approaches) that has to adapt and react to maintain the shared state and consistency of the game, the dynamic scripting approach would aid in selecting the appropriate shared state distribution strategy and decisions for dynamic interest management for efficient distribution, scalability and load balancing. Dynamic scripting has been proven to be very efficient for online adaptation of behaviours in games and requires very few trials for learning and therefore is a good candidate for development of a prototype system to evaluate content adaptation and state distribution for mobile multiplayer games.

4 Conclusions

This paper presented some of the issues related to multiplayer games on heterogeneous mobile devices. We presented several questions that we are trying to address in the context of multiplayer gaming on mobile devices and briefly provide an investigation of networking issues in mobile games, software architectures for supporting online games, approaches for scalable shared state distribution and content representation in games. Further, we discussed the use of dynamic scripting approach as an integral part of the adaptation system that will be used for content adaptation and shared state distribution for mobile games. This would allow for selecting appropriate representation, encoding and transmission scheme for the content depending on the device capabilities and constraints associated with the device. Further evolution of the scripts would be used for efficient shared state distribution and dynamic adaptation of the networking topology. In future we plan to investigate the set of constraints that would form part of the rule base and how weights are assigned to these. We plan to develop a prototype system to test the effectiveness of this technique for mobile devices. This would include some level of detail modelling for geometry, using client-server approach for transferring geometry and using client-sever or peer to peer approaches for sending game updates and maintaining shared state. We also plan to test several protocols such as Bluetooth 2.0, wifi and Wimax for communication between the devices.

References

[1] Alborghetti etal. 2004. "A united scalable framework for on-line gaming". http://www-artemis.int-evry.fr/Artemis/Research/OLGA/OLGA0.html (accessed 10th October 2006).

[2] Chu C. D., Humphrey M. 2004. "Mobile OGSI.NET: grid computing on mobile devices.*Fifth IEEE/ACM International Workshop on Grid Computing.*"pp. 182 – 191.

[3] Smed J, Kaukaranta T, Hakonen H. 2002. "Aspects of networking in multiplayer computer games." *The Electronic Library*, 20(2):87–97.

[4] Yu A, Vuong S.T, 2005. "MOPAR: a mobile peer-to-peer overlay architecture for interest management of massively multiplayer online games. *Proceedings of the international workshop on Network and operating systems support for digital audio and video NOSSDAV '05*" pp. 99 -104.

[5] Budke D, Farkas K etal. 2006. "Real-Time multiplayer game support using QoS mechanisms in mobile ad-hoc networks. *WONS 2006 : Third Annual Conference on Wireless On-demand Network Systems and Services"*. Pp 32 – 40.

[6] Phan T, Huang L, Dulan C. 2002. "Challenge: Integrating Mobile wireless devices into the computational grid. *Proceedings of the 8th annual international conference on Mobile computing and networking"*. Pp 271 – 278.

[7] Andersson A, Thoren M. 2005. "Zigbee, a suitable base for embedded wireless development?" http://db.s2.chalmers.se/download/masters/master_030_2005.pdf

[8] Wibree.com http://www.wibree.com (accessed 15th October 2006).

[9] Wikipedia http://en.wikipedia.org/wiki/Bluetooth (accessed 16th October 2006).

[10] Sreenivas H, Ali H. 2004."An Evolutionary Bluetooth Scatternet Formation Protocol. *Proceedings of the Proceedings of the 37th Annual Hawaii International Conference on System Sciences"*.

[11] Riera S M, Wellnitz O, Wolf L. 2003. "A Zone-based gaming architecture for ad-hoc networks. *Proceedings of the 2nd workshop on Network and system support for games (NETGAMES '03)"*. Pp 72 – 76.

[12] Abichar Z, Peng Y, Chang J M. 2006. "Wimax: The emergence of wireless broadband. *I.T. professional.*"pp 44 – 48.

[13] Fourty N, Val T, Fraisse P, Mercier J. 2005. "Comparative analysis of new high data rate wireless communication technologies "from WIFI to WIMAX. *Joint International Conference*

on Autonomic and Autonomous Systems and International Conference on Networking and Services - (icas-icns'05) ". Pp 66.
[14] Cronin E, Filstrup B, Kurc A. 2001. "A Distributed Multiplayer game server system." http://warriors.eecs.umich.edu/games/papers/quakefinal.pdf (accessed 20th October 2006).
[15] Pellegrino J D, Dovrolis C. 2003. "Bandwidth requirement and state consistency in three multiplayer game architectures. *Proceedings of the 2nd workshop on Network and system support for games (NETGAMES '03)*". Pp 52 – 59.
[16] Singhal S, and Zyda M. 1999. *Netwroked Virtual Environments: Design and Implementation.* Addision Wesley
[17] Morse K. 2000. "An Adaptive, Distributed Algorithm for Interest Management"; *PhD Thesis*, University of California, Irvine
[18] US Defence Modelling and Simulation Office. 1998. High Level Architecture (HLA)- Interface Specification, version 1.3
[19] Macedonia M, Zyda M, Pratt D, Brutzmann D and Barham P. 1995. "Exploiting Reality with Multicast Groups: A Network Architecture for Large-Scale Virtual Environments"; *IEEE Computer Graphics and Applications,* 15(3): 38-45
[20] Miller D and Thorpe J A. 1995. "SIMNET: The Advent of Simulator Networking", *Proc. of IEEE,* 83(8): 1114-1123
[21] Greenhalgh C and Bendford S. 1995. "MASSIVE: A Distributed Virtual Reality System Incorporating Spatial Trading", *Proc. of 15th International conference on distributed computing systems (DCS 95)*, IEEE Computer Society, 27-35
[22] Epic Games 1999. *The Unreal Networking Architecture.* World Wide Web, http://unreal.epicgames.com/Network.htm
[23] Yu A and Vuong S T. 2005. "MOPAR: A Mobile Peer-to-Peer Overlay Architecture for Interest Management of Massively Multiplayer Online Games", *in proc. of International Workshop on Network and Operating systems Support for Digital Audio and Video,* pp: 99-104
[24] Liu E, Yip M and Yu G. 2005. "Scalable Interest Management for Multidimensional Routing Space", *in proc. of the ACM symposium on Virtual Reality Software and Technology,* pp: 82-85
[25] Kumar P and Mehdi Q. 2006. "Recursive Interest Management For Online Games", *in proc. of 8th International Conference on Computer Games (CGAMES),* Louisville, KY, USA

[26] Clark J H 1976. "Hierarchical Geometric Models for Visible Surface Algorithms", Communications of the ACM, 19-10, 547-554, October 1976.

[27] MPEG (Moving Picture Experts Group) – 4 [Online]. Available: http://www.chiariglione.org/mpeg/standards/mpeg-4/mpeg-4.htm

[28] ISO/IEC 15444-1:2000: Information technology – JPEG 2000 image coding system – Part 1: Core coding system.

[29] Real Video: [Online] Available: http://en.wikipedia.org/wiki/RealVideo
[30] DivX: [Online] Available: http://en.wikipedia.org/wiki/Divx
[31] Katz R H 1994. Adaptation and mobility in wireless information systems. *IEEE Personal Communications*, 1(1):6–17, 1994.
[32] E. de Lara, D. S. Wallach, and W. Zwaenepoel. 2001 Puppeteer: Component-based adaptation for mobile computing. In *Proceedings of the 3rd USENIX Symposium on Internet Technologies and Systems*, San Francisco, California, Mar. 2001.
[33] Fox A., Gribble S. D, Chawathe Y, and Brewer E. A.1998. Adapting to network and client variation using infrastructural proxies: Lessons and perspectives. *IEEE Personal Communications*, 5(4):10–19, Aug. 1998.
[34] Lum W. Y.and. Lau F. C 2002. A context-aware decision engine for content adaptation. *IEEE Pervasive Computing*, 1(3):41–49, July 2002.
[35] Narayanan D., Flinn J., and Satyanarayanan M. 2000. Using history to improve mobile application adaptation. In *Proceedings of the 3rd IEEE Workshop on MobileComputing Systems and Applications*, Monterey, California, Dec. 2000.
[36] WAP Forum. Wireless application protocol architecture specification, Apr. 1998. Available at: http://www.wapforum.org/what/technical/arch-30-apr-98.pdf.
[37] Mohomed I, Cai J H, Chavoshi S, Lara E 2006. Context-Aware Interactive Content Adaptation. *In Proceedings of the 4th International conference on Mobile systems, applications and services*, Uppsala, Sweden
[38] Smith J. R., Mohan R., and. Li C.-S 1998. Content-based transcoding of images in the Internet. In *Proceedings of the IEEE International Conference on Image Processing*, Chicago, Illinois, Oct. 1998.
[39]. Smith J. R, Mohan R., and Li C.-S.1998. Transcoding internet content for heterogeneous client devices. In *Proceedings of the IEEE International Symposium on Circuits and Systems*, Monterey, California, May 1998.
[40] Bickmore T. W.and Schilit B. N. 1997. Digestor: Device-independent access to the World Wide Web. *Computer Networks and ISDN Systems*, 29(8–13):1075–1082, 1997.
[41] Spronck P. 2005. "Adaptive Game AI"; *PhD Thesis*, University of Maastricht, The Netherlands

Mobile and Multiuser Games

Network Latency in On-Line Gaming: An Engineering or a Psychological Problem?

Conor Linehan[+], Bryan Roche[+], Séamus McLoone[°] and Tomás Ward[°]

[+]*Department of Psychology,*
National University of Ireland Maynooth,
Maynooth, Co. Kildare, IRELAND

[°]*Department of Electronic Engineering,*
National University of Ireland Maynooth,
Maynooth, Co. Kildare, IRELAND

Abstract: Ongoing research attempts to find engineering-based solutions to the problem of network latency in multiplayer computer games. However, few studies have been conducted to examine the end-users' experience of latency from a psychological perspective. The current study examines the roles of network latency and game complexity on the subjective experience of participants playing a specially designed computer game. Results suggest that participants prefer complex over simple games, regardless of the level of latency experienced. These findings suggest the possibility of a psychological solution to some of the negative effects of network latency. It is suggested that by manipulating Relational Complexity, it may be possible to maintain a satisfactory gaming experience in the presence of latency.

Keywords: Networked Multiplayer Games, Latency, Playability

I. INTRODUCTION

Distributed Interactive Applications, (DIAs) such as shared whiteboards and multi-player computer games, may be described as virtual environments that allow real-time collaboration and co-operation between geographically dispersed users. Each individual interacts with their own local representation of the environment and the application attempts to maintain a consistent representation of that environment to all users at all times. However, in practice this is often impossible to achieve, due to the distances and information transfer speeds involved [1]. Thus, participants often see slightly different events at different times. This problem is known as inconsistency and is particularly destructive to the experience of online game playing [2], [3].

Much recent research has been conducted in an attempt to find engineering-based solutions to this problem (i.e. [4]-[6]). While such work will undoubtedly help combat the detrimental effects of network latency on consistency in DIAs, it may also prove beneficial to examine the end-users' experience of this latency from a psychological perspective. Such research may help to inform us of the sufficient limits of improvements in technology needed to combat network latency. Moreover, such research may help us to identify means by which we can ameliorate the negative affects of latency by using psychological technology in the construction of games in the first instance. The results of a psychological investigation, therefore, may improve our understanding of game playing behaviour in general and guide both engineering research and game development. In addition it may shed light on playability and gaming experiences in general – an aspect of the industry that lacks rigorous analysis.

The current research approaches online games in terms of a series of cognitive challenges or problems to be solved. From this perspective, game players earn high scores by responding appropriately to each challenge presented within the game. In more technical terms, we conceive these cognitive challenges in terms of a psychological process known as stimulus equivalence [7, 8]. Stimulus equivalence is one of the simplest examples of problem solving and may be described as the following; if any one stimulus *A* is the same as any other stimulus *B*, and *B* is the same as a further stimulus *C*, then *B* is the same as *A*, *C* is the same as *B*, *A* is the same as *C* and *C* is the same as *A*. While stimulus equivalence may appear simpler than the problem solving typically required in game playing, it has been proposed as the basis for all complex human behaviour such as language, cognition and problem solving [7] and thus provides a solid starting point for the current research program.

II. DEVELOPMENT

A. Stimulus Equivalence Training Phase

The study was divided into two stages which we will refer to as the stimulus equivalence training phase and the game phase, respectively. Each phase required the development of a standalone computer program which was programmed using *Microsoft Visual Basic 6.0* software. The stimulus equivalence phase involved the development of a program for training two five member equivalence classes among a range of stimuli (i.e., *A1-B1-C1-D1-E1* and *A2-B2-C2-D2-E2*) using a matching-to-sample procedure. The actual stimuli used were nonsense syllables and coloured shapes, but are represented here in alphanumeric form for simplicity. In this procedure, one stimulus (the sample) was presented at the top of a screen. Another two stimuli (comparisons) were presented at the bottom of the screen, and the participant was required to choose which of these two stimuli goes with the sample. Corrective feedback was given after a choice was made. For example, on one trial a sample stimulus *A1* was presented along with two comparison stimuli *B1* and *B2*. If the participant chose *B1*, the screen cleared and they were presented with the word 'correct'. If the participant chose *B2*, the screen cleared and they were presented with the word 'wrong'. Feedback remained on-screen for one second before the next trial was presented.

Training was conducted in blocks of 20 trials, in which the participant was required to respond correctly to 19/20 trials before advancing to the next block (this criterion is standard in stimulus equivalence research [8]). Four training blocks of this kind were trained sequentially: A-B, B-C, C-D and D-E. Once training was successfully completed, participants were presented with the game phase.

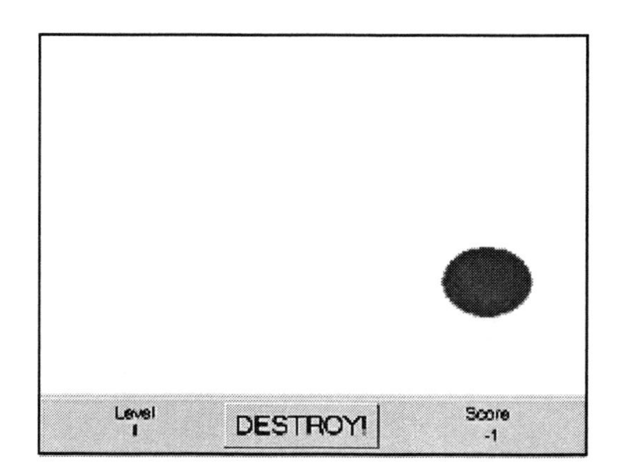

Fig. 1. Screenshot from Level 1 of the game.

B. The Game Phase

The game phase involved presenting subjects with a specially designed computer game consisting of three levels. All levels had the same user interface, as depicted in Fig. 1. Level 1 was a training level in which participants learned how to use the interface and gain high scores in the game. In Level 1, stimuli *A1* and *A2* from the stimulus equivalence training and testing phase comprised the game characters. Participants were instructed that one character could be destroyed to earn points while the other character could be saved to earned points. Characters were destroyed by clicking on an on-screen 'destroy' button and saved by clicking on the character itself. The participants' score was displayed in the bottom right hand corner of the screen. Importantly, characters increased in size rapidly in order to simulate movement towards the screen. If no response was made within 2 seconds, the screen cleared and a point was deducted from the total displayed on the computer screen.

Level 2 was similar to Level 1, with the exception that no score was displayed and the characters used were the *C1* and *C2* characters from the stimulus equivalence training phase. Importantly, these stimuli had never appeared on-screen with the *A1* and *A2* stimuli before. Thus participants had to infer, in the absence of any feedback from the score indicator, which of the characters had to be saved in order to earn points and which had to be destroyed.

Level 3 was identical to Level 2, with the exception that the *E1* and *E2* characters from stimulus equivalence training and testing were presented. Again, participants had to solve the problem of which character was to be saved and which character was to be destroyed, in the absence of any feedback. Importantly, Level 3 was considered to be more difficult than Level 2. In order to respond correctly to characters in Level 2, the participants had to rapidly recall the relations between the A stimuli presented in Level 1, the B stimuli which were not presented in any game level, and the C stimuli presented in Level 2. In Level 3, participants had to rapidly recall further relations between the C, D and E stimuli in order to respond correctly to the *E1* and *E2* stimuli in the same manner as the *A1* and *A2* stimuli, respectively.

Simulated network delays were inserted on one quarter of all trials presented in Levels 2 and 3 of the game phase. These delays were designed to functionally simulate the effects of network latency. Specifically, on a delayed trial, the interface was unresponsive to users' actions, impairing the ability of a participant to make a response within the appropriate time frame. Two separate game types were created, one in which delays lasted 0.5 seconds and one in which delays lasted 1 second. 0.5 second delays were assumed to be detrimental to game playing experience [9], while 1 second delays were assumed to have an even higher negative impact on user experience.

A questionnaire, which forms part of the Day Reconstruction Method (DRM) [10] was presented after each level of the game, as a subjective measure of both positive and negative attitudes towards that level. Importantly, the DRM has been validated with a sample of 1018, so the scale in question may represent a reliable subjective measure for the current study.

III. EXPERIMENT

Twenty two participants were recruited, all of whom were undergraduate students. Eleven of these were male, while eleven were female. Participants were promised a payment of €5 upon reaching a high score in the game. The experiment employed a 2x2 mixed between-within participants design (as depicted in Table 1). The main variables were the length of simulated delay in each game, and the level of complexity across the levels of the game. The first variable was manipulated across participant groups as participants either played the short delay or long delay games. The second variable was manipulated within groups, i.e. all participants were exposed to both levels of the game.

	Low Complexity	**High Complexity**
Short Delay	1	2
Long Delay	3	4

Table 1. A representation of the four experimental conditions employed in the study.

There were three dependent measures; participants' score on each level of the game, and their subjectively rated level of both Positive and Negative Affect. Positive and Negative Affect are constructs statistically derived from responses to the DRM questionnaire, which was presented after each level of the game [10].

IV. RESULTS

All participants passed the stimulus equivalence training phase and advanced on to the game phase. None of the twenty-two participants failed to pass the Level 1 training level in the game phase. Mean scores were calculated for all conditions in the study (see Table 2). There was no consistent pattern of higher mean total correct responses in either game or in either level within games. However, it must be noted that the highest mean total correct responses score was for Level 3 of the Long Delay game. That is, participants achieved the highest scores in the most difficult and highly delayed game. Thus, effective playing appears not to have been affected by delay or complexity.

	Low Complexity	High Complexity
Total Correct Responses		
Short Delay	25.7	23.7
Long Delay	22.8	26.5
Positive Affect		
Short Delay	5.7	8.1
Long Delay	5.5	6.5
Negative Affect		
Short Delay	7.5	5.3
Long Delay	6.7	5.1

Table 2. Mean scores on all measures employed in the study.

As expected, Mean Positive Affect ratings were higher on both levels of the short delay game than in the corresponding levels in the long delay game, suggesting that subjects preferred the games with shorter delays. However, mean Negative Affect ratings were also found to be higher on both levels of the short delay game than in the corresponding levels in the long delay game. These results are contradictory, suggesting that further work must be undertaken to better understand the impact of different increments in delay on game enjoyment.

Mean Positive Affect ratings were higher in Level 3 than Level 2 in both the delay and non delay games, suggesting that participants preferred the more complex levels of the game. Correspondingly, Mean Negative Affect ratings were also lower in Level 3 than Level 2 in both the delay and non delay games.

A mixed between-within subject's analysis of variance was conducted to explore the impact of Relational Complexity and Level of Delay on participants' Total Correct Responses made during game play, as well as their ratings of each game type for Positive and Negative Affect. The results of this analysis are presented in Table 3. Relational Complexity had a significant effect on participants' ratings of Negative Affect. Specifically, participants found the later, more complex levels of the game significantly less negative than the earlier, less complex levels. In addition, there is a trend of higher Positive Affect ratings for Level 3 over Level 2, although this effect is not significant. Relational Complexity did not have a significant effect on Total Correct Responses. In addition, Delay Level had no significant effect on any measure employed in the experiment.

	Wilks' Lambda	F Value	P Value	Eta Squared
Total Correct Responses				
Complexity	0.999	0.023	0.882	0.001
Delay	N/A	0.00	0.99	0.00
Interaction	0.987	0.270	0.609	0.013
Positive Affect				
Complexity	0.883	1.253	0.308	0.117
Delay	N/A	0.178	0.678	0.009
Interaction	0.972	0.273	0.764	0.028
Negative Affect				
Complexity	0.674	4.598	0.024*	0.326
Delay	N/A	0.045	0.834	0.002
Interaction	0.993	0.070	0.933	0.007

Table 3. Results from mixed between-within subjects ANOVA, testing for the effects of Delay Level and Relational Complexity on the dependent variables of Total Correct Responses, Positive and Negative Affect. Those marked with an asterisk represent significant results.

V. CONCLUSIONS

A number of conclusions can be drawn from the current preliminary results. Firstly, the finding that Delay Level had no significant effect on any measure employed in the experiment suggests that increased length of delay does not significantly affect game players' enjoyment of, or performance at, a game. This finding provides a contrast to a number of other studies which have investigated the effects of network latency [1, 9]. However, this finding does not necessarily suggest that simulated network delays have no effect whatsoever on participants' enjoyment of and performance at a game. Rather, this finding may merely suggest that 1 second delays do not affect participants' enjoyment of and performance at a game any more than 0.5 second delays do. It is clearly a difficult matter to ascertain the degree to which enjoyment of a game is affected by increments in delay. More specifically, delay may reach a critical, as yet undetermined threshold, beyond which its negative impact increases negligibly or not at all. It remains for future research to identify whether this is the case and the relevant threshold that may apply.

Secondly, in the current study network latency was modeled as a fixed interval of either 0.5 seconds or 1 second. It may be argued that, given that participants could predict the length of each delay suffered, the delays could have been perceived as a particular challenge of the game, rather than a nuisance or problem with the game. In practice, network latency is rarely, if ever, predictable and typically oscillates erratically during game play. It has been suggested that this oscillation in network latency, known as jitter, is much more destructive to the game playing experience than fixed delays [9], such as those modeled in this study. Thus, future work must attempt to better understand the role of jitter on user experience in online gaming.

Thirdly, it must be noted that very different results may be obtained by using different types of games in a similar study. The game used in the current study has been contrived for experimental purposes and may lack some ecological validity when compared to modern online games. However, it must be remembered that any serious psychological investigation into game playing must employ games where all features are being simultaneously controlled or manipulated. This is difficult to do with commercial games that have not been specifically designed for this purpose.

Fourthly, Relational Complexity had a significant effect on participants' ratings of Negative Affect, where the more complex levels of the game were rated as significantly less negative than less complex levels. In addition there is a trend of higher Positive Affect ratings for the more complex levels. Thus, if future studies establish more firmly that network latency is indeed detrimental to the game playing experience, we may be able to compensate for this by manipulating complexity, thereby maintaining a satisfactory gaming experience. For example, more relationally complex games could allow for fractionally slower game play, without any loss of enjoyment from the end-user's perspective. Of course, some game players will still want to play games involving the rapid presentation of stimuli and strict time demands on responding. However, these findings provide a starting point for a psychological intervention for the problem of network latency in DIAs.

Finally, Relational Complexity did not have a significant effect on Total Correct Responses. This finding is interesting because it shows that score achieved during game play, and enjoyment of a game, are not directly correlated. High scores are not necessarily what game players find reinforcing.

It would appear that a thorough psychological study can reveal the dynamic features of an enjoyable game and provide the technology to increase those levels of enjoyment. For this reason, the current research agenda and its preliminary findings should be of interest to psychologists working in technological fields and also to engineers, games designers and marketers of on-line games. More generally, bringing rigorous psychological methods to bear on existing engineering problems may prove to be an exciting and fruitful strategy for future research.

ACKNOWLEDGEMENTS

This work is supported by Science Foundation Ireland and Enterprise Ireland - grant no. IRCSET/SC/04/CS0289.

REFERENCES

[1] I. Vaghi, C. Greenhalgh, and S. Benford, "Coping with inconsistency due to network delays in collaborative virtual environments," *Proceedings of the ACM symposium on Virtual reality software and technology, 1999,* pp 42 – 49.

[2] T. Yasui, Y. Ishibashi and T. Ikedo, "Influences of network latency and packet loss on consistency in networked racing games", *Proceedings of 4th ACM SIGCOMM workshop on Network and system support for games*, pp 1-8, ACM Press, Hawthorne, NY, 2005

[3] J. Aronson, "Dead Reckoning: Latency Hiding for Networked Games", *Gamasutra.com, September 19, 1997* http://www.gamasutra.com/features/19970919/aronson_01.htm. Viewed 07.09.2006.

[4] D. Marshall, D. Roberts, D. Delaney, S.C. McLoone, and T. Ward, "Dealing with the Effect of Path Curvature on Consistency of Dead Reckoned Paths in Networked Virtual Environments," *IEEE Virtual Reality Conference (VR2006), Alexandria, VIRGINIA, USA, 25-29 March, pp. 299-300*

[5] D. Delaney, S. McLoone, and T. Ward, "A Novel Convergence Algorithm for the Hybrid Strategy Model Packet Reduction Technique," *IEE Irish Signals and Systems Conference, Dublin, Ireland, 1-2 September 2005, pp. 118-123.*

[6] Yu-Shen Ng, "Designing Fast-Action Games For The Internet", *Gamasutra.com, Sept 5, 1997.* http://www.gamasutra.com/features/19970905/ng_01.htm. Viewed 07.09.2006.

[7] S.C. Hayes, D. Barnes-Holmes, and B. Roche, (Eds.) *Relational Frame Theory: A Post-Skinnerian Account of Human Language and Cognition.* New York: Kluwer Academic/Plenum Publishers, 2001.

[8] M. Sidman, *Equivalence relations and Behaviour: A Research Story.* Boston: Authors Cooperative, 1994.

[9] D. Delaney, P. Meeneghan, T. Ward and S.C. Mc Loone, "Examining user performance in the presence of latency and jitter in distributed interactive applications," *Proc. IEE Irish Signals and Systems Conference, Belfast, N.Ireland, June/July 2004,* pp. 323-328.

[10] D. Kahneman, A. B. Krueger, D. A. Schkade, N. Schwarz, and A. A. Stone, "A Survey Method for Characterizing Daily Life Experience: The Day Reconstruction Method ", *Science, Vol 306, Issue 5702,* 1776-1780 , 3 December 2004.

AUTHOR BIOGRAPHIES

Conor Linehan is currently a research fellow on a Science Foundation Ireland funded project entitled 'Exploiting psycho-perceptual effects to combat latency in Distributed Interactive Applications'. In this research he is examining the psychological effects of network latency on the experience of on-line gaming. He is also examining means by which the complexity of on-line games interacts with delay as an ameliorative or exacerbating influence on the enjoyment of on-line gaming. This research is conducted within the framework of a modern behavioural theory of human language, cognition and complex behaviour, known as Relational Frame Theory.

Bryan Roche is a lecturer in psychology at the National University of Ireland, Maynooth. His primary research interest is human language and the role of language processes in the development of clinical disorders and in human development more generally. He is the author of over 60 scientific papers and has contributed to several edited books on the topics of human language, clinical and forensic psychology. He is co-author of the book *Relational Frame Theory: A Post-Skinnerian account of human language and cognition,* with Steven C. Hayes and Dermot Barnes-Holmes.

Tomas Ward is a member of the distributed interactive applications group at the NUI Maynooth. His main interests are in assistive technology and data management techniques for distributed shared applications. Spare time is spent on pushing out his personal best on Konami DrumMania V.

Dr. Séamus McLoone is a member of the distributed interactive applications group (DIAG) at the Department of Electronic Engineering in the National University of Ireland Maynooth. His research interests vary from multiple model approaches to nonlinear system identification, to reducing and masking the effects of latency in distributed interactive applications.

A Psycho-Perceptual Comparison of the Dead Reckoning and the Hybrid Strategy Model Entity State Update Prediction Techniques

Séamus McLoone, Alan Kenny, Tomás Ward and Declan Delaney

Department of Electronic Engineering,
National University of Ireland Maynooth,
Maynooth, Co. Kildare, IRELAND
E-mail: seamus.mcloone; akenny; tomas.ward@eeng.nuim.ie

ABSTRACT

Distributed Interactive Applications (DIAs) typically employ entity prediction mechanisms in order to reduce the number of packets sent between clients across the network. This in turn counters the effect of network latency and can improve the consistency of the distributed application. Dead Reckoning (DR) is currently the most commonly used entity state prediction mechanism but a more recent technique called the Hybrid Strategy Model (HSM) has been proposed in the research literature. This alternative method has been shown to further reduce the number of update packets required to maintain a consistent state in a DIA. However, there is a distinct lack of end-user perceptual analysis of these techniques. In other words, does the HSM method improve the gaming experience of the user compared to DR? A reduction in packet count may improve issues with latency but can adversely degrade the modelling quality and therefore the overall level of consistency is unknown. Hence, this paper proposes the novel use of user perception as a means to determine the quality of a given entity state update mechanism. Here, we compare DR and HSM from a user perceptual viewpoint by collecting linguistic feedback on short scenes recorded from a racing game. Details of the experiment and the obtained results are presented within.

Keywords – Distributed Interactive Applications, Entity Update Mechanisms, Psycho-Perceptual Analysis, Dead Reckoning, Hybrid Strategy Model

I INTRODUCTION

One of the main aims of a distributed interactive application (DIA) is to maintain a high level of consistency amongst the client participants. This is of particular importance in the gaming world where networked multiplayer games are becoming more and more dominant. However, issues such as network latency and jitter are causing major concerns as they conspire to reduce the level of consistency. As a result, it is desirable to minimise the number of packets that must be sent across a network in order to assist in the maintenance of a consistent view for each remote user. This counters the effect of latency in the network and therefore can improve the consistency achieved. Various methods for achieving this reduction in packets exist, including entity state prediction mechanisms, area of interest management, data compression and dynamic load balancing [1 - 6].

One of the most popular techniques used to date is the entity state prediction mechanism known as Dead Reckoning (DR). This was formalised in the IEEE Distributed Interactive Simulation (DIS) standard [3] and has become the standard for commercial games, such as Doom, Quake and Tribes II. Dead Reckoning is a method of predicting a user's future actions based on their dynamics, which results in the transmission of less data to remote nodes.

Another, more recent, entity state prediction method has been proposed in the research literature. This method is known as the Hybrid Strategy Model (HSM) and differs from DR by using a priori knowledge of user behaviour to build a set of strategies by which to model the user [4, 5]. It is purported that this method outperforms DR by significantly reducing the number of update packets required to maintain a consistent state in the distributed application [4]. However, there is currently a distinct lack of psycho-perceptual analysis of such mechanisms. In other words, there is no analysis available to determine if the HSM or the DR mechanisms perform better from a user's viewpoint. What is the impact on the gaming experience of the end-user as a result of these mechanisms?

A reduction in packet count may improve issues with latency but, unfortunately, this can also adversely degrade the performance quality of the underlying predictive models and, as a result, the overall level of consistency remains largely unknown. Hence, this paper proposes the novel use of user perception to subjectively compare and contrast the DR and HSM prediction techniques. This involves collecting linguistic user feedback from a series of short video recordings from a racing game. The analysis of this data is presented later.

The rest of this paper is structured as follows. The next section provides a brief description of the DR and the HSM methods. Section III details the design and implementation of the experiment used to collect information pertaining to the end-user perceptual experience. The obtained data is then analysed and discussed in section IV. Finally, the paper ends with some concluding remarks and suggestions for future work in section V.

II DEAD RECKONING AND HYBRID STRATEGY MODEL

For the convenience of the reader, a brief description of the Dead Reckoning and the Hybrid Strategy Model entity state prediction techniques are now presented. The basic convergence algorithm used in each case is also given. At this stage, it is important to mention that these methods rely on an underlying error threshold value that determines when an update packet needs to be transmitted. There are two different threshold metrics that can be used and both of these are also briefly described.

A. Dead Reckoning (DR)

Under DIS, once an entity is created the information pertaining to this entity is transmitted to all participating remote nodes. Each remote node then attempts to predict this entity movement based on its trajectory data. There are many ways in order to extrapolate a player's position. The most basic and common of these is to set the new position to the transmitted position and the new velocity to the transmitted velocity, which is known as first order DR. Another common DR technique is to use the transmitted position and velocity along with the transmitted acceleration information.

The local node also keeps a model of itself under DR, which is continually compared to its actual position. Once the actual position differs from its predicted position by a set amount, known as its error threshold, an update is sent to all the remote nodes informing them of its updated trajectory. Once the remote nodes receive this new information they update their models to reflect the latest transmitted data. In this paper, we simply make use of the basic first order DR model. Further information on Dead Reckoning can be found in [3, 7].

B. Hybrid Strategy Model (HSM)

HSM is a novel prediction mechanism that uses a priori knowledge of user behaviour to build a set of strategy paths. The hybrid strategy approach involves dynamically switching between a DR model and one of a number of strategy models. The distance from the actual point to the various models is continuously calculated. When the entity movement is within a defined threshold value of one of the strategy models then that strategy model is employed to describe the entity movement. If no suitable strategy models exist, then the DR model is used by default. The HSM implemented in this paper employs a simple switching mechanism, switching instantaneously between the most suitable models. Further information on the operation of the HSM and generating appropriate strategy paths can be found in [4, 5].

C. Convergence

One of the key problems with predicting a remote entity's position is that once the updated position has been received, the remote entity's position has to be rapidly corrected. If the remote entity is moved directly into the new position this can result in a disjoint and unnatural behaviour from the user. Convergence is an attempt to naturally blend the incorrect current player trajectory into the updated player trajectory. Here, we employ a basic convergence routine.

In the case of DR, when an update packet is received, a linear set of points is generated that connects the current position to a future predicted position. This latter value is based on the received updated position and updated velocity values. The intermediate path is then played out with increased velocity. With HSM, the convergence involves a blending of the underlying strategy paths using a suitable weighting function. Initially, the weighting favours the current strategy path before quickly moving towards the actual strategy path. Further detail can be found in [8].

D. Error Threshold Metrics

Two different error threshold metrics can be employed in both DR and HSM. The first is known as *spatial* and is simply determined by the spatial difference between the actual and modelled position of an entity's motion. The alternative threshold metric is known as *time-space* and uses local absolute inconsistency measures in determining when an update is required [8]. In simple terms, the time-space error is calculated as the integral of the modelling error over time, i.e. the area under the modelling error curve. These two metrics can be used separately or together in the form of a hybrid metric, as outlined in [9].

In this paper, the DR and the HSM methods are analysed from a user perceptual viewpoint. Both error threshold metrics are considered in each case. The next section outlines the design and implementation of the experiment used to obtain the user perceptual feedback.

III EXPERIMENTATION

A. Video Clips

In order to obtain the required feedback, a set of video clips was created. This was achieved by recording the movements of a 'bot', i.e. a computer controlled entity, under various conditions. The first video clip was used for benchmarking purposes and consisted of the bot's motion under ideal conditions, i.e. the values of latency, jitter and error threshold were all set to zero. Each subsequent video consisted of the bot modelled with either DR or HSM

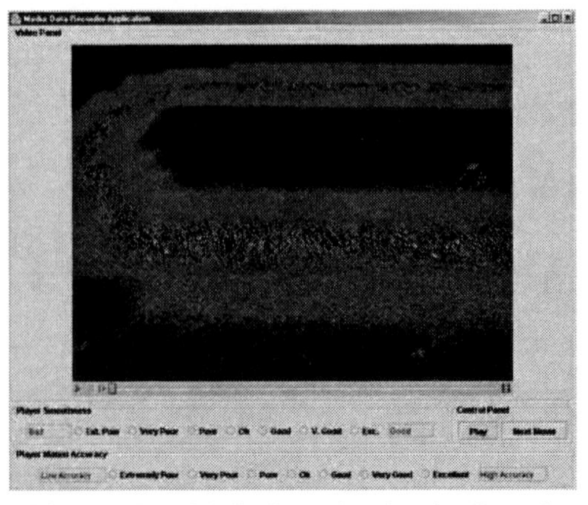

Figure 1: Java Media Recorder showing Part of elliptical racing Track

using various error threshold metrics and values. In these clips, the bot's motion was subject to latency of 200ms. Jitter was set to ±10% of the latency value. These values reflect typical network conditions [10]. Various subjects were then asked to compare the bot's motion with the perfect one.

An elliptical racing course was chosen for simplicity, as shown in Figure 1. This was created using the Torque Game Engine [11]. Here, the game measurements, such as the spatial distance, are calculated in Torque Game Units (tgu). As a reference point, the track used in this experiment is approximately 100 tgu in width and 250 tgu in length.

The main strategy path used for the HSM approach in this paper was generated from analysing a number of path traversals and choosing the one that represented the most common behaviour. Additional strategies are then generated in real time based on their distance from the main strategy. If this distance exceeds a pre-defined limit, than the DR model is employed. The base strategy model used here is effectively the centre path of the track. This is a simple implementation of the HSM approach. In less spatially restricted scenarios the development of strategy models may be non-trivial.

Finally, the various games scenes were recorded as AVI files using FRAPS (http:// www.fraps.com), a utility designed for recording game footage.

B. User Feedback

The goal of this experiment was to perceptually compare the DR and HSM methods for various error metrics and threshold values. In order to achieve this, feedback relating to these models had to be obtained, specifically in terms of how accurate a subject perceived the model to be relative to the perfect scenario. Previous experimentation [12] revealed that in the case where a bot followed a particular path accurately but appeared to be slightly 'jumpy' in its motion, subjects rated this as very poor in terms of accuracy. In an attempt to alleviate this problem, users were asked, in this experiment, to provide separate feedback on both the smoothness and accuracy of the bot's motion.

Linguistic variables were used to obtain subject feedback. This avoided the problem of having to assign an exact numerical value to a given level of accuracy or smoothness. The following linguistic variables were used: *Extremely Poor*, *Very Poor*, *Poor*, *Okay*, *Good*, *Very Good*, *Excellent*. Seven variables were used in accordance with the fact that, as humans, we can reliably perceive up to 7 different states [13]. The test application used in this experiment is shown in Figure 1.

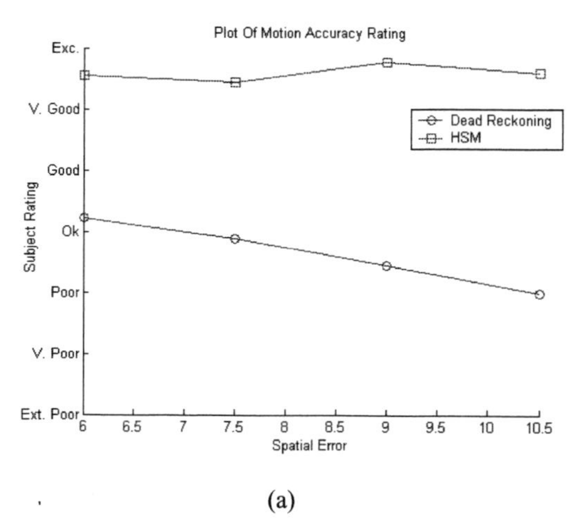

(a)

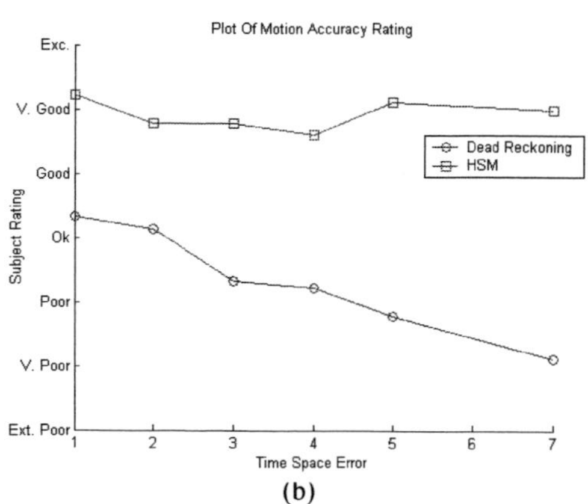

(b)

Figure 2: Average Motion Accuracy rating for DR and HSM when (a) a spatial and (b) a time-space error metric was employed

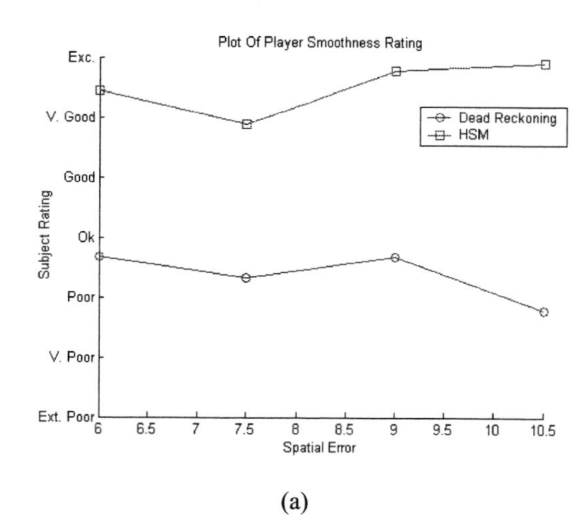

(a)

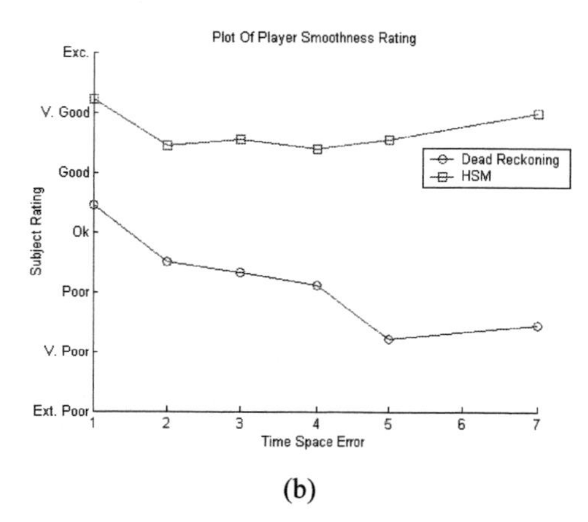

(b)

Figure 3: Average Player Smoothness rating for DR and HSM when (a) a spatial and (b) a time-space error metric was employed

C. Experimental Setup

Prior to the start of the experiment, each subject was given an explanation of the task in hand, and were also shown a demonstration video. The tests began once the subject felt confident that they understood the requirements. The experiment consisted of the subject watching a video clip once and then, on completion, rating it in terms of Player Smoothness and Motion Accuracy.

Each experiment consisted of a total of 28 video clips - 6 perfect play-outs, 20 unique models and 2 duplicates. Each video lasted about 20 seconds and the entire experiment lasted approximately 15 minutes. Subjects were only told that the first video clip was perfect.

IV ANALYSIS AND DISCUSSION

A total of 10 subjects took part in this experiment, consisting of 6 males and 4 females, ranging in age from 15 to 35 years. All subjects had some level of experience with using a computer, while 6 had some experience with computer games and 4 had experience with networked games.

DR and HSM were both examined using spatial error threshold values ranging from 6 to 10.5 tgu and time space threshold values ranging from 1 to 7 tgu. The relationship between these two metrics is explored in detail in [9].

Figure 2(a) represents the average motion accuracy obtained for the various spatial threshold values for both entity state prediction mechanisms, while Figure 2(b) represents similar results for different time space threshold values. Figures 3(a) and 3(b) present similar results for player smoothness.

It is worth noting that these results are based on a small number of participants. Nevertheless the results obtained are a fair reflection of the performance of both the DR and the HSM for the given set of video clips.

The results show that the rating for DR falls below acceptable between 6 and 8 tgu for both the player smoothness and motion accuracy. On the other hand the HSM exhibits much higher ratings, obtaining a '*very good*' rating for all the measured thresholds. This shows that not only does HSM result in less packets being generated than DR, but also maintains a much higher perceptual rating. Interestingly, at the highest tested error threshold, 10.5 tgu, HSM only generates one packet of data but still remains more than acceptable to the end user. However, this simply reflects the simplicity of the underlying track as well as the high accuracy of the models used as part of the HSM approach. Nevertheless, the same analogy extends to more complex situations provided that suitable and accurate models can be determined for use in the HSM technique.

Like the spatial error threshold, HSM also outperforms DR when using the time space error threshold. The acceptance rating for DR rapidly falls below acceptable levels between 2 and 3 tgu for both the player smoothness and motion accuracy. However, the HSM maintains a rating of approximately '*very good*' throughout.

It is worth noting that HSM performed slightly worse when using a time-space threshold metric compared to when it used a spatial threshold one. The former results in sending more update packets, which is purported to improve absolute consistency [9], yet this is not evident in the obtained results. The results here suggest that updating too frequently can lower the end users experience as they notice the entity having to correct its position more often and these corrections are regarded as inaccurate.

Another point of note rising from these results relates to the operation of the HSM. As previously stated, HSM attempts to choose the best available strategy model for a given circumstance. If no appropriate model exists then a DR model is employed by default. Error threshold values are normally static, i.e. they are fixed to a constant value prior to runtime. Therefore, the HSM strategy models and its associated DR model would end up with the same error threshold. Clearly this experiment shows that different models require different error thresholds in order to get the best packet rate to maintain the overall end user experience. In essence the error threshold should be dynamically chosen depending on the current model employed. From the work presented here, a strategy model could have a significantly larger error threshold, regardless of error metric, than a DR model.

V CONCLUDING REMARKS

This paper has shown how psycho-perceptual measures can be employed as a useful means to compare different entity update mechanisms. Here, Dead Reckoning and the Hybrid Strategy Model approaches were compared from an end-user's viewpoint. Both spatial and time space threshold metrics were considered for both techniques.

HSM was shown to give far better perceptual ratings than Dead Reckoning for both the spatial and time space error threshold. HSM also requires less update packets to be transmitted across the network. Therefore, the results confirm that for this particular application, namely an online racing game, that HSM is far better suited to delivering a good end user experience. In fact HSM appears to give very good results even at the highest error threshold for this type of application. Other applications, such as fast paced First Person Shooter (FPS) games, have more intense interaction and may require tighter thresholds. Nevertheless it would be expected that HSM would still perform better than DR. This requires further investigation.

Finally, for the HSM, it is proposed that dynamically choosing an error threshold based on the current model would result in the best possible end user experience, while minimizing the number of update packets. Future work will look at this issue also.

ACKNOWLEDGEMENTS

This work is supported by Science Foundation Ireland and Enterprise Ireland - grant no. IRCSET/SC/04/CS0289.

REFERENCES

[1] Delaney, D., T. Ward and S. McLoone. "On consistency and network latency in distributed interactive applications: A survey - Part I." *Presence: Teleoperators and Virtual Environments* 15(2), pp. 218-234, April 2006.

[2] Delaney, D., T. Ward and S. McLoone. "On consistency and network latency in distributed interactive

applications: A survey - Part II." *Presence: Teleoperators and Virtual Environments* 15(4), pp. 465-482, August 2006.

[3] IEEE. *IEEE Standard for Distributed Interactive Simulation - Application Protocols IEEE Std 1278.1-1995* IEEE, 1995.

[4] Delaney, D., T. Ward and S. Mc Loone "Reducing Update Packets in Distributed Interactive Applications using a Hybrid Model". *16th International Conference on Parallel and Distributed Computing Systems, August 13-15*, Reno, USA, pp. 417-422, 2003.

[5] D. Marshall, D. Delaney, S. McLoone and T. Ward, "Exploring the spatial density of strategy models in a realistic distributed interactive application", DS-RT'04, Budapest, Hungry, 2004.

[6] S. Singhal and M. Zyda, "Networked virtual environments: design and implementation.", ACM Press SIGGRAPH Series, Addison-Wesley, Reading, Massachusetts, 1999.

[8] D. Delaney, S. McLoone and T. Ward, "A novel convergence algorithm for the hybrid strategy model packet reduction technique", *IEE Irish Signals and Systems Conference*, Dublin, Ireland, 1-2 September, pp.118-123, 2005.

[9] Roberts, D., D. Marshall, S. McLoone, D. Delaney, T. Ward and R. Aspin "Exploring the use of local inconsistency measures as thresholds for dead reckoning update packet generation". *Distributed Simulation and Real Time Applications*, Montreal, Canada, pp. 195 - 202, 2005.

[10] T. Defanti and R. Fraser, Teleimmersion in the grid: blueprint for a new computing infrastructure, San Francisco, CA, USA, Morgan Kaufmann Publishers Inc. pp. 131-155, 1998.

[11] Lloyd, J. "The Torque Game Engine", Game Developer Magazine, 11 (8), pp. 8-9, September 2004.

[12] A. Kenny, S. McLoone, T. Ward and D. Delaney, "Using User Perception to Determine Suitable Error Thresholds for Dead Reckoning in Distributed Interactive Applications", IEEE Irish Signals and Systems Conference, Dublin, Ireland, 2006.

[13] G. Miller, "The magic number 7 plus or minus 2", Psychological Review, USA, 1956.

AUTHOR BIOGRAPHIES

Dr. Séamus McLoone is a member of the distributed interactive applications group (DIAG) at the Department of Electronic Engineering in the National University of Ireland Maynooth. His research interests varies from multiple model approaches to nonlinear system identification to reducing and masking the effects of latency in distributed interactive applications.

Alan Kenny graduated from NUI Maynooth in computer science and software engineering in 2004. Having spent a short stint working as a web developer he returned to the University to study a PhD in the area of psycho-perceptual measures in networked games.

Dr. Tomas Ward is a member of the distributed interactive applications group at the NUI Maynooth. His main interests are in assistive technology and data management techniques for distributed shared applications. Spare time is spent on pushing out his personal best on Konami DrumMania V.

Declan Delaney received his B.E. and M.Eng.Sc. from University College Dublin in 1991 and 1998 respectively. His PhD was awarded in 2005 by the National University of Ireland, Maynooth. From 1992 to 2000 he worked as a software developer and subsequently as project manager. At present he works in the area of Knowledge management for an Italian multinational, ENI and is based in Milan, Italy.

Using Perceptual Feedback To Determine Time-Space Threshold Values For Dead Reckoning

Alan Kenny, Séamus McLoone, Tomás Ward and Declan Delaney

Department of Electronic Engineering,
National University of Ireland Maynooth,
Maynooth, Co. Kildare, IRELAND
E-mail: akenny; seamus.mcloone; tomas.ward @eeng.nuim.ie

ABSTRACT

Entity state prediction mechanisms are used in order to reduce the number of packets required to maintain a consistent state in a Distributed Interactive Application (DIA). Typically in the case where the entity is representing a participant in a networked game this is achieved by continually comparing the output of a prediction algorithm against a player's actual state. The state usually comprises position and orientation information in such cases. If the error exceeds a pre-defined threshold value, then an update packet is transmitted, which contains the player's latest trajectory information. However, obtaining a suitable threshold value remains one of the key challenges that face such entity state prediction techniques. Furthermore, these methods can employ two different threshold metrics. These are *spatial*, which exploits distance measures, and *time space*, which uses both time and distance measures. While a spatial threshold value can be arguably determined based on a prior knowledge of the gaming environment, it remains difficult, at best, to obtain a corresponding value for the time space threshold metric.

This paper proposes the novel use of user perception as a suitable means to solve the aforementioned problem. Here we employ the most common entity update mechanism, namely *dead reckoning*, and use perceptual feedback to determine suitable threshold values for both spatial and time space threshold metrics. This involves collecting linguistic feedback on short scenes recorded from a racing game. This technique is compared and contrasted with an alternative method whereby equivalent spatial and time space threshold values are obtained based on a common measure of inconsistency. Details of the experimentation and an analysis of the results are presented within.

Keywords – Distributed Interactive Applications (DIAs), Psycho-Perceptual Measures, Dead Reckoning, Spatial Error Threshold, Time Space Error Threshold

1. INTRODUCTION

Distributed Interactive Applications (DIAs) have to continually deal with the limitations of their underlying networks, i.e. latency, jitter and network congestion. As a result, it is desirable to minimise the number of packets that must be sent across a network in order reduce the possibility of remote users having an inconsistent view. To achieve this, prediction mechanisms are used to model remote entities.

One of the most popular techniques used to date is the entity state prediction mechanism known as dead reckoning. This was introduced in the IEEE Distributed Interactive Simulation (DIS) standard [1] and has become the standard for commercial games, such as Doom, Quake and Tribes II. Dead reckoning is a method of predicting a user's future actions based on their dynamics, which results in the transmission of less data to remote nodes. The most basic of these is to set the new position and velocity to the transmitted position and velocity, which is known as first order dead reckoning and is employed in this paper. Further information on dead reckoning can be found in [1,2]. Other packet reduction techniques used in DIAs include the area of interest management, Hybrid Strategy Model, data compression and dynamic load balancing [3-6].

One of the key factors in all entity update methods is when to send the updated information. For a dead reckoning model an update is sent once a certain tolerance value has been exceeded. This value is known as the error threshold. Typically this threshold value is arbitrarily chosen and generally reflects what 'appears' to be appropriate with respect to the underlying application.

Traditionally the most popular error metric has been spatial distance. Spatial distance compares the distance between a player's actual position and their local model. If the distance exceeds the error threshold value then an update is sent. The spatial metric is popular as it is simple to implement and the game environment can be used as a reference point to determine suitable error thresholds. For example, a narrow racing track may require a tighter threshold than a wide track, as an entity leaving the track would be apparent sooner on the narrow track.

However, the spatial metric does not take the duration of an error into consideration, which led to the development of the time space metric [7]. For example, if the model continually has an inaccuracy just below the error threshold the spatial metric will allow this error to continue indefinitely. As the time space metric takes the duration of an error into consideration it will eventually send an update packet to correct this scenario, resulting in greater overall consistency.

Time space error refers to the cumulative spatial error over time. Figure 1 shows the time space error over one time period, where D represents the spatial distance error. Effectively this is the area under the curve between the local player's actual position and the local model over time. Similar to the spatial metric, the cumulative error is then compared to an error threshold. The biggest problem with the time space metric is determining a suitable error threshold. Unlike the spatial metric the environment alone cannot be used as a reference point for potential thresholds.

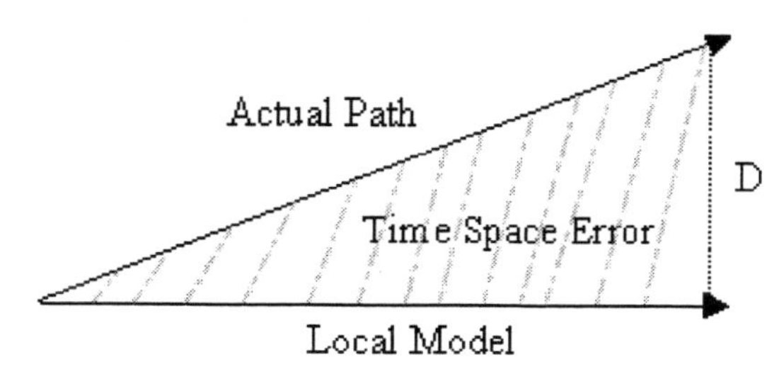

Figure 1: Time Space Metric Error

This paper proposes the novel use of perceptual feedback to determine equivalent spatial and time space error thresholds. We describe an experiment that collects relevant user perceptual feedback. From the collected perceptual feedback a lookup table is generated, for equivalent spatial and time space thresholds. Recent research has proposed a method of determining equivalent threshold values based on a common measure of inconsistency, namely the mean squared error [8]. A similar lookup table is generated using the mean squared error. The results for the two methods are compared and some possible outcomes are discussed.

The remainder of the paper is structured as follows. Section 2 details the design and implementation of the experiment used to collect information pertaining to the end-user perceptual experience. The resulting data is then analysed and discussed in section 3. Finally some conclusions and suggestions for future work are given in section 4.

2. EXPERIMENTATION

This section details the design and implementation of the experiment used to gather user perceptual feedback. The primary design goal was to examine the performance of the dead reckoning model for both spatial distance and time space error metrics.

2.1 *Video Clips*

In order to obtain the required feedback, a set of game-like video clips was created. This was achieved by recording the movements of a computer controlled entity or 'bot' under various conditions. The first scenario was created under ideal conditions, with no error or latency, and was used as the benchmark video. Each subsequent video consisted of the bot modelled with dead reckoning under various error thresholds. The user was then asked to compare the models with the original benchmark video. Feedback from our previous work [9] suggested that subjects find it difficult to continually recall the benchmark video. As a result the benchmark video was repeated after every four model videos. The latency was set to 200ms, with random jitter set to between ±10% of the latency value. These latency and jitter values were chosen as it has been shown that the average transmission times fall within the region of 200ms [10].

One of the main challenges encountered in designing this experiment was the creation of a suitable track for the bot to race around. In order to avoid subject fatigue during the experiment, due to long video durations, the track had to be relatively short. This resulted in an elliptical course being chosen. The Torque Game Engine [11] was used to create the track and scenarios used in this experiment. Most of the game measurements, such as the spatial distance, are calculated in Torque Game Units (tgu). As a reference point the track used in this experiment is approximately 100 tgu in width, 250 tgu in length and the two straight sections are about 30 tgu wide. Finally, the various games scenes where recorded as AVI files using FRAPS (http://www.fraps.com), a utility designed for recording game footage.

2.2 *User Feedback*

Previously our work in [9] highlighted bot smoothness, or 'jumpiness', as being a challenge in rating a video clip. A bot may be very accurate but nevertheless appear to 'jump' from time to time, which resulted in lower ratings. As a result users were asked to rate the model using two measures, its smoothness and motion accuracy. It was hoped that this would result in more realistic results for the motion accuracy score.

Linguistic variables were used to obtain subject feedback. The player smoothness and motion accuracy variables were rated as *Extremely Poor, Very Poor, Poor, Okay, Good, Very Good* and *Excellent.* A seven-point linguistic scale was chosen in order to avoid difficulties in quantifying specific levels of accuracy and it has been shown that humans can reliably distinguish between seven distinct states [12].

Subject feedback from our previous experiment indicated that staying focused for the duration of an experiment was difficult. In order to avoid this, the duration of the experiment was kept under fifteen minutes and subjects were asked to give continuous feedback about the overall quality of the scene, both player smoothness and motion accuracy. The continuous feedback was recorded on a discrete sliding scale from *Poor* to *Good.* A smaller scale was chosen for the continuous feedback in order to make it quick and easy for subjects to update their score. This also gave a greater level of interaction in the experiment, which more closely resembles the experiment source material, and would potentially allow for closer examining of a scene to determine when and for how long a subject's perception was altered. The application used in this experiment is shown in Figure 2.

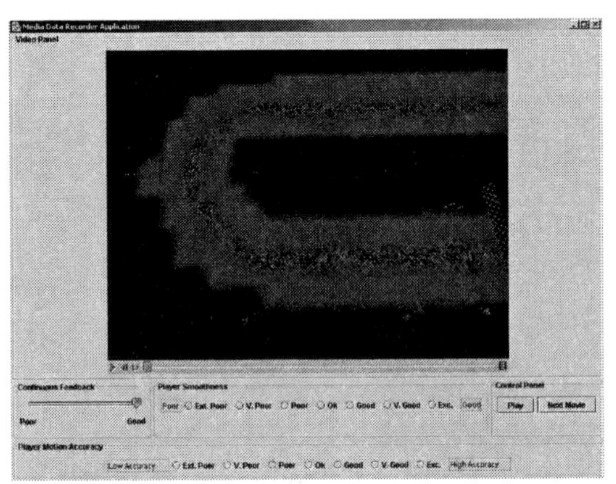

Figure 2: Java Media Data Recorder playing the Elliptical Racing track

2.3 *Experimental Set-up*

Before the experiment began each subject had the task explained to them and were shown a demonstration video to illustrate the tasks involved in the experiment. In order to avoid biasing the results, the difference between the two error metrics was not explained to the subjects. The tests began once the subject felt confident they understood the requirements for the experiment. The experiment consisted of the subject watching a video clip once, whilst giving continuous feedback. In addition, at the end of each video, participants were asked to rate Player Smoothness and Motion Accuracy.

There was a total of twenty-eight video clips per experiment. A demonstration video was also shown to participants to ensure that they understood the experiment. Six of the experiment videos were benchmark videos, twenty were unique models and two were duplicates. Each video lasted approximately twenty seconds and the entire experiment lasted approximately fifteen minutes.

3. ANALYSIS AND DISCUSSION

A total of ten subjects took part in this experiment, consisting of six males and four females, ranging in age from fifteen to thirty five. All subjects had some level of experience with using a computer, while six had some experience with computer games and four had experience with networked games.

The spatial thresholds used in the experiment were 6, 7.5, 9 and 10.5 tgu. These thresholds were chosen as our previous work indicated that the perceptual ratings would fall below acceptable within this region. A more explorative set of time space error thresholds were chosen, specifically 1, 2, 3, 4, 5 and 7 tgu.

3.1 *Experimental Results for Discrete Feedback*

This section is representative of the data collected from the subjects' ratings after viewing a video and does not take continuous feedback into consideration. Figure 3 represents the perceptual rating for the motion accuracy. For the four spatial thresholds, 6, 7.5 9 and 10.5 tgu, the perceptual rating is extracted from the graph in Figure 3a. These perceptual ratings are then applied to the motion accuracy scores for the time space metric in Figure 3b. For example, Figure 3a highlights the perceptual rating for the spatial threshold of 7.5 tgu, which has a rating just above *ok*. The equivalent perceptual rating in Figure 3b gives a time space error of 2.35 tgu. From this information a perceptual lookup table can be generated that relates equivalent spatial and time space thresholds, which can be seen in Table 1.

It should be noted that the data for time space graph is not entirely smooth. This is most likely a result of the relatively low number of participants and should be taken into consideration when analysing these results. Increasing the number of participants should ameliorate this issue.

For comparison purposes, a lookup table is also determined according to [8]. The mean squared error is calculated by summing the absolute spatial inconsistency at every time interval and taking its average over the total time. Larger error thresholds will naturally result in larger mean squared errors. Figure 4a shows the mean squared error for the spatial metric. The mean squared error for each of the four threshold values is highlighted. Figure 4b highlights the mean squared error for the time space threshold. By taking the corresponding spatial mean squared error and plotting it on this graph, equivalent spatial and time space thresholds can be determined and a lookup table generated. Table 2 represents the lookup table generated from Figure 4 and excludes the spatial threshold of 10.5 as it goes beyond the region covered in Figure 4b.

Interestingly only the smallest equivalent threshold in Table 1 corresponds to it's equivalent in Table 2, with values of 1.6 and 1.8 tgu respectively for the spatial threshold of 6 tgu. It is possible that for above average perceptual ratings the lookup tables will match. In this case both the spatial and time space graphs are likely to exhibit a steeper decline in perceptual rating, from *excellent* to just above *ok*, for a spatial threshold from 0 to 6 tgu.

However, for large error thresholds there does not appear to be a correlation between the two lookup tables. For example, a spatial error of 7.5 gives a time space error of 2.35 in Table 1 and 4.1 in Table 2, which is a reasonable difference. It should be noted that the perceptual rating has a defined scale; from *excellent* to *extremely poor*, while the mean square error does not and will continue to grow as the error threshold increases. In other words, no matter how large the error threshold gets the perceptual feedback would be limited to *extremely poor* while the mean squared error would become very large.

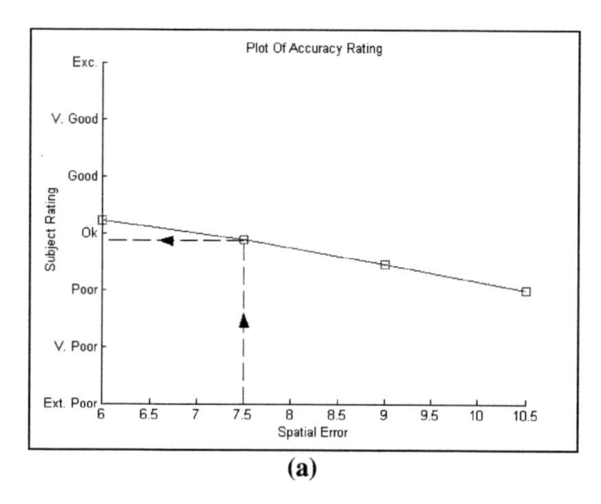

(a)

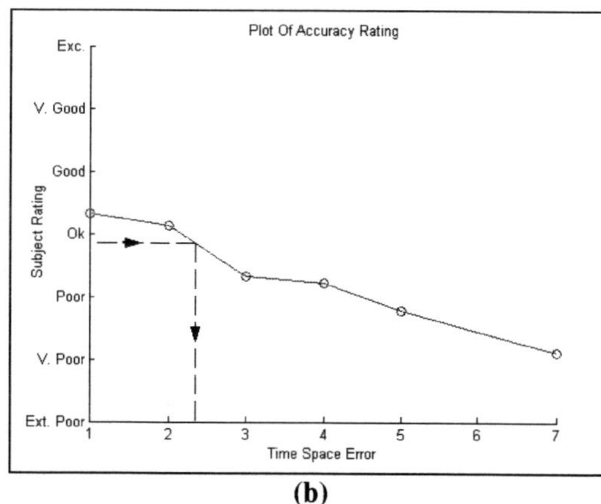

(b)

Figure 3: Plot of the Motion Accuracy Rating for the **(a)** Spatial and **(b)** Time Space metrics

Spatial	Perceptual Rating	Time Space
6	Just Above Ok	1.6
7.5	Just Below Ok	2.35
9	Between Ok/Poor	2.85
10.5	Poor	4.5

Table 1: Lookup table for Perceptual Ratings

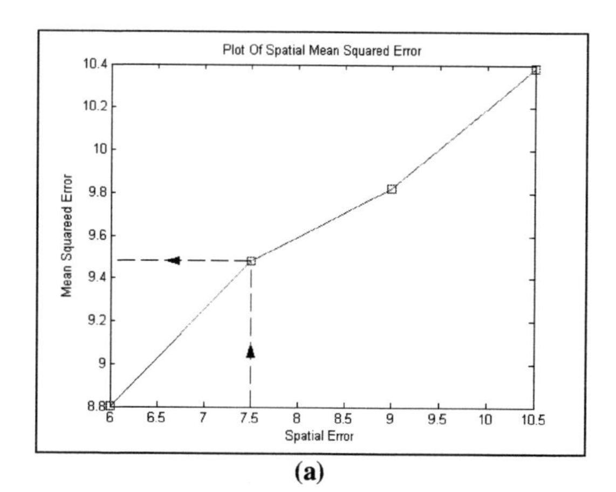

(a)

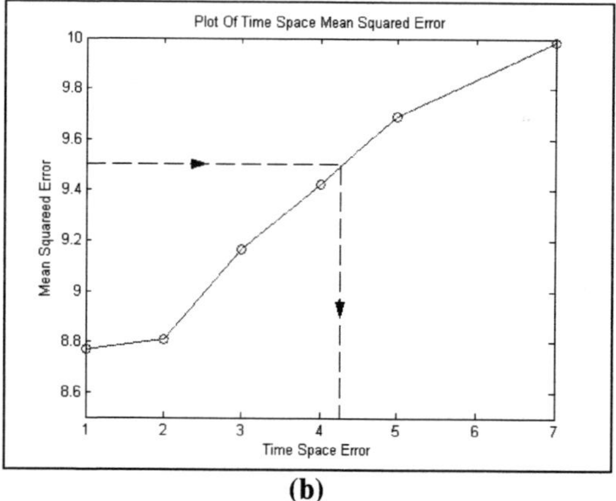

(b)

Figure 4: Plot of the Mean Squared Error for the **(a)** Spatial and **(b)** Time Space metrics

Spatial	Mean Squared Error	Time Space
6	8.8	1.8
7.5	9.5	4.1
9	9.8	5.9

Table 2: Lookup table for Mean Squared Error

Ultimately it is the region that garners above acceptable error thresholds that is of use to developers. The mean squared error can theoretically generate equivalent time space values for very large spatial thresholds, but they would result in poor end user experience and therefore be undesirable. Therefore it is of most interest to examine the relationships between the error thresholds that garner above acceptable perceptual ratings. Clearly future work is required to examine if smaller thresholds will produce similar lookup tables.

Additionally, previous work suggested that the perceptual rating would fall below acceptable around 8 tgu for a fast paced entity using a spatial metric [8]. In this experiment the motion accuracy falls below acceptable just before 7.5 tgu, which is in keeping with our previous findings. The entity used in this experiment was slightly slower than that of our previous work and as a result slightly lower acceptable spatial threshold is to be expected.

3.2 *Experimental Results for Continuous Feedback*

This section focuses on the continuous data collected during each video. The results are compared to those presented in Section 3.1. During each video the continuous feedback could be at one of three ratings, *Poor*, *Ok*, or *Good*. The average percentage time per each score was calculated for each scenario and is shown in Table 3.

Scenario	Good %	Ok %	Poor %
Spatial 6	55.72	38.59	5.68
Spatial 7.5	58.08	27.46	14.44
Spatial 9	54.58	34.01	11.4
Spatial 10.5	50.16	26.46	23.36
Time Space 1	70.87	26.69	2.42
Time Space 2	54.86	35.3	9.82
Time Space 3	51.17	24.5	24.31
Time Space 4	52.44	26.08	21.46
Time Space 5	48.69	15.51	35.78
Time Space 7	49.92	15.35	34.72

Table 3: Breakdown of the Average Time Duration for each Continuous Rating Scenario

As expected the amount of time with a *poor* rating increases as the thresholds increase. Interestingly for the spatial metric the amount of time with a *poor* rating never goes above 24%, whereas for a time space threshold anything above and including 3 tgu gives a higher percent for the *poor* rating. Surprisingly the amount of time with a *good* rating remains high regardless of metric or threshold, generally above 50%. Analysing the data further reveals that most of the negative ratings occur around the two corners of the track. A high rating is maintained during the straights and into the early part of each bend.

Despite spending a relatively long period of time with an acceptable rating, a subject may rate the player smoothness and motion accuracy scores as unacceptable. For example, a spatial error of 9 tgu gives a perceptual rating of *poor* for the motion accuracy but the continuous feedback is rated as acceptable 90% of the time. This would indicate that if a large enough error occurs in a simulation, even for a small amount of time, it significantly impacts an end user's experience. This highlights the need for appropriate error thresholds. If an error threshold is chosen on the grounds that it 'appears' suitable, without any research into the end user experience, then it may be acceptable for a large proportion of the time but still be considered a bad system and ultimately be dismissed by potential users.

4. CONCLUDING REMARKS

This paper has shown how psycho-perceptual measures can be used as a tool to garner feedback on various entity update scenarios. Dead reckoning was examined for both spatial and time space metrics under various error thresholds. The resultant perceptual feedback was analysed, which highlighted some interesting issues.

In keeping with our previous work, the perceptual acceptability for a spatial metric falls between 6 and 7.5 tgu for this application. A perceptual lookup table was created that outlined equivalent spatial and time space thresholds. Similarly, the mean squared error for both the spatial and time space metrics were calculated. The two lookup tables were then compared.

Except for the smallest threshold value the two lookup tables did not match. For large error thresholds the finite nature of the perceptual scale results in an upper limit on the potential perceptual rating, whereas the mean squared error can always increase. This results in a perceptual graph that will decrease until it reaches its upper limit, *extremely poor*, whereas the graph for the mean squared error will always increase. Interestingly the smallest threshold value appears to match. This may indicate that, for above acceptable ratings, the lookup tables will match, which would be the area of most interest to developers. Future work will examine smaller error thresholds to determine if this is the case. It is, to a degree, irrelevant to calculate the mean squared error for large error thresholds if it is going to be considered extremely poor by the end user.

Finally the continuous feedback data was analysed. As expected larger error thresholds resulted in more time with a *poor* rating. However, for both metrics, the amount of time with at least an acceptable rating never falls below 64%, yet the resulting player smoothness and motion accuracy scores were considered unacceptable. It appears large errors, even for a relatively small period of time, result in dissatisfaction for the end user. Error thresholds that are arbitrarily chosen may work most of the time but may ultimately result in a poor end user experience. Also as such thresholds are typically static, there is a need for research into adaptive error thresholds, which future work will focus on.

5. ACKNOWLEDGEMENTS

This work is supported by Science Foundation Ireland and Enterprise Ireland under grant no. IRCSET/SC/04/CS0289.

6. REFERENCES

[1] IEEE (1993). "IEEE Standard for distributed interactive simulation – application protocols", in IEEE Std 1278 –1993, I.C. Society, New York, 1993.
[2] Aggaraval, S., H. Banavar, A. Khandelval, S. Mukherjee and S. Rangajan, "Accuracy in Dead-Reckoning based multiplayer games", SIGCOMM'04 Workshops, Oregon, USA, 2004.
[3] Delaney, D., T. Ward and S. McLoone, "On consistency and network latency in distributed interactive applications: A survey - Part I." Presence: Teleoperators and Virtual Environments 15(4), August 2006, pp 218-234.
[4] Delaney, D., T. Ward and S. McLoone, "On consistency and network latency in distributed interactive applications: A survey - Part II." Presence: Teleoperators and Virtual Environments 15(4), August 2006, pp 465-482.
[5] Delaney, D., T. Ward and S. McLoone, "Reducing update packets in distributed interactive applications using a hybrid model", 16th International Conference on Parallel and Distributed Computing Systems, Reno, USA, 2003, pp 417-422.
[6] Singhal, S., and M. Zyda, "Networked virtual environments: design and implementation.", ACM Press SIGGRAPH Series, Addison-Wesley, Reading, Massachusetts, 1999.
[7] Zhou, S., W. Cai, F.B.S Lee and S.J. Turner "Time-space Consistency in Large Scale Distributed Virtual Environment", ACM Transactions on Modeling and Computer Simulations, 14(1), January 2004.
[8] Marshall, D., S. McLoone, T. Ward and D. Delaney, "Statistical Determination of Hybrid Threshold Parameters for Entity State Update Mechanisms in Distributed Interactive Applications", Forthcoming publication in DS-RT'06, Spain, 2006.
[9] Kenny, A., S. McLoone, T. Ward and D. Delaney, "Using User Perception to Determine Suitable Error Thresholds for Dead Reckoning in Distributed Interactive Applications", IEEE Irish Signals and Systems Conference, Dublin, Ireland 2006, pp49-54.
[10] Defanti, T. and R. Fraser, Teleimmersion in the grid: blueprint for a new computing infrastructure, San Francisco, CA, USA, Morgan Kaufmann Publishers Inc. pp. 131-155, 1998.
[11] Marshall, D., D. Delaney, S. McLoone and T. Ward, "Exploring the spatial density of strategy models in a realistic distributed interactive application", DS-RT'04, Budapest, Hungry, 2004, pp 210-213.
[12] Miller, G., "The magic number 7 plus or minus 2", Psychological Review, USA, 1956.

7. AUTHOR BIOGRAPHIES

Alan Kenny graduated from NUI Maynooth in computer science and software engineering in 2004. Having spent a short stint working as a web developer he returned to the University to pursue a PhD in the area of psycho-perceptual measures in networked games.

Dr. Séamus McLoone is a member of the distributed interactive applications group (DIAG) at the Department of Electronic Engineering in the National University of Ireland Maynooth. His research interests vary from multiple model approaches to non-linear system identification to reducing and masking the effects of latency in distributed interactive applications.

Dr. Tomas Ward is a member of the distributed interactive applications group at the NUI Maynooth. His main interests are in assistive technology and data management techniques for distributed shared applications. Spare time is spent on pushing out his personal best on Konami DrumMania V.

Declan Delaney received his B.E. and M.Eng.Sc. from University College Dublin in 1991 and 1998 respectively. His PhD was awarded in 2005 by the National University of Ireland, Maynooth. From 1992 to 2000 he worked as a software developer and subsequently as a project manager. At present he works in the area of Knowledge Management for an Italian multinational in Milan.

Does Reducing Packet Transmission Rates Help to Improve Consistency within Distributed Interactive Applications?

Damien Marshall, Séamus McLoone, Tomás Ward and Declan Delaney

Department of Electronic Engineering,
National University of Ireland Maynooth,
Maynooth, Co. Kildare, IRELAND
E-mail: dmarshall, seamus.mcloone, tomas.ward@eeng.nuim.ie

ABSTRACT

Networked games are an important class of distributed systems. In order for such applications to be successful, it is important that a sufficient level of consistency is maintained. To achieve this, a high level of network traffic is often required. However, this can cause an increase in network latency due to overloaded network hardware, which, ironically, can have a negative impact on consistency. Entity state prediction techniques aim to combat this effect by reducing network traffic. Although much work has focused on developing predictive schemes, there has been little work to date on the analysis of their true impact on the consistency of the system overall. In this paper, we identify an important performance-related characteristic of packet reduction schemes. It is demonstrated that there exists an optimal packet transmission region. Increasing or decreasing network traffic above or below this level negatively impacts on consistency. Based on this characteristic, it is proposed that predictive schemes exploit this optimal point in order to maximise consistency by efficiently utilising the available resources.

Keywords – Distributed Interactive Applications, Networked Games, Entity Update Mechanisms, Dead Reckoning, Consistency

I INTRODUCTION

Network games, a part of a larger class of applications known as Distributed Interactive Applications (DIA), have become extremely popular and commercially successful in recent years. At their core, they involve multiple participants collaborating and competing within a virtual environment, even though those participants may be located at geographically separate locations. Popular examples of networked games include first person shooters, such as Counter Strike, and massively multiplayer online games, such as World of Warcraft.

In order for interaction between participants within the virtual environment to be fruitful, it is important that a sufficient level of consistency is maintained in real time. Consistency is the degree to which each participant experiences the same worldview [1-2].

Achieving a fully consistent world state generally requires a large amount of network traffic as changes to the world made locally need to be communicated to all participants. However, excess network traffic can overload the underlying network connecting participants, resulting in increased network latency, jitter and packet loss due to swamped network hardware [3]. This then negatively impacts on world consistency as changes to the virtual world take extra time to propagate between participants.

Other work has focused on solving this issue, examining means of reducing network traffic, thus improving network conditions, while still maintaining a sufficient level of consistency. One popular method of doing this involves predictive models. Under this approach, information regarding entity dynamics, such as acceleration and velocity, are transmitted between participants. Each participant then uses this data to model the future behaviour of other participants. An update is not transmitted until the model and actual behaviour differ by a predefined error threshold. Examples of this approach include dead reckoning and the Hybrid Strategy Model [4-5]. In both cases, spatial difference is traditionally used as the error threshold metric.

In such techniques, there is a tradeoff between the error threshold and the underlying consistency that can be achieved. Lowering the error threshold, for example, will increase consistency as the model will be more accurate due to increased updates. Ironically, this may cause a resultant decrease in consistency, as the resultant increase in network traffic negatively affects the performance of the network and application. To date, however, we have no firm understanding of this tradeoff.

In this work, we highlight a key performance characteristic related to this tradeoff. Using a testbed developed in an industry standard games engine known as Torque [6], the amount of network traffic transmitted between participants operating in a typical home environment is varied. It is demonstrated that there is an optimal region of packet transmission rate. Increasing transmission rates above this region introduces inconsistency due to latency caused by overloaded network hardware. Such a situation necessitates the use of packet reduction techniques such as dead reckoning. On the other hand, reducing the rates below this region means that available capacity is being underutilised, which causes inconsistency, due to less information being transmitted in the form of less packets.

Based on this result, we propose that packet reduction schemes such as dead reckoning should take this characteristic into account during their execution, so as to optimally use available resources.

The rest of the paper is structured as follows. In Section II, we present some brief background information on network latency and entity state predictive schemes. In Section III, the test network environment for the experiment is described, and results collected using this testbed are outlined and analysed in Section IV. We conclude the paper in Section V.

II COMBATING LATENCY

One of the greatest limiting factors in achieving consistency within DIAs is network latency [1-2]. Network latency is the time taken for data to travel between a transmitter and receiver on the same network [7]. The problem of dealing with latency in DIAs is confounded by the variation in latency over time, known as jitter [8].

The causes and effects of network latency and jitter within DIAs have been well researched [9-10]. There are 4 main factors that contribute to latency:

1. Propagation delay – time to transmit a packet over the wire. Subject to speed of light delays
2. Transmission delay – time taken to serialize the data onto the wire.
3. Nodal delay – time to decide on a route for a packet at each router
4. Queuing delay – delay caused by waiting at overloaded network hardware.

Techniques that tackle the issue of latency and jitter tend to primarily concentrate on the reduction of network traffic so as to ameliorate the effects of queuing delay. A popular method of achieving this is predictive schemes, such as dead reckoning and the Hybrid Strategy Model [2-3].

Much work has analysed the performance of various predictive techniques. Roberts et al. propose an alternative to the standard spatial error threshold used in dead reckoning, known as time-space error threshold [11-12]. It is demonstrated how this technique improves consistency in comparison to traditional dead reckoning, at the expense of increased network traffic. The pre-reckoning algorithm, proposed by Duncan et al., improves on standard dead reckoning by providing a technique that detects likelihood of breaches of the error threshold, resulting in improved consistency [13]. Lee et al. propose a scheme under which the spatial error threshold value is increased based on distance between entities, resulting in less network traffic being transmitted between participants that are not close to one another within the virtual world [14]. The Hybrid Strategy Model (HSM) improves the dead reckoning predictive model by taking long-term user behaviour of an entity within a set environment into account [15]. This long-term model is known as a strategy model, and can include information detailing how an entity navigates a winding corridor, for example. This approach was shown to require fewer packets than dead reckoning, whilst maintaining an equal or greater level of consistency.

All the approaches outlined above allow a certain level of inconsistency for a resultant decrease in network traffic. However, none of these approaches take the capabilities of the underlying network into account in their operation, meaning that such approaches may be performing sub-optimally. This issue arises, as there is no firm understanding of how the relative reduction or increase in network traffic transmitted will actually impact on the overall consistency of the virtual environment.

To analyse this issue, a number of network trials were conducted using an industry standard engine known as Torque. The network setup for these trials is described in the next section.

III EXPERIMENTATION

Each experiment was carried out over a LAN using two desktop computers. Both test computers had equal specifications. Each computer also ran a copy of Torque, which was modified in two key ways to facilitate the experimentation. Firstly, the default client/server architecture was modified to operate in a peer-to-peer fashion, in order to emulate the architecture of applications that use packet reduction techniques such as dead reckoning. Secondly, the engine was extended to include full logging of both local and remote client information.

Both clients were connected via a network bridge running NetDisturb software, as shown in Figure 1. Net Disturb allows for the emulation of Wide Area Network limitations, such as latency and queuing delays, within a Local Area Network environment [16].

Using Net Disturb, we emulated the capacity of a home ADSL connection with an upstream bandwidth of 256kb/s. However, given that only 2 participants were involved in each experiment, this would mean that each participant had a full 256kb/s bandwidth, which is unrealistic. To compensate for this, we scaled the bandwidth down to 14kb/s, so as to emulate the performance of hosting 18 distinct clients. No limit was set on the buffer size, meaning that no packets could be lost due to buffer overflow.

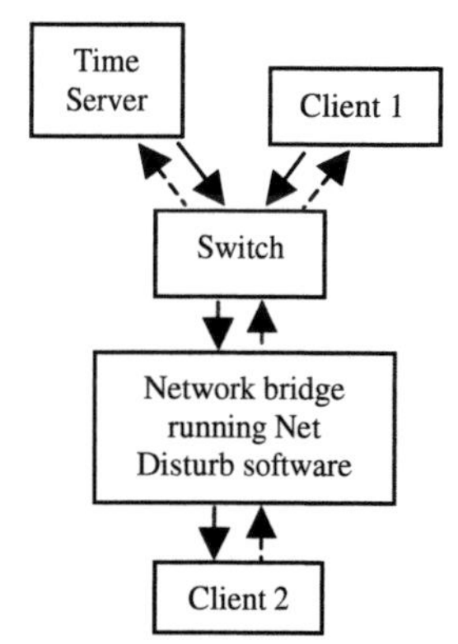

Figure 1. Overview of the network setup

Upon entering the virtual environment, each participant first contacted the other and initiated communication. Next, each participant synchronised his or her time with that of the "Time Server". This was done so as recorded information could be accurately compared offline following the experiments. The experiment then began. The goal in the environment was to navigate a racetrack, and reach the end position before the other participant. A plan view of the test scenario is shown in Figure 2. The

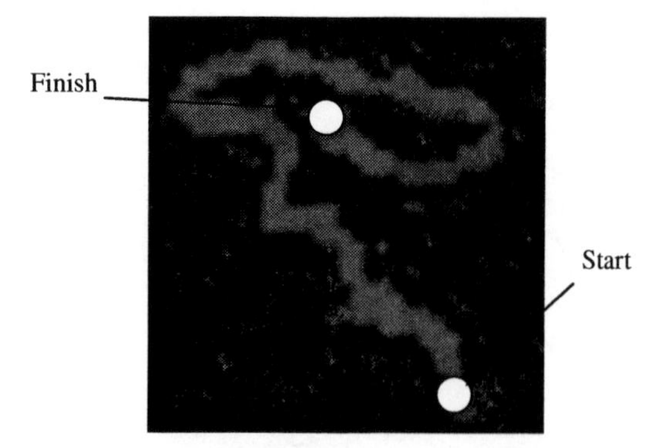

Figure 2 Plan view of test environment

packet transmission rate was varied per experiment, beginning at 2 packets per second (PPS), and incremented by 2 up to 24 PPS. All data collected during each experiment was then compared offline using Matlab. The spatial inconsistency, which is the Euclidean difference between the local and remote position of a client, was calculated at each time step. As it is impossible to guarantee that data will be recorded at the exact time on both machines, each local data point recorded was compared with that which has the closest time stamp. The maximum difference in compared timestamps was 2ms. The average spatial inconsistency was then calculated for the entire experiment.

IV RESULTS AND DISCUSSION

Analysing the data collected during the experiments described in Section III, the tradeoff between packet transmission rate and consistency is evident, as shown in Figure 3. Here, the average spatial inconsistency in Torque Game Units (TGU) is plotted against increasing packet transmission rates for a single set of participant trajectories.

As can be clearly seen from Figure 3, there is a region between approximately 18-22 PPS, within which average spatial inconsistency is at its lowest level. This is the optimal region of packet transmission rates, as increasing or reducing network traffic above or below this level only serves to negatively impact on consistency.

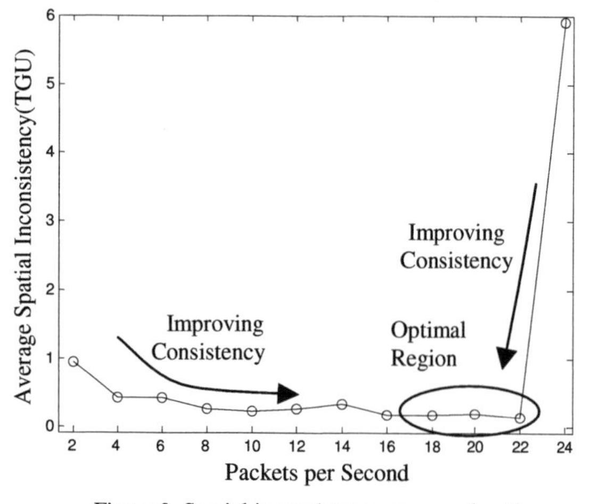

Figure 3. Spatial inconsistency measured as the packets per second increases

To the left of this region, inconsistency is being unnecessarily introduced due to modelling error. As the bandwidth being consumed within this region is well below that of the available 14kb/s, no extra network latency is caused by excess packet transmission. In such a case, it is worthwhile transmitting extra packets, so as to improve consistency. The typical behaviour exhibited within this region is shown in Figure 4. Here, a section of a single user local and remote path is shown when a transmission rate of 2PPS is used, along with the spatial inconsistency arising from a different section of the course. From Figure 4(a), it can be seen how the remote behaviour deviates from that of the local behaviour until an update is received, at which point, the two are reconciled. This is further evident from Figure 4(b). Note how the spatial inconsistency increases between updates, then returns to zero when an update is received.

Currently, predictive packet reduction schemes do not take this result into account. Their use, therefore, may result in an inefficient use of available resources. Based on this, we propose that such schemes incorporate a dynamic threshold, which can be scaled based on application and network parameters, so that packet transmission rates match that of the optimal region. The location of this optimal region will vary based on the nature of the application.

In the optimal region, the average bandwidth being consumed is approximately 13.5kb/s, which is just below that of the available bandwidth. Any increase above this level will overload the available bandwidth, leading to increased network latency. The impact of this increase on consistency is obvious from Figure 3, where it can be seen that inconsistency increases dramatically above 22 PPS. Consistency is improved in this case by reducing network traffic. Such a scenario necessitates the use of packet reduction schemes, such as dead reckoning. However, as demonstrated by the previous result, network traffic should not be reduced below the optimal region.

We further highlight the impact of network traffic at this end of the spectrum of transmission rates by analysing a single user trajectory, shown Figure 5(a) and (b). Figure 5(a) shows the local and remote trajectory for a packet transmission rate of 24PPS whilst figure 5(b) shows the spatial inconsistency arising from a different section of the course. Comparing Figure 5(a) and Figure 4(a), the effect of the extra packets is apparent. The remote behaviour is now indistinguishable from that of the local behaviour. However, examining the spatial inconsistency in Figure 5(b), the true impact of the higher transmission rates and network latency can be seen. In this case, the average bandwidth usage is 16kb/s, 2kb/s greater than the available bandwidth. However, as the NetDisturb buffer does not overrun, latency within the overloaded network continually increases, as the buffer grows larger. This has the knock on effect of continually increasing spatial inconsistency. Although this trend is evident from Figure 5(b), as shown by the broken straight line, there are occasions where the spatial inconsistency value decreases. The reasons behind this will now be discussed.

On the straight sections of the course, as shown in Figure 6, the remote position remains at a distance behind the local position due to network latency. The Euclidean distance measure used to calculate inconsistency works well in this case, and inconsistency has a value of d. As the

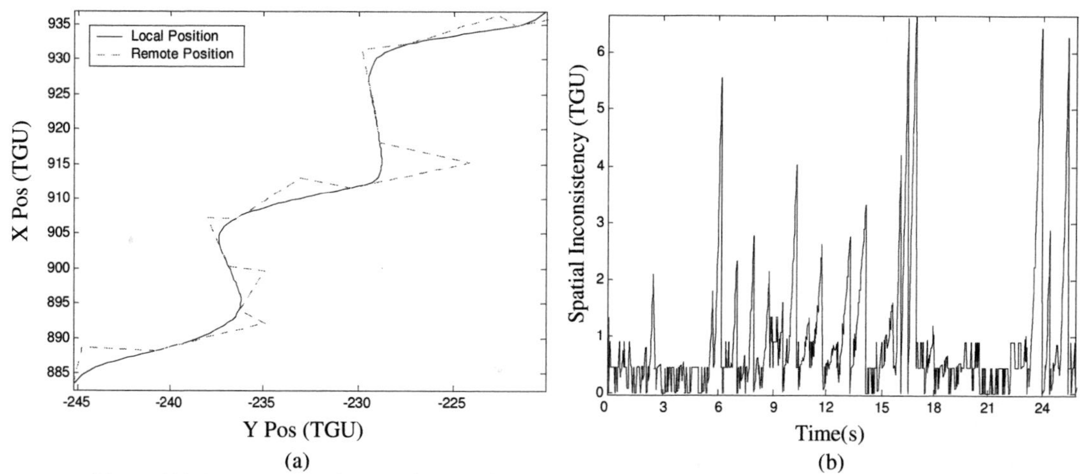

Figure 4(a) An example trajectory showing the local and remote positions when a transmission rate of 2PPS is used (b) Spatial inconsistency for a section of the course

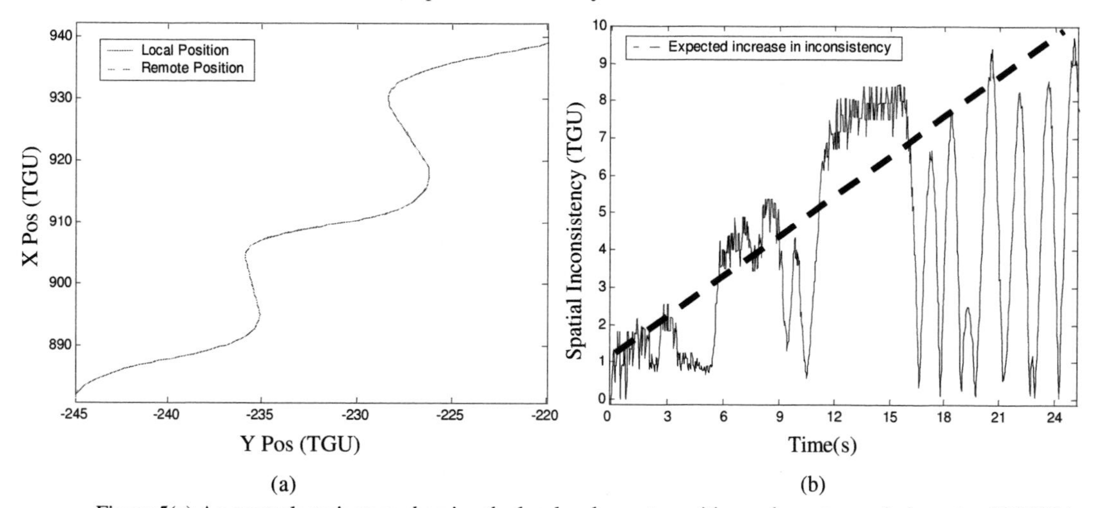

Figure 5(a) An example trajectory showing the local and remote positions when a transmission rate of 24PPS is used (b) Spatial inconsistency for a section of the course

entity navigates a corner the distance around the curve between the two positions is still given by *d*. However, as we are using Euclidean distance, the inconsistency measured at this point is actually *d'*, which is smaller than *d*. Upon reaching the straight section of the track again, the inconsistency is once again correctly measured as *d*. This demonstrates a shortcoming in the spatial measure of inconsistency, a solution to which is outside the scope of this work.

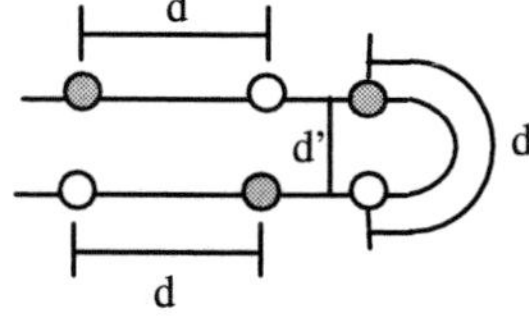

Figure 6. As the player navigates the course, the measured inconsistency can vary due to the nature of the inconsistency metric

V CONCLUDING REMARKS

In this work, the tradeoffs between network packet transmission rates and consistency were investigated, in order to analyse the true impact of packet reduction schemes on the performance of Distributed Interactive Applications. Using the Torque games engine, converted to operate in a peer-to-peer fashion, a number of network trials were conducted.

Results collected from these trials highlight an important performance related characteristic of packet reduction. There exists an optimal transmission rate region, within which average inconsistency is at it's lowest. Increasing the packet transmission rate above this point means that inconsistency is introduced due to network latency. Such a scenario requires the use of predictive schemes, such as dead reckoning. Reducing the rate below this level however, introduces inconsistency unnecessarily, without providing any subsequent improvement in network latency. Using these results, a shortcoming of the traditional spatial inconsistency measure was also demonstrated.

Based on this work, we propose that predictive schemes take this optimum packet transmission region into account, so as they can operate in an efficient manner. Such a scheme could use a threshold value, as with other predictive schemes. However, the value of this threshold could be scaled based on application attributes, in order to maintain a packet transmission rate that lies within the optimal region for that application. This is the focus of future work.

ACKNOWLEDGEMENTS

This work is supported by Science Foundation Ireland and Enterprise Ireland - grant no. IRCSET/SC/04/CS0289.

REFERENCES

[1] Delaney, D., T. Ward and S. McLoone. "On consistency and network latency in distributed interactive applications: A survey - Part I." *Presence: Teleoperators and Virtual Environments* 15(4),August 2006, pp 218-234.

[2] Delaney, D., T. Ward and S. McLoone. "On consistency and network latency in distributed interactive applications: A survey - Part II." *Presence: Teleoperators and Virtual Environments* 15(4),August 2006, pp 465-482.

[3] Roehle, B. (1997). "Channeling the data flood." IEEE Spectrum 34(3). p.p 32-38. 1997

[4] IEEE. IEEE Standard for Distributed Interactive Simulation - Application Protocols IEEE Std 1278.1-1995 IEEE, 1995

[5] Delaney, D., T. Ward and S. Mc Loone "Reducing Update Packets in Distributed Interactive Applications using a Hybrid Model". *16th International Conference on Parallel and Distributed Computing Systems, August 13-15*, Reno, USA, pp. 417-422, 2003.

[6] Lloyd, J. "The Torque Game Engine", Game Developer Magazine, 11 (8), pp. 8-9, September 2004.

[7] S. Singhal and M. Zyda, "Networked virtual environments: design and implementation.", ACM Press SIGGRAPH Series, Addison-Wesley, Reading, Massachusetts, 1999.

[8] Blow, J.. "A look at Latency in Networked Games." Game Developer **5**(7): 28-40, 1998.

[9] Bolot, JC. "End-to-end packet delay and loss behavior in the internet" *SIGCOMM '93: Conference proceedings on Communications architectures, protocols and applications*, San Francisco, California. pp: 289 - 298

[10]Vaghi, I., C. Greenhalgh and S. Benford. Coping with inconsistency due to network delays in collaborative virtual environments. Symposium on Virtual Reality Software and Technology (VSRT '99), London, England, ACM, pp. 42-49.

[11] Roberts, D., D. Marshall, S. McLoone, D. Delaney, T. Ward and R. Aspin "Exploring the use of local inconsistency measures as thresholds for dead reckoning update packet generation". *Distributed Simulation and Real Time Applications*, Montreal, Canada, pp. 195 - 202, 2005.

[12] Zhou, S., W. Cai, F. B. S. Lee and S. J. Turner. "Time-space Consistency in Large Scale Distributed Virtual Environment." *ACM Transactions on Modeling and Computer Simulation (TOMACS)* 14(1):pp. 31 - 47,2004

[13] Duncan, T. P. and D. Gracanin "Pre-reckoning algorithm for distributed virtual environments". *Winter Simulation Conference*, New Orleans, Louisiana, 2003, pp. 1086-1093.

[14] Lee, B.-S., W. Cai, S. J. Turner and L. Chen. "Adaptive Dead Reckoning algorithms for distributed Interactive Simulation." *International Journal of Simulation* 1(1-2):pp. 21-34,

[15] Delaney, D., T. Ward and S. Mc Loone "On Reducing Entity State Update Packets in Distributed Interactive Simulations using a Hybrid Model". *Proceeding of the 21st IASTED International Multi-conference on Applied Informatics, February 10-13*, Innsbruck, Austria,pp. 2003

[16] NetDisturb Website, ZTI http://www.zti-telecom.com/pages/main-netdisturb.htm. Accessed 21 Sept 2006.

AUTHOR BIOGRAPHIES

Damien Marshall graduated with a B.Sc degree (Computer Science and Software Engineering) in 2003. He then joined the Distributed Interactive Applications Group, and completed his M.Sc in January 2005. Shortly afterwards, he began his Ph.D. Currently, his work examines the various factors of consistency in distributed interactive applications.

Dr. Séamus McLoone is a member of the distributed interactive applications group (DIAG) at the Department of Electronic Engineering in the National University of Ireland Maynooth. His research interests varies from multiple model approaches to nonlinear system identification to reducing and masking the effects of latency in distributed interactive applications.

Dr. Tomas Ward is a member of the distributed interactive applications group at the NUI Maynooth. His main interests are in assistive technology and data management techniques for distributed shared applications. Spare time is spent on pushing out his personal best on Konami DrumMania V.

Declan Delaney received his B.E. and M.Eng.Sc. from University College Dublin in 1991 and 1998 respectively. His PhD was awarded in 2005 by the National University of Ireland, Maynooth. From 1992 to 2000 he worked as a software developer and subsequently as project manager. At present he works in the area of Knowledge management for an Italian multinational, ENI and is based in Milan,

Games Design & Aesthetic approaches

CREATING GAMES WITH FEELING

A.Cavan Fyans and Graham McAllister
Sonic Arts Research Centre
Queen's University Of Belfast
E-mail: afyans01@qub.ac.uk

KEYWORDS

Haptics, multi-sensorial games, development environments.

ABSTRACT

This paper presents a novel approach for the creation of computer games where the user can actually feel and manipulate objects in the 3D environment. Haptics (the sense of touch), is commonly used in virtual reality simulations such as tele-operation (the control of remote systems), however to date, games have not typically been targeted for development. By taking two existing products; a game engine (Unity) and a commercial haptics device (a PHANTOM Omni), a plug-in has been developed to link these technologies together. The resulting system allows anyone, with even modest programming skills, to create a computer game which allows the user to feel 3D objects in the environment. The paper will discuss how Unity allows for the rapid prototyping of games, how this plug-in was developed, and finally how haptics can be used in future computer games. By introducing this extra modality channel into computer games (in addition to visuals and audio), it is hoped that this technology could lead to a new genre of games.

INTRODUCTION

The stimulation of our senses in computer games has historically been limited to the visual and auditory channels. Therefore, games designers are aiming to create believable, immersive environments using only two of our five input senses. Of our remaining senses, only haptics (touch) has been exploited, and even then, only to a limited extent in computer games, typically through the use of rumble features on joypads or steering wheels. Recently, amBX have developed peripherals which are designed to augment the gaming and film experience by controlling lighting and fans (air flow) in the user's physical environment.

Computer games are becoming increasingly more complex and as a result, they need to convey more information to the user. Hence, the field of HCI for computer games has become of great interest to games designers, to ensure that they can convey the in-game status accurately and in real-time. By also employing the haptic sense, games designers could use this sensory channel to encode appropriate information, thus avoiding overload in the visual or auditory channels.

Previous work in the field of haptics and computer gaming is limited and for the most part unpublished. A small example of what developers have made is documented on SensAble's (Developer of the Phantom Omni) website. Through their developers competition, '3D Touch Developers Challenge', entries were submitted which encompassed gaming, education and music. One of the winning developments was one of the two gaming entries, a multiplayer sports game 'Haptic Ball', where up to eight players could compete each using a haptic device, adding the extra element of touch to the existing sound and visual environment of the game. The second game 'Haptic Mini Golf' takes a similar route in giving the player physical feedback of the course and golf club they are using. Outside of these examples there is limited available research in the haptic gaming area, possibly due to the nature of creating games in this context, involving extensive graphical and game programming (eg openGL and C++) with the addition of the haptic device programming. Small research projects have been undertaken in haptic device development, 'The Plank' (Verplank et al. 2002) was a project based on creating simple haptic controller from an old disk drive and using the result for live sound manipulations. Another similar project was 'A Development Of a High Definition Haptic Controller' (Akahane et al. 2005) where research was conducted to develop high definition haptic control for realistic force feedback. These projects while still related to the haptics and gaming area have no real link to computer gaming. It could be down to the extent that prototyping (in the current state of haptic game development) an idea or testing a game concept is not a simple task and would require a skilled programmer or development team to bring basic concepts to life and from this there are few published examples of projects in haptics and 3D gaming.

The approach discussed in this paper is unique for two main reasons:

- The system couples a commercial games engine with a haptics device. By using the Unity commercial games engine the user can create games in a development environment.
- The ease of creation of haptic 3D environments. Unity is a games creation environment which is ideal for rapid game development. As the use of haptics in computer games is still a new field, being able to easily create experimental haptics games may lead to successful concepts more quickly.

The remainder of the paper will discuss how the system was developed (the plug-in) and present ideas for future work.

BACKGROUND

The system proposed in this paper consists of two major components; Unity and the PHANTOM Omni. Each of these components will now be discussed.

Unity

Unity is a games creation system for Mac OS X that allows for the rapid design and development of computer games. It runs on Mac OS X and once the game is completed, can be published to Mac, Windows, a web browser or a Dashboard widget, all from the same code base.

Unity is a unique product in that it allows the game designer to construct their game world in a highly visual approach. Assigning properties to objects (such as physics) is typically done by clicking on the game object and then adding the desired property. The effects of this can be tested immediately and if they're not what was intended, can easily be changed. In this way, Unity encourages the designer to experiment with the settings of the game world constantly through the development period, making the game fun to develop and easier to test.

One of the major features of Unity is an extensible plug-in architecture which allows developers to extend the built-in functionality by allowing for the creating and linking in of external libraries. This plug-in architecture was used to bridge between the custom game code and the PHANTOM API. Figure 1. shows the Unity development environment.

Figure 1. Unity games creation environment from OTEE

Phantom Omni

SensAble manufacture several variants of their PHANTOM haptics controllers, the Omni is aimed at the consumer end of the market, however it is still prohibitively expensive to most users (approximately $2000). The device offers 6 degrees of freedom allowing the user to accurately touch and manipulate objects in 3D space. Most importantly, the device is capable of applying forces which can be programmatically controlled to create a range of effects. The user interacts with the PHANTOM by gripping the pen-like device to control the on-screen cursor in the virtual environment. Figure 2. shows the PHANTOM Omni from SensAble.

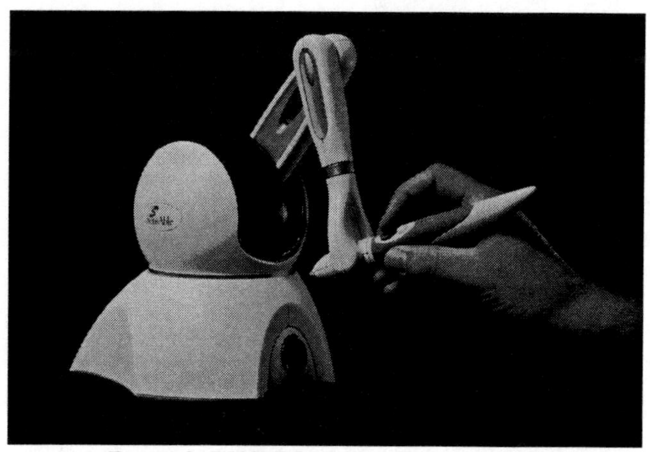

Figure 2. PHANTOM Omni from SensAble

The next section shows how The phantom Omni library was implemented into Unity enabling developers to utilise the full haptic control functions within games or virtual environments.

DEVELOPMENT

This section details the development of the plug-in and how it can be used to create a game.

Plug-in Development

This section discusses specifically the implementation details of the plug-in and how the PHANTOM Omni API is accessed from within Unity.

Development of a C++ plug-in from the Phantom Omni API that incorporates all the available control and haptic feedback functions

The method for executing C++ code from within Unity is through converting the standalone C++ code/application into a '.bundle' file. A bundle is dynamically loadable code in which individual methods can be executed individually, the bundle simply makes the C++ code importable into other environments (Unity) that do not directly support the C++ language. The Phantom Omni API has two main libraries for development provided by Sensable; Haptic Device Application Programming Interface (HDAPI), used for gathering precise control values and direct rendering of force in the haptic device, and Haptic Library Application Programming Interface (HLAPI), aimed at building 3D haptic environments and generating limited control effects such as friction or gravity.

Force rendering with the haptic device is processed through the scheduler, essentially a secondary thread of processing that iterates at around 1000Hz. This ensures forces generated or any transitions between forces are smooth and no resolution is noticeable. Device calls (force rendering or gathering position information etc) are all conducted within 'haptic frames', where information between the Phantom Omni and the computer are synchronized through stacking events until the end of a haptic frame. The calls work on two systems; synchronous calls, a 'one shot' call back method used to return instance information, and asynchronous calls, executed at every tick of the scheduler and used to render the haptic feedback.

Implementing all the HDAPI and HLAPI methods in a '.bundle' requires putting each task in a method of its own, where when called it can be passed required variables and performs the 'scheduler' task that is required. For the asynchronous scheduler calls information is passed to them through global variables implemented in the C++ code; for example the force is set through setting the values of a three dimensional vector that the asynchronous scheduler method checks at every 'tick'. The synchronous tasks are a lot easier to command and are called simply with a method containing the desired scheduler method for each event (friction, spring effect etc).

Implement the plug-in within Unity, gaining access to all the C++ plug-in methods from Unity.
Once the desired methods are implemented in the bundle this can be imported into Unity as a plug-in. In Unity all of the methods in the '.bundle' file can be called as external methods through a call to the external bundle file from a C# script:

[DllImport('bundle filename')] public static extern methodReturnVariable methodName();

This imports the method and implements it as a method within the C# class it was called from, this can be called the same way as any method in the same class. In the same way as internal method's variables can be passed both ways between the C# script and the C++ plug-in, so values like the force to be applied or the position of the device can be transferred.

Game Development

This section discusses creating 3D haptic environments and the implementation of the Phantom Omni's control and feedback.

Developing the haptic feedback system
The main aim of creating a 'generic' feedback system was so that a developer using Unity could implement the Phantom Omni in any environment created in Unity and instantly have (if desired) force feedback and the ability to feel any object instantly. The method implemented to enable the user to feel the surface of virtual objects utilises Unity's collision system. Through having a 'collider' sphere (of a slightly larger size) attached to the player sphere, a collision method could be called as soon as the 'collider' sphere touched another object in the simulation. This system works on the 'player' controlling a sphere of any size within the environment. The designer may want to implement other shapes or designs for the 'player's' virtual object and to this aim the collider sphere can easily be exchanged with, for example, a cube collider. By making the size of the collider slightly bigger then the player sphere this meant that collisions were 'pre-empted' and through this the virtual collision would be synchronised with the haptic feedback of the collision (when the player object touch another object visually the physical feedback would be synchronised). As soon as a collision was detected by the collider, a 'ray' was then cast towards the location of the collision at every iteration in Unity until the object has no contact with a surface. The cast ray returns all of the collision information including the distance that is then translated linearly to the force required in the device to provide the effect of the player touching the surface.

Creating a Game
With the entire HL and HD API's now implemented and accessible from within Unity, a scaling system was implemented to scale all of the incoming control numbers to a more manageable scale (-1 to 1). Then several 'general purpose' control scripts were created that could be edited depending on the environment they were applied to or the desired application, giving instant access to haptic control from a Unity scene. With these 'general' scripts available they can be linked to player object(s) in any haptic environment created in Unity and mapped to any control system the designer requires. With this flexibility of control, individual aspects of the control (the rotation of one joint or only the position in the x plane) can be implemented as well as utilising the entire control or feedback system. With the development of the haptic feedback system enabling users to feel virtual surfaces, creating an environment the user can feel is very straightforward. The script containing the calculations for the force to be applied when the player comes into contact with a surface has to be attached to the player object, and any surface the developer wants to be felt has to have a 'rigid body' attached and instantly the user can touch the surface of the objects. With the addition of Unity's ability to import models made in the majority of 3D modeling programs (Maya, Cheetah, Blender, Cinema 4D etc.) then the developer is not restricted to primitives only. This ability enables the developer to create any custom environment or object in the modeling software and import it into unity and instantly be able to touch, feel and manipulate the imported object.

PROTOTYPES

Touching Virtual Surfaces

This demonstration primarily showcases the ability to touch and manipulate virtual surfaces with the Phantom Omni. It demonstrates that expansive 3D environments can easily be created in Unity utilising the full 3D movement of the haptic device and combining this with the ability to generate forces so that the user can feel the environment as they manipulate it. The demonstration gives the user control of a small sphere in an environment filled with different surfaces to show different haptic environment reactions. Some surfaces are rigid and cannot be moved whereas others will move freely when pushed or will be heavy to move. Figure 3. shows a screenshot of the prototype.

Figure 3. Touching virtual surfaces prototype

Crane Control

The 'Crane Demonstration' gives the user 3D control of a crane arm in an enclosed environment where the objective is to pick up and move boxes within the environment. The concept behind this prototype is to demonstrate the HLAPI 'effects' that can be easily implemented into a created 3D environment. In this example the friction effect is used to translate the feeling of the mechanical crane arm movement directly to the user through the haptic device. In the same manner, when the user picks up a box the weight of the box and subsequent drag on the crane arm is physically represented as well as the visual representation. Again this also demonstrates the ability to design visually attractive games and environments with ease. Figure 4. shows a screenshot of the prototype.

Figure 4. Crane control prototype

Turret Control

In this application of the Phantom Omni within Unity the user is placed in control of a turreted gun with the aim of destroying all the objects in the scene in the specified time. The friction effect is also implemented here in a different guise to the crane demonstration, the friction (through the haptic device) physically reproduces the effect of turning a turreted gun, adding 'weight' to the movement. The force of the recoil of the gun when a shot is fired is also implemented into the environment alongside feeling the force of the exploding objects through physically shaking the controller. This demonstration also utilises the sound functions of Unity and shows the simplicity of adding sound as well as visual stimuli into the haptic environment. Figure 5. shows a screenshot of the prototype.

Figure 5. Turret control prototype

CONCLUSIONS

Through the application prototypes it is clear that the implementation of the Phantom Omni within the gaming engine Unity as a haptic controller is successful. From the conducted development of this project, the intended outcome of creating a plug-in to promote easy creation of immersive haptics environments has also been successful and from the demonstrations the project has proven that implementing the Phantom Omni within such 3D environments is now a simple task and the device can easily be translated to different environments and applications with full haptic feedback. With the demonstrations the project has shown some of the capabilities of utilising the HDAPI and HLAPI from within Unity and being able to quickly implement them in the environments to reach new and innovative methods of control, haptic feedback, and expression in modern computer gaming.

FUTURE WORK

From initial evaluations, where users were asked to explore the environments using a 'think aloud' method of capturing their experience and thoughts on the demonstration system, one area of further work is the implementation of haptic force calculations. Users stated that the haptic feedback for the surface of virtual objects could be improved. With further development on this application of the plug-in, it could be used in a variety of ways by future developers; games/environments could be created for blind and visually impaired people with the full ability to touch and feel the environment they are in, games involving intricate surface interaction would be easy to implement through unity and the Phantom Omni plug-in.

It should be stressed that the aim of this project was to implement the Phantom Omni within Unity (develop the plug-in), this has been successful and several prototypes have been developed to show how it could be used in the creation of games and interactive environments.

The developed ability to create immersive haptic environments with the Phantom Omni and Unity is a novel development system in terms of 'creating' an easy to use development engine (specifically aimed at gaming) where vast 3D environments can be created very simply and in which the haptic device is easily implemented and feedback controlled. This has created the ability for further developers to easily progress (into or through) the field of haptics and computer gaming or virtual haptic environments. This also opens up the world of haptic environment creation through (as stated) the development of an easy to use 3D environment creation engine, and because of this, further projects in haptic environments can be undertaken without the need for extensive C++ and openGL coding knowledge and typical game development timeframes. With the easy creation of immersive 3D environments in Unity for games or haptic simulations, future developers can concentrate more on the concept of a game or environment and can rapidly construct working prototypes to develop ideas further rather then have to spend the time trying to code expansive 3D environments and complex force calculations.

REFERENCES

Akahane, K. Hasegawa, S. Koike, Y. "A Development Of a High Definition Haptic Controller." In Proceedings of the first Joint Eurohaptics Conference and Symposium on Haptic Interfaces for Virtual Environment and Teleoperator Systems 2005.

AMBX, http://www.ambx.com, 2006.

OTEE Unity, http://www.otee.dk, 2006.

SensAble, http://www.sensable.com, 2006.

SensAble 3D Challenge, http://www.sensable.com/newsevents/pressreleases/pr-080205A.asp

Verpunk, B. Gurevitch, M. Matthews, M. 2002. "The Plank: Designing a Simple Haptic Controller." In Proceedings of the 2002 NIME Conference.

Cavan Fyans has just completed an MA in Sonic Arts at the Sonic Arts Research Centre in Belfast. Previously he has completed a BSc in Music Technology at Queen's University Belfast. 'Creating Games With Feeling' was submitted as a Dissertation for the MA in Sonic Arts, other projects and research conducted recently by Cavan relate to a similar area of innovative interaction with computers for computer games, interactive environments and music.

Graham McAllister is a lecturer in Music Technology at the Sonic Arts Research Centre, Queen's University Belfast. His research interests include computer games design, HCI and usability. He has recently completed a three-month industrial placement period at computer games technology company Over The Edge in Denmark.

Interface Design Requirements For Playing Pong With A Single Switch Device

J. Gilligan, B. Mac Namee and P. Smith

Abstract— **Motivated by a desire for increased accessibility in digital games, in this paper we consider the design requirements for an interface to a variation of the game Pong for single-switch users. We consider the issues in the design of accessible interfaces for games and propose a set of interface configurations for playing Pong, using this as a proof of concept for more elaborate games.**

***Index Terms*—Games, interface design, accessibility, assistive technology, switch access, selection grids, scanning**

I. Introduction

As the world market for computer games expands, increasing attention is being focussed on games accessibility. In its mission statement the Game Accessibility special interest group (GA-SIG) of the International Game Developers Association state that it intends to "*develop methods of making all games genres universally accessible*" [8]. This reflects other world wide accessibility initiatives such as the Web Access Initiative (www.w3.org/WAI) [9], and the Universal Design philosophy [12].

Thus, motivated by this desire for increased accessibility, and as a proof of concept for more elaborate games, we consider the design requirements for an interface to a variation of the Pong electronic game for single switch users. Switch devices are one of the major alternative input technologies to computers for people with disability.

This paper will begin by briefly introducing the game of Pong. This will be followed by an in-depth discussion of switch technologies. Following on from this design configurations required both to make switch access suitable to Pong and to make the Pong interface suitable to switch control. Finally, we will propose a scheme through which Pong could be made available to single-switch users, and extrapolate on what is required to make other games available to switch users.

II. Pong

Although there is some argument as to who first created a ball and paddle video game, we can be certain that the electronic game Pong was released in 1972 by the ATARI corporation, at the time headed by Nolan Bushell. A screenshot of an early version of Pong is shown in figure 1. Pong was released both as a coin-operated arcade machine and as a home system and became one of the first games to reach a mass audience. The success of Pong is largely attributed to its simplicity [7].

The concept of Pong is simple. A small ball moves across the screen, bouncing off the top and bottom edges. In the two player version, each player controls a paddle which can move up and down. The objective is to position the paddle so it hits the ball and returns it to the other side. The opposing player must then anticipate the likely position of the ball and try to hit it back to the other participant. A score is awarded when the opposing player misses.

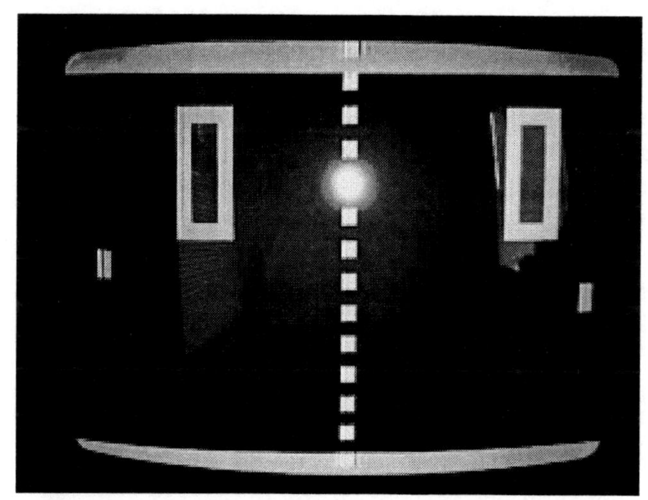

Figure 1: A screenshot of an early version of Pong

Over the years there have been many clones of Pong. There In this report we will consider a single player version in which 'the court' is enclosed by top, left and right walls off which the ball can bounce. The player controls a paddle at the bottom of the screen which can be moved from left to right and the object of the game is to keep the ball in play, with scores being awarded for each successful hit. A diagram showing the layout of this version of Pong is shown in figure 2.

J. Gilligan is with the School of Computing at the Dublin Institute of Technology, Dublin, Ireland. (e-mail: John.Gilligan@ comp.dit.ie).

B. Mac Namee is with the School of Computing at the Dublin Institute of Technology, Dublin, Ireland. (e-mail: Brian.MacNamee@ comp.dit.ie).

P. Smith. is with School of Computing and Technology at the University of Sunderland, Sunderland, U.K.

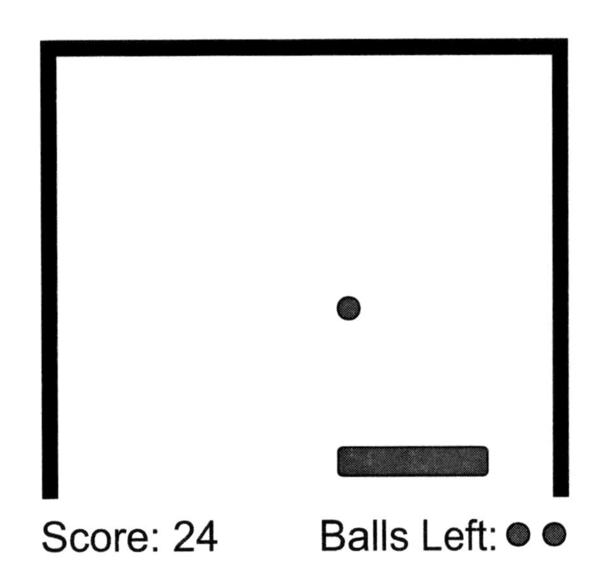

Figure 2: A simple illustration of the proposed single player Pong clone

While Pong may seem an unusual choice to work with - there are countless more sophisticated games currently available - it has a number of compelling advantages. Firstly, although Pong is relatively straightforward, with its relatively fast pace it does offer enough complication to allow exploration of the important issues surrounding accessible games. Furthermore, the ubiquity of Pong style games means that even those unfamiliar with modern digital games will not feel out of their depth with a Pong clone. In fact, there is also a growing body of thought that suggests that simple, or *casual*, games offer the greatest potential for growth of the digital games industry [13]. And finally, as our work will focus on single switch control, we require a game with simple control requirements.

III. SWITCH ACCESS

A switch is simply a make-or-break electrical circuit used by those disabled people who are incapable of using conventional computer input devices such as the keyboard and mouse [6, 11]. The switch is placed on or near the muscle group over which the user has most control, in some cases just an eyebrow. Figure 3 shows an image of the Jelly Beamer™ wireless switch.

Many types of switch are available from the standard hand-controlled switch to sip/puff switches which involve a tube connected to a switch which is activated by a change in air-pressure caused by sipping or blowing. Switches can be activated by most muscle movements, with newer ones even controlled by thought alone [4]!

Switch access as a means of input to a computer works in association with on screen grids of items to be selected. This collection is known as the *selection set.* This is placed in a separate window and can comprise text and graphic items. The window can be positioned anywhere on the screen and always appears on top of any other application windows.

Figure 3: The Jelly Beamer™ wireless switch

Switch access works by selecting appropriate items on the grid through a process known as *scanning*. Each item in the selection set is highlighted in sequence. The length of time for which an item is highlighted is known as *scan delay*. A press of the switch will select the currently highlighted item. Scanning is characterised by the switch configuration used, the manner and order in which the highlighter moves through the items in the selection set (*scan movement*) and by how items on the computer screen are sequentially highlighted - one after the other, until the user chooses one by pressing the switch (*scan method*). Figure 4 shows a sample selection grid used to enter text into a word processor.

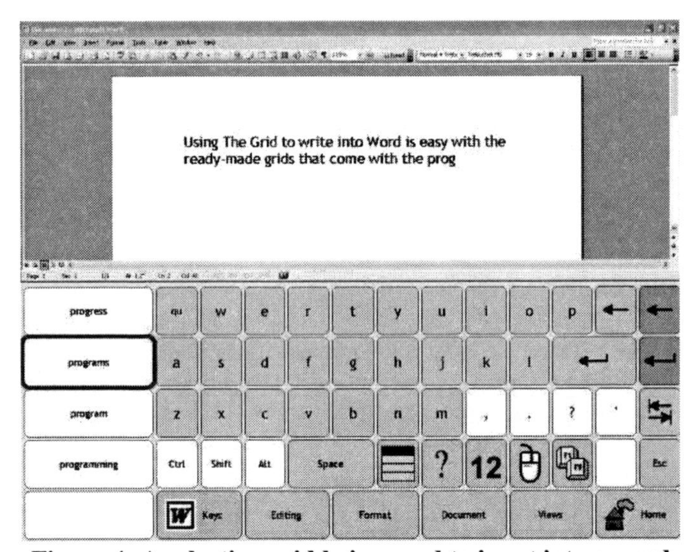

Figure 4: A selection grid being used to input into a word processor

The following section will describe the considerations which must be kept in mind in order to allow switch control of a Pong clone.

IV. PONG AND SWITCH ACCESS DESIGN CONFIGURATIONS.

The game Pong places a number of functional requirements on the user. The most important of these are as follows:

- The player must be able to control the paddle through an input device.
- The player must be able to react quickly enough to effect paddle movement in the time interval in which the ball is within the playing area.
- The player must possess enough spatial awareness to

understand the relative positions of the ball and paddle to each other.

- The player must anticipate the likely position at which the ball will arrive at the paddle plane of movement and move the paddle there beforehand - this involves projecting the path of the ball as it bounces through the angles of the playing area.

Using a switch device also places a further set of functional requirements on the user. To use a scanning system, a switch user must be able to [5]:

- Make a choice from a field of options.
- Watch/listen and wait until the choice is highlighted by the scanning box or advance through choices until they arrive at the choice.
- Activate a switch to select their choice.

Successful switch use involves issues such as volitional and reliable movement, anxiety control, and cognition [2, 5, 11].

How the switch system is configured can significantly affect performance. For example, the choice of scanning method demands different abilities [1] which individual users may have to varying degrees.

The design of the grid significantly impacts on performance. Decisions must be made as to the grid layout, item size, shape, colour, spacing, presentation and so on [5, 11].

In the next section we will look at how some of these switch design choices can impact on the accessibility of Pong.

V. Switch Interface Design Issues for Pong

Most accessible design philosophies place the user at the centre of development. The choice of switch is determined by the functional limitations of the user and can impact on the consequent usability of the game. So, there are a number of important considerations which must be made in determining an appropriate control scheme for the game of Pong.

For example, a standard Pong player requires reasonable function of sensing size, form and contour using both eyes for objects close to the eye. If an eyelash switch were used it may interfere with the user's view of the playing area and the ball and paddle. This in turn could reduce the user's effectiveness in assessing the relative position of the ball in space in relation to the paddle. Similar considerations for other switch locations for which, for example, the user may have to turn their head away from the screen.

Maybe most importantly switch access is slow. Even for less complex grid traversals, the accumulation of scan delays amounts to a slow selection process [1]. This must be accounted for when setting the speed of the ball, as the ball should not move so fast as to reach the paddle line quicker than the time it takes to make the required number of paddle moves.

Also, switch systems involve a selection grid. This adds another element to the screen layout of the game. While the game is playing the switch user is forced to change their focus from the path of the ball to the selection grid while making a paddle move. Again this introduces another layer of complexity and both the speed of the ball and the design of the selection grid should account for this.

The presentation of items in the selection grid is an important area in which switch access can be facilitated. The larger the item size the easier the item is to target and select. However, this increases the size of the grid which in turn encroaches onto the space allowed for the playing area. By reducing the size of the playing area it can leave the ball with a shorter path to travel. This might leave the user with less time to move the paddles to the required positions.

Scan methods (i.e. how the item is selected) also affect user performance. Nisbet and Poon [11] outlines the functional demands that different scan methods (such as Autoscan and Userscan [3]) place on the user. Some of these may be in conflict with the requirements of Pong.

For example, in Autoscan the highlighter moves automatically between items. This places the onus on the user to wait until the required grid item is highlighted. Pong also requires the user focus attention on the playing area and its constituent objects at the same time. Thus, the user is required to shift attention between the grid and the playing area and at the same time carry out the multiple tasks of controlling grid selection and the Pong paddle. Switch users may not have sufficient capacity to carry out multiple tasks simultaneously or to divide attention between differently sited stimuli. These difficulties may result in increased stress and anxiety on the part of the user.

Another consequence of the dual focus imposed on switch users of games is that there may not be correlation between the direction of grid traversal and the direction of the paddle. It is an added burden on the player to control a paddle moving up and down in a vertical plane through grid selection involving left to right traversal in the horizontal plane. This involves complex control and coordination of counter intuitive voluntary movements. Grid traversal and paddle movement should be similar in so far as is possible.

Following on from these issues the next section will suggest a number of possible solutions for making Pong more accessible to single switch users.

VI. Proposed Solutions

Based on all of the considerations discussed in the previous sections we now propose a number set-ups for single switch controlled Pong. There are three different configurations, two of which use a selection grid which appears in a separate window to the actual Pong game, and one of which uses a selection grid which integrated into the game itself.

A screenshot of the first proposed configuration is shown in figure 3. In this scenario the Pong window is positioned above a smaller window which contains the selection grid for switch control. Here the selection grid has only two options – to move the paddle left or to move the paddle right. When a user selects either one of these options the paddle would move a pre-determined amount in the appropriate direction. This configuration would use an Autoscan-based scan method in which the arrows are continually highlighted one after another allowing the player make repeated selections.

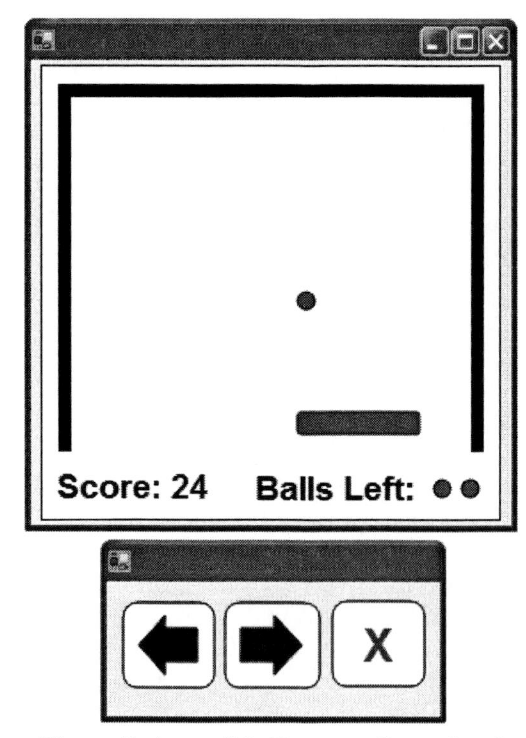

Figure 5: Accessible Pong configuration 1

The obvious concern over this configuration is that it would take an unacceptable amount of time for the user to successfully move the paddle as they must make repeated choices. This difficulty inspires the second proposed configuration.

In the second proposed configuration a third choice is added to the selection grid used by the player. This time the selection grid offers choices to go left, go right and stop, as shown in figure 4. In this configuration the left and right choices are alternately highlighted until the user makes a selection. However, this time once a selection is made the paddle moves continuously in that direction. While the paddle is moving the selection grid changes to only offer the stop option, which when selected stops the paddle. At this point the selection grid reverts to alternately offering the left and right choices.

The advantage of this proposal over the previous offering is that it will allow the player move the paddle more fluently, making the game more playable. However, there is still the difficulty that the player must shift their attention between the selection grid window and the game window. The final proposed configuration addresses this problem.

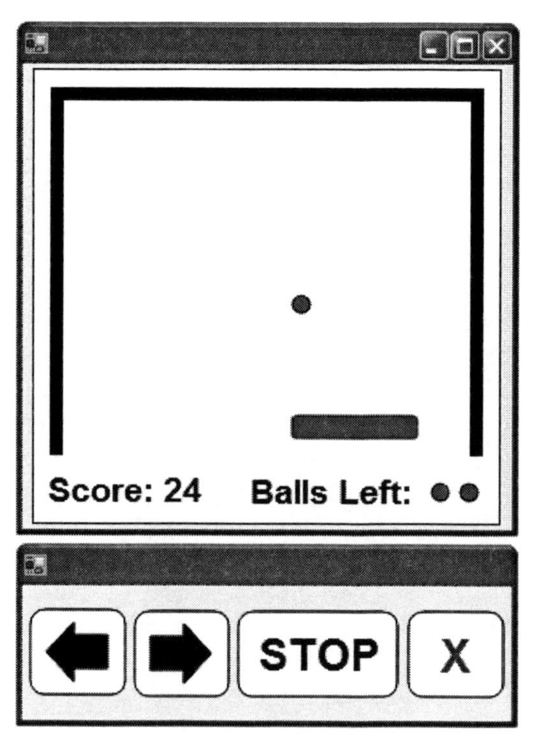

Figure 6: Accessible Pong configuration 2

The final proposed configuration does not use a selection grid in a separate window, but rather integrates the selection grid into the play area itself. This configuration is illustrated in figure 5. This time two options are initially offered to the player by right and left arrows which flash alternately at either side of the paddle (shown in figure 5(a) and 5(b)). Once the player selects a direction the paddle moves continuously in that direction until the player chooses the newly offered stop option (figure 5(c)) which stops the paddle.

This configuration has the advantages that movement selection should be relatively fast and that the player's attention does not need to shift between two different windows. However, the major drawback is that the selection mechanism has to be built directly into the game. Ongoing work is exploring a number ideas to solve this problem. For example, it is proposed that a game could offer an accessibility layer which would allow external programs overlay graphics onto the game window to facilitate accessible control, assuming that the game exposed enough information to allow sensible positioning of the control graphics. This would allow games be built without major consideration for accessible control, while allowing any number of accessible control schemes be built onto the game after release.

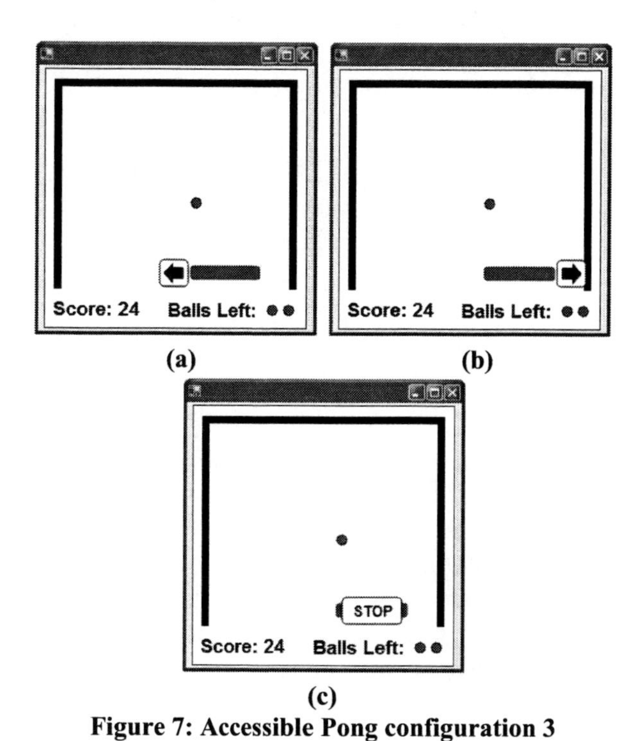

Figure 7: Accessible Pong configuration 3

VII. CONCLUSIONS & FUTURE WORK

In this paper we have reviewed some of the issues surrounding single switch access to computer games, particularly focusing on how the game Pong would be implemented for single switch users. It is clear from the above that switch access is a complex issue with considerations arising both for the design of the switch control and the design of games themselves. We have proposed a set of configurations for switch control of Pong that attempt to address these. It is clear from this initial review that very flexible designs are required.

Within the domain of switch access there are many other variations and considerations, for example set-ups for younger players, multi-switch configurations and different selection grid layouts and these form the basis of our plan for future work. As is accepted best practice [10] it is also intended to perform an extensive set of tests of the proposed configurations with switch users.

REFERENCES

[1] J. Angelo, "Comparison of Three Computer Scanning Modes as an Interface Method for Persons with Cerebral Palsy". American Journal of Occupational Therapy, 46 (2), p217-222. (1992)

[2] J. Angelo, "Factors Affecting the Use of a Single Switch with Assistive Technology Devices", Journal of Rehabilitation Research and Development Vol. 37 No. 5. (2000)

[3] D. Colven & T. Detheridge, "Common Terminology for Switch Controlled Software", ACE Centre Oxford. (1990)

[4] D. Colven & S. Judge, "Switch Access to Technology a Comprehensive Guide", ACE Centre Oxford. (1996)

[5] A.M. Cook & S.M. Hussey, "Assistive Technologies: Principles and Practice", Baltimore: Mosby. (1995)

[6] A.M. Cook& S.M. Hussey, "Assistive Technologies: Principles and Practice", 2nd Ed, Baltimore: Mosby. (2002)

[7] J.C. Herz , "Joystick Nation: How Videogames Ate Our Quarters, Won Our Hearts, and Rewired Our Minds", Little, Brown & Co. Inc. (1997)

[8] Internationl Games Developers Association Accessibility Special Interest Group, "Accessibility in Games: Motivations and Approaches" (2004) [www.igda.org/accessibility/IGDA_Accessibility_WhitePaper.pdf]

[9] Irish National Disability Authority, "Guidelines for Web Accessibility". (2006) [accessit.nda.ie/guidelineindex_1.html]

[10] S. Iwarsson & A. Stahl, "Accessibility, Usability and universal Design – Positioning and Definition of Concepts Describing Person Environment Relationships, Disability and Rehabilitation, 2003;25, p57-66. (2003)

[11] P. Nisbet & P. Poon, "Special Access Technology", The CALL Centre, University of Edinburgh. (1998) [www.callcentrescotland.org]

[12] W.F.E Preiser & E. Ostroff, "Universal Design Handbook", McGraw-Hill. (2001)

[13] H. Wen, "Analyze This: Will 'Casual' Games Dominate the Future of the Industry?", Gamasutra, August. (2006) [gamasutra.com/features/20060803/wen_01.shtml]

John Gilligan is a lecturer in computer science at the School of Computing in the Dublin Institute of Technology in Dublin, Ireland and former member of the scientific committee for the Association for Advancement of Assistive Technology in Europe Conference 2003.

Dr. Brian Mac Namee is a lecturer in computer science at the School of Computing in the Dublin Institute of Technology in Dublin, Ireland with a significant research interest in digital games.

Prof. Peter Smith is the head of the School of Computing and Technology at the University of Sunderland.

Computer Game Accessibility: From Specific Games to Accessible Games

Roland Ossmann[1], Dominique Archambault[2] and Klaus Miesenberger[1]

[1] Institute Integrated Study
University of Linz
Altenbergerstr. 69, 4040 Linz
Linz, Austria

[2] Université Pierre et Marie Curie
9, quai Saint Bernard
Paris 5, France

E-mail: roland.ossmann@students.jku.at

KEYWORDS
Games Accessibility, Disabilities, Special Needs, Assistive Technologies, Guidelines.

ABSTRACT

Computer games are very important for learning, teaching and entertainment. Therefore they are one of the most challenging applications concerning accessibility, and usability for people with disabilities. Equal access is especially critical in the context of playing together and in groups. This paper describes the different kinds of disabilities. It will show the state of the art in games accessibility research and development, the relations to software accessibility and techniques and methods which could be applied to make games accessible. Tools and guidelines for the support of game developers will also be part of this paper. Mainstreaming accessibility efforts will be discussed as the challenge of future development.

INTRODUCTION

Computer games have become an important part in child and youth culture, but they are also played by adults. To give people with disabilities the chance to have access to games should be seen as an important issue for better inclusion and participation. Due to this access by assistive technologies (e.g. screen readers, alternative in/output devices) should be supported by games and new methods and tools for the game design and development should support better access for all.

Types of Disabilities

Disabilities (or impairments) in terms of different requirements towards accessibility support are classified in four main categories:

Visual Impairments
Visual impairments covers blindness, low vision and colour blindness. They ask for flexibility in terms of screen output adjustments, keyboard access to the interface and in addition speech/sound output.

Auditory Impairments
Auditory impairments cover deafness and hard of hearing. Problems in language understanding and usage might also as a consequence of hearing problems. Alternative access to audio information, easy to understand information and reduced complexity are key elements for accessibility of this group.

Mobility Impairments
Mobility impairments cover paralysis (disordered muscle control), neurological disorders (problems transmitting impulses to muscles), repetitive stress injury (result of repeating motions over a long period of time), lack of mobility (e.g. by arthritis) and lack of steadiness (gradual loss of muscle tone). They ask for support of alternative input techniques (e.g. non-mouse based interaction) and for possibilities to adjust timing settings.

Cognitive Disabilities
Cognitive disabilities cover the main topics memory loss, attention deficit disorder and dyslexia (learning disability). The range of cognitive disabilities is wide, but most of the symptoms attend to the three mentioned impairments. In a similar way like for auditory disabilities reduced complexity and an easy to understand style of language use are important.

ACCESSIBILITY

Games accessibility should be seen as a follow up activity to areas like software[1], hardware[2] or web accessibility[3]. Besides basic similarities game accessibility must take specific differences into account.

Computer Access

Assistive technologies enable people with disabilities

[1] http://www-306.ibm.com/able/guidelines/
[2] http://www.tiresias.org/guidelines/
[3] http://www.w3c.org/wai/

to use a computer. They have to use specific devices or assistive software, or the combination of the two. A large variety of cases exist, depending on the impairment and the ability of the user. Nevertheless the use of assistive technologies requests that the software respects a certain number of accessibility rules.

Software Accessibility

To use special devices and/or software, in most cases it is necessary that applications respect a certain number of rules. Indeed some devices using alternative modalities request some specific data like alternative texts for graphical contents.

But it is not enough that the application respects accessibility standards. In most cases the contents must be accessible too. For instance in the case of websites, the contents must comply with the Web Content Accessibility Guidelines, which were published by the Web Accessibility Initiative of the W3C. (Chisholm et al. 1999)

Accessibility of Games

Accessibility in games is a more complex problem then software accessibility or web accessibility. In normal software, the work is often highly structured and the work steps are quite often repeating. And in normal software products, there is no need to react in real time.

Furthermore it is not enough to find a technical way to make a game accessible, the result must be as interesting and as useable as the original game. So one of the most important rule in the development of accessible games is, that an accessible game must still be a game. (Bierre et al. 2005; Archambault et al. 2005)

SPECIFIC GAMES

To handle the special needs of the impaired players, new ways of interacting and communicating have to be found. This starts with the topic of how to navigate a blind user thru a mace and might end with the question how can a person, who can not use his/her hands, control a car racing game. This section will give an overview about computer games, who already deals with this topic, some of them with special assistant technologies, some without.

Audiogames

Audiogames are games, where all the (graphical) output is done over audio output. The main target group are visual impaired people. No additional hardware (excepting a sound card and speakers) is needed to play these games.

Tactile Games

Tactile games are games, where the inputs and/or the outputs are done by special tactile boards or by Braille displays. In (Archambault et al. 2005) is the description of a tactile game for blind children, called "Reader rabbit's Toddler", where the children can feel the buttons they can press in connection to the action they activate.

Internet Games

The internet is on the one hand an interesting place for the publishing of games, because it is platform independent and the game needn't be installed, on the other hand the (limited) technologies of the web browsers and the internet makes the game development to a special challenge.

GAME ACCESSIBILITY

Specific Games which are Accessible to Everybody

The first step is to start from specific games and to move towards universally accessible games, games designed for all. (Grammenos et al. 2006) describes a Space Invaders game designed in that perspective.

In the TiM project, the Blindstation was developed as a platform allowing to support any kind of specific device (Sablé and Archambault 2003).

Mainstream Game Accessibility

The first famous publication that waked up the mainstream game developers and was showing them that it is possible and necessity to include more users to the mainstream games, was a whitepaper from IGDA, the International Games Developer Association. Inside IGDA is the Games Accessibility Special Interest Group (GA-SIG), which has published this whitepaper about games accessibility. (IGDA 2004)

From the TiM project, (Archambault et al. 2005) shows a set of rules that are necessary to design a game "that works" for visually impaired people.

THE GAMES ACCESSIBILITY INITIATIVE

The aim of the games accessibility initiative, or also called Active Game Accessibility (AGA) is, to give game developers tips, hints and tools for the development of accessible computer games. To reach this goal, two main projects are under development: the first project are guidelines for the development of accessible computer games and the second project is a descriptive language for the connection of (alternative) input/output devices with the game engine and the providing of additionally inputs and outputs.

The AGA-initiative itself is a (loose) cooperation between universities and companies dealing with the topic of (games) accessibility.

Guidelines for the Development of Accessible Computer Games

As basis for out work, there are two main research works in the area of guidelines for games accessibility. The first work is a section in the already mentioned IGDA whitepaper. (IGDA 2004)

The other main work is done by the Norwegian IT company MediaLT. MediaLT has developed a set of guidelines (MediaLT 2004), which were the basis for further development of our guidelines.

Our guidelines have five main categories: level/progression, input, graphics, sound, and installation and settings.

The guidelines have, beside the rules itself, a categorisation in three classes of priorities: *must have* (priority 1) for rules which have to be fulfilled that a game is accessible for a group of disabilities, *should have* (priority 2) for rules which are a big help for the listed group and *may have* (priority 3) for rules which make the game easier to play for a group.

Furthermore there are the four already mentioned groups of disabilities: visual, auditory, mobility and cognitive disabilities. These disabilities are allocated to the priorities, e.g. one rule can have priority 1 for visually impaired people and priority 3 for auditory impaired people.

The working and publishing media for the guidelines is a web page. The web page was chosen to give project partners and interested persons the possibility to add ideas and comments to the rules and hints. More information about the development process of the guidelines is published at (Ossmann and Miesenberger 2006).

The development process of a first version of the guidelines (GL) is nearly finished. At the moment we add code samples and best practice methods to help the game developers to fulfil the rules of the guidelines easily.

Guidelines Contents

This section describes the five main categories of the guidelines and their content to give an overview.

Level/Progression
This aim of this section is to give the developers an idea about finding the right level of difficulty that the game is a challenge and not being too complex or too simple. These goals can be reached by offering progression from simple to more difficult and/or from beginner to advanced levels. A training mode could help beginners to learn how to handle the game. The use of simple language and not mixing up different languages are also as important as the providing of meta information to every scene/object.

Input
This section shows the problems and there methods of solving these problems in the area of game inputs. The main issues here are allowing inputs from alternative controls and devices and allowing the use of several different input and output devices simultaneously. Also giving immediately feedback after every input and the reduction of different inputs to minimum supporting different kinds of handicapped gamers are important issues. Furthermore sensitivity and error tolerance are covered in this section.

Graphics
The graphical presentation and the customisation of graphical output are discussed in this section and possible solutions are offering choices for the screen resolution, the size of objects and graphical details of the objects. The colour and contrast of all objects (buttons, menus, background, text ...) should also be adjustable. Moreover it should be possible to switch graphic elements off/on to help people with concentration problems.

Sound
This section is all about sound issues and the way of dealing with it in games. This covers topics like explanations of pictures and actions, background music and effects that can be switched off/on. Also offer choices for speed, duration, voices and volume for different auditory information. Furthermore all audio information should optional displayed as (synchronised) subtitles.

Installation and Settings
The last section of the guidelines gives hints about the installation, the settings and the game menu. This covers an easy installation of the game, preferably without changing system files, because this can affect screen readers or other assistive technologies.

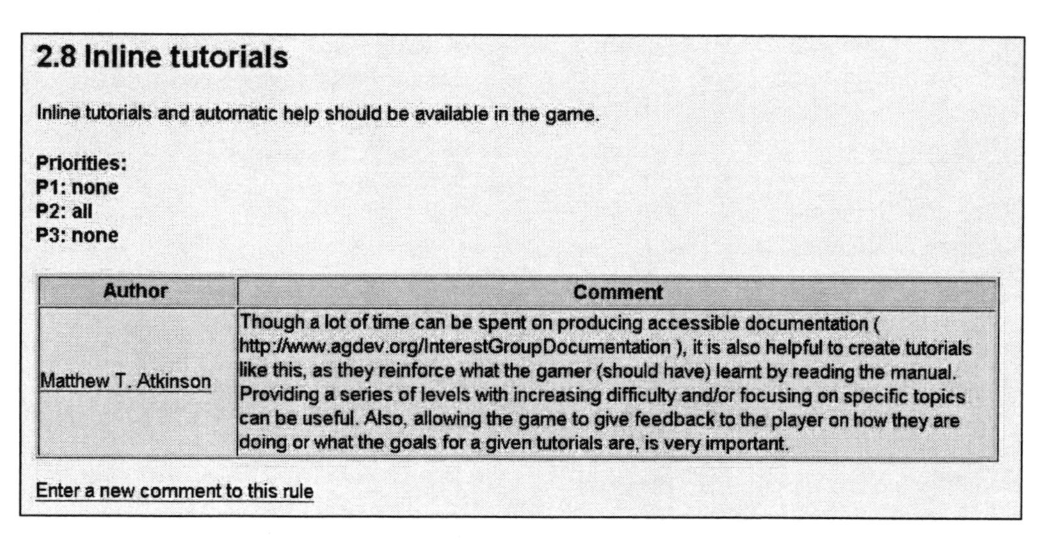

Fig. 1. Screenshot of the Guideline Tool

Also saving settings for different kind of gamers should be available.

Figure 1 shows one rule of the GL (about inline tutorials), the categorisation in the priorities and a comment given to this rule. The guidelines can be found at **`gameaccess.medialt.no/guide.php`**.

Descriptive Language

The Descriptive Language (DL) helps the game developers during the game design process to fulfil parts of the rules of the game development guidelines. The DL connects (alternative) input/output devices with the game engine with the possibility to use several input devices simultaneously and present the game output on several output devices. This means that, as example, the game player can decide if he/she wants to have all graphical objects presented on screen, described over speaker or be on both output devices.

Additionally covers the DL the option for an extensive configuration of the game, so that the game can be customised to the special needs of a (disabled) person. This configuration ranges from game speed to the number of opponents to many other game options, depending on the kind of game. The DL should not only be used to develop new, accessible games, it also should help to make games, already being published, accessible.

First Prototype

The research and development of the DL is at the beginning of a longer research process. At the moment, a first prototype of the DL was included in a simple game (an open source implementation of TicTacToe). The process to include the DL into TicTacToe to make the game accessible was divided in three parts of extending and adapting the input behaviour, the output behaviour and the game configuration. These steps are required to provide the support of different I/O-Devices and the simultaneously use of these devices.

After this preparation of the game, the DL itself was integrated in the game. The language defines all needed inputs (in the test case the four directions and hit) and the devices, which can be used for this inputs. The devices and there facilities (e.g. definition of a joystick: two axis and two buttons) are defined in an external device definition file and just being included where it will be needed. Furthermore it defines the output devices, which can be used with the option to set properties for the devices like the font size on screen or the loudness for the speakers.

The DL is written in XML-Schema and the output of this schema is a XML-file which makes the mapping between the game engine and the input/output devices and covers the game configuration.

The aim is to have a collection of different schemas for the different kinds of computer games in combination with the different kinds of disabilities. The following code sample shows parts of the XML-file of the first test case (TicTacToe)

```
<Inputs>
  <Hit>
    <Keyboard>
      <kbr_enter/>
      <H/>
    </Keyboard>
    <Mouse/>
    <Joystick>
      <js_butt1/>
    </Joystick>
  </Hit>
...
```

Description of the code sample: The “Hit” operation in the game can be done with the keys ‘Enter’ and ‘h’ on the keyboard, with the mouse or with ‘button 1’ on the joystick. From this it follows that the game must support keyboard, mouse and joystick.

A special topic and one of the next steps of the development of the DL is the game menu at the beginning of the game and during the game. On the one hand accessible computer games need a lot of customisation to fulfil all the special needs for the different kinds of persons; on the other hand, configuration must be easy and simple, so that it can be handled by everyone.

The future aims are different tools to generate the DL by selecting the kind of game and the group of disabled people for which this game should be accessible and generate parts of the game source code out of the DL.

CONCLUSION

It will not be possible to make every computer game accessible to all people. But in the last years a lot of projects and initiatives started. Games accessibility has become a serious issue for game developers (e.g. IGDA). Now it is the time to move from the individual developed accessible games to the mainstream. Automatic tools will help the game designers by the development to fulfil guidelines and rules so that the games will be accessible for as many people as possible.

Nevertheless research for new methods of getting input, navigating in the game and representing the output (on different devices) not ended yet. And accessible computer games muss still be games so that children and adults enjoy playing them.

REFERENCES

Archambault D., D. Olivier and H. Svensson. 2005. "Computer games that work for visually impaired children". In Proceedings of the 2005 HCI International Conference, (Las Vegas, USA, 2005) 8 pages (proceedings on CD-Rom).

Bierre K., J. Chetwynd, B. Ellis, M. Hinn, S. Ludi and T. Westin. 2005. „Game Not Over: Accessibility Issues in Video Games". In Proceedings of the 2005 HCI International Conference, (Las Vegas, USA, 2005) 10 pages (proceedings on CD-Rom).

Chisholm W., G. Vanderheiden and I. Jacobs, eds. 1999. "Web Content Accessibility Guidelines 1.0". **www.w3.org/TR/WAI-WEBCONTENT/**

Grammenos D., A. Savidis, Y. Georgalis and C. Stephanidis. (2006). "Access Invaders: Developing a Universally Accessible Action Game". In Proceedings of the 10th International Conference Computers Helping People with Special Needs (Linz, Austria, Jul. 12-14 2006). Springer, Berlin, 388 - 395.

International Game Developers Association (IGDA). 2004. "Accessibility in Games: Motivations and Approaches". **http://www.igda.org/accessibility/IGDA_Accessibility_WhitePaper.pdf**

MediaLT. 2004. „Guidelines for the development of entertaining software for people with multiple learning disabilities". **http://www.medialt.no/rapport/entertainment_guidelines/index.htm**

Ossmann R. and K. Miesenberger. 2006. „Guidelines for the Development of Accessible Computer Games." In Proceedings of the 10th International Conference Computers Helping People with Special Needs (Linz, Austria, Jul. 12-14 2006). Springer, Berlin, 403 – 406.

Sablé S. and D. Archambault. 2003. "Blindstation: a Game platform adapted to visually impaired children" In: Proceedings of the AAATE'03 Conference (Dublin, Ireland, September 2003). IOS Press, Amsterdam. 232-236.

SHORT BIOGRAPHY

Roland Ossmann is since 2004 a PhD student at the University of Linz, Institute for Integrated Study. His topic is games accessibility. During his study work he developed guidelines and tools for computer game designers. Furthermore he created a homepage about games accessibility, attends and co-organized workshops and meetings about this topic. First publication and presentation about guidelines for computer game designers at the 10th International Conference on Computers Helping People with Special Needs in 2006.

Computer Games in Supporting Children's Visual-Spatial Intelligence in Teaching and Learning Environment

Maizatul H. M. Yatim
Games Group
Dept. of Simulation and Graphics
Faculty of Computer Science
University of Magdeburg,
39106 Magdeburg, GERMANY
maizatul@isg.cs.uni-magdeburg.de

Khairul Anuar Samsudin
Dept. of IT Education
Faculty of ICT
Sultan Idris University of Education,
35900 Tg. Malim, MALAYSIA
khairul@ftmk.upsi.edu.my

Abstract

The educational software has tremendous value especially for helping to nurture children's intelligence. It is about time the educational technology looks into what have been offered by another increasing technology - the computer games. We present the significance of visual-spatial intelligence among children, especially in the domain of teaching and learning, which underpins the computer games technology. We relate the connection between children intelligence and the usage of educational games. Additionally, this paper will explore the potential impact of computer games on children that will embrace their visual-spatial intelligence and how these will affect the design and development of children educational software.

1. Introduction

In today world, technology has taken over many of primitive tasks that were values in former times. Our society has been transformed due to speed in mathematical computation, electronic communication, and the availability of information, which all achieved through technology. The emerging elements of computer culture have captured human attention in all aspects of lives, ironically, computers are changing the way we learn, communicate and collaborate. For children, computers have become their toys and many believe that children are very passionate and motivated when it comes to computer technology.

The benefits of introducing computer technologies allow the exploration of new concepts and ideas and schools have become one of the learning institutions to integrate technologies in teaching and learning. In this paper, we, as the educator would highly recommend that the children must have frequent access to advanced multimedia technologies.

Our starting point is that learning is shaped based on relationships between teacher and student, and the relationship between learning and memory. Memory is the link based on learning and retaining information, together with the cognitive process of applying what you have learned. Cognitive is defined as the mental process of knowing, while memory is defined as the mental of retaining and recalling past experiences.

Somehow, people often think of intelligence as quickness of thought or propensity for flashes of insight. But, the main key ingredient of intelligence may be the ability to juggle lots of possibilities in the mind. And all these, depends on the brain's systems for holding and processing words, object, or ideas in memory (to be precise, working memory).

In this paper, we will relate the connection between children intelligence and the usage of educational games. To be precise, we will look upon the used of computer games by children that will embrace their visual-spatial intelligence and how these will affect the design and development of children educational software.

How can by playing computer games encourages visual-spatial ability among children, and more importantly, how can they value and enhance this ability in order to build children's self-esteem and engagement towards learning? How can computer games act as teaching and learning tools? How can computer game helps children in understanding relationships and recognizing underlying concepts that are closely related to problem solving and conceptual skills required for knowledge such as science and mathematic?

2. Multiple intelligence

In general, human intelligence can be described as the ability of an individual to acquire knowledge and apply the knowledge in the environment which they evolved. Studies have shown that general intelligence can be passed down at least 50 percent heritable from generation to generation ([2][6]. However, human intelligence changes since the emergence of environmental, globalization and technological migration factors in modern society. A great importance has been placed on human ability and intelligence to allow human to function in modern society.

One of the theories underlying constructivist learning theories is Multiple Intelligences by Howard Gardner [7]. In his theory of Multiple Intelligences, he discussed the role of intelligence in learning and learning is shaped by innate intelligences. Since his original listing of intelligences in 1983, Gardner and his colleagues has added up three particular possibilities of intelligences to concluded additional intelligences to the list of the original seven intelligences. These intelligences are logical-mathematical, linguistic, musical, spatial, bodily-kinesthetic, interpersonal, intrapersonal and with additional intelligences, naturalist, spiritual and existential intelligence. He explains these intelligences can be adapt and adopt especially for educators in appreciating, recognizing, and nurturing the diversity of intelligences among children.

According to Gardner's theory, IQ test and traditional academic tasks cannot judge student's ability to learn. This theory support doing group work on multimedia products and assigning students group roles based on their type of intelligence. One of the intelligences that will be discussed in this paper is spatial intelligence or visual-spatial intelligence. It means the ability to perceive the world visually and can recreate things after seeing them. Taking into consideration, the definition of spatial, according to Gardner, involves the potential to recognize and use the patterns of wide space and more confined areas.

3. Visual-spatial intelligence

One of the important skills to used to get information from the environment and integrate them with other senses is visual information processing. It is done with incorporating integrated information with past experiences, motivation and the new information in order to understand the meaning of the situation. It is very important especially when we are learning, remembering things, having good hand-eye coordination and integrating visual information with thing we do in life such as driving, listening to the music and others.

Visual information processing can be broken into three components which are visual-spatial skills, visual analysis skills and visual integration skills. This paper will only look into visual-spatial ability. But the main point is, these skills work together and always build upon each other to help human in their lives.

Visual-spatial ability is about the way an individual perceived objects and relatively reporting the information and its relationship with environment surrounding them. This ability is very important especially for children who are still beyond their still-developing abilities. In their early years, children with high visual-spatial intelligence, think in pictures and images. They perceived the environment as a whole and store the information in a non-sequential way. This will make their internal imagery becomes more creative and imaginative.

Spatial awareness ability gives the children skills in drawing pictures, doing puzzles, mazes, and any tasks that requires fine-motor manipulation. Furthermore, spatial ability involves the manipulation of information presented in a visual, diagrammatic of symbolic form in contrast to verbal, language-based modality. In additional to imaginary, spatial representations also include diagrams, drawings, maps and models.

4. Visual-spatial learners in children

People who learn and think in images have one filing system of pictures in their brains that symbolize words and information. People who think this way learns more holistically compare to those who are linear or auditory sequential processing (steps-by-steps fashion). Visual props such as graphic, paper and crayon, computers, mnemonic method, cartoons and much more, can enhance the educational experience for every learner either they are visual-spatial or auditory-sequential.

But, visual-spatial learner got most of the advantages and they learn by observation. They have good memory skills in remembering what they see because they have excellent 'right-hemispheric' brain talent that produce skills in art, geometry, multiple dimension thinkers, music, creativity, design, creation and invention.

Since we need thinkers who are creative, imaginative and diversify in any areas, we should concentrate on the young ones. The children are our next generation leaders and one of the ways to mole and design a good leader is to create the future leaders starting from their young age. Skills such as visual-spatial skills are born together with the child but we can also teach these skills to the children.

4.1. Teaching visual-spatial skills to children

Mitchell and Burton [10] argue that the use of toys may afford opportunities for children to exploit and develop their spatial skills. The foundation for science and mathematics is built through play and the use of toys can develop visual-spatial ability for children to exploit their visual-spatial skills [12]. The importance of playing in facilitating the development of high achievement in these fields cannot be underestimated. Various experiences should be planned to provide opportunities for the development of each of these skills. Others claim that suitable experiences such as playing Lego or puzzles, painting and drawing, and mapping activities can provide opportunities for enhancing and expressing spatial ability [3].

Children are natural pattern finders. Therefore, they are ideally suited to the types of experiences in gifted programs and activities. Activities such as playing construction toys, taking note combining words and drawing images, reading using phonics and mnemonics, using visual props (crayon, clay and cartoon) and also using technology (computer and early keyboarding), can help the children to gained visual-spatial ability. Others, such as, brain-pop or brainstorm activities, drawing to illustrate a story, designing Web pages, presentation or create brochures (layout design), electronic field trip, computer-aided design or using digital imaging program, can also be done as teaching and learning materials in schools. In summary, activities that are more on pictures and images are the most suitable activities to teach and enhance visual-spatial intelligence among children.

Technology is here to stay. Multimedia opens the world of learning to children in a way that is amazing to watch. In multimedia, space includes the area occupied by the elements that make up the multimedia product, as well as the space that surrounds the product, such as on Web open-environments. It is the openness and the potential for navigation in many directions that allows user movement to expand beyond linear, hierarchical structure of traditional media. Other examples of spatially-oriented activities are playing electronic games or computer simulation games [5].

5. Computer games

Firstly, we would like to define the meaning of electronic games. Electronic games are games that are played using consoles (arcade games, Sony's PlayStation, Microsoft's XBox or Nintendo's GameCube), handheld devices (mobile phone, Sony's PSP, Nintendo's GameBoy) and computers. In this paper, the term computer games refer to games that been played using personal computer.

Everything we do is spatial. So do computer games. Playing computer games, including any other console games (also know as video games) is a complex activity involving all sorts of variables that are underlying in the game design itself. For years, educators and education game-developers are looking for ways to increase learner productivity beyond schools and workplace. According to Dr. James Paul Gee [8], a professor of Curriculum and Instruction, the game developer and educators are trying to engage the students to learn something that is difficult and takes a lot of commitment, and these problems can be solved only with good learning tools, such as games.

Perhaps, one of the biggest challenges facing educators today is to engage students in an active learning environment. Educators need to explore new and exciting ways of engaging students in the course content. Additionally, electronic games encourage communication by facilitating cooperation. How can electronic games (including computer games, video games, and console games) be the tools that can make the learners learn and produce a good way of thinking in problem solving and decision making.

Visual-spatial ability can be taught by observation people. Children approach the computer by observation how adult way and act with computer, manipulate the mouse, clicking the icons or selecting the undo features just by watching [13]. For many years, children enjoy the 'A-Ha!' moments of discovery, invention and problem solving. These moments usually occurred especially when watching adult playing computer games. In certain instances, computer games can reinforce concepts and inspire curiosity among children. Computer games are also a great way to engage the players in way that suit their various learning styles and intelligences. When using computer games, it is worth considering which learning styles and multiple intelligences they used. But, what kind of games (genre) that are suitable to increase visual-spatial ability among children?

In a study of computer gaming, Aarseth [1] has noted that the representation of space is the defining factors in computer games. Given the importance of spatial representation and the variety of spatial forms within and across the computer game genres, more studies are needed to understand how these spaces are constructed and experienced by players.

Taylor [11] in her paper published in Gameology Web site, she used three (3) video games as representative of spatial experience within their respective gaming genres - *Super Mario Brothers*, *Metroid* and *Resident Evil: Code Veronica*. She also discussed throughout the world of these games, many different portrayals of space and spatiality are created. These include how code, music and perspective all add to the creation of lived, representational space. Even though these games were released in different eras of computer games development and carried under different genres, they all share different levels of spatial development, which is allowing the player to experience the game's space.

There are also games for children such as *Girls' Super Dunk* that is designed to measure player's reaction time that is the total time it takes the player to respond to a sound by clicking the mouse. The reaction time is important in listening, speaking and reading skills. This game motivates the player to increase auditory attention and processing in order to improve their games score each time they play.

Other examples of children's games are *ABC Gulp* that focuses on learning letter names and *Bear Wear* that is a letter-sound relationship game that helps children as their pre-reading activities. Games such as *Thomas and Friends - The Great Festival Adventure* can helps children with both computer skills and simple educational ideas like matching shapes and colours, sizing, counting and following instructions. It also helps with early eye-hand coordination and is educational whilst fun.

Finally, the edutainment and instructional games should be designed carefully to keep children occupied and engaged for around hour and hour. Educationist games developer do believes that by just playing catch, players can improves eye-hand coordination in other tasks. The question here is whether or not computer games can support spatial intelligence.

6. Supporting visual-spatial Intelligence using computer games

Traditional teaching techniques are designed for the learning style of sequential learners. Concepts are introduced in a step-by-step fashion, practiced with drill and repetition, assessed under timed conditions, and then reviewed. This process is ideal for sequential learners whose learning progresses in a step-by-step manner from easy to difficult material.

By way of contrast, spatial learners are systems thinkers-they need to see the whole picture before they can understand the parts. They are likely to see the forest and miss the trees. They are excellent at mathematical analysis but may make endless computational errors because it is difficult for them to attend to details. Their reading comprehension is usually much better than their ability to decode words.

One experimental study [9] showed that children's experiences of spatial relations in game worlds are constituted by two different phases - the represented room and the possibilities to navigate. Once again, concepts are quickly comprehended when they are presented within a context and related to other concepts. Once spatial learners create a mental picture of a concept and see how the information fits with what they already know, their learning is permanent. Repetition is completely unnecessary and irrelevant to their learning style.

It's a good idea to match the user interface to the game architecture. A spatial reasoning game works better with spatial input and output structures. A verbal reasoning game works better with verbal input and output structures. Most of the player inputs were all geared toward moving pieces around on a map. Now, the designer was required to support both keyboard input and mouse input.

It should have been child's play to devise an intuitively system for moving units with the mouse. Click on the unit you want, drag to the location you want him to go to, and release the mouse. What could be simpler? As programmers, we speak to the computer through the keyboard, so we are all fast touch typists. We tend to view the keyboard as the primary input device. This problem is especially pronounced with programmers steeped in the folklore of the MS-DOS environment. Despite years of experience that prove the utility of mouse-based input, despite the steady evolution of all systems towards the GUI user interface paradigm, there are still die-hards in computing business who insist that the keyboard is the king of all input devices and that the mouse is fundamentally inferior. The keyboard is faster, they insist; the mouse is clumsy.

The debate between keyboard and mouse has become a norm in the computing industry. For us, it all depends on the balancing used and understand of the usage of application architecture. The users' expertise and experience will aid the interface design decision and furthermore, will impact the user's judgement on the best input device. The keyboard is without question the fastest and cleanest way to input verbal information. But the other side of the coin is that the mouse is the fastest and cleanest way to input spatial information.

At this point, some people will protest that they find cursor keys faster than the mouse for designating spatial locations in, say, a text file. We suspect that these people have lots of experience with the keyboard and little with the mouse. Yes, it takes a little time to become proficient with a mouse. But it takes a lot longer to become proficient with a keyboard. And my own experience as a heavy user of both mouse and keyboard is that the mouse is the fastest way to move around, especially while playing game (depends on which computer games). This is also has to do with the questions of which categories of users fits you the most - expert or novice?

The important point here is that a good designer will match the input device to the nature of the information being entered. Recently, we are playing EyeToy games (Sony Computer Entertainment Europe) with children. Together with four children in Sultan Idris University of Education, Malaysia, we spent six hours a week (for three weeks) playing and enjoying ourselves. The game that we played is called *EyeToy: Play 3*, which can be played up to four persons, aged three and above. Together with the four children, we played almost 50 fun and original EyeToy mini-games including *Beach Volleyball, Boot Camp, Bowling, Fed the Cat* and others. The players enjoyed the games, battling it out on-screen at once and experience the excitement they have never felt before.

Being released in 2004, a number of interesting issues revealed regarding spatial knowledge acquisition of children in using and playing EyeToy mini-games. Although we enjoyed playing it but the children are facing difficulties in assessing and controlling the game. The game needs the players to understand the space within the game because most of the game control is inside the game itself. By using the motion-camera known as EyeToy USB Camera with a PlayStation 2 console, the players (children) has to move all parts of their body in order to play, instead of only used their hands to handle the gamepad (as usual).

Aarseth [1] claims that game worlds are best understood as allegories of space. Game worlds are often landscapes that 'promise more then they keep'. For example, in a game it is possible to represent some mountains far away at the horizon that the user cannot interact with. Thus, there is a conflict between the represented space and the opportunities to move in the game world. Coming back to the study, Sony's EyeToy relies on a camera to work as a result in field of vision. It is a new revolution controller for gameplay but yet should take into depth perception by players especially for children. They having trouble and sometimes gets confused as to what it is supposed to be watching.

According to Del Grande [4], children's understanding of spatial symbols systems should be developed first. The foundation skills such as eye-motor coordination, figure-ground perception, perception constancy, position-in-space perception, perception of spatial relationships, visual discrimination and visual memory, are needed to create and interpret spatial symbol system based on spatial perception. In the case of EyeToy, just because the camera detects motion and generates collision detection from it, sometimes the camera won't detect a certain spot. This is usually due to a lack of lighting on the particular player's part and can be easily corrected.

Bottom line, EyeToy may be a camera but it is also like your average computer game in that the mini-games are best enjoyed with other people. Uniquely, EyeToy is perfect for parties and can nurture children's gameplay towards increasing their abilities in spaces and spatial intelligence. Perhaps, the ability of visual-spatial in computer games can be used in schools or at home to enhance children's skills and intelligence.

Figure 1. Children and adults are experiencing playing EyeToy's mini-games

7. Conclusion

In the traditional school situation, the atmosphere is often hostile to visual-spatial learners and their skills. The students are visual, whereas instruction tends to be auditory: phonics, oral directions, etc. The students are gestalt, 'A-Ha!' learners and can be taught out of order, whereas the curriculum is sequential, with orderly progressions of concepts and ideas. The students are usually disorganized and miss details, whereas most teachers stress organization and attention to detail. The student is highly aware of space but pays little attention to time, whereas school functions on rigid time schedules.

As educators, again, we do belief that computer games offer a good solution to develop skills since most children are more easily engaged themselves in games. Perhaps the most valuable thing we can focus is how to make learning experiences more fun and educational by using computer games. Educators need to ensure that they adequately prepare our students with the essential tools to succeed in the global community of today.

Any skills in which these young people experience success should be encouraged and nurtured. Their skills, interests and hobbies may lead to careers in adult life. We need individuals with highly developed visual-spatial abilities for advancement in the arts, technology and business. These are the creative leaders of society. And those children with highly spatial ability skills always end-up as designers. We need to protect their differences in childhood and enable them to develop their unique talents in supportive environments at home and at school.

8. Acknowledgement

We would like to thank all our colleagues at Sultan Idris University of Education; parents and the children involved, without whose cooperation this study would not been possible.

9. References

[1] Aarseth, E. Allegories of Space: The question of spatiality in computer games. In Eskelinen, Markku Koskima, Raine (eds) *CyberText Yearbook 2000*. Jyvaskyla, Finland, 2001.

[2] Bouchard, T. J. McGue, M. Familial studies of intelligence: A review. *Science*, 212:1055-1059, 1981.

[3] Brosnan M.J. Spatial ability in children's play with Lego blocks. *Perceptual and Motor Skills*, 87:19-28, 1998.

[4] Del Grande, J. Spatial sense. *Aritmetic Teacher*, 37(6):14-20, 1990.

[5] Diezmann, C. M. Watters, J. J. Identifying and supporting spatial intelligence in young children. *Contemporary Issues in Early Childhood*, 1(3):299-313, 2000.

[6] DiLalla, L. F. Development of intelligence: current research and theories. *Journal of School Psychology*, 38:3-7, 2000.

[7] Gardner, H. *Intelligence reframed: Multiple intelligences for the 21st Century*. Basic Books, NY, 1999.

[8] Gee, J.P. *What video games have to us about learning and literacy*. Macmillan, Palgrave, 2004.

[9] Linderoth, J., Lantz-Andersson, A. Lindstrom, B. Electronic exaggerations virtual worries: Mapping research of computer games relevant to the understanding of children gameplay. *Contemporary Issues in Early Childhood*, 3(2):226-250, 2002.

[10] Mitchell, C. E. & Burton, G. M. Developing spatial ability in young children. *School of Science and Mathematics*, 84:395- 405, 1984.

[11] Tailor, L. N. Toward a spatial practice in video games. http://www.gameology.org/node/809 *Retrieved on 10 September 2006*.

[12] Tracy, D. M. Toys, spatial ability, and science and mathematics achievement: Are they related? *Sex Roles*, 17:115-138, 1987.

[13] Tracy, D. M. Toy-playing behavior, sex-role orientation, spatial ability, and science achievement. *Journal of Research in Science Teaching*, 27:637-649, 1990.

Short Biography

Maizatul H.M. Yatim is a PhD student in the Games Design and Development program at University of Magdeburg. Her research interests focus on the development of games programming for children, combining with educational and children psychology (cognitive) fields.

Khairul Anuar Samsudin is a PhD student currently enrolled at the Faculty of Creative Multimedia, Multimedia University (Malaysia). His research focuses on improving spatial ability through computer-mediated engineering especially in drawing instruction and currently, he is waiting for his thesis defence.

Intelligent agents and Gamebots

A Multiagent System for Monitoring and Analysing the Game of Risk

Patrick Person, Hadhoum Boukachour, Michel Coletta, Thierry Galinho and Frédéric Serin

LITIS (Laboratoire d'Informatique, de Traitement de l'Information et des Systèmes)

25 Rue Philippe Lebon

76058 Le Havre Cedex

E-Mail: Patrick.Person@univ-lehavre.fr

ABSTRACT

This paper presents the design and the realisation of a multilayer multiagent system for the analysis of situations and intentions. Our system is applied to the game of Risk because it is suited for crisis management. It represents the pointed out situation, evaluates the situation, takes into account past situations. We have developed agents using semantic features, proximity measure, ontology, dynamic clustering and case-based reasoning. This multiagent system is dynamic in order to be able to take into account the changes in the description of the evolving situation. The current situation is represented by a layer of factual agents which is fed by the semantic features constituting the atomic data elements of the situation. The aim of the set of factual agents is both to be a real snapshot of the situation at any time and to model the evolution of the situation dynamically.

KEYWORDS

Multiagent system, game of Risk, ontology, semantic features, factual agents, proximity measure.

I. Introduction and Context

This paper develops the architecture of our multiagent multilayer system adapted to the analysis of situations and intentions in the game Risk (Risk is a registered trademark).

As a team, the starting point of our research at the end of 2000 was a multiagent system (MAS) in a context of crisis management in an oil plant [2] [6]. The reader will find a detailed historical background in [14].

The aim of this work is to apply our computer-assisted decision support systems to the managing of the crisis present in the game of Risk. This system deals which the data representation of the current situation and analyses its evolution. Such a system can represent the pointed out situation but also its evaluation. Evaluating the situation can be done by determining the potential consequences that it could generate. This process can be carried out by taking into account past situations whose consequences we know. Then we use reasoning by analogy based on the following assumption: if a given situation A looks like situation B then it is probable that the consequences of situation A will be similar to those of situation B.

Case-based reasoning (CBR) [12] is a methodology of resolution of problems being based on the re-use of past experiments for solving new problems. Decision support systems are one of the most promising applications of CBR. The capacity of resolution of a problem by human beings and the corresponding ability of information processing systems are put in synergy. The memory of both is reinforced mutually to take part in the problem resolution.

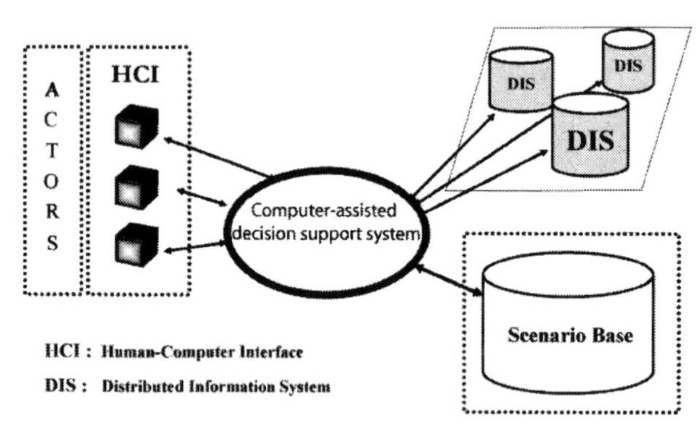

Figure 1: General Architecture

Our work is within the framework of the computer-assisted decision support systems having to evaluate a dynamic situation [7] [15]. The situation under scrutiny generates dynamic parameters which vary all the time. The system must be dynamic in order to be able to take into account the changes in the description of the evolving situation. This requires a system able to be reconfigured when necessary, thus benefiting from a sufficiently flexible and adaptive architecture. Complexity and dynamics of the situation to be treated, lead us to choose multiagent system paradigm for its modeling [11]. We are interested in developing a multiagent architecture allowing the implementation of dynamic and incremental CBR for the evaluation of dynamic situations [3]. This architecture allows to compare the situation under scrutiny with past situations stored in a case base in real time [16]. Using this dynamic and incremental case-based reasoning, our objective is to find, as rapidly as possible, the cases in the base which look like the situation in progress in order to anticipate its consequences as well as possible.

II. Multi layer architecture

The objective of the architecture is to allow an evaluation of the potential evolution of a current followed situation, by implementing dynamic and incremental case-base reasoning. The core of the system is structured with layers of agents [13]. It is made up of three layers of multiagent systems in which the agents are of different types:

- the lowest layer: factual agents;

- the intermediate layer: synthesis agents;

- the highest layer: prediction agents.

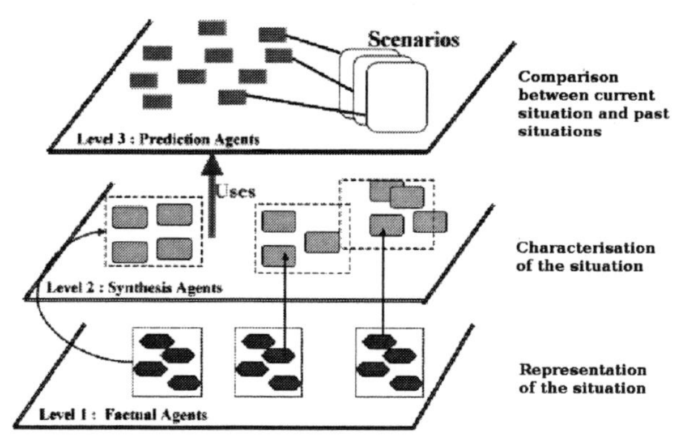

Figure 2: Multilayer Architecture

A. Factual Agents Layer

The current situation, in our context, is represented by a layer of factual agents. This layer of agents is fed by the semantic features which constitute the atomic data elements of the situation. Each factual agent encapsulates a semantic feature.

Moreover, each factual agent must make measurement of its evolution in the time available. More precisely, these measures allow to take into account the evolution of the agent in its organisation in relation to the semantic feature which it carries. Indeed, we suppose that the more one factual agent will be reinforced in the organisation, the more the data element it represents will have to be taken into account in the evaluation of the current situation. This strengthening depends on a measure of similarity between semantic features which can take into account semantic, temporal and space points of view based on ontology [4] [5]. Thus, some elements entered into the system at an early stage, can be proven irrelevant while others, entered later can finally be taken as representative of the analysed situation.

The past situations are modeled in scenarios gathered in a database of scenarios. For each past situation, the associated scenario characterises the decisive aspects of the evolution of the situation. At this point, a decisive aspect is called a fact (carried by one or more semantic features) which has played an effective role in the way in which the events have unfolded. Each scenario thus contains a temporal list of semantic features associated with the significant aspects of the situation. An agent of prediction is associated with its scenario.

The description of the significant aspects of the current situation is carried out by a layer of agents located between the layer of the factual agents and the one of the prediction agents: synthesis agents will be described in the following paragraph.

In the Risk case study, we distinguish two kinds of scenarios: the first one helps detect a global attempt like "reaching a player's final objective", the second one focuses on local conquests as for example "preparations for the conquest of Australia".

B. Synthesis Agents Layer

The purpose of these agents is to offer an overall picture of the organisation of factual agents making the comparison between the current situation and past situations easier. This layer takes part in the phase of development of the target case of the case-base reasoning. The difference with traditional CBRs is to manage a dynamic and incremental development. The goal of the synthesis agents is to compare the agents or groups of factual agents with each other. The synthesis agents use internal indicators of the factual agents to identify some groups of agents which have one or more very close indicators. The existence of such groups can be significant of decisive points in the current situation and then can be exploited at the level of prediction agents. The role of the synthesis agent is to build, dynamically, these groups of agents which we will call clusters. To do this we propose a dynamic clustering of the agents described in [8]. Each cluster will evolve in time according to the behaviour of the factual agents which it contains. It can possibly grow if new factual agents have similar characteristics to those of the cluster. If on the contrary, some factual agents of the cluster end up evolving to a point that they leave their place within the cluster, the cluster may decrease until it disappears.

C. Prediction Agents Layer

The role of the population of prediction agents is to build a continuous and incremental process of recollection for dynamic situations. The goal of a prediction agent is to evaluate the degree of resemblance between the current situation and its associated scenario continuously. There are as many prediction agents as scenarios in the base if this one is plane. In the case of a hierarchical base, a prediction agent can then be associated to a family of scenarios rather than to one scenario only. To evaluate the resemblance to its own scenario, each agent of prediction is based on the result of the dynamic clustering factual agents made by the prediction agents.

III. Focus on the representation MAS

A. *Summary of the Game of Risk*

Risk is a game of strategy in which a player must occupy all the territories on the board, eliminating all other players, thus conquering the world (version 1), or reach a goal according to his or her objective card (version 2). Rules, tricks and strategies are detailed in [17].

B. *Class Diagram of the Game Design*

We consider the following seven classes: Player, Territory, Continent, Army, Card, Dice, and Battle (cf. Fig. 3). Each territory has adjacent territories. Each continent is subdivided into several territories. A player owns armies, an army occupies a territory.

A battle indicates the "current" attack between two territories. The campaign defines three of the four states of a player: deploying armies, attacking opposition, fortifying territories. The fourth one is a turn waiting.

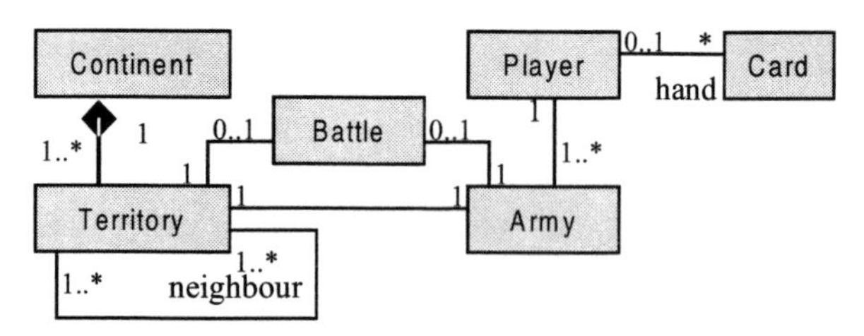

Figure 3: Class Diagram of the Game Design

We have simplified the observed world ; the design is finally composed of four classes: Player, Territory, Army, and Continent. From this model, we have determined our elementary information called semantic features.

C. *Semantic Features*

Semantic features (SFs) are sent to our MAS; they are elementary information. Each semantic feature (SF) is regarded as a fact. Comparisons between semantic features will be done using an ontology associating a proximity measure.

Each SF is a list of parameters, it represents elementary information, its structure is inspired by the memento Gamma's design pattern. Complete information translates both particular and partial aspects of an observed situation. It produces a set of SFs.

The designing of the SFs allows the obtaining of a homogeneous structure in the studied information system. This homogeneity is of primary importance because it allows establishing comparisons between SFs.

We need to define the set of the observations sent to our system. A basic semantic feature will be defined by its XML document type definition:

<! ELEMENT SF (SELECTOR, QUALIFICATION, VALUE)>

A composite semantic feature (CSF) could associate a few couples of *qualification-value* to one *selector*.

The game of Risk study allows us to define the dedicated types of objects according to our class diagram.

The different types of objects issuing from the study can take two identified values: player and territory. Phenomena or actions corresponding to battles are not taken into account. These types of objects are regarded as descriptions of a persistent situation (at least until it is invalidated by new information).

We define various qualifiers and their associated values. Some qualifiers are shared by the territories and the players ("colour", "power"), some others are specific to territories ("continent", "owner") or to players ("nbTerritories").

The value associated to the qualifier can be qualitative value and identified by its type or quantitative value.

Managing comparisons between the quantitative qualifiers necessitates the definition of a scale

The typing of a qualitative qualifier permits to define the set of the possible values in order to be able to establish rules of comparisons described clearly and formally in an ontology.

Qualifiers have a representation close to the attributes representation in a class, that is for example, the colour of a player or the power of a territory.

Thus, the following example, <player> <selector>blue</selector> <nbTerritories>0</nbTerritories> <step>0</step> </player> shows that the blue player had 0 territory at the beginning of the game (step 0).

D. *Creation of an Ontology*

Agents have to communicate with each other therefore they must share the same language and vocabulary. This is evident according to FIPA communicative acts [18]. However, we define our own vocabulary and semantics for the content of the semantic features. This means defining an ontology.

We have created different ontologies to represent the relationships between terms. These terms are included in the semantic features; they are territory names, player identities, qualifier terms...

1) Proximity

The proximity is useful to be able to have a distance between two SFs. We aim to lay out one or several functions which compute the distance in a formal way. Establishing distances between SFs makes it possible to reinforce or to weaken the factual agents carrying the SFs. We limit the properties of the distances to define our proximities and we adopt dissimilarities (dissimilarity does not respect the property of the triangular inequality).

We distinguish three types of proximities: time proximity (Pt), spatial proximity (Pe), and semantic proximity (Ps). The global proximity between two SFs multiplies these three proximities together.

We introduce time proximity to take into account that the more distant two events are, the smaller the proximity is. For spatial proximity, the same reasoning is applied. We can speak about time and spatial distances; they are not dissimilarities.

These two proximities (for time and space) are sigmoid functions, except that they do not take negative values into account. They are written to remain on the interval [0, 1]. Using sigmoids has the following five advantages: its continuity, its derivability, the knowledge of its primitive, its definition on entire (including negative values) and its symmetry in zero.

The definition of a semantic proximity is related to the definition of one ontology. Proximity between two semantic features SF1 and SF2 provides a value on [-1, 1]. For example, Ps (SF1, SF2) = 0.8 signifies that the two SFs are relatively close semantically speaking. Such measurement of proximity must relate to an ontology. This ontology is represented by elements in relation the ones with the others.

Scale represents the size of an object (i.e. cardinality). All distances are related to a scale. For example, the distance between territories is specific to the game of Risk.

For the proximity computation, the used reference value is the 0 that is to say the neutral action of the arriving SF. If the value is different from 0, it intervenes in the computation of the strength of the factual agent. Restricting values in a given range permits to apply the strategy to any problem independently of the real values (i.e. 0=Neutral, 0,4=Quiet Close, 0,7=Close, 0,9=Very Close, 1=Equal). Negative values mirrors positive ones (replacing close by different) [9].

2) Factual Agents for Risk

The multiagent system responsible for dealing with the representation of the current situation is made of factual agents. The aim of the set of factual agents is both to be a real snapshot of the situation at any time t and to model the evolution of the situation from a time t_i to t_{i+n} dynamically. This double aim is achieved by the design of factual agents. Three principal indicators and a semantic feature are embedded within a factual agent.

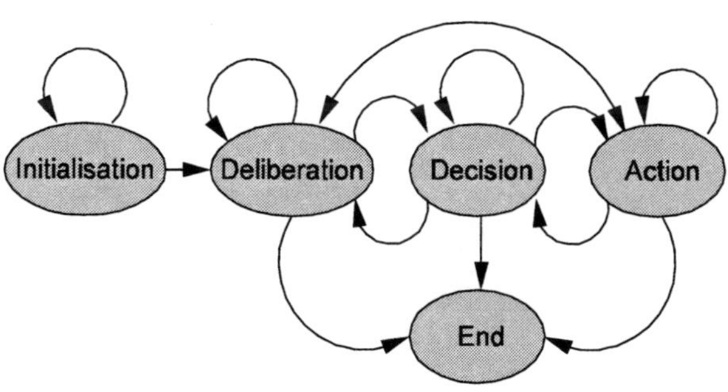

Figure 4: Generic Automaton of a Factual Agent

One fundamental hypothesis of our research is that a situation – and its evolution in time – can be represented by semantic features. From an outside view of the global system, a semantic feature is a compound of fields. The inside view is richer: when a semantic feature comes into the system, it is stamped by the time of arrival and it is categorised. This last point implies that the behaviour of the agents is different depending on the type (category) of semantic feature.

All factual agents have three main internal variables, an automaton and an acquaintance network. The shape of the automaton is derived from a generic automaton; the way the variables are used and computed together with the reaction of the acquaintance network depends on the type of semantic feature. Figure 4 shows the generic automaton of a factual agent.

From the analysis of the game of Risk we identified two categories of semantic features:

– The first category deals with the number of territories of a given player. Because there are six different players, this type is called "player".

– The second type is concerned with the colour and the strength of an army for a given territory. Because there are 42 territories, this type is called "territory".

The three principal internal variables are named "pseudo-Position", "pseudo-Speed" and "pseudo-Acceleration" to mimic the physician's world. The "pseudo" prefix is used here to emphasize that it is not a real mathematical speed or acceleration: we consider a fixed variation of time of one between two evolutions of semantic features related to the same territory. For type "territory", we also experimentally decide to influence the speed directly in a slightly different way from its counterpart in physics. If an army A1 conquers a new territory T against an army A2, we add the number of regiments lost by A2 and the number of regiments of army A1 on T instead of computing only the delta of the regiments. There is no mathematical justification for that formula but it seems to represent the dynamic of the evolution better and gives accurate results for all experiments.

The internal variables are used as a threshold for allowing a transition from a state to another inside the automaton. Figure 5 shows the specific automaton of type "territory" and conditions of transitions.

The acquaintance network is defined by the union of friends and enemies. Two factual agents are friends (enemies) if and only if the comparison of their semantic features returned by the proximity measure is strictly positive (negative). The acquaintance network of each agent is permanently updated as friends and enemies may change with time. When a transition in the automaton occurs to state "Decision" or "Action", agents broadcast messages to help friends and attack enemies by influencing their internal variables. This possibly leads to some change in the state of the automaton of the agents receiving a message.

The current implementation is developed in Java. Screen shots and discussion about the monitoring of the behaviour or the knowledge of factual agents could be found in [14]

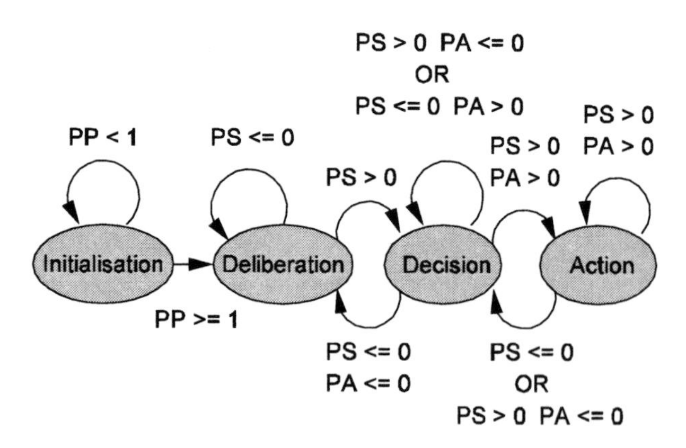

Figure 5: Specialized Automaton ("territory")

IV. Conclusion

The architecture of our multiagent multilayer system is adapted to the design and the realisation of the system for intentional analysis of the Risk. We are developing new tools for a complementary analysis and design. For example, we introduce two new indicators whose definitions are generic and independent of the application. These indicators must reflect the kind of evolution of the internal ATN of an FA. The satisfactory indicator is a valuation of the success of an FA in reaching and staying in state Action which is, by design, the ultimate aim of an FA. The constancy indicator will represent the tendency of a given FA to transit both from a state to a different state and from a state to the same state inside the ATN. The computation and a comprehensive description of these generic indicators can be found in [10]. Some specific graphic tools for analysing the behaviour of the representation MAS were created and tested. The plan is to include parts of these tools later in the intelligent user interface. A dynamic internal view of the data representation MAS, a static view of the same MAS, a dynamic Gantt chart focusing on indicators and an animated cartogram which is a fusion of the static view of the MAS with the pseudoPosition indicators of FAs were developed. The aim of animated cartograms is to provide a synthetic view of the situation for users [10].

References

[1] Bertin J.C. and Gravé P. 2004, "Didactic ergonomics and Web-based materials design", *communication in CALICO 2004*, Carnegie Mellon University, Pittsburgh, USA.

[2] Borodzicz E., Aragones J. and Pidgeon N. 1993 "Risk communication in crises: meaning and culture in emergency response organizations". in *European Conference on Technology & Experience in Safety Analysis and Risk Management*, Roma.

[3] Boukachour H. 2002 Système de veille préventive pour la gestion de situations d'urgence: une modélisation par organisations d'agents. Application aux risques industriels. PhD Thesis, University of Le Havre.

[4] Boukachour H., Simon G., Coletta M., Galinho T., Person P., Serin F. 2002, Preventive Monitoring Information System: a Model Using Agent Organizations *SCI2002*, Orlando, USA.

[5] Boukachour H., Galinho T., Person P., Serin F. Towards an Architecture for the Representation of Dynamic Situations, IC-AI2003, 659-664, Las Vegas, USA, 2003.

[6] Cardon A. Modéliser et concevoir une machine pensante : approche de la conscience artificielle, Vuibert, 2004.

[7] Carlsson C., Turban E., DSS : directions for the next decade, Decision Support Systems, Vol.33(2), 105-110, 2002.

[8] Coma R., Simon G, Coletta M. 2003, "A multiagent architecture for agents clustering" *Agent Based Simulation ABS'2003*, Montpellier.

[9] Galinho T. and Serin F., 2004. "Semantic Features and Factual Agents: A Model to Represent Changeable Situations", *ESM2004, 18th European Simulation Multiconference*.

[10] Galinho T., Coletta M., Person P., Serin F. Dynamic Representation of Information for Decision Support System, 8th international Conference on Entreprise Information, ICEIS'2006, Proceeding of Artificial and Decision Support System, pp 156-163, Paphos, Cyprus 2006.

[11] Jennings N., Wooldridge M. and Sycara K., 1998, "A roadmap of agent research and development". *Autonomous Agent and Multiagent Systems*, 1(5), p 7-38.

[12] Kolodner J. 1993, *Case-based reasoning*, San Mateo CA : Morgan Kaufman.

[13] Marcenac P. 1997, Modélisation de systèmes complexes par agents. *Techniques et sciences informatiques*, p 1013-1037.

[14] Person P., Boukachour H., Coletta M., Galinho T., Serin F. From Three MultiAgennt Systems to One Decision Support System, IICAI'05, 2856-2875, Pune, India, 2005.

[15] Power D.J, A Brief History of Decision Support Systems, Editor, DSSRessources.COM, http://DSSResources.COM/history/dsshistory.html, last retrieved May 2006.

[16] Simon G., Boukachour H., Towards a MultiAgent architecture for dynamic case-based reasoning, IKEDS'04, Porto, Portugal, 2004.

[17] http://www.thegamesjournal.com/articles/Risk.shtml, last retrieved March 2006, http://www.tuxick.net/doc/riskfaq.html, last retrieved March 2006.

[18] http://www.fipa.org, last retrieved March 2006.

Evolving Tactical Behaviours for Teams of Agents in Single Player Action Games

Darren Doherty

Department of Information Technology
National University of Ireland, Galway
darren.doherty@nuigalway.ie

Colm O'Riordan

Department of Information Technology
National University of Ireland, Galway
colm.oriordan@nuigalway.ie

Abstract

In this paper, we describe an architecture for evolving tactics for teams of agents in single-player combative 2D games using evolutionary computing (EC) techniques. We discuss the evolutionary process adopted and the team tactics evolved. The individual agents in the team evolve to have different capabilities that combine together as effective tactics. We also compare the performance of the evolved team against that of a team consisting of agents incorporating the built-in AI of the environment.

1 Background

One of the main roles of AI in computer games is to incorporate 'intelligent behaviour' in the artificial agents so as to enhance the playability of the game for the human player. The motivation behind this is to prevent the behaviour of the non-playable characters (NPCs) in the game from becoming predictable, as occurs frequently in games that rely on scripting and finite state machines (FSMs) to describe their NPCs' behaviour.

Action games are a genre of games where conflicting groups of agents are competing in a hostile environment with the primary goal being to eliminate the opposition. One category of these games is the "shoot-em up" genre, where agents use some form of projectile weapon to attack the enemy from a distance. As tactics are highly dependant on the situation (i.e. terrain, team supplies, enemy movement, etc) it is very difficult for game developers to manually code the tactics for the NPCs. In order to imitate a tactical behaviour, a broad understanding of the situation is needed [4].

In this paper, we create an architecture to develop team tactics for a combative 2D game using genetic programming (GP) techniques. We aim to use this architecture to evolve novel and effective combat tactics that can be used by teams of enemy NPC agents in a single-player, 2D "shoot-em up" style gaming environment. We aim to develop an architecture that can automatically create effective team tactics for a 2D combative computer game setting.

2 Development

This research builds upon previous research [2] in which a team of agents was evolved to perform as well as a designed team of agents. The designed team used the built-in AI of the gaming environment to define their behaviour. In the previous research, the evolving teams consisted of five agents and were evaluated by playing them against another team of five agents using the built-in AI of the game engine. In this research, we propose to evolve a team of five game agents against a single intelligent agent. This single agent has infinite ammunition and a health level equivalent to that of the team of five agents. This type of environment was chosen as it shares many similarities with the single-player "shoot-em-up" genre of games, where the single intelligent agent can be viewed as the human player in a single-player game. Thus, the tactics evolved using this environment should be effective for use by teams of enemy NPCs in single player combative computer games.

As each individual team unit has only one fifth the health of the single intelligent enemy agent and much less firepower available to it, it would be highly unlikely that five agents working in isolation would defeat the enemy agent. The five team units must therefore work together as a collective group and display tactical team behaviour in order to outwit and overcome the single intelligent enemy unit.

2.1 Gaming Environment

The simulator is built on the 2D *Raven* game engine created by Matt Buckland [1]. The environment consists of an open 2-dimensional space, enclosed by four walls with another small wall in the center. The five agents will begin the game from the bottom center of the map facing the enemy agent and enemy agent will start the game from the top center of the map facing the five team agents. Agents can navigate from their current position to any other position on the map by using the A* algorithm to find the shortest path. Items are also placed on the map at locations that are equidistant from both the team starting points and the enemy starting point. These items consist of shotguns, railguns, rocket launchers and health packs, all of which can be used by both the team agents and the enemy agent during the course of the game. If an item is picked up by an agent during the course of the game it will disappear from the map for a short time before it respawns and can be used again.

2.2 Game Agent AI

The single enemy against which the team will be evolved is a fit autonomous agent whose behaviour is based on the goal-driven agent architecture as described by Buckland [1].

The goal-driven agent architecture uses a hierarchy of goals to define an agents behaviour. Goals can be either atomic (define a single task or action) or composite (made up of several subgoals). Composite goals are broken down into subgoals of a simpler nature, hence a hierarchical structure of goals can be created for any game agent to define its behaviour.

The way the enemy agent decides on which goal to pursue at any given time is based on intermittent desirability checks. Each goal has a hardcoded desirability algorithm associated with it that is used to calculate how desirable it would be to pursue that goal under the current circumstances. The goal with the highest desirability score gets chosen as the unit's current behaviour. The behaviour of the evolving team's units is also based on this goal-driven agent architecture. However, the way in which they decide what goal to pursue is based on their evolved decision-making tree.

2.3 Evolution of Team Tactics

In order to evolve the team tactics, we have adopted a genetic programming approach as it has the potential for uncovering novel team behaviours for the NPCs. Using a GP tree representation also means that the behaviours of the teams can be analysed and later reused in game design. The chromosomes used in the GP comprise five separate GP trees, one for each agent in the team that defines the manner in which the agent decides what actions to perform when following the tactic (i.e. the decision-making tree referred to in the previous section). There will be 100 individual teams or chromosomes in the population and the simulation will be run for 90 generations. Five games are simulated for each individual team chromosome in the population in each generation and the results averaged so as to give a more accurate representation of a team's fitness as there is a degree of randomness within the gaming environment. So a total of 45000 games must be simulated throughout a single run of the GP.

2.3.1 GP Node Sets

We use a strongly-typed GP in order to constrain the type of nodes that can be children of other nodes. Our simulator consists of five node sets in total:

Action node set: The nodes that constitute this set define the goals the agent should pursue or actions it should perform (e.g. attack the enemy) but also include the *IF statement* node.

Conditional node set: There are 7 conditional nodes in this set that can be combined to form the conditions under which an action is to be performed.

Positional node set: Nodes in this node set are all terminal nodes that represent vector positions on the map to which the agents can move; namely, the positions of the enemy and the agent's nearest ally and a position directly behind the enemy.

Environmental parameter node set: This node set consists of parameters taken from the gaming environment that will be checked during the decision making process of the evolving agent. Such nodes include an agent's current health, the distance to an agent's nearest ally, the distance to its enemy and the agent's ammunition supplies for each weapon in it's inventory.

Numerical node set: This node set defines arithmetic operators and constants.

There are a total of 39 different types of node across the five node sets that can be combined to describe an agents decision-making tree. The trees created from the evolutionary process can reach a maximum depth of 17 and hence the search space of possible trees is vast.

2.3.2 Team Fitness Evaluation

To evaluate how a team performed in a given simulation, the fitness function must take a number of factors into account: the health remaining of both the enemy and ally teams after each of the five games in the simulation, the duration of each game and the length of the chromosome (i.e. number of nodes in the decision-making trees of the team agents). The basic fitness is calculated as follows:

$$RawFitness = \left(\frac{(5 * (Games * TSize * MaxHealth - EH) + AH)}{Games * TSize * MaxHealth}\right) + \left(\frac{AvgGameTime}{Scaling * MaxGameTime}\right)$$

where EH and AH is the total amount of health remaining for the enemy agent and for all five ally units respectively (averaged over five games). $TSize$ is the number of agents in the evolving team, $Games$ is the number of games played (i.e. five) and $MaxHealth$ is the maximum health an agent in the game can have. As we are focusing on evolving tactics capable of defeating the enemy, more importance is attached to the change in the enemy agent's health than the corresponding change in the ally team's health. This term is also the factor which distinguishes most between the teams in the early generations of the simulation, helping the GP to get a foothold in the search space.

The fitness function is further expanded to take into account the duration of the games in the simulation. As a general rule, the longer a game lasts, the longer the team survives the enemy attack and the better they are performing. $AvgGameTime$ is the average running time of the five games in the simulation and $Scaling$ is a variable to reduce the impact the game time has on the fitness of a team. Here $Scaling$ is set to 4 so the maximum value that can be added to the teams fitness is 0.25. This occurs if the team lasts the full game time. In our simulation, the maximum value $RawFitness$ can be is 6.25.

The length of the chromosome is taken into account in the fitness calculation to prevent trees from bloating.

$$StdFitness = (6.25 - RawFitness) + \frac{length}{lengthFactor}$$

The $lengthFactor$ parameter is a value used to limit the influence the length of the chromosome has on the fitness and is set to 5000 for these experiments. The fitter the team the closer the value $StdFitness$ is to zero.

Once fitness scores are calculated for all teams in the current generation of the population; we then use these scores to probabilistically select chromosomes (i.e. teams) from the present generation that will be used to make individuals for the next generation of the population.

2.3.3 Team Selection Process

Selection is performed in two phases. The first is a form of elitism where m of the best n individuals from each generation are retained by reproducing them into the new generation unaltered. For these experiments, three copies of the best individual and two copies of the next best individual are retained in this manner. This ensures that the fittest members of the population are not destroyed or lost.

The second method of selection is roulette wheel selection, which selects chromosomes from the current generation probabilistically based on the fitness of the chromosomes. Each individual is assigned a section of the roulette wheel proportional to its fitness in relation to all other individuals in the population. Any chromosomes selected in this manner are then subjected to crossover and mutation operators before being inserted into the next generation.

In order to add more diversity and prevent premature convergence of the population, there is also a 2% chance for completely new chromosomes to be created and added to the population each generation rather than selecting from the current population.

2.3.4 Team-based Crossover

The crossover operator used here is the same as that used in previous research [2]. The operator, first proposed by Haynes [3], involves selecting a random five bit mask that decides what units of the parent team chromosomes are to be altered during crossover. A '1' indicates the unit is copied directly over into the child chromosome and a '0' indicates the unit is to take part in crossover with the corresponding unit of the other parent chromosome, before being placed in the child chromosome.

Following the selection of the bit mask, a random crossover point is then chosen within each unit to be crossed over. The node at the crossover point in each corresponding unit of the two parents must be from the same node set in order for a valid crossover to take place (e.g. a subtree with its root as a conditional can only be swapped with a subtree whose root is also a conditional).

2.3.5 Team-based Mutation

Following the possible application of crossover, mutation is then applied to each chromosome with some relatively low probability (0.05). There are two kinds of mutation operators used in this research:

In the first form of mutation, known as swap mutation; a node is randomly selected from one of the five units of the chromosome. The subtree at the selected point is then deleted and the node is replaced with a new random node from the same node set and a new random subtree is grown from this new node.

The second mutation operator randomly selects two of the five units of the chromosome to take part in the mutation. A random point is then chosen in each of the unit's trees for the tactic being evolved and the subtree at that point is swapped between the two units. This mutation operator is akin to performing crossover between two units within the same chromosome.

3 Results

In these experiments, the team of evolving agents generated a number of solutions capable of defeating the single intelligent enemy agent.

The graph in Figure 1 plots the fitness of the best GP/team of the population for each generation of a typical run. Note that fitness values closer to zero are better.

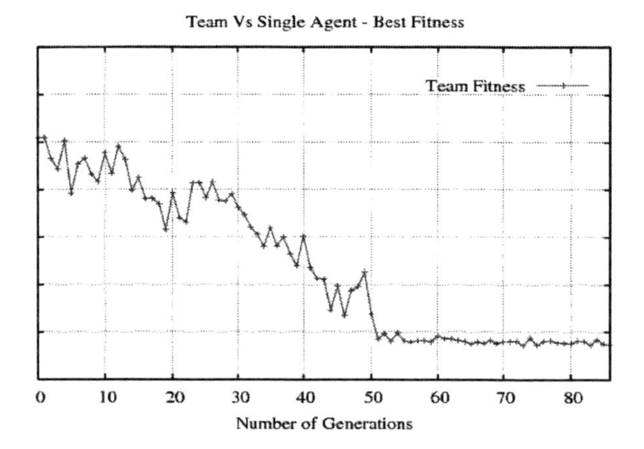

Figure 1: Plot of best fitness over run of GP

Here we can see an significant improvement in the team's performance over the course of the evolution. At generation 51 we see the best fitness begin to plateau as the good solution found at this generation quickly spreads throughout the population causing convergence.

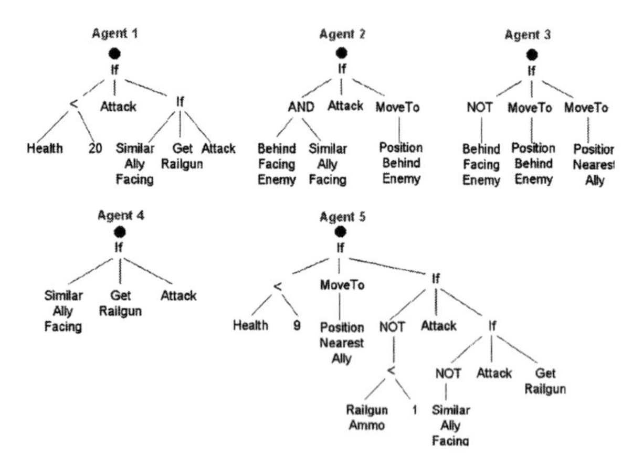

Figure 2: Behavioural trees of evolved team agents

Figure 2 shows a sample result from a typical GP run. In this solution, we can see the exclusive behaviours of the team members that allow it to display group rather than individual rationality, a common attribute of the more fit solutions that emerged. If we analyse the behaviours, we can see that two of the team members act as decoys (agents 2 and 3) and distract the enemy by running at the enemy, whilst the other three offensive team members collect ammunition and weapons before attacking the enemy simultaneously with the collected weapons. In this solution the two decoy team members nearly always get killed, as they sacrifice themselves for the good of the team. The actions of the decoy agents here do not appear individually rational but their behaviour is essential to the success of the team. Group rationality is a key element to the effective execution of any team-based tactic.

If we look at the subtrees of individual agents within a team, a number of interesting behaviours can be seen. For example, an agent might check its ammunition supplies for a given weapon during the course of the game and search for more ammunition for that particular weapon if needed; otherwise it would attack the enemy.

Another interesting behaviour that emerged in a number of solutions is that, during the course of a game, a team member would check if it is facing the same way as its nearest ally and if so go off and search for a item, otherwise attack the enemy. This behaviour is intuitive in a sense, as the ally could provide covering fire for the agent if needed while the agent gathers ammunition or health. This behaviour emerged in a number of the more fit solutions in numerous different runs of the GP. It can be seen displayed here by agents 1, 4 and 5 of the team shown in Figure 2.

To demonstrate the effectiveness of the evolved team behaviour, a series of experiments were carried out: one involved simulating 100 games of the team of evolved agents against the single enemy agent and the other involved simulating 100 games where a team of generic agents played the single enemy agent. (Note that the generic agents have the same AI as the single enemy agent)

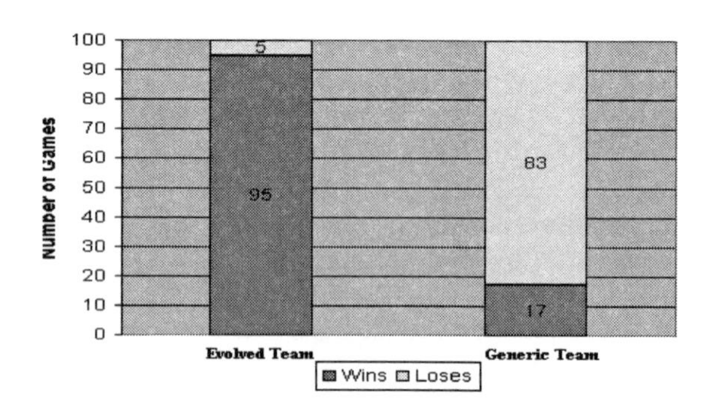

Figure 3: Results of experiments

From this we can see that the evolved, team rational behaviour significantly outperforms the combined behaviour of a team of five generic individually rational agents for the given problem. Even though the generic team consists of individually fit agents whose behaviour is hand-coded by a game developer, the combined efforts of the team is not enough to overcome the single enemy agent on the majority of occasions. This is due to the fact that all five generic agents reason in a similar manner so the behaviour of one is comparable to another. They do not combine to fill specific roles within the team in an attempt to defeat the enemy, unlike the agents of the evolved team. This group rationality of the evolved team is the key to its success as is the case many real world tactical situations, e.g. a military offensive on an enemy base.

4 Conclusions

As discussed earlier, the simulator did manage to evolve a number of solutions capable of defeating the single generic agent. These evolved solutions displayed intelligent group behaviour, where the individual efforts of the team members combine to outwit and overcome the enemy. These evolved behaviours also outperform a team of generic agents at executing the same task.

Here we have presented a useful test-bed for exploring the potential for genetic programming to evolve useful, novel behaviours for teams of NPCs in computer games. The team tactics evolved in these experiments have the potential to be used by teams of enemy NPCs in single-player combative games, where the single enemy agent can be viewed as the human player.

In future experiments we hope to introduce more environmental parameters and add new agent actions/goals to the genetic program in an attempt to evolve more intricate behaviours for use in more complex environments. For example, allow agents to make use of walls as cover from enemy attack. We could also evolve individual aspects of the tactics first and reuse these as elements of our node sets in future experiments.

We would like to introduce a communication element into the evolutionary environment to provide a mechanism to allow the evolving agents to explicitly coordinate their behaviour. We believe this will permit the team to display more human-like, responsive behaviour. For example, warn allies of enemy threats or call for backup.

Acknowledgment

The primary author would like to acknowledge the Irish Research Council for Science, Engineering and Technology (IRCSET) for their assistance through the Embark initiative.

References

[1] M. Buckland. *Programming Game AI by Example*, chapter Goal-Driven Agent Behaviour, pages 379–415. Wordware Publishing, Inc, 2005.

[2] D. Doherty and C. O'Riordan. Evolving agent-based team tactics for combative computer games. In *AICS 2006 17th Irish Artificial Intelligence and Cognitive Science Conference*, 2006.

[3] T. Haynes, S. Sen, D. Schoenefeld, and R. Wainwright. Evolving a team. In E. V. Siegel and J. R. Koza, editors, *Working Notes for the AAAI Symposium on Genetic Programming*, Cambridge, MA, 1995. AAAI.

[4] C. Thurau, C. Bauckhage, and G. Sagerer. Imitation learning at all levels of game-ai. In *Proc. Int. Conf. on Computer Games, Artificial Intelligence,Design and Education*, pages 402–408, 2004.

Author Biography

Darren Doherty (pictured left) was born in Letterkenny, Co. Donegal, Ireland in 1984. He received the BSc degree in Information Technology from the National University of Ireland, Galway in 2005. He is currently undergoing a Ph D. degree in the field of Computer Game Artificial Intelligence and is funded for such by the Irish Research Council for Science, Engineering and Technology. His research interests include evolutionary computation, artificial intelligence and computer game development.

Colm O'Riordan (pictured right) lectures in the Department of Information Technology, National University of Ireland, Galway. His main research interests are in the fields of agent based systems, artificial life and information retrieval. His current research focuses on cooperation and coordination in artificial life societies and multi-agent systems.

POSH Tools for Game Agent Development by Students and Non-Programmers

Cyril Brom[†], Jakub Gemrot[†], Michal Bída[†], Ondrej Burkert[†], Sam J. Partington[‡] and Joanna J. Bryson[‡]

***Abstract*— Agent based systems are becoming popular outside the agents research community, among biologist, artists and in the game industry. Yet tools are lacking that facilitate non-expert agent developers building complicated agents for modelling and systems. As a part of our own agent-based research programmes we have been developing such tools. In this paper, we review the progress made, highlighting issues of usability. Examples of agents developed in these tools are also given, with an emphasis on intelligent virtual combat agents situated in Unreal Tournament.**

***Index Terms*— AI, Dynamic Planning, Life-Like Characters, Programmability, Accessible AI**

I. Introduction

Building intelligent systems, like programming systems in general, is hard. While some principles such as modularity are widely agreed upon, even highly related questions such as how to integrate these modules back into a coherent system, are not. Standard multi-agent system techniques are formal and highly distributed but unnecessarily complicated for modular systems where the extent of the system is well bounded, as when it composes a single autonomous agent like a game character or robot. The problem of this complexity becomes apparent when one tries to hire ordinary or even exceptional programmers to create AI systems. Yet the ideal for the games industry would be if skilled story writers for interactive dramas could directly create — or even prototype or adjust — the characters they design into their narratives.

We have been working on the developing and extending the notion of reactive or *dynamic plans* as the key integration technique for an intelligent system. The advantage of these plans is that they can be developed from simple sequences of actions and prioritised lists of goals — skills accessible to most people as they are fundamental to everyday planning and scripting.

Based on this approach, we have developed several complex, apparently cognitive agents, as well as tools that facilitate such construction. In this paper, we review our progress in developing these tools, with a particular focus on their educational aspects. Examples of agents developed in the tools will be also given, primarily VR game-playing agents situated in the video game Unreal Tournament (UT) [32], although related systems have been and are being developed for applications from autonomous robots to scientific social simulations. In this paper, the review of each advance will necessarily be brief, however we reference more complete descriptions of the individual projects which have been published elsewhere.

Our primary objectives for this paper are to present an overview and to summarise our main lessons learned to date. We start with detailing the toolkits' requirements, continue with describing our methodological approach, and then describe the tools themselves, including example agents.

II. Goals and Related Work

Currently, our main target audiences for our toolkits have been undergraduate computer science students (Prague) and graduate-level researchers in social and behavioural sciences (Bath). For both groups of users, we hope that by engaging them in directly exploring agency we will contribute to both their understanding of their discipline and at the same time provide them tools to be used in their future employment. Building agents situated in dynamic, potentially antagonistic environments that are capable of pursuing multiple, possibly conflicting goals not only teaches students about the fundamental nature and problems of agency but also encourage them to develop or enhance programming skills. Although academics are our most readily accessible testers, we expect our techniques to be of use to professionals from artists through games engineers. Many of our tools are available freely on line, and we have recently installed basic bug tracking facilities. In essence we want to expand access to AI as a tool for research, entertainment and education.

Toolkits to meet this aim must fulfill several requirements:

1) They must provide tools for facilitating agent development. These tools must allow for making *simple things simple, and complex things possible*. In other words, a non-programmer should be facilitated in building simple agents, while more experienced developers should be able to increase their agents' complexity or capabilities. The best way to meet these desiderata is with a modular architecture, iterative design practice and an easy-to-cope-with integration technique. Auxiliary tools such as a debugger or a graphical behavioural editor should also be available.
2) In a related point, toolkits should facilitate rapid prototyping, so that a writer or creator can try a number of different scenarios quickly, and so that a full character with a number of goals and/or scenes can be fleshed out in a reasonable amount of time.
3) They should provide a graphical virtual environment. Visualisation is vital to understanding agency. Most people have a great deal of difficulty reasoning about

[†]Department of Software and Computer Science Education, Charles University, Prague 118 00, Czech Republic

[‡]Artificial models of natural Intelligence, University of Bath, Bath BA2 7AY, United Kingdom

the consequences of interacting parallel goals and behaviours in a single agent; how an agent will operate with a three dimensional, real-time world, where actions once committed cannot be recalled; and particularly with how interacting agents can influence and interfere with each other, even in simple ways such as attempting to take the same physical location. Visualisation at least assists with debugging, and sometimes established social reasoning makes recognition if not prediction of problems relatively straight forward. The visualisation environment can either be provided built-in, or as a stand-alone application with a provided API.

There are several commercial, relatively user-friendly toolkits which at least begin to fulfil these requirements available. For example, AI.Implant [3], a middleware for building complex computer game agents, or Behavior [29], which is a Softimage plug-in for controlling behaviour of virtual actors in movies. Such systems tend to be too expensive for academic and entry-level purposes.

Several purely educational toolkits exist for learning programming by means of agents, such as Alice [2]. Unfortunately, these allow for building only simple agents with entirely scripted behaviour. NetLogo is a popular tool for agent-based modelling, partly because it meets the rapid-prototyping desiderata above. It has also recently become extendible due to a Java API [33]. However, this does not facilitate creating engaging single VR agents, which we see as a powerful and vital mechanism both for creating truly animal-like systems and holding the interest of the average (rather than the exceptional) student. Similar problems hold for agent development toolkits specially intended for artists, such as Movie Sand BOX [19].

Robust and formally well-founded tools for agent development do exist, such as the general-purpose Jack [17], or the powerful cognitive modelling languages like Soar [28] and ACT-R [4]. However, it is not easy for entry-level programmers to create engaging human-like agents in these architectures. Further, even for professional programmers, building intelligence in such 'heavy' systems takes a good deal of time. Such systems also tend to take too much CPU for complex societies or game play.

Thus there is still a need for systems which provide accessible development of virtual-reality animal-like and humanoid characters, but also allow extensions into full programming languages. What we propose as a basic starting point is a system built on the high-level yet powerful dynamic programming language python. Python is a scripting language which allows for rapid prototyping, yet it has access to extensive libraries which allow for powerful and detailed computation. Beyond this though, agent building requires special idioms or design patterns, and a character-based AI development platform should provide for these.

III. Approach: Behavior Oriented Design

We have taken as a starting point Behavior Oriented Design (BOD) [10, 11]. This is a modular technique that draws both from object-oriented design (OOD) and behavior-based AI (BBAI), with additional features for integrating an intelligent system. From BBAI, BOD takes the principle that intelligence is decomposed around expressed capabilities such as walking or eating, rather than around theoretical mental entities such as knowledge and thought. Each module supports a related set of expressed behaviours called *acts*, whatever sensing is necessary to control such acts, and whatever memory and learning is necessary to inform and disambiguate such sensing and acting. For example, the act of going home requires being able to sense and recognise the current location, which requires remembering previous routes or some other form of map. A diversity of standard machine learning techniques can be included inside a single agent: BOD supports efficient learning by allowing per-module specialization of techniques and representations.

From OOD, BOD takes both the object metaphor (BOD modules are built as objects in an object-oriented language such as Java, C++, CLOS or in the present case python) and an agile, iterative development process [c.f. 5]. BOD consists of two sets of heuristics. The first are for the initial design of an agent, and the second are for recognising — after a period of development — optimisation opportunities for simplifying the agent's code. In other words, BOD encourages regular refactoring so that the agent remains as easy to expand and maintain as possible. Details of these heuristics can be found elsewhere [10, 12].

The core of this simplification process is a good mechanism for integrating the behaviour modules that compose an agent. Modular decomposition has no benefit if the process of making certain the modules can execute without interfering with each other is more complicated than building a homogeneous architecture would have been in the first place. Unfortunately, this problem plagued early BBAI approaches such as subsumption architecture [9] and spreading activation networks [22], making them difficult to scale. BOD provides a relatively simple action-selection mechanism for providing behaviour arbitration, which we describe next.

A. POSH Action Selection

BOD uses Parallel-rooted, Ordered, Slip-stack Hierarchical (POSH) dynamic plans for action selection. These allow the specification of an agent's goals and priorities, or in other words the contexts in which an agent acts. The primitives of these plans are the acts supported by the library of behavior modules just described (referred to as *the behavior library*), as well as set of sense primitives provided by the same library. These sense primitives inform the plans at decision points about the current context. *Context* here is both environmental (e.g. visible food, heard enemies) and internal (e.g. remembering the way home, feeling hungry or happy.)

Besides these two primitive types, there are three types of POSH planning aggregates: simple sequences, competences and drive collections. The *sequence* functions as expected; the drive collection is a special form of competence that serves as the root of the plan hierarchy, we return to this below.

The *competence* is the core of a POSH plan. It is an instance of a fundamental AI design pattern, which we refer to as a *basic reactive plan* [10]. This is essentially a small, prioritised set of productions. A *production* is a condition-action pair which forms the core of most expert systems and cognitive modelling architectures. The idea is that AI can be described as a look-up of an action based on the current context[1]. The problem is that specifying such context in sufficient detail to be unambiguous for an agent with multiple goals in a complicated, dynamic environment is either tedious and cumbersome (for a human programmer) or computationally intractable (for machine learning or planning.) By using a hierarchical structure, we can assume we know a large amount of the context by the fact we are even considering this particular plan fragment. For example, the agent has already realized that it is hungry and there are bananas around, now it just needs to peel one. Thus a competence only needs to express how to consummate one particular subgoal. By assuming the rules are prioritised, we can further assume that for any particular step of the plan, no better action closer to consummating goal is a available, or it would already have been executed. Thus for each potential action, the only thing that the context needs to describe is not whether it *should* be performed, but rather only whether it *can* be.

Because POSH plans are hierarchical, each 'action' as described above in a competence may be primitive acts supported by the behaviour library, or they may in fact be another competence or a sequence. At the root of this hierarchy is a special competence called a *drive collection* which is executed on every program cycle to ensure that there is no more important goal the agent should be attending to than the one it is currently attempting to complete. The drive collection also supports enough state such that goals can be pursued in coarse-grain parallel. Thus an agent could for example stand up every few seconds and look around, while spending most of its time concentrating on building a fire.

To small extent, POSH plans resemble languages built upon BDI architecture, e.g. JACK Agent Language [17]. However, POSH is especially designed for non-agent experts, which means that it does not have some advanced BDI features (e.g. pre-defined meta-level planning), but on the other hand it is easier for the intended audience to cope with. What makes it easy to design is that all of its aggregates can be designed initially as sequences. Competences are however capable of executing actions out of sequence (skipping or repeating elements) as needed to respond appropriately to the uncertain consequences of behaviour in a dynamic environment.

IV. Platforms

Based on the BOD approach and the POSH action selection mechanism, we have created three development systems fulfilling the requirements outlined in Section II. The first two each consist of two applications — first a pyPOSH action selection engine that implements a POSH mechanism and allows for BOD design [20], and second an environment for running experiments. The first of these pairings is BOD/MASON, which allows artificial life simulations. The second, Pogamut, is a platform integrating pyPOSH with the Unreal Tournament 3D environment and providing several development tools. The third system, IVE (for "intelligent virtual environment"), is a stand-alone application which is a complete simulator of large virtual worlds inhabited by tens of virtual humans [7]. We describe these three systems below.

A. PyPOSH and BOD/MASON

PyPOSH[2] is a POSH action selection mechanism built in the python language. It can be edited with the standard POSH plan editor, ABODE, and can be connected to any arbitrary system or virtual environment, e.g. a robot or an agent-based modelling tool. We have recently integrated pyPOSH with the agent-based modelling toolkit MASON [21], producing BOD/MASON [13]. This has two advantages: for novice agent programmers, it provides a platform and basic behavior libraries for simulating animal-like behaviour — BOD/MASON comes with a sheep/dog demo illustrating how different agents can be created with different POSH plans and the same behavior library. For agent-based modellers, BOD/MASON supports making more elaborate or individuated agent intelligence than most platforms, such as MASON on its own or NetLogo.

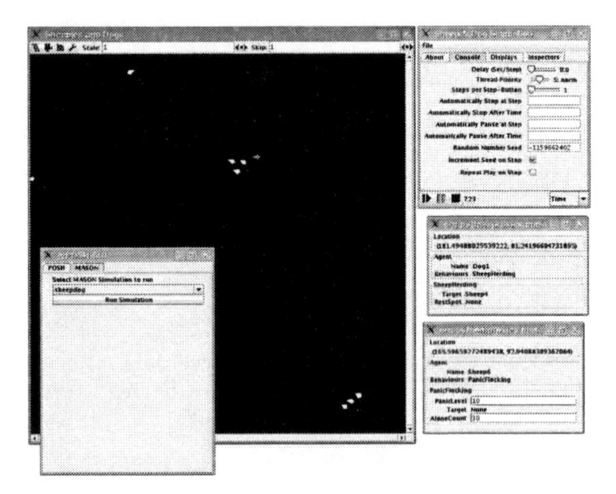

Fig. 1. A screenshot of BOD/MASON running the sheep/dog demo.

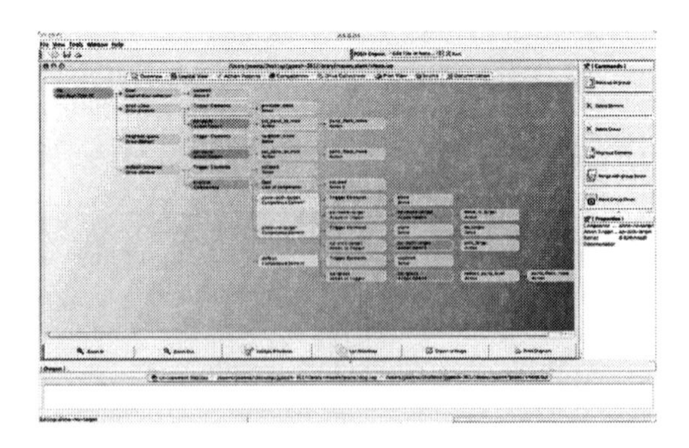

Fig. 2. A screenshot of ABODE editing a sheep's POSH plan.

[1]Many machine-learning approaches to AI make the same assumption and call the lookup structure a *policy*, which they attempt to learn.

[2]pyPOSH and ABODE can be downloaded from http://www.bath.ac.uk/comp-sci/ai/AmonI-sw.html. The pyPOSH distribution includes BOD/MASON and also another set of UT libraries (not Pogamut), which are described further below.

B. Pogamut

To provide additional tools facilitating games development, we have developed Pogamut[3] middleware and integrated it with pyPOSH and UT via the Gamebots interface [1]. The system architecture is depicted in Fig. 3. Each agent is treated as a triple (*avatar*, *behaviors*, *plans*), where *avatar* is merely a body driven in UT, *behaviors* are the set of behavioral modules in python maintained by Pogamut and *plans* is the set of plans by which pyPOSH controls behavioral modules.

The following tools are included in Pogamut:

- a simple agent management system,
- a debugger and a development environment for controlling agent's properties and communication with the environment (Fig. 4),
- a graphical editor for behaviors and dynamic plans called ABODE (Fig. 4), and
- a set of auxiliary class and basic behaviors, e.g. the navigation module.

The system can manage multiple agents simultaneously and can be easily plugged into another virtual environment, provided only with a gamebots-like interface (API) to that environment.

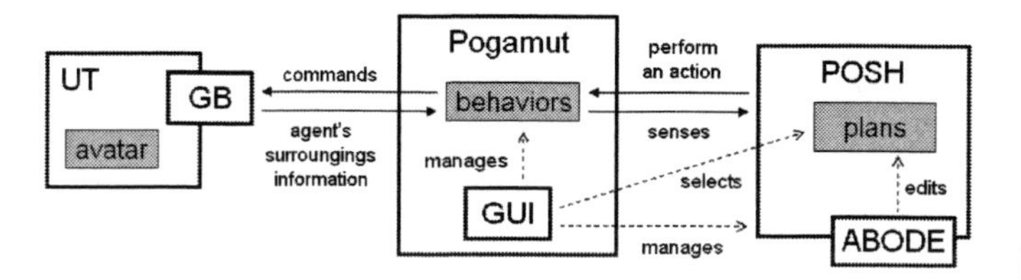

Fig. 3. Pogamut system architecture.

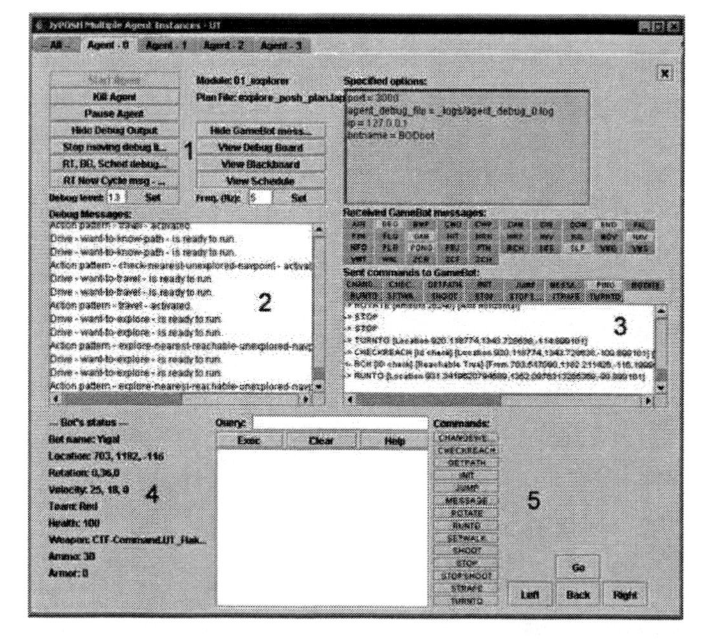

Fig. 4. Pogamut GUI: 1—the control pane. 2—the POSH log. 3—the Gamebots communication log. 4—the agent's properties. 5—the manual command pane.

[3]Pogamut can be downloaded from http://carolina.mff.cuni.cz/~gib/. UT99 should be bought; it costs about 10 Euro.

In academia, UT with Gamebots have been used in several research projects already [18, 23], which makes it valuable for comparing AI approaches from different laboratories. The goal of Pogamut is to extend it to create a platform that can be used extensively by students and new programmers.

C. IVE

IVE[4] is a stand-alone Java framework and middleware supporting development of virtual human-like agents [7] (Fig. 5). IVE itself already includes development tools, i.e. a debugger, a neat GUI, and the action selection engine, which is based on a POSH extension. Virtual environments as well as behaviour of agents is specified in external XML and Java files.

IVE is specifically intended for simulations of large environments, which is its most notable distinction from pyPOSH / Pogamut (one can control hundred of actors in IVE, for example). There are several non-trivial issues stemming from large environments [detailed in 7] and the most features of IVE are designed to cope with these. These include:

- IVE uses the level-of-detail technique for automatic simplification of the simulation in unimportant places. Contrary to its typical use in the domain of computer graphics, we exploit this for simplifying the space and actors' behaviour [30].
- IVE exploits a knowledge representation that allows for adding new objects and actions into the environment in the runtime and for controlling actors both as autonomous agents or from a centralised director.

IVE is not the only recent work using LOD for behaviour [see e.g. 24]. Unlike other approaches, our technique is applied directly to the planning mechanism, which allows for gradual and robust simplification of the simulation that to our knowledge has not been addressed previously. For example, in our bar-drinking scenario, we allow for 4 degrees of detail of bar behaviour for each bar actor.

IVE can be used (and is being used) *as is*, both as a research and an educational platform. Current research includes:

- investigating level-of-detail AI techniques,
- simulating a virtual company
- augmenting IVE with a *drama manager* for the purpose of an educational virtual game in civics. Drama manager is a component for controlling agents' top-level goals according to a given story-plot (specified by Petri Nets as detailed in [8].)

V. Example Projects

We have been using BOD-based systems on variety of projects, from controlling mobile robots to simulating primate task learning. In this section, we illustrate the systems' potential on three projects concerning gaming agents' AI. We start with a description of a gaming agent capable of juggling multiple goals that plays capture the flag. Next we describe an agent with an emotional module, which extends POSH action selection with an additional control layer. Finally we illustrate that our approach can be scaled for synchronising

[4]IVE can be downloaded at http://urtax.ms.mff.cuni.cz/ive.

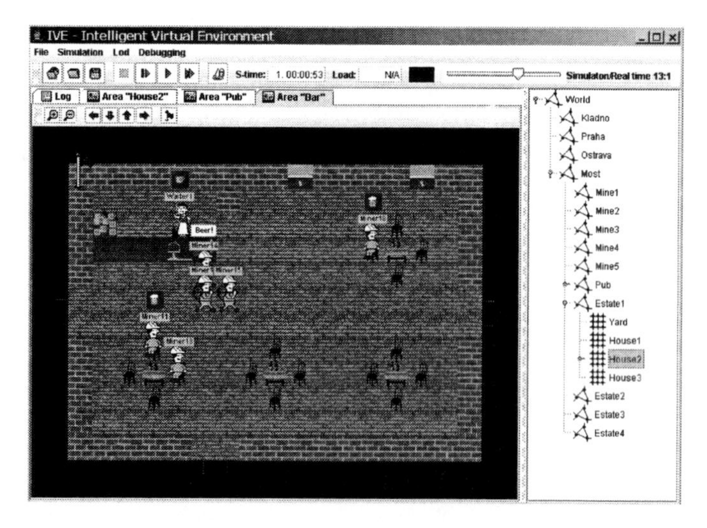

Fig. 5. A screenshot from IVE restaurant scenario. Miners and a waiter are depicted. Notice, there are tens of such actors in the scenario and yet the simulation runs on a single PC in a timely fashion. The pane on the right depicts the world structure.

two gaming agents. All these projects have been conducted by undergraduate students, which illustrates the tools' accessibility and educational potential.

A. Capture the Flag

The goal of this project was to test whether BOD scaled well for the agents acting in complex gaming environments, as well as ensuring that undergraduates can learn to use BOD. The full iterative development of this capture-the-flag gaming agent for Unreal Tournament is documented elsewhere [26]. The agent was coded using python and pyPOSH [20] directly, not with Pogamut. A slightly modified version of this agent (which can play in two-person teams) is currently distributed with pyPOSH.

Partington wrote a two-layer behaviour library, consisting first of four modules for expressed behaviour: *movement* and *combat* (behave as per their names), *status* (contains state regarding health level, weapons held etc.) and the class containing some *primitives* for UT communication. Additionally, there are three modules dedicated to maintaining internal state useful for more than one of the expressed behavior modules (e.g. information about position). He also developed one of the most intricate POSH plans to date (see Fig. 6) which allowed the agent to both attack and defend as necessary, sometimes at the same time (e.g. strafing an attacker while returning a flag to base). However, some of the complexity of the final bot plan was unnecessary — dedicated to timing out outdated memories. This indicates we need to clarify idioms dealing with memory and time to improve the BOD framework.

B. Emotional gaming agent.

In modern games, the key feature is agents *believability*, which simply stated means *the extent to which the players think the agents look and behave how the players expect.* It includes whether the agent acts like a human (if it is human-like), perceives only things a human could perceive, etc. Note,

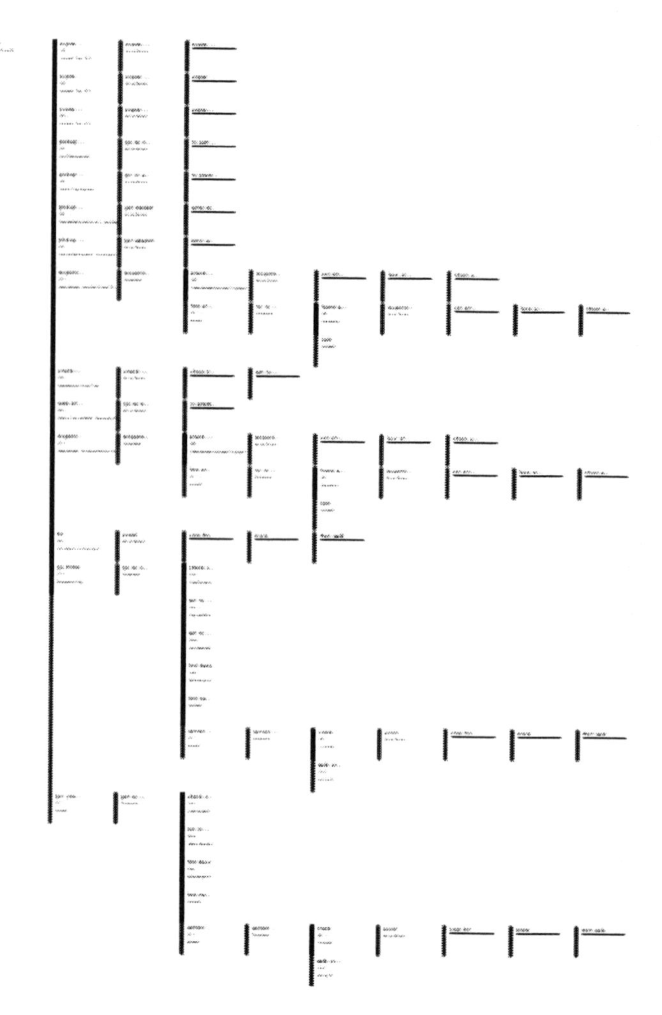

Fig. 6. A high-level view of Partington's capture-the-flag POSH plan showing the extent and limits of plan depth necessary for a complete game agent. Plan details, while not legible here, are available elsewhere [26]; the complete plan is also included in the (free) pyPOSH download.

however, that believability is more related to imitation than to rational reasoning or psychologically plausibility.

The hypothesis behind this project was that expressing emotions at the behavioural layer (i.e. not only by facial changes) may increase believability of a first-person shooter (FPS) game agent. We developed the emotional UT agent using the Pogamut platform. An emotional module is added in the BOD architecture. The module is based on Champandard's model [16], which is intended for such game agents. Champandard's model is partially based on Plutchik's psychologically grounded model [27]. Champandard also prototyped an emotional game agent, however ours is more elaborate.

The emotional model uses eight emotions in complementary pairs: *pride – shame*, *fear – anger*, *joy – sorrow*, *amusement – weariness*. It also exploits moods, feelings and sensations, which are other affective states of "minds". The outcome of the emotional module is threefold. First, different emotions enforce different dynamic plans (and thus behaviors). Second, emotions influence agents' properties (i.e., shooting accuracy). Third, the agent gesticulates and comments on the situation according its emotional state.

Preliminary tests reveal first that the model is too complicated and overly psychologically plausible for the purpose of a UT agent. Since a typical UT agent lives for tens of seconds, the agent does not have five minutes for grief, even if that is more human. Second, we have realized that it is hard to parameterise the model without habituation, which is a form of adaptation to repetitive stimulation by increasing probability of ignoring it. Although POSH supports primitive habituation, neither our nor Champandard's model works with it. Appropriate dynamics are vital even for a simple, non-plausible emotional model [31], thus BOD should also probably be extended with an pattern for supporting such state. Third, it was extremely simple to layer emotions upon pyPOSH as well as implement different plans for expressing different emotions, which demonstrated scalability of the basic BOD architecture. We now plan to simplify the model and to conduct a psychological study of players playing against agents with and without emotions.

C. Agent Twins

Several FPS platforms include a *team deathmatch* mode, where agents and players fight in teams against each other. Although agents in one team might cooperate, this is not always the case. In recent FPS games, cooperation often occurs accidentally as an 'emergent' phenomenon only. The goal of this project was to develop agent twins that cooperate in a decentralised manner (i.e. each twin is self controlled; there is no leader) and test whether the cooperation is fruitful. Additionally, we wanted to verify POSH/BOD approach in a multi-agent scenario[5]. The twins have been developed on the Pogamut platform. Generally, they cooperate in two ways: (a) they perform some tactical operations, and (b) they inform each other about positions of objects and other agents. Finally, we have tested the twins of type (a), and (b), and the twins that do not cooperate at all in the deathmatch against each other and against original UT bots (who do not cooperate).

The tests surprisingly showed that cooperation by information passing (b) was fruitful, but that of tactical operations (a) was not. We think the reason is that our cooperation was intended to be plausible. However, the deathmatch in UT is not plausible at all; UT is not a realistic combat simulator. We have stumbled here on another "plausibility — believability" tension. We have also demonstrated that tests themselves can be easily managed in the Pogamut system, since pyPOSH is flexible enough to allow for simply switching on/off different behaviours and types of cooperation.

We have also shown that POSH does not cope well with expressing of certain more complicated behaviours, particularly the human adult capacity for finishing (or at least putting into order) a current task when motivation has switched so that another task is now the primary goal. This is a basic problem for dynamic planning. See [6] for details; some of these are being addressed in IVE.

We plan to conduct a study for more than two agents and to augment this work with some aspects of centralised reasoning and classical planning, which has recently attracted gaming industry attention (e.g. [25]). The project is detailed in [15].

[5]The version of pyPOSH currently distributed includes a two-agent (offence and defence) team version of Partington's UT code, developed at Bath by Steve Couzins.

VI. Summary; Present and Future Work

In this paper, we briefly introduced several agent-based development tools — BOD/MASON, Pogamut and IVE. These are systems which provide entry-level development humanoid and animal-like characters, which can be used by students and other non-professional programmers. The systems are extendible, grounded in standard programming languages. We have demonstrated this in the described research. This scalability is a notable distinction from similar toolkits.

We have at least a dozen finished students' projects using these platforms, and more in progress. These projects not only demonstrate that the systems can be used by the students, but also verify that BOD and POSH, which the projects and platforms are built upon, are accessible, flexible and scalable. We have also used the platforms for education of non-AI experts (including artists).

In addition to the observations made earlier on improving BOD and/or POSH, current limitations of our systems include that we have not tested the platforms extensively on non-AI experts yet. In IVE, we do not have a neat editor yet, which makes specifying new virtual worlds and behaviour of agents slightly complicated for non computer scientists. The editor is current work. In Pogamut, perhaps the main problem is that it relies on Gamebots interface [1], which limits the amount of information passed from UT. Additionally, Gamebots code is not well optimised and has several bugs. Rewriting Gamebots is another work in-progress; we have already fixed some of the bugs. We also plan to incorporate Gamebots UT 2007.

Acknowledgement.

This work is partially supported by several grants. For Cyril Brom and Prague GA UK 351/2006/A-INF/MFF and "Information Society" 1ET100300517. For Joanna Bryson and Bath the EPSRC GR/S79299/01 (AIBACS). Jan Drugowitsch and Tristan Caulfield have assisted with BOD/MASON as developers and Hagen Lehmann as a naive tester.

References

[1] Adobbati, R., Marshall, A. N., Scholer, A., and Tejada, S.: Gamebots: A 3d virtual world test-bed for multi-agent research. In: Proceedings of the 2nd Int. Workshop on Infrastructure for Agents, MAS, and Scalable MAS, Montreal, Canada (2001)

[2] Alice 3D Authoring system. Alice v2.0. Carnegie Mellon University. Project homepage: http://www.alice.org/ [4th Aug 2006]

[3] AI.implant. EngenuityTechnologies, Inc. Product homepage: http://www.biographictech.com/ [4th Aug 2006]

[4] ACT-R. A cognitive architecture. ACT-R Research Group. Carnegie Mellon University Project homepage: http://act-r.psy.cmu.edu/ [11th Aug 2006]

[5] Extreme Programming Explained: Embrace Change. Addison Wesley (1999)

[6] Brom, C.: Hierarchical Reactive Planning: Where is its limit? In: Proceedings of MNAS: Modelling Natural Action Selection. Edinburgh, Scotland (2005)

[7] Brom, C., Lukavský, J., Serý, O., Poch, T., Safrata, P.: Affordances and level-of-detail AI for virtual humans. In: Proceedings of Game Set and Match 2, Delft (2006)

[8] Brom, C., Abonyi A.: Petri-Nets for Game Plot. In: Proceedings of AISB: Artificial Intelligence and Simulation Behaviour Convention, Bristol (2006) III, 6–13

[9] Brooks, R.: Intelligence without reason. In: Proceedings of the 1991 International Joint Conference on Artificial Intelligence, Sydney (1991) 569595

[10] Bryson, J.: Intelligence by Design: Principles of Modularity and Coordination for Engineering Complex Adaptive Agents. PhD thesis, Massachusetts Institute of Technology (2001)

[11] Bryson, J., Stein, A.L.: Modularity and Design in Reactive Intelligence. In: Proceedings of IJCAI'01 (2001)

[12] Bryson, J.: The Behavior-Oriented Design of Modular Agent Intelligence. In: Mueller, J. P. (eds.): Proceedings of Agent Technologies, Infrastructures, Tools, and Applications for E-Services, Springer LNCS 2592 (2003) 61-76

[13] J. J. Bryson, T. J. Caulfield, and J. Drugowitsch, "Integrating life-like action selection into cycle-based agent simulation environments," in *Proceedings of Agent 2005: Generative Social Processes, Models, and Mechanisms*, M. North, D. L. Sallach, and C. Macal, Eds. Chicago: Argonne National Laboratory, October 2005.

[14] Bryson, J.J., Prescott, T.J, Seth, A.K. (edited conference proceedings): Modelling Natural Action Selection: Proceedings of an International Workshop. AISB, UK (2005)

[15] Burket, O.: Unreal Tournament Twins. Bachelor thesis. Charles University in Prague, Czech Republic (2006) (in Czech)

[16] Champandard, A.J.: AI Game Development: Synthetic Creatures with Learning and Reactive Behaviors. New Riders (2003)

[17] JACK toolkit. Agent Oriented Software Group. Project homepage: http://www.agent-software.com/shared/home/ [4th Aug 2006]

[18] Kaminka, G. A., Veloso, M. M., Schaffer, S., Sollitto, C., Adobbati, R., Marshall, A. N., Scholer, A. and Tejada, S., "GameBots: A flexible test bed for multiagent team research," *Communications of the ACM*, 45(1):43–45 (2002)

[19] Kirschner, F.: Movie Sand BOX. Project homepage: http://www.moviesandbox.com/ [4th Aug 2006] (2006)

[20] Kwong, A.: A Framework for Reactive Inteligence through Agile Component-Based Behaviors. Master's thesis, Department of Computer Science, University of Bath (2003)

[21] S. Luke, G. C. Balan, L. Panait, C. Cioffi-Revilla, and S. Paus, "MASON: A Java multi-agent simulation library," in *Proceedings of Agent 2003: Challenges in Social Simulation*, D. L. Sallach and C. Macal, Eds. Argonne, IL: Argonne National Laboratory, 2003, pp. 49–64.

[22] Maes, P. The agent network architecture (ANA). In: SIGART Bulletin, 2 (4) (1991) 115-120

[23] Muñoz-Avila H., Hoang H.: "Coordinating Teams of Bots with Hierarchical Task Network Planning," in *AI Game Programming Wisdom I*, S. Rabin, Ed. Charles River Media, Inc., Hingham, Massachusetts (2006)

[24] O'Sullivan C., Cassell J., Vilhjálmsson H., Dingliana J., Dobbyn S., McNamee B., Peters C., Giang T. "Level of Detail for Crowds and Groups," in *Computer Graphics Forum*, 21(4):733–742 (2002)

[25] Orkin, J.: 3 States and a Plan: The AI of F.E.A.R. Game Developer's Conference Proceedings. San Francisco, CA (2006)

[26] Partington, S.J., Bryson, J.J.: The Behavior Oriented Design of an Unreal Tournament Character. In: Proceedings of IVA'05, LNAI 3661, Springer (2005)

[27] Pluchick, R.: Emotion: A Psychoevolutionary Synthesis. Harper and Row, New York (1980)

[28] Soar architecture. University of Michigan, USA. Project homepage: http://sitemaker.umich.edu/soar [4th Aug 2006] (2006)

[29] Softimage/Behavior. Softimage Co. Avid Technology. Homepage: http://www.softimage.com/ [4th Aug 2006]

[30] Serý, O., Poch, T., Safrata, P., Brom, C.: Level-Of-Detail in Behaviour of Virtual Humans. In: Proceedings of SOFSEM 2006: Theory and Practice of Computer Science, LNCS 3831, Czech Republic (2006) 565–574

[31] E. A. R. Tanguy, P. J. Willis, and J. J. Bryson, "A dynamic emotion representation model within a facial animation system," *The International Journal of Humanoid Robotics*, 2006.

[32] Unreal Tournament. Epic Games, Inc. Product homepage http://unrealtournament.com [4th Aug 2006]

[33] Wilensky, U. NetLogo. Center for Connected Learning and Computer-Based Modeling. Northwestern University, Evanston, IL. Project homepage: http://ccl.northwestern.edu/netlogo/ [4th Aug 2006] (1999)

Cyril Brom is a PhD candidate situated at Charles University, Prague. His research interest is in modelling artificial environments and behaviour of human-like artificial agents. Additionally, he teaches courses on modelling and computer games development and supervises about a dozen undergraduate students, whose theses concern gaming AI. He holds Magister (Master equivalent) in computer science and optimisation from the Faculty of Mathematics-Physics, Charles University in Prague.

Jakub Gemrot is a Magister (Masters equivalent) candidate situated at Charles University, Prague. His interests are artificial environments and software engineering. He holds a Bachelors in computer science from the Faculty of Mathematics-Physics, Charles University in Prague.

Michal Bída is a Magister (Masters equivalent) candidate. His interests are artificial intelligence in computer games, especially those featuring 3D virtual environment, artificial emotions and psychology. He holds Bachelor in computer science from Faculty of Mathematics-Physics, Charles University in Prague.

Sam Partington undertook a major evaluation of Behavior Oriented Design as part of studies at the University of Bath. His interests include both the practical and theoretical aspects of this methodology and of AI in general. Having obtained a BSc from Bath in 2005, he currently works in Software Development for RM Consultants, a company in Abingdon, Oxfordshire, UK.

Ondrej Burket is a student of the masters program at Charles University, Prague. His main interest is in gaming artificial intelligence, his last work concerned a couple of cooperating agents in UT. He holds Bachelor degree in general computer science from the Faculty of Mathematics-Physics, Charles University in Prague.

Joanna Bryson lectures computer science at the University of Bath; she founded her research group there in 2002 following a postdoc in the Primate Congitive Neuroscience Laboratory at Harvard. Her research interests include increasing access to building intelligent systems and using these techniques to model intelligence as found in nature. She holds a BA in Psychology from Chicago, Masters in AI and Psychology from Edinburgh, and a PhD from the MIT AI Laboratory.

Is Agent-Oriented Programming Ready for Computer Games? *

Juan Reverte, Abel Bernabeu, Francisco Gallego, Faraón Llorens
Department of Computer Science and Artificial Intelligence
University of Alicante
Ctra. San Vicente del Raspeig s/n, Alicante, Spain
{jreverte,abelbg,fgallego,faraon}@dccia.ua.es

keywords. Agent-Oriented, Software Paradigms, Methodology, JADE

Abstract

Despite of the fact that computer games technology has evolved incredibly in many areas, we still feel some lack of innovation about design and programming paradigms used by software engineers in the Computer Games industry. Although new interesting paradigms have been proposed by academics, the industry still remains using Object-Oriented modelling and programming as it was more than ten years ago.

Our work focuses on applying the Agent-Oriented paradigm to Computer Games directly, so as to obtain feasibility and performance results. For our purpose we use the JADE Agent-Oriented platform which complies with the FIPA standard and it is open source.

We have developed 3 proof-of-concept games of different genres to probe their feasibility and measure their performance. Our results show that there are several genres of games which could benefit from Agent-Oriented Programming because of its distributed nature, for instance, MMORPGs.

1 Introduction

Computer Games are quite young: the very first Computer Games were born approximately 35 years ago. During these years the technological revolution has been incredible, especially in the area of graphics. Nevertheless, in spite of this revolution, patterns used in the development of games have not evolved so much.

At the very beginning, games where developed by one or two people at most, using assembler language directly, with almost no design phase at all. Those games were pretty simple like Pong or Frogger, and they did not have enough requirements to set up a development cycle for them. The hardware evolution gave enough power to use high-level languages for games and structured programming appeared in the trenches in the eighties. Development time grew from days/weeks to months, and developer groups of 3 up to 8 or 10 people started their journey. Assembler was not forgotten, but its use started to be relegated to kernel routines.

Once again, in the early nineties, the hardware revolution lead game development to the next stage. Structured Programming was progressively replaced by the Object-Oriented paradigm. Assembler language continued to decrease in use in favor of design and algorithm-level optimizations and improvements. Greater groups started to create greater and greater games and 3D graphics engines led the industry to its height.

Now some games are completely distributed applications needing to address new issues like scalability for supporting an increasing number of players, interoperability between complex software components and highly heterogeneous communications. The communications are heterogeneous in the sense of not being just constrained to the strict roles assignment of the classical client/server model, where there is just a unique centralized authority for informing the state of the game. Now some clients can make tasks of game state management in order to reduce the load of the game server or interaction latencies.

In the last decade, lots of new software development paradigms have been presented in the academic field in order to solve those problems. The Internet is guilty of the present revolution and the Agent-Oriented paradigm is the one which has been born in its lap. This new paradigm arises with the aim of profiting from the spread nature of the net to power up computers and communications to the next level. Nevertheless, developers are still distrusted about this new manner of thinking. Although the potential benefits of Agent Oriented Modeling are clear and substantial, it is still

*This work has been supported by the spanish Generalitat Valenciana, project number GV05/165

not proven that this benefits outperform the potential development costs.

The Agent-Oriented paradigm is widely used in academic fields and has many applications [1][2]; nevertheless its performance for the use by the general public has not been proven. This work aims to evaluate the feasibility and performance of the Agent-Oriented paradigm in the field of Computer Games [3][4]. Moreover, we pursue not only establishing present measurements, but also obtaining conclusions about future possibilities of making breakthroughs by using this technology. In summary we will try to find a symbiosis between games and Agent-Oriented programming. All the experiments we present in this paper are conducted using the Java Agent-Development Framework (JADE, [5]).

In this paper the work that we have done at the University of Alicante using JADE as a platform for multiplayer games is explained. Section 2 gives a short explanation about what Agent-Oriented Programming and JADE are. Section 3 details the 3 games that have been developed, their general concepts, their problems and the reasons for implementing them. Section 4 shows the data collected during the experiments, with a visual representation to give them a practical utility. Finally, section 5 presents a discussion about the viability of making games using JADE, and illustrates the conclusions of our work and ideas which will act as guidelines for future research.

2 Agent-Oriented Programming

There is a huge variety of definitions of Agent, but the one we think to be more complete is the one given by [6]: "Agents are computational systems that inhabit some complex dynamic environment, sense and act autonomously in this environment, and by doing so realize a set of goals or tasks for which they are designed". That is to say, the agents incorporate behaviour to their actions. This is the principal difference between objects and agents.

The Object-Oriented languages have the necessary elements to code common tasks done by agents. Nevertheless, when complex internal states and communication between the objects are needed the agent oriented programming can be a better alternative. The agent concept adds to the objects a dynamic dimension, because each agent has his own objectives and rules. Thinking in agents has even more sense when they are part of a multi-agent system where they cooperate or compete with other agents.

Agent-Oriented Programming is totally aimed to take advantage from communications in computer networks. The idea of running several agents, each one in a different computer, is inherent to the paradigm. This means that programmers do not have to worry about network issue, and they can concentrate their effort in the system itself. Agent-Oriented Programming also takes into account agent distribution across computers (the deployment) and hides the nasty details about agent migration (an object could not easily travel across computers while an agent can). These are the main advantages which Agent-Oriented Programming gives to developers.

A lot of organizations are involved in the development of protocols and tools for Agent-Oriented Programming. The Foundation for Intelligent Physical Agents (FIPA)[7] is an international association created with the objective of produce specifications of generic agent technologies. In order to promote interoperability between agent platforms, a number of standard Message Transport Protocols (MTPs) have been defined by FIPA. On the other hand, there exist different development environments to build agents systems: Zeus ([8]), RETSINA ([9]) and AgentBuilder ([10]) among others. For our tests we have used the JADE platform, which is described next.

2.1 JADE Overview

JADE (Java Agent Development Framework) [7] is a FIPA compliant agent platform. JADE is written in Java and offers different advantages for the developers of multi-agent systems:

- Distributed environment.

  JADE is composed of several run-time agent containers, each one of them running on a Java Virtual Machine. Each container provides services for one or more agents. This allows us to distribute agents by different computers connected by a network, balancing between them the load of the system.

- A FIPA platform for the execution of agents and the management of communication between them.

  In JADE all agents communication is performed by messages following the FIPA protocols. The GUID (Global Unique Identifier) allows referencing uniquely an agent and is independent of the agent location. The GUID is automatically assigned by the the platform at agent creation time. When the agents are executed in the same platform, JADE uses internal message transport protocols (IMTPs). Each agent have an incoming message queue whose messages can be filtered by different fields such as sender, ontology or performative.

- A set of packages for the programming of these agents.

  In JADE, agents reactions are implemented by means of behaviours. These behaviours are execution threads and they are the core of the agent. JADE uses one thread per agent instead. The behaviours are executed in a round robin policy among all behaviours (one per agent every time) available in the queue. There exists three big types of behaviours:

1. One-shot: They are executed instantaneously and only one time.
2. Cyclic: They are always executed while the agent remain alive.
3. Generic : Their code is executed depending the status of the agent.

All these characteristics can be used for programming a simple videogame, especially the network capabilities. In the next sections we will explain the three games which we have implemented and we will show the parts in which the use of Agent-Oriented programming has been more usefulg.

3 Games battery

In order to conduct our evaluation of the Agent-Oriented paradigm and the JADE platform we choosed to develop a battery of games of increasing complexity. The development process should allow us to acquire knowledge of the tools, methodology to be adopted and problems derived of its use.

Instead of inventing new game concepts and looking for original play modes we prefered to develop common genres. This decision was adopted in order to be able to extract results of general interest and saving the long time needed to develop very unique game concepts, since we wanted to focus our work on the software architectures.

Three games of increasing complexity were chosen, each one more resources demanding than the previous one. During the experimentation the machine-resources consumption was measured. We hope our results will be useful for evaluating the convenience of using JADE in more resources-demanding games, in addition to the intrinsic advantages of using the Agent-Oriented paradigm. The three chosen games were:

- Battleships
- Galaxians.
- Micro MMORPG

3.1 Battleships

This one is based on the traditional board game. A player can create a new game or joining a game already created by another player, in such a way that several players can compete. Their common objective is sinking their opponents' boats until all the opponents but one has got all his boats sinked.

The playing turn is rotatory assigned by a neutral entity not controlled by any player in order to avoid any cheating. The fact that the turn is rotatory assigned assures that two players will never be allowed to alter the game state simultaneously.

Our chosen game was simple but still useful as a first step towards testing the capabilities of JADE. The architecture is build as an agenthood of entities having all the basic elements of a common JADE agent: a user interface (in instance based on Swing), an Agent class implementation, mechanisms of communication with other agents and some behaviours.

We can summarize the requisites of the system as follows:

- A server entity allows players to look for and create games on the net.
- On any game board one or more players can play.
- The dimensions of the game board as well as the number and type of the boats will be decided by the players.

These specifications conditioned a design with three types of agents (see figure 1):

- Player Agent: He creates the games and plays them.
- Board Agent: He maintains the game state and manages the turns of the Player Agents.
- Server Agent: He creates new games, registers the active ones and transfers incoming players to the corresponding Board Agent.

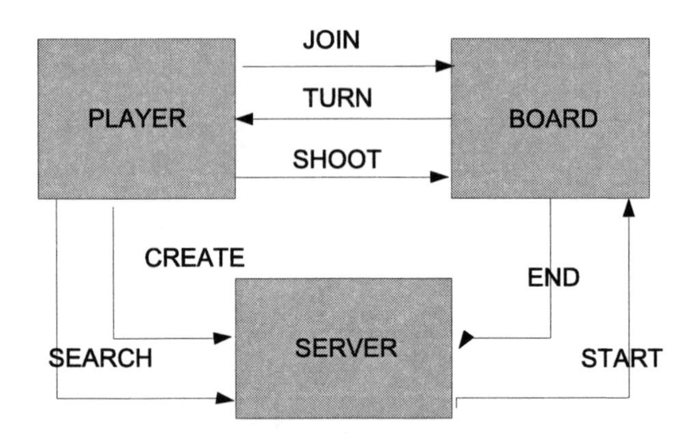

Figure 1. BattleShip scheme

3.2 Galaxians

The original Galaxians game was one of the first games to appear on the market. A fleet of alien space ships gradually comes down from the top of the screen while the player controls his ship at the bottom line of the screen trying avoid colliding with the aliens or destroying them before the they reach the bottom of the screen. In addition, since Internet is our primary target, the Galaxians game that we developed (see figure 2) admits the multiplayer game mode through a network.

Additionally to the JADE capabilities already proven with the Battleship game, this game adds the need of modifying the world state in real time. Several players must be able to modify a shared world and be aware of the modifications done by other players imposing a new level of difficulty to our software architecture.

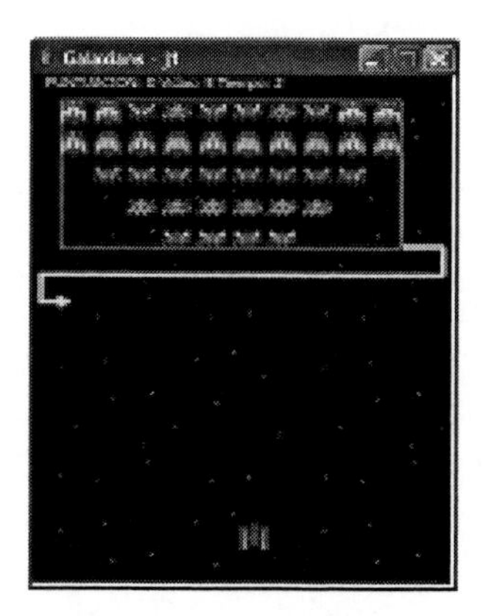

Figure 2. Ship movement

This time, the number agent classes will be 4: Enemy, Alien, Player and Server. The Enemy Agent creates an Alien Agent for each individual alien. Its objective is to move all the Aliens from their starting position at the top left corner of the screen to the bottom left corner. The Aliens have a fixed position with respect to each other and move simultaneously as a block without breaking their rank. They move as a block because individual movement would create too many messages. At random intervals during the game an Alien breaks rank to dive-bomb the player and then returns to his position (if he does not get destroyed by a player shot).

The difficulty in this game lays in the synchronization between the player perception (what he is seeing on his monitor) and what is actually happening. This happens because instances of agent classes are executed as independent processes in separate machines. Therefore, each machine has a local copy of the world in which the game takes place; these copies, obviously, must be as similar as possible. Meaning that if an Alien moves within the limits of his local world, then the rest of the agents must be informed so that they can update their own local worlds.

3.3 Micro MMORPG

The intention in this 3rd game was that the agents had an important weight as characters within the game, therefore, increasing the processing load. The ideal type of game for these tests is denominated Massive Multiplayer Online Role Playing Game or MMORPG. In this type of game many players enter in a continuous virtual world and interact among them and with the environment. In these games hundreds or even thousands of individual agents interact, each representing a different role within the game (an old man, a horse, a troll, a salesman and so on). In this case, if each role is handled in an independent manner by an instance of an agent class, the processing load on the system can be completely distributed. Thanks to this, virtual worlds can be created of a much greater size and with a greater amount of simultaneous characters.

The design specifications of this game can be summarized as follows:

- Server Agent: There only exists one for each virtual world. It handles the information about the players, characteristics, state of play, scores, characteristics, etc. It is responsible for maintaining the continuity of the virtual world, and hence the game.
- World Agent: One exists for each zone of the map into which the world is divided. This makes it easy to add new zones to the game and, additionally, each zone can be executed in a different machine, so increasing the distribution.
- Player Agent: He has all the common actions to create any game character, independently of who it is controlled by. From him derive all the types of players that could be used in the game. In our example game the derivatives are: Agent Jugador, Agent Monstruo, and Agent Personaje No Jugador (Controlled by the IA).

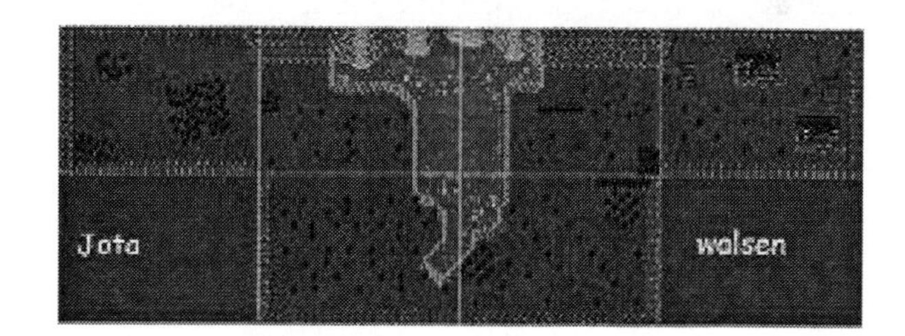

Figure 3. Map of the game

4 Experimentation

Our objective is to prove the feasibility of developing games with JADE. After running the three proposed concept tests, performance results were obtained for each test.

These results were generated using different tests carried out according to the type and characteristics of each game.

The term "connect time" is given to the time lapse between the instant in which the player creates or searches for a game in the server and the instant in which the result is received by the player. We will distingish if the player has created, looked for or aggregated him to the game. The tests have been made using a WLAN (54 Mbps) connection.

4.1 Tests for Battleship Game

Because the players act "in turns" large scale communication between them is not necessary. For this reason, in this game we have measured the time that passes from the moment an agent shoots until the moment a result is received. This provides an idea of the speed of answer that the player will perceive.

4.1.1 Test 1: The machine that is used as the server is also used by the player who creates the initial match, and is joined by another player using a different machine.

- Connect time from Local Player, creating match 39,23 ms.
- Connect time from Remote Player, searching match 58,73 ms.

The player using the server does not have any time problem, as he receives the answers in an average time of 23.53 ms. Nevertheless, the remote player has a pair of peaks of answer of 5 s, which gives an average answer time of 569 ms (half a second). These peaks take place 2 or 3 times per game which could make the average time erroneous, for this reason we also calculated the medium time which gave a value of 21.51ms for the local player and 26.58 ms for the remote player, satisfactory readings so that players do not lose the sensation of interaction.

4.1.2 Test 2: Creation of two simultaneous games

- Connect time for Local Player, creating match 90,98 ms.
- Connect time for Remote Player, searching match 5378,36 ms.

In this case, the games are created simultaneously, which explains the delays (see figure 4). The average response time for local player was 21,74 ms and 20,13 ms medium, whereas the remote player was 256,22 ms average and 21,02 ms medium.

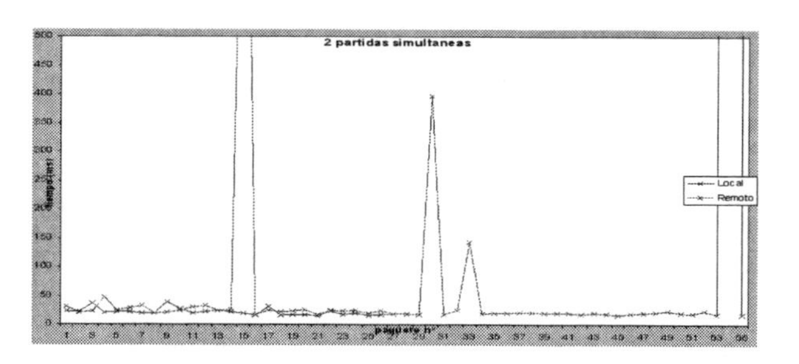

Figure 4. Resulting wait times with two games running simultaneously

4.2 Tests for Galaxians

With this game, the aim of the tests is to discover the differences between the transmission times of a message (in this case the death of an Alien agent) to all the agents in the game. The message is sent by the player who killed the Alien to the enemy agent who then communicates it to the other agents and to the Alien. Our interest is centered in knowing the time needed for the message to be received by all players: when an Alien dies he must disappear from the screens of all the other players as soon as possible.

In order to obtain the graphs the average time was calculated for a message of the death of an Alien to be received by all the implied agents and we have subtracted the individual time for each agent. We have repeated the measurement for the death of each Alien. With this data we represent the time difference with respect to the ideal reception time (0).

4.2.1 Test 1: The local player creates the game; the remote player joins.

- The time of life of the REMOTE player is 21.88s, 422 packages sent and received, average of 19.3 packages per second.
- The time of life of the LOCAL player is 23,74 s , 463 packages sent and received, average of 19,5 packages per second.
- The time of life of the ENEMY is 24,02 s , 319 packages sent and received, average of 13,3 packages per second.

In the figure 5 we can see the plot of a number of latency times in the arrival to all the Player agents of the Alien-death notifications. We can observe that less than 100 ms are needed to get all the Player agents informed of an Alien death.

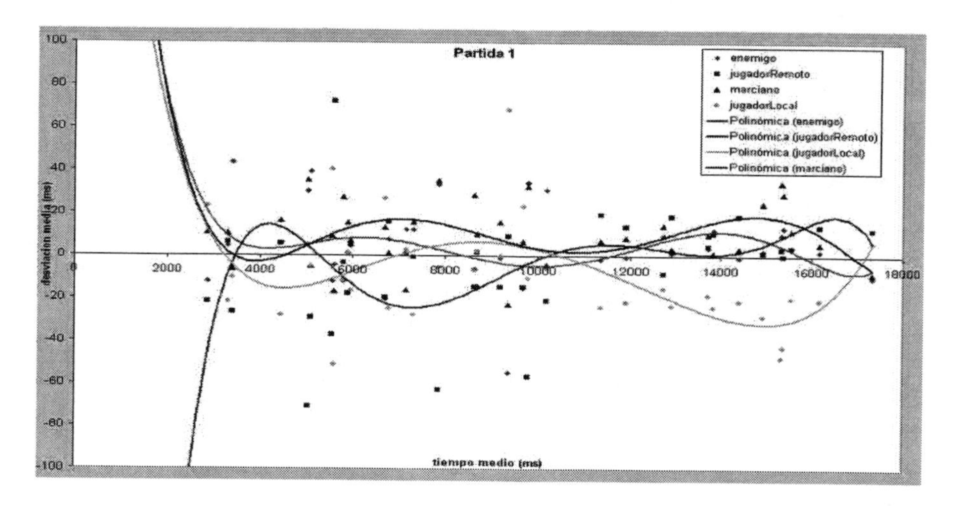

Figure 5. Latency times in the arrival of Alien death messages to all the player Agents.

4.2.2 Test 2: The remote player creates the game, the local player joins.

- The time of life of the REMOTE player is 30,24s , 600 packages sent and received, average of 19.8 packages per second.
- The time of life of the LOCAL player is 25,67 , 467 packages sent and received, average of 18.1 packages per second.
- The time of life of the ENEMY is 30,91s , 339 packages sent and received, average of 10,9 packages per second.

Results from this game are very similar to the previous game, with respect to the tendency of the lines. Nevertheless, now the time necessary to inform all of the agents of the death of an Alien is approaching 200 ms.. This is because it is the remote player who creates the game and lodges the Enemy Agent, and also the reason for message conflicts.

4.3 Tests for Micro MMORPG

This game has certain similarities with the Galaxians game but now the trajectories are not previously defined and can change randomly throughout the game. In addition to the fact that there can be hundreds and thousands of agents in one game, that must also know the position of all the other agents.

In order to avoid the passing of positional messages back and forth between the agents creating saturation, all the other agents receive only an advice of our movement intentions, that is to say, our present position, destination position and speed of movement. The other players have to make predictions based only on this information as they are only informed again if the vector speed of the player in movement changes.

The aim of these tests is to see the level of synchronization between the agents. Can the user see the rest of agents in their real location? In order to respond to this question we are going to represent the view that each agent has of the rest of agents that he wishes to know their location (see figure 6).

In the graph, the circles show the real position and the crosses the position estimated by the other characters. As we can see, the synchronization is not perfect, but it is more than acceptable given that the maximum difference in the graph representing the X coordinate is only 20 pixels.

The peaks that appears between seconds 73 and 77 are due to a change of zone of the player. Therefore, synchronization messages were not sent to the rest of the agents, who imagined that the original movement continues, until they were informed of the change of screen.

When two agents begin a battle they send each other messages of attack every half a second. This can result in them not receiving the synchronization movement messages from the rest of the agents in time and getting them unsynchronized until the next message.

5 Conclusions

In this paper we have exposed some of the limitations of the present methodologies of programming applied to the world of computer games. Agent-oriented programming is proposed as a possible change of methodology for a future where Internet will be the undoubted protagonist. We have used 3 small computer games with increasing resource requirements as concept tests to study the viability of the change. The platform used for these experiments was JADE.

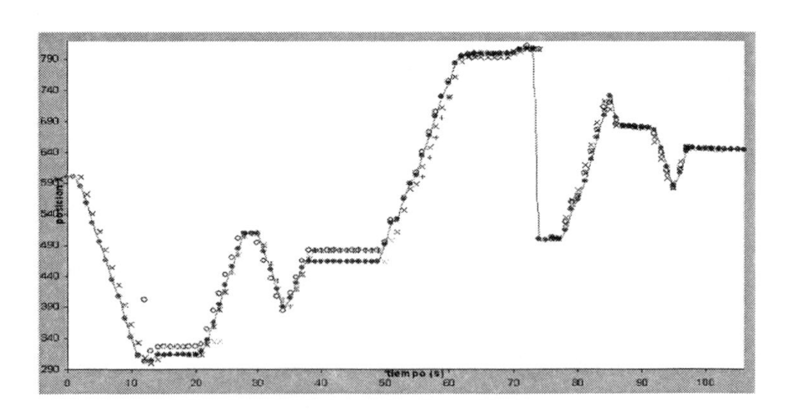

Figure 6. Predicted player position related to the real one

After the experiments, analysis of the results and conclusions reveals them to be more positive than expected. In spite of having to run the 3 games in JADE, and being accustomed to an interpreted environment such as Java, the performance has not been affected alarmingly. In the network test, although we had protocols added for the communication between the agents, the results demonstrate that the difference is not appreciable, even in games like the Mini MMORPG, where the amount of agents implies an increase of the bandwidth for the increasing amount of messages.

On the other hand, the advantages noted during the experiments of the agent-oriented programming were:

1) Greater development speed of the games once the programming paradigm is controlled. Being at an optimum level, the concepts to be treated treat appear more natural, especially the communication.

2) Distribution of process with a practically zero development cost. Being part of the actual paradigm means that the mere fact of designing classes of agents instead of classes of objects takes an implicit distribution of the load; something that in the Object Oriented paradigm would require an additional effort.

3) Simple design for the scalability of the system. To be able to duplicate agents with the same simplicity as duplicating objects in other languages makes the system scalable without added design effort. This is very desirable for servers that control thousands of simultaneous players.

Naturally, not all of the results are positive, although the disadvantages found will surely be resolved in the near future. The origins of the major problems lie in the difficulty of debugging of agent orientated systems because they are inherently distributed and powerful debugging tools are still unavailable. Another problem is the lack of development-methodologies of reusables agents, unlike Object Oriented Paradigm, where design patterns exist.

Our final conclusion is that JADE is a suitable platform for experimentation but, at the present time, for the development of commercial Computer Games that operate at the maximum capacity of each machine, the development of a similar platform in C++ or another recognised language would be interesting. We believe that Agent-oriented paradigms represent an evolution created by the Internet, and this evolution must be incorporated slowly to allow it to mature.

Acknowledgement

We want to specially thank Francisco Luis Morote Malaga and Juan Manuel Sabater Guillo for their work and effort developing the three games presented here.

References

[1] Bigus J., Jennifer B. (2001): Constructing Intelligent Agents using Java. Wiley Computer Publishing.

[2] Bellifemine F., Poggi A., Rimassi G.(1999) JADE: A FIPA-Compliant agent framework, Proceeding Practical Applications of Intelligent Agents and Multi-Agents (http://sharon.cselt.it/projects/jade)

[3] Morote, F. L. (2006): Agentes inteligentes y videojuegos escalables: JADE, vision del jugador. Master Thesis. Departamento de Ciencia de la Computacion e Inteligencia Artificial. Universidad de Alicante.

[4] Sabater, J. M. (2006): Agentes inteligentes y videojuegos escalables: JADE, vision del servidor. Master Thesis. Departamento de Ciencia de la Computacion e Inteligencia Artificial. Universidad de Alicante.

[5] Vitaglione, G., Quarta, F., and Cortese E. (2002): Scalability and Performance of JADE Message Transport System In AAMAS Workshop, Bologna, 2002.

[6] Maes, P. Agents That Reduce Work and Information Overload. Software Agents. Cambridge, MA: MIT Press. 1997.

[7] FIPA - Foundation for Intelligent Physical Agents. http://www.fipa.org.

[8] Collis, J. and Ndumu, D.: Zeus Technical Manual. Intelligent Systems Research Group BT Labs. British Telecommunications. (1999)

[9] Sycara, K., Paolucci, M., van Velsen, M. and Giampapa, J. The RETSINA MAS Infrastructure. Accepted by the Journal of Autonomous Agents and Multi-agent Systems (JAAMS).

[10] Reticular Systems Inc AgentBuilder An Integrated Toolkit for Constructing Intelligent Software Agents. (1999) http://www.agentbuilder.com

BIOGRAPHY

Juan R. Reverte graduated in computer science in 2005 at the University of Alicante. He is Actually scholar and PhD student and works as researcher and programmer in the Screaming Racers videogame project. His current research interests are in the fields of Intelligent Agents, Multi-Agent Cooperation, Computer Games and Evolutionary Computing.

Abel M. Bernabeu is a game programmer with some experience in the field of computer graphics. Between 1999 and 2005 he studied Computer Engineering in Alicante University (Spain). In the last years he has been doing some independent research in computer graphics, mainly in the LOD field. Currently he is working at I3A Group of Alicante University where he develops some software tools used by the group in their research activity.

Francisco J. Gallego works as assistant professor at Alicante University and has long experience in designing and programming Computer Games. Francisco Gallego read his MSc Thesis in Computer Science in 2003 at the Alicante University and is currently working on his PhD Thesis about Neuroevolution, Generic Machine Learning and Computer Games. His research interests cover the fields of Human-Level AI, Computer Games, Game-AI, Machine Learning, Neural Networks, Genetic Algorithms, A-Life and Bayesian Programming. He is a member of the AEPIA (spanish society for AI research).

Faraón Llorens was born in Spain in 1961. Received a degree in Computer Science from Polytechnic University of Valencia in 1993 and a PhD from Alicante University in 2001. Since 1994 has been linked to the Alicante Universtiy, where currently is a cathedratic. His research activity has been centered in the field of artificial intelligence (logics, reasoning, vision and intelligent agents) and the application of the digital technologies to the education (didactics of computing, intelligent tutoring...). He is a member of the AEPIA. Since January of 2005 he is vice-chancellor of "Technology and Educative Innovation" at Alicante University.

Graphics & Visualisation (1)

Virtual Reality Games for Motor Rehabilitation

M. Ma[1], M. D. J. McNeill[1], D. Charles[1], S. McDonough[2] and J. Crosbie[2]
[1] School of Computing and Information Engineering,
[2] Health and Rehabilitation Sciences Research Institute,
University of Ulster,
Northern Ireland
E-mail: mdj.mcneill@ulster.ac.uk

KEYWORDS

Serious games, Virtual Reality (VR), rehabilitation.

ABSTRACT

Dynamics provides realistic motion of virtual objects by simulating the behaviour of virtual objects and their responses to external force and torque based on the laws of physics. It has been successfully applied in various fields such as engineering, medicine, training, and high-quality 3D games, but few VR therapy systems currently support physics. This paper presents opportunities for applying physics simulation techniques in post-stroke VR therapy and discusses their potential therapeutic benefits to upper limb motor rehabilitation. A framework for physically-based VR rehabilitation systems is described which consists of functional tasks, such as grasping and catching, and game scenarios designed to encourage patients' physical activity. Activity takes place in hihly motivating, physics-enriched virtual environments where collision response, gravity, restitution, and kinematics are simulated and factors such as gravity and restitution can be scaled to adapt to individual patient's abilities.

INTRODUCTION

The use of Virtual Reality (VR) technology and computer games in motor rehabilitation has been shown in the literature to be an effective way of providing enjoyable and motivating tasks which can be graded to facilitate the rehabilitation process. To date the application of VR to rehabilitation has focussed extensively on using the technology to encourage patients to practise active functional tasks in virtual environments. Many studies have identified the benefits of using VR in rehabilitation to improve balance, endurance, dexterity, speed and range of motion (Viau et al. 2004, Holden et al. 2005).

Currently, most VR applications in rehabilitation simulate real life activities such as grasping and manipulating objects or performing everyday tasks e.g., pick-and-place virtual objects (Viau et al. 2004, Kuttuva et al. 2005), shop in a virtual mall (Rand et al. 2004), or cross a street (Katz et al. 2004). These VR systems help patients enhance improve functional ability and realise greater participation in community life. However, object animations in most VR therapy systems are pre-rendered and hence not realistic in terms of physical simualation. This paper reports on our system for stroke rehabilitation which supports physically-based modelling.

DYNAMICS IN VR THERAPY

Physically based simulation creates realistic motions of virtual objects based on the laws of physics. The behaviour of virtual objects and their responses to external force and torque are simulated in a physically realistic manner. Physics simulation models objects with physical properties, such as mass, inertia, barycentre, joint limitations, restitution and surface friction - it can make objects in virtual worlds not only *look real* but *act real*. Typical dynamics simulation includes collision detection (CD) and the simulation of gravity, friction force, torque, kinematics in motor actions, fluid and cloth. Physics can be applied to rigid bodies or deformable bodies (e.g., human tissues). Rigid body dynamics plays an important role in VR motor rehabilitation and is especially needed when dextrous manipulation of virtual objects is concerned. Here we focus on rigid body dynamics including mechanics and kinematics.

Physically-based simulation has been successfully used in various fields such as engineering (Li et al. 1998, Pohland et al. 2002), medicine, training, education, interactive games and vehicle and surgery simulation (Müller and Teschner 2003), but currently few VR therapy systems support physically based simulation beyond simple collision detection. In many VR therapy systems, broad phase collision response where approximate collisions between objects are detected is the only aspect of physics which is supported.

The advantage of using VR in clinical settings is that by virtue of its programmability, environments and the type and difficulty of tasks can be modified according to the user's capacities and therapeutic goals. Physics simulation provides more flexibility on experiment configuration in which not only object positions, orientations, size can be modified but also gravity, restitution, force and torque damper, joint limitations, etc. can be reliably modified, thereby providing the potential for a very individualised set of rehabilitation exercises to be created. These exercises can then be reliably recreated over a period of several weeks or months and patient outcome can be assessed. The addition of physics to the VR therapy may increase patients' experience of immersion in Virtual Environments (VE), which may in turn increase engagement and activity enjoyment and thereby improve rehabilitation.

The Rutgers Arm upper-extremity rehabilitation system (Kuttava et al. 2005) trains arm/shoulder movement through a sequence of pick-and-place exercises and a 'Breakout3D' game. Since the system only uses one sensor attached on the user's wrist and doesn't use a dataglove to sense hand movements, the grasping and release is achieved by a proximity-action triggering facility, i.e., when the virtual hand is in the proximity of the object, a predetermined grasping action is triggered; a release action is triggered once the virtual hand is at the edge of the target box. If the user opens his hand, the grabbed object will not be released and drop as in the real world, since the grasping and releasing animations are predetermined. Broad phase collision detection algorithms in the Breakout3D game allow the user to use a prismatic paddle to hit a ball in a particular direction and destroy a number of blocks placed on a game board.

Kurillo et al. 2005 present a '3By6' fingertip force input device to measure the fingertip forces and torques of thumb, index and middle fingers, and apply them in a virtual environment aimed at the rehabilitation of hand function for stroke patients, doing tasks such as opening a safe, filling and pouring water from a glass, and playing with an elastic torus. In the grasping task, the object is grasped when two or three fingers in opposition are in contact with the object.

This paper discusses various aspects of physically-based simulation before presenting a framework for VR therapy for motor rehabilitation incorporating both functional tasks and game activities. The integration of dynamic simulation with conventional clinical therapy and game-like scenarios adds richness to the virtual environment which has the potential for improving patient outcome.

PHYSICS FIDELITY AND LEVEL-OF-DETAIL

It could be argued that an aim of immersive VR is to simulate as far as possible the range and intensity of stimuli that human senses detect and interpret in perceiving the natural world, which leads to a quest for photorealism, 3D audio, haptic and even olfactory feedback. Previous VR research has focussed extensively on achieving high visual fidelity to improve the sense of presence experienced by people in the virtual world. Relationships between graphic realism and perceptual realism have been investigated and many studies (Riva et al. 2003, Hwang et al. 2004) have identified visual factors of fidelity that affect presence in VR such as stereoscopy, bodily interaction, head tracking, field-of-view, shadow, geometric detail (i.e. polygon numbers of objects), texture resolution, illumination models, and object motion.

While many researchers have reported on perceptual response to physically-based simulation in general VR systems there has to date been little reporting of physically-based VR therapy systems. It may be the case that accurate physics simulation in VR therapy systems does not improve patient outcome, but, equally, physically based simulation may prove beneficial. We suspect that support for realistic physics within a VE simulation will increase the feeling of immersion that the user experiences, which may result in better engagement and subsequently, improved rehabilitation. These are the issues we are addressing with this research.

Physics Fidelity

Physics realism can be displayed by both visual and haptic modalities. Many physically-based VR systems use haptic devices, such as PHANTOM, VTI CyberGrasp, and SPIDAR (Sato 2001), to render force feedback which contributes to realism by adding kinaesthetic perception. There is a distinction between physics and haptics. Haptics is an efficient way to present physics force feedback. Feedback of physics simulation includes visual, auditory display (e.g. sound effects of impact), and haptics. Haptic feedback can be partially substituted by a low-cost alternative such as visual force feedback where the haptic information is simulated through visual cues presented to the user.

Borst and Indugula 2005 proposed a spring model to simulate collision response in realistic virtual grasping where sensor data acquired from the dataglove, i.e., the "tracked hand", are suspended when a collision is detected, and unrealistic hand motion such as the virtual hand penetrating a virtual object is therefore avoided. Visual feedback is improved by keeping the virtual hand outside of the object, though the visual feedback no longer accurately represents the real hand movements. Crison et al. 2004 use pseudo-haptic feedback in technical training of milling. Resistance in the milling process is simulated by changing the ratio of the speed of hand movement (control) to the speed of the virtual object manipulated in the simulation (display). When a milling tool (the virtual object controlled by an input device) is carving a workpiece, the control/display ratio is modified and the speed of the tool is decreased on the computer screen to simulate the resistance. A strong resistance of the material is associated with large deceleration of the tool on screen. These are typical examples of using visual feedback substitution for haptics in physics simulation.

Consider the pick-and-place task in the Rutgers Arm system (Kuttava et al. 2005). In a physics-based simulation the object will fall from the hand if the user opens his hand during transportation and drop on the table top; it will probably bounce once or twice, usually rotating as it bounces, before coming to rest. Accurate physics simulation, however desirable, is nonetheless computationally demanding and may not be necessary for all applications. Users may not care about or be sensitive to all aspects of a physics simulation. The fidelity of a physics simulation may be compromised in order to reduce computational cost, provided the user is either unable to detect the difference or is unaware that the physics in the virtual world is not *correct*. O'Sullivan et al. 2003 propose a set of probability functions that could be used to evaluate the visual fidelity of a physically based simulation.

The quality of physics that is required in a simulation is application specific. In the cognitive and affective domains of learning, high physical fidelity is not always required, such as situations where the focus of training is more on attitudes. However, in medical simulation such as surgery planning and training, high quality physical fidelity is so important that without it the skills acquired in the virtual world may not transfer to the real one.

Research suggests that physics fidelity may be important for motor rehabilitation. Viau et al. 2004 compared movement kinematics of identical tasks of reaching, grasping, transporting, placing and releasing a ball in a real and a virtual environment. Their results showed that there is a slight change in motor patterns when grasping and placing a ball in the two reality conditions for both healthy subjects and hemiparesis patients with motor deficits, which was mainly due to lack of collision handling in the VE. Their interpretation of the results is that both healthy subjects and individuals with motor deficits used similar movement strategies in pick-and-place tasks in the two conditions, and they concluded that training of arm movements in VR may be a valid approach to the rehabilitation of patients with motor disorders. However, the results also suggest that physics simulation in VR rehabilitation may reduce the difference of movement strategies in the virtual and real world, which may be an important factor in the transferability of virtual skills to the real world.

Physics Level-of-Detail

Level of Detail (LOD) is a useful construct for managing graphic complexity across many scales. In many VR systems, a virtual object often has multi-resolution representations and the graphics system makes real-time decisions about which representation to render, according to criteria such as the distance of the object to the camera. When the object is close to the camera a higher LOD representation is rendered, and when it is far away from the camera a low LOD model (or 2D imposter) is used. This has been proved to be an effective optimization strategy in real-time computer graphics (Hamill et al. 2005). The different requirements for physics fidelity in various application domains suggest that incorporating similar algorithms for physical simulation may be equally useful. This could be supported by having multiple collision representations, for example, or multiple articulations in a jointed system. Hubbard 1996 describes a system whereby polyhedra are approximated by spheres for time-critical collision detection, resulting in an algorithm which maintains real-time performance as objects become more complicated.

In many physics-based VR systems objects have several different collision representations. For example, bounding volumes are used for low physics LOD (broad phase CD), and polygonal meshes for high physics LOD (narrow phase CD), so that under circumstances where detailed collisions are not necessary, computation efficiency is enhanced by reducing physics accuracy. It can be used on terrain collision, object-to-object CD, and avatar-to-object CD. We extend this concept of broad and narrow phase CD across the whole physics simulation.

Physics LOD involves Levels of Articulation (LOA) when applied to jointed systems like vehicles and virtual humans. For instance, a low LOA virtual human may be based on a 6-joint skeleton, and a higher LOA virtual human can have 18 or even 71 joints (H-Anim 2006). Carlson and Hodgins 1997 describe how level-of-detail switching in a game with multiple dynamically simulated legged creatures effects both the outcome of the game and also the viewer's perception.

Physics LOD can not only adapt to distance of the object to the camera, focus of attention, and application domains, but also apply to certain events. Consider a car with a bounding volume collision model for low physic LOD simulation, and a high physics LOD collision model as a collection of individual rigid bodies (e.g. mirrors, bumper, fenders, grilles, doors, hoods, trunk, lights, and tyres). As the car collides with something and is broken into pieces, low physics LOD is replaced by higher physics LOD, and rigid bodies representing car parts are scattered around as if by the force of the collision.

PHYSICS ENGINES

In order to bring realistic dynamics into virtual environments and make virtual objects behave as the user would expect they would from their experience in the real world, either simulation software supporting physics must be developed from scratch or, an existing software library (or 'physics engine') can be integrated with the simulation software.

There are several physics engines available, many of which have been successfully used in commercial games. Havok Physics (Havok 2006) is a stable commercial solution that has won several awards and is used in many commercial games. To our knowledge, Havok only provides commercial licences for their engine. Ageia PhysX (Ageia 2006) (formerly known as Novodex), Open Dynamics Engine (ODE 2006) and Newton Game Dynamics (Newton 2006) are probably the most widely used solutions due to low cost (all are free for non-commercial use) and good performance, both of which are platform independent with a C++ API. Ageia PhysX is widely used by commercial game developers, e.g., Epic Games (Unreal) and Ubisoft. In addition, Ageia PhysX provides hardware accelerated physics via a Physics Processing Unit (PPU). ODE is an open-source library for simulating rigid body dynamics. It is also used in many games, 3D authoring tools (e.g. Softimage, Vizard) and simulation tools.

ADAPTIVE REHABILITATION

Rehabilitation needs to be targeted to the individual needs of patients. Patients have a wide range of abilities and tasks which are impossible for some can be trivial for others. It is usual to tailor a stroke rehabilitation session to individual patients according to the type of injury (left/right hemiplegia) and their capabilities. Typically this is done by assessing the patient in a number of standardised tests prior to the rehabilitation session. The therapist can then create a suitably challenging set of exercises for the patient. This is a time-consuming part of the physiotherapist's duties, as constant monitoring is required to ensure the tasks remain adequately challenging throughout the sessions, which typically last for several weeks.

Adaptivity

Adaptation is one technique that VR therapy systems can exploit to suit such a group of users with a wide range of abilities. In order to maintain patient motivation, rehabilitation tasks should be set at an appropriate level of challenge. Also, for the patient to stay engaged in the process, he or she should experience a feeling of immersion in the virtual environment. Charles et al. 2005 applied flow theory to adaptive game design, and they suggested that the game should find a balance between the annoyance of an activity that is perceived as trivial and the frustration of one that is perceived as too difficult. This is even more important in the context of VR motor rehabilitation due to the repetitive nature of the exercises and the limitations of the users (patients).

A physiotherapist will typically design motor therapy exercises for a patient based on a number of factors, including the patient's age, gender, culture background, usual handedness, and his or her medical condition (e.g., time since stroke, left or right hemiplegia and cognitive, sensory, and motor abilities based on standardised tests such as the Line Cancellation Test). Not only the difficulty level of the exercises but also the body parts activated during the task may be adapted to individual patient's needs. For example, tasks may be developed to train a specific movement such as wrist extension in order to increase range of motion or endurance of the wrist joint. This data, taken together, forms an individual patient profile which can then be used to initially configure the system to present a suitably challenging, individualised rehabilitation session. Various elements of the simulation can be configured from this profile data, including the number and type of objects, their sizes, speed, mass, distance between objects and the patient, distance of object transportation etc. Additionally, data collected during the rehabilitation session can be used to further improve the patient experience. Such in-session data (e.g., the time taken to perform a task or achieve a goal in a game, the accuracy rate or stimuli-response time) can be used to evaluate the initial configuration of the system. If tasks are not being successfully completed then the objects or game elements in the simulation should be configured to make them easier. Objects can be made larger (easier to grasp), for example, or moved closer to the patient (easier to reach). Alternatively, if activities are being completed much too quickly it may be that the activity is too easy for the patient, and corresponding changes can be made to make the task more challenging.

The ability to dynamically adjust the difficulty of the simulation is a key benefit since in addition to offering a tailored solution which suits the patient's individual needs it also decreases the dependence on human therapists to monitor and provide similar solutions.

User Profiling

We have constructed a patient model using traditional symbolic classifiers based on patients' age, time since stroke, left/right hemiplegia, impairment and functional measurement, and hemispatial neglect. Table 1 below shows the profile of three patients participating in the study: their age, gender, time since stroke, usual handedness, left or right hemiplegia, Motricity Index (MI) for impairment measurement, and Action Research Arm Test (ARAT) for functional measurement. For each patient, three MI and ARAT scores are given, representing their status before training, post training, and 6 weeks after training. Patients 1 and 3 have only mild deficit, while patient 2 has a moderate deficit.

	Patient #1	Patient #2	Patient #3
Age	76	62	42
Gender	M	F	M
Years since stroke	4	4	1
Usual handedness	R	R	R
L/R hemiplegia	L	L	L
MI	77,77,81	62,73,77	77,79,77
ARAT	3,6,11	4,11,19	54,53,54
Hemispatial neglect?	None	None	Left-sided

Table 1: Examples of patient profiling

A FRAMEWORK FOR PHYSICS-BASED VR REHABILITATION

Figure 1 shows our framework for VR post-stroke motor rehabilitation.

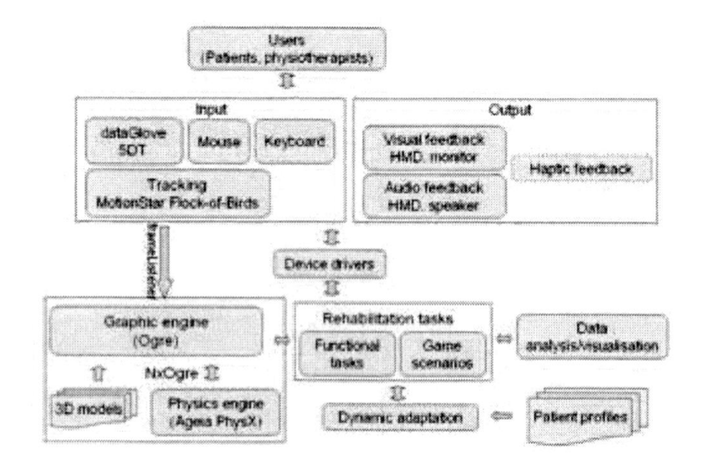

Figure 1: VR therapy framework

Game simulations have been added to functional tasks such as wrist extension, reaching, grasping and catching. The system allows users to interact with virtual objects in real-time through multiple modalities and to practise specific motor skills. Users of the system are stroke patients with motor deficits and physiotherapists who, as operators, are responsible for initialising the system and controlling the scripting of tasks. Input devices include ordinary devices, mouse and keyboard for operators and a range of real-time motion tracking devices - two 5DT Ultra DataGloves which capture finger flex and hand postures; Ascension MotionStar wireless magnetic sensors allow tracking of the patient's hand, arm and upper body movements.

Output involves visual, audio and haptic modalities. The dual output visual interface includes a desktop monitor for operators and a head-mounted display (HMD) for patients.

Haptic interface is a possible extension of the system but it is not our current concern.

The device drivers interface the specialised hardware with the software components which include a 3D graphic engine based on OGRE (Ogre 2006), dealing with loading of mesh data, rendering, scene management and the user interface, and a rehabilitation engine which creates functional (task-based) or non-functional (game-based) activities. We use Ageia PhysX to handle dynamics simulation, e.g., articulated structures, robust CD, and friction/contact modelling. A wrapper called NxOgre (NxOgre 2005) is used to integrate PhysX with OGRE. The databases consist of mesh data of 3D models and patient profiles which may be used to automatically adapt the tasks to specific therapeutic needs.

The dynamic adaptation part of the system uses patient profile data to select tasks and initially configure the difficulty level of the tasks and the game. This continues in-session, as all patient interaction with the system is recorded and analysed for in-game adaptation (discussed in more detail later in the paper). The data analysis module enables visualization of patients' movement trajectories and displays joint angles, range of movement and velocities. Currently this occurs off-line, after the rehabilitation session has finished.

Functional Training

The 3D position and orientation of the user's hand, elbow, and shoulder are sampled via using three magnetic sensors. Sensor 1 is placed on the volar aspect of the hand, at the base of the head of the 3rd metacarpal bone, Sensor 2 is placed on the posterior aspect of the elbow, just above the olecrannon process, and Sensor 3 is placed on the anterior aspect of the shoulder, on the greater tuberosity of the humerus.

In the functional training part we simulate a virtual kitchen where subjects are asked to manipulate virtual objects of various shapes and sizes at different locations, such as a typical pick-and-place task by reaching and touching a start marker, grasping a virtual cup, and placing it on a saucer some distance away (Figure 2). When the virtual hand, controlled by the tracking sensors and data glove, intersects with any object in the VE, an auditory signal is played and the object changes colour to indicate success (collision between hand and object detected). For example, when the hand touches the start mark, the patient will hear "Okay". Then the patient reaches and grasps the cup and hears "Okay", and when the cup collides with the goal mark, i.e., the user places the cup on the saucer, the patient will hear applause indicating a successful trial is completed. Patients use the hand of their hemiplegia side to perform the task.

A catching task has also been developed, where the user holds a virtual basket with either one hand or two (for bilateral upper limb training) to catching falling oranges which fall at random onto a target area (Figure 3).

Figure 2: A functional 'pick-and-place' task

The position/orientation of the virtual basket is controlled by a sensor attached either on the user's hand if one hand is used to perform the task, or on a real object, a real basket, for example, which the user holds with both hands. If the patient tilts the basket, he or she may not able to catch the oranges and the ones already in the basket may fall to the ground. The target area on the x-z plane, the falling speed of oranges (controlled by simulating gravity in the virtual environment), the time between oranges falling and the size of oranges and the basket can all be adjusted to suit individual patient's needs.

Figure 3: A functional catching task

All sensor data is recorded to disk, allowing post-therapy visualisation of the trajectories and analysis of joint angles, velocity, acceleration and range of movement

An Adaptive Game for Motor Rehabilitation

We have developed an adaptive VR "whack-a-mouse" game for upper limb stroke rehabilitation as shown in Figure 4. The mouse appears at a random location on the table top, stays there for a certain number of seconds (the actual time it stays still depends on the patient profile), and then re-appears on another part of the table. While the mouse is stationary the patient tries to hit it using a virtual hammer which is controlled by the position and orientation of sensor 1 on the patient's hand. This simulation encourages faster, grosser and less accurate movement than the functional task described earlier. It has also been designed to improve patient's visual discrimation and selective attention, important aspects of stroke rehabilitation where the patient exhibits hemi-spatial neglect.

Figure 4: A 'whack-a-mouse' game

Initial configuration of the game is done automatically based on the profile of the player. For example, the game will be configured to be easier for patients with serious upper extremity motor impairment, i.e., the mouse will stay still for a longer period of time for them than for patients with minor motor impairment. The locus of stimuli will also depend on if a) the patient has right or left-sided hemiplegia and b) if the patient exhibits hemi-spatial neglect. For left-sided hemiplegia patients, the random positioning of the mouse is biased towards the right; similarly for the left. If the patient also exhibits hemi-spatial neglect this bias can be increased. It is important that patients are given a chance to familarise themselves with the game and not be presented initially with something that is too difficult, which could lead to disengagement. Therefore we tend to be conservative with the initial setup.

Patients will learn as they play and their progress of learning may be different. Therefore, the configuration that we use at the beginning of the game may no longer be appropriate as the game proceeds. The length of time that the mouse is stationary and the locus of mouse and dog adapts dynamically to patient performance. The mouse appears more frequently in the quadrant where the patient has more misses and seems to have difficulty due to either motor deficit or attention deficit.

There are, therefore, a number of adaptive elements of the game which change dynamically according to how well or badly the user is performing. The game has been programmed to enable automatic progression between three levels (Beginner, Intermediate and Expert) under preset conditions. At the Beginner level the time that the mouse is stationary is set automatically according to the patient profile. At the Intermediate level, the time adapts to the patient's performance (to begin with, the speed is the same as in the beginner level). The game progresses according to a simple accuracy test based on the number of mice hit and the number missed, where

$$accuracy = miceHit / (miceHit + miceMissed)$$

When the accuracy rate drops below a certain threshold, the length of time that the mouse remains still for increases which has the effect of slowing the game, making it easier; and when the accuracy rate exceeds a certain threshold, this time decreases, making the game harder. The Expert level contains both a mouse and a dog which appear simultaneously: patients must hit as many mice as possible and try to avoid hitting the dog. Hitting a mouse increases the score by one, but hitting a dog decreases it by one. This aspect to the game forces patients to search for and hit only the mouse when both mouse and dog are present, in order to improve visual discrimination and selective attention, which can be important aspect to patient rehabilitation particularly for patients with hemi-spatial neglect.

The player, level of game, score, and adapted speed are shown in the upper-right corner of the screen to give the user real-time feedback. Overall performance data such as score, accuracy rate, and the length of game-play sessions are also shown to the user when the game is over or on entry to the next level, and this data is also written to the user profile. The next time the patient uses the system this information will be used to configure the game. Further, the physiotherapist can analyse this data to assess how the patient is progressing over a number of sessions. Besides the performance feedback, multiple sensory feedback is given. When a mouse is hit, it squeaks and its colour changes to red, and when a dog is hit, it barks and its colour changes to red. To create an element of competition, but also to give feedback to the patient, the user can view the highest scores of all the users and also his or her personal best scores of each game level.

Discussion

The system has been tested with respect to the user experience in a number of ways which have been previously reported (McNeill et al. 2004, Crosbie et al. 2005). In a group of 10 healthy individuals and 10 stroke patients, all participants indicated a generally favourable experience using the system. The main difference between the two groups tested was their level of perceived exertion, as measured by the Borg Scale (Borg 1982). Another two case studies in 3 week trials were conducted (Crosbie et al. 2006), and a randomized control trial to compare this VR based therapy to standard care is ongoing.

CONCLUSION

This paper has shown how digital games can contribute to an VR motor therapy system which provides motivating tasks that can automatically adapt to individual patient's capabilities. We discussed the potential for the integration of physics simulation techniques into VR games for upper limb motor rehabilitation and the relationships between physical and perceptual realism of VR therapy. A physically based VR framework with adaptive game configuration based on data collected before-game and in-game was described which is currently being used by a number of hemiplegia patients with various levels of severity. Initial feedback is very positive, with patients reporting that they enjoy playing the game. Further work is necessary to determine just how much the introduction of physics into the game simulation actually influences patient outcome, but we believe that digital game technology has much to offer rehabilitation systems.

REFERENCES

Ageia, "Ageia PhysX SDK", http://www.ageia.com 2006

Borg, G. V., "Psychophysical bases of perceived exertion", *Medicine and Science in Sports and Exercise*, Vol 14, pp 377-381, 1982

Borst, Christoph W. and Arun P. Indugula, "Realistic Virtual Grasping", *VR '05: Proceedings of the 2005 IEEE Conference on Virtual Reality*, Washington D.C., pp. 91-98, 320, 2005

Carlson, Deborah A. and Jessica K. Hodgins, "Simulation Levels of Detail for Real-time Animation", *Graphics Interface '97*, Wayne A. Davis, Marilyn Mantei and R. Victor Klassen (Eds), Canadian Human-Computer Communications Society, pp 1-8, 1997

Charles, Darryl, Michael McNeill, Moira McAlister, Michaela Black, Adrian Moore, Karl Stringer, Julian Kücklich and Aphra Kerr, "Player-centred game design: player modelling and adaptive digital games", *DIGRA2005: Proceedings of the Second International Digital Games Research Conference*, pp 285-298, Vancouver, Canada, June 2005

Crison, F., A. Lécuyer, A. Savary, D. Mellet-D'Huart, J.-M. Burkhardt and J.-L. Dautin, "The use of haptic and pseudo-haptic feedback for the technical training of milling", *Proceedings of EuroHaptics 2004*, June 2004

Crosbie, J. H., S. M. McDonough, S. Lennon and M. D. J. McNeill, "Development and testing of an immersive virtual reality based rehabilitation system for the upper limb after stroke: the user's perspective", *Proc. of the 4th International Workshop of Virtual Rehabilitation*, Catalina Island, California, U.S.A., September 2005

Crosbie, J. H., S. M. McDonough, S. Lennon and M. D. J. McNeill, "Virtual reality as a training device for movement rehabilitation in the upper limb after chronic stroke: Two case studies", *Proc. of the 4th World Congress on NeuroRehabilitation*, Hong Kong, China, February 2006

H-Anim, "Humanoid animation", http://www.h-anim.org 2006

Hamill, J., R. McDonnell, S. Dobbyn and C. O'Sullivan, "Perceptual Evaluation of Impostor Representations for Virtual Humans and Buildings", *Computer Graphics Forum (Eurographics 2005)*, M. Alexa and J. Marks (Eds), 24(3), September 2005

Havok, "Havok Physics", http://www.havok.com 2006

Holden, M. K., T. A. Dyar, L. Schwamm and E. Bizzi, "Virtual Environment-based Telerehabilitation in Patients with Stroke", *Presence - Virtual Rehabilitation*, M. Alexa and J. Marks (Eds), 14 (2), pp 214-233, 2005

Hubbard, P. M., "Approximating polyhedra with spheres for time-critical collision detection", *ACM Trans. Graphics*, 15(3), pp 179-210, ACM Press, 1996}

Hwang, J., A. Rizzo and G. J. Kim, "Space Extension: The Perceptual Presence Perspective", *Proc. of ACM SIGGRAPH International Conference on Virtual Reality Continuum and its Application in Industry (VRCAI 2004)*, Chicago, U.S.A., June 2004

N. Katz, H. Ring, Y. Naveh, R. Kizony, U. Feintuch and P. L. Weiss, "Interactive Virtual Environment training for safe street crossing of right hemisphere stoke patients with unilateral spatial neglect", ICDVRAT2004: Proceedsings of the Fifth International Conference on Disability, Virtual Reality and Associated Technologies 2004, Oxford, UK, 2004.

Kurillo, G., M. Mihelj, M. Munih and T. Bajd, "Grasping and manipulation in virtual environment using 3By6 finger device", *Proc. of 9th International Conference On Rehabilitation Robotics (ICORR)*, Chicago, U.S.A., June 2005

Kuttuva, M. R. Boian, A. Merians, G. Burdea, M. Bouzit, J. Lewis and D. Fensterheim, "The Rutgers Arm: An Upper-Extremity Rehabilitation System in Virtual Reality", *Proc. of the 5th International Workshop on Virtual Rehabilitation (IWVR05)*, Catalina Island, California, U.S.A. pp 94-103, 2005

Li, Y. F., Wang, J. G. and Ho, J. K. L., "Using physics based models in virtual reality for dynamic emulation of robotic systems", *Proc. of Computer Graphics International*, Catalina Island, California, U.S.A., June 1998

Matthias Müller and Matthias Teschner, "Volumetric Meshes for Real-Time Medical Simulations", *Proc. of 7th Worksh. Bildverarbeitung für die Medizin*, T. Wittenberg, P. Hastreiter, U. Hoppe, H. Handels, A. Horsch and H.-P. Meinzer (Eds), Springer-Verlag, pp 279-283, March 2003

McNeill M. D. J., L. Pokluda, S. M. McDonough and J. Crosbie, "Immersive virtual reality for upper limb rehabilitation following stroke", IEEE International Conference on Systems, Man and Cybernetics, pp 2783-2789 October 2004

Newton Game Dynamics, http://www.newtondynamics.com 2006

NxOgre, http://www.nxogre.org 2006

O'Sullivan, Carol, John Dingliana, Thanh Giang and Mary K. Kaiser, "Evaluating the visual fidelity of physically based animations", ACM Trans. Graphics, 22(3), pp 527-536, ACM Press, 2003

OGRE, "Object-oriented Graphics Rendering Engine", http://www.ogre3d.org 2006

Open Dynamics Engine (ODE), http://www.ode.com, 2006

Pohland, K., Berssenbrugge, J., Krumm, H. and P. Ebbesmeyer, "Virtual Reality-Based Dynamics Simulation of Virtual Prototypes, *Proc. of 22nd Computers and Information in Engineering Conference, ASME DETC*, Montreal, Canada, Oct 2002

Rand, D., N. Katz, N., Shahar, M., Kizony, R. and Weiss, P. L., "The virtual mall: development of a functional virtual environment for stroke rehabilitation", *Abstracts of the 55th Annual Conference of the Israeli Association of Physical and Rehabilitation Medicine*, 2004

Riva, G., F. Davide and W.A. IJsselsteijn, "*Being There: Concepts, effects and measurements of user presence in synthetic environments*", IOS Press, Amsterdam, 2003

Sato, M., "Evolution of SPIDAR", *Proc. of the 3rd Virtual Reality International Conference (VRIC), Laval Virtual*, Laval, France, May 2001.

Viau, A., A. G. Feldman, J. McFadyen and M. F. Levin, "Reaching in reality and virtual reality: a comparison of movement kinematics in healthy subjects and in adults with hemiparesis", *Journal of NeuroEngineering and Rehabilitation*, 1 (11), 2004

BIOGRAPHY

Dr. Minhua Ma is currently a postdoctoral Research Associate at the School of Computing and Information Engineering in the Faculty of Engineering and has over 8 years research experience in 3D animation, Virtual Reality, and computational linguistics. She received her Doctorate from the School of Computing & Intelligent Systems, University of Ulster, U.K. in 2006, MSc in Computing Science from the University of Newcastle upon Tyne, U.K. in 2001, BA and MA in Linguistics from Shanghai Normal University, China in 1995 and 1998 respectively. Her principal lines of work have been published in over 15 peer-reviewed scientific journals as well as conference proceedings. She has been involved in a number of interdisciplinary projects, e.g., Comparison between Normal Persons and Cleft Lip and Palate Patients after Operation between Linguistics Institute, SNU and Department of Cleft Lip, Shanghai Ninth People's Hospital, and her Ph.D. project Automatic Conversion of Natural Language to 3D Animation integrated Natural language Processing with 3D animation. She has received grants from the NICHSA for her work on Virtual Reality. Her current research interests include Virtual Reality in games and rehabilitation, 3D animation, virtual human animation, and Natural Language Processing. She has a keen interest in interdisciplinary research.

Advanced Real-time Animation

Dr. Mark Leeney
Letterkenny Institute of Technology
mark.leeney@lyit.ie

Darragh Maloney
Letterkenny Institute of Technology
darragh.maloney@lyit.ie

Abstract

3D computer games with animated characters are restricted to the animations provided by an animator. Treating the animations as a series of digital signals allows digital signal processing techniques to be applied with the aim of decreasing the workload of an animator while allowing the character to interact better with its environment. These techniques involve treating an animation as a continuous signal, sampling it, passing it through a low pass filter and then subtracting the low passes to get band passes. The band passes can be altered before summing them to get back an altered animation. Timewarping animations is also discussed with the aim of better improving the combination of animations and poses. This paper explores a method for having a character perform different animations using only simple base animations and discrete poses incorporating a multiresolution and timewarping approach.

Keywords: Computer animation, timewarping, motion blending, motion filtering.

1 Introduction

Computer games have progressed a long way in pretty much every aspect since they began in the early 80's. They are more complex to play, graphically more appealing, bigger, longer and have better multiplayer implementations. Along with this, they can simulate the real world more accurately than ever. This is most obvious with lighting and physics. Where realism tends to fall down though is in level design where the levels are made to fit a character. Ledges are all the same height so the character can climb on them, or boxes are all the same size so the character can jump onto them. This can lead to dull levels and hence dull gaming. The reason for this uniformness is having variable level objects requires many various character animations to produce smooth interactions. However, this is a lot of work for an animator and it increases the storage and operational overhead for the game. This paper explores a method for having a character perform different animations using only simple base animations and discrete poses.

1.1 Related Work

In their paper, Motion Warping, Witkin and Popović [6] describe a technique for taking animations produced from motion capture and morphing them into new animations. By adding in new keyframes or poses, they created realistic and new motions. They also treat animations as time based signals. However, their method didn't suit a real time application due to the way the new keyframes were specified.

Bruderlin and Williams [1] detail how to filter an animation and perform Digital Signal Processing (DSP) operations on it. They base their approach on multiresolution filtering, a process applied to images to reduce noise. They mixed this filtering with time warping based on shape blending to create an offline method for animation warping.

2 Animation Architecture

There are two main types of computer animation: prerendered and real time. The prerendered is best showcased in films such as Toy Story or Shrek with real time animation being the norm for computer games. The difference lies in how the animations will be used. For a film, the animation will only be used once, so it can be tweaked to suit its environment. However, in a game, an animation can be used an unspecified number of times, for example, a simple walk animation or jump animation will be used throughout a platform game. A simplified look at the animation architecture of a game is shown in Figure 1.

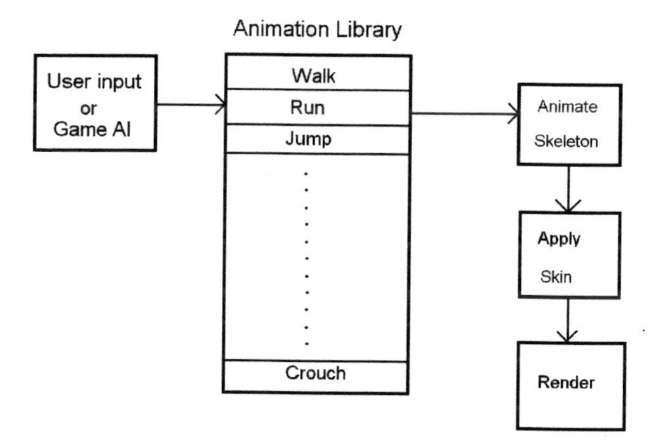

Figure 1. Diagram of animation architecture.

A library of animations is created, either through motion capture, or by an animator using a package like Maya or 3D Studio Max. An event occurs, caused either by the user or the game AI that will request an animation to be played. This will animate a skeleton. The skeleton is then 'skinned' with the appropriate mesh which is then rendered (see [3] for details). The skinning procedure is a topic in itself, this paper doesn't deal with it, instead focusing on animating the skeleton.

Having a large library of animations means the character can call on a large range of different motions. However, what happens if a motion that isn't in the library is required? If our character approaches a door that is too low to walk through, but big enough that using the crouch motion would leave too much head room as to look awkward? The standard way around this is not to build such doors into a level, leading to levels having a uniform feel.

Figure 2. A skeleton with a skin applied to it.

What this paper addresses is a method to take a animation and a pose and to blend them to produce an new motion, that is not in the animation library, at run time. If we have a door of non standard height, we provide a pose of the character walking through the door with a stooped appearance. Or if we have a handrail along a flight of stairs, we can provide some poses with the character having his hand on the rail. This will result in the character walking on the stairs with a hand on the rail, instead of just walking along as normal. The character is able to respond to the environment it is in, giving a more realistic finish and making game levels less uniform.

2.1 Skeletal Animation

Like any skeleton, a skeleton for computer animation is made up of bones, however it is not necessary to have a 1 to 1 mapping of real bones to animation bones in order to produce convincing results. There are 35 bones in the skeleton used for this research. The number of bones will vary depending on the character being developed – a fish character may have only a spine and 2 bones for fins, while a horse character will have more bones as it is a more complex creature.

The bones are stored as quaternions. While a 4x4 matrix could be used, quaternions take up less space and give better, smoother results when being interpolated. The only real disadvantage to using quaternions is they are harder to understand.

An animation as stored in the animation library will consist of a series of key frames – discrete poses with an associated time. To play the animation, the system calls a function to return the position and rotation of all the bones in turn, at a given time. Normally the time specified will not match the time of a keyframe, so the result is an interpolation of the two closest keyframes. This is a linear interpolation (LERP), which, if not done quick enough can can result in varying amounts of rotation being applied to the bones. This appears as a limb moving with a speed alternating between slow and fast. There are two solutions to this. Calling the LERP function often enough means this speed variance is too small to be noticed. As modern games operate between 30 and 200 frames per second, and with the LERP operation being called every frame, this is the solution used. The alternative solution is to use spherical liner interpolation (SLERP). This has a slightly higher overhead, but will give a constant velocity for the rotations.

The stored animation can be thought of as a series of signals. To illustrate, think of viewing a walking character side on. Looking at a specific point, eg. the knee it can be thought of as moving up and down with respect to the ground, or like a point having displacement along the vertical y axis. Over time this point will map out a signal like a sine wave. Similarly two other signals, with a smaller amplitude will exist for the x and z axis.

The motion for a skeleton is given by the rotations applied to its bones. The rotations can be thought of as signals. Using the same approach as Bruderlin and Williams[1], these signals can be subjected to DSP.

3 Methodology

The method described is more complicated than would appear necessary at first glance. To have an animation morph into a pose and then morph back to the animation, the obvious method is to interpolate the two. This is called a blend. It will give a smooth transition, but not one that is acceptable. While the motion of something like reaching out with an arm will look realistic, looking at the legs or other limbs, they can tend to float or drag across the ground – this is known as footskate. Time warping is needed to eliminate footskate when hitting a pose while walking in a natural looking fashion. There are three main parts to the warping algorithm: sampling, filtering and timewarping.

3.1 Sampling

The system is designed to take a pose and an animation and warp them together. We set a warp time – the amount of time to warp to the pose and back to the original animation. The animation is sampled for the duration the warp is to take place. Only the rotations are sampled, as the positions, which give the length of a bone, don't change. The rotations are converted from quaternions to Eularian angles (henceforth referred to as Eulers), as quaternions are hard to work with, and this was beyond the scope of the research. This gives three signals, one each for the x, y and z axis – for each bone in the skeleton. Importantly, the x values of the points on the signals shown are the times of the sample and the y values are the rotations at that time. With 35 bones per character, this gives 3 x 35 = 105 signals per animation. The signals are sampled at 15Hz, giving 1575 samples per animation per second of warp time. So reducing from quaternion's to Eulers has the advantage of meaning there is less data to be processed.

This conversion is not without its overhead though., as a property of quaternions is that a negative quaternion and a positive quaternion will give the same rotation. However, they will produce different Eulerian representations. This problem occurs with the thigh bones of the skeleton.

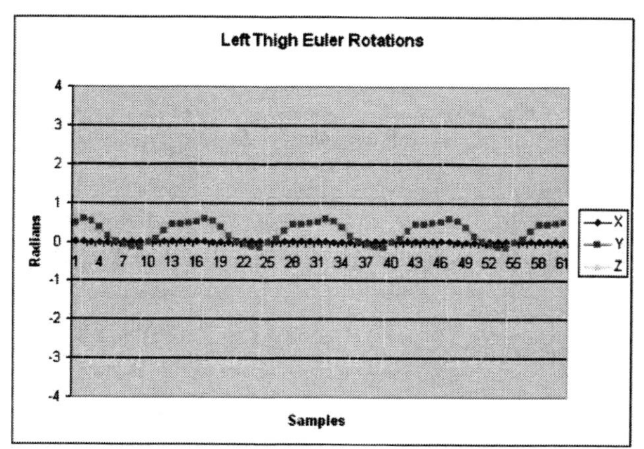

Figure 3. The yellow signal is an Eulerian version of a quaternion flipping around π.

When the signal in Figure 3 is passed through a filter, or through the warping process, the jump from -π to π becomes a problem. The jump is removed by comparing each sample with the previous sample and seeing if the difference is greater than 2π radians. If it is, there is a jump in the signal. The jump is eliminated by multiplying the sample by -1. The resulting correct signal is shown in Figure 4.

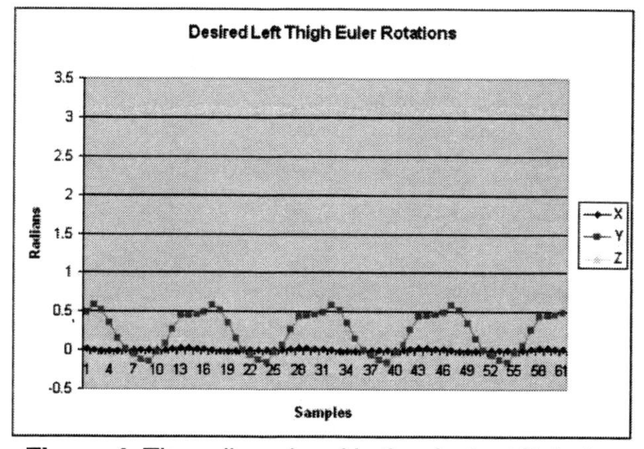

Figure 4. The yellow signal is the desired Eulerian version of the signal shown in Figure 3.

3.2 Filtering

Following Bruderlin and Williams [1], a system was developed to incorporate multiresolution filtering. This can be thought of as an equaliser, as commonly used in audio processing, but used for animation in this case. In [1], the purpose of the filter is to be able to adjust animations before timewarping to give a better result. The goals of implementing such a filter for warping an animation with a pose are similar. However, the actual use of the filter in this project is to enhance the resulting warped animation after the timewarping.

In audio signals, the low frequencies contain the bass - the general sound, and the high frequencies contain the treble, or the detail. Motion is somewhat similar - the middle frequencies contain the general motion, with the high frequencies containing the detail of the motion.

Passing the animation through successive low pass filters results in several low pass versions of the animation, each with less detail than the low pass before it. Subtracting consecutive low passes from each other gives band passes – see Figure 5.

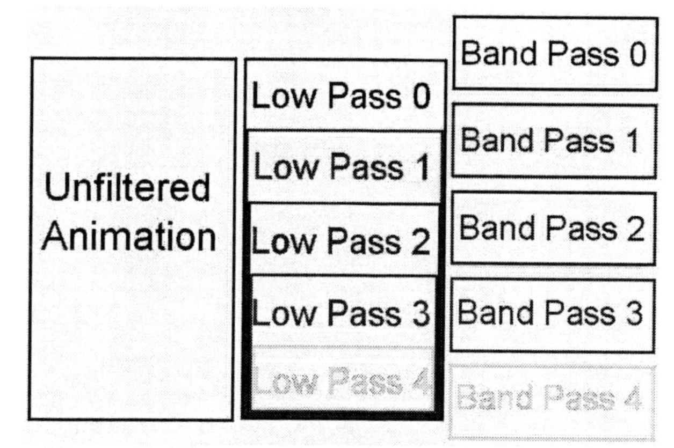

Figure 5. Diagram illustrating an animation being split into Band Passes.

These band passes can be summed to recreate the original animation. However, if a band pass is scaled before it is added, it will alter the animation. Scaling the lower pass bands positively exaggerates the general shape of the animation; scaling them in a negative direction will restrict the general shape of the animation. Along with this, scaling the higher band passes will cause the character to appear twitchy and nervous. This filtering method can be used to remove noise from the final timewarped signal. An example of some filtered signals is shown in Figure 6. For a detailed discussion on the implementation of the filter see [1].

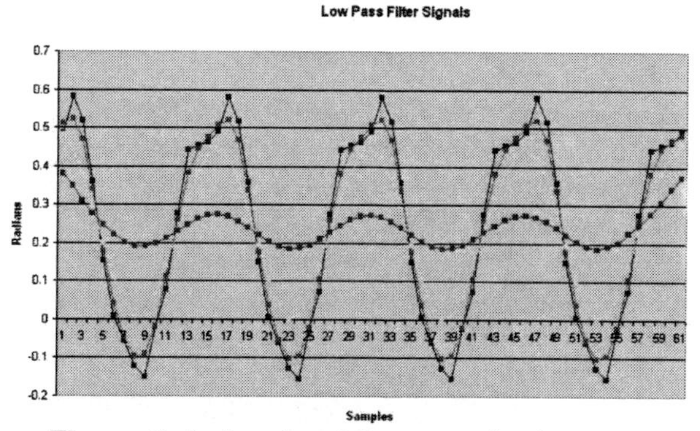

Figure 6. A signal and 3 successive low pass versions of the signal.

3.3 Time Warping

A blend is taking a frame of one animation and combining it with a frame from a second animation to create a frame of a third animation. The problem with this is if the second animation doesn't synchronize with the first animation regarding the general motion of the limbs, the result can be very restricted or static. A good example is that of foot plants, where a walking/running combination can cancel each other out resulting in a still pose for the characters legs (if the running character has a leg at the highest point of its motion while the walk animation has a leg on the ground, the blend gives the in between, resulting in a hovering motion). The character can then be seen to slide across the ground with no walking motion.

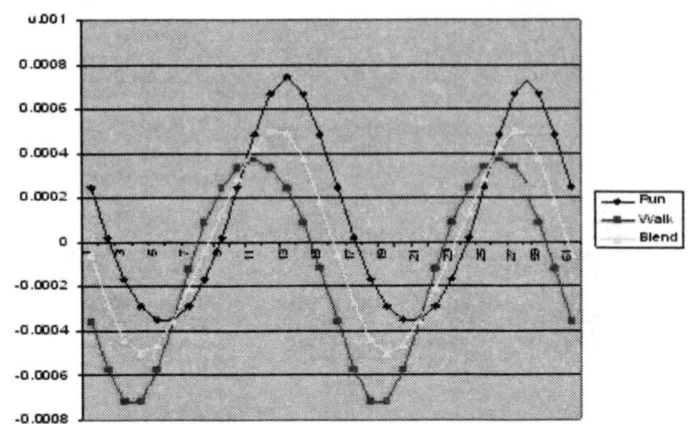

Figure 7. A blend between a walk and a run. The resulting yellow signal is reasonable, regarding phase and amplitude. This is due to the walk and run signals almost synchronizing.

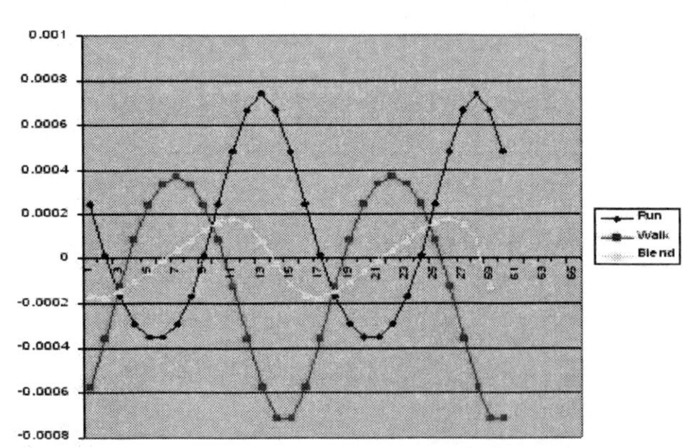

Figure 8. If the walk and run signals are out of synchronization, the result is lifeless. It's amplitude is too small and its phase doesn't match up.

A different blend that first of all synchronize the two animations before blending is required. This is called timewarping. The goal of timewarping is to put one animation into a suitable position before blending to give results that won't be 'canceled out'.

The algorithm used is based on Sederbergs [2] shape blending algorithm but changed slightly to suit the implementation. Each animation signal is treated as if it was a physical piece of wire, and it is to be bent to the shape of the corresponding blended signal with minimum effort. This operation has two parts, bending and stretching. With bending, three consecutive points on each signal are passed through a function that will calculate how much work it will take to have the set of points from the animation signal bend from its current shape to the shape of the three points from the blended signal. With stretching, only two points are needed from each signal, and the work calculated is the work needed to stretch or shrink the two points from the animation signal to the same length as the two points from the blended signal.

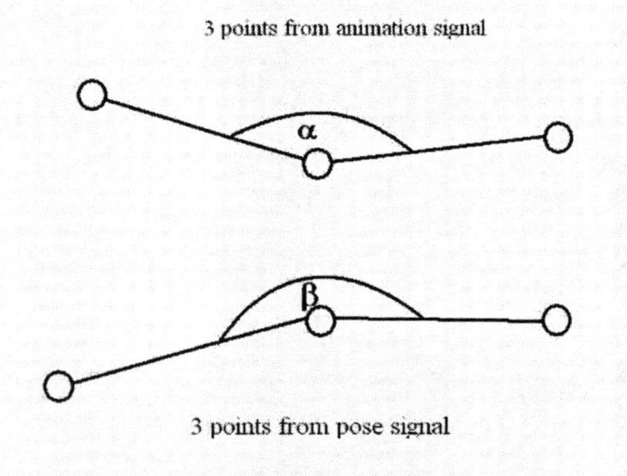

Figure 9. Work is calculated to have the angle between the 3 animation signal points (α) equal to that between the 3 pose signal points(β).

This process is carried out for all corresponding signals. This means the three animation signals for each bone are matched up with the 3 pose signals for each bone. The matching process can be represented by a graph which will get the optimal least work match for 2 signals.

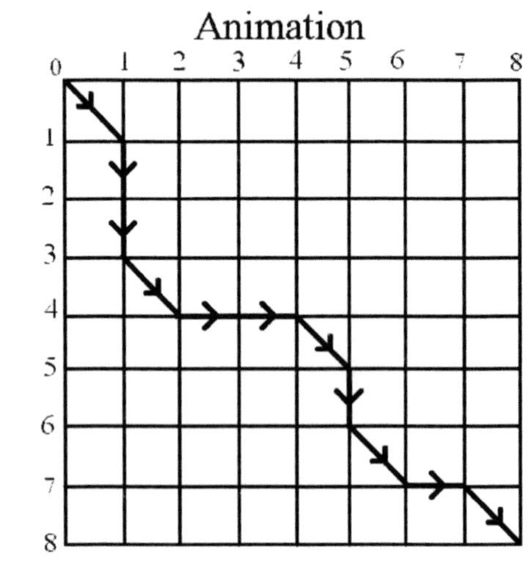

Figure 10. Graphing out the least work correspondence between the Animation signals and the Blend signals.

As expected, the greater the distance between two points the more expensive the stretching, and the greater the angle between three points the more expensive the bending is.

Having computed the cost at every node on the graph, the cheapest route is mapped out from [0,0] to the opposite corner. Where the route between two nodes is diagonal, the corresponding point on the warped signal has the same point as the animation signal. A horizontal path means multiple points of the animation signal map to one point on the pose signal, so the resultant signal is an average of these animation points. A vertical path means one point of the animation signal maps to x samples on the pose signal with the resultant signal getting x points from a B-Spline around the point on the animation signal.

4 Results & Conclusions

As discussed, timewarping is necessary to synchronize 2 animations before blending them. The timewarping implementation works well, as shown by Figure 11 – where a walk motion is timewarped to match up with a run motion before blending. The resulting blend has the correct phase and amplitude, as shown in Figure 12.

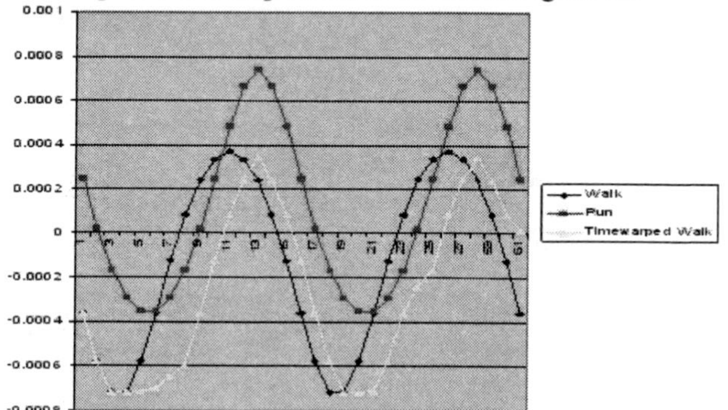

Figure 11. The blue walk signal has been timewarped to synchronize with the pink run signal, resulting in the yellow timewarped signal.

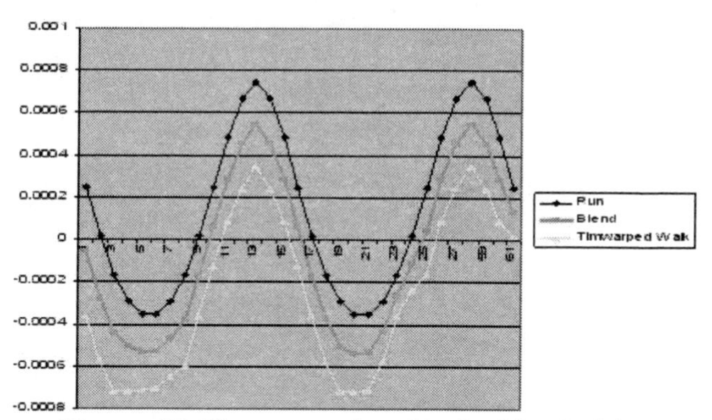

Figure 12. The green signal is the blend of the timewarped walk (yellow) with the run (blue).

Timewarping a pose to synchronize with an animation or vice versa is different. Recall that the goal of this project is to warp a pose with an animation. A pose signal appears as a flat line – much like a DC signal in electronics. So shifting it to the left or right by timewarping results in the same signal. Warping a pose with a walk signal by means of a 50/50 blend results in a motion that looks like a stiff walk, whilst only getting half way towards the pose, see Figure 13.

At this point, filtering and then scaling up the band passes will possibly exaggerate the motion back to its normal scope, however, there is a better more efficient method to get the same result, discussed in the next section.

4.1 Pose Specific Motion Warping

There is a significant improvement to be had over what has been presented so far. Noting that the aim of

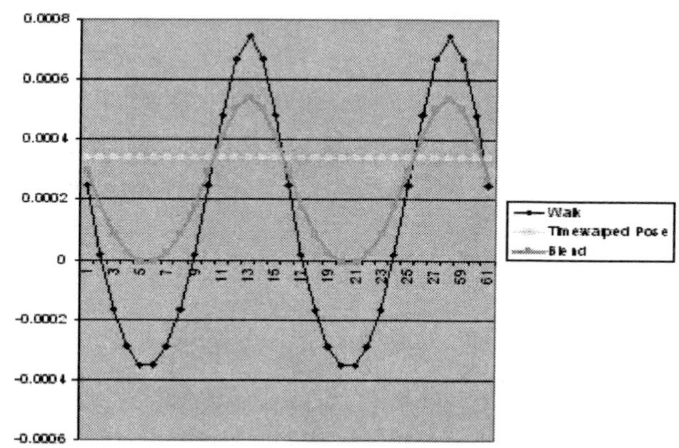

Figure 13. A 50/50 blend between a pose (yellow) and a walk (blue) gives a constrained result shown in green.

timewarping is to synchronize two animations, and that the DC nature of a pose cannot be synchronized in the normal sense, timewarping doesn't serve any particular purpose in this instance. Instead, the animation is shifted so it oscillates about the pose signal, giving the result shown in Figure 14.

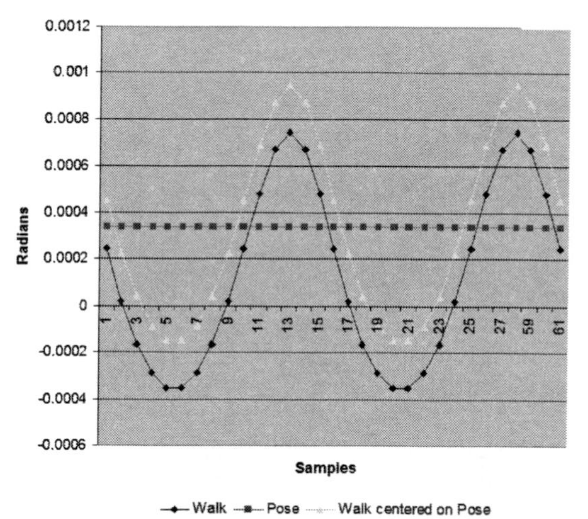

Figure 14. Shifting the blue walk signal to oscillate about the pink pose signal gives a result with the correct phase and amplitude.

This produces a better result than timewarping and then shifting, as there is no footskate in the resulting animation (When timewarping with a pose – footskate is introduced). At the same time, the result has both the movement of the original walk, and the rotation needed to meet the pose. Removing the timewarping also removes most of the work required to warp the pose and the animation. Calculating the grid is quite expensive. As an illustration of this, at 35 bones per character, and with 3 signals per bone, 135 grids must be calculated. A 4 second interval with 15 samples per second, means 4 x 15 x 135 = 8100 memory allocations. For each of these, a cost must be calculated - at a glance it can be seen that its not a cheap method, especially when the goal is to have it completed in the space of 4-5 frames (60 fps gives 0.016 seconds per frame). Compare this to doing a shift on a signal - get the average value of the walk signal, find the difference between the first point of the walk and pose signals and then add this difference to every point on the walk signal. There is no need to allocate temporary memory, work out bending or stretching costs, or find grid paths. This leads the process to be cheap enough to develop for use in a real time environment.

5 Further Research

In section 3.1 it's stated that although quaternions are used to apply rotations, they are converted to Eulers for the animation warp. This was mainly a result of quaternions being hard to work with . A further development of the project would be to remove this conversion and keep everything in quaternions. This would have the added benefit of reducing the overhead as the conversion is not without its cost.

Another area of related research involves implementing the process with an engine and defining the parameters for when a warp is enacted, and what needs to happen to break out of the warp back to an animation before the warp has ended.

6 Acknowledgments

We would like to thank Instinct Technologies, for their time, support and resources. Our gratitude also goes to Enterprise Ireland for funding to carry out this research.

7 References

[1] Bruderlin, A., Williams, L. Motion Signal Processing. In *International Conference on Computer Graphics and Interactive Techniques Proceedings* (1995) pp 97 – 104.

[2] Sederberg, T.W, Greenwood, E. A Physically Based Approach to 2-D Shape Blending. In *Computer Graphics 26* (July 1992) pp 25 – 34.

[3] Watt, A., Policarpo, F. 3D Games Animation and Advanced Real-time Rendering. (2003) Chpt 7 – 11.

[4] Dunn, F., Parberry, I. 3D Math Primer for Graphics and Game Development. (2002) Chpt 7 – 10.

[5] Maestri, G. Digital Character Animation 2 Volume 1. (1999) Chpt 6.

[6] Witkin, A., Popović. Z, Motion Warping. In *Computer Graphics Proceedings, Siggraph*. (1995).

Interactive Generation of Cities for Real-Time Applications

George Kelly, Hugh McCabe
Institute of Technology Blanchardstown, Ireland
george.kelly@itb.ie, hugh.mccabe@itb.ie

Abstract

We present a design for a city generation system for use in real-time 3D applications such as games. Our goal is to create an interactive application that uses procedural techniques to create road and building geometry.

1. Introduction

A successful city generation system should be capable of producing varied, detailed and realistic results. Additional goals for our system include the following:

- Accessibility – input data such as geo-statistical data should not be prerequisite to using the system.
- Interactivity – the system should be capable of fully autonomous generation but also facilitate interactive control when required.
- Real-Time – for efficient rendering techniques like culling, paging and level of detail should be implemented.

Our design is comprised of three major components: *primary road generation, secondary road generation* and *building generation.* A standalone application integrates the components and provides access to the algorithm controls.

2. Method

The primary road generation component utilises templates [2] that encapsulate common city road network patterns. These templates are applied to a terrain in the form of a graph. The edges of the graph can be automatically deformed by terrain characteristics such as gradients, water levels and other obstacles. The resultant road network graph is editable using an interactive 3D interface. Streets can be added, deleted and moved, using junctions as control points for manipulation.

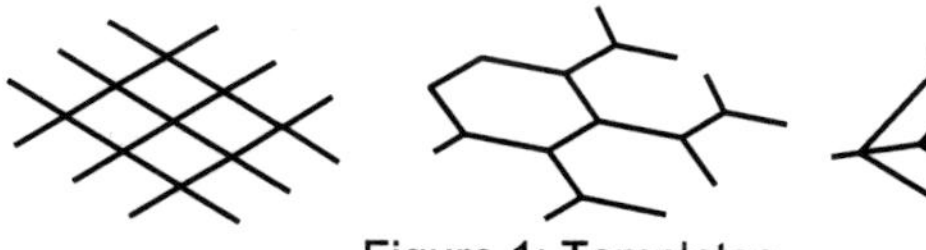

Figure 1: Templates

Cells resulting from the division of the city by the primary road network form the basic units upon which the secondary road generation component operates. A technique based on L-systems, similar to that used in [1], is employed. Global and local parameters can be adjusted for the generation algorithms, resulting in citywide or localized changes.

Buildings can be placed on the lots created from the secondary road network. These can be constructed using a generative grammar [3] that supports several distinct building usage types including commercial, industrial, and residential.

Real-Time rendering is possible in our design via the provision of a number of optimization features:

City cell paging is a concept similar to terrain paging, the primary road network forms a skeleton for the city and the secondary road network cells within can be pre-emptively generated and loaded on demand.

Geometry generation: Building structures can be generated at run time providing a substantial reduction in memory usage by storing simple generation data rather than complex geometry.

Level of detail: As a result of geometry generation several variants of buildings can be constructed depending on the instantiation parameters used.

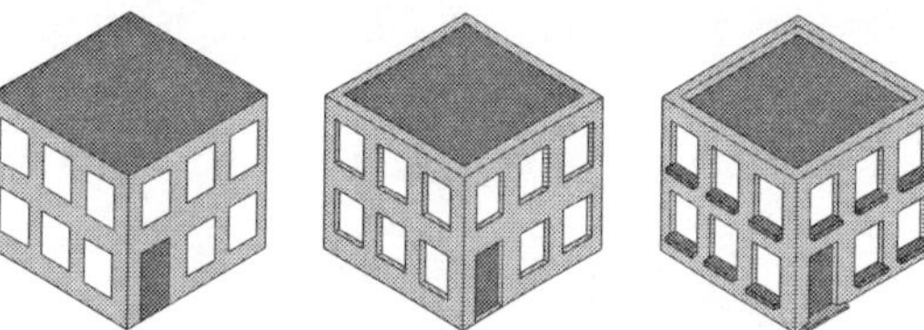

Figure 2: L-system building iterations

L-systems refine a basic model into a complex one over a series of iterations. A range dependant level of detail can be provided by including a parameter that specifies the number of iterations proportional to the distance between the camera and building.

3. Results and Conclusions

At present an interactive application has been built that implements the primary road generation component, allowing generation from templates and interactive editing. Current work involves implementing L-systems for secondary road generation and generative grammars for building generation.

References

[1] PARISH, Y. I. H., AND MULLER, P. 2001. Procedural modeling of cities. In SIGGRAPH 2001, Computer Graphics Proceedings, ACM Press / ACM SIGGRAPH, E. Fiume, Ed., 301–308.

[2] SUN, J., YU, X., BACIU, G., AND GREEN, M. 2002. Template based generation of road networks for virtual city modeling. In VRST-02, ACM Press, H. Sun and Q. Peng, Eds., 33–40.

[3] WONKA, P., WIMMER, M., SILLION, F., AND RIBARSKY, W. 2003. Instant architecture. In Proceedings of ACM SIGGRAPH 2003, Eds., vol. 22(3), 669–677.

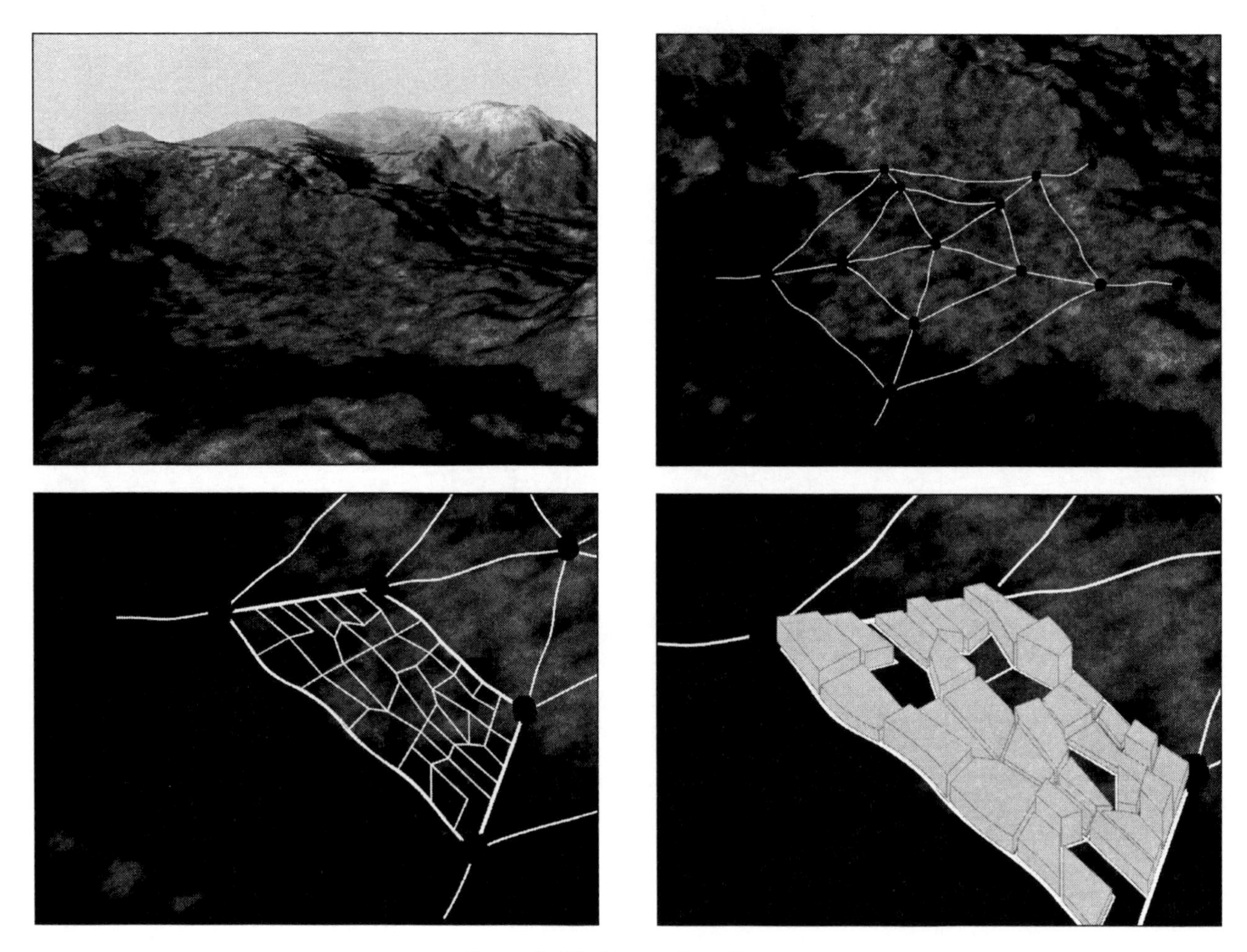

Figure 3: City Generation Stages

Immersive visual and audio world in 3D

Patrice Bouvier, Pascal Chaudeyrac, Raphaël Loyet, Benoit Piranda, François de Sorbier de Pougnadoresse

Université de Marne la Vallée, Institut Gaspard Monge and Equipe SISAR
{bouvier, pchaudey, piranda, fdesorbi}@univ-mlv.fr

Abstract

This article presents the approach we followed for the creation of our virtual reality room, both from the hardware point of view and the software one.

Our main goal, to build a virtual reality room as cheap as possible and easily transportable, was constrained by our knowledge of the mechanisms of human perception. Like any virtual reality system, our room aims to immerse the user in a place where he will be able to feel the presence of the virtual objects and his self-presence in the virtual environment. To recreate this dual feeling of presence we use the less intrusive as possible sensory interfaces and the most natural and intuitive motor interfaces.

We achieve this goal by diverting the user's attention to the application itself. We present applications in various fields : art, games and archaeology.

Keywords: virtual reality, immersion, presence, spatial auditory display

1. Introduction

The aim of a virtual reality system is to immerse one or more users in an artificial environment where he will feel and interact in real-time thanks to sensory and motor interfaces. The experience will have to be credible enough to gull user's senses in order to create, the ultimate goal, a feeling of presence of the virtual objects, but also a feeling of his presence in the virtual environment. This will be the only condition for the user to accept to take part of the game.

Among the classic virtual reality systems, let us quote the CAVE [CNSF*92] and the Workbench [KBF*95]. The Cave Automatic Virtual Environment, is composed of a small room of roughly five square meters, where each wall and the ground are screens on which are displayed synchronised images. The Workbench is a virtual work environment composed of two perpendicular screens, a liquid crystal display which provide depth perception, a head motion capture device and a six degrees of freedom stylus to manipulate objects. At last another method is to use a head mounted display (HMD) with liquid crystal display.

Those solutions are both very expensive and/or hardly transportable. Targeting different objectives, the Sisar team of Marne la Vallée University has built a virtual reality room with consumer grade components. Our objective is to dispose of an installation at low cost and easily transportable. It allows us to test various user interfaces, as less intrusive as possible, and different visual and sound rendering in order to immerse the user more and more.

After a brief outline on the methods used for visual and sound immersion we'll focus on our interfaces managing the interactions. Finally, before we conclude, we'll present some of our realizations. It is important to note that proposing applications with a strong focus on the playful aspect, build on a strong scenario or bearer of feeling help to forget the interfaces and develop a feeling of presence.

2. Immersion

Within the framework of our virtual reality room, the immersion of the user is based on the visual rendering in 3D based on stereo-vision and a 3D sound environment reproduced thanks to an 8.0 sound system. After a brief theoretical reminder, we'll describe these devices.

2.1. 3D visual display

From a visual point of view, the immersion of a user is based on three fundamental points: the field of view of the installation, the depth perception and the real-time display of the virtual environment. The first point is easily solved by respecting a correct ratio between the distance separating the user and the screen, and the screen's dimensions (see figure 1). For the second point, depth perception is created by stereoscopic images [Oko]. They simulate the human vision, that is based on the perception of a scene through two different points of view: each eye having a specific image. This is this rule that the stereoscopic system (see figure 2), the usage of filters and polarizing glasses, targets to recreate. The two images are the result of two OpenGL processing of the same scene; these images are afterward displayed with two video-projectors equipped with polarizing filters. The separation of the two images on the same screen is made with polarizing glasses.

Figure 1: *Our 6x3 meters screen.*

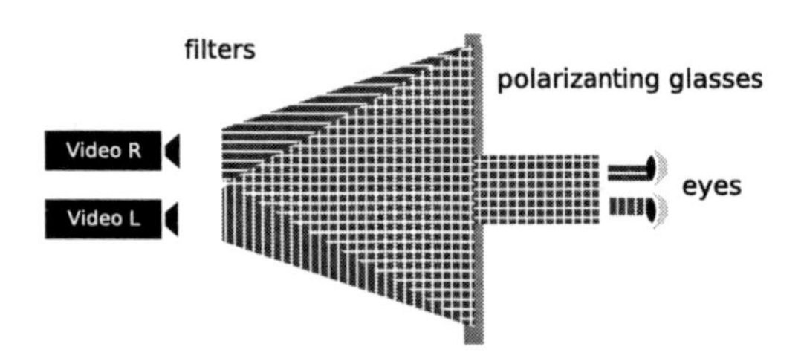

Figure 2: *Stereoscopic system.*

The usage of a home-made 3D engine allows us a total control of the parameters. Among others, the management of the distance between the two cameras, or their orientation allows us to adapt the quality of the depth perception according to the distance of the user. Our room, made with large audience transportable material has been employed during the last "Journée du Patrimoine" in a theater (see section 6). The management of these parameters allowed us to switch easily between a public of 200 people sitting on terraces and a unique user at 2 meters from the screen.

Another great point of a home-made system is that it allows us to switch easily from a hardware solution to another so that it is possible to experiment algorithms linked to recent evolutions on graphical cards. The massive use of shaders programs [Ros] in our rendering algorithms allows us to guaranty a satisfying framerate without making concessions on the visual effects that are essential to the immersion. For example, the usage of shader-based blur algorithms [PdSdP04] allows orienting the regard of the user to relevant zones, but also gives a bit of rest to the observer's eyes and increases his visual comfort (see figure 3).

Figure 3: *Blur in virtual scene.*

2.2. Spatial sound

2.2.1. Theory

First of all let us remind that the audible range of frequency for human ears is going from 20Hz to 20kHz. In 1907 Lord Raleigh [RS07] defined the Duplex theory on the sound perception in three dimensions. This theory approximates human head to a sphere with two holes diametrically opposed representing the ears. Besides the case where the sound source is located on the median plane between the two ears, the distance from the sound to the ipsilateral and contralateral ears are different. This difference, because of the transit time, is the source of the interaural time delay (ITD). However the ITD is only effective [Bla97] for frequencies above 1500Hz†. Below this frequency, the waves aren't disturbed by obstacles of the size of a human head. It's interesting to note that the ITD occurs particularly for the localization of sounds with fast attack. For continuous sounds or whose attack is slower, the brain will use the interaural phase difference (IPD) that match the difference of phase at each

† That corresponds to a wave-length of about 22cm, that is the width of the head

ear. Above 1500Hz the interaural level delay (ILD) starts to operate. Due to their wave-length these waves bounce on the head so they are largely declined (through diffraction) or not transmitted to the contralateral ear. According to Carlile [Car96], an attenuation of 40dB if obtained for a frequency of 3kHz.

The theoretical limit of the Duplex theory is that it makes us think we hear in 3D because we have two ears. To get convinced let us study the case of a person who is deaf of one ear, we will talk about monaural audition, it is possible for this person to localise a sound in three dimensions [WK97]. It rely on the learning of extended spectral signatures, not only determined by the sound itself but also by it's relative position regarding the auditor. Those spectral variations are based on interferences caused by the shoulders, the head and the pinna [Bat67]‡. This ability also contributes in classical cases of binaural audition to ripen the localization, to simplify the distinction front / rear and to locate sounds on the median plane. These interferences can be simulated thanks to Head Related Transfer Functions (HRTF) which are used with headphone reproduction. In order to be complete let us add that a priori knowledge of the source position increases the precision of detection.

It is possible to affirm that hearing is a multimodal sense, indeed, human unconsciously performs small movements of the head. By tightening the ear, he tries to obtain other sound pictures of the scene and so ripen the precision of detection. Moreover we feel sound waves with all the body, notably low frequencies that are more felt than heard.

Let us note that there are strong interactions between image and sound perception, here are two examples: Ventriloquism and McGurk effect [MD76] where vision of lips articulating a syllable whereas the sound emitted is another syllable makes the person recognize a third syllable different from the 2 others.

2.2.2. 3D sound reproduction device

As we have told in the introduction we are looking for the less intrusive interfaces, that is why we decided to make the sound spatialization with speakers rather than headphone which can become telling and a source of discomfort. We found the following advantages: no need to use generic HRTF which are by definition not those of our user. His ability to locate could taper off. As we've told in last paragraph, the user performs some unconscious movements of the head to ripen the localization. These movements will be executed, so we should use a very fine tracking to reflect these variations into the HRTF, so it gives the feeling that the sound comes from inside his head. The sound is a wave that is also felt by the foot, the bones and the body. It is impossible to simulate the very low frequency sounds that are more felt than eared.

‡ The shape of he pinna makes affect sounds with frequencies above 2000Hz.

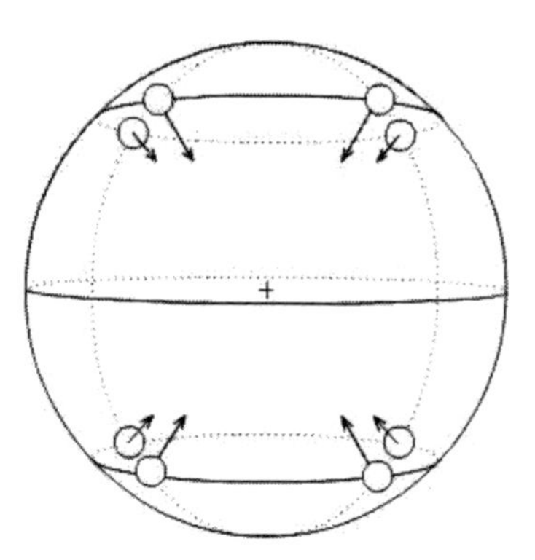

Figure 4: *Position and direction of the speakers on the sphere.*

Hearing is an omnidirectional sense, so it is natural to represent the sound space by a sphere with user's head as the center. To keep the fact that the system has to be easily transportable, we have decided to use only 8 speakers at the corners of a cube defined inside this sphere (see figure 4). However it's clear that whith more loudspeaker the reproduction would be more accurate. Our system would allow us to locate the origin of the sound on the plane defined by three speakers.

2.2.3. Our system

The spatialisation of the sounds uses a Terratec 7.1 sound card, which was originally designed to make a planar spatialisation (front centre, front right, front left, surround right, surround right, rear left, rear right and sub-woofer). This configuration has been modified to an 8.0 system that creates a 3D space for the sound. The eight speakers have all the same characteristics and are placed at the corners of a cube, the sound recreated is not a hi-fidelity sound, because no sub-woofer is used, but a great part of the audible spectra (15 Hz - 22 kHz) is reproduced.

Three sound libraries have been tryed on Linux, the firsts of a higher level than the third, OpenAL [Opea], FMOD [FMO] and Jack-it [Dav]. Both have systems to read and seek inside a sound file and they all provide buffers to manage communication between audio elements. OpenAL and FMOD provide ready-to-use API which play sounds through a classical sound system such as stereo or 5.1 using planar localization because no third dimension can be transmitted to the user. With Jack-it it is possible to share concurrent§ sound buffers with low latency between audio applications and devices. The eight speakers have been defined

§ Operating at the same time

as independent devices and algorithms managing the spherical spatialization have been written. The main advantage of Jack-it compared to Alsa or OSS is that it manages an optimized mix of the buffers before sending them to the device. The main drawback is that none of the high level elements such as the sample rate conversion, the management of interleaved audio files, the Doppler, the attenuation of some frequency according to the distance or the reverberation linked to the environment of the sound.

The aim of the spatialization is to place a sound source in a 3D environment, so there is no need to read stereo interleaved files, all files used by the system are mono WAV files.

The sample rate conversion have been made with time variant filters structure [PM96] that has the advantage to integrate the interpolation and decimation processes in the filter so that it provides a really optimized filtering for real-time applications. The conversions have been implemented for the classical frequencies: 44.1 kHz (CD quality), 48 kHz (DAT quality) and 96 kHz (studio quality). This module have been implemented in order to import easily sounds to the software, and to be compatible with the majority of the sound cards operating on Linux.

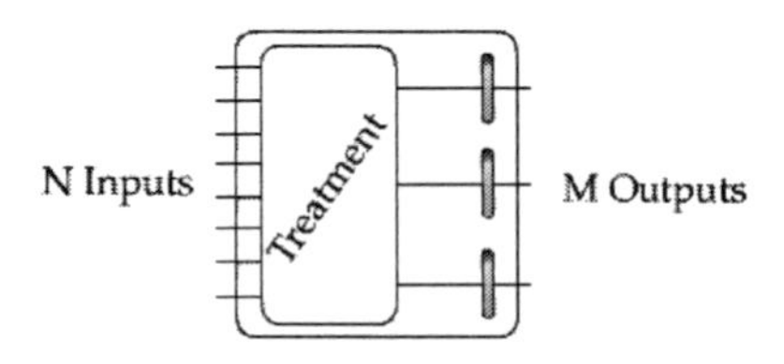

Figure 5: *Representation of a LADSPA module.*

The modules of spatialization have been implemented thanks to LADSPA [LAD]; it is a simple API to develop audio modules that can be seen in figure 5. These modules have N inputs that can be muted and M Outputs. On each output the level can be checked (to display a vu-meter for example). The processing is the part that determines the modifications to sounds and / or the links between inputs and outputs. Many free modules have been implemented with this structure including a great collection from Steve Harris [Har]. Reverberation has been used to create some ambiances depending on the location of the scene; a great reverberation is used to simulate a cathedral or a dream, a small one for a very small room or to give the user a felling of confinement.

A LADSPA low-pass filter has been used to simulate the attenuation of high frequencies according to the distance between the user and the sound.

The module of spatialization is the last step of the sound precess, as shown in figure 6. It takes one input, the sound coming from the reverberation module, and has eight outputs linked to the devices on the sound card.

The position of the speakers and of the sound is converted

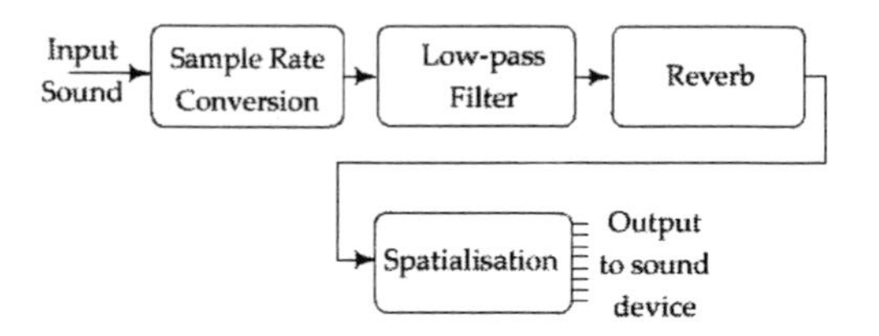

Figure 6: *Operations applied to a single sound.*

from Euclidian space to spherical space with the head of the player as origin in both real and virtual worlds.

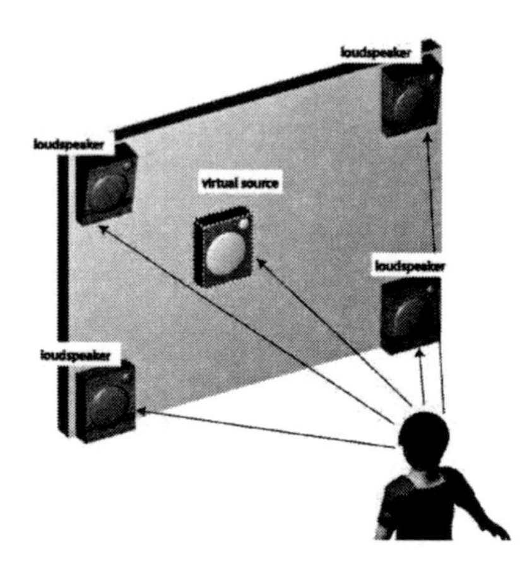

Figure 7: *Amplitude panning.*

The output level for a speaker i $h_{i,vol}$ is calculated this way: The sound position is defined by $(s_\rho, s_\phi, s_\theta)$ with s_ρ the distance, s_ϕ the zenith and s_θ the azimuth. The eight speakers' positions are defined by $(h_{i,\rho}, h_{i,\phi}, h_{i,\theta})$. The zenith and azimuth are then compared and if the following condition is true,

$$\{\frac{-\pi}{2} \leq h_{i,\theta} - s_\theta \leq \frac{\pi}{2}\}\{\frac{-\pi}{2} \leq h_{i,\phi} - s_\phi \leq \frac{\pi}{2}\}$$

Then the next relation is used to defined the amplitude panning :

$$h_{i,vol} = s_{vol}.|\cos(h_{i,\theta} - s_\theta)|.|\cos(h_{i,\phi} - s_\phi)|$$

s_{vol} is the volume of the source. At last s_ρ allows to modulate the sound volume functions of the distance between the virtual source and the user.

2.3. Synchronization of visual and sound events

It's central for the success of a virtual reality application, that the different sensory events are synchronous and to preserve the causality link between user's actions and system's reactions. That's why our system used 2 threads, the main thread manages the inputs (capture of the LEDS) and the graphical part of the application. When the user or an object moves on the scene a message is send via a FIFO to the audio thread. When a message is received, the audio thread checks if the sound is too far from the player, in this case, the sound isn't played and the corresponding output is muted. If the sound enters in the listening zone, the process (see figure 6) start. If the sound was already in the listening zone, only the calculation of the spatialization will be made.

3. Interaction

The virtual reality room is fit out which two cameras located in such manner that they can capture every user's movements. Those cameras, calibrated with the OpenCV [Opeb] library, permit to extract the position in 3D of electroluminescent diodes places on the polarizing glasses of the user or on various interface objects such as a pen. We can observe that the LED on the glasses (see figure 8)enable to deduce head's position and movements of the user and therefore user's interest center. An horizontal variance of the head more significative is associate to user's will to move in the scene. Our acquisition system being based on diode detection, it's easy to change any common object into a tool for virtual reality. For example (see figure 9) two small welds can transforms an inoffensive child's gun to a redoubtable weapon of precision in our room or an old paintbrush becomes a tool of the XXIth century.

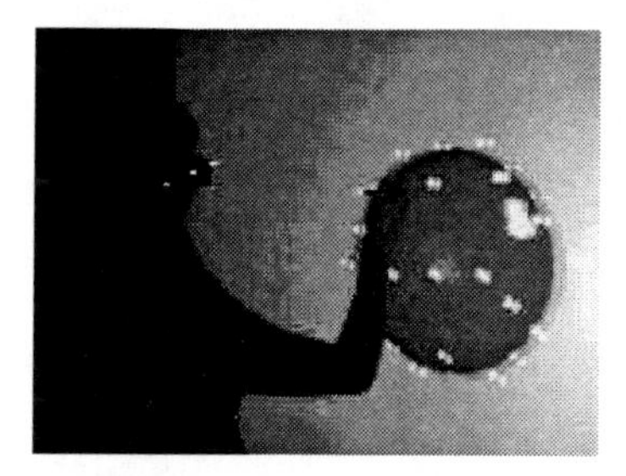

Figure 8: *LED on glasses.*

The freedom of interfaces choice can permit to propose either an original interface that implies an adaptation time or an easier one using common tools to be as intuitive as possible. In both cases, the tool must be adapted to be as transparent as possible in the users mind.

4. Applications

One of the first experiment we have set up in our virtual reality room is the extraction of depth information from art paintings, synthesized in the form of a depth map and rendered in the room. This incursion in arts has also led to an original new tool for virtual painting in four dimensions.

Figure 9: *Example of tools.*

Coats of paint are melted when the virtual brush come over older layer, if not dry, integrating the time factor. Always in the field of art, the Amorphous Ubiquity [AP04] is a real time interactive installation where the user is immersed in a perpetually moving 3D maze, the motion of the maze being determined by the user's motion and speech.

A project in collaboration between the city of Serris, an archaeological team and SISAR has led to the creation of a virtual Merovingian environment whose data are based on vestiges discovered on the site of the city. In addition to the ability for the city to communicate on it's history, this reconstitution is seen by the archaeologist as a completely new way to emit and to evaluate historical hypothesis.

The virtual reality room allows also to play 3D movies filmed with a device consisting of two calibrated cameras next to each others. The restitution imply a precise synchronization of the video-projectors.

The Puppet is an application that allows to manipulate an avatar. The extraction from a video flow of the user's profile on a white background is done in real time. The skeleton is then analyzed to interpret the user's will and the avatar is activated accordingly.

The last application using our virtual reality room is an interactive game similar to the famous adventure game MYST [MYS] (see figure 10). The main goal is to move from a scene to another solving puzzles and riddles. The user has a panoramic stereoscopic vision of each scenes. Our new method is different from usual methods in the sense that we don't project the three dimensional objects onto the screen. Our method is composed of three stages. First, we generate a very realistic scene using a rendering and modeling software like 3DSMAX. Then we calculate three dense sets of pictures that represent three different 360ř points of view of the scene. These last ones are used to create the panoramic of the scene. Finally we project them on three cylinders. The steroscopic vision rendering is achieved choosing the right pair of cylinders.

Figure 10: *A ludic application.*

5. Conclusion

In this article, we have presented our virtual reality room, its main qualities are its low cost, its mobility and its evolutivity. Apart from the screen, it is only constituted of consumer grade elements. From a computer science perspective, we have made the choice of using open source softwares, available under Linux.

The interest of this device is to allow the visual and auditive immersion of the user and, by the mean of sensors, its intuitive interaction with the environment.

For electronic games, this room allows new types of gameplay and amplify the players sensations. Moreover virtual reality does not limit to stimulating in an independent manner, the different senses of the user, but has to offer a multi-sensorial perception. The aim is there to propose new sensations, of intersensoriality, quasi synestesical.

References

[AP04] ALMIRON M., PIRANDA B.: Ubicuidad amorfa. *CiberArt Bilbao 2004* (avril 2004).

[Bat67] BATTEAU D. W.: The role of the pinna in human sound localization. In *Proceedings of the Royal Society* (1967), vol. 168, pp. 158–180.

[Bla97] BLAUERT J.: *Spatial Hearing, Revised edition.* The MIT Press, Cambridge, MA, USA, 1997.

[Car96] CARLILE S.: Virtual auditory space: Generation and applications. *New York: RG Landes* (1996).

[CNSF*92] CRUZ-NEIRA C., SANDIN D. J., FANTI T. A. D., KENYON R. V., HART J. C.: The cave: Audio visualexperience automatic virtual environnement. *Commun. ACM Siggraph 35(6)* (1992), 64–72.

[Dav] DAVIS P.: Jack audio connection kit. http://jackaudio.org/.

[FMO] Fmod. http://www.fmod.org/.

[Har] HARRIS S.: Swh plug-ins. http://plugin.org.uk/.

[KBF*95] KRUEGER W., BOHN C., FROHLICH B., SCHEUTH H., STRAUSS W., WESCHE G.: The responsive workbench. *IEEE Computer 28*, 7 (1995).

[LAD] Linux audio developer's simple plugin api (ladspa). http://www.ladspa.org/.

[MD76] MCGURK H., DONALD J. M.: Hearing lips and seeing voices. *Nature* (December 1976), 746–748.

[MYS] Myst 3 : exile. http://www.myst.com/.

[Oko] OKOSHI: *Tree-dimensional imaging techiniques.* Academic Press Inc.

[Opea] Open audio library (openal). http://www.openal.org/.

[Opeb] Opencv. http://www.intel.com/technology/computing/opencv/.

[PdSdP04] PIRANDA B., DE SORBIER DE POUGNADORESSE F.: Simulation de flou en synthèse d'images stéréoscopiques pour la réalité virtuelle. *AFIG 2004* (2004).

[PM96] PROAKIS J. G., MANOLAKIS D. G.: *Digital Signal Processing, principles algorithms, and applications.* Prentice Hall International Editions, 1996.

[Ros] ROST R. J.: *OpenGL Shading Language.* Addison Wesley.

[RS07] RALEIGH L., STRUTT J. W.: Our perception of sound direction. *Philosophical Magazine* (1907).

[WK97] WIGHTMAN F. L., KISTLER D. J.: Monaural sound localization revisited. *J. Acoust. Soc. Am 101* (February 1997), 1050–1063.

Figure 11: *A ludic application.*

Graphics & Visualisation (2)

Line-Triangle Test for Collision Detection and Response in Soft Bodies

Jaruwan Mesit
jmesit@cs.ucf.edu

Ratan K. Guha
guha@cs.ucf.edu

School of Electrical Engineering and Computer Science
University of Central Florida, Orlando, Florida 32826

KEYWORDS

soft body collision, animation, spatial subdivision, spatial hashing

ABSTRACT

Soft-body models are common in games to simulate cloth or elastic objects. To realistically simulate soft-body objects, collision detection and response is required. In addition, soft-body models must re-arrange their internal structure to react to the collision. This paper presents a new collision detection and response algorithm which can simulate a variety of soft-body material behaviors ranging from stiff to elastic. In this approach, a line-triangle intersection test is used for collision detection and force propagation is used for collision response. Implementation and experiments using the algorithm show that complex deformable objects composed of thousands vertices can be animated at interactive speeds.

1. INTRODUCTION

Soft-body, or deformable, objects in games and simulations include flags, banners, cloaks, rubber or elastic walls, trampolines or bounce pads, and semi-solid surfaces such as slime. Soft-body objects impose additional complexity to collision computation over solid-body objects due to: (1) changing collision detection boundaries, and (2) collision response that requires change of the solid body internal structure.

Deformable models have had some recent research attention [6, 30, 26, 32], many of which utilize a mass-spring system. Mass-spring systems can be classified as either finite-element methods (FEM) or long-element methods (LEM). Bounding volume hierarchies have been developed to speed up intersection tests of close bodies. For example: bounding spheres [14, 15], axis-aligned bounding boxes (AABBs) [2, 31], oriented bounding boxes (OBBs) [16], quantized orientation slabs with primary orientations (QuOSPOs) [11], and discrete-oriented polytopes (K-DOPs) [19], octtree [25], BSP tree [27], brep-indices [3], k-d tree [13], bucket tree [8], hybrid tree [20] , BVIT [28], and uniform space subdivision [31]. There are also collision detection algorithms for large environments such as I-COLLIDE [4] and CULLIDE [9].

In order to simulate realistic collision response [12, 25, 17] in deformable objects, a basic idea is to use discrete-time simulations. Penalty forces are generated to eventually separate deformable objects that are colliding. The function of penetration depth represents the distance and the direction of vertices in deformable objects. Additionally, response force is considered as a function of the relative velocity of colliding structures and their penetration depth. Many penetration depth approaches focus on specific problems in large penetration. However, these methods are not suitable to our algorithm.

The method proposed in this paper extends existing deformable modeling techniques by incorporating efficient ways to compute the contact surfaces in colliding objects. For computational efficiency a mass-spring system is used. As a result large environments of at least 10 thousand faces of deforming primitives can be simulated at interactive speeds.

1.1 SOFT BODIES

This section explains the modeling of soft-body behavior with a pressure force. The model in this paper is based on the classic soft body method presented in [22]. Pressure force is represented as a vector. Matyka and Ollila [22] computed pressure force vector by applying pressure at particular point to the normal vector of that surface, since pressure force is always acting in a direction normal to the surface. The expression for pressure at a specific point is:

$$\vec{P} = P \cdot \hat{n}\left[\frac{N}{m^2}\right]$$

where P is a pressure value, $\hat{n}$ is a normal vector to surface where the pressure force is acting, m^2 is a surface area, and N is a force dimension. Pressure forces can be evaluated with $\vec{P}$ multiplied by $A[m^2]$ which is the area of the surface. The equation becomes:

$$\vec{F}_P = \vec{P} \cdot A[m^2]$$

Note that a larger force might generate a smaller pressure if it is distributed in a wider surface area. In contrast, a smaller force can create a larger pressure if the area is smaller. The value of P is from thermodynamic approximation known as ideal gas approximation. In the Clausius Clapeyron equation:

$$PV = nRT$$

where V is volume of the body, n is gas mol number, R is ideal gas constant, and T is a temperature. Then, the pressure can be generated by the temperature and volume of the soft-body as:

$$P = V^{-1}nRT$$

It is assumed that the temperature does not change while volume of a soft body changes.

1.2 EULER INTEGRATION

The following notation will be used throughout the paper.

Geometry

$v^i_0 \ldots v^i_n$ are the positions of vertices for object i.

m^i is the mass of object i.

Direction

${}_n ve^i_k$ is the velocity of v^i_k at time n.

${}_n n^i_k$ is the normal vector of v^i_k at time n.

${}_n f^i_k$ is the force of v^i_k at time n.

Note: k is vertex number of object i

For forces that are applied to the objects:

1) Rigid body has one external force.

${}_n f_g$ is the external force (gravity)

2) Flexible body has one external force and one internal force.

${}_n f^i_g$ is the external force (gravity)

${}_n f^i_s$ is the internal force (mass spring

${}_n f^i_k = {}_n f^i_g + {}_n f^i_s$ +Pressure force ($\vec{P}$)

Euler 1st order integration is used to simulate the soft bodies for ease of implementation. Each time step in the animation is computed by the interval from frame to frame. From Euler 1st integration we have:

$$dve^i_k/dt = f^i_k / m^i$$
$$dve^i_k = f^i_k \, dt/m^i$$

Next,

$${}_{n+1}ve^i_k = {}_n ve^i_k + ({}_n f^i_k/m^i)\, dt$$

Then,

$${}_{n+1}v^i_k = {}_n v^i_k + {}_{n+1}ve^i_k \, dt$$

Using integration, the position of each vertex in the flexible object is computed. Then collision detection and collision response will be applied.

2. ALGORITHM OVERVIEW

For collision detection and collision response of dynamically deforming bodies in a large environment, four steps of collision detection and collision response algorithm proceed as follows:

(1) *Multi-level Subdivided Bounding Box* (Multi-level SB): All soft bodies are surrounded by a bounding box (AABB) for tracking. Two points, a minimum and a maximum, define the bounding box. Then, the bounding box is subdivided to n-levels of sub-division. A 3-level subdivision is used for this simulation.

(2) *Box Hash Function (BHF)*: The box hash function is applied to each point that we use to create the subdivided bounding box. One subdivided bounding box has 8 points. Each point is hashed and given hash index by box hash function. A list of subdivided bounding boxes is put in hash table related to hash index. Then, the contact surface is computed from vertices that belong to subdivided bounding box in the lists of hash table. Multi-level SB Collide and the box-hash function which are further detailed in [24].

(3) *Collision for Flexible Models (CF)*: A line-triangle intersection test detects collision. To reduce high computation in triangle-triangle intersection, we use multi-passes of line-intersection. Using the line-triangle intersection, there are two possibilities: 1) one line from one triangle interferes in another triangle 2) two lines from one triangle intersect with another triangle. A triangle intersects with another triangle if and only if there is one or two lines in the triangle intersecting with another triangle.

(4) *Collision response (CR):* For soft bodies, the objects change shape dynamically in response to its typical environment. Response is handled by using

normal vector at the surface of colliding object and response is provided accordingly.

2.1 MULTI-LEVEL SUBDIVIDED BOUNDING BOXES (Multi-level SB)

Step one of the algorithm is tracking with multi-level subdivided bounding boxes. Each object is surrounded by an axis aligned bounding box (AABB). A minimum point and maximum point are calculated to bound the soft body. The AABB is subdivided in to 2^n regions, where n is level of subdivision (see detail in [24]).

2.2 BOX HASH FUNCTION (BHF)

We use a **Box Hash Function (BHF)**. The idea is to use **BHF** and hash to 8 points that we use to create the subdivided bounding box. To facilitate hashing, initially a hash table is created which is based on grid size. The formula is:

```
Index = ( floor(Grid.min.x / length) * xprime+
          floor(Grid.min.y/ height) * yprime +
          floor(Grid.min.z / width) * zprime)
          % bucketsize;
```

where length is grid length, height is grid height, width is grid width, grid.min.x, grid.min.y, and grid.min.z are
minimum points of each grid, xprime, yprime, and zprime are any prime number for x, y, and z. Next, the **BHF** is applied to 8 points of the subdivided bounding box. Since there are 8 points, [0..7], in one subdivided bounding box, the **BHF** is:

```
HashIndex = (floor(point[0..7].x /length) *
             xprime+
             floor(point[0..7].y /height) *
             yprime +
             floor(point[0..7].z /width) *
             zprime) % bucketsize
```

where xprime, yprime, and zprime are any prime number for x, y, and z , length, height, and width are length, height, and width of grid cell.

2.3 MULTI-PASS LINE-TRIANGLE INTERSECTION

All particles in the subdivided bounding boxes which are in the same hash index will be passed to the next step to find if the objects are colliding or not. Three passes of the line intersection test are as follows:

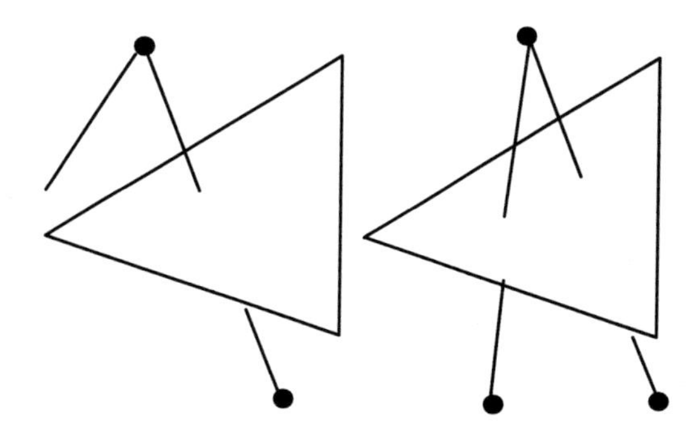

Figure 1: *Two examples of line intersection; one line is intersecting with a triangle (left) and two lines are intersecting with a triangle (right) (black dots represent the particle points)*

First pass: The algorithm takes first line of the triangle in 3D space. Then, it finds if the first line is penetrating the triangle or not. If so, the collision occurs and then finds the intersection point. The algorithm continues to the second pass

Second pass: the algorithm takes second line of the triangle. It checks again if the second line is interfering with the triangle or not. If so, the collision happens and calculates the intersection point. Incase the first line and second line are interesting with triangle, the algorithm stops. On another hand, algorithm continues to next pass if either first or second line is intersecting.

Third pass: The algorithm take the third line and check for intersection test as describe in first pass and second pass

To test for line and triangle intersection, first we compute the point of intersection between line and plane. Next, we check if the point is in the triangle or not by using Barycentric coordinates. For a 3D plane, we drop the component in which the plane normal has the biggest absolute value. If the point is in the triangle, the point of intersection is returned. If not, the line is not intersecting with the triangle. section. Next the intersection point is passed to the to next step, which is collision response.

2.4 COLLISION RESPONSE

Collision response for soft bodies in most analytical methods is based on penalty forces. The methods calculate response forces based on penetration depths to resolve colliding objects. However, those methods are not appropriate for our soft body representation. To simplify the algorithm, we use a method for response based on contact surface and the intersection point. There are two cases.

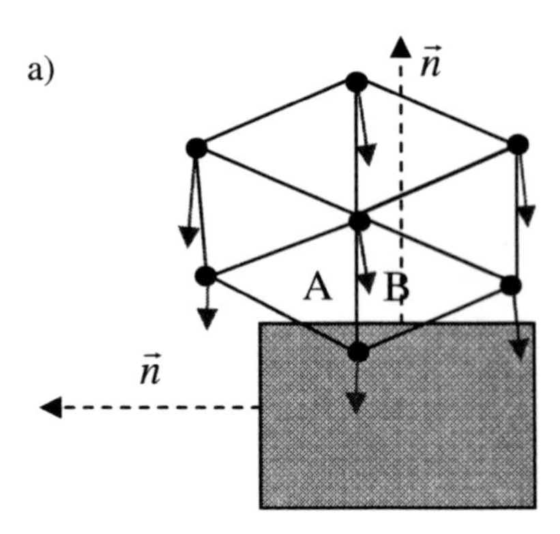

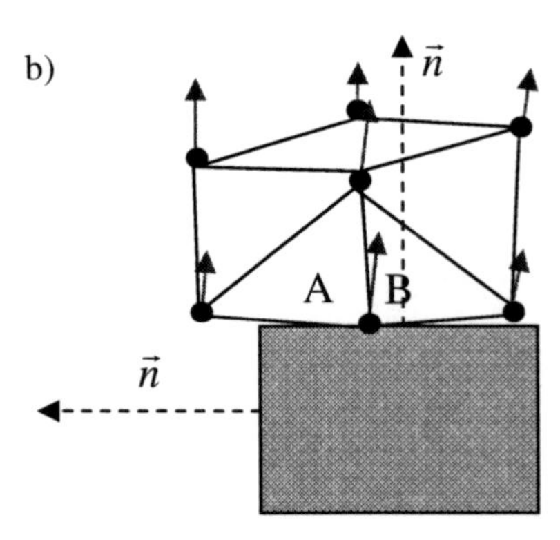

Figure 2: *a) collision detection algorithm detects the collision between soft bodies and another object surface (dark vectors represent velocities of the particles and dashed vector represent normal vector of the surface) b) collision response pulls back the position of the particle to object surface.*

In first case (figure 2), there is only one intersecting surface. The position of particle is changed to be at the intersection point of line. If there are more than one intersection lines for that particle, we take the smallest distance between particle and intersection point. Then, we move the position of the particle to the intersection point. The velocity of the particle will be calculated form normal vector at that surface.

In the second case (figure 3), there are two intersecting surfaces. We keep track of the first surface and second surface. Then the position of the particle will be pulled back to the corner between those two surfaces. The velocity of the particle will be computed by the average of normal vector from those two surfaces.

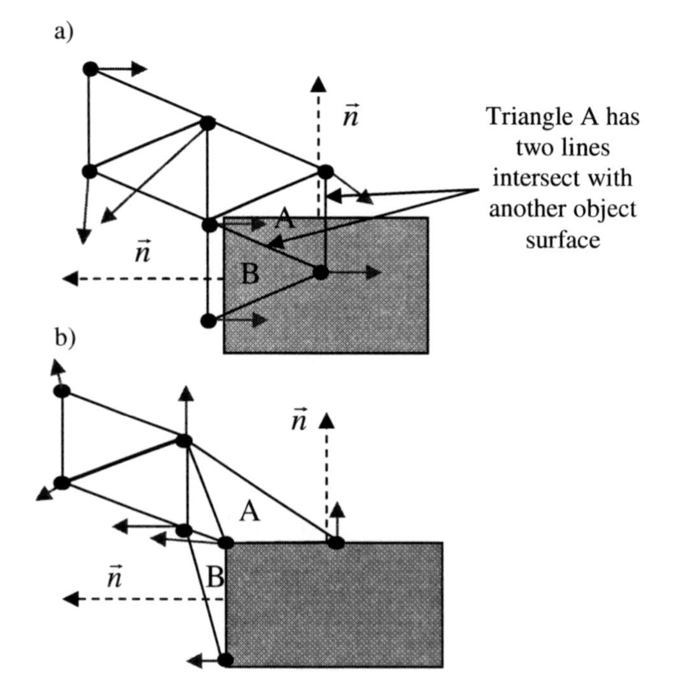

Figure 3: *a) our collision detection algorithm detects the interference between two objects: (again dark vectors represent velocities of particles, dot vectors represent normal vectors at the particular surfaces) b) our collision response pulls back the velocities of the particles by the normal vector of the surfaces.*

3. EXPERIMENTS

The simulation was implemented in Visual C++ with OpenGL. It ran collision detection in soft bodies up to 10,000 vertices at more than 30 frames per second on Pentium4 3.2 GHz Laptop with Nvidia GeForce Go 6800 GPU. Clearly this is more vertices than required for most games, but the simulation was done to test the limits of the algorithm. Figure 4 shows the collision detection between two dynamically deformed soft bodies. The gray spheres represent the colliding points between those two objects.

From the results, 2480 faces of soft bodies can detect collision at 120 frames per second. Figure 5 is a comparison of using our collision response and without collision response. The soft body bouncing with the ground is shown in figure 5a. Figures 5b and 5c illustrate that (b) some particles of the soft body are passing through the ground, then in (c) the particles colliding with ground are pulled up above the ground when collision is detected. For this simulation, frame rate is captured at 80 frames per second. Figure 6 shows soft bodies that are falling down from the top to the bottom and colliding with another sphere at 45 frames per second.

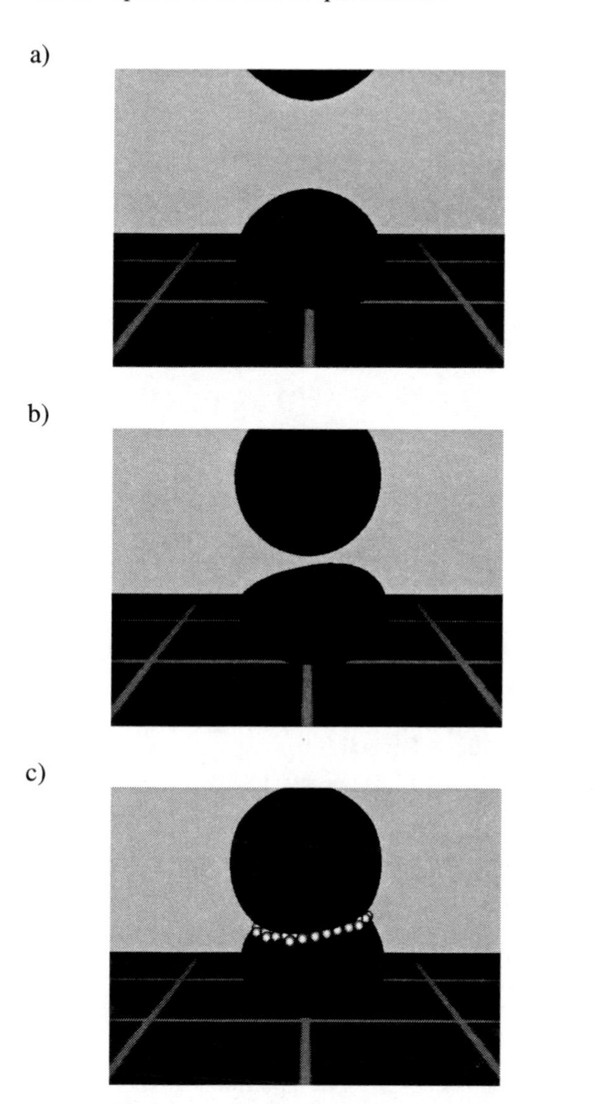

Figure 4: *Two deformable objects are colliding; the gray sphere presents the colliding surfaces that have been captured by our collision detection algorithm; the simulation is captured at frame 100, 200, and 300 shown in a), b), and c) respectively*

Figure 7 and 8 present the comparison between our multi-level SB collide with collision response and spatial hashing proposed presented in [31]. 10k faces of soft bodies are simulated and animated from frame 1 to frame 2000 measured in frame per second (FPS) with the same number of collision. The performance in figure 7 is decreasing when the frame number is increasing while the performance in figure 8 is slightly decreasing. Both show that our proposed method is more efficient than normal spatial hashing method.

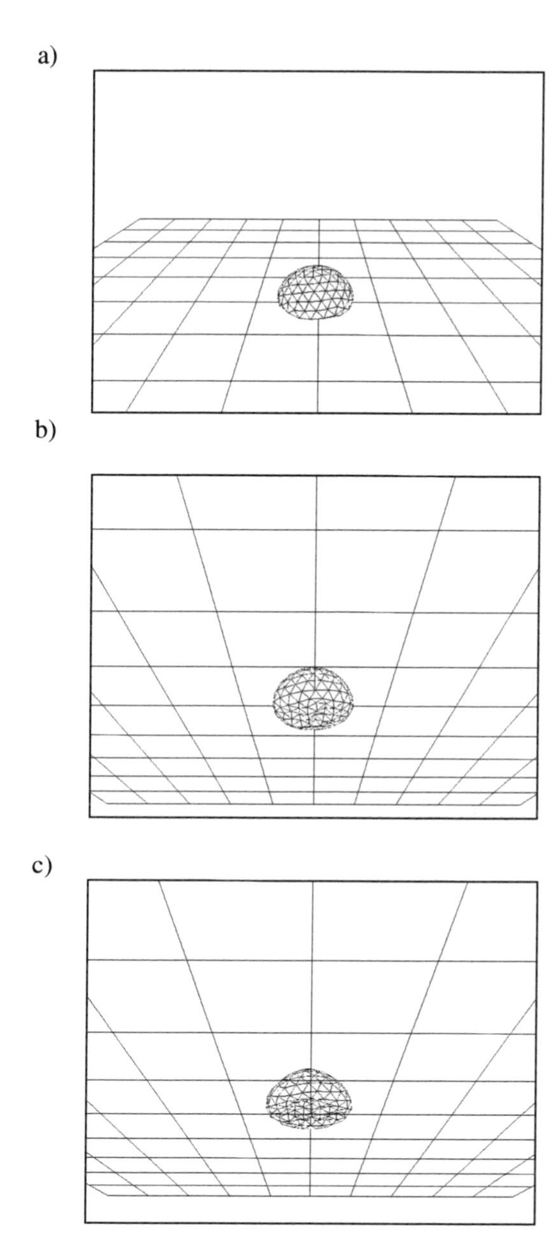

Figure 5: *a) a soft body is colliding with the ground (eye poison is set to look above the object and the direction is set to look down to the object and ground, b) some particles colliding with the ground are passing through the ground without collision response algorithm, c) some particle colliding with the ground are not passing through the ground with our collision response (eye position is set to look below the ground and direction is set to look up to the ground in b and c)*

a)

b)

c)

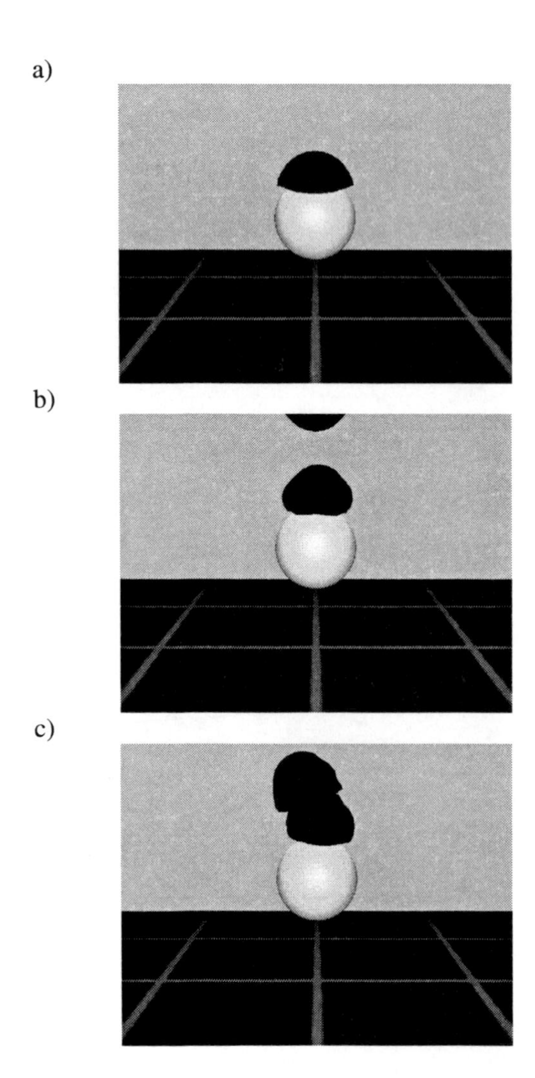

Figure 6: *our deformable objects are falling down from the top to the bottom and colliding with one sphere; again the deformable objects are modeling by our modeling algorithm and detecting the collision by our collision detection algorithm shown in a), b), and c) respectively*

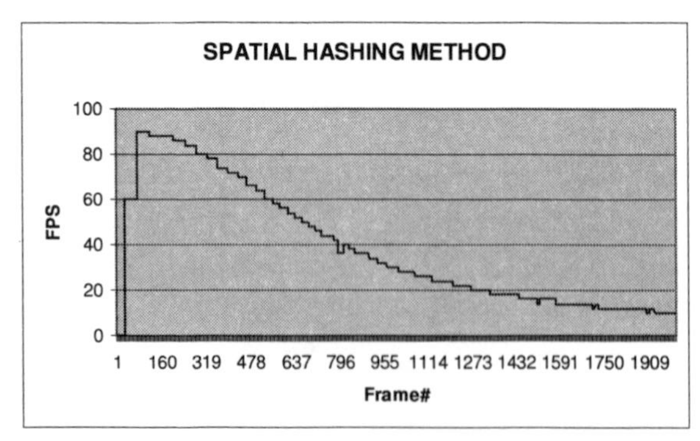

Figure 7: *Performance of the collision detection by spatial hashing*

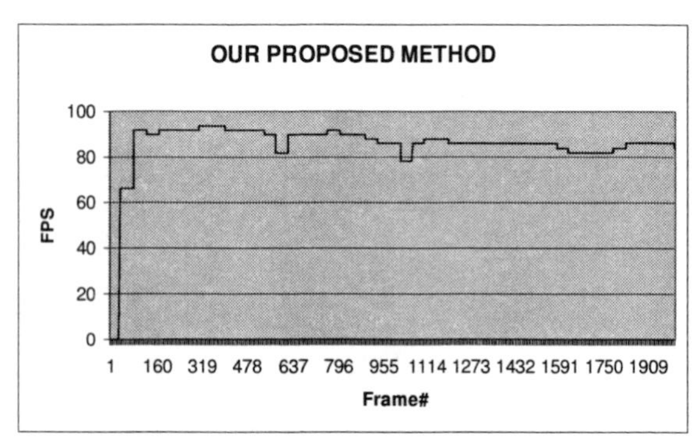

Figure 8: *Performance of the collision detection by our proposed method*

4. CONCLUSION AND FUTURE WORKS

In 3D games and simulations collision detection and collision response of soft bodies is a significant problem. Since soft bodies are composed of possibly thousands of moving particles, it becomes time consuming and adds additional complexity over regular, solid-body collision detection. To speed up collision detection and collision response, we propose a line-triangle intersection test to extend Multi-Level SB Collide. Several passes of line-triangle intersection give accurate results for collision detection and collision response in soft bodies. There are four main steps in the algorithm: *Multi-level Subdivided Bounding Box, Box Hash Function, Collision for Flexible Models and Collision response.* Experimental results show that our algorithm is efficient method for real-time collision detection and collision response in soft bodies for real time gaming.

There are several ways to extend this research. The first is to simplify the operation process to optimize the algorithm. The second possibility is to use a tree structure to determine the area of collision in the object body and perform the collision detection in the overlapped area to reduce time complexity. And finally to create additional, suitable test cases to compare with other algorithms.

REFERENCES:

[1] Balaniuk, R. and Salisbury, K. 2002. "Dynamic simulation of deformable objects using the Long Elements Method," *Haptic Interfaces for Virtual Environment and Teleoperator Systems*, pages 58–65.

[2] Bergen, G.V.D. 1997. "Efficient Collision Detection of Complex Deformable Models Using AABB Trees." *Journal of Graphics Tools 1997*, vol. 2, Issue 4 (Apr.): 1-13.

[3] Bouma, W. and Vanecek, G. Jr. 1991 "Collision Detection and Analysis in a Physical Based Simulation." *Eurographics Workshop on Animation and Simulation 1991* (Vienna) 191-203.

[4] Cohen, J.D., Lin, M.C., Manocha, D., and Ponamgi, M. 1995. "I-COLLIDE: An Interactive and Exact Collision Detection System for Large-Scale Environments." *Proceedings of the 1995 symposium on Interactive 3D graphics 1995* (Monterey, CA, United States) 189-196.

[5] Cotin, S., Delingette, H., and Ayache, N. 1999. "Real-time elastic deformations of soft tissues for surgery simulation," *Visualization and Computer Graphics, IEEE Transactions on* , Vol. 5 Iss. 1 , pages 62–73.

[6] Debunney, G., Desbrunz, M., Caniy, M.-P., and Barrx, A. 2000, "Adaptive simulation of soft bodies in real-time," *Comp. Anim.*, pages 133–144, May 2000.

[7] Erickson, J., Guibas, L.J., Stolfi, J., and Zhang, L. 1999 "Separation-Sentitive Collision Detection for Convex Objects." *Proceedings of the tenth annual ACM-SIAM symposium on Discrete algorithms 1999***,** Baltimore, Maryland , 327 – 336.

[8] Ganovelli, F., Dingliana, J., and O'Sullivan, C. 2000. "Buckettree: Improving Collision Detection between Deformable Objects." *In Spring Conference in Computer Graphics SCCG 2000* , Bratislava, 156-163.

[9] Govindaraju, N.K., Redon, S., Lin, M.C., and Manocha, D. 2003. "CULLIDE: Interactive Collision Detection Between Complex Models in Large Environments using Graphics Hardware." *Siggraph Eurographics Graphics Hardware 2003* (San Diego, CA, Jul. 26-27).

[10] Gottschalk, S., Lin, M.C., and Manocha, D. 1996. "OBB Tree: A Hierarchical Structure for Rapid Interference Detection." *Preceeding of ACM Siggraph 1996* (New Orleans, Louisiana, Aug. 4-6), 171-180.

[11] He, T. 1999. "Fast Collision Detection Using QuOSPO Trees." *Proceedings of the 1999 symposium on Interactive 3D graphics*, (Atlanta, Georgia, Apr. 26-29) , ACM 1999 55-62.

[12] Heidelberger, B., Teschner, M., Keiser, R., Müller, M., Gross, M. 2004. "Consistent Penetration Depth Estimation for Deformable Collision Response" *VMV 2004* Stanford, USA, November 16–18.

[13] Held, M., Klosowski, J.T., Mitchell, J.S.B. 1995. "Evaluation of Collision Detection Methods for Virtual Reality Fly-Throughs." *Proceedings Seventh Canadian Conference on Computational Geometry 1995*, 205–210.

[14] Hubbard, P.M. 1995. "Collision Detection for Interactive Graphics Applications." *IEEE Transactions on Visualizationand Computer Graphics 1995*, **1**(3):218–230.

[15] James, D. L. and Pai, D.K. 2003. "Multiresolution green's function methods for interactive simulation of large-scale elastostatic objects," *Transactions on Graphics (TOG)*, Vol. 22 Iss. 1.

[16] James, D.L. and Pai, D.K. 2004. "BD-tree: Output-Sensitive Collision Detection for Reduced Deformable Models." in *Proceedings of ACM SIGGRAPH 2004*, (Los Angeles, CA ,Aug 8-12).

[17] Kim, Y.J., Lin, M.C., and Manocha, D. 2002. "Incremental Penetration Depth Estimation Between Convex", *Proceedings of the 2002 ACM SIGGRAPH/Eurographics symposium on Computer animation*

[18] Kim, Y.J., Lin, M.C., and Manocha, D. 2004. "Incremental Penetration Depth Estimation between Convex Polytopes Using Dual-Space Expansion", *IEEE Transactions on Visualization and Computer Graphics*,vol. 10, no. 2.

[19] Klosowski, J.T., Held, M., Mitchell, J., Sowizral, H., and Zikan, K. 1998. **"**Efficient Collision Detection Using Bounding Volume Hierarchies of k-DOPs." *IEEE Transactions on Visualization and Computer Graphics*, vol4 issue 1(Jan.) : 21-36.

[20] Larsson, T. and Akenine-Möller, T. 2001. "Collision Detection for Continuously Deforming Bodies" *In Eerographics 2001*., Manchester, UK, 325-333.

[21] Matthew Moore, M. and Wilhelms, J. 1988. "Collision Detection and Response for Computer Animation", *Computer Graphics*, Volume 22, Number 4.

[22] Matyka, M. and Ollila, M. 2003. "Pressure Model of Soft Body Simulation," *SIGRAD2003, November 20-21.*

[23] Mesit, J.; Guha, R.;Hastings, E., 2004 "*Optimized Collision Detection For Flexible Objects*". International Conference on Computer Games: Artificial Intelligence, Design, and Education CGAIDE2004.

[24] Mesit, J.; Guha, R.;Hastings, E., 2006 "Multi-level SB collide: collision and self-collision in soft bodies". International Conference on Computer Games: CGAMES2006.

[25] Moore, M. and Wilhelms, J. 1988. "Collision Detection and Response for Computer Animation" *In proceedings Computer Graphics SIGGRAPH 1988* , 22(4):289-298.

[26] Nixon, D., and Lobb, R. 2002. "A fluid-based soft-object model," *Comp. Graph. and App., IEEE* , Vol. 22 Iss. 4, pages 68–75, July-Aug. 2002.

[27] Naylor, B., Amatodes, J.A., Thibault, W. 1990. "Merging BSP Trees Yields Polyhedral Set Operations." *In proceedings Computer Graphics SIGGRAPH 1990* ,24(4):115–124, 1990.

[28] Otaduy, M.A. and Lin, M.C. 2003. "CLODs: Dual Hierarchies for Multiresolution Collision Detection." *Proceedings of the Eurographics/ACM SIGGRAPH symposium on Geometry processing 2003* (Aachen, Germany, Jul. 27-31), 94-101.

[29] Rabaetje, R. 2003. "Real-time simulation of deformable objects for assembly simulations," *Proceedings of the Fourth Australian user interface conference on User interfaces,* Vol. 18.

[30] Teran, J., Blemker, S., Ng Thow Hing, V., and Fedkiw, R. 2003. "Cloth & deformable bodies: Finite volume methods for the simulation of skeletal muscle," *Euro. Symp. on Comp. Anim. (SIGGRAPH Proc.)*, pages 68–74.

[31] Teschner, M., Heidelberger, B., Müller, M., Pomeranets, D., and Gross, M. 2003. "Optimized Spatial Hashing for Collision Detection of Deformable Objects." *Vision, Modeling, and Visualization 2003*. (Munich, Germany, Nov. 19-21).

[32] Witkin, A. and Baraff, D. 1993. "An Introduction to Physically Based Modeling," *SIGGRAPH Course Notes.*

Line-Triangle Test for Collision Detection and Response in Soft Bodies

Jaruwan Mesit
jmesit@cs.ucf.edu

Ratan K. Guha
guha@cs.ucf.edu

School of Electrical Engineering and Computer Science
University of Central Florida, Orlando, Florida 32826

KEYWORDS

soft body collision, animation, spatial subdivision, spatial hashing

ABSTRACT

Soft-body models are common in games to simulate cloth or elastic objects. To realistically simulate soft-body objects, collision detection and response is required. In addition, soft-body models must re-arrange their internal structure to react to the collision. This paper presents a new collision detection and response algorithm which can simulate a variety of soft-body material behaviors ranging from stiff to elastic. In this approach, a line-triangle intersection test is used for collision detection and force propagation is used for collision response. Implementation and experiments using the algorithm show that complex deformable objects composed of thousands vertices can be animated at interactive speeds.

BIOGRAPHY

Ms. Mesit has been a Ph.D. student at University of Central Florida since 2002. She got her M.Sc. in computer science and B.Sc. in computer science from NIDA (National of Development Administration) and Rajabhat Institute Phetchaburi Thailand, respectively. She is working as a graduated research assistant with Dr.Ratan Guha. Her research area is computer graphics in collision detection for flexible objects such as cloths, soft body, and water.

Dr. Ratan Guha is a professor at the department of Computer Science, University of Central Florida, with primary interests in Computer Networks, Distributed Computing, Distributed Simulation, and Computer Graphics. He received his Ph.D. from the University of Texas at Austin, and his M.Sc. in Applied Mathematics, and B.Sc. with honors in Mathematics from the Calcutta University, India.

Real Time Single Scattering Effects

Venceslas Biri
Gaspard Monge Insitute - University of Marne-la-Vallée
6 cours du Danube,
F-77700 SERRIS
Email : biri@univ-mlv.fr

Abstract— **Rendering mist, haze or fog remains a challenge in current computer graphics since it is intrinsically a 3D problem. While the attenuation caused by fog is easy to implement, single scattering effects such as glows and shafts of light, that increase considerably the realism, are harder to render in real-time. This paper addresses the rendering of such effects along with volumetric shadows induced by shadow casters in the participating media. Whereas techniques related to shadow maps have been explored when rendering with single scattering, this paper proposes a real-time algorithm using the philosophy of shadow volumes, including volumetric shadows. With a spatial coherence method, simple shaders and an intensive use of the stencil buffer, we render the shadow planes in a back to front order to obtain the correct volumetric shadows. Therefore our method is easy to integrate in a graphics engine using the shadow volume technique since it requires only a little additional texture memory and is implemented with simple shaders. Realistic images can be produced in real-time for usual graphic scenes and at a high level framerate for complex scenes, allowing changes in the properties of participating medium, animations of objects and even light sources movements.**

Keywords— **Single scattering, Real Time, Hardware rendering**

I. Introduction

If light scattering has been intensively explored, from Blinn in 1982 [1] to Sun et al. [2], it is mainly because it greatly enhances the realism of virtual scenes and can greatly improve the graphic quality of computer games. Indeed, the light scattering occurs everywhere in a scene and therefore is intrinsically a 3D phenomenon. For example, look at the differences between the Figure 1.a rendered classically and the Figure 1.b where the contributions of a participating medium have been added. In the first picture, it is not clear where the lights are while they can be roughly located in the second. Nevertheless, the Figure 1.c shows that, in some cases, rendering only the participating medium is not enough. In order to increase realism, we must render the volumetric shadows. Volumetric shadows are the shadows that cast objects in the participating medium itself. They greatly contribute on the presence in a virtual world. Here, the representation of shadow volumes is necessary to obtain a realistic image and understand clearly that a light stands inside the amphora.

A simple and common way to model light scattering is to handle the attenuation due to participating medium and consider the multiple scattering of light as homogeneous and constant over the scene. This is the OpenGL fog model which is popular since it only needs a fog color and is handled automatically by graphic cards. Figure 1.a is a perfect example of this technique. Despite its great speed, this model poorly represents all the effects induced by light scattering. On the other hand, methods seeking for great realism have investigated the computation of the multiple scattering of light through the medium. But due to this goal, these methods are very slow since they need Monte Carlo or finite element techniques.

In this paper we investigate the complete single scattering illumination model. In this local illumination approach, only the first scattering of light in the medium is taken into account. The remaining scattering of light is considered as homogeneous and constant all over the scene, like in the OpenGL fog model. The originality of the model is the introduction of the **indirect single scattering**. Indeed, we will call **direct single scattering** the effect of the first scattering of light along view rays. The **indirect single scattering** is the same effect but along illumination rays of any point of scene. Our contributions in this paper are :

- **Define an analytic and comprehensive formulation of light scattering along view rays and illumination rays**. Based on a angular formulation of the radiative transfer equation, we present a way to use precomputed 2D table to compute directly these contributions.
- **Integration of the volumetric shadows**. We build a method based on the shadow volume technique and using spatial coherence strategy, allowing the rendering of volumetric shadows in the scene, especially discernable around light sources.
- **Hardware implementation**. Except for the determination of object's silhouette, all the work is done in hardware. We store our precomputed 2D tables in textures and use simple shaders to render the illumination of objects and participating media. The rendering of volumetric shadows also involves an intensive use of the stencil buffer.

Our goal is to design an algorithm that can render accurately participating media, including effects like light beams in foggy or smoky scenes. Our method is not restricted to isotropic participating media which can be lit by one or several, static or moving, point light sources since no precomputation is done involving either lights or camera. Our technique produces high resolution images and takes into account volumetric shadows, cast by occluders contained in the media. With very few

Fig. 1. The same scene lit a. (left) classically, b. (center) with single scattering and c. (right) with single scattering and volumetric shadows. Who could say precisely where are the lights in the left picture ? This is obvious in the right picture

texture memory cost, but using intensively graphics hardware, our method can render images at a high frame rate and is real-time for classical graphics scene. Our method is also easy to implement in traditional graphics engines since it follows the same strategy than the shadow volume algorithm, and use only shaders and textures. Therefore, it is straightforward with our method to obtain animations where objects or even light sources can move.

II. Related Work

The representation of participating media has been a real challenge for years. We can easily divide all these studies between the single and the multiple scattering methods. The last ones try to compute all light reflections and inter-reflections inside the medium, whatever the number of these reflections. Despite their realism, they suffer from excessive computation time due to the complexity of light exchanges occurring in these cases. Therefore these approachs are not suitable for our goal and we will focus on methods considering only the single scattering case.

These techniques [9], [12], [15]–[17] approximate multiple reflections of light as a constant ambient term and consider only the first scattering of light ray in the direction of the camera. This assumption allows a direct rendering of the illumination of the medium which is more suitable for interactive rendering. Visualization is often done by ray tracing or ray marching. View rays are followed to gather the participating media contributions. Unfortunately, these methods [18], [19] are far from being real-time on a conventional desktop computer. With the growing capacities of graphics hardware, the real-time problem has been investigated.

Two approaches can be used to achieve this goal : volume rendering or direct representation. In order to add the volumetric shadows, the first approach will naturally use shadow maps techniques whereas the second is implicitly shadow volumes oriented [20]. Volume rendering is a classic solution to render a participating medium which is a volume de facto. Methods like [3]–[7] represent density or illumination in voxels encoded into 2D or 3D textures. Accumulation techniques using textured slices or virtual planes are then used to display the result. These methods could produce nice images of clouds or gas, but, in addition to requiring a lot of texture memory, they are not suitable for shafts of light where sharp edges exist. Special methods are defined to render beams and shafts of light precisely and most of them [11]–[14] use volume rendering techniques along with sampling shadows in shadow maps. Unfortunately, they suffer from artifacts due to the sampling. Dobashi et al. [15] present a very elegant solution to solve this problem using specialized adaptive sampling for shadows. They obtain an interactive rendering of participating media without aliasing or artifacts. However the image resolution remains low since the method is expensive in terms of fillrate. Moreover, the method works only with static lights due to the precomputation of shadow maps and only addresses the direct single scattering.

Method	Volume rendering	Direct computation
Direct single scattering	[3] [4] [5] [6] [7]	[8] [9] [10]
+ Indirect single scattering	none	our method and [2]
+ Volumetric shadows	[11] [12] [13] [14] [15]	our method

TABLE I

Overview of previous work on single scattering

The algorithms belonging to the second approach compute directly on every point of the scene the contribution of the participating medium. It is well adapted to classical graphics engines since it consists in one more rendering of the scene. In this case, methods like [8], [9] use participating medium boundaries, or special virtual planes, combined with vertex and fragments shaders. Other methods focus on the rendering of the atmosphere [10]. Despite their speed and simplicity, all these methods consider only the direct single scattering. The most advanced method of this group is proposed by Sun et al. [2] and is the first to consider the effects of the indirect single scattering. Unfortunately, it does not take shadows into account, even though it is real-time. Our work belongs to this group but is the only one of them to integrate direct single scattering, indirect single scattering and volumetric shadows. Compared to our own work presented in [21], we present here an hardware implementation along with the representation of the indirect single scattering which are major improvements.

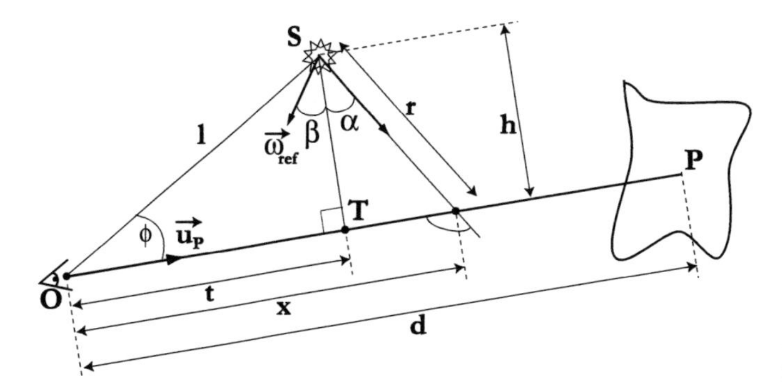

Fig. 2. Notations for our model

III. THE SINGLE SCATTERING ILLUMINATION MODEL

In this section, we will present an analytic formulation of the single scattering illumination model. We will mainly focus on in-scattering since absorption, emission, multiple scattering and out-scattering are really simple to integrate. We start in the following developments with the angular formulation we presented in [21], [22], and that were finely used by [2], work we review and extend here to obtain the complete illumination model of single scattering. Our developments consider only homogeneous participating media defined all over the scene and point light sources, assumed to be isotropic.

A. Single scattering along a ray

Considering a view ray immersed in a participating medium, the radiance L observed along $\vec{u_P}$ from a point P can be written (see Figure 2) :

$$L_{\vec{u_P}} = L_{dss}(\vec{u_P}) + e^{-k_t OP} L(P) + L_a e^{-k_t OP} + L_{oiss}(\vec{u_P}) \quad (1)$$

where L_{dss} is the direct single scattering and $L(P)$ the radiance of P attenuated by both absorption and out-scattering. k_t is the extinction coefficient, sum of the absorption coefficient and the diffusion coefficient, properties of the participating medium. The third term represents both emission and multiple scattering inducing a constant radiance L_a along the ray. The last term is the object indirect single scattering.

Now we focus on the radiance of P that can be written :

$$L(P) = L_{iss}(P) + e^{-k_t SP} L_d(P) + L_a e^{-k_t SP} \quad (2)$$

L_{iss} is the indirect single scattering received on point P and $L_d(P)$ an usual direct illumination, like Phong model, that is attenuated by absorption and out-scattering. The third term is once again the contribution of emission and multiple scattering on the illumination ray.

Then, only L_{dss} and L_{iss} remain unknown. They both are the contribution of the first light scattering along, respectively, a view ray and an illumination ray. First of all, we will investigate the general contribution of this first scattering along a ray before to see its application on view rays and illumination rays. The integral transfer equation, presented in [23], gives the incoming radiance L_{ss} in direction $\vec{u_P}$ stopped at vertex P and seen from O (see Figure 2) :

$$L_{ss}(\vec{u_P}) = \frac{k_t \Omega}{4\pi} \int_0^d \frac{I_S(\alpha+\beta) e^{-k_t x} e^{-k_t r}}{r^2} p(\alpha + \frac{\pi}{2}) dx \quad (3)$$

In this equation x, r, d, h are geometrical factors and Ω is the albedo, i.e. the fraction between the diffuse coefficient and the extinction coefficient of the medium. p is the phase function expressing for any incoming direction the ratio of light following the ray direction. Finally, I_s is the directional intensity of the source computed relatively to the reference direction $\vec{\omega_{ref}}$. Equation (3) expresses the in-scattering which is responsible for the subtle effects of atmospheric scattering.

The previous equation can be simplified [21], [22] using the angle α to minimize the dependency of the integral to it. Using the variable change $x = t + h.\tan(\alpha)$, t and h are constant along the ray, we can obtain (see the annexes) :

$$L_{ss}(\phi, d, l) = \frac{k_t \Omega e^{-k_t t}}{4\pi h} \int_{\gamma_0}^{\gamma_d} I_S(\alpha+\beta) p(\alpha+\frac{\pi}{2}) e^{-k_t h \frac{\sin(\alpha)+1}{\cos(\alpha)}} d\alpha \quad (4)$$

where

$$\gamma_0 = -\frac{\pi}{2} + \phi = atan(\frac{-t}{h})$$

$$\gamma_d = atan(\frac{d - lcos(\phi)}{lsin(\phi)}) = atan(\frac{d-t}{h})$$

B. The direct single scattering

In the case of view rays, the point O is the position of the camera. Therefore, the distance between O and S remains constant whatever the view ray considered. The only variables in the equation (4) are the angle ϕ and the distance d. For an isotropic light, this equation becomes :

$$L_{dss}(\phi, d) = \frac{k_t \Omega I_S e^{-k_t t}}{4\pi h} \int_{\gamma_0}^{\gamma_d} p(\alpha+\frac{\pi}{2}) e^{-k_t h \frac{\sin(\alpha)+1}{\cos(\alpha)}} d\alpha \quad (5)$$

If we denote :

$$\Gamma(\lambda, \gamma) = \int_0^{\gamma} p(\alpha+\frac{\pi}{2}) e^{-k_t \lambda \frac{\sin(\alpha)+1}{\cos(\alpha)}} d\alpha \quad (6)$$

the direct single scattering could be written :

$$L_{dss}(d, \phi) = \frac{k_t^2 \Omega I_S}{4\pi} \frac{e^{-k_t t}}{k_t h} \Big[\Gamma(k_t h, atan(\frac{d-t}{h})) - \Gamma(k_t h, atan(\frac{-t}{h})) \Big] \quad (7)$$

This particular formulation is well suited to optimize the shader that computes the direct single scattering. Note that the 2D function Γ is purely numerical and only depends on the shape of the phase function. It can therefore be precomputed and stored in a 2D table. Figure 3 shows two examples for isotropic phase function and mie-hazzy phase function.

C. The indirect single scattering

Inspired by [2], we also compute the illumination of vertex P due to the light scattering all over the scene. The indirect single scattering can be written (see Figure 4) as follows :

$$L_{iss}(P) = \int_{\theta=0}^{2\pi}\int_{\phi=0}^{\pi} L_{ss}(\phi, d_{\phi,\theta}, l) f_r(\vec{u_c}, \vec{u_v})(\vec{u_c}.\vec{n})d\omega \quad (8)$$

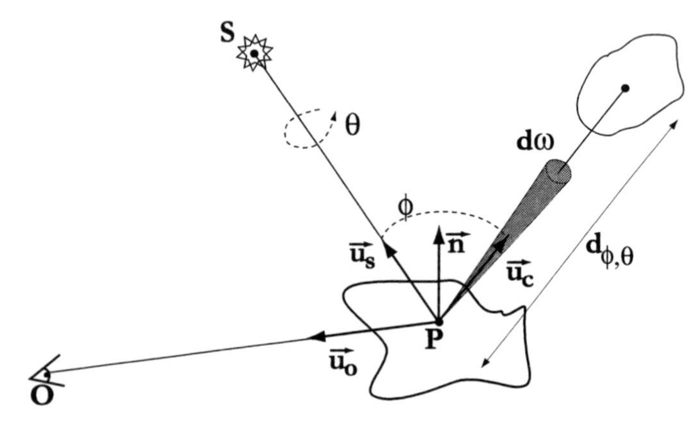

Fig. 4. Notations for Lambert illumination model

The first difficulty is to obtain for each direction $\vec{u_c}$ the distance $d_{\phi,\theta}$. This distance has been arbitrary fixed at ∞ in [2] but this is a coarse approximation. Nevertheless, it is necessary if we want to avoid too much complexity. So we will make the same assumption and take, $d_{\phi,\theta} = \infty, \ \forall\phi, \theta$.

First of all, consider the Lambertian case where the function f_r is the diffuse reflectivity of the surface k_d. We then have :

$$L_{iss}(P) = k_d \int_{\theta=0}^{2\pi}\int_{\phi=0}^{\pi} L_{ss}(\phi, \infty, l)(\vec{u_c}.\vec{n})sin(\phi)d\phi d\theta \quad (9)$$

Thanks to the symmetry on θ, we can choose the spherical coordinates centered on P such that $\vec{n} = (sin(\phi_n), 0, cos(\phi_n))$ (cf.Figure 4) and write :

$$L_{iss}(P) = k_d \int_{\phi=0}^{\pi} L_{ss}(\phi, \infty, l)\left[\int_0^{2\pi} cos(\phi_n)cos(\phi)d\theta + \int_0^{2\pi} sin(\phi_n)sin(\phi)cos(\theta)d\theta\right] sin(\phi)d\phi$$

It remains after integration :

$$L_{iss}(P) = 2\pi k_d \int_{\phi=0}^{\pi} L_{ss}(\phi, \infty, l)cos(\phi_n)cos(\phi)sin(\phi)d\phi$$

Now we can substitute L_{ss} with equation (4) to obtain :

$$L_{iss}(P) = 2\pi k_d cos(\phi_n)\int_{\phi=0}^{\pi} \frac{k_t^2 I_S \Omega}{4\pi l} g(l, \phi)cos(\phi)d\phi$$

with

$$g(\lambda, \phi) = \frac{1}{\lambda}\int_{\phi-\frac{\pi}{2}}^{\frac{\pi}{2}} p(\alpha + \frac{\pi}{2})e^{-\lambda\frac{\cos(\alpha-\phi)+1}{\cos(\alpha)}}d\alpha$$

And finally we have :

$$L_{iss}(P) = \frac{k_t^2 \Omega I_S}{4\pi}\frac{2\pi k_d cos(\phi_n)}{k_t l}\Gamma_L(k_t l) \quad (10)$$

with

$$\Gamma_L(\lambda) = \int_0^{\pi} cos(\phi)\int_{\phi-\frac{\pi}{2}}^{\frac{\pi}{2}} p(\alpha + \frac{\pi}{2})e^{-\lambda\frac{\cos(\alpha-\phi)+1}{\cos(\alpha)}}d\alpha d\phi \quad (11)$$

The Phong model is much more difficult and we need the reparametrization of Ramamoorthi et al. [24]. It gives use the following equation :

$$L_{iss}(P) = k_s \int_{\theta=0}^{2\pi}\int_{\phi=0}^{\pi} L_{ss}(\phi', \infty, l)cos^n(\phi)sin(\phi)d\phi d\theta$$

where n is the shininess and k_s the specular reflectivity of the surface. ϕ and θ are defined relatively to the axe $\vec{u_r}$. ϕ' is the angle formed by vector $\vec{u_s}$ and $\vec{u_c}$ (see Figure 5). We can choose the base to have :

$$\phi' = acos(cos(\phi_S)cos(\phi) + sin(\phi)cos(\theta)\sqrt{1 - cos^2(\phi_S)})$$

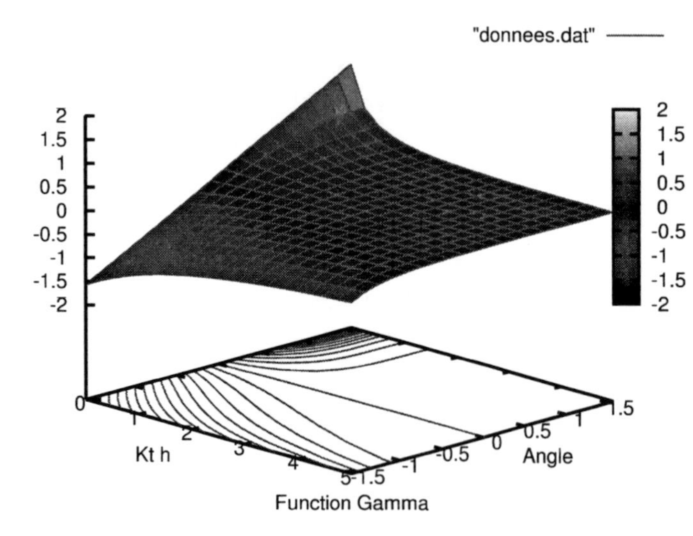

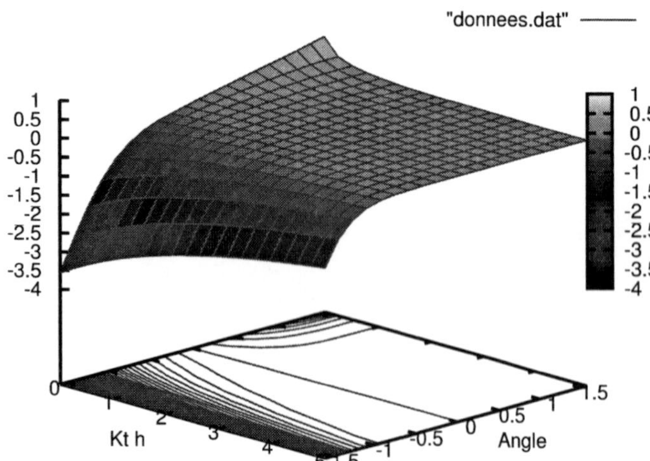

Fig. 3. The Γ function for isotropic and hazzy phase function

Therefore, the equation will be :

$$L_{iss}(P) = \frac{k_t^2 \Omega I_S}{4\pi} \; \frac{k_s}{k_t l} \; \Gamma_P(k_t l) \tag{12}$$

with

$$\Gamma_P(\phi', \lambda) = \int_0^{2\pi}\int_0^{\pi}\int_{\phi'-\frac{\pi}{2}}^{\frac{\pi}{2}} p(\alpha+\frac{\pi}{2}) e^{-\lambda \frac{\cos(\alpha-\phi')+1}{\cos(\alpha)}} cos^{\eta}(\phi) d\alpha \tag{13}$$

D. Shadows on view rays

We want to integrate now the effect of occlusions along any view rays. Equation (7) describes the particular case where the view ray remains totally lit. In order to integrate shadow volumes, we need to consider more general cases, illustrated in Figure 6. Indeed, the ray must be split into lit and shadowed parts. In this example, the medium contribution along the ray is split into two parts on OA and BP. Using the laplace formula, it is straightforward to see that equation (7) becomes :

$$\begin{aligned} L_{dss}(d, \phi) &= \frac{k_t^2 \Omega I_S}{4\pi} e^{-k_t t} [\Gamma(k_t h, \gamma_P) - \Gamma(k_t h, \gamma_B) \\ &\quad + \Gamma(k_t h, \gamma_A) - \Gamma(k_t h, \gamma_O)] \end{aligned} \tag{14}$$

IV. Hardware Implementation

A. Overview of our method

Our algorithm is easy to implement. We present here the 5 steps of this method and we will precise for each step if the computation is done by CPU or by GPU.

1) (CPU) The silhouettes of every moving shadow caster are computed. If the light source is moving, every silhouette needs to be recomputed.
2) (GPU) Scene is rendered using the conventional polygonal rendering method to obtain the direct illumination and the indirect single scattering. Surface shadows can be obtained using shadow planes algorithms [20], [25]. The stencil buffer now contains lit areas of the scene. An ambient fog is added to take into account both absorption and multiple scattering.
3) (GPU) Scene is rendered once more time and direct single scattering is computed for each vertex of the scene. Depth test is set to equality. Only lit parts of the scene are rendered thanks to the stencil buffer.

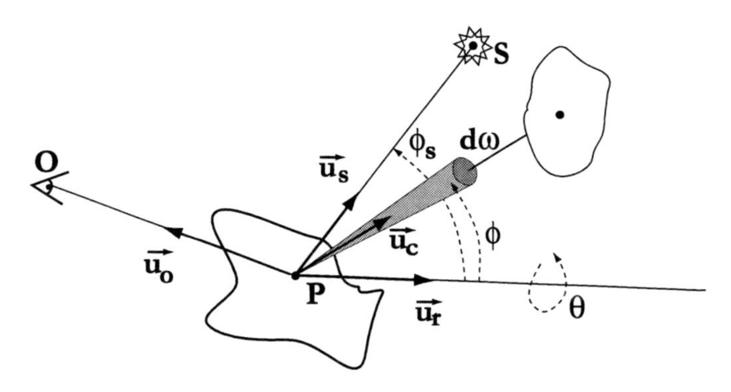

Fig. 5. Notations for Phong illumination model

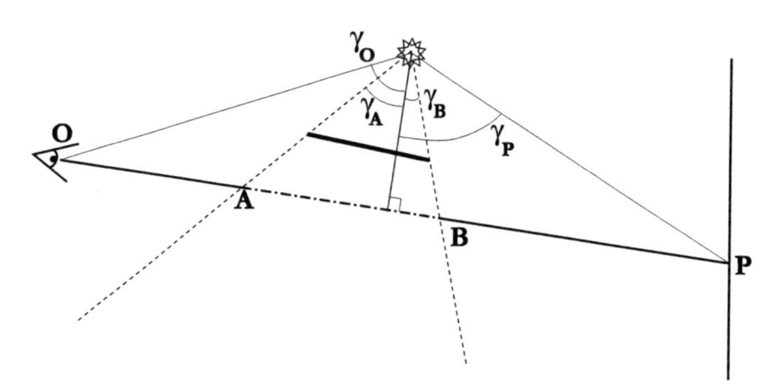

Fig. 6. Case of a partially shadowed view ray

4) (CPU) Shadow planes determined by the object's silhouettes are sorted in a back to front order.
5) (GPU) Shadow planes are rendered in that precise order. The depth test function accepts only planes that are closer to the camera. Front facing planes add their contribution when back facing planes subtract them. Stencil function is set to allow fragments if the stencil is equal to 1 for front facing planes and 0 for back facing ones. Front facing planes always decrement the stencil buffer and back facing ones always increment it.

All stages have to be done for each light source. As in [25], a initialization stage is done to obtain the ambiant lighting and the first depth map. Each stage is detailed in the following sections.

B. Computation of silhouettes (step 1)

In our algorithm, we select some objects to be shadow casters. Their silhouettes are easily computed by determining all edges of their mesh common to a front-facing triangle regarding the light position and one back facing it. Then all these edges are linked together if possible, and stored in a loop list. In order to obtain correct silhouettes, we need well designed closed triangular meshes (2-manifold) for which connectivity information are available. These conditions for the shadow casters are the ones indicated in [25]. Shadow planes are infinite quads formed by a silhouette edge and the light position. They are constituted by the two edge's vertices and two other points, projections of the previous vertices to infinity toward direction : light position - vertex [20]. They are oriented toward the unshadowed area of the scene. As we need to compute the medium contribution on all shadow planes, it is wise to use shadow plane silhouettes rather than the shadow planes of all little triangles. Of course, if the light does not move, only moving shadow caster silhouettes have to be computed. Finally, if the input geometry is modified by graphics hardware, using displacement mapping for example, a solution to obtain silhouettes of all objects quickly and accurately can be found in [26].

C. Rendering the scene (step 2 and 3)

The second and third steps of the algorithm compute the illumination on surfaces. This can be done using one or

```
varying vec4 posInScene;
// coeff_milieu.rgb = light_intensity.rgb*albedo.rgb*coef_extinct^2/4*PI
// coeff_milieu.a  : extinction coefficient
uniform vec4 coeff_milieu;
uniform vec4 poslght; // Light position
// integralRange (min,max,max-min)
uniform vec4 integralRange;
uniform sampler1D monarctan;
uniform sampler2D integrale;
uniform sampler2D depthtex;

void main() {
  vec4 facteurs,resultat;
  float rayDist ;
  vec3 rayDir;
  // facteurs.x = -t
  // facteurs.y = h
  // facteurs.z = alpha0
  // facteurs.w = alphad

  // View ray computation
  rayDir.xyz = posInScene.xyz;
  rayDist = length(rayDir);
  rayDir /= rayDist;

  // -t computation
  facteurs.x = -dot(poslght.xyz,rayDir);
  // h computation
  facteurs.y = length(poslght.xyz + rayDir * facteurs.x);

  // alpha0 et alphad computed thanks to atan texture
  facteurs.z = (facteurs.x/(facteurs.y*20.0)) + 0.5;
  facteurs.z = (texture1D(monarctan,facteurs.z)).r;  // atan(-t/h)
  facteurs.w = (rayDist+facteurs.x)/(facteurs.y*20.0) + 0.5;
  facteurs.w = (texture1D(monarctan,facteurs.w)).r;  // atan(d-t/h)

  // Ldss computation
  resultat.a = coeff_milieu.w*facteurs.y; // Kt h
  resultat.b = facteurs.z;                    // alpha0
  resultat.r = texture2D(integrale,resultat.ab).r;
  resultat.b = facteurs.w;                    // alphad
  resultat.g = texture2D(integrale,resultat.ab).r;
  resultat.rg = resultat.rg*integralRange.zz + integralRange.xx;

  // Final depth test
  rayDir.x = gl_FragCoord.x/1024.0;
  rayDir.y = gl_FragCoord.y/1024.0;
  rayDir.z = texture2D(depthtex,rayDir.xy).x;
  if (gl_FragCoord.z <= rayDir.z + 0.0001) {
    gl_FragColor.a = (resultat.g - resultat.r)/ facteurs.y;
    gl_FragColor.rgb = coeff_milieu.xyz * exp(-coeff_milieu.w * rayDist) * gl_FragColor.a;
  }
  else {
    discard;
  }
}
```

Fig. 7. Shader for L_{dss} computation

two rendering of the scene depending on the ability of the graphic cards to handle large shaders. Indeed, the number of instructions in the shader for both indirect single scattering and direct single scattering computations could exceed the capacity of the graphic card.

We show in Figure 7 and 8 the two GLSL fragment shaders used for steps 2 and 3 and which "implement" respectively equation (1) and (7). These shaders, and the corresponding steps, can be grouped together if possible. Note that we use a shader for any kind of participating medium of the scene. The two shaders need four textures : a 1D texture used as a lookup table for arctangent function, a 2D texture representing the function Γ defined in (6), 1D texture to store the Lambertian function (11) and finally one for the Phong function (13). Note that in equations (7), (10), (12) the first fraction could be a uniform variable and the second fraction could be computed directly by the shaders. Moreover we have avoided the direct computation of $atan$, cos or sin functions in these shaders,

```
varying vec3 lightDir,eyeVec,normal;
varying float att;
uniform vec4 coeff_milieu; // Same as the first shader
uniform sampler1D gamma_lambert;
uniform sampler2D gamma_phong;
// integralRange.x : Minimum value of Gamma L
// integralRange.y : Range of Gamma L
// integralRange.z : Minimum value of Gamma P
// integralRange.w : Range of Gamma P
uniform vec4 integralRange;

void main()
{
  // facteurs.r = l then kt * l
  vec4 facteurs,resultat;
  vec3 N = normalize(normal);
  facteurs.r = length(lightDir);
  vec3 L = lightDir/facteurs.r;

  float lambertTerm = dot(N,L);

  if(lambertTerm > 0.0) {
    // Standard computation of lambertian and phong illumination
    color += att * gl_LightSource[0].diffuse * gl_FrontMaterial.diffuse * lambertTerm;

    vec3 E = normalize(eyeVec);
    vec3 R = reflect(-L, N);
    float dre = max(dot(R, E), 0.0);
    float specular = pow(dre,gl_FrontMaterial.shininess);
    color += gl_LightSource[0].specular * gl_FrontMaterial.specular * specular *att;

    // ISS lambert
    float dist = length(eyeVec);
    facteurs.r *= coeff_milieu.w;
    facteurs.g = texture1D(gamma_lambert,facteurs.r/10.0).r*integralRange.y+integralRange.x;
    resultat.a = 6.2831853*lambertTerm*facteurs.g/facteurs.r;
    resultat.rgb = gl_FrontMaterial.diffuse.rgb*resultat.a;

    // ISS phong
    if (dre>0.0) {
      facteurs.g = facteurs.r/10.0;
      facteurs.b = dre;
      resultat.a = texture2D(gamma_phong,facteurs.gb).r*integralRange.w+integralRange.z;
      resultat.rgb += gl_FrontMaterial.specular.rgb*resultat.a/facteurs.r;
      gl_FragColor.rgb = facteurs.gbb;//*resultat.a;
    }
    color.rgb += coeff_milieu.rgb*resultat.rgb*exp(-coeff_milieu.w * dist)*att;
  }
  gl_FragColor = color;
}
```

Fig. 8. Shader for L_{iss} computation

and preferred simple scalar products and texture lookups.

D. Sorting the shadow planes (step 4)

Before rendering all shadow planes, we have to make sure that we will not render shadow planes, or part of them, that are themselves in shadow. If we do not care about this problem, it will create artifacts we call shadow in shadows, shadow planes that are in shadow must not be rendered. Then, we render the shadow planes, back- or front-facing, in a "back to front" order and use the stencil buffer to avoid the drawing of shadowed shadow planes.

E. Rendering the shadow planes (step 5)

It remains to render the shadow volumes, i.e. to take into account the equation (14). We still have the stencil we have obtained in the stage 2. Shadow planes are rendered in the order defined in the previous stage. The same pixel shader of Figure 7 is used for the shadow planes. The only difference is blending : front facing planes add their contribution when back facing planes subtract them.

Taking into account correctly the shadow in shadow problem requires the use of the stencil buffer. The key idea is to draw only the planes that constitute the boundary between

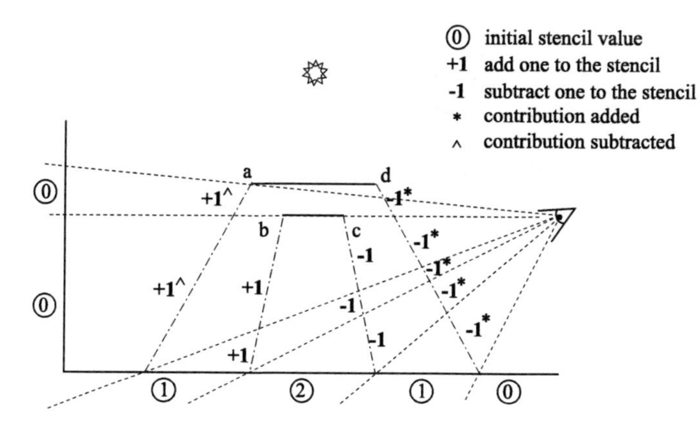

Fig. 9. Use of the stencil buffer in the rendering of shadow planes

lit volumes and shadowed ones. This can be done using our ordering and the value stored in the stencil. We define the stencil test such that front facing planes pass the stencil test if its value is one, representing shadowed area, and back facing ones passes if it equals zero, value representing lit area. Ideally the back (resp. front) facing quads should always add (resp. subtract) one to the stencil buffer if it passes depth test. Unfortunately, the stencil test is before the depth test so we have to do our own depth test in the pixel shader. Thus, we only draw shadow planes that make the shadow volume boundaries. The indicated strategy works if the camera is in the light. A slightly different strategy can be used when the camera is in shadow but the philosophy remains the same.

V. Results

The previous algorithm has been implemented on a standard computer using a 2.6 GHz processor and an ATI 9800 PRO graphics card (which is an old card now!). All images and videos we present have a 800x600 resolution. First of all, we point out, in Figure 10 the influence of each part of our single scattering illumination model. In this example, we have not considered the multiple scattering to concentrate on the other effects. On the top row, the first column shows the directe illumination of surfaces. The second column adds the direct single scattering. This effect highlights slightly all lit surfaces. Therefore, if we don't consider shadow volume, discontinuity in the illumination can occur between lit and shadowed areas, like in the bottom of the jug. After the shadow volumes rendering, illustrated in the third column, the discontinuities disapear. All these pictures have been rendered with indirect single scattering, that introduces subtle modifications : dimming of the specular highlights on the vase and brightening of darker region.

We also present some snapshots of our animations. The first image in Figure 11.a. is a simple scene, where a pen is bumping in front of two lights. It illustrates a classical situation where well design 3D objects are moving and casting shadows. Here the shadow planes are really intricated. This scene is rendered at more than 30 fps, including direct single scattering, indirect single scattering and of course volumetric shadows rendering. The image in Figure 11.b is a snapshot of an animation presenting two point light sources, including one that moves, in a complex scene containing about 100 000 triangles. The last picture 11.c is another snapshot from an animation where camera moves and properties of the participating medium evolve. The table II presents the FPS compared to the number of triangles of those scenes.

scene	without iss with dss and shadows	with iss, dss and shadows	number of triangles
fig. 11 .a	31	30	14 785
fig. 11 .b	10.5	10.2	110 014
fig. 11 .c	7.6	7	136 266

TABLE II

FPS COMPARED TO NUMBER OF TRIANGLES

VI. Conclusion

We have presented in this paper a complete single scattering illumination model along with a new algorithm able to render the main part of this model. It considers a single participating medium recovering the scene and lit by one or several, eventually dynamic, point light sources. Our algorithm is fast enough to handle more than 30 frames per second for moderately complex scenes. It implements the direct single scattering, the indirect single scattering and, most of all, volumetric shadows along with surfacic shadows. Our method can be implemented in programmable graphics hardware, and compared to volume rendering approach does not need a lot of texture memory. Therefore it can easily be integrated in any graphics engine. We also have to point out that our algorithm does not create the aliasing effect we can have with volume rendering techniques thanks to the use of the exact shadow planes.

The perspectives are numerous but two developments seems promising :

Relax assumptions : So far we consider only isotropic point light and homogeneous participating media. We have made satisfying preliminary work about animating several bounded participating media and it could be a way to handle heterogeneous medium. Directional light source are easier to handle than point light and will not be a problem. The real challenge is the integration of directionnal point light sources.

Make it soft ... and quick : An other way to obtain more realistic image will be to consider soft shadows, for surfacic shadows but also for volumetric shadows. Fortunately, our work is well adapted to algorithm such as [27] since it uses shadow volumes. Finaly, note that no optimization have been done to render the scenes. We believe that occlusion culling, frustum culling and clustering would greatly speed up our algorithm.

Acknowledgment

We thank Pascal Lecocq for the developments done in his thesis about this subject and wish him a excellent career in Spain. We also thank Leonie Van Royeen for her english review.

Fig. 10. Insight of the influence of the different contributions. The first column is the result after step 2, the second presents the addition of the direct single scattering and the third adds the volumetric shadows

Fig. 11. Some snapshots of our animations. a. (left) a simple scene with a pen flying between two lights. b. (center) A complexe scene with two lights c. (right) A more complex scene

REFERENCES

[1] J. F. Blinn, "Light reflection functions for simulation of clouds and dusty surfaces," in *SIGGRAPH '82: Proceedings of the 9th annual conference on Computer graphics and interactive techniques*. New York, NY, USA: ACM Press, 1982, pp. 21–29.

[2] B. Sun, R. Ramamoorthi, S. Narasimhan, and S. Nayar, "A practical analytic single scattering model for real time rendering," in *proceedings of SIGGRAPH'05, Computer Graphics*, vol. 24 (3), 2005, pp. 1040–1049.

[3] U. Behrens and R. Ratering, "Adding Shadows to a Texture-based Volume Renderer," in *proceeding of 1998 Symposium on Volume Visualization*, 1998, pp. 39–46.

[4] R. Westermann and T. Ertl, "Efficiently Using Graphics Hardware in Volume Rendering Applications," in *proceeding of SIGGRAPH'98, Computer Graphics*, 1998, pp. 169–177.

[5] J. Stam, "Stable Fluids," in *proceedings of SIGGRAPH'99, Computer Graphics*, 1999, pp. 121–128.

[6] R. Fedkiw, J. Stam, and H. Jensen, "Visual Simulation of Smoke," in *proceedings of SIGGRAPH'01, Computer Graphics*, Aug. 2001, pp. 15–22.

[7] M. Nulkar and K. Mueller, "Splatting with Shadows," in *proceedings of Volume Graphics 2001*, 2001, pp. 35–49.

[8] R. Mech, "Hardware-Accelerated Real-Time Rendering of Gaseous Phenomena," in *Journal of Graphics Tools*, vol. 6(3), 2001, pp. 1–16.

[9] N. Hoffman and A. Preetham, "Rendering Outdoor Light Scattering in Real Time," 2002.

[10] S. O'neil, "Accurate atmospheric scattering," in *GPU Gems 2*, A. Wesley, Ed., Mar. 2005.

[11] Y. Dobashi, K. Kandea, H. Yamashita, T. Okita, and T. Nishita, "A Simple, Efficient Method for Realistic Animation of Clouds," in *proceedings of SIGGRAPH'00, Computer Graphics*, Aug. 2000, pp. 19–28.

[12] Y. Dobashi, T. Yamamot, and T. Nishita, "Interactive Rendering Method for Displaying Shafts of Light," in *proceeding of Pacific Graphics 2000*, 2000, pp. 31–37.

[13] C. Everitt, "A Fast Algorithm for Area Light Source Using Backprojection," 2002, www.r3.nu/cass/shadowsandstuff.

[14] S. Lefebvre and S. Guy, "Volumetric Lighting and Shadowing NV30 shader," 2002, lefebvre.sylvain.free.fr/cgshaders/vshd/vshd.html.

[15] Y. Dobashi, T. Yamamot, and T. Nishita, "Interactive Rendering of Atmospheric Scattering Effects Using Graphics Hardware," in *proceeding of Graphics Hardware 2002*, 2002.

[16] T. Nishita, Y. Miyawaki, and E. Nakamae, "A Shading Model for Atmospheric Scattering considering Luminous Distribution of Light Sources," in *proceedings of SIGGRAPH'87, Computer Graphics*, vol. 21(4), 1987, pp. 303–310.

[17] N. Max, "Efficient Light Propagation for Multiple Anisotropic Volume Scattering," in *proceedings of 5th Eurographics Workshop on Rendering*, 1994, pp. 87–104.

[18] N. Foster and D. Metaxas, "Modeling the motion of a Hot, Turbulent Gas," in *proceedings of SIGGRAPH'97, Computer Graphics*, Aug. 1997, pp. 181–188.

[19] H. W. Jensen and P. Christensen, "Efficient Simulation of Light Transport in Scenes with Participating Media using Photon Maps," in *Proceedings of SIGGRAPH'98, Computer Graphics*, Aug. 1998, pp. 311–320.

[20] T. Heidman, "Real Shadows Real Time," in *IRIS Universe*, vol. 18, 1991, pp. 28–31.

[21] V. Biri, D. Arquès, and S. Michelin, "Real Time Rendering of Atmospheric Scattering and Volumetric Shadows," in *Journal of WSCG'06*, vol. 14(1), Feb. 2006, pp. 65–72.

[22] P. Lecocq, S. Michelin, D. Arques, and A. Kemeny, "Mathematical approximation for real-time rendering of participating media considering the luminous intensity distribution of light sources," in *proceedings of Pacific Graphics 2000*, 2000, pp. 400–401.

[23] R. Siegel and J. Howell, *Thermal Radiation Heat Transfert*, 3rd ed. Hemisphere Publishing, 1992.

[24] R. Ramamoorthi and P. Hanrahan, "Frequency space environment map rendering," in *proceedind of SIGGRAPH '02*, vol. 21(3). New York, NY, USA: ACM Press, 2002, pp. 517–526.

[25] C. Everitt and M. Kilgard, "Practical and Robust Shadow Volumes," 2003. [Online]. Available: http://developer.nvidia.com/object/robust_shadow_volumes.html

[26] S. Brabec and H. Seidel, "Shadow Volumes on Programmable Graphics Hardware," in *proceedings of Eurographics'03*, vol. 22(3), 2003.

[27] U. Assarson and T. A. Mller, "A Geometry-based Soft Shadow Volume Algorithm using Graphics Hardware," in *proceedings of SIGGRAPH'03, Computer Graphics*, vol. 22(3), 2003, pp. 511–520.

Crowd Creation Pipeline for Games

R. McDonnell[†1], S. Dobbyn[1] and C. O'Sullivan[1]

[1]Interaction, Simulation & Graphics Lab, Trinity College Dublin, Ireland

Abstract

With the increase in realism of games based in stadiums and urban environments, real-time crowds are becoming essential in order to provide a believable environment. However, realism is still largely lacking due to the computation required. In this paper, we describe the pipeline of work needed in order to prepare and export models from a 3D modelling package into a crowd system. For our crowd, we use a hybrid geometry/impostor approach which allows thousands of characters to be rendered of high visual quality. We use pre-simulated sequences of cloth to further enhance the characters appearance, along with perceptual metrics to balance computation with visual fidelity.

1. Introduction

In the games industry, real-time crowds are increasing in popularity due to the emergence of new level of detail (LOD) techniques. Currently, the humans that occupy crowd systems in games use skinned meshes for their clothing, often resulting in rigid and unnatural motion of the individuals in a simulated crowd. While there have been advances in the area of cloth simulation, both offline and in real-time, interactive cloth simulation for hundreds or thousands of clothed characters would not be possible with current methods. We addressed this problem in previous work by devising a system for animating large numbers of clothed characters using pre-simulated clothing.

In Dobbyn et al. [DMK*06], we added realism to our crowd simulations by dressing the individuals in realistically simulated clothing, using an offline commercial cloth simulator, and integrating this into our real-time hybrid geometry/impostor rendering system ([DHOO05]). We have also improved the quality of the impostors in the system by using perceptual metrics described in [HMDO05, MDO05, MDSC06] in order to drive the impostor rendering. In this paper, we discuss the necessary steps to advance from a single character in a modelling package such as 3D Studio Max, to a perceptually guided crowd of thousands of clothed characters in a real-time system. This useful step by step guide will enable others to incorporate pre-simulated deformable clothing and perceptual metrics into their crowd systems. Our results show a system capable of rendering large realistic clothed crowds in real-time.

† Rachel.McDonnell@cs.tcd.ie

2. Pipeline

We present the pipeline of work needed to achieve real-time crowds of clothed characters. In [MDSC06] we performed a rigorous series of psychophysical experiments in order to determine the most appropriate representations to use for depicting the deformations of cloth. We found that a hybrid combination of impostor and detailed geometry meshes would be most suited to our purpose since participants were unable to tell the difference between this type of crowd and a crowd containing all high resolution geometry.

The system is an extension of the crowd system detailed in [DHOO05], and this paper describes all of the alterations necessary to convert that crowd of skinned characters, to a crowd of characters with deformable clothing.

There are three main stages in the pipeline process (see Figure 1):

1. Stage 1: Model Prepping: The first stage involves modelling the character and adding a suitable animation for use in a crowd. The character's clothes are then constructed and fitted, and finally simulated in response to the underlying motion. Our novel technique detailed in [DMK*06] for constructing a cyclical cloth animation is also applied here.
2. Stage 2: Exporting the Data: The second stage is concerned with exporting the human mesh, skeletal anima-

Figure 1: *Pipeline stages.*

tion, cloth mesh and simulation, and impostors into a suitable format for use in the system.

3. Stage 3: Crowd Rendering: The final stage involves details on how the crowd is rendered in real-time.
   The following three sections will describe the stages in detail. We also present some images of the final crowd system integrated into the Virtual Dublin Model [Ham05].

3. Stage 1: Model Prepping

Stage 1 of the process is concerned with the processing that is necessary in order to prepare a virtual character to be exported into the system.

3.1. Preparing the Human

Choosing a suitable model is the first thing that needs to be done. Characters in a crowd should look different from each other but should have the same overall style (e.g., a cartoon style character and a photorealistic character will not look good together in a crowd).

We discovered in [MDO05] that characters of lower resolution around the joints are not as capable as those with more detail of displaying subtle motion variations. Therefore, the character should be detailed enough for both realism and the accurate deformation of the mesh around the joints in order to produce good animations. However, when choosing how detailed the character will be, it should be remembered that, for a hybrid system, a number of the high level of detail characters will be displayed on-screen at one time, as well as many low level of detail characters. Therefore, the detail of the character is limited to what is achievable in real-time. Our characters ranged in detail from roughly 2000 to 9000 polygons, depending on the number of characters needed for the crowd. However, we also found in [MDO05] that the resolution that we were using for our highest characters was actually perceptually equivalent to lower resolution characters. Therefore, there is a tradeoff between the number of polygons necessary for the virtual human to look good in appearance and the number necessary for displaying subtle motion information. This should be remembered when choosing the resolution of the high resolution character. We will use the example of a female character model called *Angela* with 6500 polygons for the remainder of our description of the pipeline process.

Figure 2: *(a) material IDs assigned to mesh, (b) mesh with greyscaled textures and diffuse colours set to white, (c) mesh with skeleton fitted.*

Once a suitable character is chosen, it can be altered in one of the packages for 3D modelling. We used 3D Studio Max but any other modelling package with built-in scripting language or custom designed system could be used. *Angela* was purchased as a correctly texture mapped mesh. However, in order to prepare her for exporting, some alterations had to be made.

Depending on the method used for colour modulation for the impostors in the system, two different approaches can be used at this stage to prepare the character's mesh. The first is to group the different coloured regions of the mesh together and use different materials for each region. This method was used by Dobbyn et al. [DHOO05] for the purpose of easily specifying the different colour regions when generating the impostor images and the mesh can be rendered using the OpenGL fixed function pipeline. The second method is to apply a single texture map image to the character, with different colour regions specified in the texture's alpha channel.

This technique was used by [dHCSMT05] for the preparation stage of their characters for a crowd of low resolution geometry. For our clothed crowds, we use this approach in order to add pattern variety (detailed in Section 5.2). We will describe both techniques for completeness.

3.1.1. Grouping Triangles

The character's triangles are first organised into groups, where each group is a body part that can be coloured differently from its surrounding parts. For *Angela* we had 8 different groups: eyes, head and shoulders, arms, fingernails, legs, top, shorts, and shoes (Figure 2(a)). Each of these groups were assigned different diffuse materials or texture maps. The reason for organising the triangles in this way is that it improves rendering when exported into the real-time system, due to the minimization of OpenGL states. Also, it allows for colour modulation, as each different group can have a palette of colours assigned to it, in order to create colour variety when duplicating characters in the crowd. The diffuse colour of each material is set to white, and each texture map is greyscaled to allow for colour modulation without the loss of detail (Figure 2(b)).

3.1.2. Specifying Regions in a Single Texture Map

The alternative method is to apply a single texture map to the character. Some models are purchased with a single texture map, but if not, it can be custom designed in an application like Photoshop to suit the character. The basic idea is to combine all of the texture maps into a single compact texture map (see Figure 3(left)). The coloured areas with no detail are simply areas that have a single diffuse colour. The alpha channel of this texture is then manually encoded with different colour regions (Figure 3(right)). Since we are using a single pass to render the impostors in the system (see [DHOO05]), as many regions as the user requires can be specified at this stage. Once this custom designed map has been created, it can be applied to the character. The texture coordinates of the character need then to be matched up to the texture, which can be a time-consuming task. This matching can be accomplished in 3D Studio Max using the *Unwrap UVW* modifier.

3.1.3. Skinning and Animating

The character now needs to be skinned, in order for an animation to be applied. Typically, a biped skeleton is first fitted to the character (Figure 2(c)), and then the vertices of the character mesh are weighted and linked to the different bones of the skeleton. This can be achieved in 3D Studio Max using the *Physique* or *Skin* modifier. We used both motion capture from our Vicon system and keyframing in 3D Studio Max to obtain the animation for our character. The choice of animation depends on the type of crowd scene that is being produced. The amount of animation data also has to be restricted due to the memory limitations for the display of large crowds. In our system, an animation is typically one second long and then looped in the system to create long sequences. The animations should be cyclical in order that

Figure 3: *(left) Example of a single greyscaled texture map for Edith, (right) Corresponding alpha channel.*

flickering animation artifacts do not occur when looping the animation in the system.

The amount of floor space that can be captured using a motion capture system is often quite limited. Therefore, capturing long sequences of humans walking is difficult, unless a treadmill is used. We can typically capture about 4 steps of a human walk, so it is unlikely that a cyclical walk could be extracted. Some postprocessing is usually necessary in 3D Studio Max, where we choose one walk cycle, and paste the pose at the start frame to the end frame and try to interpolate the motion curves to make it fit without loosing too much of the individuality and naturalness of the captured walk.

3.2. Preparing the Deformable Clothing

The commercial software that we used (ClothFX [Clo]) provided tools for constructing garment segments, and for changing the different material parameters, along with accurate collision detection. We simulated many different types of clothing using this software, including silky skirts, stiff dresses, sweaters and shorts. Cloth simulation is still limited in what it can achieve, and therefore the choice of clothing and materials is often compromised depending on the animation of the virtual human. For example, a character performing a back-flip in a tight fitting long dress would not produce nice results - cloth by its nature is resistant to stretching, but not to bending. We found that a lot of tuning was necessary to produce nice cloth animations, for the human animations that we wanted.

3.2.1. Template creation

In [EWS96, KFW04, GFL03, PLAPMT02, VCMT05] and in most commercial packages, 3D virtual clothes are constructed from planar garment segments (often referred to as 'patterns', however we will not use this term to avoid confusion with the 'pattern' or motif variety detailed later). As this is the way real clothes are manufactured, virtual garments can therefore be designed to match real clothing. It also makes texture mapping particularly easy as correct texture coordinates can be obtained automatically at the planar rest state.

The shape of the segment is usually drawn by the user using splines or imported from a software package designed for cloth manufacturers like Modaris or PAD [MOD, PAD]. Seams and seam connections are then specified by the user. A seam is usually an edge on a piece of fabric and can be attached to another seam using virtual sewing threads. The planar segments are then positioned around the virtual character at approximately correct positions. A good initial position for the clothing is very important and can determine how well the clothing fits. In order to achieve this, the segments should first of all not collide with anything (the virtual character or each other). They should also be as close as possible to the virtual character's body and the sewing between seams should not penetrate the character. The start pose of the character can be changed in order to satisfy these rules; usually a T-pose is best.

Figure 4: *Fitting a garment using ClothFX.*

Once the segments and sewing are lined up, the garment can be joined along the seam lines. In [KFW04] sewing is achieved by merging the segments along the seam lines. For every pair of vertices along the seams, the matching triangles are coupled and the seams are moved halfway between the two original points, as shown in Figure 4. The segment pieces are attached and attain a shape influenced by the form of the body.

3.2.2. Material Modelling

The mass-spring model is the most commonly used technique for deforming garments. It consists of a simple particle system, where the particles correspond to the vertices on a cloth mesh. These particles are connected by different springs: structural springs for tension, diagonal springs for shearing, and interleaving springs for bending. The forces exerted by the particles are determined by the type of spring that connects them. Forces for structural springs are very large, whereas bend and shear forces are small, which can lead to contradicting effects. In order to have a more general system, the mass-spring system can be thought of as a network of interwoven threads, where a thread is a chain of structural springs. Different threads can then interact at mass points. More complex forces are necessary to model this kind of behaviour.

The Kawabata Evaluation System (KES) for fabric is a technique used in the garment industry for measuring fabric mechanical properties through normalised procedures [Kaw80]. In this system, five experiments are conducted using different instruments, and from these experiments 15 curves are obtained, which allow 21 parameters of fabric to be determined. These experiments measure shearing, bending, friction, compression, and deformation. These energies can be modelled in the particle system using a rectangular grid, where each particle interacts with its four direct neighbours.

In commercial software, coefficients that describe these 21 parameters can be changed in order to produce cloths that behave differently. For example, for a material like silk the resistance to bending would be set to low, whereas it would be set to high for a stiffer material like burlap.

Good collision detection is also necessary when modelling clothing. When clothing a virtual human with deformable garments, full and self collision detection need to be implemented in order for the clothing not to penetrate the human or itself. Commercial cloth simulation packages usually have full and self collision built-in. This is the most time-consuming task of cloth simulation, and is a major reason why real-time simulation of clothing is so difficult.

4. Cyclical Cloth Sequences

In order to prepare the clothing generated for our characters to be exported into the system, the animation had to be cyclical. As previously described, in a real-time crowd system, the characters' animations are often cyclical in nature, so that they can be smoothly linked to allow them to move in a fluid manner. Cyclical animations are commonly obtained by manually altering the underlying skeletal motion so that they loop in a realistic looking manner. However, creating looping animations for characters with pre-simulated clothing is a more difficult task, as manual cleanup of the cloth to make it cyclical is very time-consuming, particularly for very deformable items of clothing like skirts, and can result in unrealistic effects. In [DMK*06], we describe an automatic method for generating cyclical sequences of cloth simulation. This method should be used at this point before proceeding to export the animations.

5. Stage 2: Exporting the Data

At this point, we have pre-simulated the deformation of both the virtual human's skin mesh using linear blend skinning and its cloth mesh using the physical simulator, based on the motion of its underlying skeleton. The cloth and human motion sequences are cyclical and the character should also have its triangles organised into the appropriate groups or has a single texture with specific alpha mapped coloured regions. The character is ready to be exported from 3D Studio Max into files that can be loaded into the crowd system.

5.1. Exporting the Geometry

The virtual human was exported the same way as in [Dob06]. A new plug-in was written to export the keyframes of the cloth mesh. This plug-in simply stored the world-space position of each vertex with respect to the root object for each keyframe of animation in an organised manner. By pre-calculating and storing the deformation of the cloth mesh in poses, this avoids the cost of simulating the clothes at run-time. However, this also means that all animations are predetermined and cannot be changed at run-time, which limits the motion variation in the crowd.

5.2. Exporting the Impostor

Generating the impostor representation of our character involves capturing two types of images from a number of viewpoints around the model: a detail map image to capture the detail of the model's diffuse texture and a normal map image whereby the model's surface normals are encoded as an RGB value. For more information on how these images are generated and rendered in the system see [DHOO05]. This section will describe any improvements to the algorithms and the necessary changes that were made in order to incorporate deformable cloth.

Figure 5: *Mesh after each vertex has been automatically painted with an RGB value corresponding to its normal.*

Tecchia et al. [TLC02] saved on texture memory when generating impostors by exploiting the symmetric nature of the human body performing a walk animation (both the animation and the body are symmetric). They halved the memory needed by mirroring the animation: 32 samples were acquired by sampling the mesh at 16 different points along one side, and mirroring these images to produce the samples on the other side. This worked very well for skinned humans, as the human and the clothing could be made symmetric quite easily (i.e., by mirroring one side), and would remain so for the animation. This approach could not be taken for generating impostors of humans wearing deformable clothing, as the folds in cloth are rarely symmetric in nature and mirroring them would produce artifacts at run-time. We tried generating a mirrored cloth animation using tools in 3D Studio Max, but it involved too much manual tuning and the results were not convincing. Therefore, the human was sampled on both sides to create the cloth impostor images, which increased texture memory consumption, but avoided artifacts.

In [MDSC06], we performed a psychophysical experiment that determined the optimal impostor update frequency, balancing texture memory consumption with visual fidelity. We found that an update rate of 17° was necessary to produce smooth transitions for normal pedestrian characters, where as 9° was necessary for characters with large width to depth ratios. The number of impostor images to be generated at this stage in the pipeline should be chosen based on these metrics.

Incorrect back-facing polygons was another issue which arose when implementing cloth impostors. The previous impostor plug-in did not account for back-facing polygons as it was not a noticeable problem for skinned clothing, which clung tightly to the body and did not turn inside-out at any point. However, for flowing garments, this occurred quite regularly and resulted in incorrect normals in the impostor image. A simple approach was used to solve this, by testing the direction of the normal and flipping if it was back-facing.

The normal maps in [DHOO05] took considerable time to generate, as per-pixel look ups and operations were needed, so we improved the algorithm using a less computationally intensive technique. A copy of the character's mesh and cloth at the current frame was first needed. Each vertex normal was first converted into eye-space coordinates, to find the normal with respect to the camera, and then converted into an RGB colour (using the equations described in [Dob06]). Per-vertex colouring was then used to paint the RGB colours onto the vertices of the copied meshes (3D Studio Max's *VertexPaint* modifier was used to do this). These vertex colours were interpolated over the polygons, creating a character mesh with normal map colours (Figure 5). The normal map image was then generated by rendered an image of this mesh, from the current viewpoint. Per-vertex colouring and interpolating are operations that are performed very quickly, as they are supported by graphics hardware. This meant that the image could be produced almost immediately, without the need for slow per-pixel operations.

The new technique for adding hardware assisted pattern variety to the impostors that we developed in [DMK*06] involves a slightly different process for generating impostor images. The detail map image is replaced with a texture coordinate map or *UV map*. This is similar to a normal map just described. However, this time it is the texture coordinates that are converted into an RGB colour and then painted onto the vertices of the mesh. Similar to the normal map images, these images were generated for each viewpoint.

6. Stage 3: Crowd Rendering

We are finally at the stage where all data is ready to be imported into the crowd system and used to display crowds of clothed characters. A number of alterations needed to be made to the crowd system in order to incorporate our perceptual metrics and the pattern variation technique. In this section, we will first give a broad overview of how the system was written, then we will look at how each of the levels of detail were rendered and how switching was achieved. This work was based on the approaches detailed in [Dob06].

6.1. Setup

The framework was based on a perceptually driven LOD approach, whereby the viewer's perception is exploited to compute less accurate models when they would not be noticed. The highest level of detail was the mesh model and the lowest was the impostor, as previously described. The system is a C++ application running on the Win32 API, where the OpenGL rendering library is used as the core component of the rendering subsystem. The number of humans in the crowd is first specified and they are then given random initial positions in the scene. Algorithms can be implemented to make sure that no human intersects, or that they are all oriented in a certain way. Each crowd individual is then randomly allocated a human template model, and variety is added by randomly choosing a specified *outfit*, which is a set of colours for each of the different parts of the body.

6.2. Rendering the Geometric Human and Cloth Models

The system is optimised by taking advantage of the fact that crowd individuals perform a default walk animation. Previously, we used static meshes, where the deformation of the mesh is pre-calculated. However, with advancements in graphics hardware we now calculate the deformation of the mesh on the GPU using linear blend skinning. The cloth animation is stored as pre-baked poses directly from 3D Studio Max, as described in Section 5.1. The rendering speed is improved by using Vertex Buffer Objects (VBOs) to store the key-frames of animation for both human and cloth poses. The idea behind VBOs is to provide buffers (regions of VRAM) accessible through identifiers. A buffer is made active through binding (in a similar manner to display list binding). This allows graphics drivers to optimise internal memory management and also to choose the most suitable type of memory to store the buffers. At run-time, the correct VBO pose is selected and rendered, depending on the current frame of animation of the virtual human.

Adding colour variation to the mesh involves first creating different outfits, which specify the different colours to be used for each different region in the mesh. For example, an outfit for Angela would consist of: eyes coloured blue, head and shoulders coloured pale pink, arms pale pink, fingernails red, legs pale pink, top white, shorts blue, and shoes white. Many different outfits can be specified for each different template human as described in [Dob06].

As mentioned in Section 3.1, there are two techniques for setting up the virtual humans' colours. We will now describe the two corresponding techniques to colour the human at run-time.

The first technique grouped together the triangles of the different regions of the mesh and then tagged them with IDs. At run-time, the OpenGL fixed function pipeline is used for rendering the mesh, where the diffuse colour of each mesh region is changed depending on its material ID and corresponding outfit colour. This was the technique used in [DHOO05] and is suitable for meshes that will be used alongside detail mapped impostors.

The second technique is needed to match the geometry with the UV mapped impostors. This method should be used if texture variation is important to add variety, as in the case of adding different designs to clothing. This technique uses programmable graphics hardware to add variation. As described in Section 3.1, a single texture map was applied to the character, where the alpha channel of the texture specified the different colour regions. The shading sequence for the geometry is shown in Figure 6.

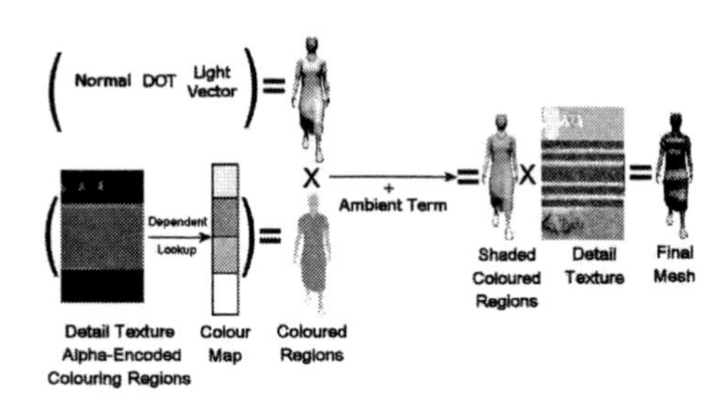

Figure 6: *Geometric mesh shading sequence.*

6.3. Rendering the Impostor

In order to render the impostor, the correct viewpoint image needs to be found. Using the camera position and the virtual humans position and direction, the most suitable viewpoint image can be calculated and retrieved from the large texture containing the pre-generated viewpoint images. This image is then mapped onto a quadrilateral. To dynamically orientate the quadrilateral towards the viewer, the amount to rotate can be calculated using the camera and virtual humans position. See [DHOO05] for detailed descriptions of the equations.

6.3.1. Switching Between Representations

Ulicny et al. [UdCT04] noted that impostors were an efficient approach for rendering crowds of far-away humans, but that their pixellated appearance when displayed close to the viewer prevented them from being used for detailed crowds. Dobbyn et al [DHOO05] solved this problem by using a hybrid impostor/geometry system, similar to that described in this paper. In crowd scenes where the humans and the camera are moving, the distance from impostors to viewer will change throughout the viewing time. Thus, a switching mechanism was employed to allow impostors to switch to geometry and vice versa when they reach a certain distance.

In Hamill et al. [HMDO05], we found a perceptual metric for the optimal pixel to texel ratio at which to switch representations, which ensures that users will not notice the switch. This ratio was one-to-one, which means that geometry can be switched to impostor representation when one of its texels is displayed on one pixel on the screen. A seamless transition is achieved by matching the pose of the impostor to the geometry at the point of switching. This technique did not need to be altered for our clothed characters, as the poses of the cloth were inherently linked to the human poses.

In [MDSC06], we validated this metric by performing a system experiment which examined participant's perception of level of detail representations in different sized crowds.

We found that participants did not notice the difference between a hybrid crowd of impostor/geometry and a crowd of all high resolution geometry, when the camera was zooming in and out of the crowd, which meant that popping between representations was not noticed.

7. Discussion

In this paper, we provided a useful step by step approach to realising crowds of clothed characters incorporating perceptual principles. This pipeline should be of use to game developers, to create and/or improve the quality of their crowds.

Our technique of adding pre-simulated clothing improved the realism of our crowd system. The visual quality of the clothed crowd is maintained by creating cyclical cloth motions to avoid discontinuous motion artifacts. Additionally, the use of the impostor's UV map complements the use of impostors with its mesh representation in a LOD crowd system, since it allows the matching of texture and colour variation between the cloth and skin. In Figure 7 we show our virtual model of Dublin city inhabited by crowds of pedestrian characters wearing deformable clothing. All of the walk cycles were captured using a motion capture system, and pattern variety was added using our UV mapping technique. This pipeline could also be used to create characters with pre-simulated hair or fur, by replacing the cloth creation stage with hair simulation.

References

[Clo] ClothFX, cloth simulation software. Size8Software, 2004.

[dHCSMT05] DE HERAS CIECHOMSKI P., SCHERTENLEIB S., MAÏM J., THALMANN D.: Reviving the roman odeon of aphrodisias: Dynamic animation and variety control of crowds in virtual heritage. *VSMM* (2005), 601–610.

[DHOO05] DOBBYN S., HAMILL J., O'CONOR K., O'SULLIVAN C.: Geopostors: a real-time geometry / impostor crowd rendering system. In *SI3D '05: Proceedings of the 2005 symposium on Interactive 3D graphics and games* (2005), pp. 95–102.

[DMK*06] DOBBYN S., MCDONNELL R., KAVAN L., COLLINS S., O'SULLIVAN C.: Clothing the masses: Real-time clothed crowds with variation. *Eurographics Short Papers* (2006).

[Dob06] DOBBYN S.: *Hybrid Representations and Perceptual Metrics for Scalable Human Simulation.* PhD thesis, University of Dublin, Trinity College, 2006.

[EWS96] EBERHARDT B., WEBER A., STRASSER W.: A fast, flexible, particle-system model for cloth draping. *IEEE Computer Graphics and Applications 16*, 5 (1996), 52–59.

[GFL03] GROB C., FUHRMANN A., LUCKAS V.: Automatic pre-positioning of virtual clothing. In *SCCG '03: Proceedings of the 19th spring conference on Computer graphics* (2003), pp. 99–108.

[Ham05] HAMILL J.: *Level of Detail Techniques for Real-Time Urban Simulation.* PhD thesis, University of Dublin, Trinity College, 2005.

[HMDO05] HAMILL J., MCDONNELL R., DOBBYN S., O'SULLIVAN C.: Perceptual evaluation of impostor representations for virtual humans and buildings. *Computer Graphics Forum, (Eurographics 2005) 24*, 3 (2005), 623–633.

[Kaw80] KAWABATA S.: The standardization and analysis of hand evaluation. *The Textile Machinery Society of Japan* (1980).

[KFW04] KECKEISEN M., FEURER M., WACKER M.: Tailor tools for interactive design of clothing in virtual environments. In *VRST '04: Proceedings of the ACM symposium on Virtual reality software and technology* (2004), pp. 182–185.

[MDO05] MCDONNELL R., DOBBYN S., O'SULLIVAN C.: LOD human representations: A comparative study. *Proceedings of the First International Workshop on Crowd Simulation* (2005), 101–115.

[MDSC06] MCDONNELL R., DOBBYN S., S. COLLINS C. O.: Perceptual evaluation of LOD clothing for virtual humans. *Proceedings of the 2006 ACM SIGGRAPH/Eurographics Symposium on Computer Animation* (2006), 117–126.

[MOD] LECTRA SYSTEMS MODARIS Version 4. http://www.lectra.com/en/pds/modaris_fashion.html.

[PAD] PAD system Inc. http://www.padsystem.com/.

[PLAPMT02] PROTOPSALTOU D., LUIBLE C., AREVALO-POIZAT M., MAGNENAT-THALMANN N.: A body and garment creation method for an internet based virtual fitting room. *Computer Graphics International Conference Proceedings, Springer Verlag* (2002), 105–122.

[TLC02] TECCHIA F., LOSCOS C., CHRYSANTHOU Y.: Visualizing crowds in real-time. *Computer Graphics Forum (Eurographics 2002) 21*, 4 (2002), 753–765.

[UdCT04] ULICNY B., DEHERAS CIECHOMSKI P., THALMANN D.: Crowdbrush: interactive authoring of real-time crowd scenes. In *Proceedings of the 2004 ACM SIGGRAPH/Eurographics Symposium on Computer Animation* (2004), pp. 243–252.

[VCMT05] VOLINO P., CORDIER F., MAGNENAT-THALMANN N.: From early virtual garment simulation to interactive fashion design. *Computer-Aided Design 37*, 6 (2005), 598–608.

Figure 7: *Example screenshots from our clothed pedestrian crowd inhabiting a virtual model of Dublin city. The city is populated by four template models processed through our pipeline.*

Serious Games & Social & humanities aspects of games (1)

Building Virtual Training System with Verbal/Nonverbal Interface Using Multiple PCs Connected with High-speed Networks

Norihiro Abe   Syunji Uchino
Kyushu Institute of Technology
680-4 Kawazu, Iizuka-shi, Fukuoka, 820-8502, JAPAN
E-mail: abe@mse.kyutech.ac.jp

Hirokazu Taki ,
Wakayama University
930 Sakaedani, Wakayama-shi,
Wakayama 680-8510, Japan

Shoujie He
Eastman Kodak Company,
Plano, Texas, USA

KEYWORDS
Training system, Virtual Reality, Synchronized real-time processing, Interface, Billiards game

ABSTRACT
Virtual reality (VR) technology has been more and more mature over the last decade. Development of a virtual environment for training purpose is considered one of the most practical applications of the VR technology. Since the VR technology involves all kinds of sensors in exchanging information between the real world and the virtual environment, it is computationally intensive in terms of data processing at an individual sensor and information integration among all the sensors. In general, the information integration has to be well synchronized in order to meet the training needs. At the same time, real-time processing capability is also considered critical. Many more practical issues could be uncovered only when a virtual training environment is actually being developed. Based on this belief, this study is experimenting on the development of a virtual environment for training billiards players. The technical difficulties encountered and the corresponding resolutions are considered beneficial to the development of other practical virtual training environments and its interface which facilitates communication between players and a training system. This paper summarizes the design and implementation details about our experimental virtual training environment and reports the algorithms for the synchronization of the information from different sources.

. INTRODUCTION

Ever since the computer was invented, a lot of things that used to be impossible have become possible and many imaginations have become the reality. Constructing a 3D world inside a computer and interacting with it have been the goals that virtual reality (VR) technology is targeted at. Over the last decade, the VR technology has become more and more mature. These days, low cost and high performance computers and the advanced sensor technologies become the driving force for the VR technology to quickly find its real-world applications. Development of a virtual environment for training purpose is considered one of the most practical applications of the VR technology.

A high-quality virtual training environment is required to offer the trainee a real-world experience while interacting with virtual objects. This includes not only the high-quality 3D graphics representation of the virtual environment and virtual objects but also the high-performance interactivity. The 3D graphics representations need to be dynamically and smoothly updated based upon the user interaction. The interactivity, on the other hand, requires well synchronized real-time processing of the sensor data. These are all computationally intensive. The limited

resources and processing power on a single PC become very difficult and even impossible to meet the needs.
In this study, a virtual environment for training billiards players has been developed. Behavior identification, 3D sound effects, and the force torque sensor feedback are identified as three essential components. The synchronization of the real-time processing of the sensor data is achieved through the SCRAM Net+.

It is not always easy for a user to communicate what he intends to the system using ordinary interface such as mouse and keyboard during a training session because the user may have to operate an input device such a PHANToM. Verbal/ nonverbal interface for helping a user specify his intention is added to the system. PHANToM can be used not only as a haptic device but also as a pointing device; it is, however, difficult to pointing at a virtual object out of reach of it. To point at an object (whether it is real or virtual) that is distant from the user, pointing action using a forefinger is usually applied along with utterance including a pronoun such as "this" or "that" instead of a noun phrase corresponding to the object.

SYSTEM ORGANIZATION

To construct a high-quality virtual training environment, it is a common recognition that there must be visual, auditory, and haptic sensors and the sensor data must be well synchronized. This study basically follows the same direction with the emphasis on the synchronization among the behavior generation using rigid object physics, 3D sound effects, and the haptic feedback. In order to do so, VORTEX, 3D-Sound Space and PHANToM are used in the construction of our experimental virtual environment.

Since it is impossible to have one PC to handle the processing of all the data, three PCs are used with each dedicated to a particular sensor or device. The three PCs are connected through SCRAM Net+. Figure 1 shows the system organization. The details are described as follows.

PC for vision

(1) Graphic rendering and simulation
(2) VORTEX – the rigid object physics engine

PC for auditory

It generates stereophonic sound using Roland 3D Sound Space and RSS Data Stream Management system.

PC for haptic computation

It is used as the user interface and returns haptic feedback through the GHOST and PHANToM

PARALLEL PROCESSING ISSUES

With the nature of the system organization, the following parallel processing related issues have been identified.

- The transmission of position data
- Presentation of haptic sensation
- Synchronization of sound effects

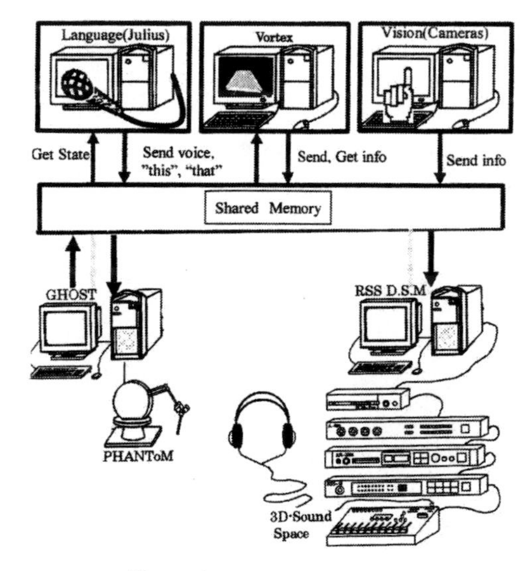

Figure.1: system organization

The transmission of position data

The three PCs are doing their jobs cooperatively by sending their data through the shared memory of the SCRAM Net+. When a user starts interacting with the VR environment, for example, the interaction is communicated to the VR environment through

PHANToM. The interaction event is then simulated by VORTEX. Based on the simulated results, RSS10 will play the sound effects and the PHANToM will react with haptic effects to the user whenever it is necessary.

The position data such as shift or rotation that are generated through the interaction with PHANToM is transmitted to VORTEX through the SCRAM Net+ with a delay of less than one millisecond. The results simulated by the VORTEX must be transmitted to the PC for a haptic reaction data computation and the PC for the processing of the 3D sound effects. All the data are written into the shared memory in the form of coordinates and a transformation matrix.

As soon as a simulation result is updated, are the updated coordinates written to the shared memory. However, since the updating of the simulation result is intermittent and non-linear, the receiver has to behave in the same way. There is a possibility that a moving virtual object passes through other virtual objects as shown in Figure 2 and thus the unexpected simulation happens.

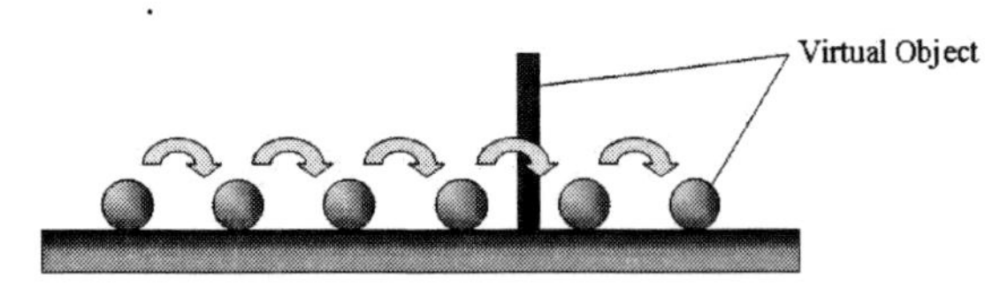

Figure.2: A penetration problem

In the rigid object physics, the impulsive force occurring at the collision is generally calculated from the inertia tensor and relative velocity based on the shape data. As velocity information is indispensable while applying the rigid object physics to objects colliding with each other, instead of updating the coordinates, updating the velocity is considered necessary.

It is, however, impossible to correctly simulate the state of a virtual object because an error slowly accumulates if the state is updated based on the velocity. Therefore, both the current coordinates and the velocity of a virtual object are considered necessary while updating the shared memory. In this case there is potentially a danger of error accumulation. For instance, right after both the coordinates and the velocity of a virtual object have been transmitted, the virtual object suddenly stops moving. In this case, its coordinates are invariant but in the PCs receiving the coordinates and velocity of the virtual object, the virtual object keeps moving.

This gives rise to the inconsistent information between two PCs in regard to the position of the virtual object. The slower the updating is, the more significant the error becomes. Because of the error, velocity is considered inadequate for the application that concerns the accuracy of locating the virtual objects. In the regular cases, using the coordinates is recommended. It is suggested to take the velocity into account as well only at the time that collision is going to happen.

Consider the situation that a moving virtual object collides with a still virtual object. In this case, a user hits a virtual billiard ball using PHANToM. The PHANToM here is the billiard cue. GHOST detects the collision of the PHANToM with a virtual billiard ball. Since the coordinates of the virtual ball is not sent to the VORTEX yet at the moment when GHOST detected the collision, collision is not happening in the VORTEX. At this moment, changing the control from the coordinates to the velocity makes it possible to apply the rigid object physics in the VORTEX.

It is necessary to transmit to the VORTEX the coordinates and velocity right before the collision occurs. This is because the collision has already occurred if the coordinates at the collision are transmitted. Figure 3 illustrates how to change the control by velocity (the right) from that by coordinates (the left). Not coordinates at the time collision were detected but the ones one step before (just before collision) and velocity are transmitted to the PC for VORTEX.

It was a concern that inappropriate movement may happen due to the skipped coordinates update for one time interval. The experimental results show that the movement within one time interval is so tiny and the haptic simulation in GHOST is repeated 1000 times per second and thus nothing unnatural is noticeable.

This technique makes it possible to change control from that using coordinates to that using velocity at the best timing and vice versa. As a result, applying rigid object physics at collision becomes possible while keeping precise operation

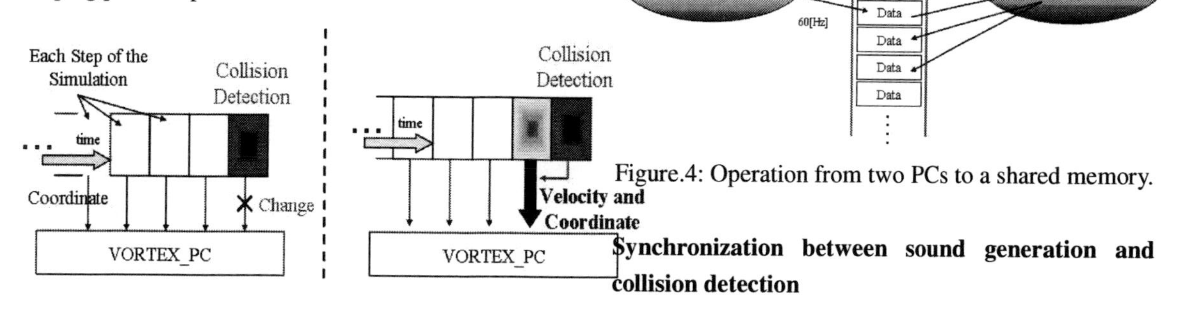

Figure.3: How to change process

Figure.4: Operation from two PCs to a shared memory.

The presentation of haptic sensation

When performing parallel computation in a real time simulation, it is necessary to run simulation while maintaining synchronization between two PCs. Processor speed in two PCs are so different from each other that it is difficult to synchronize them as the time taken in each process are quite different.

VORTEX needs at most 60 Hz but GHOST does 1000Hz. The smooth presentation of touching sense is generally required at least from 200 to 300 Hz. If VORTEX were synchronized with GHOST, smooth touching sense is difficult to return. To ensure that GHOST gets enough velocity to return smooth haptic feeling, asynchronous execution of two PCs is proposed.

Figure 4 illustrates how the data is exchanged through the shared memory system. It shows how VORTEX and GHOST are accessing the shared memory along the time axis. Since GHOST is running at high processing speed, it writes data into the shared memory with high frequency, but reads data out from the shared memory only after VORTEX has finishing writing. Therefore, although it is parallel computation, accessing data asynchronously makes it possible to let the individual PC perform its own job without affecting others.

Synchronization between sound generation and collision detection

In a general sound revitalization instrument, when a sound is being generated, it is impossible to revitalize several sound effects simultaneously. Any new revitalization command is simply ignored until the current sound effect has been fully generated. Because of this limitation, when more than one sound effects are needed in a short period such as the simulation of the repeated collision, none of the sound effects will be generated. In addition, when multiple objects collide with each other at the same time in the real world, a loud sound will be heard. With the current limitation, instead of a loud sound, a monotonous sound will be generated.

In the system, when virtual balls collide in an extremely short period, the sounds accompanying with the collision are considered as a unified sound. When more than one virtual ball collide with each other, the sound effect is generated by recording in advance the real sound accompanied with the collision of the real balls in the real world and then replaying the recording. Different levels of sounds are also recorded in advance according to the velocities of virtual balls. Each sound must be recorded as short as possible so that the recording could be repeatedly replayed as needed.

CONSTRUCTION OF VR SPACE

In order to offer a real-world experience to the players, the virtual space must be made with high interactivity. In general, if a simulation is only for a simple scenario, it is sufficient to build only one VR space.

This system, however, is constructed with 3 PCs and each of the PCs is handling visual, auditory and haptic sensations, respectively. Since each of them is handling different type of tasks and thus the time spent is largely different. If we build only one VR space which includes everything, in the case that a particular PC spends extra long time to finish its task, the other two PCs will have to be idling during that period of time. In this study, in order to speed up the overall processing, instead of one VR space, three VR spaces are constructed with each on one PC. Since each individual VR space is handling one type of tasks (visual, auditory, or haptic), only the data related to the particular sensor or device is held in the memory. The memory usage could be reduced substantially.

Figure 5 illustrates the information needed for each of the VR spaces. The PC for vision space keeps track of the coordinates of virtual objects. The PC for sound space locates the existence of the player and also the sound sources so that the virtual sound could be generated to the best effect. The PC for haptic sensor has to keep track of all data of all the virtual objects including the cue, stand and balls for detecting the collision between the cue and virtual objects.

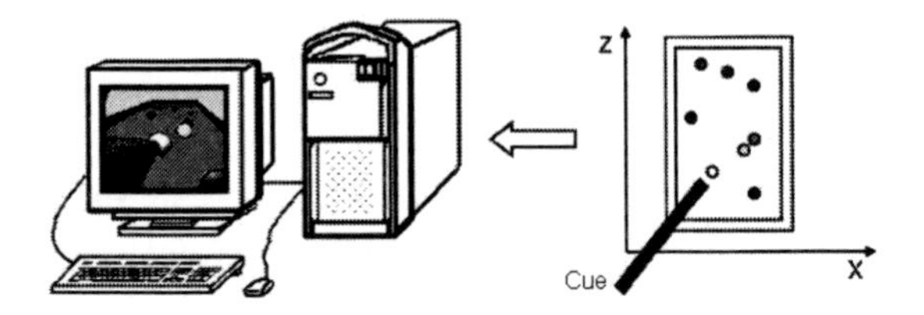

Figure.5-1: Vision space

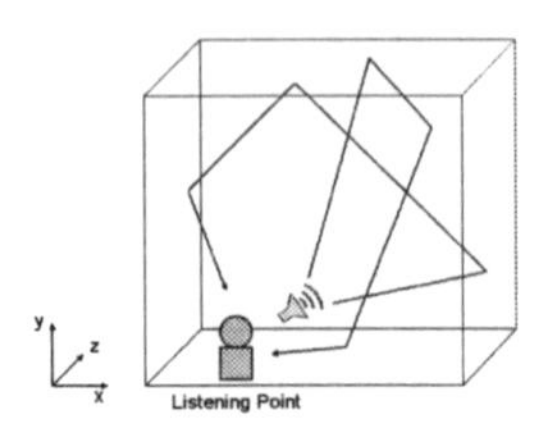

Figure.5-2: Sound space

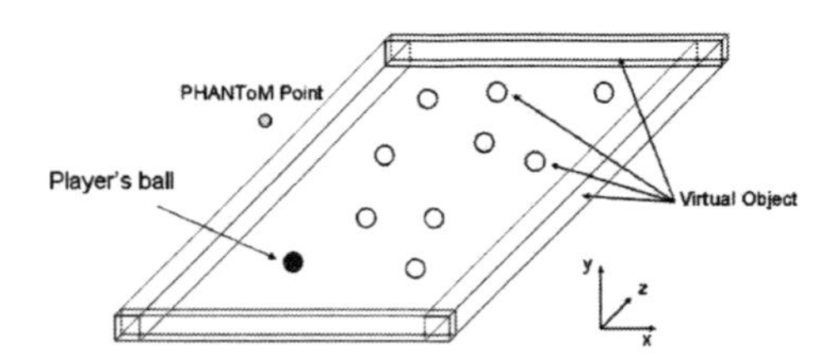

Figure.5-3: Haptic space

Although there are three separate VR spaces, the player needs to feel like interacting with a single VR space. Otherwise, the player will not have the real-world experience. This requires synchronizing the three VR spaces seamlessly. This is achieved through the SCRAM Net+. When one VR space has changes, the updates will be written into the shared memory of the SCRAM Net+. The information in the shared memory will be read by the other VR spaces. By controlling each VR space separately, the visual, auditory and haptic sensations are eventually synchronized.

FLOW OF PROCESS

Figure 6 shows the outline flow of a system,

1. The visual, auditory and haptic simulation is started at each PC.
2. Each VR space is constructed.
3. When a user operates a cue, GHOST acquires the coordinates and posture of PHANToM through SCRAMNet+, and detects collision detection between a cue (PHANToM) and a ball which is hit with the cue. And haptic feedback is returned to the user via PHANToM and the collision information is written into SCRAMNet+.
4. VORTEX reads coordinates of the object whose position is changed and updates simulation. As a result, as soon as the collision is detected, the result will be written to the SCRAM Net+. Finally, it visualizes the virtual world on a display. The same process is repeated (Hereafter this is regarded as one cycle).
5. RSS10 acquires the name, coordinates and velocity of a set of virtual objects which collided from the SCRAM Net+ and then generates stereophonic sound and output the sound effects.

VORTEX and GHOST at the acquisition of data do not have to wait for the other output in order to access the SCRAM Net+. This makes it possible for both of them to guarantee the updating frequency of simulation. The above, however, is a basic regular flow. The other special cases such as switching from coordinates to the velocity and other information exchanging are performed only when it is needed.

A flow of a vision system

1. In addition to a transformation matrix of PHANToM, collision information is also collected. GHOST detects whether there is a collision between PHANToM and a virtual object.
2. If the collision is detected with GHOST, the control is switched to be velocity-based. The SCRAM Net+ is accessed again in order to get coordinates and velocity of PHANToM right before the collision.
3. After setting the coordinates and velocity of PHANToM right before the collision with the object, the control that prevented PHANToM from updating coordinates must be canceled. It transmits information to make PHANToM write its coordinates hereafter.
4. The simulation is updated again and in order to make collision between PHANToM and an object by all means happen at this step, once again control is changed back to the coordinates-based mode from the next step.
5. Updated coordinates of all virtual objects and current cue coordinates are written to the SCRAM Net+

A flow of an auditory system.

1. Access the SCRAMNet+ and read all the updated information from VORTEX. The information includes the coordinates of all virtual objects and a position of PHANToM.
2. Check if collision among virtual balls or with the frame of the billiards board is detected with VORTEX. Also check to see if a virtual ball has been hit with the cue.
3. When collision is detected, the number of collision and information concerning pairs between objects colliding with each other is acquired in order to select the sound source for the generation of the sound effects.
4. After a sound source is selected, sound generation command in MIDI is transmitted to Roland Sound Space.

A flow of haptic system

1. Once the haptic space is constructed, the coordinates of virtual objects will be transmitted into the haptic space. Note that the coordinates of the virtual objects are all simulated by VORTEX.
2. Not only coordinates and the posture but also the velocity of PHANToM are acquired, and they are stored in memory to make it possible to use them when VORTEX switch the control to from coordinates-based mode to the velocity-based one.
3. If collision has been detected before, the transmission of the current PHANToM coordinates is restrained in order to make VORTEX shift to the velocity-based control mode. During that time, the SCRAM Net+ does not allow any data to be written until VORTEX finished reading velocity information. Here it is examined whether VORTEX has updated its state or not.
4. In the case that it has not been examined yet after collision, the transmission of new coordinates will not be done. Only PHANToM coordinates are updated. Collision analysis among virtual objects will not be completed because there is the possibility of consecutive collisions.
5. When it is not examined or when collision does not happen yet, collision detection is performed. If there is collision, collision information and the coordinates and velocity stored right before are transmitted.

VIRTUAL BILLIARDS GAME

A virtual billiards game is selected to evaluate the method proposed in this paper. Figure 6 shows a cue controlled with PHANToM.

The game starts from the opening break shot. When a player hits his cue ball put on a pool table with his cue,

Figure.6: User interface

it will collide with the rest of balls. But it is too difficult to precisely simulate the collision occurrence among balls. Ordinarily, they seem to collide against each other almost simultaneously, but such a collision does not happen really. More than two balls may collide simultaneously and the collision is observable using a high-speed video camera but Vortex cannot detect such a collision happening in extremely short time but only some of collisions are detectable. Consequently precise collision sound generation is also impossible. The current system just simulates behavior of balls after collision occurrence based on the detected collision and the real impulsive sound occurred by the real opening break shot is replayed. The way for the later simulation of the game will be shown in the followings.

When a cue ball is hit toward the group of balls, some balls may be fallen into pockets, and others are scattered on a pool table. Changing the position of a cue ball is not allowed according to the rule. When a player changes, the player must appoint the location of his cue ball. The player designates it by touching with PHANToM the point on a table where he wants to locate his cue ball. However, the player cannot appoint the location out of reach of PHANToM. In the case, if the player has only to point at the location where he wants to put his cue ball with a forefinger while saying "puts it here", then the interface system detects the position, and it is moved within the reach of PHANToM. Then the player hits with PHANToM the cue ball put in the appointed location.

We have already constructed an interface system that allows us to communicate with virtual environment using both voice and action pointing at a virtual object. It is used as interface to specify the position of a cue ball.

The player is allowed to change his position relative to the arrangement of a pool table when he judged that he couldn't hit a cue ball at the current situation. The location of PHANToM being fixed, the direction to hit a cue ball is restricted and it is difficult to change the direction of a virtual cue in comparison with a real one. Furthermore, in a real billiard a trial hit is permitted as far as a cue does not hit a cue ball. So a trial hit must be allowed with PHANToM. At the point where a player pulls back a stylus of PHANToM to hit a cue ball, he is asked if he wants a trial or not. This makes it possible for a player to examine the result of a trial and to change the positional relation between a cue ball and PHANToM if it not adequate. Of course, position change of a cue ball is not permitted when the same player hits the cue ball in succession. Only modification of a table position is allowed which makes it possible to change the position of a player and/or his attitude. Immediately after a player took turns, a player is permitted to change both its position and that of a cue ball.

The table is translated when a player tells the system "change position" while pointing at a point on a table in which he wants to locate PHANToM. At the point where a player thought that he has done practice enough, trial session finishes by informing the system of the end of a trial.

.

Now players can enjoy virtual billiards, but they must acquire the right way to hit a cue ball to enhance the technique and abilities of billiard game. A hemisphere of a ball is divided into five regions as shown in Figure 7. Naturally C point of a cue ball must be hit to make it go straight, and to make it curve R or L point must be hit. If you want to get it spin, you should hit point B. Whenever a player hits a cue ball, not only the portion of the cue ball hit with a cue, velocity and direction of the cue but also the trajectory of the ball and other balls collided with it are also recorded. It is also possible to record the collision information among balls including a cue ball in the similar way; only the record concerning a cue ball is kept. Referring to this information, a player can confirm actually how he operated a cue. Repetition of trials will play a vital role that helps a player enhance his abilities. However, at present we do not examine the effect by subjects test.

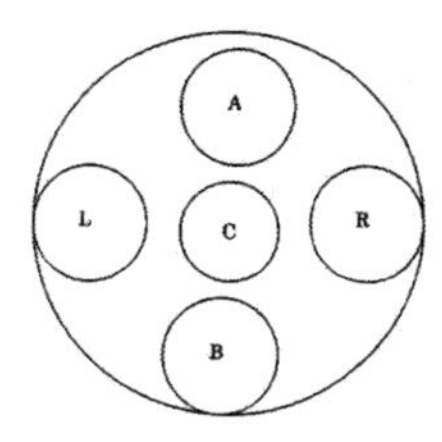

Figure 7, A hemisphere of a billiard ball

Improving processing speed by parallel computation.

The processing speed of each PC is measured. The time taken to complete one cycle of process using each PC is measured 100 times and the maximum and the minimum of the results were recorded. Processing speed when a single PC manages 3 jobs was measured afterwards.

Experimental result

It is understood that large amount of processing time can be reduced by parallel computation. It is difficult to perform 3 jobs with a single PC because both haptic and auditory rendering are not fully realized as shown in Table 1. On the other hand, each PC exploiting parallel computation achieves enough iteration necessary for giving a user high reality.

Table 1: Comparison between processing speed

Task	Time [ms]	Frequency[Hz]
vision	16-20	48-60
auditory	8-12	83.3-120
hap tics	3.6-5.1	196-277
All of them	25-31	32-40

Evaluation of the system

Ten subjects were asked to operate a virtual billiards game and to evaluate the validity of visual, auditory and haptic sensation and how much they are synchronized. Results are shown in Figure.8 and Figure.9. Figure 8 implies that good evaluation is obtained concerning both auditory and haptic sensation. It can be considered that parallel computation succeeded in constructing VR space in which haptic sensation synchronizes with auditory one. But evaluation on visual sensation was not so good. Concerning behavior of virtual objects, high reality is attained as simulation is performed based on rigid object physics. Rendering system provided with VORTEX does not have enough functions which GL offers and cannot draw any shadows of virtual objects. It is still necessary to evaluate how close the current behavior is to the real billiards game. In terms of improvement, at the very least, the friction factors need to be incorporated in the future

Figure 9 shows that enough synchronization among them is established. One of the goals of this study is to make the real-time processing possible while dealing with the different type of sensor data. In that sense, the experimental results are positive.

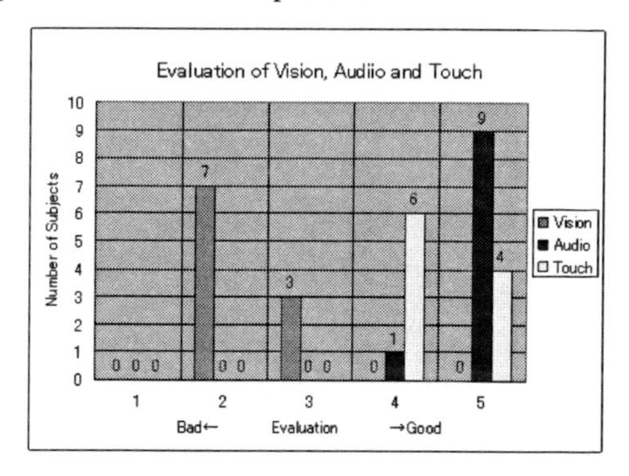

Figure8: Evaluation on visual, auditory and haptic sensation.

CONCLUSIONS

Game construction with high reality is obtained by integrating rigid object physics, haptic feedback and stereophonic sound system. For developing a system with much higher reality than that realized in this study, the operability which gives a user the feeling as if he were playing a real game is necessary. One of promising ways is to build a Mixed Reality system permitting a user to hit a virtual ball with a real cue. The system needs not only installing both position sensors on the body and impact generation device on the tip of the real cue, but also technique realizing complete registration between real and virtual environment permitting a user to hit a virtual ball with a real cue.

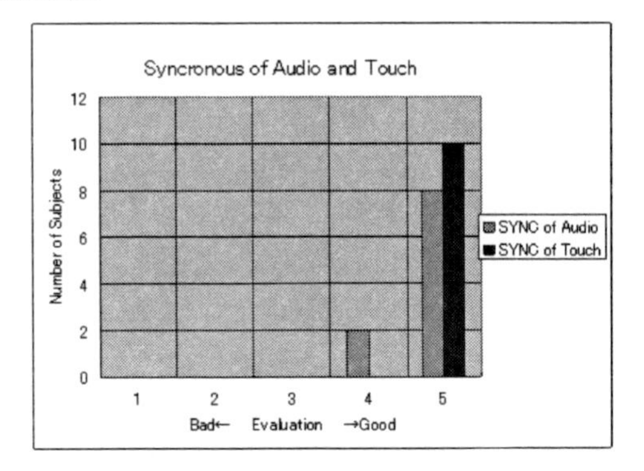

Figure.9. Evaluation of synchronization among three sensations.

Acknowledgment

We greatly appreciate the aid of Ministry of Internal Affairs and Communications (MIC) and the Grant-in-Aid for Scientific Research.

REFERENCES

Abe, N., Takamura, Y., Tanaka, K., Taki, H., He, S.:2006, "TOWARDS PRACTICAL VIRTUAL TRAINING ENVIRONMENT THROUGH VR TECHNOLOGY",. European Conference on Modeling and Simulation

Dragovi´c, V., Radnovi´c. M. "Geometry of Integrable Billiards and Pencils of Quadrics", Journal de Math´ematiques Pures et Appliqu´ees

Jebara, T., Eyster, C,. Weaver, J. Starner, T., Pentland, A. 1997. "Stochasticks: Augmenting the Billiards Experience with Probabilistic Vision and Wearable Computers", Proc. of the Intl. Symposium on Wearable Computers,

Matsuura, H,, Abe,N., Tanaka, K., Taki, H. 2006. Hiroaki Matsuura, Norihiro Abe, Kazuaki Tanaka, Hiroaki Taki, Shoujie He : Virtual Air Hockey Game Allowing Two Players to Fight thorough Network, Journal of Computational Information Systems, pp. 583-591, 2006

M.Doi, T.Takai, and K.Chihara. "VR american football simulator with cylindrical screen", *Lecture Notes in Computer Science*, No. 1834, pp. 286–293.

Pan, Y., Abe, N., Tanaka, K., Taki, H. 2004. "The Virtual Debugging System for Developing Embedded Software Using Virtual Machinery", Proc. of Embedded and Ubiquitous Computing, International Conference (EUC 2004), pp.85-95, Aizu Japan.

Smith, R. 1998. "Intelligent Motion Control with an Artificial Cerebellum.", Ph.D. thesis in July 1998, department of Electrical and Electronic Engineering at the University of Auckland, New Zealand.

Shinya Matsui 2004 "MR Billiard : Training System of Billiard" Master's Thesis, Nara Institute of Science and Technology, NAIST-IS-MT0251113

T. Ohshima, K. Satoh, H. Yamamoto, and H. Tamura."AR2 Hockey A case study of collaborative augmented reality". *CVVRHC*, pp. 78–85.

Watanabe, Y., Norihiro Abe, Abe, N., Tanaka, K., Taki, H., Yagi T., 2005, "Multimodal communication system allowing man and avatar to use voice and beck", 3rd International Conference on Information Technology and Applications (ICITA'2005), pp.161-166

Dynamic Difficulty Adjustment in Game-Based Intelligent Tutoring Systems

Stephen Howell and Tony Veale

Abstract – **Computer games which utilize lexical resources allow players to experience games focusing on their linguistic abilities. They can also add an educational dimension where language skills can be assessed. An effective game should immerse the player in a state of flow. An effective educational tool should tailor the difficulty of the material presented to that this state of flow is uninterrupted. We present a game-based Intelligent Tutoring System and show the effects of adding a dynamic difficulty adjustment module.**

Index Terms – Flow States, Intelligent Tutoring Systems, Dynamic Difficulty Adjustment, Word Games

I. Introduction

The Development of educational language games that use lexical resources like electronic dictionaries and large text corpora presents both opportunities and challenges to the game developer. Any game may acquire scholastic material and present it to a player, but unless the game is entertaining and engaging, most players will simply lose interest. To allow players to achieve *a state of flow* in educational games, such games must adapt to the player's ability in real-time, to gives them an incentive to keep playing. As a valuable corollary, the rate of adaptation also supplies detailed student profiling data to those educators who employ games as part of their teaching process.

We have developed a number of educational computer games that employ data derived from lexical resources such as Wikipedia (the open-source, and constantly growing, on-line encyclopaedia) and WordNet, an electronic dictionary and thesaurus (Miller 1995). One of these games is a compound-term recognition game for second-level students. The current target audience is English native speakers between the ages of 11 to 17. The game is a brick-stacking exercise in which falling bricks contain words that indicate how the bricks are best stacked: those brick combinations that form a known compound-term, like "roast" + "beef" or "honey" + "bee", obliterate each other to yield a bonus score, while those that do not combine in this way eventually stack up to clog the game screen. This game, named *BuzzWords*, was designed to be an effective Intelligent Tutoring System (ITS) in the domain of vocabulary-learning, but the conceptual nature of the core combination paradigm means that BuzzWords is as much about idea combination as word combination. As such, it gives rise to many variants that prove to be educational in domains other than language (such as mathematics, science, and history).

ITS are traditionally designed in a modular fashion (Woolf 1992, Shute & Psotka 1998), typically combining a domain module with a student module, a tutor module and a communications module (essentially the user interface manager). BuzzWords follows this structure also, with some minor modifications to reflect the game-based focus of its design.

A typical game of BuzzWords proceeds as follows: A player identifies himself/herself to the system and chooses a starting level of play, ranging from 'Easy' to 'Medium' and 'Difficult'. The student is then presented with a series of brightly coloured word bricks that fall down from the top of the screen. As these fall, the player has a few seconds to manoeuvre the brick into a desirable location on the brick pile below. The player's goal is to drop the falling word-brick on top of any brick that contains a complementary word that, when combined in any order, forms a vertically stacked compound-term. This newly formed compound will then vanish and the player's score is increased. A higher score is given to a compound-forming stack-up if it is judged by the game to be the best match the student could have achieved with that particular move.

Other wrinkles make the game more strategically interesting. For instance, if the player drops a word in such a way that it is horizontally adjacent to a word-brick with which it can form a compound term, the falling brick will become stuck to this horizontal match and possibly prevent access to other bricks beneath it later in the game. As one might imagine, there is a certain amount of manual dexterity involved in BuzzWords, but we are primarily interested here in testing the student's ability to mentally match compound terms, and thus ideas, than their in testing either their dexterity or geometric abilities.

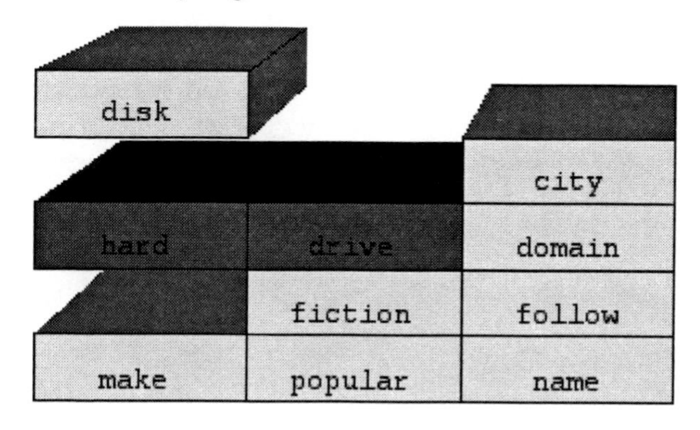

Screenshot: A small portion of the game window showing two horizontally placed bricks "hard drive" which have become stuck, hindering the player's access to 'make'. The falling brick 'disk' will remove this lock as it will create the vertically stacked compound noun "hard disk".

II. Creating a state of Flow

In order to create and maintain a state of immersion in the game, that is, a state of 'flow', BuzzWords also incorporates a Dynamic Difficulty Adjustment module. Flow was originally described by Csikszentmihalyi as a state which gives rise to intense concentration in a task, such that an actor experiences a loss of his/her sense of time. Particularly relevant to a state of flow is a harmonious

* Both authors are with the School of Computer Science and Informatics at University College Dublin, Ireland (email: {stephen.howell, tony.veale}@UCD.ie}.

balance between the ability of a person in this state relative to the perceived difficulty of the task (Csikszentmihalyi 1992). It follows that tasks which are either too difficult or two easy will not give rise to states of flow since participants cannot readily lose themselves in such tasks.

In game terms, this implies a state where the player becomes deeply involved with a game, possibly losing track of time while desiring to continue playing indefinitely. In order to maintain such a state of flow, a process for automatically personalizing the game's difficulty level to individual players becomes necessary. Traditionally, this adjustment is made when the player first enters the game, by means of a simple menu choice. However, this process can also be performed during the game, so that the difficulty level adjusts to the level of ability exhibited by the player as the game progresses.

Several researchers have studied both states of flow and dynamic difficulty adjustment (DDA) in the context of computer games (e.g., Johnson & Wiles 2001, Draper 1999, Jones 1998). This research has practical outcomes, and games have also been built which attempt to place the player in a state of flow by adapting to their particular abilities (Chen 2006).

DDA has also been utilised in mainstream games (Sweetser & Wyeth 2005, Bailey & Katchabaw 2005), but less scrutiny has been given to the use and effects of DDA in an educational game context.

BuzzWords employs DDA to challenge players with relevant compound terms at the appropriate level of language difficulty as their play progresses, in such a way as play does not become so difficult as to cause players to abandon the game. Most game-based DDA systems take the approach of limiting supplies of key inventory items such as health or ammunition (Hunicke & Chapman 2004). Another common approach is to speed up the rate of player interaction with the environment (e.g. by increasing the rate of enemies encountered, or their speed and accuracy). However, these tactics do not have an obvious analogy in game-based ITS. Thus, after experimenting with a number of game styles, it was decided to use DDA purely as a device for adapting the perceived difficulty-rating of compound terms, and not to speed up the rate of fall or impose other challenges on the player.

III. Intelligent Tutoring Systems

As mentioned above, ITS systems are normally designed with modules reflecting the roles a successful ITS needs to fulfil. Our ITS was designed with game play and assessment as priorities, so the design of a system with instructional priorities would taken a slightly different form. We detail here the design and development considerations which went into the various modules.

A. Expert Module

The expert module in BuzzWords comprises the complete set of English compound terms that the game can recognise. These were derived from the contents of the WordNet electronic dictionary. The set of compound terms has been filtered to remove obviously non-English terms (such as Latinate terms, biological names and obscure scientific terms). Also, as the target audience of the games are second-level students, some slang and most sexual terms are also filtered. This was done by a combination of human identification of undesirable terms, and automated cross referencing with previous categorised terms from resources such as Wikipedia. Although geographical terms and historical figures can be filtered as well, it was decided that they added a certain gravitas to the game. There remain approximately 36,000 compound terms in the list at present.

B. Tutor Module

The tutor module contains knowledge of how 'difficult' a particular compound noun is, in regards to any other compound term. To ground a metric for difficulty, we used a web-frequency value (Shamma *et al.* 2004, Modjeska *et al.* 2003) to suggest a measure of word familiarity. This requires an automated query system to take every compound term known to the expert module obtain a hit-count from a search engine like Google. These values are converted via a logarithmic scale into a series of values between 10 (most common) and 80 (least common). Table 1 presents a representative sampling of words positioned along this scale.

Noun 1	Noun 2	Difficulty
mail	order	23
national	park	23
first	step	24
news	story	24
street	address	25
booking	agent	25
big	brother	25
cash	advance	26
news	agency	26
estate	agent	26

Table 1: A sample of compound nouns with web frequency difficulty ratings

Using this difficulty rating, the tutor module can determine that 'news agency' has a greater difficulty than 'news story'. During a game the player may have a choice of dropping 'news' on 'agency' or 'story'. Although they will receive a score by choosing either, the former will reflect more positively on their language level and thus on their score.

C. Student Module

The student module is designed to analyse the placement decisions a player-student makes during a game. This data is used to build a model of the student's knowledge and ability. This model is then used in conjunction with the tutor module to perform dynamic difficulty adjustment.

Each time a student has the opportunity to match a word to a number of possibilities, the actual choice is recorded against the best choice that could have made, and whether there are any lower scoring but still valid choices available. This data in aggregate gives us a view of how the student played the game, and it can be later used to 'play back' the game for instructional purposes.

D. Communications Module

The communications module is the user interface to the ITS, which in this case is a computer game. BuzzWords has been developed with an emphasis on the structure of the graphical-user-interface by using Java in conjunction with the Processing graphics library (Fry & Reas 2004).

The Processing library was chosen because it allows developers to concentrate on game design and play functionality. Processing also has the ability to deploy to both web and to the desktop, and can and target Windows, Mac OS and Linux using both Java2D or OpenGL Processing allows developers to switch seamlessly between 2D and 3D interfaces, depending on the capabilities of the target platform.

The game design is modular, with a number of manager classes controlling the game data in play and a number of classes dealing with extracting and analysing the compound term data. The DDA classes are designed to be independent of the target game, and can be easily deployed in a completely different game.

E. Dynamic Difficulty Adjustment

The Dynamic Difficulty Adjustment (DDA) component is designed to facilitate the optimal flow state for a given player while simultaneously determining the player's compound-term recognition level, as measured by the difficulty levels described previously. The game invokes the DDA component each time the player makes a brick placement, whereupon the DDA determines if it should adjust the difficulty level. Since the DDA mechanism does not know the player's actual level of competence, any adjustment to the game's difficulty level is essentially done via hill-climbing, using the player's on-screen successes or failures as a search gradient. The DDA module thus examines all the placements made since the previous level change, and computes the highest possible score the player could have scored, comparing this optimal score to the score actually achieved. Depending on the result, the player may find the difficulty level decreasing (if they have consistently failed to match any or very few compound terms on the previous level), staying the same (if they matched some but not most falling bricks) or increasing (if they made the best match in nearly every case).

BuzzWords attempts to find the player's natural ability as quickly as possible, which is to save, in as few moves as possible. To test this ability, batteries of software agents are used to play the game independently. Each agent has a pre-determined competence-level at which it would perform optimally if the game were to provide stimuli at the same difficulty level. For example, we expect an agent with a competence level of 20 to achieve an optimal score in a game that operates at difficulty level 20, since this is the point at which the player can accumulate the greatest expected return for each correct brick placement. Our test thus comprises multiple agents playing BuzzWords continually, starting from various initial difficulty levels. Each game played by an agent is recorded, and aggregate data is compiled from each agent's individual performance. A small sample of 3 agent-tested games is given below. It shows the decline, increase or steady-state nature of the game's difficulty-level under the influence of the DDA for each game. With a large deployment of agents playing at different levels, the effect of using the DDA module can be analysed in greater detail.

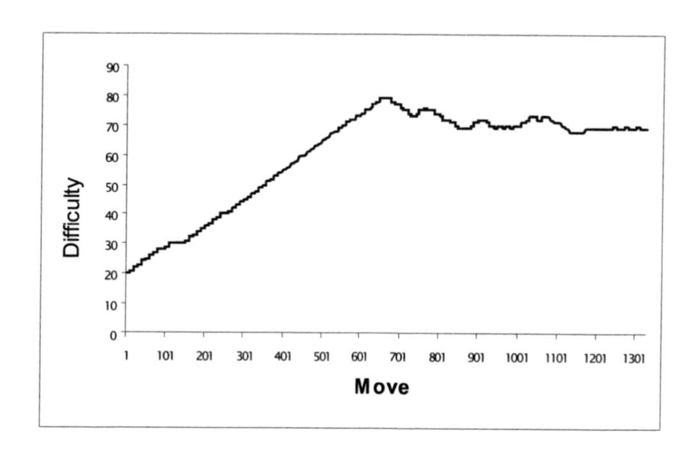

Fig 1: An agent with an ability level of 75 starts at 20 (difficulty-level = easy).

The success or otherwise of each game-playing agent's brick placement decisions is determined by a probability function which takes into account the pre-assigned competence level of each agent, the game-level it is currently playing at, and the particular game stimuli which are currently in play. An agent is not penalised if there is no high scoring move it can make in a given circumstance. As each test game progresses and each agent is forced to make successive brick placements, one can expect to see the DDA module adjusting the game's difficulty level so that it approximates the competence level of the agent. For instance, in Fig 1 above, an agent with a competence level of 75 (very high) starts the game at difficulty level 20 (easy). This means that the DDA must continually raise the difficulty level from 20 to 75 (without explicitly knowing that 75 is indeed the correct goal) if the agent is to achieve a simulated state of flow. We can see from Fig. 1 that it takes approximately 1000 moves (brick placements) for the DDA mechanism to home in on a flow-conducive setting.

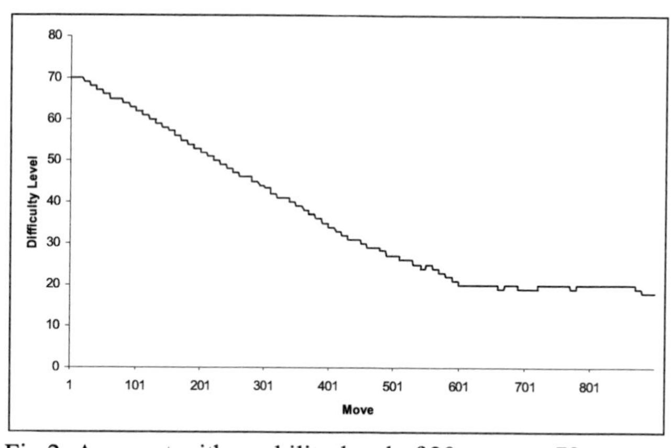

Fig 2: An agent with an ability-level of 20 starts at 70.

Fig 2 illustrates the contrary effect, in which an agent starts the game at a difficulty level much higher than it's true competence. The goal of successive DDA adjustments is to lower this difficulty level until it begins to plateau around the agent's competence level of 20; Fig. 2 illustrates that in this case around 600 brick placements are required to reach a flow state.

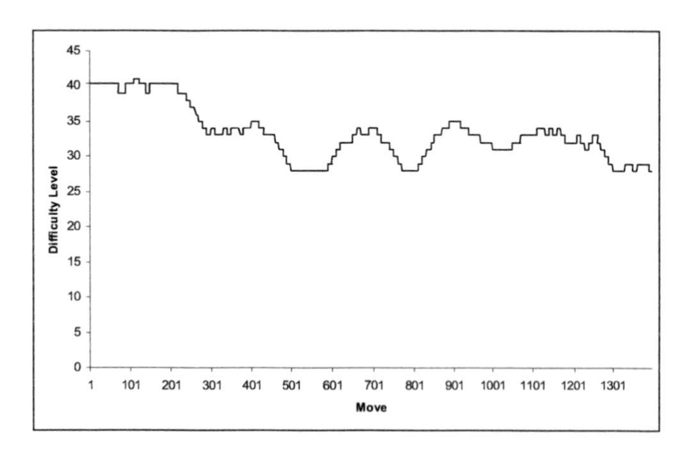

Fig 3: An agent with a ability-level of 30 starts at 40.

In the game reported by Fig 3, an agent starts at a difficulty-level that is slightly too challenging (a difficulty-level of 40 versus a competence-level of 30). As such, the DDA does not modify the difficulty level significantly, and begins to oscillate around the target level of 30 after about 400 brick placements.

IV. Conclusions

The DDA can adjust the stream of compound terms so that a player of a given level is continually challenged, but not frustratingly so. More importantly, the use of DDA in tutoring systems enables more complex feedback than a mere score to be given to the end-user (both student *and* educator). The workings of DDA are dependent on the tutor module providing valid difficulty ratings for a given stream of game stimuli, whether the compound terms of BuzzWords or other ITS learning-objects. By using software agents to test these workings, one can see the DDA module adjusting the game difficulty level in real-time to reflect the choices made by the player.

A further modification to the tutor module is proposed which would replay the game at various points to the student (or teacher who sets the game as a test). This module could serve as a backseat driver of sorts, instructing the player of better placements that could have made at a particular juncture and allowing players to establish a better starting point for future games.

We expect that a more sophisticated ITS platform can be developed via continuous refinement of the DDA algorithm as it arises from further student testing. This platform will present a variety of game styles via its communication module, and a variety of dynamically generated data from disparate corpora via its expert and tutoring modules. The goal, of course, is to allow educators with neither the requisite programming skills nor game design abilities to easily deploy a range of different games in their particular subject area. As student interest and immersion in entertainment technologies such as educational computer games increases, such a platform becomes an important tool for an educator who needs to combine entertainment technologies with traditional pedagogical tools.

The authors would like to thank Enterprise Ireland, who funded this research through a Commercialization Fund grant.

References

Bailey, Christine and Katchabaw, Michael (2005). "An experimental testbed to enable auto-dynamic difficulty in modern video games". *Proceedings of the 2005 GameOn North America Conference*

Chen, Jenova (2006). MFA Thesis: "Flow in Games". *University of Southern California*

Csikszentmihalyi, Mihaly (1990). "Flow: The Psychology of Optimal Experience". *Harper Perennial*

Draper, S.W. (1999). "Analysing fun as a candidate software requirement". *Personal Technology* 1999 vol.3 pp.117-122

Fry, Ben & Reas, Casey (2004). Ph.D. Thesis: "Computational Information Design", MIT Media Laboratory.

Hunicke, Robin, Chapman, Vernell (2004). "AI for Dynamic Difficulty Adjustment in Games". Northwestern University.

Johnson, Daniel & Wiles, Janet (2001). "Effective Affective User Interface Design in Games". *Conference for Affective Human Factors Design 2001.*

Jones, Marshall G. (1998). "Creating Engagement in Computer-based Learning Environments". *The University of Memphis.*

Miller, G. (1995). "WordNet: A Lexical Database for English." *Communications of the ACM,* 38 (11).

Modjeska et al. (2003)." Using the Web in Machine Learning for Other-Anaphora Resolution." *Proceedings of the 2003 Conference on Empirical Methods in Natural Language Processing.*

Shamma D. A., Owsley S., Bradshaw S., Hammond K., (2004). "Using Web Frequency Within Multimedia Exhibitions". *ACM Multimedia 2004.*

Shute, Valerie J. & Psotka, Joseph (1998). "Intelligent Tutoring Systems: Past, Present and Future". *Defence Technical Information Center.*

Sweetser, Penelope & Wyeth, Peta (2005). "GameFlow: A Model for Evaluating Player Enjoyment in Games". *ACM Computers in Entertainment.*

Woolf, B. (1992). "AI in Education". *Encyclopedia of Artificial Intelligence,* Shapiro, S., ed., John Wiley & Sons, Inc., New York, pp. 434-444.

5 Keys to More Effective Educational Games
A systematic Approach to Emotionally Sound Games

Patrick Felicia[1], Ian Pitt[2]

University College of Cork

ABSTRACT

The authors propose a framework to facilitate the integration of serious games in primary teaching and to increase their educational effectiveness. Using well-known Instructional Software Design methodologies coupled with an awareness of users' personality will increase knowledge transfer from games to school settings.

CR Categories and Subject Descriptors: I.3.6 [Computer Graphics]: Three-Dimensional Graphics and Realism- Virtual reality; K.3.1 [Computers and Education]: Computer Uses in Education – Computer Assisted Instruction

Additional Keywords: games, computer-assisted instruction

BIOGRAPHY

Patrick Felicia is a PhD student in University College of Cork. He is currently focusing on exploring the ways in which games can accelerate the learning process.

1 INTRODUCTION

In the last 30 years, a new generation of students and workers has emerged: the digital natives. This generation processes and accesses information randomly, plays video games, uses digital devices and often needs to be motivated to perform tasks (Prensky, 2001). However, schools and training settings have not evolved accordingly, and as a result their educational material is often not adapted to the needs of this new generation.

1.1 Games are Powerful Educational Tools

Video games are very popular among digital natives regardless of their age or gender (Pratchett, 2005; Entertainment Software Association, 2004). They represent a powerful entertainment medium where users can take part in social activities, exploration and informal learning (Gallardeau, 2005; Prensky, 2004). They represent the most popular form of story-telling (or digital story-telling) involving dynamic open-ended environments where the story unfolds according to players' actions. Kort (2005) reminds us that story telling remains the most ancient form of instruction through which knowledge was passed from generation to generation. Since the introduction of formal education, learning has lost its emotional dimension and thus the power of story telling. Video games include many aspects of drama and story telling such as physical, verbal, political and economic conflict, direct or indirect conflict or interactions between characters (Crawford, 2003). They have the ability to motivate, to offer problem-solving situations and a rich range of interaction between users (e.g.: Multi-player Online Games). As such, video games provide an ideal medium for instruction.

1.2 The Introduction of Video Games in Schools

The educational effectiveness of games has been proven in various domains such as the military (e.g. America's Army) and the training of fire fighters. However, when it comes to schools, the introduction of video games in the curriculum has been much slower. Commercial Off The Shelf (COTS) games are being used primarily to increase pupils' motivation and interest. Pupils do learn from those video games, however, evidence of their effectiveness is often anecdotal (Squire, 2002; Cannon-Bowers, 2006). Furthermore, most of those games do not match the constraints set by school environments (time, users' literacy, curriculum, etc.). Some questions still need to be answered:

- How can we evaluate the effectiveness of educational games?
- How can we design them to suit school settings?
- How do emotions affect learning in educational games?

The authors propose the PLEASE model to facilitate the introduction and effectiveness of educational games in schools using an instructional design approach coupled with an awareness of the user's personality and emotions.

In the second and third sections, the authors relate their experience of developing an educational game, Math Quest, and explain how users' personalities have affected the learning outcome. Following this, they further describe issues raised by teachers and the evaluation of educational games in school settings.

In the fourth section, the authors investigate the theoretical basis underpinning the influence of emotions and personalities on learning using both the Big 5 and the Myers-Briggs Type Indicator (MBTI) models.

2 THE EXPERIENCE OF MATH QUEST

In June 2006, Math Quest, a Java3D-based video game, was created to enhance secondary schools pupils' Mathematics skills.

2.1 Analyzing the Needs of Students and Teachers

Prior to developing the game, a meeting was setup with the teachers to assess their needs in terms of educational content, format and students' motivation. Following this meeting, a post-survey was carried out in the school to collect information on students' gaming experience.

41 pupils aged between 13 and 14 (2nd and 3rd year) took part in the survey. The results were as follows:

- 56% of the students played video games. 34% of the pupils just did not like video games.
- Most of the players preferred (in order of preference) role-playing games, educational games and first person shooter.
- 29.7% of the pupils played at least once a week
- 47% of the pupils had been playing video games for more than a year.
- When asked about game qualities, pupils identified the game play and discovering new levels as the most important features.
- 23% of the players already had experienced with educational games but only 20% of them found those games entertaining (educational games were often perceived as boring).
- When asked how they would obtain help in the game, 28% of the pupil said they would ask their friends, only 11.2% would read the booklet, 3.4% would read the help available in the game and 3.4% would try until they find the solution.

Results from this survey were then used to design the educational game.

2.2 Designing the Game

2.2.1 Post-Survey Results and Teachers' Interviews

The constraints imposed by both students and school settings were as follows:

[1] e-mail: pf2@csmail.ucc.ie
[2] e-mail: i.pitt@cs.ucc.ie

- Easy learning curve game play (only 56% of the pupils used to play video games)
- Diversity of levels and sound
- Help provided primarily by experienced peers (28% of pupils would ask their friends how to play the game).
- Completion of the game in less than 40 minutes.

To meet the expectations listed above, the game was developed around a First Person 3D maze where users have to find the exit to proceed to the next level. Throughout the maze, users need to solve equations to open doors.

2.2.2 Overall Structure of the Game

The game includes an Intelligent Tutoring System (ITS) with two distinct modules:

- The expert module is responsible for the educational strategy
- The student module holds information about the student (actions, skills, etc.)

The expert module is in charge of monitoring students' progress and providing just in time intervention. It includes methodologies to solve linear equations, to detect pupils' reasoning errors and to perform remedial actions. The educational strategies used by the expert module are based on a course book that pupils use during the year and also on teachers' hints.

The student module records details about students' progress and skills. It is updated throughout the levels and provides necessary information to the ITS to detect weaknesses and to trigger corrective actions.

2.2.3 Game Flow

When a user approaches a door, she is presented with an equation to solve. The solution can be entered in the form "x=...". Each time an answer is entered the system provides feedback, highlighting what the user has done well and letting her know what could be done next. The system does not overload the user with information; instead, to keep the user confident and motivated, one hint is given at a time.

After several unsuccessful attempts to find the solution, the system offers help (voice and text message); if the user accepts the help, the system provides step by step hints, highlighting what the user has done well so far and the next step.

The strategy used to solve the equation is the same as the one covered by students' Mathematics books. This is to ensure that knowledge gained during the game will be directly applicable in the classroom.

In the first level, the instructional system observes the student's answers when solving equations. Successful entries and errors are recorded. Solving an equation is broken down into a set of 6-7 steps. Each of those steps is identifiable as a skill and associated with a success rate. At the end of the level, the system can detect which skill needs to be improved (if the success rate is less than 85%).

In the next levels, when the user approaches a door, the question she has to answer is based on the skill previously evaluated as low. Every subsequent equation will be designed to help the user improve this skill until it has been mastered (success rate greater than 85%).

The same applies to any other skill evaluated as insufficient by the expert module. Once the user masters each of the steps involved in solving an equation, the system promotes the user's autonomy by asking her to decide what step/strategy to apply at a certain stage of the equation solving. The question could be as follows:

If you had the following expression: 4X+2-2 = 6-2, what would you do?

1. Add -2 to each side
2. Divide each side by 4
3. Calculate 2-2 and simplify the left side of the equation

2.2.4 Implementation

It was decided that pupils would act as helpers for the game. Teachers pointed out that since 4th and 5th year pupils got on well with students taking part in the pilot study (2nd and 3rd), they would be perfectly suited for the task. Four of those pupils tested the game and gave assistance to their younger peers during the pilot study.

The pilot group was divided into two subgroups: Group A and Group B.

- Students who belonged to Group B played a placebo version of the game where there was no educational content.
- Pupils who belonged to Group A played a game that contained educational material covering linear equations.

2.2.5 Experimental Settings and Evaluation

Each session was structured as follows:

- Teachers and designers welcome pupils.
- Pre-test in the classroom for 5-10 minutes.
- Pupils are sent to the computer lab.
- Designers demonstrate the game mechanics for five minutes.
- Designers and teachers answer pupils' questions.
- Pupils play the game for 30 minutes, supervised by both teachers, game designers and helpers from 4th and 5th year.
- After the game, pupils return to the classroom where they do a post-test and fill out a questionnaire.

2.3 Results Analysis and Lessons Learnt

2.3.1 Post-test Results

The post-test results were as follows:

	Group A	Group B
Average Mark Before playing	35.44%	66.67%
Average Mark After playing	60.46%	57.50%
t-test	p> 0.05 (Not significant)	
Mann-Whitney test	p> 0.05 (Not significant)	

Table 1: Post-Test Results

Group A, which played the educational game, increased their marks by 25.02 % whereas for group B, the average mark dropped by 9.17%. Even if the effect of the video game on the first group is obvious, the statistical evaluation reveals that we can not guarantee with 95% of certitude that the introduction of the educational game has increased the average marks for group A.

The authors believe there was slight confusion for the Group B during experiments, which corrupted some of the results and their statistical analysis.

2.3.2 Post-Survey Results

A post-survey was given to students belonging to Group A. It assessed the extent to which the game had improved their confidence in solving equations. The results were as follows:

- 68% of the pupils felt that the game had helped them to understand how to solve equations.
- 80% felt that the game should be used more often in their school.
- 71% were willing to use the software at home.

The post-survey also showed that most pupils found the game was fun to play, and challenging. However, they asked for more levels, and for some of them, an increased level of difficulty.

3 OBSERVATIONS AND LESSONS LEARNT

The observations made during the pilot study influenced our vision of requirements for educational games and led to the creation of a new model: the PLEASE model.

3.1 Student Behaviors and Personalities

During the pilot study, we found that behaviors often differed between students and influenced greatly in what way, how much and how fast they learnt from the educational game. The game was based on repetition and reinforcement, however, as stated by Gagne et al. (1992), repetition of a task, even if it can help the retention of information, is not essential. Instead, the internal state of the leaner (or previous learned capabilities) ought to be accounted for (e.g.: prior learning, motivation, self confidence, etc.).

We observed a range of student behavior which we categorized as follows: extraverted students, introverted students, tense students, confident students, 'careless' students and sometimes a combination of several behaviors. Each of these groups showed a particular approach to learning and to using the educational game.

As predicted by the survey, most students did not use the help during the game; they obtained information through the presentation made by the game designers and later on, from peers or teachers. Some students, tried to *'game'* the system (instead of reflecting upon solving the equations, they were trying every possible solution until it worked) which prevented them from understanding the underlying methodology involved in solving equations. According to Schank et al. (2001) such behavior is quite common in educational software. They advise designers to keep students focused on their task, to provide realistic and motivating contexts. They believe that providing a sufficiently complex system that leaves no room for lucky guesses should counteract such behaviors. However, despite the fact that the system implemented most of those features (headphones, immersive environment, solving equations as a condition to go further in the game, only correct answer is accepted), it did not prevent users from trying to game the system. The authors suspect that, regardless of the content, some pupils are more inclined to display such behavior because of their personality and approach to learning in general.

Some students enjoyed working on their own or sharing their experience with other pupils. The former seemed to get on better and complete the game earlier. Some students exhibited very competitive behavior, often communiating with other pupils and comparing their progression.

Finally, some students appeared tense using the game. They would not ask for help, even from their peers when facing a situation they could not overcome. Reasuring them helped them progressing further in the game. On the other hand, confident students seemed to perform better, whereas those who felt insecure or less confident using the software encountered more problems.

These observations suggest that the degree of success for each student was often based upon their previous skills and willingness to learn but primarily on their personality and learning style.

3.2 Promoting Autonomy

The strategy used by the ITS involved providing progressively more autonomy in their learning activities. They learn first how to perform tasks and then learn to decide how to sequence those tasks. The authors believe that this strategy has influenced greatly the pilot study results (68% of the pupils reported that the software had helped them to understand how to solve equations).

3.3 Issues Raised by Teachers

Discussions with teachers revealed some of their concern regarding the introduction of educational games in the classroom:

- The possibility of customizing the content
- The educational strategy used in the game
- Ease of installation
- Completion time
- Ease of use

Most COTS games do not offer such features, making their integration in the classroom more difficult. Of course, some of them have a genuine educational potential, but unless their content can be adapted to teachers' needs, they are very unlikely to be widely used in schools (Van Eck, 2006).

3.4 Evaluating Educational Games and Knowledge Transfer

Serious game designers still find it difficult to evaluate the effectiveness of serious games (Squire, 2002) and to transfer effectively the knowledge learnt in the game to daily life. Most of the evidence is anecdotal and refers to pupils' comments on their experience. No study has proved the long-term impact of such games on academic results (Mitchell & Savill-Smith, 2006). This is predictable as most of the Commercial Off the Shelf (COTS) games are not initially designed for schools and therefore do not fit into their evaluation procedures. Their design is often focused on increasing motivation rather than on measurable educational effectiveness.

To enhance the effectiveness of Math Quest, several actions were taken:

- The educational content was based on the Irish Mathematics curriculum. It ensured that the methodology used in the game would be applicable outside the game. The knowledge gained within the game could then be directly evaluated.

- Each step needed to solve an equation was identified and formalized in the game. This made it easier to identify where users encountered difficulties and allowed appropriate remedial strategies.

- The format of the questions used within the game was the same as the one used in the pre and post tests.

3.5 Summary

The results of the pilot study have been encouraging. They have shown the importance of tailoring the game to school settings to facilitate evaluation and enhance knowledge transfer. Promoting learners' autonomy by progressively developing their meta-cognitive skills seemed to have influenced the results positively. The authors also feel that adopting a systematic approach (Analysis, Design, Development, Implementation and Evaluation) as well as including both teachers and students in the design process has been highly beneficial.

The most striking observation was that users' personalities and emotions can play a key role in the way they benefit from an educational game. Whereas fear or anger prevented pupils from enjoying the learning experience, positive and confident learners often performed better.

4 5 KEYS FOR MORE EFFECTIVE EDUCATIONAL GAMES

To address issues faced by serious games developers, the authors propose the PLEASE model based on the following features:

- **P**ersonality and **L**earning Styles
- **E**motions to accelerate learning
- **A**utonomy
- **S**ystematic Approach
- **E**valuation

4.1 Account for Personalities for a Tailored Learning Experience

The PLEASE model accounts for users' personalities and learning styles. It tailors the learning environments to users' cognitive and emotional needs. The following sections explain the benefits provided by this model based on the Big 5 and MBTI models, for each personality type on a cognitive and emotional level.

4.1.1 Theoretical Basis

The process of seeking and processing information is both a cognitive and emotional process linked to subjects' personalities (Heinström, 2003). The 5-factor model, one of the most widely accepted models of personality, categorizes subjects' personalities as: neuroticism (prone to anxiety), extraversion, openness (open to new information), competitiveness and conscientiousness (hard worker). The impact of personalities on information processing is explained further.

- Subjects who belong to the 1st category (neuroticism) consider lack of time as a barrier. They need to increase their control and it is better to show them documents that confirm previous knowledge or ideas.

- Subjects who belong to the 2nd category (extraversion) show a preference for thought-provoking documents. They tend to privilege social activities and seek information through peers (teachers for guidelines and peers for feedback). They also like discussions or documents that bring new perspective to their area. However, they do not tend to be systematic and they do not perform deep analysis of the material or learn from it in a way that can be measured in marks.

- Subjects who belong to the 3rd category (openness) need to search a broad range of information (not only one source) and tend to be curious. They are eager to find information and therefore they are open to accidental discovery. They are also open to new information to question it. On the other hand, conservative students (low level of openness) prefer clearly and recently written documents recommended by teachers. For such subjects, it is important to promote invitational and open information at the initiation stage.

- Subjects who belong to the 4th category (competitiveness or low level of agreeableness) show a base for skeptical and critical thinking. They also show impatience during learning activities.

- Subjects who belong to the 5th category (conscientiousness) are characterized by their ability and willingness to work hard to achieve their goal. They are ready to seek, analyze and reconsider information. On the other hand, easy going students (low level of conscientiousness) tend to be impulsive, easily distracted, careless and hasty. They have a predilection for information that confirms their previous knowledge and their choice is often guided by a need for a quick answer.

This suggests that unless designers take users' personalities into account, the information delivered and the way it is delivered could have opposite effect to that intended.

4.1.2 Personalities and Learning According to the MBTI Model

The Big 5 model is primarily used in academic research whereas the MBTI model, created in 1962, is applied to counseling and management training and is therefore more practical. It is often associated with learning styles.

The Myers Briggs Type Indicator model measures Extraversion-Introversion (E-I), Sensing-Intuition (S-N), Thinking-Feeling (T-F) and judgment-Perception (J-P).

There is a correlation between the two models (Mc Crae & Costa, 1989): E-A and S-N are strongly related to Extraversion and Openness (respectively -0.74 and 0.72) whereas T-F and J-P are more weakly related to Agreeableness and Conscientiousness (respectively 0.44 and -0.49). The emotional stability dimension of the Big 5 is largely absent from the MBTI.

According to Briggs-Myers et al (1985) there is a correlation between the MBTI model and students' learning styles:

- Extraverted students learn by explaining to other students, they enjoy working in groups. Teaching methods such as TAPP (Thinking Aloud Paired Problem) or Nominal Group Method provide optimal educational outcomes for them. For the former method, teachers ask questions, provide quiet time for students, choose the student explaining and the listeners; explanations are then given by the former, questions are asked for clarification and teachers critique some of the answers. Extraverts find solitary activity difficult but they excel in activity involving interaction between people and visible results.

- Introverted students seek to interconnect knowledge relevant to the subject in hand; chunking, grouping and interconnecting is valuable to introverted students. They learn best through quiet mental reflection, prefer reading, lectures and written work over oral work. They prefer independent work and need sufficient time to process information.

- Sensing students prefer linear, structured and organized information. The *What Must be Known* (WMBK) and *Application-Theory-Application* (A-T-A) strategies can be successfully used. Sensing students primarily learn through their senses, and because they are very practical, they like to learn material related to real-life situations.

- Intuitive students tend to prefer discovery learning. They focus on general concepts. They see the big picture and also tend to forget about the details unless they relate to a pattern. They enjoy new material, and find repetition boring once they have understood the pattern. Ideal environments for them allow for creativity and provide them with many different ways to solve problems.

- Thinking students like clear course and topic objectives (precise, action-oriented, etc.). Using the Bloom taxonomy (Ryder, 2005) can be a good way to define course objectives in this case. Those students are usually good at problem solving and enjoy feedback on their objective achievement.

- Feeling students enjoy working in harmonious groups, they feel rewarded when they can help others but they can have difficulty when the material does not relate to people, human values or relations.

- Judging students learn better when color-coding is used and when they are asked to analyze organize and respond. Judging students sometimes reach conclusions too quickly and it is advisable to challenge their knowledge, to encourage them to consider pros and cons of the answer and to consider alternative solutions.

- For perceptive students, it is good to break down the main goal into sub-goals and eventually provide deadlines to keep them on target. They prefer to gather as much data as possible before making a decision. They are stimulated by new material and work best when they understand the reason for an assignment (relevance).

4.1.3 Consequences for Game Design

The Big 5 model, and indirectly the MBTI model, show how the difference in pupils' personalities affects how they learn. It also allows instructors to tailor their teaching style to students needs. The PLEASE model accounts for personalities and learning styles and includes instructional strategies to maximize learning outcomes accordingly. The table below summarizes instructional strategies included in the PLEASE model.

N	Refer to previous knowledge Do not use time as a limiting/constraining factor
E	Use thought provoking content Promote systematic approach Promote social learning and social activities in general Learn by Explaining (See smart machines)
O	Provide different sources of information Promote Curiosity and Exploration Use patterns and open-ended content with different ways to solve a problem.
O-	Use clear and recently written documents recommended by teachers and linear content
A	Use material that relates to people, human values (e.g.: SIMS) Promote harmonious environment
A-	Promote critical thinking Use clear objectives Promote problem solving Provide feedback on achievement (score, time, etc)
C	Provide different sources of information
C-	Question users' answers, ask for alternative solutions

Table 2: Personalities and Instructional Strategies

(N: Neuroticism, E: Extraverted, O: Openness, A: Agreeableness, C: Conscientiousness, -:low level of)

4.2 Emotions to Accelerate Learning

As mentioned previously, learners had a different approach to using Math Quest according to their personalities. Games represent a rich sensory and emotional experience, and it seems that users' emotions affect their ability to learn from a game. Whereas some were held back by negative feelings such as fear or angriness, others had a more positive approach to the educational game and benefited more from it. Also, players seemed to experience a cycle of emotions through which they learnt: frustration (wrong solution), doubt (wondering why their solution was wrong) and joy (when they found the solution).

The following sections explain how emotions are included in the PLEASE model to motivate, reassure and immerse the user.

4.2.1 Emotions Accelerate Learning in a Safe Environment

Positive and negative emotions are necessary for learning. According to the FEASP model (Fear Envy Angriness Sympathy Pleasure - Astleitner, 2000), learning can be improved by decreasing negative feelings such as fear, envy or anger and by increasing positive feelings such as safety and pleasure. It recommends that instructors should assess emotional issues before and during instruction. It also provides a set of instructional strategies to increase positive feelings such as: using Q&A, displaying success statistics, using anger buttons, using synchronous and asynchronous communication tools, collaborative learning tools and play like activities.

On the other hand, regardless of the learner's initial emotional state, a learning experience is often emotionally dynamic because the learner feels various emotions: curiosity, fascination, surprise, anxiety, confusion, bewilderment, frustration, anguish, chagrin, hope, perplexity, elation, satisfaction, and confidence. Experiencing a mix of feelings is necessary to progress, to make sense of our experience and to accelerate the learning process (Kort, 2005).

The idea of experiencing a mix of positive and negative feelings and the ones developed in the FEASP model are, however, not contradictory. The FEASP model focuses on the learning environment (not on the content), providing safety, collaboration opportunities, a reduction of users' frustrations and a feeling of fairness. It allows learners to experience a mix of feelings but in a safe and controlled environment.

4.2.2 Motivation and Learning

The ARCS model (Keller & Kopp, 1987) addresses motivation while learning. Partly inspired by Gagne's model, it promotes Attention, Relevance, Satisfaction and Pleasure. Keller believes that to address learners' motivation, instructors ought to know their needs in terms of: the value of the instructional program to the user, the benefits from the training program and the interest of the user in the topic.

4.2.3 Flow Theory and Intrinsic Motivation

A flow state refers to a state where an individual is highly motivated by an activity she is involved in, regardless of the difficulty or challenge she is facing (Csikzentmihalyi, 1990). Many factors can contribute to a flow state such as: clear goals, appropriate level of difficulty, challenge, curiosity or fantasy. In a flow state, one experiences a sense of serenity, timelessness and increased self-confidence.

4.2.4 Summary

The following table summarizes the key features promoted by the main emotionally sound educational games.

ARCS	FEASP	FLOW	Kort
Attention Relevance Confidence Satisfaction	Decrease Fear, Envy and Anger Increase Sympathy and Pleasure	Clear goals Adjusted difficulty Intrinsic Motivation Timeless Involvement	Curiosity Satisfaction Confusion Disappointment Frustration Determination Hopefulness

Table 3: Emotions and Instructional Design

The PLEASE model uses video games as rich emotional experiences to accelerate learning in a safe and motivating environment.

4.3 Autonomy and Scaffoldings to Maintain User in ZPD

The Zone of Proximal Development (ZDP) is a concept developed by Lev Vygotsky (Riddle & Dabbagh, 1999). It refers to the ability of an educational system to make a learner progressively more independent. The key is to teach learners and keep knowledge within their reach. Ultimately, learners develop meta-cognitive skills and become totally independent in their learning activities. Autonomy is one of the 5 keys of the PLEASE model. The following sections explain how autonomy is promoted in the model by increasing confidence and motivation, by creating cognitive disequilibriums, and by implementing educational scaffoldings.

4.3.1 Learning and Autonomy

4.3.1.1 Increase Confidence and Motivation

To reach full autonomy, pupils need to be confident about using their knowledge and skills. The authors believe that confidence can be increased by positive emotions (feedback, safe environment, etc), a relevant content and in-game evaluation process (using same format as school tests).

To maintain learners motivation, educational software must promote intrinsic motivation and create a flow state. This can be achieved by clear goals, an adjustable difficulty level, challenge, curiosity arousal and fantasy.

4.3.1.2 Cognitive Disequilibrium

Creating Cognitive disequilibrium can be an efficient way to further learners' acquisition. This process can be helped or accelerated by specific emotions such as frustration, *"ahah"* moments, etc.

Kort (2005) refers to this disequilibrium as non-monotonic teaching where learners go through different set of emotions. Schema theory also promotes cognitive disequilibrium. A *"Schema"* corresponds to a learner's internal representation or understanding of her surrounding environment. It is based more on the learner's experience than on "raw intelligence" and allows interpretation, prediction and understanding. The schema is *"updated"* with new knowledge. Learners can take the new input without modifying their schema (accretation), modify their internal (inadequate) schema according to new information (tuning) or create a new schema that addresses the inconsistencies between the old one and the new knowledge. Feltovitch et al. (2001) warn us that users can develop cognitive shield, by constructing strategies to maintain their misconceptions despite of evidence that they are incorrect.

4.3.2 Using a Systematic Approach to Maximize the Environment and Scaffoldings

Creating educational games following well known Instructional System Design techniques such as the ADDIE model provides a systematic approach and helps in effectively analyzing the needs of teachers and pupils, but more importantly in making the most of the school environment (collaboration with peers, teachers, limited time allocated to IT, etc.). According to Gagne et al.(1992), external conditions must be looked after to ensure that they facilitate a successful learning outcome.

For example, the Analysis and Implementation phases of the ADDIE model account for teacher training, students' comments and description of constraints. To introduce games in schools it is essential that teachers have a good understanding of the game itself. It allows them to interact better with pupils and also to lead essential debriefing sessions in which pupils can relate their experience. Teacher training also removes the technological/generation barrier between them and the children. Omitting this phase can have a negative effect on the introduction of games in the classroom.

The ADDIE model represents a sound base for educational software development. It is a widely used model that has the potential to address most of today's educational game pitfalls. It is an iterative instructional design process based on learners' needs and governed by learning outcomes. It accounts for the environmental constraints through needs assessment, problem identification and task analysis, and includes an evaluation process to determine the adequacy of the instruction. However, it does not account for users' emotions and some issues related to game design (aesthetics, game play, etc.).

This section has explained the strategies included in the PLEASE model to promote users' autonomy and ensure positive learning outcomes. It has also emphasized how the instructional approach used in the PLEASE model helps teachers and developers to make the most of the educational environment.

4.3.3 Facilitating Evaluation

The evaluation of education games should be an integral part of the game design and be thought of at an early stage. Defining assessment methods inside and outside the game maximizes the chances of knowledge transfer. Building an educational game with a systematic approach in mind helps to define and assess clear, measurable and achievable objectives. Discussions with teachers also help defining objectives and methods for evaluation. For example, the format of the questions used in Math Quest was the same as the one used in the pre and post-tests. The progression of players within the game was directly linked to their mathematical proficiency.

The PLEASE model accounts for evaluation as an important factor for knowledge transfer in educational games and promotes the use of instructional design and the involvement of teachers at an early stage, to establish clear, achievable and measurable objectives.

5 CONCLUSION

The PLEASE model offers a bridge between Instructional Design and Game Design, allowing educational games to benefit from a solid systematic approach while accounting for users' emotional state and personality. It is essentially based on personality traits and brings a new dimension to game and instructional design by addressing the needs inherent to learners' personalities and learning styles at both cognitive and emotional levels.

The table below summarizes the different concepts included in the PLEASE model.

P	Personality Aware
L	Learning Styles are accounted for
E	Emotions to accelerate learning
A	Autonomy to maintain user in ZDP
S	Systematic Approach to maximize the environment
E	Evaluation built-in to maximize knowledge transfer

Table 4: The PLEASE Model

6 FUTURE IMPLEMENTATIONS

Since the pilot study held in June 2006, three additional Cork secondary schools have showed interest in taking part in a wider study to assess the effect of educational Games on pupils' Mathematical skills. A modified version of the Math Quest game will be offered to them in order to assess the PLEASE model.

REFERENCES

Marc Prensky (2001), Digital Natives - Digital Immigrants, On the Horizon, Internet: http://www.marcprensky.com/writing/Prensky%20Immigrants%20-%20Part1.pdf.

Pratchett (2005), Gamers in the UK, Digital Play, Digital Lifestyles, BBC, Internet: http://crystaltips.typepad.com/wonderland/files/bbc_uk_games_research_2005.pdf.

Entertainment Software Association (2004), Essential Facts about the Computer and Video Game Industry, Internet: http://www.theesa.com/files/EFBrochure.pdf.

Lisa Gallardeau (2005), Spontaneous Communities of Learning: Learning Ecosystems in Massively Multiplayer Online Gaming Environments, Internet: http://www.gamesconference.org/digra2005/papers/bbcbceff7f24a397c76489b7d4c78bad.doc.

Marc Prensky (2004), How Kids Learn to Cooperate in Video Games: A Lesson for Parents and Teachers, Internet: http://www.sensiblesoftware.com/articles/a/How-Kids-Learn-to-Cooperate-in-Video-Games-A-Lesson-for-Parents-and-Teachers.html

Barry Kort (2005), Presentation of the IEEE Education Society, Cognition, Affect, and Learning, available at: http://web.media.mit.edu/~bkort/Short-Talk.html

Chris Crawford (2003), On Game Design, New Rider Games.

Kurt Squire (2002), Cultural Framing of Computer/Video Games, Internet: (http://www.gamestudies.org/0102/squire/).

Jan Cannon-Bowers (2006), Gaming for Food, Internet: http://www.scholastic.com/administrator/feb06/articles.asp?article=Opinion.

Gagne, R., M., Briggs, L., J., Wager, W., W. (1992), Principles of Instructional Design 4th edition.

Schank, R., Neaman, A. (2001), Motivation and Failure in Education Simulation and Design.

Van Eck, R. (2006), Learning Through Gaming, Internet: http://72.14.221.104/search?q=cache:ahBejFvUtAkJ:www.tasscc.org/presentations/annual_2006/Van_Eck.pdf+Richard+Van+Eck+zone+of+proximal+development&hl=en&ct=clnk&cd=1&client=safari.

Mitchell, M., Savill-Smith, C. (2004), The Use of Computers and Video Games for Learning , Internet: http://www.m-learning.org/docs/The%20use%20of%20computer%20and%20video%20games%20for%20learning.pdf.

Heinström, J. (2003), Five Personality Dimensions and their Influence on Information Behavior, Internet: http://informationr.net/ir/9-1/paper165.html

McCrae, R., R., Costa, P., T. (1989), Reinterpreting the Myers-Briggs Type Indicator From the Perspective of the Five-factor Model of Personality.

Briggs-Myers, I., McCaulley, M. (1985), A Guide to the Development and Use of the Myers-Briggs Type Indicator.

Martin Ryder (2005), Instructional Design Models, Internet: http://carbon.cudenver.edu/~mryder/itc_data/idmodels.html#prescriptive.

Astleitner, H. (2000), Designing Emotionally Sound Instruction: The FEASP-Approach, Internet: http://www.springerlink.com/openurl.asp?genre=article&id=doi:10.1023/A:1003893915778.

Keller, J., Kopp, T. (1987), An Application of the ARCS Model of Motivational Design.

Csikszentmihalyi, M. (1990), Flow : The Psychology of Optimal Experience.

Riddle, M., Dabbagh, N. (1999), Lev Vygotsky's Social Development Theory, available at: http://chd.gse.gmu.edu/immersion/knowledgebase/theorists/constructivism/vygotsky.htm.

Feltovitch, P., J., Coulson, R., L., Spiro, R., J. (2001), Learners (Mis) understanding of Important and Difficult Concepts: A Challenge to Smart Machines in Education.

Serious Gordon: Using Serious Games To Teach Food Safety in the Kitchen

B. Mac Namee, P. Rooney, P. Lindstrom, A. Ritchie, F. Boylan & G. Burke

***Abstract*—This paper will describe the development of Serious Gordon, an interactive digital game developed to tech the basics of kitchen food safety to workers in industries dealing with food. The motivations driving the development of the game will be described as will the development process itself. An initial evaluation of the game, from both a technical and pedagogical point of view, will be presented as will conclusions on the viability of using a commercial game engine for the purpose of developing educational games.**

***Index Terms*—Serious games, education, food safety**

I. Introduction

RECENTLY there has been huge growth in interest in serious games, and in particular their use for education [17]. While it is certainly true that using games (and in this paper we refer exclusively to digital games) for education is nothing new, the relatively recent trend in which commercial game developers open up their technology for modification has brought things to a new level. Now developers of serious games can use the sophisticated technology of their mainstream counterparts to create environments which exhibit a level of realism that was previously only possible for those working with budgets that stretched into the millions.

In this paper we will describe the development of *Serious Gordon*, a prototype game developed to teach the rudiments of kitchen food safety to workers in industries dealing with food. The paper will begin with a short introduction to the areas of serious games and game-based learning. This will be followed by a brief synopsis of the key aspects of kitchen food safety that the game sets out to teach. Next, the development of the game will be described. A preliminary evaluation of the usefulness of the game has been carried out and this is described before, finally, some directions for future development both of this and other related projects are laid out.

Manuscript received September 28, 2006.

B. Mac Namee is with the School of Computing, Dublin Institute of Technology, Kevin St., Dublin 8, Ireland. (e-mail: Brian.MacNamee@ comp.dit.ie)

P. Rooney is with the Learning Technology Team, Dublin Institute of Technology, 14 Upper Mount St., Dublin 2, Ireland. (e-mail: Pauline.Rooney@ dit.ie)

P. Lindstrom is with the School of Computing, Dublin Institute of Technology, Kevin St., Dublin 8, Ireland.

A. Ritchie is with the School of Computing, Dublin Institute of Technology, Kevin St., Dublin 8, Ireland. (e-mail: Andrew.Ritchie@student.dit.ie).

F. Boylan is with the Learning Technology Team, Dublin Institute of Technology, 14 Upper Mount St., Dublin 2, Ireland. (e-mail: Frances.Boylan@ dit.ie)

G. Burke is with the School of Food Science and Environmental Heath, Dublin Institute of Technology, Sackville Place, Dublin 1, Ireland. (e-mail: Greg.Burke@dit.ie)

II. Serious Games & Digital Game-Based Learning

The term *serious games* [16] refers to games designed to do more than just entertain. Rather, serious games, while having many features in common with more traditional games, have ulterior motives such as teaching, training, and marketing. Although games have been used for ends apart from entertainment, in particular education, for a long time, the modern serious games movement is set apart from these by the level of sophistication of the games it creates. The current generation of serious games is comparable with main-stream games in terms of the quality of production and sophistication of their design.

The modern serious games movement can be said to have begun with the release of *America's Army* (www.americasarmy.com) in 2002 [18]. Inspired by the realism of commercial games such as the Rainbow 6 series (www.rainbow6.com), the United States military developed America's Army and released it free of charge in order to give potential recruits a flavour of army life. The game was hugely successful and is still being used today as both a recruitment tool and as an internal army training tool.

Spurred on by the success of America's Army the serious games movement began to grow, particularly within academia. A number of conferences sprung up and notably the Serious Games Summit became a part of the influential Game Developer's Conference (www.gdconf.com) in 2004.

Some other notable offerings in the serious games field include *Food Force* (www.food-force.com) [4], a game developed by the United Nations World Food Programme in order to promote awareness of the issues surrounding emergency food aid; *Hazmat Hotzone* [3], a game developed by the Entertainment Technology Center at Carnegie Mellon University to train fire-fighters to deal with chemical and hazardous materials emergencies and *Yourself!Fitness* (www.yourselffitness.com) [16] an interactive virtual personal trainer developed for modern games consoles.

However, education still holds the greatest potential for serious games, with proponents of their use arguing that they hold enormous potential as learning tools [21, 23]. One argument for the use of games in education is that the multi-sensory environment offered by virtual gaming worlds caters for multiple learning styles (e.g. visual, auditory and kinaesthetic) [10].

Another argument is that in training settings where learners need to acquire a skill or competence, games provide extensive opportunities for drill and practice (where learners master skills or information through repetitive practice) thereby reinforcing information retention [17]. In particular, the micro-worlds of games allow educators to create learning activities that may be too dangerous or costly to replicate in the classroom [11]. For example, in a gaming environment, students can "blow" circuits, mix lethal chemicals or make mistakes in a surgical procedure without killing a real-life patient. Thus, gaming affords new opportunities for learning which are not available in traditional media.

In addition to facilitating the acquisition and retention of information, it is argued that games also hold considerable potential for developing higher order skills such as critical thinking, strategic thinking, problem solving, team work etc [23]. Simulation and adventure games, where students are immersed in a virtual world and assume a specific role within this world, allow this by creating a constructivist learning environment (where students construct their own knowledge and create their own meanings in a social process) [21]. For example, at the Carnegie Mellon University in Pittsburgh, a video game called *Peacemaker* (www.peacemakergame.com) allows players to assume the role of the Israeli prime minister or the Palestinian president. Within their role, the player makes various political decisions, their ultimate aim being to achieve a ceasefire [22]. In another UK study, researchers found that games such as SimCity (www.simcity.com) and RollerCoaster Tycoon (www.rollercoastertycoon.com), where players create societies or build theme parks, developed players' strategic thinking and planning skills [2].

Thus, such complex games hold considerable potential as a learning tool. On one level games can be seen as embodying behaviourist learning principles – where learners acquire and practice a range of skills and competencies while receiving regular feedback in an engaging, highly interactive and safe environment. On another level, more complex games allow learners to develop higher order skills in a constructivist learning environment by embodying various pedagogical strategies including experiential learning [12], problem-based learning [20] and situated learning [13]. In addition, many games are highly social, the clearest example being massively multiplayer online games (MMOGs). In such games, thousands of players are playing online simultaneously at any given time, interacting in virtual worlds with their own economies, cultures and political systems. Such games allow players to experiment with new identities, develop social skills and experience effective (and often ineffective) social practices in a range of political, social and cultural environments. In essence they allow players to experience and become part of a community of practice, which according to Lave and Wenger [13] is crucial for effective learning.

However, the results of using games as teaching tool are not all positive. Much of the so called *edutainment* software produced results in nothing more than boring games incorporating what is termed *drill-and-kill* learning. Arguments have been put forward that this is due to the fact that these educational games are designed by academics who do not have a true understanding of the science and art of game design. So, while the products might be educationally sound as learning tools, they do not fulfill 'gaming' criteria [19, 23]. It also stands to reason then that games for the education market that are designed solely by gamers are also destined to fail in achieving their overall objective. The answer, as summed up in [23], "*...is not to privilege one arena over the other but to find the synergy between pedagogy and engagement in digital game based learning*".

Research has shown that for a serious game to be successful, the overall structure of the game, and the instructions provided to play it, should be kept simple so as to minimise the time spent learning the rules of the game [17]. Such an approach also ensures a clear route through the game with constant access to information that aids navigation. The nature of the challenge, the levels of the challenges and the methods of scoring need to be varied, but effective games must provide feedback so as to encourage a focus on the process in hand as well as the performance achieved. A constant cycle of hypothesis formulation, testing and revision needs to be built in [23], as it gives the user a chance to correct and learn from errors made. And, most importantly, the structure of the game must suit the learning objectives and outcomes set out during the planning stage.

These were the considerations that drove the development of Serious Gordon. The following section will briefly touch upon the aspects of kitchen food safety which the game sets out to teach.

III. Food Safety in the Kitchen

EC Regulation 852/2004 [5] (transposed into Irish law under the Food Hygiene Regulations 1998 [8] and SI 369 2006 [9]) reinforces the requirement "*that food handlers are supervised and instructed and or trained in food hygiene matters commensurate with their work activity*". Therefore, food safety is an essential component of the training undertaken by anyone embarking on a career in the food industry.

The Food Safety Authority of Ireland has devised training guides [6, 7] which cover the principles of food safety at three levels:

- Guide to Food Safety Training: Induction Skills (food service, retailers and manufacturing sectors) [6]
- Guide to Food Safety Training: Additional Skills (food service, retailers and manufacturing sectors) [6]
- Food Safety Skills for Management (food service, retailers and manufacturing sectors) [7]

The first of these guides - Guide to Food Safety Training:

Induction Skills [6] – was used as the content basis for Serious Gordon. The guide lists a set nine competencies which workers must demonstrate in order to safely handle food. These are as follows:

1. Wear and maintain uniform/protective clothing hygienically.
2. Maintain a high standard of hand-washing.
3. Maintain a high standard of personal hygiene.
4. Demonstrate correct hygiene practice if suffering from ailments/illnesses that may affect the safety of food.
5. Avoid unhygienic practices in a food operation.
6. Demonstrate safe food handling practices.
7. Maintain staff facilities in a hygienic condition.
8. Obey food safety signs
9. Keep work areas clean.

Serious Gordon sets out to teach the importance of these skills. The following section will describe the development of the game, the starting point of which was this list of competencies.

IV. Development of Serious Gordon

This section will describe the development of Serious Gordon, which was undertaken by a multi-disciplinary team at the Dublin Institute of Technology (DIT) in Dublin, Ireland over the Summer of 2006. The discussion will begin by outlining the learning objectives which were the genesis of the project, followed by the development of the script and game scenario and finishing with a short description of the development of the game itself.

A. *Learning Objectives for Serious Gordon*

The overall aim of the Serious Gordon project was to teach the basics of kitchen food safety required of both food and non-food handlers in the food service, retail and manufacturing sectors, as set out in [6]. This document centres around the nine *induction skills* given in the previous section. In order to demonstrate that they understand how to handle food properly an employee must be able to display each of these skills.

The guide provides further details of each skill by outlining how the employer should demonstrate each one to their employees, as well as listing the resources or supports that employees may need to help them demonstrate good food practices. These nine skills steered the design of Serious Gordon, inspiring all of the tasks the player must undertake during the game. Essentially, demonstration of these nine skills are the learning objectives expected of a player after playing the game to completion.

B. *Script and Level Design*

So that this game achieved each of its learning outcomes in a concise and effective manner, it was vital that a structure for the game, in the form of a very detailed storyboard, was set out quite early in the project and agreed between both the game designers and developers. Furthermore, it was extremely important that the factors in the design of serious games, as outlined in section 2, were kept in mind at all times. Briefly, these are that the controls and rules of the game are kept simple, that a clear route through the game is presented to the player at all times and that useful feedback is presented to the player after all challenges have been completed (either passed or failed).

During an initial meeting between all of the parties involved in the design of the game (including persons with expertise in the areas of education, game design and food safety) the different possible scenarios for the game were considered. After much discussion a broad outline of the game was agreed upon. It was decided that the game would be a realistic simulation of a restaurant environment in which the player, playing from a first-person perspective, would take the role of a kitchen porter arriving for their first day at work. Over the course of the game the player would be given a number of different tasks to complete, each of which would relate back to the aforementioned list of nine induction skills. Some of the tasks discussed in the initial design stages included choosing the correct uniform for a particular job from a selection of different options, correctly moving deliveries from a truck outside the restaurant to the kitchen's various store rooms and dealing with workplace disasters such as injury and sickness.

As a means to provide a clear route through the game and provide useful feedback to the player at all times, a chef character was introduced whose part would be to welcome the player to work, give guidance on what tasks the player had to carry out and offer feedback on the player's success or failure in these tasks. Throughout the game the chef character would also drop nuggets of information relating to the nine induction skills into their conversations with the player.

To begin with, a specification was written for each of the characters in the game outlining their name, their personality and their general appearance, given their role in the kitchen environment. The characters included the player, the chef and two commis-chefs who also worked in the restaurant. The game's storyboard was then built around these characters outlining, in great depth, the learning outcomes to be achieved in each individual scene of the game, the tasks that the player needed to undertake in each scene so as to achieve the specific learning outcomes in question, a detailed description of the exact environment in which each scene would take place and finally the characters involved in each scene and the appropriate interactions and dialogue that needed to occur between them. During the group's weekly meetings, the storyboard was constantly referred to and often updated as the first draft of each scene of the game was reviewed and edited so as to ensure that the learning outcomes were achieved as effectively as possible.

As each scene was finalised, so was the associated dialogue. The dialogue for serious games is always functional with its sole purpose being to pass on vital information in a concise and natural manner, and is used primarily as either a bridge from one part of the game to the next or to explain to the player what the next part of the game involves.

Serious Gordon is set predominantly in the kitchen of a small restaurant. In order to make the game environment as true to life as possible the design of this fictional kitchen was based on a set of real kitchen plans, which are shown in figure 1.

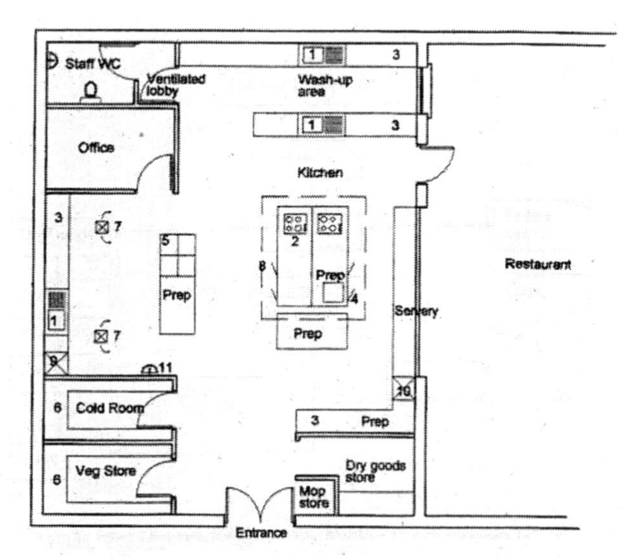

Figure 1: The floor-plan on which the kitchen in Serious Gordon was based

However, with the notion of *virtual fidelity* in mind [1], the design of the game environment did not rigidly stick to the real world version of the kitchen. Virtual fidelity suggests that simulations need only remain true to the real world in so much as this enhances the experience of the users of a the simulation. A good example of this is that virtual environments need to be designed with a much larger amount of empty space than real world locations so as to avoid users feeling claustrophobic [15].

Similarly, in designing the game environment great lengths were gone to in order to make the game environment appear to stretch beyond the boundaries of the restaurant, and yet at the same time coral the player within this smaller space without their noticing. It has been shown that this approach to game design aids immersion in that the player believes themselves to be part of a larger world [15].

C. Implementing Serious Gordon

The full-time development team on Serious Gordon consisted of two developers who worked on the game over a period of approximately 10 weeks in the summer of 2006. This small team was augmented by experts in the areas of food safety, education and games. Shortly after agreeing upon the initial storyboard for the game it was decided that the best approach would be to set it in a realistic 3D environment played from a first-person perspective. It was felt by the team the sense of immersion for players achieved by this sort of game would best aid the learning process [21].

Due to the scale of the project, and the time limits involved, it was established early on that the development of a complete game engine would not be feasible. Rather, the best option was to use an existing game engine to create the game. After investigating a number of options Valve Software's Source Engine (www.valvesoftware.com), developed to create Valve's Half Life 2 (www.halflife2.com) was selected for the project. The Source engine has a number of compelling features which include highly realistic physics modeling, the capacity for sophisticated scripting and the existence of an active and helpful community of professional and amateur developers. The challenge in using the Source Engine was that it was designed for developing a game so different to Serious Gordon and it was unclear whether it could be successfully turned to this new purpose. A screenshot of Half-Life 2 is shown in figure 2 to illustrate this point!

Figure 2: A screenshot of Half-Life 2 for which the Source Engine was developed

With the engine agreed upon the team's developers set about creating a series of proof-of-concept scenarios in order to experiment with the requirements of each learning task set out in the storyboard. This was an extremely useful stage in the development as it highlighted aspects of the Source Engine which would need work in order to turn it to the task of developing an educational game. As each proof-of-concept scenario was developed the entire team was brought together to determine how well this scenario matched the learning outcomes it set out to achieve. In this way the cycle of repeated hypothesis formulation, testing and revision outlined in [23] was adhered to.

After the proof of concept development phase was complete, focus switched to developing the complete game. Serious Gordon is essentially script driven, with the chef character leading the player through a series of learning tasks and responding to the player's efforts to complete these tasks. Again, throughout the development of the full game the *hypothesize-test-revise* cycle was used in order to ensure that while achieving the learning outcomes set out, the game remained playable and, as much as was possible, enjoyable.

The choice of Valve's Source Engine put a range of invaluable tools in the hands of Serious Gordon's development team. The most important of these was the Hammer Editor which is the tool used to develop the game's environment and to add all of the scripting to this environment. Hammer allows developer's relatively easily create sophisticated virtual worlds, fill these with authentic objects and populate them with characters that react to the actions of a player. A screenshot of the interface to the Hammer editor is shown in figure 3.

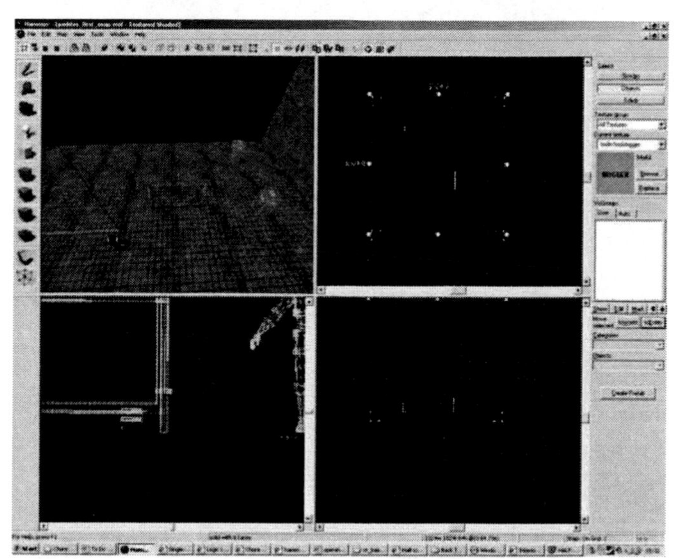

Figure 3: A screenshot of the Hammer editor used to create the world of Serious Gordon and script the behaviours of its characters

While the Hammer editor proved an extremely useful tool, it was not without its problems. The first of these was that the assets pre-packaged with the editor are those used in Half-Life 2 and so were much too grimy and industrial for use in the modern restaurant environment required in Serious Gordon. This meant a range of custom textures and objects had to be developed which put a considerable burden on the small development team. Secondly, the level of scripting required by Serious Gordon, and the free-flow nature of some of its scenarios pushed the scripting capabilities of the Hammer editor to their limits which caused some further development difficulties.

The second tool used heavily in the development of Serious Gordon was Valve's FacePoser, a tool used to choreograph game sequences that controls facial expressions, lip synching and body gestures. A screenshot of Faceposer being used is shown in figure 4. Although Faceposer proved a somewhat unreliable tool to work with, the results possible with it lend a great deal of realism to a game's characters.

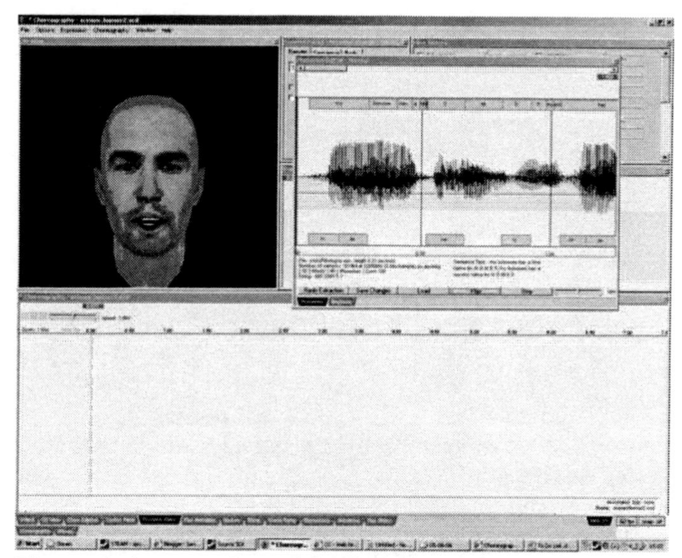

Figure 4: A screenshot of the Faceposer tool

As well as using the Source Engine development tools in developing Serious Gordon, a number of major additions were also made to the functionality of the engine itself, which involved making changes to the engine's code-base. The first of these was the addition of an inventory system. The Source Engine does not have the capacity for players to pick up objects and give them to other characters in the manner that was required by the Serious Gordon story board, so this had to be built into the engine. The functionality developed was used in scenarios where the player had to retrieve specific objects for the chef and also by a clothing system introduced through which the player could choose to wear clothes appropriate to their current tasks.

The second major addition to the Source Engine was a change to the interface system in order to allow players perform puzzle based interactions. A good example of this is a game sequence in which the player have to wash their hands correctly before entering the kitchen. In this scenario, after choosing to interact with a sink object, players are shown a dialogue box indicating that the available actions (shown on buttons) are to wet their hands, use the soap and dry their hands. Only by indicating the correct sequence of tasks (wet hands – use soap – wet hands – dry hands) can the player successfully complete the task. A screenshot of this simple scenario is shown in figure 5.

This addition to the Source Engine was developed in such a way that the available set of options and the consequences of certain sequences of choices by a player could all be defined in a simple data file making the technique easily extensible. The addition of simple puzzles made some learning scenarios extremely easy to implement in a way that players, particularly those unfamiliar with games, could easily understand.

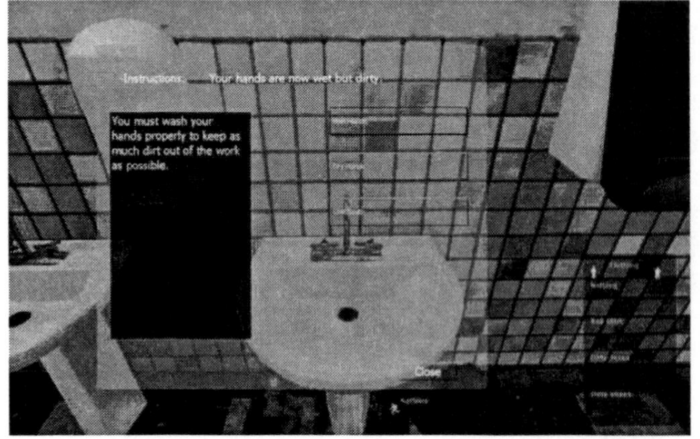

Figure 5: The customisable puzzle capacity added to the Source Engine

In spite of the difficulties in turning the Source Engine to a purpose leagues apart from that for which it was designed, the development of Serious Gordon is considered by the team to be an overall success. A series of screenshots of the game are shown in figures 6 (a) – (c). All of the learning scenarios set out in the original storyboard have been implemented, for the most part as originally intended. Taken together they constitute an engaging learning experience which holds the learner's attention long enough to teach the basics of food safety in the kitchen in a novel fashion. The following section will discuss some basic evaluation experiments undertaken in order to quantify how successful the game is as a learning tool.

(a)

(b)

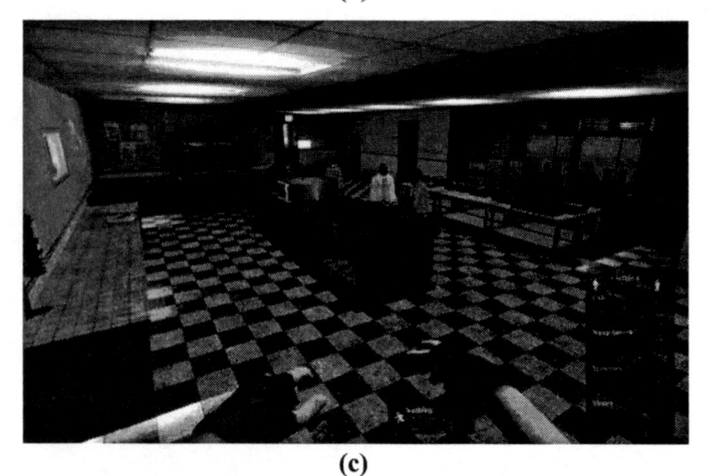

(c)

Figure 6: (a) Serious Gordon's chef. (b) The wash room environment. (c) The kitchen environment

V. EVALUATION

Initial evaluations of Serious Gordon have been carried out which aimed to evaluate the game from a technical and pedagogical perspective. To this end, a small focus group of ten participants was selected, each with varying levels of experience using serious games. Before playing the game, participants were asked to complete a questionnaire which aimed to determine (a) their previous experience of using games/serious games and (b) their prior knowledge of food safety and the nine induction skills listed in [6].

After an initial brief orientation session, participants were then asked to play the game from start to finish. On completion of the game, participants were asked to complete a final questionnaire/test which aimed to evaluate (a) the participant's experience of using the game – e.g. did they find it difficult to navigate or confusing? – and (b) how many of the learning outcomes had been achieved by the participant as a result of playing the game.

These initial evaluations of the game proved highly positive. Technically, users found the game easy to navigate and control – orientation information provided alongside the game proved very helpful in this regard.

Pedagogically, the game proved successful in its aim of teaching learners induction skills required as part of food safety training [6]. Participants' responses showed that they had acquired much of the knowledge and skills as listed in the learning outcomes for the game. In addition, participants found the game a much more stimulating and motivating environment in which to learn skills which were normally taught through the use of text books. This correlates with the experiences of other educators using serious games as part of the education process [14].

Plans for further, more comprehensive, evaluations are still in progress. It is intended that the game will be used initially by first year students in culinary arts programmes at DIT, with the game being offered in the future to other students, including part-time students working as full-time employees in the food and hospitality industry. It is hoped that through these evaluations, significant feedback will be obtained which will allow the development team to further develop and refine the learning environment of Serious Gordon.

VI. Conclusions & Future work

This paper has described the development of Serious Gordon, an educational game created to teach kitchen food safety to workers in industries dealing with food. The game was built upon Valve Software's Source Engine and showed that, in spite of some difficulties, the engine could be successfully turned to the purpose of creating serious games.

The game was developed in a manner to conform with the best practices outlined in the literature dealing with serious games, and in particular educational games. The major challenge in this regard was to achieve a successful balance between the competing goals to teach and to entertain. An initial evaluation has shown that this goal has been largely achieved.

There are two major strands planned through which to build on the work described here. The first of these is to perform a much more extensive series of evaluation experiments, and in this way fine tune the Serious Gordon experience. The second is to develop further projects which tackle the other levels of food safety as set out by the Food Safety Authority of Ireland [6].

Acknowledgment

Acknowledgement to John Tully MA (Creative Writing), Library Assistant, DIT.

References

[1] N.I. Badler, R. Bindiganavale, J. Bourne, J. Allbeck, J. Shi & M. Palmer, "Real Time Virtual Humans", In Proceedings of the International Conference on Digital Media Futures. (1999)

[2] British Broadcasting Corporation, "Video Games Stimulate Learning, BBC NEWS. (2002) [news.bbc.co.uk/1/hi/education/1879019.stm]

[3] S. Carless, "Postcard From SGS 2005: Hazmat: Hotzone - First-Person First Responder Gaming", Gamasutra. (2005) [www.gamasutra.com/features/20051102/carless_01b.shtml]

[4] R. DeMaria, "Postcard from the Serious Games Summit: How the United Nations Fights Hunger with Food Force", Gamasutra. (2005) [www.gamasutra.com/features/20051104/demaria_01.shtml]

[5] European Parliament, "Regulation (EC) No 852/2004 of the European Parliament and of the Council of 29 April 2004 on the Hygiene of Foodstuffs", European Parliament. (2004)

[6] Food Safety Authority of Ireland, "Guide to Food Safety Training: Level 1 - Induction Skills and Level 2 - Additional Skills for Food and Non-Food Handlers (Food Service, Retail and Manufacturing Sectors)", Food Safety Authority of Ireland. (2006) [www.fsai.ie/publications/training/guide_to_food_safety_training_L1andL2.pdf]

[7] Food Safety Authority of Ireland, "Guide to Food Safety Training: Level 3 - Food Safety Skills for Management (Food Service, Retail and Manufacturing Sectors)", Food Safety Authority of Ireland. (2006) [www.fsai.ie/publications/training/guide_to_food_safety_training_L3.pdf]

[8] Government of Ireland, "Food Safety Authority of Ireland Act, 1998", Government of Ireland. (1998) [http://www.fsai.ie/legislation/related/FSAI_act_1998.pdf]

[9] Government of Ireland, "Statutory Instrument S.I. No. 369 of 2006: European Communities (Hygiene of Foodstuffs) Regulations 2006", Stationary Office Dublin. (2006) [www.fsai.ie/legislation/food/eu_docs/Food_hygiene/SI369_2006%20.pdf]

[10] D.C. Jones "Scavenger Hunt Enhances Students' Utilization of Blackboard", MERLOT Journal of Online Learning and Teaching 2 (2) p86-99. (2006) [jolt.merlot.org/Vol2_No2_Jones.htm]

[11] J. Kirriemuir, "The Relevance of Video Games and Gaming Consoles to the Higher and Further Educational Learning Experience", Joint Information Systems Committee. (2003) [www.jisc.ac.uk/uploaded_documents/tsw_02-01.rtf]

[12] D.A. Kolb, "Experiential Learning: Experience as the Source of Learning and Development", London: Prentice-Hall. (1984)

[13] J. Lave & E. Wenger, "Situated Learning: Legitimate Peripheral Participation", Cambridge: Cambridge University Press. (1991)

[14] W. Lewis Johnson, H. Vilhjalmsson & S. Marsella, "Serious Games for Language Learning: How Much Game, How Much AI?" in The 12th International Conference on Artificial Intelligence in Education2005, Amsterdam (2005)

[15] A. Määtä, "Realistic Level Design for Max Payne", In Proceedings of the 2002 Game Developers Conference (GDC 2002). (2002)

[16] D. Michael & S. Chen, "Serious Games: Games That Educate, Train, and Inform", Course Technology PTR. (2005)

[17] A. Mitchell & C. Savill-Smith, "The Use of Computer and Video Games for Learning: A Review of the Literature", Learning and Skills Development Agency. (2001) [www.lsda.org.uk/files/PDF/1529.pdf]

[18] D.B. Nieborg, "America's Army: More Than a Game", Transforming Knowledge into Action Through Gaming and Simulation, SASAGA. (2004) [www.gamespace.nl/content/ISAGA_Nieborg.PDF]

[19] D. Oblinger, "Simulations, Games and Learning", EDUCAUSE Learning Initiative. (2006) [www.educause.edu/ir/library/pdf/ELI3004.pdf]

[20] M. Savin-Baden & C. Howell Major, "Foundations of Problem-Based Learning", Berkshire: Open University Press. (2004)

[21] D.W. Shaffer, K.D. Squire, R. Halverson & J.P. Gee, "Video Games and the Future of Learning", Phi Delta Kappan 87 (2) p104-111. (2005) [coweb.wcer.wisc.edu/cv/papers/videogamesfuturelearning_pdk_2005.pdf]

[22] C. Thompson, "Saving the World, One Video Game at a Time", The New York Times July 23 2006. (2006)

[23] R. Van Eck, "Digital Game-Based Learning: It's Not Just the Digital Natives Who Are Restless", EDUCAUSE Review 41 (2) p16–30. (2006) [www.educause.edu/apps/er/erm06/erm0620.asp]

Dr. Brian Mac Namee is a lecturer in computer science at the School of Computing in the Dublin Institute of Technology in Dublin, Ireland. Brian received a PhD from Trinity College, Dublin in 2004 and worked in industry as a research and development engineer before joining DIT. Brian has a significant research interest in digital games.

Pauline Rooney currently works as an eLearning Development Officer with the Learning Technology Team at the Dublin Institute of Technology. She is currently in the latter stages of a Doctorate of Education (EdD) specialising in serious games and learning.

Patrick Lindstrom graduated with a first class honours in computer science from the Dublin Institute of Technology in 2006 and is currently perusing a career in software architecture at Datalex Ltd., Ireland.

Andrew Ritchie is a 3rd year student in computer science at the Dublin Institute of Technology, Ireland and has a passion for games.

Frances Boylan works as an eLearning Development Officer with the Learning Technology Team, Dublin Institute of Technology. After working as a primary school teacher for a number of years she returned to Trinity College Dublin to undertake the Masters in Education programme, specialising in Educational Management. She followed this with a Masters in Science (IT in Education), researching online learning and the implications of Learning Style Theory on the design and development of online distance education courses. She is currently pursuing her Doctorate (EdD) with the University of Sheffield.

Greg Burke is a lecturer at the Dublin Institute of Technology School of food science and environmental health.

Serious Games & Social & humanities aspects of games (2)

SimPort: a multiplayer management game framework

Jeroen Warmerdam[1,2], Maxim Knepflé[1,2], Rafael Bidarra[1], Geertje Bekebrede[3], Igor Mayer[3]

[1] Faculty of Electrical Engineering, Mathematics and Computer Science
Delft University of Technology
P.O. Box 5031
2600 GA Delft, The Netherlands

r.bidarra@ewi.tudelft.nl

[2] Tygron – Serious Gaming & Media
Brasserskade 50
2612 CE Delft, The Netherlands

j.warmerdam@tygron.nl
m.g.knepfle@tygron.nl

[3] Faculty of Technology, Policy and Management
Delft University of Technology
P.O. Box 5015
2600 GA Delft, the Netherlands

g.bekebrede@tbm.tudelft.nl
i.s.mayer@tbm.tudelft.nl

Keywords

Serious games, Management games, Multiplayer games, Game framework, Port Planning

Abstract

The serious games industry needs game engines, or frameworks, that have been developed specifically with this sector in mind. This paper discusses the criteria that such engines need to adhere to in order to support viable solutions. These criteria are illustrated on the basis of SimPort, a novel multiplayer management game framework. SimPort has shown to be very powerful, functional and easy to use in the development of MV2, a game module simulating a major expansion project, the Maasvlakte 2 area, of the Port of Rotterdam in the Netherlands [8]. In addition, from MV2 real-life usage so far, players and tutors have concluded that this game is not only rather educational, but also a lot of fun to play.

1 Introduction

Playing computer games is becoming an increasingly popular activity in day-to-day life. This has led to consider the use of games for purposes other than simple entertainment, like education, management, decision and policy-support.

As serious games become a normal activity, different genres will appear and become accepted as such. This paper focuses on the Management Game genre (Section 2), briefly describing the current state-of-the-art. The core of the paper discusses the necessity for specific game engines that simplify and speed up the production of Management Games, and presents SimPort as an example of how this has been realised [10] (Section 3). Subsequently, some choices that were made during the production of SimPort are presented (Section 4)

Next, a description of how the engine evolved into its current state is presented, (Section 5), together with a practical evaluation of how real-life players experienced a game created with this engine. Finally, we draw some conclusions (Section 6).

2 Management Games

It is important to define what exactly the relevance of playing management games [9] is. For many decades, computers have assisted management somehow, but the role of computer games is essentially different. First this difference will be addressed, followed by an explanation of the aforementioned importance.

2.1 Decision visualisation

A well-known application of a computer system during the production and design of a complex system is the Decision Support application. Turban described a Decision Support System (DSS) as follows: *"an interactive, flexible, and adaptable computer-based information system, especially developed for supporting the solution of a non-structured management problem for improved decision making. It utilizes data, provides an easy-to-use interface, and allows for the decision maker's own insights."* [7].

When creating a management game, it is important to avoid that the players get the feeling that they are dealing with a DSS; instead, it should always be apparent that they are playing a game. If this is not handled properly, not only are the benefits that a game has over a DSS lost, the benefits that a DSS has also remain unachieved. To avoid this, a designer should opt for a computer game that does not necessarily support the player in making decisions. Instead, he should create a game that visualises the results of players' choices as they are made. By visualising the results, players see the effects of their choices and become more immersed in the game.

2.2 The rise of management games

The benefits of playing serious games with management teams have often been highlighted. Elsewhere, we have argued that designers and managers need to have a better understanding of complex system behaviour. To this end, they can benefit from experiencing the long-term behaviour and unanticipated and sometimes undesirable consequences of their complex system design before it has been implemented. The ability to manage complexity begins with an awareness of and insights in the nature of complex systems. Direct experience of what can happen or what can go wrong is often very effective for raising awareness and insights. Nevertheless, in most cases, such direct experience is difficult to obtain from real infrastructures or other real-world systems without possibly serious consequences. Therefore, games are a good substitute because they can generate learning experiences in a relatively fast and safe manner. [4]

It is important to realise that there is an increasing trend to use Management Games in a large variety of settings. Therefore, it is crucial that the development and production of such games be facilitated and assisted by adequate tools and techniques.

3 Architecture

This section deals with the benefits of an engine for serious games. For this, the SimPort Framework is used as an example.

3.1 Benefits of a serious games engine

The production time of a serious game is often shorter than that of the average entertainment game, because the subject of the game, the client and the message that it conveys are, themselves, limited by time constraints. This is one of the major factors that hold the visual quality of the serious games back from their entertainment counterparts. As a result, developers of serious games will need to use an existing game engine, or framework, if they want to keep to this short production time, while still delivering a fairly decent looking game.

The entertainment industry has provided developers with several game engines to produce their games, most of which come at a very steep price. These engines allow developers to focus their production on factors that make their game unique, and handle basic aspects like walking and collision detection for them. Much of this functionality will not be used in a serious game and, instead, a lot of time will still be spent on developing serious game-specific elements.

A game engine that has been targeted at serious game developers will do the same as the entertainment equivalent, except that (i) it also delivers those elements that are not present in entertainment games and (ii) it leaves those elements out that are not necessary. The former allows for more interesting development as developers can get to the actual game creation, while the latter makes for a cleaner and lighter package.

3.2 The Framework

The Framework needs to provide a number of features for it to be useful. For example, to allow for multiplayer sessions, all network communication needs to be handled by the Framework. Also, it needs to be expandable, to allow for development of game specific elements. The SimPort Framework fulfils both of these criteria. In this subsection both the server side and the client side of the Framework are described.

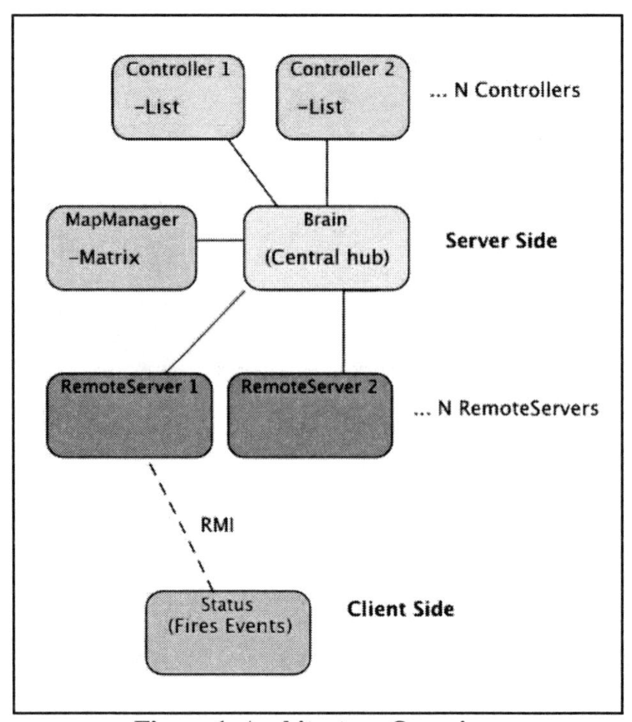

Figure 1. Architecture Overview

3.2.1 The Server

The SimPort Framework has been set up from the beginning as a multiplayer game framework, and combines a number of general-purpose parts. Functions like saving a game session to Extensible Markup Language [2] (XML) data and the handling of concurrency problems are typically done the same way for every possible game implementation. This provides the designer the freedom to concentrate on the more game-specific elements of the game. A central controller object, called the Brain, allows the game developer to attach game specific Controller object. The game designer can extend a Controller object at will, to his own liking in order to make it suitable for his specific needs. Each Controller contains a list that can be filled with game specific objects extending the Item objects. By means of annotation [3], it can be defined which variable in the Item extending object should also be saved to XML data. An example of such a controller is the CustomerControl. It can have methods like "contact this customer" and keep a list of all the customers. There is also a MapManager if the game contains a map of its world. When the Framework is started these controllers will be initialized and the data in the list is filled from a saved XML file. The Framework also synchronizes the data in these lists with the client computers.

Besides the controllers, a server object must be extended. This object is a Remote Method Invocation [1] (RMI) object and is used by the clients to give their commands. Each method can connect to a controller in this way to execute commands in a manner that is concurrently safe.

3.2.2 The Client

The Framework can have multiple clients connected to it that do not necessarily have to have the same functionality. One client can be projecting a view of the game world to a wall, without other interactions, while another client can be used as the game interface for the players. Each of these clients has a Status object containing synchronised data from the server. One of these data instances is an abstract map. The developer has the option of implementing a game specific extension of this map. The extension defines the way the map is displayed. The Framework takes care of the actual rendering and updating. Any other client-side objects can subscribe to the Status object to receive game-wide updates.

The core of the client-side Framework is fairly rigid, as it has a wide range of built-in basic game interaction. Around this core the majority of the features are customizable. A central manager arranges the order in which the game progresses through different states. The developer can add states to this controller and control the different phases that the game moves through. This allows e.g. for customisation of introduction movies, evaluation screens and menu structures.

4 Implementation choices

The production of a game framework touches on many different subjects, because many different problems need to be solved. It is important to stay flexible, so as not to limit the range of applicability. On the other hand, it is important to moderate this flexibility so that developers have the tools they need to focus on the core of their games.

This section details two of the major choices that were made in the design and implementation of the SimPort game framework. Though these subjects are not the only choices that were made, they are two of the more interesting ones: (i) the Level Of Detail strategy chosen, and (ii) the manner in which data is kept synchronized between the clients and the server, by means of versioning.

4.1 Level of Detail strategy

One of the features that makes the client side of the SimPort Framework so interesting is the possibility to navigate through a three dimensional representation of the game world. This added functionality brings with it a certain level of complexity as the world is rendered. The framework tries to limit the load of this rendering as much as possible by a so-called Level Of Detail (LOD) strategy. Objects that are further away from the viewer need less detail for them to stay visually pleasing. The goal of a good LOD strategy is to be intelligent about what LOD is chosen for each object.

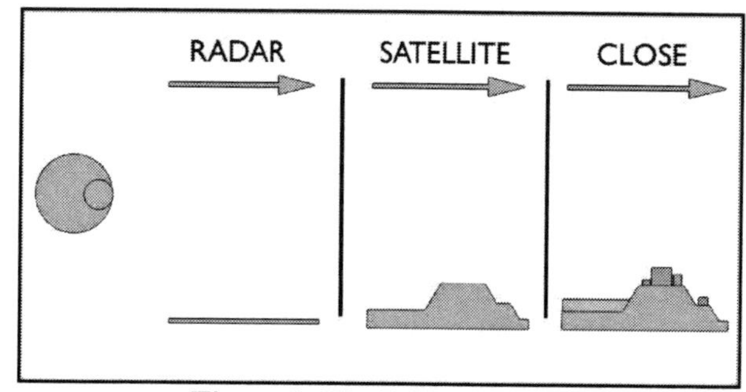

Figure 2. The LOD strategy

The current solution entails two views of the map. The first is an overview, as though the player was looking at a planning map. Company buildings and terrains area visible as outlined areas, with no structures visible. As the player comes closer, the view changes to something resembling a satellite view. The texture of the terrains becomes visible, as does the water, but still no buildings are visible.

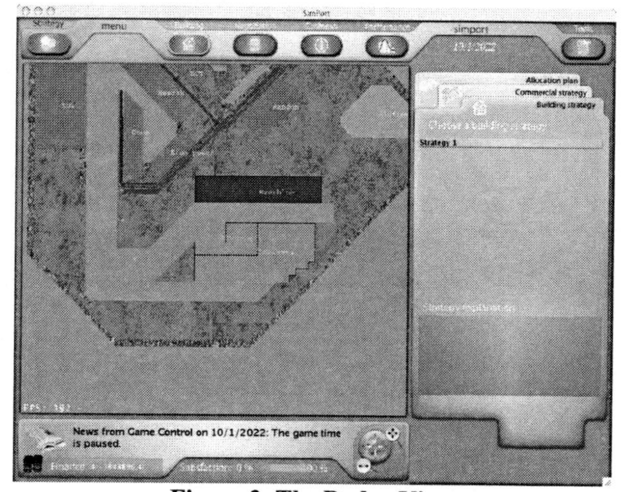

Figure 3. The Radar View

The radar view is nothing more than a textured square, greatly reducing the necessary calculations. The satellite view adapts according to the more traditional LOD strategies, as the map is broken up into smaller scene elements, which are only rendered when they are on the screen. This strategy works well, because when the view switches, not the entire map but only a part of it is visible.

The buildings in the world are handled by a very basic LOD strategy. When the viewer is far away from the building, the building is not shown at all. Only when the view comes close enough do the buildings become visible. As the framework goes through further iterations the same strategy that is used for the map can be used on the buildings, allowing for a more gradual transition from invisible to fully visible.

4.2 Versioning

The need for keeping versions of objects in the game is apparent. These objects are located in lists in the Controllers and map matrix. All objects have in common that they extend the Item object. An Item keeps track of its version number and the object's ID, which is also its position in the list. Each Controller also keeps an overall list version number.

To update to the latest version a client computer sends a version request to the server. To keep traffic to a minimum the client sends only one array containing integer numbers. The first integer represents the client's overall version status. This number is calculated by summing up all version numbers of each list and the map matrix. At the server side this overall number is compared to an overall server number. If these are not the same an update must have occurred, because if an object's number is updated the version number of the list is increased as well. When the to be updated list is found, the system cycles through it and takes out the objects with a version number higher than the client's version number. Finally the updated objects are sent back in small lists to the client. In most cases this results in comparing two numbers and sending a predefined array of integers. In case of an update only the updated object are sent. This can be different for each client computer. It is also possible for a client's Status object to make a subscription to only receive list updates or map updates. This is particularly useful, for example, in a controller application where no map is needed.

When the client's Status object is up to date, it is time to let the game know. Firing custom events to different parts of the game, containing the total list, does this. The map has a special event containing only the updated blocks.

5 SimPort Evaluation

In the previous sections we explained the importance of a serious game engine and introduced the SimPort Framework. This section will briefly describe how this engine came into existence and what its role can be in the serious game sector.

The creation of SimPort was triggered by the production of the game SIM Maasvlakte 2 (SimMV2), which, in turn, inspired the production of SimPort and its SimPort MV2 module.

5.1 The Past – SimMV2

In late 2004 Delft University of Technology and the Port of Rotterdam combined their efforts to create a game about extending the port of Rotterdam. This resulted in the first version of SimMV2 in the summer of 2005. In this game three players build the new port extension in 30 years simulated time.

The initial target audience where port experts. But students at the University also proved to be a good audience resulting in an actively played game. The game was initially setup as exclusively web-based, using mostly Flash [5] and Java Enterprise [6] in a web browser, therefore with very limited capabilities. More features where being requested conflicting with the already growing limitations and network overhead. The need for a new version became clear.

5.2 The Present – SimPort MV2

In late 2005 the two lead programmers of SimMV2 founded a new company called Tygron, and started construction of the next generation called SimPort. Having detailed knowledge of the possibilities and limitations of the SimMV2 game, they came up with a new framework. SimPort is totally built in Java [6] from bottom up, giving it more possibilities. The framework makes it possible to develop more serious games in shorter time. SimPort is not limited at all to the port area in Rotterdam but other ports can also be played. Furthermore, the application is not browser-based anymore, and supports 3D graphics and GUI, while maintaining LAN and web-based networking.

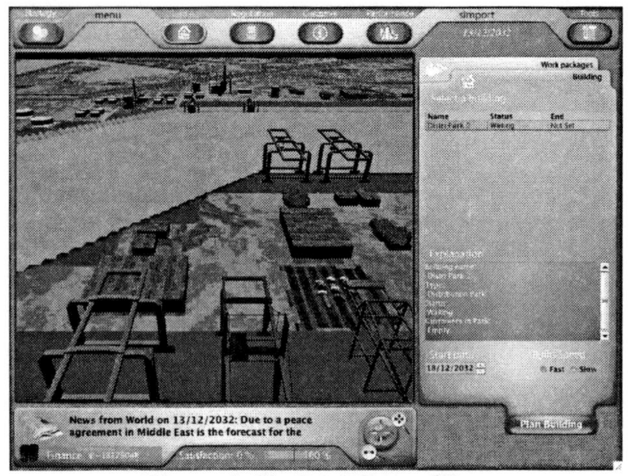

Figure 4. SimPort Game View

At the moment SimPort is ending its development cycle and the first games are being played at the University. In late 2006 the first commercial version will be released

5.3 Real-life experiments

SimPort and its predecessor have both been used in real-life situations. "Preliminary findings (...) suggest that the game is of high quality, that players enjoy it and find it educational and instructive" [4] was the evaluation after the first few sessions of SimMV2 and the first life test session of SimPort as raised similar reactions. The game's original target group was experts, but it has shown its worth in other situations too.

Figure 5. Players at Work

Observations during the game and the results from questionnaires indicate that generally the players very much enjoyed the game. The game's degree of immersion was fairly good: players had to be urged to stop for a lunch break a couple of times, and then found that they had come back early to start playing again. The active presence of two contacts from the Port of Rotterdam in one of the student sessions seemed to engage the students even more and improve their performance. It triggered interesting discussions and interactions between the professionals and the students, and also demonstrated the value of the game for education and training [4].

With a serious game like SimPort MV2 it is easy to fall into a simulation/decision support mood. It is important to have the players be caught in the gaming attitude, to achieve the learning benefits of playing the game. Players were very active during every phase of the game, and they fell into their respective roles easily. A game needs to be enjoyable and SimPort MV2 has definitely succeeded in this.

6 Conclusions

The increasingly widespread use of computer games for purposes other than entertainment, so-called serious games, is finding an important niche in a variety of management applications. However, the design and development of such games cannot follow the same long production cycles of current commercial entertainment games. Therefore, all tools and techniques that help to concentrate on the central management game and simulation aspects are more than welcome by the serious game developers. In this paper we described a platform independent game framework that was specifically developed for this purpose. As such, it is especially suited for developing new management games, as it avoids having to start from scratch each time.

The framework was first utilized in the implementation of the SimPort MV2 module, a multiplayer game simulating the expansion process of the Port of Rotterdam along a period of 30 years. This game has been played several times by students and professionals together at the Delft University of Technology, Erasmus University and the Port of Rotterdam.

Out of these real-life experiments, players said they considered the game of high quality, they enjoyed it and found it quite instructive. Student players emphasized that they learned much about the complexity of the port project, while professionals stressed that the game can enhance communication and cooperation with the authorities of the Port of Rotterdam. But probably most important of all is the fact that the game provided an opportunity for professionals and students to look at the future of a complex project in an engaging and entertaining way.

7 Acknowledgements

The authors wish to thank the Port of Rotterdam for its continuous support and knowledge in developing these new games. Especially we wish to thank Anne-Kirsten Meijer, Jan-Willem Koeman, and Maurits van Schuylenburg for their contributions.

Edwin Branbergen and Hasso Schaap, students at the Faculty of Industrial Design at TU Delft, for developing the user interfaces of the SimPort game. Alexander Hofstede, colleague at the Faculty of Technology, Policy and Management (TBM) at TU Delft, for his outside expertise and help during stressful times.

We also wish to thank Gijs Buijsrogge and Teun Veldhuizen for assisting in the design of the original game SimMV2 basis of SimPort.

8 References

1. Pitt, E. and McNiff, K., 2001. Java.rmi The Remote Method Invocation Guide, Addison-Wesley, Edinburgh Gate UK
2. Extensible Markup Language (http://www.w3.org/XML/): XML Standard website.
3. Annotations (http://www.developer.com/java/other/article.php/3556176): Website on how to make custom annotations.
4. Bekebrede, G. and Mayer, I. (2006) 'Build your seaport in a game and learn about complex systems', J. Design Research. pp 2 & 25.
5. Flash (http://www.macromedia.com): Macromedia Flash website.
6. Java (http://java.sun.org): Sun's Java development website.
7. Turban, E. (1995). Decision support and expert systems : management support systems. Englewood Cliffs, N.J., Prentice Hall.
8. Port of Rotterdam (2004). Projectorganisatie Maasvlakte 2, Project initiatie document (Project Organization Maasvlakte 2, Project initiation document). Rotterdam, Port of Rotterdam: pp 87.
9. Duke, R. D. and J. L. A. Geurts (2004). Policy Games for Strategic Management: Pathways into the unknown. Amsterdam, Dutch University Press.
10. Mayer, I., Bockstael-Blok, W. & Valentin, E. (2004) A building block approach to simulation. An evaluation using Containers Adrift, In: Simulation and Gaming, 35 (1) pp 29-52. ISSN: 1046-8781.

9 Biography

Jeroen Warmerdam is an MSc student in the faculty of Electrical Engineering, Mathematics and Computer Science of Delft University of Technology, The Netherlands. He is co-founder of Tygron – Serious Gaming & Media and has been working on the SimPort project after starting its development during his BSc project.

Maxim G. Knepflé is an MSc student in the faculty of Electrical Engineering, Mathematics and Computer Science of Delft University of Technology, The Netherlands. He is co-founder of Tygron – Serious Gaming & Media and has been working on the SimPort project after starting its development during his BSc project.

Rafael Bidarra is assistant professor Geometric Modelling at the Faculty of Electrical Engineering, Mathematics and Computer Science of Delft University of Technology, The Netherlands. He graduated in electronics engineering at the University of Coimbra, Portugal, in 1987, and received his PhD in computer science from Delft University of Technology in 1999. He teaches several courses on computer games within the CS programme 'Media and Knowledge Engineering', and leads the research work on computer games at the Computer Graphics and CAD/CAM Group. His current research interests in this area include procedural and parametric modelling, and advanced techniques for animation and path finding. He has published many papers in international journals, books and conference proceedings, and has served as member of several program committees.

Geertje Bekebrede is a PhD researcher in the faculty of Technology, Policy and Management at Delft University of Technology, the Netherlands.

Igor S. Mayer is an associate professor in the faculty of Technology, Policy and Management at Delft University of Technology, the Netherlands. He is also a director of the Delft Rotterdam Centre for Process Management and Simulation (www.cps.tbm.tudelft.nl). He is a co-founder and board member of Saganet – the Netherlands' Simulation and Gaming Association - and a member of the Netherlands Institute of Government (NIG).

MACSIM: Serious Gaming in Crisis Management via Script-based Simulation

T. Benjamins, drs. and Dr. L.J.M. Rothkrantz
Man-Machine Interaction Group
Faculty of Electrical Engineering, Mathematics and Computer Science
Delft University of Technology,
The Netherlands

***Abstract*— Experiments in crisis management are expensive and difficult to realize. There is also a lack of training facilities in real crisis environments. Serious games and simulation can provide an alternative. We developed a system that provides serious game for crisis management. It is called MACSIM (Multi Agent Crisis Simulator Interpreter and Monitor). It is composed of the following components: First a software based platform for dynamic simulating of disasters. We designed a communication infrastructure that allows agents participants in the simulation to exchange messages. Every agent is able to observe the results of crisis events, process these events using dynamic scripting (based on XML files) and initiate appropriate actions. The decision making process is distributed among autonomous agents. We developed a first prototype. The design and test results will be described in this paper.**

Keywords: gaming, serious gaming, simulation, crisis management, multi agent systems

I. Introduction

IN recent years we observe an enormous growth in the scale and complexity of the terrorist attacks and natural disasters. It proves that the existing infrastructure and crisis management is unable to face the challenges of such events. There is a need for additional research, training methods and training facilities. But to set up a test in real life crisis situation is far from trivial. To research for example communication and corresponding infrastructure during terrorist attacks or flooding is infeasible. Software from the game industry can be applied to crisis context, to provide a virtual simulation environment for research or an interactive method for training in the field of emergency response.

In general games are designed for entertainment. Our application domain is more serious. To play a game on terrorist attacks can be very exciting and joyful for the players. But if rescue employees as fireman and police and first aid employees use the game for training, the ultimate goal is to have better trained people to help more victims. So the games will be employed for serious goals.

CGAMES 2006 Dublin - The 9th INTERNATIONAL COMPUTER GAMES CONFERENCE

For many years disasters are simulated for training and research. Disasters are generated using a fixed script, based on an XML file. In serious gaming dynamics scripts are used. Serious games are interactive. Users can change the order of the crisis events and the environment has to be adapted taking care of the reactions of the user.

Games are usually based on a phantasm script and generate a phantasm world. Serious games are supposed to have a high reality and presence value. Players should experience the environment as a real world and should get the feeing that they are part of this world. So in serious gaming the environment is not full of dragons and ghosts. And the actions are modeled after human behavior. In the current serious game it is possible to simulate an explosion of a chemical plant. The toxic cloud spread out according to the law of physics. And in case of a fireman flushing a fire should result in a decrease of the fire.

Recently the COMBINED (Chaotic Open world Multi-agent Based Intelligently NEtworked Decision-support Systems) project [10] was finished, which was an initiative of DECIS-labs, in combination with several Dutch research partners, including TU Delft, The university of Amsterdam, TNO, Thales and several Fire departments (NIFV), . The goal of this project was to design systems that consist of human actors and artificial agents. These agents work together to achieve their common goals, even if this means they are functioning in chaotic circumstances. Examples of other work in this field can be found in [11] and [12].

Our research conducted for MACSIM fits in the framework of the COMBINED project and had three main goals: to create a crisis environment in which different crises can be simulated by means of an event generator, to create a communication layer through which agents can exchange messages, and to create intelligent software agents that move around in the crisis world. This crisis world should be the basis simulation and training based on serious gaming.

At this moment game software is available which can be used for serious gaming. This software provides tools to build a realistic environment and to design bots with realistic behavior. We decided to develop our own software. First software tools are not freely available. Games which are able to generate realistic crisis events are not well developed. Next our focus was how to design the communication between agents and to model agents. In future implementation iterations gaming software will be used to design 3D-graphic visualization to represent the data currently available in side the simulation world.

This paper will have the following structure: In section II we will introduce the world model for MACSIM. The related literature and sources of research will be discussed in Section III. Section IV will be dedicated to introducing the designed software components and the way external software components like JADE and Jess was included. In the Evaluation section (Section V) an example of a testing scenario is given, and finally we end this paper with a conclusion.

II. RELATED WORK

At this moment we observe an explosion of serious games initiatives, tools and games. Many of them are developed in the military domain. "America's Army" and Darwars Ambush are on of the most popular serious games. Another example is "Incident Commander" which teaches incident management for multiple scenarios's, including terrorist attacks, and natural disasters. Both games are built on the top of other games, using the game engine. America's Army is built on top of Unreal engine and Darwars Ambush on top of Operation Flash Point. In this section we will further restrict ourselves to the simulation and games which are on the basis of our research.

The US government organizations EPA (Environmental Protection Agency) and NOAA (National Oceanic and Atmospheric Administration) have made a very easy-to-use gas dispersion modeling tool called ALOHA (Arial Locations Of Hazardous Atmospheres) [6] . It is able to model chemical releases and has some advanced features in modeling. ALOHA has been designed for people with crisis response duties, so after an incident they can get a fast overview of what is going on and what will be the situation in the upcoming hour.

A program that is especially dedicated to real time simulation is the program REALTIME, which is made by Safer Systems [7]. Once a branch of DuPont de Nemours, one of the leading chemical companies in the world, it is now an independent company that is dedicated to chemical risk estimation and chemical simulation. REALTIME is a program that is used by a lot of chemical companies for determining the consequences of an incident that just happened. It can also be used as a simulator.

Hazmat: Hotzone is a simulation that uses video game visualization techniques to train first responders about how to respond to emergencies concerning hazardous materials. It is currently in the development stage at the Entertainment Technology Center at Carnegie Mellon University in collaboration with the Fire Department of New York. Hazmat: Hotzone is still in development and is estimated to be completed in Spring 2007 [8].

Another project focused on crisis situations is the Rescue project. We agree with the researchers on the following statements as can be found on the project website [9]: The response to different types of crises in a timely and effective manner can reduce deaths and injuries. It is also important to contain or prevent secondary disasters, and furthermore try to minimize the resulting economic losses and social disruption. The drillsim simulator, which is a part of the CAMAS (Crisis assessment, mitigation and analysis)-testbed [13] is a multi-agent crisis simulator in which crisis response roles (e.g., evacuation) can be played by game participants. The simulator models different response activities at both tactical and operational levels, and model the information flow between different crisis response agencies. External components can be inserted at different interfaces between these activities or at some point of the information flow in order to study the effectiveness of research solutions in disaster management and tested for utility in disaster response. In addition this simulator can integrate real life drills into a digital simulation.

III. MODEL

To describe the concepts in MACSIM, we have devised a World Model that is divided into three parts (see Figure 1), being the Real World, the Observed World and the Crisis Center. Through these parts of the world model we will explain the MACSIM concepts.

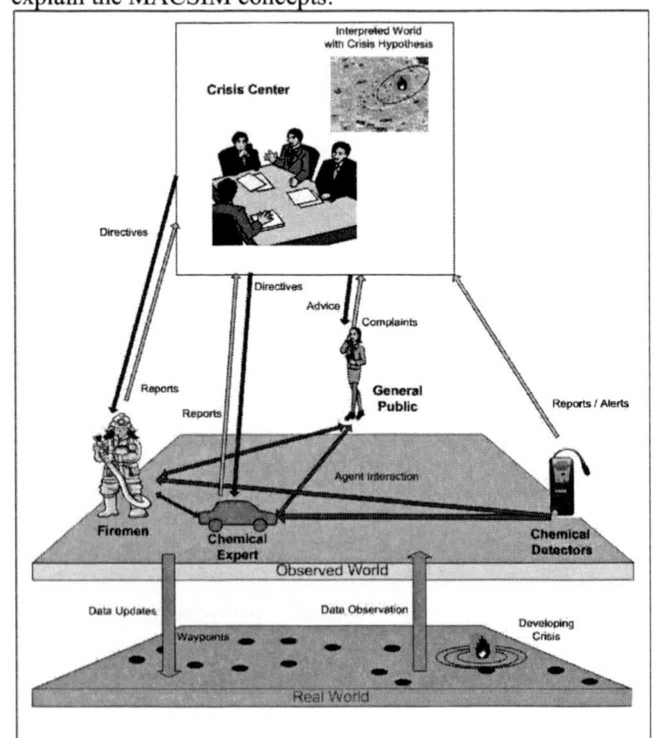

Figure 1: Global Overview of MACSIM

Real World

The first world is called the Real World. We consider the Real World to be a simulation of the real world, that is, a model of the real world good enough to fit our needs. In this world there are a lot of waypoints. Waypoints are considered to be data storage with information about the area directly surrounding a certain point. This data can also be updated. These waypoints contain a lot of data that the agents walking through the area use to gather information about the crisis at hand. Those waypoints are located all through the area. The main reason we use waypoints is because of the reduction of computational complexity that is achieved when we only have to calculate physical properties for a limited number of points in the world instead of for every possible coordinate in the entire area. As long as the computations for a certain point are reasonably accurate it will serve our purpose very well. While the simulation lasts, the physical properties of a waypoint are subject to change.

Observed World

The second world is called the Observed world, because it is in this world all the agents see the events unfold and report about it to the Crisis Center or to other agents. In the Figure we can see that the different agents can report things to each other. Also they can complain or report observed effects of events to the crisis center.

In the Observed World operate all different types of agents that have one thing in common: They observe the world. But because they are all have a different perspective on the world, they interpret the effect of certain event differently, and therefore also react differently to those effects. This leaves room for flexible interpretation of situations that in real life is one of the key characteristics of crisis response.

In the observed world operate different types of agents that all have their own view of the situation. This is visualized more clearly in Table 1.

Table 1 Agents and corresponding Actions

	Sensors	Observers	Professionals	Decision Makers
Message passing	Reporting	Reporting Receiving	Reporting Receiving	Ordering Reporting
Reasoning	N/A	Common Knowledge	Analysis based on experience	Analysis Incoming Information
Tactical Actions	N/A	N/A	Orders to peers	N/A
Operational Actions	N/A	N/A	Job-Related Response	Orders to Crisis responders

The table contains the following agents:

- ***Sensors***: Devices that are placed inside the world to report to other agents what is going on over there. This could be gas detectors, or smoke detectors or more intelligent devices reporting through intelligent combinations of sensory input.
- ***Observers***: The innocent bystanders that mind their own business but when something happens in the environment get involved in the crisis. They can be victims, but also complain about certain physical properties that cause them to have medical problems.
- ***Professionals***: These agents have to perform a job during a crisis situation and all their actions are based on performing that job as good as possible. Furthermore they maintain contact with the crisis center and give aid and information about what is going on to innocent bystanders. Examples of this kind of agents are Firemen and Chemical Experts.
- ***Decision Makers***: Decision Makers have the intention to control and to be in charge of certain professionals in the field. They are the ones politically responsible for the crisis response effort and therefore it is absolutely vital that they make good decisions. Based on either their own observations (a commander in the field) they form an interpretation of the world in which their decision will have to meet their responsibilities.

Crisis Center

All information acquired in the Observed World is being sent to the Crisis Center. The Crisis Center will be able to either inform the agents in the world about what's going on or it will send directives. The crisis center has to determine what is going on in the real world based on the views that the agents in the observed world have of it. It has to make a reconstruction of the facts given by the observing agents. Based on this a hypothesis of the crisis situation is formulated.

If they have a theory about the crisis, the Crisis Center can decide whether or not action should be taken and if so, what kind of action. This means that they can request Professionals to check out a current location about what is going on. If the investigations of those Professionals give enough evidence that there is a problem, they could order further units to go to the presumed location and aid in the crisis response effort. Also advice to the general public is being given about the situation.

Communication

The data flow between different components of MACSIM can be organized in a view as shown in Figure 2. In this view we can distinguish a Simulation Layer, Agent Middleware, an agent layer and one or more GUI's. It gives a clear overview of the flow of information and in which way it is being transferred to the components in the system.

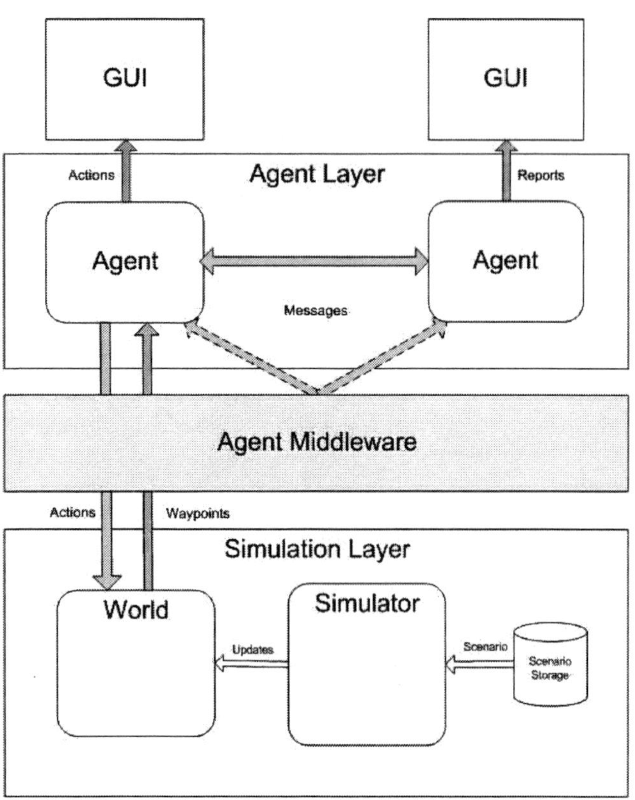

Figure 2: Global Overview Communication

The Simulation Layer contains scenario storage. In this storage scenarios are being kept. A scenario can be acquired from the storage by the Simulator. The Simulator is in charge of simulating crises and for that it needs scenarios. Those scenarios are being transformed into a script internally by the simulator. A script is basically a timeline with a start time and an end time and certain events that can take place in the world in between. The simulator is processing those events and this usually means that as a result of a certain event the world is modified in one way or another, i.e. the simulator is updating.

When the world is being updated, the agents in the world should be notified, because they have to sense changes in the world caused by the events. This is where the agent middleware comes into play. The agent middleware takes care that the agents in the simulation are receiving the updates of the world. The agents are receiving this information via agent middleware of because they are supposed to be autonomous. This means that the agents are supposed to work as independently as possible. Therefore other components should not have direct access to the agents, because that would imply some sort of ownership that does not fit inside the concept of independent agents.

In the meantime, the agents are receiving data updates of the world in the form of waypoints. If these agents sense this data they can process and reason about it. Based on this reasoning the agents initiate actions. Those actions might have an effect on the world or not, but this is of course depending on the type of action that is the result of the agent's reasoning.

Besides reading waypoint data, the agents are also capable of sending messages to other agents. In the diagram the blue arrow indicates this, but it would be more accurate to connect the arrows via the agent middleware. This is because of the same reasons of agent independency. Those messages are being sent to other agents through the agent middleware as well. The agent actions that have an effect on the world are being propagated back again to the world to implement the changes. This requires a synchronicity scheme that ensures that the simulator applying the script to the world knows about the updates by agents, so it can update the world again according to the most recent changes.

Finally the users of MACSIM will be able to view agent actions and play a certain part of an agent inside the scenario. This means that the agents will have to have some sort of GUI because otherwise the user will not notice their actions. If they have received or sent a report, then its GUI must also be showing those, for information purposes.

Architecture

A global overview of the MACSIM system is given in Figure 3. These are all the components that can be distinguished from a global perspective.

Simulation component: In this component a simulation of the concerned area can be given. The physical properties on a location (x,y,z) on time t can be read, and in this version of the program this means for instance fire, gas dispersion and explosions. For the gas dispersions formulae that are being used in commercial available software are used, the Gaussian Plume Model, to be exact. The simulation will be simplified to reduce computing complexity and design issues, because creating a scientifically valid simulation could be a full master project on its own, and as the purpose of this system was to create a design proof of concept, a slimmed-down version of the simulation will be available, to prevent the development from this component to overshadow the development of the reasoning engine.

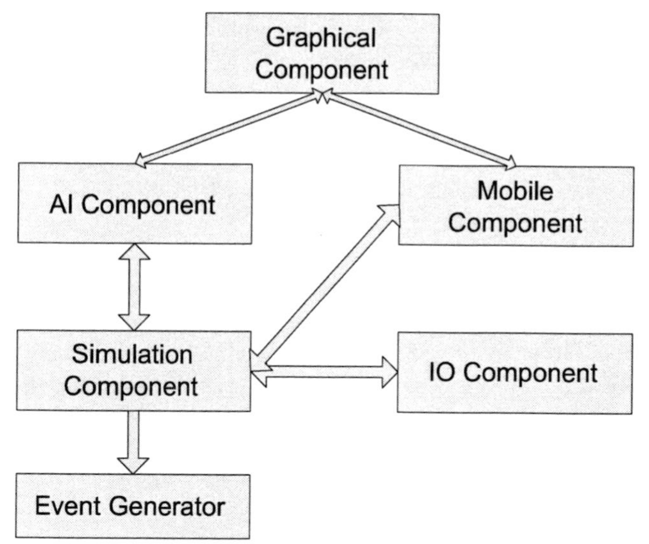

Figure 3: Component Architecture

Event Generator: This event generator should be able to generate crisis events, which is an XML-based script. When the script unfolds, events are being launched and those events have their effect on the simulation environment. This event generator in the future should work in two ways: first it generates events from a predefined script; secondly it should be able to generate new events as the participants in the simulator respond to the system. Based on the time schedule it will be decided which ones of these two forms of scripting will be available in the first version of MACSIM.

Graphical component: The graphical component of this program will consist of several user interfaces. One user interface will be used to setup the scenario, and simulation parameters. Another Interface will be used as a representation of what is going on at the crisis center. It will also contain a graphical representation of the area that will show the incoming reports of the people that are currently in the simulation area.

AI-component: This component will consist of a knowledge based system that, based on decision rules that are derived from first-hand experience from experts and real-life complaints from people that smell gases, helps in deciding what probably is the most realistic scenario that is currently happening. This is of critical importance in the first stages of the development of a crisis, when not much information is known and a first hypothesis can be made through a knowledge-based system. Inside the knowledge based system the agent has several hypotheses available. These hypotheses are represented as frames or sets of properties and rules and actions. Each moment that new knowledge arrives, on a scoreboard the scores for each different frame are placed. The frame that is triggered the most is the frame or hypothetical event that is chosen as most probable event. This could mean that also information is coming in that is conflicting with the hypothesis, but as long as the information rejecting the current hypothesis is not convincing enough, the current hypothesis is being maintained. If there is enough conflicting information to reject the hypothesis, then another more probable hypothesis frame is chosen. Therefore a different set of knowledge will become available and this means also different actions that will be performed by that specific agent (see Figure 4).

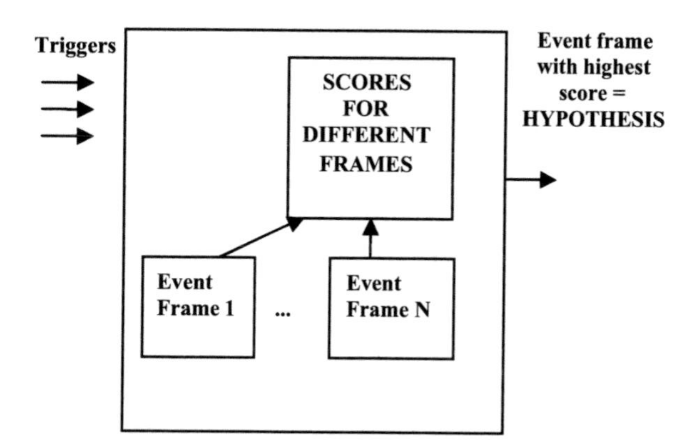

Figure 4: Frame-based Hypothesis Forming

Mobile component: In the future, the crisis response components should also be able to be used in real life (no simulation) and for this, a mobile component should be created that can be run on a handheld pc, that enables user participants to create reports based on an icon based application such as ISME [14]. These reports are then treated in the same fashion as other reports, and can be used in the system in the same way to help determining what the most probable crisis situation my be.

I-O component: This component will take care of the regular file IO operations that might be necessary inside the system, such as loading and saving files. Examples could be loading and saving of scripts, or saving or saving graphical representations while running.

IV. Implementation

The design for MACSIM was made in Java and it was designed in such a way that it was:

- ***Expandable***: Being a research object, the system should be able to incorporate new features that could improve the functionality of the system but are currently not yet in the scope of the system. In the design we should take care that we design as 'open' as possible, to facilitate future work on the system.

- ***Not memory consuming***: The agents that are at a certain location must get the data they need as fast as possible, so their observing and interpreting of the data does not get delayed.

- ***Without too much hard coded data***: Being a simulation, the system relies on a lot of mathematical, physical and empirical constants. It should be avoided to include those constants in java code, because this would mean that if they should be changed for some reason, that people have to dig in the Java source to change whatever they want. It is more preferable to read constants from text or XML files, where they are being imported by the system and can be edited easily for future use.

- ***Operating on JADE***: With JADE being one of the leading platforms for multi-agent programming, it was decided that the simulation should run on JADE, to facilitate running of system on mobile devices in the future.[5]

In Figure 5 MACSIM is being described as a series of Java software components that are independent parts of the system and exchange information during the course of a simulation. In the crisis center component in Figure 5 the reasoning mechanism Figure 4 is used. In some of these components external open source software components like JADE and Jess were used. In the description of each component the use of that particular tool will be described.

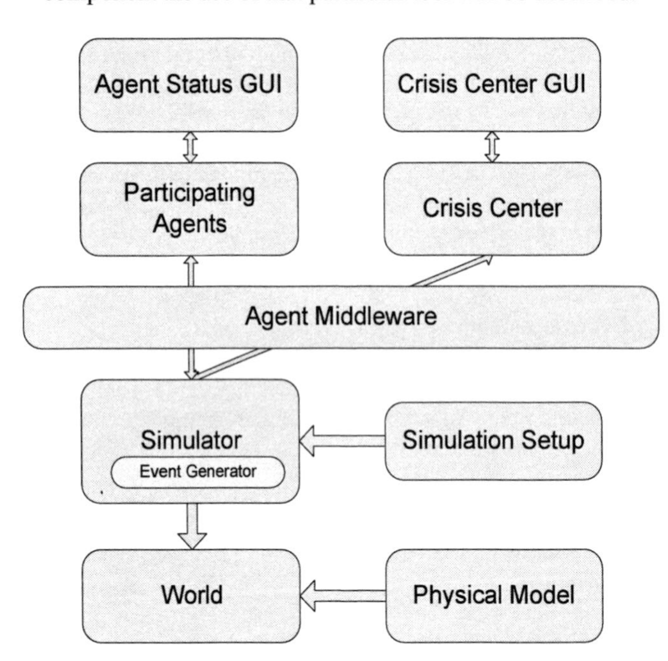

Figure 5: Software Component Decomposistion

Simulator: This is the main component of the program, where the simulation is being set up and run. The startup and all necessary parameter checking are done here. From here all the other necessary components are started. The simulator ensures that the agents receive the waypoints that the agents need to correctly observe the world. By passing the essential data via the agent middleware ensures the agents in the field receive the appropriate data.

World: the simplification of the world for which we are making simulations. We cannot incorporate everything that is in the real world into our world model. Because of complexity and performance reasons we make the world in which a scenario is developing as simple as possible. The World consists of waypoints which contain the values that the agents observe.

Physical Model: The collection of models that enable the events to impose changes inside the world. These are mainly a set of formulae that can be changed or added when necessary. The formulae are designed in such a way that they can be replaced by more advanced counterparts very easily.

Event Generator: This component makes sure that events, that are part of a scenario, are executed in the right way. This means that the event generator takes care of updating the world model in the fashion that a particular event requires. It uses the formulae available in the Physical Model to update a particular event. There are as many Event Generators as there are active events in the simulator. Whenever according to the scenario a new event needs to be launched, a new event generator is started that takes care of updating the waypoints with data relevant to that event.

Simulation Setup: In this window all the properties of a certain simulation can be edited, loaded and saved. After the user is satisfied with the scenario, it can be stored and executed. Things like starting time, ending time, number of participating agents can be set up in this GUI. It is really up to the creativity of the programmer and the complexity of the simulation presented how much parameters and details can be set.

Agent Middleware: The agent middleware ensures that the messages that are sent between agents are being processed correctly. Also the updates of the world are processed so that the agents have them at their disposal. MACSIM uses JADE as Agent middleware, which is a very popular platform for the programming of multi-agent systems.

Participating Agents: These are the key elements in the system. They are the main characters in the simulation and as the scenario unfolds, the characters respond to the changing situation. The agents can communicate with each other about the current status, and they can use reasoning for making decisions about what they should do the next. Participating agents can also contact the crisis center. For communicating, they use JADE agent messaging, through FIPA compliant ACL Messages [5]. These messages contain information that is based on a Java-Based crisis ontology developed by Siska Fitrianie [2]. For reasoning they use a knowledge base. As a knowledge base Jess is being used for its easy interaction with Java objects, such as the ontology elements inside Fitrianie's crisis ontology.

Crisis Center: during a crisis, a crisis center is usually being set up to coordinate the crisis response effort. Here all the information about the crisis comes in and is being interpreted by the people who are there. The crisis center interprets all the messages that are coming in and based on rule-based reasoning, they create orders for their subjects that can be sent by using agent messages. They issue commands to the participating agents that are in the field, based on the information that they get from all available sources. This information is being stored inside something that is called an interpreted world. This is an interpretation of what the crisis center believes is going on inside the world. In real life, the interpreted world is usually some sort of real or digital map onto which status information is being added. Based on what they see on the map, the crisis team decides what to do. The decision making functionality described in Figure 4 is implemented in this component.

Interface during simulation (Agent Status GUI and Crisis Center GUI): During the simulation the agents are making all kinds of decisions, and a lot of communication is exchanged as well. We want to keep track during run-time of what is going on in the world, so we need some way to eavesdrop on the communication during a crisis. In quite the same way that communication during a flight is being recorded, the agent communication will be shown on a user interface while the simulation is running. Besides that, for the agents that the user identifies with during the simulation, agents can be controlled and agent actions can be initiated from this GUI. For the participating agents, the status of the agent is being shown. As a visual component of the crisis center, an icon-based crisis map will be used, that is able to show incoming crisis messages on top of a map of a crisis area. This was made using components from another application called 3MNews, designed by Iulia Tatomir [4].

V. EVALUATION

For testing MACSIM, simulations had to be run, and for simulations we needed scenarios. These scenarios are script-based. This means that a scenario consists of an XML-based script. A script is a combination of a time and an event with the source location of the event added to it. In this way the event generator knows exactly what to do to update the world based on that event.

To test the simulation we had to define some test scripts to evaluate the system. At this point the simulation consists of automated predefined actions based on the observation of effects of script-generated predefined events. Later on this will evolve into a more dynamic form of scripting, in which game players can initiate actions themselves and scenarios can be changed as a result of those actions.

The first minutes of an example test scenario could look like the contents of Table 1:

Table 2: First minutes of Example Scenario

Time	Event + Location	Agent	Possible Action
14:00	Fire starts at (X,Y)	General Public	Run Away + Report trough GSM or SMS
		Sensor	Activation smoke alarm + reporting to Crisis Center
		Crisis Center	Sends a call to Fireman about developing situation.
		Professional (Fireman)	Receives a call from Crisis Center to go to (X,Y) and is on his way
14:02	Fire develops	General Public	Complaint to Crisis Center about developing smoke
		Professional (Fireman)	While on its way to (X,Y) receives info from crisis center that fire is developing
14:04	Explosion	General Public	Report to Crisis Center about damage and casualties and a loud bang
		Crisis Center	Order extra units of Firemen and Police to (X,Y)
14:05		Professional (Fireman)	Arrives at (X,Y) and starts extinguishing fire
		Professional (Policeman)	Receives order from Crisis Center to seal off crisis area around (X,Y)

VI. CONCLUSION

With the development of MACSIM we have devised a system that is able to simulate crisis situations based on scripts. For this purpose a crisis generator component, a communication layer and intelligent agents were developed and tested and although further testing is still needed, first result look very promising.

An advantage of this system is that it enables us to add new physical models, new intelligent agents and new types of crisis events very easily; also existing components can be updated very fast.

As an open simulation platform, MACSIM offers a lot of room for further development. The first additions planned for the near future are the use of gaming software for the creation of graphical components for 3D graphics and more sophisticated algorithms for agent reasoning, like Bayesian belief networks. When more features become available, there will inevitably also be a need to visually represent these new features. Therefore the existing user interface will be upgraded to improve the visual experience and sense of presence for the user that runs the simulation. At this point the user interface just shows message traffic, but real time crisis simulation of course is something that cannot do without a realistic visual representation.

Furthermore, the design offers enables adding more advanced reasoning algorithms. In all cases where new intelligence/ knowledge has to be added or intelligence/ knowledge should be updated, it is important to have discussions with the domain experts during the development process to get useful first-hand experience and information that can be represented in rules, behaviors and agent actions. The rules in this way will also become better and more sophisticated.

REFERENCES

[1] Ernest Friedman-Hill. Jess in Action. Manning, 2003.

[2] S. Fitrianie and L.J.M. Rothkrantz. The represenation of the world. Technical report, TU Delft, 2006.

[3] L.J.M. Rothkrantz. Interactive Simulation in Disaster Management (ISDM). 2006.

[4] I. Tatomir. 3MNews - Message-based Multimodal News. Technical report, TU Delft, 2006.

[5] Fabio Bellifemine, Agostino Poggi, and Giovanni Rimassa. Jade: a fipa2000 compliant agent development environment. pages 216–217, 2001.

[6] EPA and NOAA. ALOHA User's Manual, 2004.

[7] SAFER Systems Inc, SAFER REALTIME/TRACE Technical Manual.

[8] Hazmat: Hotzone project website, (http://projecthazmat.org)

[9] The Simulator project website, (http://www.ics.uci.edu/~projects/drillsim/)

[10] COMBINED Project Website, (http://combined.decis.nl)

[11] B. Tatomir, L. Rothkrantz and M. Popa, "Intelligent system for exploring dynamic crisis environments", Third International Conference on Information Systems for Crisis Response and Management ISCRAM 2006, May 2006.

[12] P. Klapwijk L.J.M. Rothkrantz, "Topology Based Infrastructure for crisis situations", Third International Conference on Information Systems for Crisis Response and Management ISCRAM 2006, May 2006.

[13] S. Mehrotra, C. Butts, D. Kalashnikov, N. Venkatasubramanian, K. Altintas, Haimin Lee, J. Wickramasuriya, R. Hariharan, Y.Ma: CAMAS: A Citizen Awareness System for Crisis Mitigation. University of California, Irvine

[14] Paul Schooneman. ISME - Icon based System for Managing Emergencies. Master's thesis, TU Delft, 2005.

Using the Source Engine for Serious Games

Andrew Ritchie, Patrick Lindstrom, and Bryan Duggan
School of Computing,
Dublin Institute of Technology,
Kevin St., Dublin 8.

Email: andrew.richie@student.dit.ie
patrick.lindstrom@gmail.com, bryan.duggan@comp.dit.ie
http://seriousgordon.blogspot.com/

Keywords

Serious Games, Source SDK, Half Life 2, Valve, Food Safety, Food Hygiene, Restaurant Kitchen.

Abstract

In the paper we describe our work in using the Source engine from the game Half Life 2 to develop a *serious game* - Serious Gordon. Serious Gordon is used to teach principals of food safety and food hygiene in a restaurant kitchen environment. The target users of Serious Gordon are students of catering in the DIT Faculty of Tourism and Food. The paper describes the formation of the Serious Gordon team and the development of a story for the game. It continues with a description of the features from Half Life 2 that we retained and those that we removed for the game. We then describe the process we undertook to implement the game including a description of the tools we used. We conclude with a brief evaluation of the project and present future work.

1. Introduction

The Source Engine is an award winning 3D game engine developed by Valve Software [PC Gamer, 2004; PC Zone, 2004; IGN.com, 2006]. It is regarded as one of the most advanced games engines on the market supporting such features as realistically simulated physics using the Havok engine, DirectX 9.0 support including High Dynamic Range lighting, skeletal animation, sound systems and many other features [Valve, 2006]. It is the engine that the successful game Half Life 2 is built on. The source engine comes with the Source SDK which can be used to build game mods. The SDK is freely available to owners of the Half Life 2 game and provides access to the tools used by Valve themselves to create the Half Life 2 series of games, Day of Defeat Source, Counter Strike Source and upcoming games including Portal and Team Fortress 2. It is also used by many independent developers including Ritual the creators of SIN: Episodes and Arkane the developers of the game Dark Messiah [Ritual, 2006; Sin, 2006; Arkane, 2006].

This paper describes our work developing the "Serious Gordon" project. The aim of Serious Gordon was to test the feasibility of using the Source engine to develop a *serious game*. Serious games are games that have non-entertainment purposes such as education or training [Johnson *et al*, 2004]. Serious Gordon is a game that can be utilized as an aid in teaching food safety in a restaurant kitchen in a unique, safe and fun environment. The target users of Serious Gordon are students of catering in the DIT Faculty of Tourism and Food. Using a game engine, our aim was to simulate situations that could not be recreated safely and easily in the real world. In Serious Gordon the player takes the role of a new junior employee in a restaurant kitchen and is given a number of tasks such as changing into appropriate clothing, observing personal hygiene, first aid and storing deliveries of food in the correct locations.

2. Specification & requirements gathering

To develop the project, a team of domain experts was first assembled to address the technical and pedagogical aspects of the project. The team consisted of experts in three areas, from three faculties in DIT:

- Software development
- Learning technology
- Food safety

To implement the project, a number of candidate developers were interviewed and two undergraduate students with significant games development experience were recruited and retained for the summer of 2006. The students employed an iterative prototyping methodology to develop the system. In other words, the team proceeded on several fronts - requirements gathering, research and development of prototypes in parallel [Fullerton *et al.*, 2004].

The development of a "story" for the game posed an interesting challenge that was unfamiliar to the student software team. The Serious Gordon project required that a player interacting with the game would achieve a set of learning outcomes, whereas the students were used to thinking of gaming outcomes in terms of scores, end of level bosses and so on.

This game story was considered to be core to the development of a game that delivered the learning outcomes and so several weeks of meetings with food safety experts took place to develop realistic scenarios for the game. These meetings had input from experts in not only Food safety but also in learning technology. The *script* for the game went through many revisions, as the team developed an awareness of the capabilities and limitations of the Source engine. Iterative prototypes were developed to test games concepts.

The story of Serious Gordon places the player in the role of a new employee in a restaurant kitchen. The player starts the game similarly to a real restaurant employee by observing certain personal hygiene pre-requisites and dressing appropriately. The player then has to respond to an accident which requires them to administer first aid to a fellow employee. They then are required to stack food deliveries into appropriate locations in the kitchen - for example by placing frozen food in the freezer and chilled food in the chill room. Throughout the game the player receives feedback on their activities from the "head chef" (Figure 6). Once the story was finalised, the assets (maps, models, animations, sounds and so on) in Half Life 2 were compared to those required by the story and the required gameplay elements had been tested the decision made that the project was feasible and could proceed.

3. Removing Half Life 2 Gameplay Components

Half Life 2 is a first person shooter (FPS) [Sanchez & Dalmau, 2004]. The Serious Gordon project only shares only the first person perspective with Half Life 2. The first step in transitioning the Half Life 2 single player experience to something that would provide a foundation for Serious Gordon was to remove gameplay elements such as Non Player Characters (NPC) that would attack the player. Weaponry carried by both the player and NPCs were also removed and most of the player health based statistics such as the players HEV (Hazardous Environment Suit), damage taking and displays were removed. Figure 1 is a screenshot from Half Life 2 giving examples of these elements.

Scripting in the Source engine is achieved by implementing modules in C++. Valve provides the full source code for the games Half Life 2 and Counter Strike and consequently modules from these games were adapted for use in Serious Gordon. In some cases changes were simple and involved removing code that instantiated existing features, such as the HEV (Hazardous Environment Suit) suit statistics. Once these features were removed the game was ready for the Serious Gordon assets to be integrated and the code to script the gameplay could be added.

Figure 1: The HUD (Heads Up Display), weapons and non player characters in Half Life 2

4. Programming Serious Gordon Gameplay

Serious Gordon was developed using several software tools, including Microsoft Visual Studio .NET 2003 for coding, Valve's Hammer Editor for mapping, modelling using Milkshape3D, choreography using Valves' Face Poser, materials creation using Photoshop CS2, sound recording using Audacity and text editors for many other features.

Developing Serious Gordon was decomposed into the core tasks identified below:

- Developing context specific physics and character interaction menus
- Developing new clothing and inventory entities
- Developing new clothing and inventory Heads Up Display (HUD) panels
- Developing information panels
- Programming player tasks
- Programming events and triggers to advance the script

The source code provides access to the Valve Graphical User Interface (VGUI) which is used by Valve to create graphical panels both inside the Source Engine and outside it in Steam (Valve's content delivery system). Figure 2 is an example from the Serious Gordon source code that draws the HUD inventory items using Source SDK API calls.`

In Half Life 2, pressing the "use key" triggers an interaction between the player and the object in front of the player in the game. Using this system, the interaction menu seen in Figure 3 was created. This menu appears when the user interacts with a wash hand basin and it allows a player to simulate washing their hands in the game.

This was implemented by adapting the class `CTextWindow` from the Source SDK. This class has a member function `OnCommand` that receives a message indicating the user interface control that generated the event. We have implemented a flexible framework that facilitates the creation of interface elements such as buttons and text messages from text files.

```
void CHudInventoryStatus::Paint()
{
 C_BaseHLPlayer *pPlayer =
(C_BaseHLPlayer*)C_BasePlayer::GetLocalP
layer();
 if (!pPlayer)
   return;

 // draw the suit power bar
 surface()->DrawSetTextColor(
m_SquadIconColor );
 surface()->DrawSetTextFont( m_hIconFont
);
 surface()-
>DrawSetTextPos(m_flIconInsetX,
m_flIconInsetY);
 surface()->DrawUnicodeChar('D');

 surface()-
>DrawSetTextFont(m_hTextFont);
 surface()-
>DrawSetTextColor(m_SquadTextColor);

 surface()->DrawSetTextPos(text_xpos,
text_ypos);
 surface()->DrawPrintText(m_wcItemName,
wcslen(m_wcItemName));
}
```

Figure 2: An example from the Serious Gordon Source code that uses Source SDK API's to draw the inventory

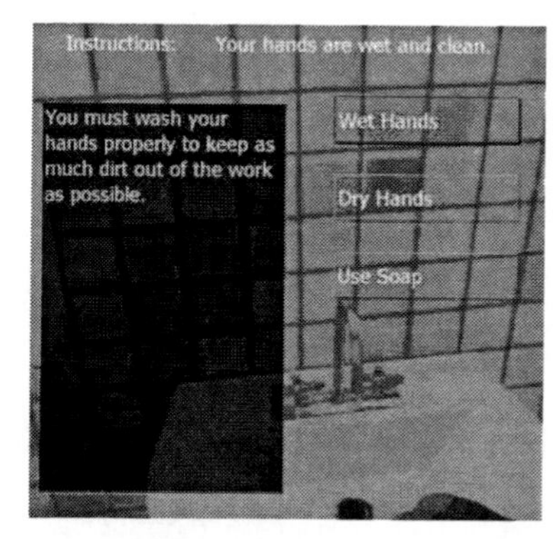

Figure 3: Interaction menu example - A player interacting with a wash hand basin.

Flexibility is again demonstrated in the approach taken in displaying the Heads Up Display (HUD). The HUD itself is derived from elements of the VGUI with Serious Gordon specific HUD elements derived from the HUD classes. Figure 4 presents the HUD from Half Life 2 and compares it with the HUD we developed for Serious Gordon. This approach provides a common look and functionality amongst HUD elements. Although the Serious Gordon elements provide different information, they do not come as a change to a player familiar with the Half Life 2 game.

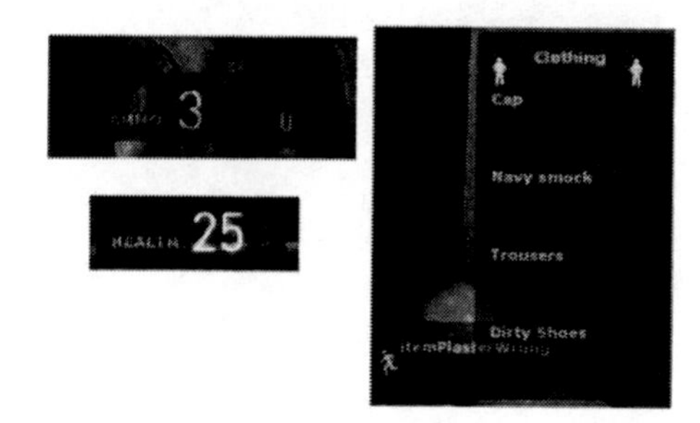

Figure 4: The Half Life 2 HUD (on the left) and the Serious Gordon HUD (on the right)

An *entity* is an object that has some kind of interaction with and exists inside the game world. The Serious Gordon entities are again all based of the existing Half Life 2 entities. HUD elements on the other hand have no interaction with the world itself and are merely indicators of specific attributes of an entity.

Model assets that did not exist in the Half Life 2 collection, such as the chef character, and kitchen implements were modeled using Milkshape3D as illustrated in Figure 5.

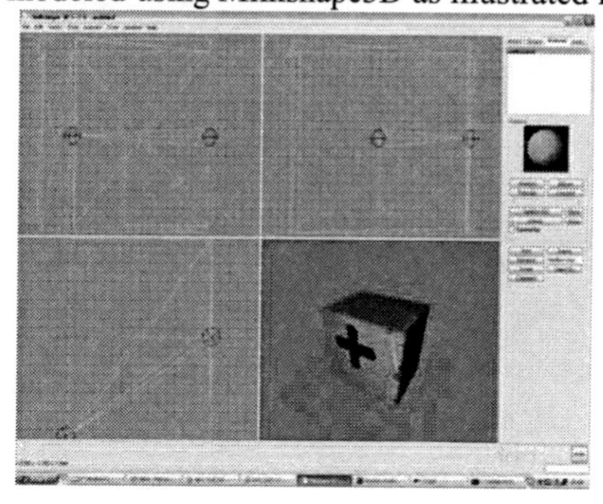

Figure 5: Editing Serious Gordon models in MilkShape3D

Meshes were created using vertex placement tools and connected to vertices with faces using the built in Face tool. Once the meshes were completed the sections were laid out onto a UV map using the Milkshape3D's built in mapping tool. A UV map maps texels on a bitmap to vertices on a 3D model. From Milkshape3D the models were exported to the Source proprietary file format, which Milkeshape3D natively supports.

The existing textures and models for Half Life 2 fit the Half Life 2 environment - a run down Eastern European city. These were brightened and cleaned to better fit into the Serious Gordon maps, by using Adobe Photoshop with a Valve Texture File plug-in. Custom models for Serious Gordon had skins created in Photoshop and then exported to the proprietary format. Some of the characters from Half Life 2 (for example the Father Gregory character from Ravenholm) were re-skinned and reused in Serious Gordon.

Figure 6: Father Gregory from Half Life 2 (left) and reskinned to make Chef from Serious Gordon (right)

Using the prewritten storyboard, dialogue was scripted for the character voices. These were recorded using the open source audio editing tool Audacity. We engaged the services of a professional voice actor from the Gaeity School of Acting to record the dialogue [Gaeity, 2006]. The actor could reproduce several speaking accents on demand and so provided the voices for several Serious Gordon game characters. The Source engine uses standard WAV files for vocals.

Source's proprietary tool, "Face Poser", was used to generate character animation and motion from voice audio files.

Valve's proprietary level editor, the Valve Hammer Editor (VHE) was used to create the kitchen and restaurant environments used in Serious Gordon. In order to accurately model the environment, the team carried out some on-site research in the college restaurant kitchen. The developers also received significant input into the environment design from the catering experts from the Faculty of Tourism and Food on the team. Our aim was to accurately simulate a real kitchen restaurant environment - a requirement unique to this type of serious game. This is obviously in contrast to a fantasy FPS like Half Life 2 which adapts elements of the real world to the gameplay.

Concessions were made however to, for example the proportions of game entities so as to make the game playable.

5. Conclusions and Future Work

The game was completed in September 2006 and was made available for download by students on the college VLE (WebCT). We carried out limited internal testing of Serious Gordon and we feel that our original project aims have been exceeded. Based on our internal testing, everyone who played the game indicated that their knowledge of food safety issues when working in a restaurant kitchen was better after playing the game than before. We therefore conclude that the Source Engine can be successfully used to create a serious game. During the development of the project, we tracked releases in the Source SDK. We did however encounter problems with tools from different releases which meant that facial animation was not incorporated into the final release of the game. The software team made all of the models for Serious Gordon and so the game retains much of the look and feel of Half Life 2.

Future work will focus on the creation of art assets to increase the realism of the game. We also hope to expand the number of learning scenarios developed and do a more structured validation of Serious Gordon by doing a usability test with first year students from the faculty of Tourism and Food.

6. About the Authors

Andrew Richie is an undergraduate student of the DIT, studying Computer Science with Games Programming. He has been interested in computer gaming from a young age and has a deep knowledge of the Source SDK from his experience as a lead developer on a number of Half Life 2 modding projects including Flanders Fields and Resitance and Liberation.

Patrick Lindstrom graduated with a first class honours in computer science from the Dublin Institute of Technology in 2006 and is currently pursuing a career in software architecture at Datalex Ltd., Ireland

Bryan Duggan is a lecturer in the school of computing at the DIT in Kevin St. He hold a first class honours degree in computer science and software engineering from the University of Dublin (studied at the DIT) and a Masters Degree from the DIT. He is presently working on a PhD with a working title of "Modeling Creativity in Traditional Irish Flute Playing". He lectures on games programming and music technology in the DIT School of Computing.

References

[Arkane, 2006] Arkane Studios Home Page http://www.arkane-studios.com/en/index.php Accessed September 2006.

[Fullerton *et al.*, 2004] Fullerton, T., Swain, C., Hoffman, S.: Game Design Workshop: Designing, Prototyping, and Playtesting Games, CMP Books. 2004

[Gaiety, 2006] Gaeity School of Acting Home Page, http://www.gaietyschool.com/, Accessed September 2006

[IGN.com,2006] PC Game of the Year 2004.

[PC Zone, 2004] PC Zone UK (Editor and Readers Choice), December 2004

[PCGamer, 2004] PC Gamer (US), December 2004

[Ritual, 2006] Ritual Home Page http://www.ritual.com/, Accessed September 2006

[Sanchez & Dalmau, 2004] Sanchez, D., Dalmau, C.: Core Techniques and Algorithms in Game Programming, New Riders, 2004

[Sin, 2006] Sin Episodes Home Page http://www.sinepisodes.com/ Accessed September 2006.

[Valve, 2006] Source Information Sheet http://valvesoftware.com/SOURCE_InfoSheet.pdf, Accessed September 2006.

"The Effect of Violent and Non-Violent Computer Games on Physiological Arousal: The Contribution of Built-In Music"

1- S. Ghorbani[1] (M.S)*

2- H. Mohammad Zadeh[2] (PhD)*

3- B. Tartibian[3] (PhD)*

*** Department of Physical Education, Urmia University, Iran.**

1- saied_ghorbani@hotmail.com
2- ha2004mo@yahoo.com
3- babak_hady@yahoo.com

Abstract
The purpose of this study was to examine the effect of violent and non-violent computer games on physiological arousal: the contribution built-in music. Participants were 50 boys' adolescents with age mean 17.48 years old (25 participants for violent group and 25 participants for non-violent group) that assigned to either Music or Silence condition. A first measurement of arousal variables (such as systolic and diastolic blood pressure, heart rate, respiratory frequency, and body temperature) was taken at the prior playing. Participants were then played for 30 minutes (music condition). Arousal variables measured in 15 minutes after start of play again, and immediately after the end of play these variables measured again. After one day, participants' exposure to computer games related to his group (silent condition), and arousal variables measured alike music condition. Result showed that the Music group had significantly higher arousal levels at during playing. These findings suggest for the first time that the auditory input contributes significantly to the physiological response found during violent computer game playing.

Keywords: Violent and Non-violent computer games-Physiological Arousal-Music

Introduction

The market for computer and video games has increased steadily in the last decade, and seems to be one of the few recession-proof sectors. According to data from NPD Fun World that measures consumer purchasing and product movement, sales of console computer and video games hardware, software, and accessories, brought in $ 10.3 billion in 2002 in the United States only, a record for the second consecutive year (John Gaudiosi, The Hollywood Reporter, Mon Feb 3, 2003) (17). Given the scope of these numbers and the prediction that computer and video games sales will continue to expand in the future, it is no surprise that a new research interest has grown into investigating what kind of effects computer and video games exert on the players.

The most dramatic effects reported were certainly those related to the aggression. Many studies reported that exposure to violent video games increase antisocial behaviors such as aggression [Anderson and Dill (2000), Anderson and Buchman (2001), Barthollow ad Anderson (2002), Buchman and Anderson (2002), Anderson and Morphy (2003), and Anderson (2003)] (1, 2, 7, 8, 5, 4). Besides effects on the aggression, many other studies have reported arousal and physiological reactions in computer and video game playing, Reported effects include increases in breath duration in children (Denot-Ledunois et al., 1998) (12) and increases in cardiovascular reactivity, blood pressure (most often systolic blood pressure), and oxygen consumption in children or adolescents (Modesti et al., 1994) (23), as well as in adults of all ages (Segal and Dietz, 1991; Mounier-Vehier et al., 1995)(28, 24), especially in those with a family history of hypertension (Ditto and Miller, 1989; Cook et al., 2001) (13,11) and in those with Type A personality (i.e., competitive individuals; Griffiths and Dancaster, 1995) (16). Cardiovascular system reactivity to video games in young men has also been taken as a reliable predictor of the future occurrence of hypertension (Markovitz et al., 1998) (21). Additionally, the finding of dopamine release during video game playing suggests that, as in the case of animals, this neurotransmitter may play a role in the anticipatory or appetitive phase of motivated behavior in humans (Koepp et al., 1998) (20). Based on these findings, video games have often been used in studies as a stressor to measure cardiovascular reactivity (e.g., Modesti et al., 1994; Cook et al., 2001) (23, 11). Yet, secretion of the stress-related hormone, namely cortisol, has rarely been measured. Few studies that have done so have mostly found either no changes (e.g., Skosnik et al., 2000) (29) or declines in cortisol secretion during video game playing (Hubert and de Jong-Meyer, 1992; Denot-Ledunois et al., 1998, in children) (18, 12). Comparing testosterone and cortisol changes in winners versus losers after a video ping-pong game, Mazur et al (1997) found an overall decline of cortisol over time for both groups (22).

Apparent conflicting results may arise from a lack of comparability between used types of video games. For example, one explanation for the effects reported on cortisol is that those latter studies have used unsophisticated and unexciting video games (e.g., ping pong games or Tetris). From this perspective, studies that have examined cortisol secretion can hardly be compared with those that have examined other measures, which have used other types of games (e.g., Ms Packman, Atari breakout, or other, unspecified games). In addition, in all of the studies reviewed but one that specified that "sound" during video game was present and "rather loud" (Modesti et al., 1994) (23), the presence or absence of music and sound has been ompletely overlooked. There are bases to postulate that music in action video games might be an important stressor. Anecdotal evidence suggests that video game designers have long acknowledged the importance of music in video games as a crucial part of gaming to enhance excitement and to draw the players into the game. More empirically, many researches focus on examining the psychological and physiological effects of music (by itself). Although such studies have mainly examined the relaxing role of music both in laboratory settings (e.g., Khalfa et al., 2003; Salamon et al., 2003) (19, 26), or in clinical populations (e.g., Field et al., 1998; Schneider et al., 2001) (14, 27), some have (often incidentally) uncovered the stressful effects of techno and rock music, i.e., the type of music found in violent computer games. At the psychological level, studies have consistently reported increases in self-ratings of aggressiveness, hostility, tension, anxiety, discomfort, and reduced caring, relaxation, and the like, after listening to rock or grunge music, with respect to silence or classical music (Burns et al., 1999, 2002) (9, 10). The purpose of this study was to specifically examine the effects of built-in music on physiological arousal levels (such as systolic and diastolic blood pressure, heart rate, respiratory frequency, and body temperature) in violent and non-violent computer games playing.

Methodology

Participants:

Participants of this study were 25 boy adolescents for each group (Violent and Non-Violent Groups) and total numbers of subjects were 50.Mean of participant's age, weight, and height were 17.6, 49.36, and 161.68 for violent group and 17.36, 50.32, and 161.04 for non-violent group, respectively. Most participants had not had any experience with computer games.

Materials and apparatus:

Counter strike software used for violent group and FIFA 2005 used for non-violent group. For the Silence condition, the (built-in) music was set to a value of 0. For the Music condition, the music was set to a maximal value.

Procedure:

Participants were asked to avoid eating for at least a half hour prior to the experiment, and to avoid intense physical exercise for at least one hour before the experiment took place. They were tested individually, and distributed in a quasi-random manner into two groups (violent and non-violent groups), which each group exposure to two different experimental conditions (Silence or Music).

Upon arrival, the participants were asked to fill a questionnaire of general information. They were then asked to sit in front of the computer (about 40cm from the screen) in a quiet room lit with soft light, where instructions were given. The participants were then instructed to put on headphones, and were allowed to practice for 5 minutes, with the possibility to ask questions to the experimenter, who remained in the room. All participants were familiarized with the game in the same condition as the experimental condition (that is, practice in Silence condition for the Silence group, and practice with Music for the Music group). Participants in the Silence group were not told beforehand that there would be no sound present. After the practice session, participants rested for 10 minutes. A first measure of arousal variables (such as systolic and diastolic blood pressure, heart rate, respiratory frequency and body temperature) was taken at the end of this period (prior playing). Participants were then left alone in the room and played for 30 minutes (music condition) Arousal variables measured in 15 minutes after start of play, again (during playing), and immediately after the end of play these variables measured again (after playing).

After one day, participants' exposure to computer games related to his group (silent condition), and arousal variables measured alike music condition.

Results

Pretest results:

Comparison the means of pretest (Independent T Test) showed that doesn't be significant difference between groups.

Comparison of prior-during-after playing:

1- Music condition: Comparison results of prior-during-after playing (One-Way Repeated ANOVA) showed that there was significant difference in the means of prior-during playing of the violent group in systolic and diastolic blood pressure, heart rate, and respiratory frequency variables, but there wasn't significant difference in the means of prior-during playing of the violent group in body temperature variable. Also, there wasn't significant difference in the means of prior-during playing of the non-violent group in arousal variables.

Also, there wasn't significant difference in the means of prior-after playing of the violent and non-violent groups in anyone of variables [Table 1, and Figures 1, 2].

Table (1) means of arousal scores (music group)

Variables	Groups	Prior playing	During playing	After playing
SBP	Violent	117.84	128.52	117.88
	Non-violent	118	118.2	118.08
DBP	Violent	77.6	87.92	77.8
	Non-violent	78.56	78.72	78.04
HR	Violent	63.16	73.92	63.36
	Non-violent	63.04	63.20	63.08
RF	Violent	20.64	25.08	20.60
	Non-violent	20.48	20.60	20.52
BT	Violent	36.956	36.946	36.960
	Non-violent	36.956	36.968	36.956

Level of Significance $P<0.05$

Table (2) means of arousal scores (silent group)

Variables	Groups	Prior playing	During playing	After playing
SBP	Violent	117.84	118.31	117.80
	Non-violent	118	118.15	118.11
DBP	Violent	77.6	78.75	77.78
	Non-violent	78.56	78.70	78.09
HR	Violent	63.16	63.90	63.50
	Non-violent	63.04	63.20	63.13
RF	Violent	20.64	21.20	20.80
	Non-violent	20.48	20.60	20.62
BT	Violent	36.956	36.959	36.962
	Non-violent	36.956	36.963	36.959

Level of Significance $P<0.05$

Figure (1) Means of violent group (Music condition)

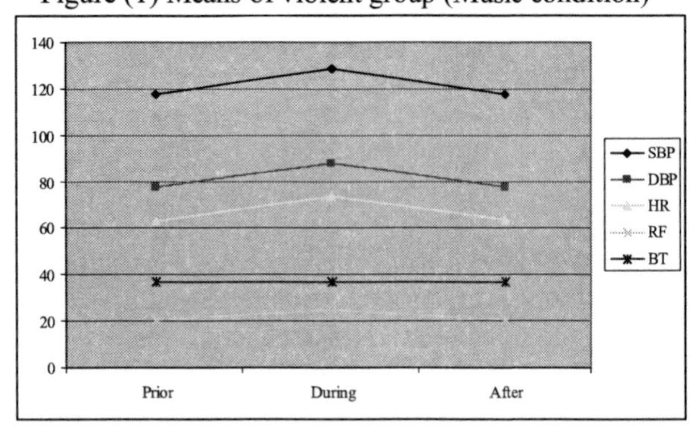

Figure (2) Means of non-violent group (Music condition)

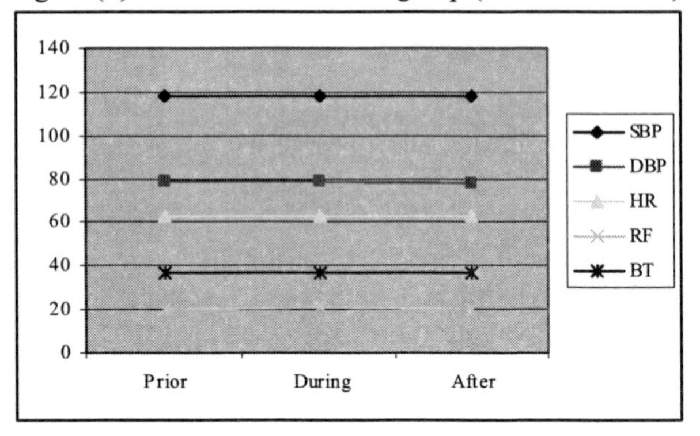

Figure (3) Means of violent group (silent condition)

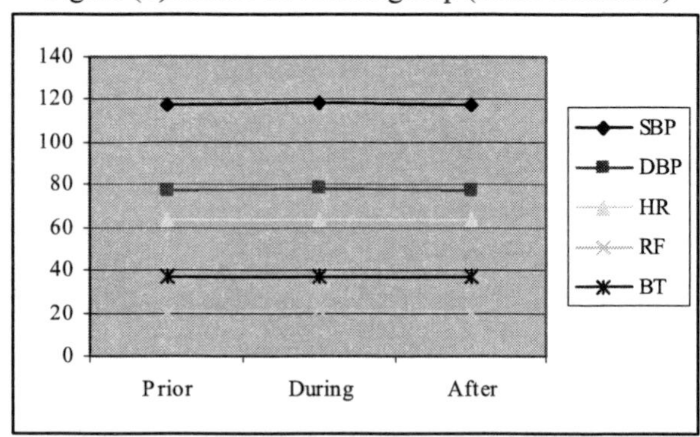

Figure (4) Means of non-violent group (silent condition)

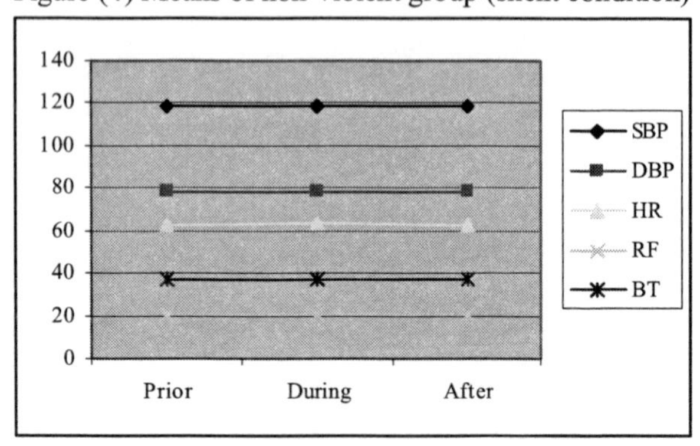

2- Silent condition: Comparison results of prior-during-after playing (One-Way Repeated ANOVA) showed that there wasn't significant difference in the means of prior-during playing of the violent and non-violent groups in anyone of variables. Also, there wasn't significant difference in the means of prior-after playing of the violent and non-violent groups in anyone of variables [Table 2, and Figures 3, 4].

Discussion and Conclusion

The purpose of this study was determining "The effect of computer games on physiological arousal: the contribution of built-in music". Our study provides the very first empirical support to the informal idea that music is an integral part of the stress generated by computer game playing.

Our findings showed that the built-in sound environment of computer games entails a measurable physiological response in the organism, which is different from the one produced under silence. These findings are in line with the ones of a previous study that examined the physiological effects of this type of music alone. Gerra et al (1998) compared the effects of listening to 30 minutes of techno vs. classical music, and found significant increases in heart rate, systolic blood pressure, and cortisol, among other measures, following techno music listening (15). Other studies have reported similar findings regarding rock and heavy metal music (e.g., Burns et al., 1999; 2002; Salamon et al., 2003) (9, 10, 26). Since techno and rock music are typical in "first-person shooter" games, which was used here and is representative of violent computer games available on the market, it is more than likely that the effects found here are representative of those that would be obtained with other games.

Violent computer and video games playing has been connected to violent behavior. An updated meta-analysis from Anderson (2004), looking at 32 independent samples and involving 5,240 participants, most of which were under 21 years of age, has revealed that exposure to violent video games similar to the one used here is significantly and causally linked to increases in aggressive behavior, cognition and affect (6). According to General Aggression Model (GAM) arousal can play an important role of the produce of aggression after playing a violent video game (3). Results of this study showed that increased arousal variables arising from playing a violent computer game turned down to initial state and there was not significant difference with initial state (prior playing). Therefore, we can tell that increasing arousal during playing a violent computer game can not be an important factor in increasing aggression, and must be searched the role of another factors.

As results of this study and another studies are showed, violent computer games resulted in significant increase on physiological arousal. But, so far has not been cleared that, would have these changes any bad long term effects on players? This is a problem that yet in this field has not been cleared up, and therefore need to longitudinal studies.

Reference:

1- Anderson, C.A and Dill, K.E. (2000) "Video games and aggressive thoughts, fillings, and behavior in the laboratory and in life" Journal of Personality and Social Psychology, 78 (4), 772-790.

2- Anderson, C.A and Buchman, B.J. (2001) "Effect of violent video game on aggressive behavior, aggressive cognition, aggressive affect, physiological arousal, and prosocial behavior: A meta-analytic review of the scientific literature" Psychological Science, 12, 353-39.

3- Anderson, C.A. and Buchman B.J. (2002) "Human aggression" Annual Review of Psychology, 53, 27-51.

4- Anderson, C.A. (2003) "Video games and aggressive behavior" Iowa State University, in press.

5- Anderson, C.A and Murphy, C.R. (2003) "Violent video games and aggressive behavior in young women" Aggressive Behavior, 29, 423-429.

6- Anderson, C. A (2004) "An update on the effect of playing violent video games" Journal of Adolescents, 27, 113-122.

7- Bartholow, B.D and Anderson, C.A. (2002) "Effect of violent video games on aggressive behavior: Potential sex differences" Journal of Experimental Social Psychology, 38, 283-290.

8- Buchman, B.J and Anderson, C.A. (2002) "violent video games and hostile expectations: A test of the general aggression model" Personality and Social Psychology Bulletin, 12, 1679-1686.

9- Burns, J., Labbe, E., Williams, K., McCall, J. (1999) "Perceived and physiological indicators of relaxation: as different as Mozart and Alice in chains" Applied psychophysiology and biofeedback 24 (3), 197–202.

10- Burns, J.L., Labbe, E., Arke, B., Capeless, K., Cooksey, B., Steadman, A., et al. (2002) "The effects of different types of music on perceived and physiological measures of stress" Journal of music therapy 39 (2), 101–116.

11- Cook, B.B., Treiber, F.A., Mensah, G., Jindal, M., Davis, H.C., Kapuku, G.K. (2001) "Family history of hypertension and left ventricular mass in youth: possible mediating parameters" American journal of hypertension 14 (4 Pt. 1), 351–356.

12- Denot-Ledunois, S., Vardon, G., Perruchet, P., Gallego, J. (1998) "The effect of attention load on the berating pattern in children" International Journal of Psychophysiology, 29 (1), 13-21.

13- Ditto, B., Miller, S.B. (1989) "Forearm blood flow responses of offspring of hypertensive to an extended stress task." Hypertension 13 (2), 181–187.

14- Field, T., Martinez, A., Nawrocki, T., Pickens, J., Fox, N.A., Schanberg, S. (1998) "Music shifts frontal EEG in depressed adolescents" Adolescence 33 (129), 109–116.
15- Gerra, G., Zaimovic, A., Franchini, D., Palladino, M., Guicastro, G., Reali, N., Maestri, D., Caccavari, R., Delsignori, R., Brambilla, F. (1998) "Neuroendocrine responses of healthy volunteers to btechno-musicQ: relationships with personality traits and emotional state" International Journal of Psychophysiology 28, 99–111.
16- Griffiths, M.D and Dancaster, I. (1995) "The effect of type A personality on physiological arousal while playing computer game" Addictive Behavior, 20 (4), 543-548.
17- http://www.aap.org/advocacy/releases/jstmtevc.htm
18- Hubert, W., de Jong-Meyer, R. (1992) In: Kirschbaum, C., Hellhammer, D.H., Read, G.F. (Eds.), "Salivary Cortisol Responses During Video-Game-Induced Success and Failure" In Assessment of Hormones and Drugs in Saliva in Biobehavioral Research. Hogrefe and Huber Publishers, Gfttingen, pp. 219–223.
19- Khalfa, S., Dalla Bella, S., Roy, M., Peretz, I., Lupien, S. (2003) "Effects of relaxing music on salivary cortisol level after psychological stress" Annals of New York Academy of Sciences 999, 374–376.
20- Koepp, M.J., Gunn, R.N., Lawrence, A.D., Cunningham, V.J., Dagher, A., Jones, T., Brooks, D.J., Bench, C.J., Grasby, P.M. (1998) "Evidence for striatal dopamine release during a video game" Nature, 393 (6682), 266-268.
21- Markovitz, J.H., Raczynski, J.M., Wallace, D., Chettur, V., Chesney, M.A. (1998) "Cardiovascular reactivity to video game predicts subsequent blood pressure increases in young men: The CARDIA Study" Psychosomatic Medicine, 60, 186-191.
22- Mazur, A., Susman, E., Edelbrock, S. (1997) "Sex difference in testosterone response to a video game contest" Evolution and Human Behavior 18, 317–326.
23- Modesti, P.A., Pela, I., Cecioni, I., Gensini, G.F., Semeri, G.G., Bartolozzi, G. (1994) "Hange in blood pressure reactivity and 24-hour blood pressure profile occurring at puberty" Angiology, 45 (6), 443-450.
24- Mounier-Vehier, C., Girard, A., Consoli, S., Laude, D., Vacheron, A., Elghozi, J.L. (1995) "Cardiovascular reactivity to a new mental stress test: the maze test" Clinical autonomic research 5 (3), 145–150.
25- Musante, L., Raunikar, R.A., Treiber, F., Davis, H., Dysart, J., Levy, M., Strong, W.B. (1994) "Consistency of children's hemodynamic responses to laboratory stressors" International Journal of Psychophysiology, 17 (1), 65-71.
26- Salamon, E., Bernstein, S.R., Kim, S.A., Kim, M., Stefano, G.B. (2003) "The effects of auditory perception and musical preference on anxiety in naive human subjects" Medical science monitor 9 (9), CR396–CR399.
27- Schneider, N., Schedlowski, M., Schurmeyer, T.H., Becker, H. (2001) "Stress reduction through music in patients undergoing cerebral angiography" Neuroradiology 43 (6), 472–476.
28- Segal, K.R and Dietz, W.H. (1991) "Physiological response to playing a video game" American Journal of Diseases of Children, 145 (9), 1034-1036.
29- Skosnik, P.D., Chatterton, R.T., Swisher, T., Park, S. (2000) "Modulation of attentional inhibition by norepinephrine and cortisol after psychological stress" International Journal of Psychophysiology, 36 (1), 59-68.

Interactive Robots, Toys and Games

Cooperative Behavior in Robot Soccer using Cognitions from Game Theory and Socionics

Birgit Koch
Department of Informatics
University of Hamburg
Vogt-Koelln-Str. 30
D 22527 Hamburg, Germany
E-mail: koch@informatik.uni-hamburg.de

KEYWORDS

Interactive Robots, Mobile Robots, Group Behavior, Intelligent Agents.

ABSTRACT

Robot soccer has proven to be an interesting and challenging test bed for research in distributed artificial intelligence, multi-agent systems and robotics. Nowadays cooperation among robots is fundamental and social considerations get more and more important not only to match the best teams in RoboCup but also to industrial robots. This paper presents some approaches using cognitions from game theory and socionics to foster cooperative behavior in robot soccer with the focus on non-communicative cooperation.

INTRODUCTION

Heinzelmaennchen are small fictive German creatures that work industriously and secretly for humans. Legend from Cologne has it that Heinzelmaennchen come out of their hiding places at night to perform the work for people whom they like. But if they are observed or disturbed they leave for good (Kopisch 1848).

Fig. 1. Heinzelmaennchen as Social Agents (Stein Collectors International 2006)

Because of the issues that arise from the embodiment of agents operating in real environments multi-agent systems consisting of robots are often called multi-robot systems (Iocchi et al. 2001).

In the last years there is a tendency to use social interaction as model for the construction of multi-agent systems. The origins of distributed artificial intelligence are the social distribution of knowledge on several intelligent and autonomous agents, the emergence of knowledge in communication between agents and its constitution over forms of coordination and exchange that are based on different social structures (Müller 1993, Gilbert and Conte 1995, Bendifallah et al. 1988, Malsch et al. 1996).

Multi-agent systems behave like a social unit from independent elements (Werner 1989) and therefore various complex and dynamic tasks can be fulfilled. Examples are the distributed information search in the internet, the simulation of swarm behavior in biology or the coordination of game and evasion maneuvers of soccer playing robots.

SOCIAL BEHAVIOR IN ROBOT SOCCER

Robot soccer has proven to be an interesting and challenging test bed for research in distributed artificial intelligence, multi-agent systems and robotics. Nowadays cooperation among robots seems to be fundamental and social considerations get more and more important to match the best teams in robot soccer.

Not only in robot soccer there are tasks that require multi robots to be accomplished. This situation arises when the robots can accomplish different functions, but also when they have the same capabilities. Moreover, even when a single robot can achieve the given task the possibility of deploying a team of robots can improve the performance of the overall system (Iocchi et al. 2001). The use of multiple robots is often suggested to have several advantages over single robot systems: problems can be solved faster, more easily, more fault-tolerant or more reliably. On the other hand, dealing with a robot group can make tasks more difficult (e.g. possible interferences between the robots and collisions with other robots).

Deciding how to act in a multi-robot environment is a challenging problem. If humans play soccer they are engaged in collaborative actions on at least two levels and in both, a balance between individual self-interest and collective endeavor must be found (Schafer 2003). On the first level, which is the main level in robot soccer, players have to collaborate with their team members. This involves the knowledge about positioning of the team members, their anticipation of actions and which player is placed best. In human soccer there is also a certain element of competition between the players of the same team. This element is missing in robot soccer teams until now. A human player would not pass the ball to another team member if he himself has a chance of success. However two competing soccer teams are not always competitors. Both teams have to observe certain rules and they sometimes add some informal ones, e.g. playing the ball over the sideline if a player of the other team is down injured (Schafer 2003).

Optimal behavior for one robot depends upon the behavior of the other robots, which may have to decide how to act as well. Multi-robot environments are therefore non-stationary, violating the traditional assumption underlying single-agent acting. In addition, robots in complex tasks like playing soccer have limitations that prevent them from acting optimally, which complicates the already challenging problem. A robot must effectively compensate for its own limitations while exploiting the limitations of the other robots.

Let us take the Fourlegged-League in RoboCup for an example. In this league a team of four identical Sony Aibo educational robots forms a team. Heterogeneity can only be given by different software control. Most of the teams use different roles in the game: goalkeeper, forward player and defender. These roles can be assigned statically to the robots. In order to support cooperative behavior in the team the social roles are often assigned to the team members dynamically according to the status of the environment, what seems to be more efficient and more robust (Nebel 2001, Stone and Veloso 1999). Using different roles helps to obstruct each other when approaching to the ball but for effective games more cooperation and coordination is necessary.

COOPERATION WITHOUT COMMUNICATION IN ROBOT SOCCER

In general, enhancing the existing approaches by social behavior (e.g. by dynamically adapting different strategies during the game) has been considered an important aspect of improving the game. In robot soccer games most of the time the robots coordinate their actions by communication via WLAN. On one hand the implementation of interaction on model-level is very comfortable but on the other hand communication consumes resources of the robot. Moreover communication might (temporarily) not be possible, be restricted to low bandwidth, or possible only over short distances. This raises the question if there is a possibility to get social behavior without communication. For getting an answer socionics and game theory can help.

Socionics is the interdisciplinary usage of methods of sociology and computer science - models, simulations, distributed agent systems - for the design and exploration of new distributed computer systems, for the study of sociological questions and for the design and research of hybrid systems (consisting of social players and software agents).

The participant model developed by Hewitt (Hewitt 1977) assumes that each component of a distributed system is closed with exception of the communication channels (to send and receive messages) and thus the component is not observable for other participants of the system. This model appears not suitable for the coordination of multi-robot systems, since there is no superior instance that has enough knowledge to transfer meaningful tasks to the participants.

In small groups that must fulfill certain tasks emergent hierarchies frequently develop, thus someone takes over the guidance of the group. This leader of the group is neither given from the beginning, nor predetermined by certain characteristics of the participants, but results from the interaction. Examples of self-organization could be soccer or rescue teams, but also teams in a company or circles of friends etc. Fundamentally the efficiency of the team increases with the result that there should be guidance, but it is not clear who takes it over. In game theory such situations are simulated with the game "Battle of the Sexes": two participants must agree on something, with one participant giving way to the other. The profit of cooperation is thereby bigger as the loss by giving way. The game deals more around the symbolism than around actual profit. Let's see an example of "Battle of the Sexes" with two robots:

Imagine two robots of the same team: Robot A and Robot B (see Fig. 2). Robot A would like to score a goal itself while Robot B would like to pass the ball to another robot of his own team who is better positioned. Both robots would prefer that their team scores a goal they only differ in the way how to score the goal. What can the robots do to come to an agreement if they cannot communicate (e.g. WLAN broke down) or if they should not use the communication channel (communication efficiency is critical particularly with scale-up in team-size)?

Fig. 2. Robot A and Robot B in the decision situation

	A scores a goal, B is inactive	B passes to C, A is inactive
A scores a goal, B is inactive	2,1	0,0
B passes to C, A is inactive	0,0	1,2

Table 1. Payoff matrix: Robot A chooses a row, Robot B chooses a column

The payoff matrix of the two robots is shown in Table 1.

The best solution for Robot A is when it scores a goal itself while B is inactive (payoff for Robot A: 2, payoff for Robot B: 1). For Robot B it is more effective when it passes the ball to another robot while A is inactive (payoff for Robot A: 1, payoff for Robot B: 2). The two situations are Pareto efficient. When both robots try to kick the ball, there is a conflict that they hinder themselves and the opponent robot may get the ball. The payoff matrix shows that this is the worst situation for Robot A and Robot B: payoff for Robot A and Robot B: 0.

This game has two pure strategy Nash equilibria, one where Robot A scores a goal directly and Robot B is inactive and another when Robot B passes to another robot and Robot A gives way to Robot B. For the first situation in the game, there is also a Nash equilibria in mixed strategies (using some probability distribution), where Robot A and Robot B do their preferred action more often than the other. For the payoffs listed above, each player does its preferred action with probability 2/3.

The coordination in robot soccer scenarios by methods that use the "Battle of the Sexes" game model must fulfill some restrictive prerequisites that render the utilization in practice more difficult: every robot has to know the environment and the preferences and options of the other robots behavior of its team.

CONCLUSION

Various aspects of cooperation in multi-robot systems have been studied intensively in the past. But non-communicative cooperation techniques are still a little explored problem in robot soccer. This paper showed some approaches of enhancing social behavior in soccer playing robot teams by the integration of research from game theory and socionics. One question is in how far the presented approaches could contribute to create cooperation in groups of robots. The answer depends on what robot soccer league one has in mind. In the simulation leagues, it seems not too difficult to realize the approaches while in the real robot leagues the capabilities of the robots are the limiting factors. As long as the capabilities (e.g. sensor inputs and interpretations) are fuzzy even the best cooperation techniques will not help. However, high flexible coordination is the key in addressing such uncertainties (e.g. cooperative sensing by a multi-robot system).

On the whole non-communicative cooperation in multi-robot systems is an interesting supplement that takes the community closer to the overall goal of RoboCup: Being able to challenge the human soccer world champion in 2050.

Perhaps we will never see any real Heinzelmaennchen for ourselves, but using the approach outlined in this paper we can have Robo-Heinzelmaennchen.

REFERENCES

Bendifallah, S.; F. Blanchard; A. Cambrosio; J. Fujimura; L. Gasser; E.M. Gerson; A. Henderson; C. Hewitt; W. Scacchi; S.L. Star; L. Suchman; and R. Trigg. 1988. *The Unnameble: A White Paper on Socio-Computational Systems*. Unpublished draft manuscript available from Les Gasser, Department of Computer Science, University of Southern California, Los Angeles.

Gilbert, N. and R. Conte. 1995. *Artificial Societies: the Computer Simulation of Social Processes*. London, UCL-Press.

Hewitt, C.E. 1977. "Viewing Control Structures as Patterns of Passing Messages." In: *Artificial Intelligence*, 8, 323-364.

Iocchi, L.; D. Nardi; and M. Salerno. 2001. "Reactivity and Deliberation: A Survey on Multi-Robot Systems." In: *Balancing Reactivity and Social Deliberation in Multi-Agent Systems*, M. Hannebauer, J. Wendler and, E. Pagello, eds. Springer, Berlin.

Kopisch, A. 1848. *All kinds of things of spirit. Maehrchenlieder, Legends and Schwaenke*. Duncker, Berlin.

Malsch, T.; M. Florian; M. Jonas; and I. Schulz-Schaeffer. 1996. „Sozionik: Expeditionen ins Grenzgebiet zwischen Soziologie und Künstlicher Intelligenz." In: *KI* 2/1996, 6-12.

Müller, J. 1993. "Einführung." In: *Verteilte Künstliche Intelligenz. Methoden und Anwendungen*, J. Müller, ed. BI-Wissenschaftsverlag, Mannheim.

Nebel, B. 2001. "Cooperating Physical Robots: A Lesson in Playing Robotic Soccer." In: *ACAI 2001*. M. Luck, et al. eds. LNAI 2086, Springer, 404-414.

Schafer, B. 2003. "It's just not cricket – RoboCup and fair dealing in contract." In: *The Law and Electronic Agents LEA03*. Unipub AS, Oslo, 33-46.

Stein Collectors International. 2006. The Coelln (Berlin) Connection, http://www.steincollectors.org/library/articles/heinzel/heinzelm.html

Stone, P. and M. Veloso. 1999. "Task decomposition, dynamic role assignment, and low-bandwidth communication for real-time strategic teamwork." In: *Artificial Intelligence*, 110(2), 241-273.

Werner, E. 1989. "Cooperating Agents: A Unified Theory of Communication and Social Structure." In: *Verteilte Künstliche Intelligenz. Methoden und Anwendungen*. L. Gasser and M.N. Huhns, eds. Vol. II, Pitman, London, 3-36.

BIOGRAPHY

Birgit Koch studied Computer Science in Germany, Spain and the United Stated. In 2003 she got the diploma in Computer Science from the University of Hamburg in Germany. Her major field of study was the utilization of robotic construction kits in schools and universities.

In 2003 she started working as a PhD student and research assistant at the Department of Computer Science, University of Hamburg, Germany. Her current research interests include teamwork in robotics with game theory, RoboCup and standards in technical education with consideration of gender aspects.

Using Interactive and Edutainment Robots to Encourage Girls in Technical Classes

Birgit Koch
Department of Informatics
University of Hamburg
Vogt-Koelln-Str. 30
D 22527 Hamburg, Germany
E-mail: koch@informatik.uni-hamburg.de

KEYWORDS

Edutainment Interactive Robots, Girls in Technical Classes, Lego Mindstorms Robots, Sony AIBO Robot Dogs.

ABSTRACT

In the effort to meet the steadily changing demands of teaching technology, new methods of learning and teaching are used by which multifarious knowledge and learning techniques can be imparted, practical skills and abilities can be developed and teamwork and creativity are encouraged. A promising attempt is the use of edutainment and interactive robots.

This paper portrays two different educational environments and shows some examples of successful utilization in classes with the focus on encouragement of girls and women in technical studies.

INTRODUCTION

In many Europe countries there is a lack of female students in technical disciplines, especially in engineering, electronics, computer science and physics. The reasons for this problem are various. Most of them deal with today's society and education, e.g. many teachers and parents still tell their daughters that technical professions are not suitable or too difficult for women. Additionally there are only few female examples in engineering disciplines.

To increase the number of women in technical fields in the long run we must first address girls. It is important to realise special projects for girls but it is even more important to introduce gender aspects in every project as the changes in society and education are more continuous.

To overcome the problems, different strategies have been employed to recover popularity in these areas of studies. These measures include presentations of technical work to girls ("Girls' Day"), mentoring projects, cooperation projects of universities and schools, etc.

Statistical studies of freshmen students at universities showed that girls and women are more attracted by interdisciplinary studies such as multimedia, medical informatics and environmental engineering compared to pure technical disciplines.

Experience shows that girls take an interest in edutainment and interactive robots and that learning by doing is an auspicious way of attract girls and women of technical subjects. Edutainment robotics - as a mixture of education, entertainment and robotics - as educational tool to introduce, teach and promote technologically based subjects seems to be one successful strategy (Druin and Hendler 2000).

For over thirty years the "Epistemology and Learning Group" of the Massachusetts Institute of Technology (MIT) has searched for correlations between learning environments and learned skills. One of the results based on the research of Seymour Papert is the idea of using robotic construction kits coupled with user-friendly programming environments (Papert 1980). Starting from the development of turtle robots and the child-friendly programming language LOGO, in 1998 the MIT and the LEGO Company came out with the first LEGO Mindstorms robotic construction kits.

While the utilization of robotic construction kits at schools was analyzed in detail and appreciated (Christaller et al. 2001, Müllerburg 2001), it was often depreciated as a toy and therefore considered irrelevant in the context of universities (Koch 2003). Using "real" robots at universities has the disadvantage of being very expensive so that many students often have to share a single robot. Additionally it can be difficult to motivate the students to work with "real" robots because the orientation time of a complex robot system often requires weeks or even months so the course is nearly over before the students have figured out all the possibilities of the robot. To avoid these obstacles in the courses at the University of Hamburg we decided to use Lego Mindstorms robotic kits for pupils and undergraduate students. The Sony AIBO robot dog has seen use as inexpensive platform for university classes, because it integrates a computer, a vision system, sensors and articulators in a package vastly cheaper than conventional research robots. For these reasons advanced students use Sony AIBO robot dogs as interactive robots in the classes.

ROBOTIC MATERIAL FOR THE CLASSROOM

To understand the relevance of using robotic construction kits and interactive robots at schools and universities it is important to know the elements contained and the possibilities of programming. In the following this is exemplified through the LEGO Mindstorms robotic construction kit and the Sony AIBO robot dog.

Lego Mindstorms Robotic Construction Kits

The LEGO Mindstorms robotic construction kit contains a programmable 'RCX-brick (Hitachi H8/3293-microcontroller with 16 KB ROM and 32KB RAM), two touch sensors, a light sensor, two motors and lots of common LEGO building bricks with gears, wheels, tyres, pins, racks, brackets and cables. Also included are an infrared sender to transmit data between the RCX-brick and a computer, the programming environment Robotics Invention System (RIS) and a construction handbook.

The RCX-brick provides three inputs for sensors, three outputs for motors or lamps, five spots for programs, a LCD-display for the output of short and simple information, four control buttons, an integrated speaker to produce simple acoustic signals and an infrared interface for communication with other RCX units or a computer. Figure 1 shows a RCX-brick with two motors, two touch sensors and a light sensor.

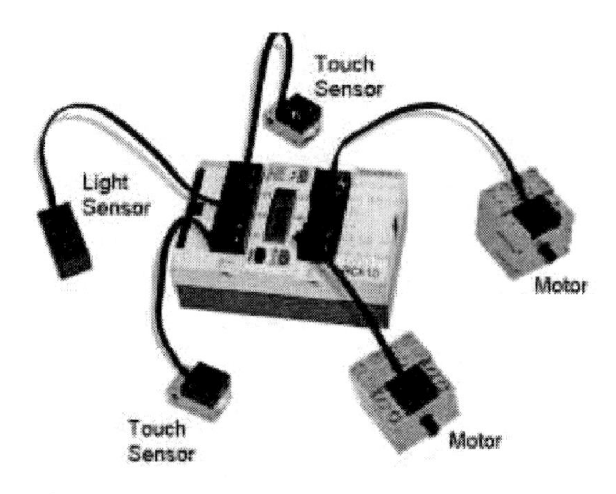

Fig. 1. RCX-brick with sensors and motors

The RCX-brick comes with the firmware installed that is necessary to communicate with a computer to load programs from the computer to the robot. Five simple programs are preinstalled so the robot can be tested immediately after just short periods of configuration. The Robotic Invention System (RIS) is a graphic-based programming environment that works with blocks. Every programming instruction is represented by one block. The blocks are joined by "Drag and Drop" in form of a chain while programming and executed in this order when the program is running. To include sensor-data of the robot, parallel chains of blocks can be used.

Besides the software RIS that comes with the LEGO Mindstorms robotic construction kit and that is directed to children and teenagers without programming skills, several other possibilities to program on an advanced level have been developed by active LEGO online-groups. Most of this software can be downloaded as freeware (Baum 2000, Baum et al. 2000, Erwin 2001, Knudsen 1999).

Sony AIBO Robot Dogs

Initially the AIBO robot dog was created by Sony robotic engineers as an interactive entertainment robot for the home, but nowadays the robots are used worldwide by academics and researchers looking for a low-cost programmable robot platform for education and research. In addition to the RoboCup domain where Sony AIBO robot dogs are used to play soccer in the Fourlegged league (Fourlegged league 2006) the robots are often used to study communication between humans and robots.

In universities the robots are often taken to support classes in artificial intelligence, mobile autonomous systems, decision and behavior processing, voice recognition, image processing and software-development.

In 2001 Sony released the AIBO-SDE (AIBO-Software Development Kit) with three distinct tools: R-CODE, AIBO Remote Framework, and the OPEN-R SDK. All of these tools are free to download and can be used for commercial or non-commercial use (except for the OPEN-R SDK, which is specifically for non-commercial use). An additional Motion Editor makes it possible for users to create motions for the robot. Since the first release of OPEN-R, several additional AIBO programming tools have been developed by university labs (AiboPet's AiboHack Site 2006, Aibo Stuff Website 2006, DogsBody & Ratchet's Domain 2006).

Fig. 2. Sony AIBO Robot Dog

EXAMPLES OF SUCCESSFUL CLASSES

The Project Roberta

The project "Roberta - girls discover robots" (Roberta Homepage 2006) is part of an initiative at the Fraunhofer Institute for Autonomous Intelligent Systems (AIS). The project plans and founds classes to design, construct and program Lego Mindstorms robots with a special emphasis on gender aspects. In toy magazines robotic kits are often related towards boys' interests, e.g. racing cards, fighting machines and space shuttles. The goal of the Roberta project is to find topics that meet the special interest of girls. According to Monika Müllerburg and Ulrike Petersen (Müllerburg and Petersen 2003) the utilisation of subjects that simulate natural phenomena (e.g. communication in bee societies or ant colonies) is a good example for such a topic since girls are more interested in the solution of environmental problems. The classes are not restricted to girls, but they are addressed to the interests of girls. Evaluations proved the positive side-effect that boys also benefit from the course concept. This is not the result in the reverse case. The evaluations also showed that "girls who participated in a short 2-hour course, do now believe - what they did not believe before - that they have the ability to become a computer expert in future if they really want to be one" (Müllerburg and Petersen 2003).

In addition to the courses the Roberta team developed educational material and made it available for teachers and tutors. Both the teaching material and the courses were evaluated by gender experts (Petersen et al. 2003). The results of this supplementary research of more than 800 participants (81% girls, 19% boys) showed that the Roberta courses achieved their goals of generating an interest in technology, encouraging the children's willingness to learn, strengthening their self-confidence, and making learning fun for them. Of the girls participating, 94% said the course was fun, 88% would recommend it to their friends, and 74% would like to have further courses. The Roberta project was even more successful in gender-sensitive courses (98%, 94%, 85%).

On the whole the results show that Roberta courses arouse interest, promote the willingness for learning and strengthen the self-confidence of the girls.

Fig. 3. A Roberta robot

Robots in classes at Summer Universities for Women in Computer Science

At summer universities for women in computer science in Germany, Austria and New Zealand (Oechtering et al. 2004) we tested different concepts of classes with edutainment robots. In most of the classes we used Sony AIBO robot dogs but sometimes also Lego Mindstorms robots. As the classes only last one week, easy to learn programming environments for the Sony AIBO robot dogs had to be used, e.g. R-Code in combination with the Motion Editor. R-Code is a scripting language that can be interpreted by the Sony AIBO robot dog. While R-Code does not allow the detailed control that the OPEN-R SDK (a C++ based programming development environment) has, what it lacks in power it makes up for in simplicity.

In the classes girls and women experimented with changes in the robots' behavior and added some new motions. Even students with no prior robotics or programming experience found it easy to program actions and create movements for the robot. Through the use of a graphical user interface in the motion editor, they could manipulate a 3-dimensional model of the robot to edit the robot's motions in a manner that resembled the editing of video footage.

One of the projects for the students was the task "Let the robots dance". The students had to take their favourite piece of music and program the robots to dance according to the music. Additionally they shot a film of their dancing robot.

The evaluation of the classes showed that most of the participating girls and women were so motivated that they wanted to have a subsequent class for advanced users (Koch and Lademann 2001) Even though in the beginning not all robot exercises in the classes worked well due to hardware and software problems the students were never frustrated to give up the class. Those problems worked rather as an incentive and challenge to go on with the class.

All the projects also worked well with participating boys. Even the task of dancing robots was very famous in groups with male students.

CONCLUSION

Education and training in technology are important requirements for the future abilities of a society. There is a decreasing interest of students in technical professions, and the rate of women in those studies and professions is still too low. Edutainment and interactive robots can be used successfully as part of a strategy to encourage girls and women to work in engineering, physics, electronics and computer science. The evaluations of the projects "Roberta" and "Robots in summer universities for women in computer science" showed that introducing robots as educational technology in classrooms to motivate girls and women can be very effective.

REFERENCES

AiboPet's AiboHack Site. 2006. Available: http://www.aibohack.com/

Aibo Stuff Website. 2006. Available: http://aibostuff.iofreak.com/

Baum, D. 2000. *Dave Baum's Definitive Guide To LEGO Mindstorms*. Apress.

Baum, D.; M. Gasperi; R. Hempel; and L. Villa. 2000. *Extreme MINDSTORMS. An Advanced Guide to LEGO Mindstorms*. Apress.

Christaller, T.; G. Indiveri; and A. Poigne. 2001. *Proceedings of the Workshop on Edutainment Robots 2000, 27th - 28th September 2000, St. Augustin, German*. GMD Report 129, GMD-Forschungszentrum Informationstechnik GmbH.

DogsBody & Ratchet's Domain. 2006. Available: http://www.dogsbodynet.com/

Druin, A. and J. Hendler. 2000. *Robots for kids: Exploring new technologies for learning*. New York, Morgan Kaufmann.

Erwin, B. 2001. *Creative projects with LEGO Mindstorms*. Addison-Wesley.

Fourlegged league. 2006. Available: http://www.tzi.de/4legged/bin/view/Website/WebHome

Knudsen, J.B. 1999. *The Unofficial Guide to LEGO Mindstorms Robot.* O'Reilly.

Koch, B. 2003. *Einsatz von Robotikbaukästen in der universitären Informatikausbildung am Fallbeispiel ‚Hamburger Robocup: Mobile autonome Roboter spielen Fußball'.* Diplomarbeit. Department of Informatics, University of Hamburg.

Koch, B. and B. Lademann. 2001. "Erfahrungen mit LEGO Mindstorms bei der Informatica Feminale." In: *Abiturientinnen mit Robotern und Informatik ins Studium, AROBIKS Workshop, Sankt Augustin, Schloss Birlinghoven, 14th-15th December 2000*, GMD Report 128, M. Müllerburg, ed. GMD - Forschungszentrum Informationstechnik GmbH, 93-95.

Müllerburg, M. 2001. *Abiturientinnen mit Robotern und Informatik ins Studium, AROBIKS Workshop, Sankt Augustin, Schloss Birlinghoven, 14th-15th December 2000.* GMD Report 128, GMD - Forschungszentrum Informationstechnik GmbH.

Müllerburg, M. and U. Petersen. 2003. "Robots and Girls – A Promising Alliance." In: *ERCIM News No. 53*, 32-33.

Oechtering, V.; S. Alder; F. Jolk; R. Klempien-Hinrichs; B. Söhle; M. Oelinger; A. Kreuzeder; A. Stiftinger; and A. Hinze. 2004. "Summer Universities for Women in Computer Science." 5th Grace Hopper Celebration of Women in Computing. Chicago, Illinois, USA.

Papert, S. 1980. *Mindstorms: Children, Computers and Powerful Ideas.* New York, Basic Books.

Petersen, U.; M. Müllerburg; and G. Theidig. 2003. *Girls and Robots - A Promising Alliance.* WIR-Konferenz: Frauen in der industriellen Forschung. Berlin.

Roberta Homepage. 2006. Available: http://www.roberta-home.de

BIOGRAPHY

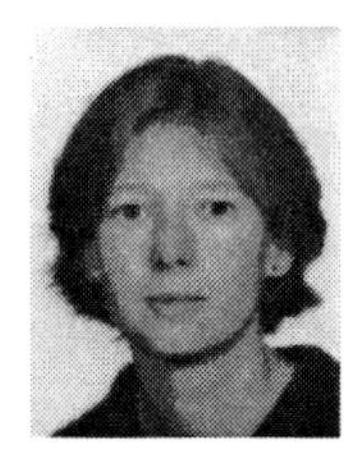

Birgit Koch studied Computer Science in Germany, Spain and the United Stated. In 2003 she got the diploma in Computer Science from the University of Hamburg in Germany. Her major field of study was the utilization of robotic construction kits in schools and universities.

In 2003 she started working as a PhD student and research assistant at the Department of Computer Science, University of Hamburg, Germany. Her current research interests include teamwork in robotics with game theory, RoboCup and standards in technical education with consideration of gender aspects.

THE REAL GUITAR HERO

Eoin Mullan
Sonic Arts Research Centre
Queen's University Belfast
Email: emullan11@qub.ac.uk

Graham McAllister
Sonic Arts Research Centre
Queen's University Belfast
Email: g.mcallister@qub.ac.uk

ABSTRACT

Recently there has been increased interest in new and novel controllers for computer games. The Guitar Hero computer game became popular by using a unique controller that resembles a guitar however guitarists desire a computer game that uses the output from a real electric guitar to interact with a computer game. Such a game would appeal to guitarists who wish to use their skills in a new way and also to guitar tutors as a means of motivating beginner students. The complexity lies in using the signal from the guitar in a way that; i) works robustly in real-time, ii) is intuitive to the player, and iii) requires skill on the players part, thereby playing the game will challenge and improve the player. Two games have been created that use the guitar's pitch value to determine what happens in the computer game. The first game listens for notes from a chosen scale to control a paddle's movement in a tennis game (Pong style). The second game listens for specific sequences of notes (licks) to be played in order to control the movements of a marble on an obstacle course. The paper will present the development of this technology and also discuss the implications for new game concepts.

INTRODUCTION

In recent years, a series of computer games have been released that have introduced novel controllers as their input method. Such examples include Dance Dance Revolution, Donkey Konga, Drum Mania, Guitar Freaks and Guitar Hero. The success of these games is largely attributed to the new controller type offered (Blaine 2005), however the associated game design is also a factor. Whilst these games offer a new type of challenge to gamers, the controllers must be designed so that a first time user will find the controls intuitive and be able to get instant results with the game. This limits the amount of subtlety that controllers can be designed to detect. Another problem is that the skills gained from playing these games are not directly transferable to any other application.

This project addresses these issues by creating two computer games that are controlled by the audio signal from an electric guitar. This system offers two key advantages; firstly it allows players to use their full skills range and expressive gestures that they have developed for their instrument. Secondly, it motivates new learners of the guitar to practice scales and other licks via an interactive and immersive game.

There are many different types of information that can be taken from a guitar's audio signal (e.g. signal strength, pitch and rhythm information) and many conceivable ways of using such information to control some of the many aspects of a computer game. Possible ways of using this information include triggering game actions and providing parameters for game actions. Three main factors were considered when deciding the sort of application that would be created.

1) Can it be implemented in a way that is robust and runs in real time? This is especially important when considering what information is to be taken from the guitar's audio signal and how this is done. There are algorithms available for extracting all sorts of information from an audio signal but not all of them can be implemented in real time and some of them extract information that may not be useful for controlling a computer game.
2) Will the game play seem intuitive to the player? The game should be designed so there is a natural relationship between what the player plays and what happens on the screen. This consideration should affect what data is taken from the audio signals and what type of game is created.
3) Will the game require skill to play? The motivation for this project is to make a game for guitarists and therefore it should require some skill to play. The information taken from the audio signal should allow the program to detect when something skilful has been played and playing something skilful should correspond to something advantageous to the player happening in the game. If this is the case more skilful players should be better at the game and this will encourage players to improve themselves.

As a result, two games have been developed that use an electric guitar as an input device, these shall now be discussed.

GUITAR GAME 1 – PONG

The main aim of Guitar Pong was to use the output signal from an electric guitar to control a paddle in the classic game of Pong.

Pong Design

The guitar-based Pong game was created through the following steps:

- Design of an algorithm to track the guitar's pitch. This must work in real-time and therefore have low latency.
- Creation of the classic Pong game that is controlled via keyboard.
- Adapting the Pong game to accept input from the guitar (via the developed pitch detection algorithm).

The game was created so the user can choose any musical key and scale with which to play the game. When the game begins, the user plays any note in the selected scale. Thereafter if they play one note lower in the scale, then their paddle will move down the screen and if they play ascending notes, the paddle moves up. Information relating to the current and previous notes played is displayed on screen.

The game was designed so two players can play against each other or one player can play against the computer.

As the graphics are quite simplistic openGL was used to manually code the environment. All physics and collisions were also be manually coded.

Pong Implementation

The Pong game development is divided into two main sections; the pitch detection algorithm and the game which uses this algorithm.

Creating a Pitch Detection Algorithm

Several known pitch detection algorithms were investigated for their suitability to this project (Middleton 2006). They belong in one of two categories:

1) The first method involves transforming the signal into the frequency domain and then looking at the constituent frequencies. This method can calculate the pitch perceived by humans even when this is different to the fundamental frequency of the signal. However, this should not be an issue with a guitar's tone and the method could be considered as being unnecessarily complex and demanding on the processor.
2) The second group of methods work with the signal in the time domain which should be easier to implement in a real-time application such as computer games.

One of these methods (de la Cuadra et al. 2001) (Brossier et al. 2004) considers that if a signal with a particular fundamental frequency is delayed by one period of that frequency and compared to the original, the two signals should match closely. If it is delayed by any other amount the two signals will not match so closely. This is the method adapted and implemented in this pitch detection algorithm.

In order to optimise the algorithm for this application it is firstly assumed that the player's guitar is in tune and therefore unless the player bends a string, they will play a pitch that matches a recognized frequency. Using this approach with the time domain algorithm discussed, when the program receives an input signal, it checks it against all of the pitches it can expect to find. For each potentially played pitch the signal is delayed by one period of that pitches fundamental frequency and compared to the original. To compare the signals, the differences between each sample of the original signal and the corresponding sample in the time shifted signal are totalled. The result of comparing the signal will be a single number and can be thought of as a measure of the likelihood that the signal being listened to is the pitch being checked, the lower the number the more likely. After all pitches have been checked the one that gave the lowest number is taken to be the note played.

This method works particularly well for this program because it is only concerned with sounds that match one of a discrete set of pitches. Processing time is not wasted checking if the sound being heard is of a pitch in between notes and this makes it a very fast method of pitch detection.

Creating the Pong Game

Firstly, the game was created so that it can be played entirely through input from the keyboard. From this base, code to implement the pitch detection algorithm was combined with code to convert the information on the pitch being played into control parameters for the game. This allows the game to be controlled in real-time by the guitarist. The diagram below shows the architecture of the game.

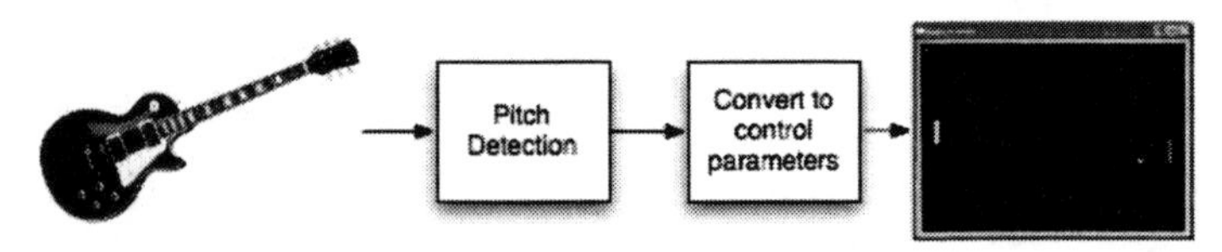

Fig. 1. Architecture of the Real Guitar Hero system.

When the game begins, a menu is displayed offering the player(s) a chance to set up the game options. Using the keyboard, they can choose to have two players playing against each other or one player playing against the computer by pressing '1' or '2'.

While the menu is being displayed the program is also listening to the audio input and if the input signal is above a certain strength it will detect the note being played, allowing the player to set up the scale they want to play with. When the game if first loaded the player is asked to play the root note of the key they wish to play in. When this note has been played the player is then shown a list of all the available scales (e.g. major, minor, pentatonic) and corresponding notes (e.g. A = Major, B = Natural Minor). When the player plays a notes the corresponding scale is picked (e.g. playing F for the key then B for the scale means the player will be playing using the F natural minor scale). Pressing the 'B' button starts the game.

When the player begins the game, they can control their paddle by using the keyboard to make it move up and down.

The program will also be listening to the audio input and if the signal is above a certain strength it will determine the note being played. This information on the note currently being played is what controls the player's paddle movement.

To make the paddle move the player must play a note from the chosen scale. When they do so, all the notes of the scale they are using are displayed along the top of the screen and the note they have just played is underlined to highlight it. Along the bottom of the screen is printed the degrees of the scale (e.g. I II IIIb IV etc for a minor scale) and again the note just played is highlighted. Another result of playing a note for the first time is that the paddle size will increase. This is to encourage players to use the audio input feature.

If the player wants to move their paddle upwards they must play the next note up in the scale from the note that has just been highlighted. If they do so, the paddle will move up and the note they just played will become the highlighted note. Similarly, to move the paddle down the player must play the next note down from the highlighted note in the chosen scale. This moves the paddle down and the new note played becomes the highlighted note.

To move the paddle up or down over a large distance the player must continue to play up or down the scale. The program only responds to one note above or below the highlighted note and therefore if any notes are missed while playing up or down through a scale the paddle will stop moving up or down. This is to encourage the scales to be played accurately.

GUITAR GAME 2 – MARBLE MADNESS

Marble Madness Design

A lick detection algorithm was created utilising the pitch detection algorithm implemented in the guitar pong game. This lick detection algorithm is able to recognise when particular sequences of notes have been played. The licks the algorithm can detect are be stored in such a way that it is easy to modify them or add in new licks.

A game was created to utilise the lick detection algorithm. It consists of a marble that must be controlled as it moves around, over and under obstacles to reach the finish or a course. Playing certain licks causes the marble to move in certain ways giving the guitar player control of the marble.

In order to make the marble as visually impressive as possible it was created using the Unity Game Engine. The Unity Engine has built in physics and collisions detection and makes it easy to create and animate detailed 3D environments.

Marble Madness Implementation

The purpose of this game was to allow the player to control a marble moving along a narrow path. This game is more advanced than the Pong-style game as the player has to perform accurate sequences of notes rather than discreet pitches.

Creating a Lick Detection Algorithm

The purpose of this algorithm is to detect when a specific sequence of notes (usually referred to as a lick amongst guitarists) has been played. To achieve this, a method is firstly needed for storing the licks to be played in the program.

The licks to be detected are all stored in a two dimensional 'note array'. One dimensions spans across the different licks and the other covers all of the notes in one lick. This array holds all of the notes of all the licks in the order which they are to be played in. The algorithm allows for expression to be input via vibrato. Another equally sized 'vibrato array' holds a value of the amount of vibrato, if any, to be played on each note in the corresponding note array position. Before the lick detection algorithm can be discussed, some improvements must be made to the pitch detection algorithm to improve its efficiency and to enable it to detect vibrato.

The pitch detection algorithm previously discussed looks at all the notes that can possibly be played by a guitar and calculates which is the most likely being played at that time. To improve the efficiency of this algorithm and to enable it to detect vibrato, it is now changed so that it checks if the note being played is one of a small group of pitches that are expected to be heard. The advantage here is that fewer pitches will be tested and hence it will process more efficiently. Also, pitches slightly higher or lower than the last pitch heard can be included in the group of pitches to be tested, meaning that the algorithm can detect a string being bent and hence if vibrato is being used.

However, with this approach there is the possibility that the pitch being played is not in the group of pitches that the program expects to hear. Therefore, there needs to be a way to determine if the most likely pitch from a group of pitches tested is actually the pitch being played. This is done by taking the 'error' of the most likely pitch and comparing it against a 'typical error' of the signal in the buffer.

The 'error' of a pitch is a measure of the difference between the signal in the buffer and the same signal shifted by one period of that pitch. Therefore the lower the error of a pitch the more likely it is to be the pitch being played.

The typical error of the signal is the average error of the frequencies 101, 241, 367 and 433 Hz. These frequencies were chosen randomly but ensuring they are not harmonically related. Therefore, even if the frequency being heard matches one of these frequencies, the typical error will not fall by a great amount. The useful characteristic of the typical error is that it rises and falls in proportion with the error of the actual frequency being played.

To determine if the most likely pitch from the group of pitches that were tested is actually the pitch being played the algorithm compares its error against the typical error of the signal in the buffer. If its error is below a certain fraction of the typical error this indicates that this is the note being played.

Having improved the pitch detection algorithm, the group of pitches to be tested is compiled, enabling licks to be detected.

Initially the guitar player will not be playing a lick and so the list of pitches being tested for is made up of the first note of all the licks that can be detected. When the first note of a lick is detected as having been played, the algorithm then concentrates on that lick. It listens for the next note until it is heard or the player is judged to have made a mistake. If vibrato is to be played on a note then the group of pitches being tested for includes several frequencies slightly higher and lower than the last frequency played (Herrera and Bonada 1998). If one of these frequencies is detected as having been played then the pitch has been slightly changed and so a measure of vibrato is increased. When the amount of vibrato reaches the amount indicated by the vibrato array then the program continues to listen for the next note in the note array.

If all notes in a lick are played then the algorithm reports the lick that has successfully been played.

One potential limitation of this lick detection algorithm is that each lick must have a unique first note. However, two different versions of a lick can be detected in the following way. If the note array contains a '-2' then the next note can be either of the following two notes in the lick array. In this case both of the notes that can be played make up the group of pitches to be tested. If one of these notes is played and the rest of the lick is successful completed the algorithm will report that the lick was successfully played and what version was played, i.e. which of the two possible notes was played as part of the lick.

The next section looks at the creation of a game that uses licks being played as a means to control what happens.

Creating the Marble game Using the Lick Detection Algorithm

The marble game was created using the Unity Game Engine. This technology makes it simple to build up a visually impressive 3D environment. The engine can enforce the laws of physics and therefore no code need be written to create a sense of gravity and to detect collisions.

As with the Pong game, this game was firstly created so that it could be played using keyboard input. A marble, to be controlled by the guitarist, was created in a simple obstacle course. Scripts were written to govern the movement of the player's marble enabling the player to move over, under and around obstacles.

The next task was to implement the lick detection algorithm in a way so that it controls the movement of the marble. For licks to be detected the audio buffer must be refreshed and the pitch determined more often than the frames of the game are updated. Therefore a program that implements the lick detection algorithm must run constantly as a separate process. Because there are to be two process running together they must communicate with each other and the following diagram shows how the inter process communication is handled.

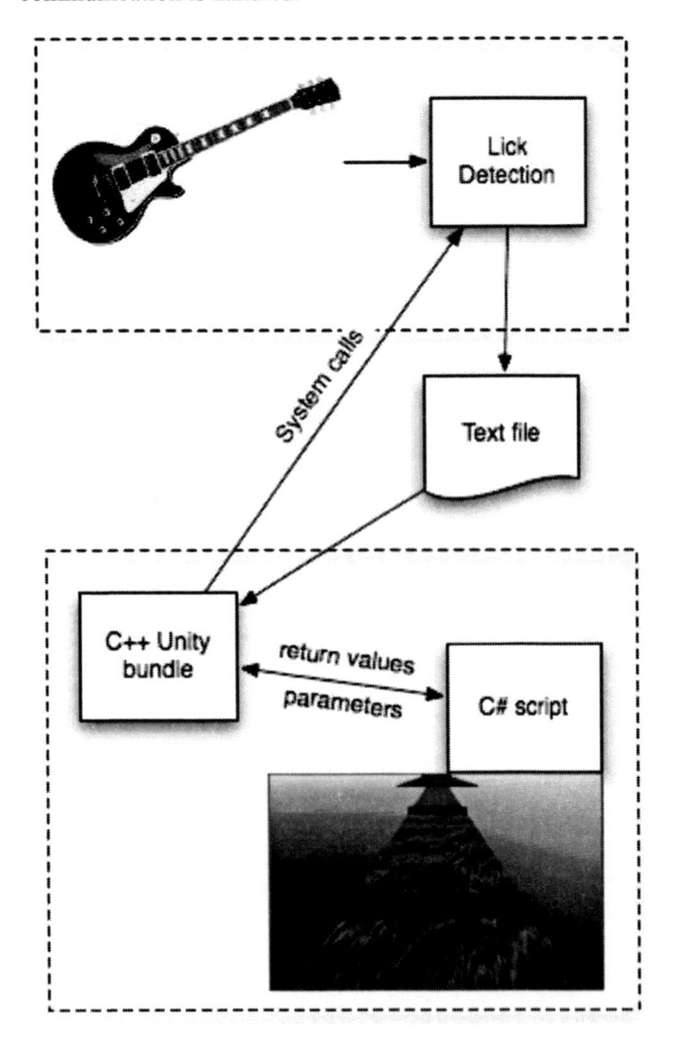

Fig. 2. Architecture of the Marble game.

All elements within the dashed box at the bottom are part of the Unity package and therefore one script can call functions from another script and variables can be passed between scripts as arguments and return values.

Communication with the lick detection program is not so straight forward and is done either through system calls or by writing data to a text file to be read by another program. Here are all the communication events in the order they would happen when the game is played under normal circumstances.

1) The Unity game starts. A startup function in Unity calls a function in the C++ Interface Bundle that starts the lick detection program through a system call.
2) When the lick detection program starts up it writes its process ID to an intermediate text file to be read by the game.
3) The game continually checks for the presence of the intermediate text file until it is created with the process ID of the lick detection program. Once it reads the process ID it stores it and deletes the file it was written in. The game will no longer looks for the lick detector's process ID.
4) As the game is being played the lick detection program is analysing the audio input to detect when a lick is played. When it detects that one has been played a message is written to the intermediate text file with an integer representing which of the licks has been played.
5) During the games execution it is constantly looking for the presence of a text file containing information on a lick that was played. When one is found the game takes the appropriate action, e.g. making the player's marble jump, speed up etc., and the text file is deleted for housekeeping. This process continues as long as the game continues.
6) When the game finishes, a function of the C++ Interface Bundle kills the lick detection program. It does so using a system call and the process ID of the program which was determined earlier.

Through these steps the guitar player is given control of the marble and a means to direct it through the obstacles in the course by playing the correct lick at the correct time.

RESULTS

The result of this project is two computer games that can be controlled entirely through playing any electric guitar and the basis on which to easily develop more such games.

An algorithm has been created to detect what note has been played on a guitar and then developed further to detect when certain sequences of notes, licks, have been played and when vibrato has been used. The algorithm allows for new licks to easily be added so that they will be detected for and for a lick to be played in two different ways.

Two games have been developed to show some of the potential of using audio input to control a computer game.

One game is an adaptation of the classic Pong. The player chooses a key and scale to use and when they start the game, playing up through the notes in the scale will cause the paddle to move upwards, and playing down through the notes in the scale causes the paddle to move down. This game requires some technical skill and playing the game will improve a player's knowledge of music theory as the scale being used is always displayed and the last note played always highlighted. The scale is displayed both in the form of the notes of the scale and the degrees of the scale, again to help improve the players knowledge of music theory.

A second game utilises the lick detection capabilities that have been developed. The game consists of a marble that must be controlled to negotiate obstacles as it advances through a course. Playing different licks causes the marble to take different actions and so playing the correct lick at the correct time will ensure success.

CONCLUSTION

For the first time, as a result of carrying out this project, guitar players can control what happens in a computer game through playing their own guitar. The games created as part of this project are simple from a game design point of view but they show the viability of using pure audio information as the sole input for a game and illustrate the potential for a new genre of games.

As discussed in the introduction other applications have been developed that use new controllers designed to look like musical instruments. However these controllers are essentially alternatively shaped joysticks. The advantage the games developed in this project offer is that their input is the signal from a real electric guitar. Guitars were designed as musical instruments with which to be expressive, not as an input device for a computer game that can be operated by someone with no previous experience or skill. Therefore games developed using the techniques of this project will appeal to guitarists who already have a level of skill and wish to use it in a new scenario.

The algorithms developed with this project are designed to detect skill on a guitarists part and even to detect an expressive gesture i.e. vibrato. This means games developed, such as those in this project can require a high level of skill, and listening to someone playing such a game could sound like an musician being expressive. Also the skills gained in playing one of these games would be transferable to situations were a guitar is traditionally played, making them appeal to beginner guitarists who want to develop their skills for traditional reasons.

Other games have been developed that use the audio signal from a microphone as a control method. However what makes this project different to those games is that the guitar is the sole input device for these games. They are targets created only for musicians. This means they can concentrate on musical ideas such as incorporating information on musical scales or requiring licks from known songs to be played.

This project has opened up many possibilities for future work and these are discussed below. However a follow up validation of this work should be the first priority. This would involve among other things investigating what worked well and what approaches could be rethought.

The advancements made in this project open up many possibilities for developing new types of games. One such type would be educational games. Tutorial games could be created that teach the user how to play for example a particular song. The application could listen to what is being played and report what is being played correctly and what needs to be practiced. It could step through a tricky lick note by note and inform the player where they are going wrong.

Another area that could be developed is multiplayer games. A game could be developed in which two guitarists play together or to sound like a jam, or a battle scenario where players take it in turns to play licks to a backing track.

As was already stated the games created with this project are quite simple and so there is clearly a lot of potential for future work in the design of the games.

There is also scope for future development in the audio input aspect of this project. Presently there are algorithms to track the pitch being played and to detect when certain licks have been played. In the future developments could be made to sense when double stops (two notes played together) have been played, or when a chord has been strummed. This would increase the amount of skill a game could require the player to have and how much a game could develop a player's skill.

At the minute an algorithm can detect how much vibrato has been played on a note but in the future it may be useful to detect the speed and width of the vibrato used. These two parameters could correspond to two control aspects of a game.

Although the time domain pitch detection currently used works well, in the future it may be worth investigating how frequency domain algorithms work. This is likely to be required if an application requires that double stops or chord hits are to be detected. It may also improve how finely small changes in pitch could be detected. Again this could enhance how much skill a game can require, making a game more challenging and more beneficial in terms of improving a player's skill.

The result of this project is that a guitar player can for first time use their own guitar to control a computer game, whilst improving their skills and knowledge of music theory.

REFERENCES

Blaine, T. (2005), The Convergence of Alternate Controllers and Musical Interfaces in Interactive Entertainment, NIME, 2005.

Brossier,P. M., Bello, J. and Plumbley, M. D. (2004). Fast Labelling of Notes in Music Signals, 5th International Conference on Music Information Retrieval.

de la Cuadra, P., Aaron Master, Craig Sapp (2001), Efficient Pitch Detection Techniques for Interactive Music, ICMC.

Middleton, G., Pitch Detection Algorithms, http://cnx.org/content/m11714/latest/ accessed Mar-06.

Herrera, P. and Bonada, J. (1998), Vibrato Extraction and Parameterization in the Spectral Modeling Synthesis Framework, DAFx.

Eoin Mullan has just completed an MA in Sonic Arts at the Sonic Arts Research Centre in Belfast. Previously he has completed a BEng in Electronic and Software Enginieering at the University of Ulster. 'The Real Guitar Hero' was submitted as a Dissertation for the MA in Sonic Arts. Eoin is about to undertake a PhD, researching Audio in Computer Games and Virtual Environments. Eoin's interests include playing and listening to music and game design and development especially relating to audio

Graham McAllister is a lecturer in Music Technology at the Sonic Arts Research Centre, Queen's University Belfast. His research interests include computer games design, HCI and usability. He has recently completed a three-month industrial placement period at computer games technology company Over The Edge in Denmark.

A Novel Humanesque Sudoku Solver

Neil Richardson
School of Computing,
Dublin Institute of Technology,
Kevin St., Dublin 8.

Email: hssa@logix.ie
Web: http://www.bio.ie/hssa

Abstract

This paper presents the Humanesque Sudoku Solver App (HSSA) [Richardson, 2006]. HSSA is a novel application designed to allow users to solve Sudoku problems. It allows the user to interact with the program to solve the Sudoku, and provide helpful hints as to the next logical step a user might take in trying to solve the puzzle. Included is a comparison of brute force methods vs. logical methods to solve Sudoku and an analysis of the HSSA Sudoku solver, and how it mimics the actions of a person, along with details of its other features.

1. Introduction

Sudoku can be dated back to the 18th Century and Leonhard Euler, famous for Euler Cycles. It began in a similar form called 'Latin Squares' which has the same 81 square layout of the common Sudoku today. Sudoku was then published in an American magazine in the 1970's, before making its way to Japan in 1984, where it got the Sudoku name, which means 'Solitary Number'. The puzzle did not attract much attention until 1986 when the mini-grids were then added, and also to reduce the numbers given initially, increasing the difficulty. This became a craze in Japan, as the number grid became the equivalent of the crossword to the west, as crosswords do not adapt well to Japanese. In 1997 a retired judge from New Zealand discovered Sudoku, and developed a computer program which would generate Sudoku puzzles. He pitched the 'new' puzzle to the Sunday Times, who began publishing Sudoku in November 2004. Within a year, Sudoku had begun to appear in every newspaper available, and has since been described as the Rubik's cube of the 21st Century [Pitts, 2005].

One particular area that was studied in creating HSSA was the methods that a person might use in order to solve the Sudoku, and how to translate these methods into functions to be run by a computer, i.e. the artificial intelligence that needed to be incorporated in the program. Programmers have put significant amount of effort into emulating humans when playing other logical games such as chess [Deep Blue, 2006], the methods used to perform this are covered in *Section 4*.

In *Section 2*, the challenges presented in solving Sudoku are examined, *Section 3* covers the general solving of Sudoku, and then *Section 4* covers the methods implemented by HSSA. *Section 5* looks at HSSA itself, and what its features are beyond solving Sudoku, *Section 6* is evaluations of the project, and finally *Section 7* details the conclusions reached and future work intended.

2. Sudoku Challenge

Humanesque Sudoku Solver App is a novel application designed to solve a Sudoku puzzle. HSSA renders the Sudoku from an xml data file with the required structure, and displays it to the user (**Figure 1**). The program will allow a user to play a Sudoku themselves, without using any of the built in solving features and the application will be able to provide them with hints for which step will be next, as they deem necessary. The application comes with 8 Sudoku of varying difficulty to exercise the program, allowing a user to start playing immediately, as well as allowing them to create and load from file, their own Sudoku to be played and solved.

The aim of HSSA is to mimic human behaviour when confronted with Sudoku and in so doing, map out a logical step by step process to solving the puzzle. It will be necessary to examine Sudoku from a point of view other than being a simple problem to be solved. The approach taken is to try and convince the user that an intelligence is at work behind the solving of the puzzle, rather than it just, being a brute force solver of Sudoku, which would not be of any benefit to teaching a person how to play. The HSSA solver solves Sudoku ranging from easy to difficult. As Sudoku is predominantly a logical puzzle, solving it can also be reduced to a logical set of processes and as such, developing an artificial intelligence technique will not be a necessary, but rather, using a set of techniques that emulates human players, the application shows how the human mind, when needed, will adopt techniques used by computers.

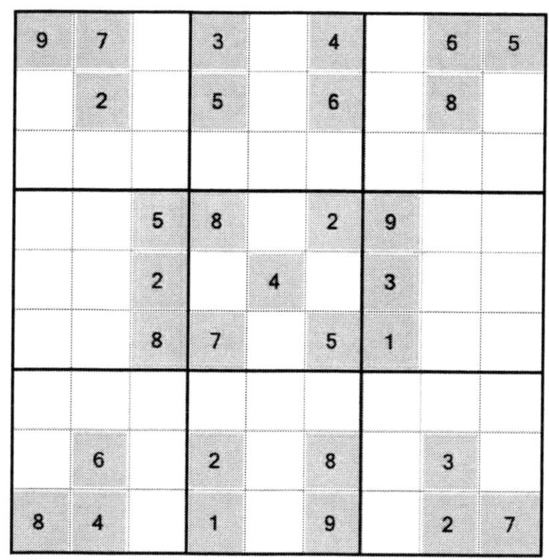

Figure 1: Typical Sudoku rendered in HSSA.

The popularity of Sudoku is helped by the fact that it is such a simple puzzle to learn and play; most people are able to pick up the basic techniques for solving one within minutes. Once someone has been taught the basics, they will often be able to work out some of the more advanced techniques themselves through solving more and more difficult puzzles. It is this logical based solving that seems to be universal, which seems to have endeared so many people to Sudoku. The fact that people from all over the world, given the same problem, will often come up with the same solution is fascinating. Once taught, people will be looking over others shoulders and pointing out what, to them, is an obvious number, but the person could have been stuck for a long time. It is the ability to be able to see the entire puzzle as a number of solvable parts, rather than one impossible piece that allows people to solve them so quickly and elegantly.

A simple internet search will show that most programs currently available are aimed to either solve Sudoku as quickly as possible or allow a user to play Sudoku. The most common technique used when solving is a brute force solver, described in *Section 3*. The challenge to this technique is to develop the code that runs fastest. The other solving technique is to use logic as described in section 4, which emulates the methods used by humans to solve Sudoku. HSSA brings these two approaches together, by allowing the user to solve Sudoku using a clean, fully featured interface, while also allowing the contrasting of various techniques used to solve Sudoku by showing the different paths taken to solve the puzzle and presenting a comparison of the time taken to run the solving algorithm. HSSA also supports larger Sudoku than the typical 9*9 Sudoku, going up to 16*16 comfortably, which allows the solving time of more complex Sudoku to be analysed.

3. Solving Sudoku

The rules of Sudoku are simple:

"Complete the grid so that every row, column and every 3x3 box contains the digits 1 to 9" [Sudoku.com, 2006]

The prerequisites for a puzzle to be a Sudoku is that there can only be one possible solution. Due to this, guessing does not have to be used to solve any Sudoku.

Solving a Sudoku is a logical process. A person looks at the available data and then based on a set of constraints looks at possible numbers to fit into each square. Usually following the Sherlock Holmes [Doyle, 1859-1930] technique of eliminating the impossible, one can find the only possible solution for a single square.

The most common technique to solving a Sudoku is known as *'slicing and dicing'* [Vorderman, 2005], this technique alone can solve some of the simpler Sudoku, and gives beginners the opportunity to ease themselves into the world of Sudoku. The basis of this technique is to use numbers already present to find where another possible number must go.

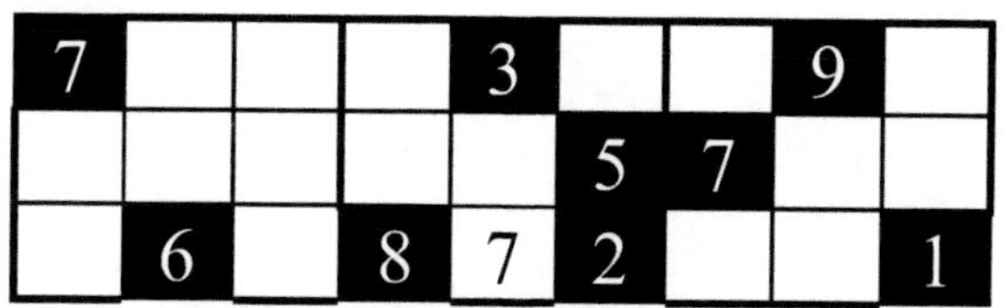

Figure 2: Slicing and Dicing Example.

In the example from **Figure 2**, the 7 with the white background is the solved number. Given that there has to be a 7 on each row eliminates the first and second row, while the middle mini-grid is the only grid without a 7. Given that the third row of the middle mini-grid already has two numbers filled in, then the 7 must go into the last remaining square.

It is this simple logic, that when applied correctly can solve every Sudoku. Other logical techniques, such as described above will be described in section 3, and when combined and adapted into code, allow a computer to solve Sudoku without random guessing.

4. HSSA Implemented Solving Methods

4.1. Brute Force Solving

Much like code breaking, the simplest way to solve a Sudoku is to guess at every possible solution, if a Sudoku was to be converted into a Tree where each node represented a possible option for each square, then the answer would be found by finding the route through the tree with the most depth (If a solution is available). Similarly if there is more than one path of greatest depth, then the puzzle is not a Sudoku, as more than one solution exists. A brute force technique will simply fill in the empty squares with numbers that don't break the rules, and only stops once either every combination has been tried, or the Sudoku grid has been fully filled. Given that a Sudoku only has one solution, this means that once the Sudoku grid has been fully filled in while following the rules, the solution has been found. Many different people have written algorithms for performing this task, as witnessed on many discussion forums, where solvers are debated, and improved [Whirlpool Forums, 2005]. For smaller Sudoku, the performance is quite acceptable, but as Sudoku get larger, the performance of these algorithms drops off geometrically. HSSA uses an algorithm developed by Craig Spitzkoff [Spitzkoff, 2006] as its brute force solver. This solver has good performance as it passes data by reference, keeping memory usage low. The disadvantages are that the algorithm will never reach an endpoint if the puzzle is not a Sudoku, meaning artificial timeouts were used when solving, and whether the solution is unique and truly a Sudoku puzzle is not calculated either, the assumption being that a user will enter a valid Sudoku currently. Improvements in this area are planned for the future.

4.2. Logical Solving

The types of logical solving algorithm used in Sudoku fall into two categories, solvers which fill in squares, and solvers which eliminate options from squares, allowing the first solvers to then fill in squares. These solvers work side by side within HSSA. When the first type of solver fails to solve a square, the second set of solvers then try and eliminate as many options as possible to allow the first type of solver to continue working. Only when both have completely failed, will a brute force solver be relied upon.

In trying to emulate human behaviour, HSSA used as its guide an off the shelf Sudoku book by Carol Vorderman [Vorderman, 2005] as a guide to the most commonly used techniques in solving Sudoku.

The ten techniques described are:

- Slicing and Dicing
- Completing Rows, Columns and Mini-Grids
- The Only One that Fits
- Completing a Row or Column when two Numbers are Missing
- Slicing and Slotting
- Writing Options
- Lone Numbers
- Looking for Single Options
- Twinning
- Triplets

Using these ten techniques, all but the most difficult of Sudoku can be solved, so the challenge was to code algorithms which would be able to perform the same functions as these techniques.

It must be noted that not every technique is applicable to all Sudoku, and some more difficult Sudoku themselves are usually unsolvable unless a particular, lesser known, technique is applied. In optimising the solver, the goal was to use the logical techniques first and only when they fail to fully solve a Sudoku, will a brute force technique be used. Given the amount of techniques available to solve Sudoku, HSSA should be able to solve any Sudoku available, even those for which the logical techniques have not yet been implemented into code, or not yet discovered.

If at all possible, the brute force solver is avoided, as especially when trying to point a direction to go to a user, the order in which they solve the puzzle will not be based in logic, but in random chance.

The solving algorithms are the Lone Number solver and the two Single Options solvers (Mini-Grid & Row and Column) [Stuart, 2006]. These algorithms were developed entirely, and work by examining each number in adjacent row, column and mini-grid and eliminating them from the square being examined. When a square then contains either one number (a lone number), or a row, column or mini-grid has only one instance of a particular number, than that square can be solved.

The eliminating algorithms are generally more complex, but people have already dedicated their time in implementing these techniques into code for others to examine. HSSA currently implements three of these solvers, Naked Pairs, Hidden Pairs and Pointing Pairs, allowing HSSA to solve most medium-difficult Sudoku using its logical solver. The algorithms behind these solvers are freely available as pseudo-code, with a particularly good webpage based example available at http://www.scanraid.com/Sudoku.htm [Stuart, 2006].

5. The HSSA

The program itself is a fully featured installable program, available free of charge from http://www.bio.ie/hssa. The program was developed in C# using the .Net 2.0 framework. The program has a fully developed user interface, with a variety of help options available to the user which show them how to use the program and how to solve Sudoku.

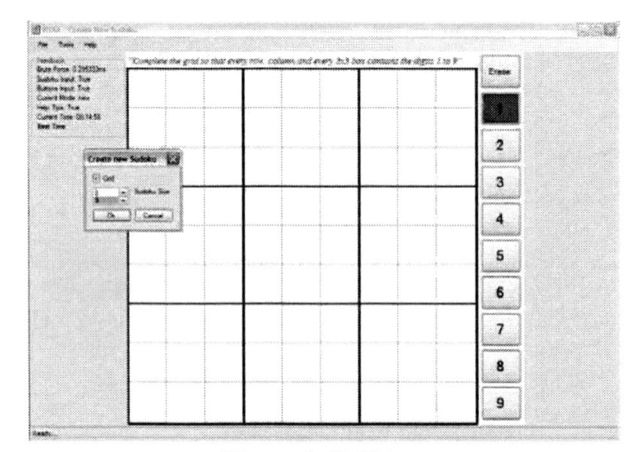

Figure 3: HSSA.

The program has four modes of operation which allow the user to perform various Sudoku activities (creating, playing, solution and solving).

Creating mode allows a user to input their Sudoku, from a paper, or book for example. The program then allows the user to save that Sudoku, and solve it in the playing mode.

Playing mode is where the user solves the Sudoku. In this mode the user can enter their answers onto the Sudoku grid. This is done by selecting the number to be input into the square on the side button bar, and then clicking on the square. The cursor changes to indicate which squares are available to enter a number, and which are part of the puzzle. If the user tries to enter a number into a row, column or mini-grid already containing the same number, then the program will not allow the number to be entered, and highlight the blocking numbers in red. This feature can be toggled on and off, but provides basic help to a user learning to play Sudoku.

Solution mode shows the brute force solver generated solution to the Sudoku. The time taken to solve the Sudoku using this algorithm is shown in the feedback box, and this mode also allows the user to re-run the solver, which will then update the time taken to solve as necessary. As the time taken to solve is stored with a Sudoku, this feature allows a user to compare time taken to solve Sudoku on different hardware.

Solving mode is where a user can learn how the logical techniques used to solve a Sudoku work. It also allows a user to solve the Sudoku using the logical solvers all in one go, so execution time can be compared with that of the brute force solver. Solving mode provides detailed help (also available on the menu bar) to the implemented logical solvers. A user is able to step through solving a Sudoku square by square, and solver by solver, with the program clearly highlighting the changes made to the grid clearly. A user can let the program work out which is the best solver to use, or can choose which solver to use next.

Besides solving Sudoku, the HSSA program also allows the user to:

5.1. Hint the user using the logical solvers
5.2. Give the user the next logically solved number
5.3. Allow the user to enter multiple options into a square
5.4. Print Sudoku
5.5. Show the user the solution to the Sudoku
5.6. Highlight mistakes made by the user
5.7. Tell the user if the Sudoku is completed correctly
5.8. Keep track of time taken to solve Sudoku
5.9. Save all Sudoku details to file including
  5.9.1. User progress in solving the Sudoku
  5.9.2. Sudoku Solution
  5.9.3. Time taken to solve Sudoku
  5.9.4. Best time taken to solve that particular Sudoku
5.10. Upgrade the program when a new release is available
5.11. Show user all options for current unsolved squares
5.12. Reset the Sudoku to start again

6. Evaluation

Evaluation of HSSA was carried out in three areas. Firstly how many of the ten techniques listed in section 4 have actually been utilised, secondly, how brute force solving and HSAA logical solving compare to each other, both in being able to solve Sudoku, and the time taken to do so, and thirdly how many types of Sudoku each technique can solve.

Each of the ten techniques has a comparable logical solver that would emulate the actions that a person would take when solving a Sudoku. The order they are presented in is also critical, as the user will often use the simplest techniques first, and only when they fail, will they employ some of the more advanced techniques needed to make progress.

As can be seen in **Figure 4**, HSSA has successfully implemented nine out of the ten techniques. HSSA has also implemented one other solving technique not covered, *naked pairs*. The solver that has not been implemented is planned for future work after some refinements have been made to the program.

Human Technique	**Implemented Solver**
Slicing and Dicing	Single Options Grid
Completing Rows, Columns and Mini-Grids	Lone Numbers and Single Options in Rows *and* Columns
The Only One that Fits	Single Options in Rows and Columns
Completing a Row or Column when two Numbers are Missing	Lone Numbers and Single Options in Rows *and* Columns
Slicing and Slotting	Pointing Pairs
Writing Options	Implemented through the Interface
Lone Numbers	Lone Numbers
Looking for Single Options	Single Options in Rows and Columns *and* Single Options in Grids
Twinning	Hidden Pairs
Triplets	Also known as Hidden Triples, not Implemented, future work

Figure 4: Implemented Logical Solvers.

The order that the techniques have been listed, and the human techniques covered, also roughly compares to the order HSSA uses to solve Sudoku, with some crossover when one solver covers multiple techniques. This allows HSSA to successfully hint the user as to the next logical step to take in solving the Sudoku, rather than a random number being filled in, which may drastically change the difficulty of the Sudoku depending on how many other squares' possibilities were reliant upon it.

The second part of the evaluation was to compare the execution time of the brute force and the HSAA logical solvers. The solvers were executed multiple times to ensure the numbers were reproducible and used the same Sudoku puzzle for both types of solver. Tests were performed on a dual core Athlon 64 4400+, 2GB RAM under 32bit Windows XP.

Sudoku Size:	9	16
Brute Force	0.33ms	68765ms
Logical	0.44ms	15.625ms

Figure 5: Brute Force vs. Logical solving time.

As seen in **Figure 5**, the difference in execution time for a 9*9 Sudoku are negligible, with both techniques showing very acceptable performance. As the Sudoku gets more complex in a 16*16 grid, where each square now has 16 options, the brute force solver slows down dramatically, taking 70 seconds to solve the Sudoku. The Logical solver meanwhile, while having an increase in solving time, is still at a very acceptable level, which would not impact upon the user.

These results can be explained by the nature of each solver. By randomly guessing, the brute force solver turns Sudoku into a game of chance, with a small number of options, solving can be done quickly, but as the number of options increases per square, and the squares increase, the amount of incorrect guesses made quickly adds up to a large amount of time, even on a modern CPU. The logical solver meanwhile, never guesses at a square, so avoids having to repeat the same loops over and over, and finishes far faster.

As implemented, the logical solver can solve most medium to difficult Sudoku, while the brute force solver can solve any Sudoku. By default, HSSA currently uses the brute force solver to work out the initial solution, and then allows the user to run the logical solver through the program. Improvements made to the program in the future will be able to improve the logical solver such that it can solve every known Sudoku, with the brute force solver used as backup if any unknown Sudoku turned up. The number of possible completely unique 9*9 Sudoku is 36,288 (2,612,736 are possible if numbers can be swapped) [Felgenhauer & Jarvis, 2005], and the number for a 16*16 or 25*25 Sudoku is many more.

Another interesting side note is that all the techniques which work on a 9*9 Sudoku, also work on a 16*16 Sudoku without modification, which is what allows HSSA to be so readily expandable for larger size Sudoku.

7. Conclusions and Future Work

This paper has described the implementation of HSSA, a Sudoku playing and solving application which is also able to show new players how to play Sudoku using the techniques described in most Sudoku books. It has been demonstrated that the program is a success in that it effectively compares the brute force method of solving a Sudoku, with a logical solving method.

It was found through the course of creating HSSA, that using a number of techniques, it was possible to create a computer program which would effectively emulate human behaviour at the task of solving Sudoku. It was an interesting experience that in order to create a logical solver for Sudoku, the best course of action was to examine the techniques used by people, then put them into code, when usually in the area of artificial intelligence, it is exceedingly difficult to have a computer almost perfectly replicate a person. It is concluded that the fact that Sudoku is a pure logic puzzle forces the player to think like a computer. The ease of which a person is able to emulate a computer is startling given the problems faced when making a computer think like a person.

The possibilities for expansion of the program are almost limitless, as besides Sudoku, there are many other logic based number puzzles which could be implemented using a humanesque approach. In the development of HSSA, a conscious decision was made at every stage to implement the code as flexibly as possible. This allows Sudoku of any size to be created within the program, with the only limit being the user interface, and the speed of a computer in solving such a Sudoku.

The main enhancement planned for the program is to change the storage method of possibilities for each square from a simple array to using a bitwise operator, allowing options to be stored by a single digit, and performing shifts left and right to add, reduce and count remaining options. This should allow a speed increase in solving Sudoku, as well as make the implemented solvers easier to follow by a developer, while also allowing other logical solvers to be implemented more easily into code.

Beyond this enhancement, other planned improvements include:

- Implementation of two distinct modes
  - Playing mode: the program as is, but without including the academic aspects.
  - Academic mode: A command line interface that allows a user to load and solve Sudoku, without being limited by an interface.
- Auto generation of new Sudoku.
- Evaluation of Sudoku difficulty.
- Testing and comparison of 64bit vs. 32bit performance.
- Implementation of design patterns to make the code more manageable and expandable.
- Further separation of logic code and UI, to allow for simple exporting to mobile or other devices.
- Multi-threaded solvers to take advantage of multi-core technology.
- Multi-threaded UI so user can view progress of a solver, and allow feedback to be given during intensive processing operations.
- 3D interface to take advantage of 3d card prevalent in PC's today.
- Checking for genuine Sudoku.
- Allowing multiple steps to be taken forward and backward through the program (currently limited to one step back).

These enhancements will occur as time permits, and when a few more Sudoku have been solved by hand...

8. About the Author

Neil Richardson is a Software Test Engineer at leading Software Company. He holds a first class honours degree in computer science from the Dublin Institute of Technology. The inspiration for this project came from a technical talk on solving Sudoku. Before beginning HSSA, he had never played Sudoku before.

9. Acknowledgements

The author wishes to thank:
June Barret for keeping the project on aim.
Ahmed El-Shimi who inspired the project.

His loving wife Di and family for support during the projects creation.
Bryan Duggan for helping to correct and enhance this paper, and encourage its creation.
Ronan Fitzpatrick for providing feedback on the paper.
The staff of DIT, Kevin St.

References

[Deep Blue, 2006] IBM Research *"Kasparov vs. Deep Blue"* http://www.research.ibm.com/deepblue/ (November 2006)

[Doyle, 1859-1930] A. C. Doyle: *"Eliminate the impossible"* Baker St, London & http://www.dailycelebrations.com/052201.htm

[Felgenhauer & Jarvis, 2005] Bertram Felgenhauer & Frazer Jarvis: *"Enumerating Possible Sudoku Grids"* http://www.shef.ac.uk/~pm1afj/Sudoku/Sudoku.pdf (June 2005)

[Pitts, 2005] J. Pitts: *"Teach yourself Sudoku"* Teach Yourself publishing

[Richardson, 2006] N. Richardson: *"Humanesque Sudoku Solver App"* Library, DIT, Kevin St.

[Spitzkoff, 2006] C. Spitzkoff: *Sudoku Solver* http://www.codeproject.com/csharp/DokuSolver.asp (March 2006)

[Stuart, 2006] A. Stuart: *Sudoku Solver* http://www.scanraid.com/Sudoku.htm (March 2006)

[Sudoku.com, 2006] Sudoku Rules: http://www.Sudoku.com/rule.htm

[Vorderman, 2005] C. Vorderman: "*Massive book of Sudoku*" Ebury Press

[Whirlpool Forums, 2005] *C++ code for Sudoku*: http://forums.whirlpool.net.au/forum-replies-archive.cfm/351170.html (November 2005)

Sound Design and Music Systems for computer games

Playing audiogames without instructions for use? To do without an instruction leaflet or without language itself.

Thomas Gaudy
Centre De Recherche en Informatique du CNAM
292, rue St Martin, Paris, France
00 332 35 62 91 79, 75003
tomgody@yahoo.fr

Stéphane Natkin
Centre De Recherche en Informatique du CNAM
292, rue St Martin, Paris, France
00 331 40 27 20 64, 75003
natkin@cnam.fr

Dominique Archambault
University Pierre et Marie Curie, Inserm U483 INOVA
9, quai Saint Bernard, Paris, France
00 331 44 27 26 10, 75005
Dominique.Archambault@upmc.fr

ABSTRACT

Audiogames, which are supposed to be accessible to the blind, have two problems related to language to be understood by most of their users : the first one is linked to an instruction reading phase, which is often essential, and the pleasure of which is often very different from the pleasure of playing the game. The second problem is even more bothersome: the major part of candidates for playing do not understand the language used by those games. In games, we can discern two approaches to learning how interactivity works: the instructions for use and the interactivity itself. So, if the purpose of a game is to learn in a friendly but challenging way how interactivity can became complex, why not first start this process from the very beginning, without the need of textual instructions ? We have therefore designed a audiogame in two versions: one with the instructions incorporated in the game, so that it is possible to play without an instruction leaflet, another without any language at all. Through the analysis of case studies in which players test those games, the version with linguistic instructions incorporated in the game appears more efficient for understanding the game and the pleasure of playing seems good. The version without linguistic instructions was properly used by two players out of five. These results, though still insufficient to prompt us to do without any language at all, encourage the improvement of the game design and sound design principles allowing a greater internationality of audiogames.

KEYWORDS

Audiogames, accessibility, interactivity, sound design, non-verbal communication

1. INTRODUCTION: AUDIOGAMES WITHOUT LANGUAGE FOR A GREATER ACCESSIBILITY

1.1 Without visual support, languages are less understandable

We want to understand how visually impaired people can easily interact with new games. There are more than 300 audiogames. The audiogames.net website [1] is great to become familiar with this type of entertainment. To have an idea of the current game styles, we can say that there are some sort of audio "Pac-man" like "Dynaman" [2], "Doom" audio remakes like "Shades of Doom" [3] and clones of "Space Invaders" like "Mudsplat" [4]. Video games that stand as standards for audio games are quite old. The reason is that the developing conditions of audio games are closer to the antique video games than the industrial developing conditions of latest video games. There are four great different kinds of audiogames: action games, exploration games, simulation games and board games (Gaudy [5]) but almost all of them are based on interaction and the understanding of this interaction. The interaction has to be accessible: it is better if these games have adjustable and attractive interfaces (Archambault [6]) so that they remain accessible to people who suffer from different sorts of disabilities. For users, the understanding of the interaction is also very difficult to master. Since users may be of any nationality, the communication process through games should not depend on a specific language but only on sounds. This is a desire for a particular design: the use of English is often deemed as sufficient for good understanding for interactivity with few instructions. But language is also an inaccessibility factor for those who cannot master it. For instance, I was able to note that most of the pupils with eye disability from the schools in Lille and Toulouse (France) have little or no knowledge of audiogames. Those same pupils seemed more familiarized with video games, which yet are supposed to be inaccessible to them. Moreover, haveing recourse to translation, which implies increasing development costs, does not enable us to target all the potential users: there are too many languages, even among the most spoken, to do all the translations.

Now, a significant part of existing audiogames requires a good understanding of interactivity principles. For this reason, the comfort given by language is tempting but, even for those who master the adequate language, can be an obstacle to amusement. For example, the audiogame "Pipe 2 Blast Chamber" [7] is very interesting but needs much reading to understand how it can be played. For players who do not master English, the game is not accessible. That is the reason why it can be advantageous, for accessibility studies or for economic needs for international distribution, to develop games, and then other kinds of software, without communication via language.

1.2 Some studies encourage the making of audiogames without language

Are audiogames without language realistic? A. Darvishi [8] confirms that an Information Technology environment using various sonorities provides support for the understanding of the interactive process. But this study does not say if sounds alone could be sufficient for proper interaction. For this reason again, the meeting between experimental research on audiogames and the field of non linguistic communication could bring interesting results. This can be a way to orientate the purpose of audiogames towards a more musical outcome: interactive music.

In this way, J.L Alty [9] points out that music is usable as the main means of communication, with three centres of interest: the communication of musical algorithms, debugging, and communication for visually impaired people. Regarding this third area, A. Darvishi [8] uses sound synthesis in a virtual environment accessible to the visually impaired people, each sound being the result of a particular configuration of the environment. One of the problems of this approach could be the very abstract result of the first contact between users and this type of software and the difficulty to communicate more concrete information. However, there are various ways of reaching a fuller level of communication.

For example, B.N. Walker [10] manages to communicate numerical data via a musical abacus. In addition to scientific studies, others ways of investigation may be very helpful. Studies of other audiogames are of course essential, but experiments with multimedia may also provide clues for non linguistic communication even if these are unfortunately inaccessible for visually impaired people. These multimedia experiments are often very abstract audiovisually and with no instructions for use. Users have to discoverer by themselves how to interact with sounds.

1.3 Learning process of video games

Several simple learning processes may be combined together for the understanding of a more complex task. Over the last years, video games have more often been analyzed by scientific studies. These new studies enable us to define the nature of games, writing processes, technologies and the cultural impact (Natkin [11]). It is easier for the player to learn a game with instructions included in the first step of the game. In this way, the players use their memory less and can practice without delay the instructions they learnt without the risk of forgetting them. Moreover, it is only when a lesson is understood by the player that the next instructions are given. A complex task may be divided into a great number of short, funny and easy-to-understand lessons often called “tutorial”.

For more complex games, we might fear that the amount of instructions could be much greater. In most cases, this is not true. Linguistic communications are sometimes used but not always. The first basic actions are explained with language and the players have to combine what they can do by themselves. The great difference with simpler games is that learning is no longer introduced before the game but incorporated in the game itself. Tutorials often have the following characteristics:

• No or very few « game over » situations.

• Players face situations that can only be resolved in a single way.

• Clues make the resolution easier. Clues may be audio, visual and / or tactile.

• There are few advantages for the player to go back.

• Players should be very interested in going further.

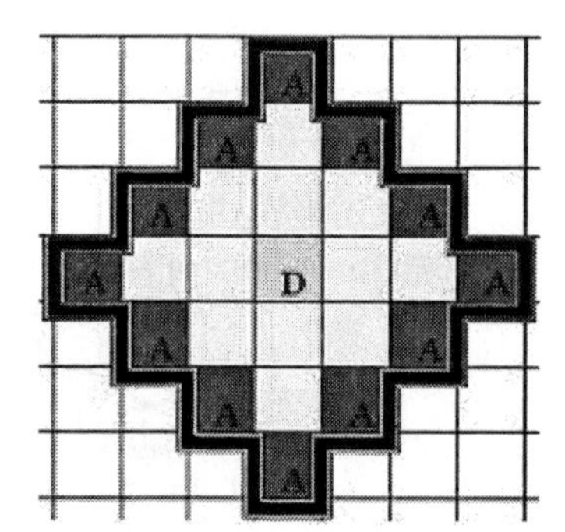

Figure2. Representation of the first level of our audio maze game: no walls, The character appears in the centre (D) and is surrounded by exits (A). No game over situation, players just have to move in any direction to reach the next level. But without visual, it can be harder that it seems. During a test before this experiment, a subject was lost in this level: he goes up and down repeatedly.

Approaching each of these characteristics from an auditory rather than a visual point of view may be of great interest (Figure 1). Consequently, there is a paradox. The number of instructions does not depend on the degree of complexity of the game. For complex games, developers are looking for other ways to make players learn and quickly enjoy themselves without being discouraged. Is the learning principle used by video games applicable to audiogames, which are still presently impeded by a not so obvious learning process, often requiring the preliminary learning of an instruction leaflet? We have tried to apply these interaction principles while designing a game that was used as the base of the following experiment.

2. EXPERIMENT

2.1 General hypothesis

Ideally, a game should be playable as soon as a player has a first contact with it during the learning phase, and without the help of someone else.

2.2 Study environment

In the game used as the base of this experiment, named “Pyvox, Musical Maze”, the player directs a character in a 70-floor labyrinthine tower, 70 floors corresponding to 70 game levels which can be explored one after other in an unchanging order. This character can also be considered as a cursor that can be moved on a grid from one square to the other.

The player can move the cursor towards target areas but obstacles block up some access paths.

The game describes the target areas as being lifts that give access to the next floor. Disregarding the semantic framework, this device enables its users to move a cursor on an area that can be explored to activate the practicalities enabling them to explore other areas.

This game is therefore a maze with a square-to-square moving system, divided into game levels, each level presenting an exit and a certain number of walls. The aim of the game is to teach the player to recognize an exit sound in order to reach it. The game also aims at bringing the player to recognize the sounds coming out of the walls in order to avoid them without hitting them. As a first contact, the game introduces the character sleeping. The keys of the keyboard almost all trigger alarm sounds. The closer the player gets to the arrow keys, the louder the alarm sounds become. The use of the arrow keys wakes the character up and the exploration of the maze can start.

2.3 Aim of the study

We want to optimize the handling of audiogames by tackling the problems linked to language in two ways: in a first way, we want the player to do without reading a manual beforehand. In a second way, we also want the player to be able to do without verbal communication.

2.4 Operational hypothesis

As a first hypothesis, we assume that linguistic instructions judiciously introduced during the course of an audiogame enable the player to learn how to master it without having to consult complementary instructions.

We assume that our game without language but including the learning principles previously suggested could be understood and properly played by at least a few people, yet without equalling the quality of the handling of the same game with explicit instructions.

2.5 Variable independent from the user

The studied system has two versions: one with incorporated linguistic instructions (Verbal condition) and the other one without any instructions (Sounds condition).

2.6 Variable dependent from the user

The game automatically counts different categories of interactions realized by the player.

• The interactions on the arrow keys (Arrows) (Figure 2), with three subcategories: The instructions amounting to a move of the character (Moving), those amounting to a collision against a wall of the maze (Hurting), those amounting to a short vocal sound effect (Singing). During the transitions between the levels, the character cannot either be moved or be knocked against a wall. This last category is mentioned for information only, for it is not directly used for the evaluation of the game versions.

• The interactions on other keys than those of the arrow keys (Wrong Keys).

The counting of these interactions enables us to provide two indicators, given in percentage and rounded off without decimal places. The first one is the efficiency of the use of the good controls employed by the game, the arrow keys, with the following formula:

Arrows / (Arrows + Wrong Keys) * 100

The second one is the efficiency of the understanding of the maze exploration principles. It depends on the formula:

Moving / (Moving + Hurting) * 100

To give an indication of the interest felt by the player vis-à-vis the game, we provide the time spent in playing. Finally, at the end of the game, we ask the player to tell us what he has understood about the game rules.

Figure3. Blind players have to find four keys between more than one hundred without any verbal instruction.

2.7 Studied population

We have preferred a more analytical approach based on case studies to a statistical approach for several reasons. First, it was not possible to gather a sample of people significant enough and with characteristics similar enough for such an analysis to be valid. Then we are not looking to quantify the proportions from which the observed game behaviours can be applied generally but rather to understand the potential causes of the behaviour with a psychology-based procedure. The testers selected for the experiment are ten persons who work in the specialized school in Toulouse (France). They are all familiarized with computers or videogames. However, they do not know audiogames, except a tester who knows an audio pinball game. Among those selection criteria, we want to mention the diversity of the profiles of male and female players. That is the reason why we will briefly indicate the level of knowledge of games, their age and their visual acuity. Each tester only does a single game on only one of the two studied devices, without preliminary training.

2.8 Instructions

In this study, the testers are not faced with the device freely, they are aware of the following details: They are going to try a game, the purpose of which is not given. The name of the game is not given to the subjects. They can play as much as they want, which was, unfortunately, not always the case. They can give up the game whenever they want to but they cannot resume it. They can adjust the sound volume with the controls indicated by the experimenter. The controls to adjust the sound volume are tested by the players. The experimenter starts the game and leaves the players to use the device until they want to stop or stop the game by themselves. The experiment being realised in a school and not in a laboratory, it happened that games were stopped because of outside events. It will be mentioned for each of the subjects whether the game was voluntarily stopped by him/her or not.

3. RESULTS

In the "verbal" condition, the highest level reached at the end of the game is the 55th whereas the lowest level is the 26th. As for the "sound only" condition, the highest level reached at the end of the game is the 29th whereas the lowest level is the first one.All the main results are reported on the table 1.

N°	Player	Experimental condition	Knowledge of game	Level reached (start at 0)	Gaming duration (minutes)	Way of ending the game ?	Efficiency of the good use of keys	Efficiency of movement	Understanding of the tested game
1	22-year-old blind woman	Verbal	Plays essentially on "Tekken III"	26	20	External event	98%	83%	Very good
2	19-year-old blind woman	Verbal	Good knowledge of various video games. Know one audiogame	29	27	By herself	98%	68%	Good but did not recognize the sounds produced by the exit
3	15-year-old visually impaired boy	Verbal	Final fantasy video games, elder scrolls…	37	41	By himself	99%	65%	Very good
4	20-year-old blind woman	Verbal	Plays essentially on Fighting games	55	128	External event	98%	78%	Very good
5	18-year-old visually impaired boy	Verbal	Good knowledge of various video game	41	62	External event	99%	67%	Very good
6	16-year-old visually impaired boy	Sound only	Good knowledge of various video games	5	4	By himself	46%	38%	Bad, but recognized a sleeping character he could wake up
7	30-year-old blind woman	Sound only	Trivial pursuit on PC	29	22	External event	93%	58%	Good but thought she was going back sometimes to the previous levels
8	13-year-old blind boy	Sound only	He has regularly been playing videogame for about one year	10	10	By himself	59%	51%	Bad, but recognized a sleeping character
9	10-year-old visually impaired boy	Sound only	Good novice videogame player	1	2	By himself	3%	100%	Bad, but recognized a sleeping character
10	14-year-old visually impaired boy	Sound only	Plays essentially on a pinball video game	29	40	By himself	90%	56%	Good

Table 1 : Main results

4. DISCUSSION

We can note that the level 29 is too difficult: three players end the game at this level. It becomes the 63rd level in the final version of the game (figure 3). None of the players of the sound condition managed to go through it.

The five first testers are used as a reference. The game has incorporated instructions and it seems to be globally well understood. The system therefore appears to work well globally as players who do not know the game can play without any outside help and without reading instructions. However, even with the incorporated instructions, some of them may not understand. Thus, the second tester explained during the final interview that she could not knowingly localise the exit as she did not understand that sounds referred to it. If we now study the testers who tried the game without linguistic instructions, firstly we note the difficulties to start the game without instructions: which keys should be used? What is the aim of the game? What do I have to do? Those questions do not have explicit answers in the version without incorporated instructions. But we also note that all the subjects were motivated enough during their first contact with the game to explore the keyboard until they found the adequate controls to truly start the game. During this first contact, the game is felt more as a sound puzzle and it seems that this device works. On the other hand, it appears that for two persons, the game went properly (figure 5) and was appreciated (testers 7 and 10) but with very personal interpretations of the scenario.

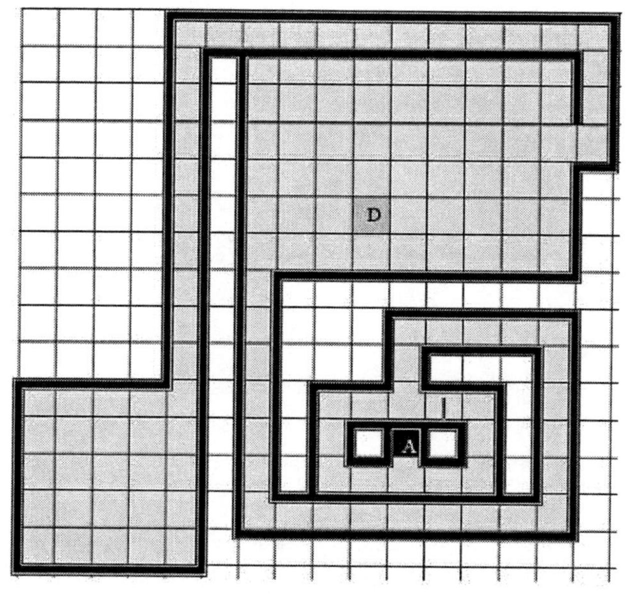

Figure3. Representation of the 29th level of our audio maze game: the character appears in D and must go out in A. Players have to properly understand the gameplay to find the audio path. It can be done easily with verbal instructions, but with a game without language, we probably need more intermediate levels.

The efficiency of their character's movement is nevertheless less good than the one of the game with linguistic instructions. The principle of the exit through sound and especially of the sound walls is less obvious and the exploring was at first much more hazardous. The test number 9 is typical of a totally misunderstanding game. The player used the arrow keys and thus started the exploring of the maze but he did not remain on these controls and gave up quickly. Testers 6 and 8 did not understand the game rules either and it seems that they got bored because the game did not give them an aim to reach after the first contact with waking up of the character by the use of the arrow keys. However, it is particularly interesting to note that in spite of these defects of understanding, their interactions enabled them to go through the first levels properly (level 5 for player 6 and 10 for player 8). If it seems too delicate to give an aim in a non-linguistic way, it would perhaps be more judicious to insist on the effects of the realised interactions. Thus, the emergence of a game scenario could be made easier. It is not possible to say to what extent such a game can be understandable and playable by a population of players. The most important thing is to note that initiating such a game can be possible but that it is much more difficult to implement. The next question is to wonder how to improve the understanding of such games for a greater international accessibility of audiogames? At our level, and following this experiment, we prefer not to do without language for the next developments for it offers obvious practicalities, but we want to implement game principles that can also be understandable by people who do not master the language used. We are here reviewing the game principles that appear to be the most important. It seems that such audiogames could have the following characteristics:

• The game must encourage players for a first interaction, whatever this first interaction might be

The first contact between players and their interface may be as a call for interaction from the game. Some games show a game over sign if the player does not interact. "Game over" situations do not seem to be a good idea because they do not encourage players if they make them understand they lost. Players may interact in very different ways with the keyboard: For this reason, any key pressed should support interaction.

• Reward the player generously for this first interaction

After this first interaction, players must be encouraged to continue. It is better for the players' motivation if they hear a progression right from the beginning. The audio reward must be clearly heard and not confused with other sounds.

• Reward each interaction, but make some rewards more important

The third contact could be a different feed back to induce the search for more appropriate behavior. The simple renewal of interaction unadapted to the continuation of the game should not be as well rewarded as previously. From this point of view, the gratification offered to tester n° 9 for the use of arrow keys is insufficient.

• Let the players choose themselves the moment to act

We have noted that it is better if the player chooses the adequate moment for interaction by themselves.

• Introduce a set of sounds that can be used as a base for a coherent interpretation of the game situation.

The first contact offered by the game makes the player hear snoring and the interaction trigger alarm sounds. All of the testers found the necessary keys for the game which woke up the character and truly started the game. Then, during the exploration of the maze, it turned out that a same collision sound could be interpreted in very different ways. This imaginative aspect which is a great strength of audiogames is also a weakness for the understanding of rules when there are no explicit instructions. To be improved, this aspect requires a deep reflection on the staging of the game

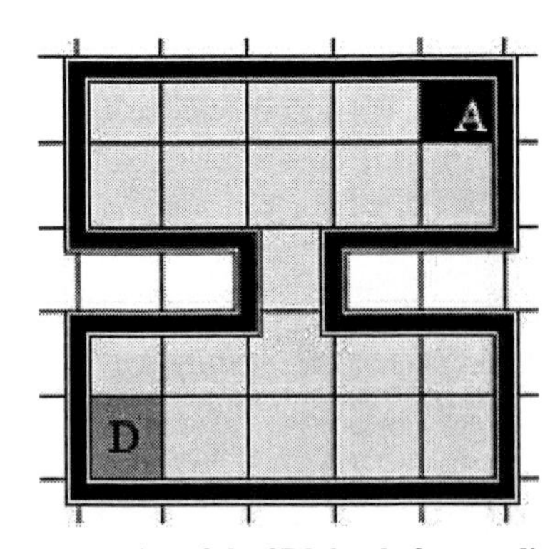

Figure4. Representation of the 27th level of our audio maze game: the character appears in D and must go out in A. Two players reached the next level, without any verbal instruction about the game. It seems easy when it is seen, but in the dark, it is more like a claustrophobic cell with a small hidden path.

We now want to know how to promote even more the distribution of audiogames. One of the best answers would perhaps be to make them more attractive to non blind players. But then, what kind of connection can these games have to the picturing? The perceiving process is very different: the visual stands enable the recognition of a great deal of information in a glimpse whereas the audio sense depends more on a temporal dimension. As a consequence it is hard to create a game that can be played either auditively or visually. For instance, the game "Shade of Doom"[3] offers an optional visual help that I could do without for the first 8 levels but which has proven very useful in order to beat the big boss. There already are a few mixed games that offer an auditive accessibility as well as a visual one, like "Terraformers"[12]. Broadly speaking, we can hope for multiplayer mixed games that would bring together both the visually impaired community and the sighted community. In this idea we are looking forward to cooperative games rather than competitive games because the later category is likely to always advantage one of the two perceiving processes.

5. CONCLUSION

We have developed and tested an audiogame for which it is not necessary to read an instruction leaflet. The principle of linguistic instructions incorporated into an audiogame enables it to be played at once, as it does in most video games. But we know that language, even though it use is optimised, is a factor of inaccessibility. Almost none of the testers in this study, although interested in games and visually impaired, had heard of audiogames. Interviews with young French testers revealed their difficulties to understand English and those games seem hardly to reach non-English speaking players. Audiogames that can do without language, like most video games, would be internationally more important. But the audiogames already do without images. Thus, a first contact with such a game without language shows difficulties for the understanding of the objective to be reached. Despite these difficulties, we managed to have all our subjects use the controls necessary for the game, at least temporarily, after an exploration phase of the keyboard, presenting itself as a kind of brain-teaser with evocative sounds. We have observed two cases of players succeeding in handling an audiogame they did not know before and that does not provide any linguistic instructions. If it is still too risky to do without the practicality of providing instructions through language, the principles of game design and sound design that enable an audiogame without language to be handled satisfactorily have to be improved to ensure better distribution of this emerging leisure.

6. ACKNOWLEDGMENTS

Our thanks to CECIAA for making a helpful partnership.

We also thank the "Institut des Jeunes Aveugles de Toulouse" and the "Ecole Regionale des Déficients Visuels de Loos", the pupils and all the staff member.

7. REFERENCES

[1] audiogames.net, http://www.audiogames.net/.

[2] Draconis Entertainment, Dynaman.

[3] GMAGAMES, Shades of Doom v1.2, 2005.

[4] TimGames, Mudsplat, 2005.

[5] Gaudy, T., Natkin, S., Archambault, D.: Classification des jeux sonores selon leur type de jouabilité, Handicap 2006 Conference, 2006.

[6] Archambault, D.: Computers for the Development of Young Disabled Children, 2002.

[7] BSG_Games, Pipe 2: Blast Chamber, PC Windows, 2002. http://www.bscgames.com/pipe2.asp

[8] Darvishi, A., Guggiana, V., Munteanu E., Shauer, H.: Synthesizing Non-Speech Sound to Support Blind and Visually Impaired Computer Users, Computers for Handicapped Persons 1994.

[9] Alty, J. L., Rigas D., Vickers P.:Using Music as a Communication Medium, 1996.

[10] Walker B. N., Lindsay J. , Godfrey J.: The Audio Abacus: Representing Numerical Values with Nonspeech Sound for the Visually Impaired, 2002.

[11] Natkin, S.: Jeux Vidéo et Médias du XXIe Siècle - Quels modèles pour les nouveaux loisirs numériques?, Vuibert, 2004.

[12] PIN Interactive, Terraformers, PC, 2002.

VOICE ATTACK RECOGNITION FOR LYRIC SINGING LEARNING GESTURE : AN ADAPTIVE VIDEO GAME INTERFACE

Jocelyne Kiss[1], Kévin Dahan[1], Sidi Soueina[2], Martin Laliberté[1]
[1]University Marne-la-Vallée, LISAA
[2]University Sullivan, Dept. of Computer Science
Kiss@univ-mlv.fr, kdahan@univ-mlv.fr, ssoueina@sullivan.edu, lalibert@univ-mlv.fr,

KEYWORDS

Tools and musicsystems for video games and virtual reality devices. Interfaces and controllers. Music system. Picture and sound recognition system. Serious games.

ABSTRACT

We will present an educational video games which propose the user to learn about his own voice attack production in order to teach him how to sing by imitation. The learning of singing, whether thought as the construction of the physical vocal pattern, or as the interpretative preparation of a piece of music, proceeds initially through observation, then by imitation of a given physical model. One of the principal difficulties in this mimetic process frequently lies in the different perceptions [1] of the singer and the listener. Without attempting to compensate directly this problem, we propose an interactive system that reacts to external data, thus facilitating the creation of a model of the singer and at the same time real-time simulation of his actions.

We hence offer, within the given framework, to create a basic virtual animation, in order to recognize the voice attack. It is important at this stage to define the nature of the work envisaged, which will not consist of an exhaustive project. We specifically intend to describe the means for encoding the vocal attack expression and its relation to the facial and sound expression, in order to translate a feeling.

We will then proceed to the development of a virtual, computer-generated lyric singer, using the process of interactive phonation as represented by a virtual actor with simplified expressions. Initially this phonation will be limited to the attack expression of a small number of phonemes. We will also predict the sound development based on this first attack. This part of the process could become the basis of further concrete developments and constitute the foundation for various potential extensions.

1. INTRODUCTION

The act of singing has been described by many performers [2] as a juxtaposition of "internal physical sensations". According to R. Miller [3], these enable the performer, to a certain extent, to escape from the problem of listening to one's self during the phonation. The majority of beginners are frequently doubtful concerning the idea that they "don't hear themselves". The teaching of singing is therefore based on the teaching of these sensations that allow accurate production of sound.

The formalization of these impressions implies using a metaphorical and visual representation in a model of the mistakes commonly made by the student as well as an ideal example. The principal difficulty in this mimetic exercise often resides in morphological differences between the model and the student. The project of using an interactive synthetic computer-generated singer does not represent an alternative for the singing coach but does however provide a systematic teaching aid that acts directly with the image and the voice of the student.

The creation of a synthetic computer-generated singer requires a restrictive definition of the action of the singer, since this is strictly influenced by aesthetic criteria and differs according to cultural practice. We will therefore limit ourselves solely to the Western practice of Italian opera that is also referred to as *Bel Canto*. Of course, we could equally attempt to define the act of singing by adopting the viewpoint of the physiologist and by taking as our departure point observations made by phoniatricians [4] on this subject.

This project also necessitates a certain degree of caution concerning the use of the term "synthetic". Clearly, by synthetic image we are referring to an image generated by a computer, either directly, or through the manipulation of a previously produced image using some kind of peripheral. In using the term interactivity what we envisage is *"a type of relation between two systems which results in the behaviour of one system modifying the behaviour of the other"* [6].

The creation of a virtual singer equally necessitates a choice concerning the methodological direction to adopt [7], which in itself leads to the initial problem of representation. Firstly, we intend to produce a comparative study intended to establish a taxonomic classification of the relationships between facial expressions and the production of sounds. Next, we will encode each of these sound-image associations according to aesthetic criteria linked to the teaching of singing. Then we will attempt to put into perspective the various possibilities created by this project.

2. ENCODING OF THE VOCAL EXPRESSION

2.1. Creation of the automaton

If we consider the computer modeling of a synthetic automaton reproducing the act of singing as a mediatory function between the concrete act of vocalisation and another, more abstract act simultaneously composed by a symbolic vocabulary and ideal objects, it would then appear that this constitutes an effective way to reach understanding of certain processes pertaining to the structure of the singing act and to artistic expression [8].

The principal difficulty in such a system resides in balancing the shares that must be accorded to the specific and inherent characteristics of this gesture and the necessary generalization. Thus we can identify an initial problem concerning the orientation of the virtual singer we wish to create, since it would be utopian, in effect, to envisage at the present stage of research a complete system capable of reproducing complete interactivity to be used in perfect staging of a particular context, the interpretation of a simple *melody*, for example. The initial presentation of the synthetic automaton resides therefore in a series of behaviour activated by the actions of the user.

In order to interpret this behavior and to translate it into data meaningful to a computer, we propose to capture the movie of the student's expression and his voice. Our automaton will be structured as presented in figure I

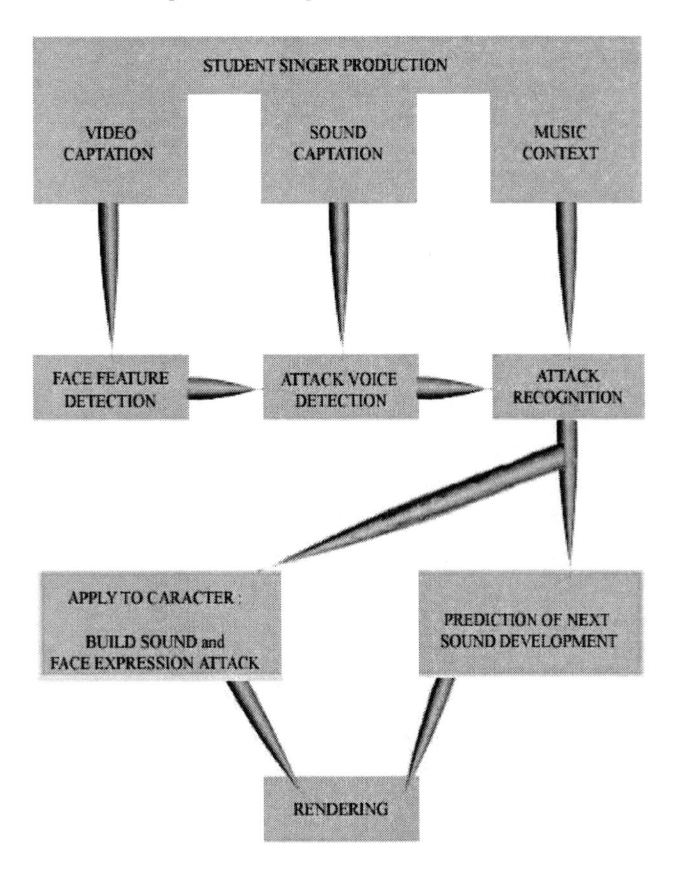

Figure I : General description of automaton

The main project is to associate visual recognition form and sound recognition in order to detect the attack form of our user. This educational video game will need a microphone and two webcam in order to get all the data needed for the inputs of our proposition.

2.2. The different conceptual orientations

If, in an ideal conception, we find ourselves in the presence of a source of sound and visual material producing events as varied as possible – this may be concretely envisaged as a library [9] of sung phonemes linked to appropriate facial expressions – and the we opt for automation of the choice of vocal expressions, we can then use to three types of "filter", which are complementary in nature.

The first "filter" could be similar to a collection of symbolic units [10] a corpus of rules resulting from a thorough analysis of the sound-image-facial expression dependency, and may lead to a systematic adaptation of an aesthetic context in terms of stage or theatre interpretation. An "interesting" automaton will naturally possess an extensible palette of options, of possibilities for decisions, of prepositional parameters, allowing wide and flexible possibilities for the creation of syntactic articulations.

It must be noted that even an exhaustive set of rules cannot reasonably be expected to explicitly render the richness of a style, and that their exclusive use present the danger of monotony, and even of predictability [11].

Consequently, the second filter will essentially be stochastic, that is to say that it will contain decisional "subfilters" based on the laws of probability and the frequency of appearance. Thus, certain stochastic laws may require that the automaton makes infinitesimal variations around a particular expression, in the canonical pronunciation of the sounds, in the frequency and velocity of the timbres produced, and so on, and that, in a general manner, these random constraints could intervene at different levels of theatrical organisation, for example in the choice of rules of coordination or of their parameters.

This complexity is due to the very nature of the recursive character of a decision-making system operating on another. Nevertheless, at this stage, even if the random modules result in unexpected changes in the sequence of facial expressions, sounds and events, the production thus automated, even in relation to symbolic units, will not correspond (except extremely fleetingly) to the particular hopes and expectations within the framework of a video game [12].

Keeping this in mind, in order to improve our automaton we will therefore need to use a third type of "filter", able to integrate stylistic characteristics inherent in a work, an author, a period or a genre, in order to accept or reject the sound sequences presented, outside of any clearly formulated analytic framework, according to an act not based on simple contingency. We can see then, that this decisional level [13] may be introduced with the help of the notion of interactivity [14], which can be constructed from the starting point of deterministic controls, or bringing random corrections.

It is equally important to note that this pragmatic conception suggests a modular construction, which presents a number of advantages. The most important of these is undoubtedly linked to current advances in robotic technology, which favours the resolution of a complex task through numerous independent units rather than through one overall calculation centre controlling all the necessary functions.

We will not envisage the production of an optimal synthetic computer-generated singer whose creation is beyond the limits of this project; instead we propose here the creation of a basic example. We will leave to one side random and connectionist interactivity, and concentrate on the creation of the basis, which, as we have explained, will be capable of extension and generalisation.

3. THE VOCALITY BETWEEN IMAGES AND SOUNDS

The creation of a vitual singer proceeds from a process of mimicry [15] stimulated to a greater or lesser degree by the real world. It would appear that there is a second fundamental problem to be considered, relating to the pertinence of the elements or parameters to be taken into account in the modeling, that is, parameters that relate not only to the descriptive field, but also to those that are the concern of expressiveness or the aesthetic intention. We then put into place a simplified elementary typology stemming from the structure of song, with a view to constitute a collection of initial considerations appropriate for defining a taxonomy of the modeling of a virtual singer[16].

The aim of this section is not so much to exhaustively study the multiple modalities of the phenomenon of the emission of sound; rather it is to develop an initial methodology capable of discovering useful extensions within the virtual conception in the domain of lyrical song. We will now describe the study of three types of sound attack, as an illustrative example of the correspondence of sound and facial expression. There are three types of attack, or commencement of vocal emission, corresponding to specific positions of the vocal chords. We normally distinguish: the soft attack, the hard attack, and the balanced attack. Each corresponds to a specific modeling [17].

3.1 The hard attack

The hard attack designate in two varieties, glottal attack and glottal occlusion, a vocal sound defined by the adduction or the tightening of the vocal chords prior to phonation. In this case the activity of the vocal muscle begins in force before the sound emission and is distinguished by its power compared to the other two fundamental types of attack. This is because the glottis closes completely and then opens suddenly as the sound is produced. This effort is accompanied by specific facial expressions although control on the part of the part of the singer can reduce these effects. The "hard" attack provokes a kind of brief congestion or even strangulation in the neck (often more visible in a male subject because of the presence of the Adam's apple) resulting in the opening of the mouth (also occasionally the forward projection of the chin) allowing the briefly stifled sound to take its place in the oral cavity and emerge. This action also produces a slight backwards movement of the head.

Figure II : Example of representation of hard attack

3.2 The soft attack

The soft attack [18] is accompanied by a respiratory flow before the emission of the sound as if the singer were preceding it with an aspirated introduction. It corresponds, especially when it is temporally drawn out, to a coming together of the vocal chords along the length of their paramedian line without obtrusion of the glottis. One sometimes observes a low level of sound emission accompanied by a powerful flow of breath.

As in the hard attack, the sound emission is accompanied by characteristic hypertonic movement of certain facial muscles that the singer can attempt to control in order to reduce the visible signs. One generally notices a tendency to exaggerate the respiratory action, forcing the singer to draw in the chest and tighten the muscles of the neck. The balanced attack corresponds to an intermediate activity between the extreme positions of the "whisper" and the "grunt". It consists of the balanced working of the larynx controlling the sound accumulations during the course of a pronounced phrase. It requires phonatory "calibration" to act rapidly in the course of a song or a discourse and this aspect concerns not only the commencement of the vocal emission but also continues throughout the declamation.

This phonatory control, which is similar to a "pre-tuning" of the activity of the emission, depends essentially on the correct management of air before the sound attack and to a lesser degree on the musculature of the larynx, which constitutes the principal voluntary contribution to its action during a sung or spoken phonation [19].

3.3 The balanced attack

The balanced attack corresponds to an ideal commencement of sound emission in which each muscle of the neck relax as if the subject were yawning. As the speech therapist B.D Wyke describes: "This process of pre-phonatory tuning involves not only the participation of the intrinsic muscles of the larynx, but also the participation of the intercostals and abdominal muscles, as well as the external laryngeal muscles. It goes into action immediately after every voluntary inspiration taken between the phrases". [20] Schematically speaking, the balanced attack is situated at an intermediate stage between the soft and hard attack.

4. RECOGNITION SYSTEM

In order to detect and to generate the user's attack, we will use a recognition system for sound and video inputs in association with a prediction system[1] based on conditional stochastic. We

[1] The conditional stochastic is defined by a universe Ω and by growing data events group $(F_t)_{t\in R}$. The conditional hoping of a random variable X_t in relation with a group F_t noted $E(X_t \mid F_t)$ is projected in orthogonal way of X_t in the Hilbert Space de Hilbert $L_2(F_t)$. Practically this interpretation in real time is not revelant because this gestion of events cannot be used for a big number of data. We need to use a simple manner

will use a traditional neural network using a learning phase, similar to an adaline.

When this training is carried out, we propose forms to it, in order to be recognized via his input cells. Let us imagine that these examples are virtually additional examples of training, i.e. one observes what the variations of weights in the connections could be, if the algorithm was being used. We can conjecture (if we omit the standards to be defined) that for examples in conformity with the training carried out, the virtual change of the weight of connections remains weak. On the contrary, a primarily singular example (within the meaning of the training carried out) will generate an important upheaval of the weights of connections of the network.

The idea is thus to make use of this measurement of virtual variations (with the direction heard previously) of weights of connections of the network, in order to provide a means of measurement of the "variation" in the nature of the environment. We could therefore, by an imitation of the structures of the "outside world", couple another network of artificial neurons with the first, so that its sensors or input cells, will not directly measure external data being fed, but the weights of connections of the first network. This device is hence being organized according to a recursive structure and then authorizes detection in the environmental changes, making it possible to evaluate a speed of change. By adding another stage, we can set up a third neuronal network whose input cells would measure the variations of the connection weights of the second network.

This third network will then give indications on the rate of changes intervening in the external world as sensed by the first network. As example, if we consider a network adaline with two input cells and one exit cell. Such a network can separate three tops from a square, without being able to solve the XOR problem. Let us call A, B, C, D the tops of a square with AC and BD as the diagonals. In order to discriminate AC from BD, the network, at training-time, will be able to reach convergence rapidly and therefore will lead to a stabilization of the connection weights. However D will be associated with B.

The impossibility of the resolution of problem XOR will profoundly impact the connection weights, and the reading of the variation of the weight of connections will permit "to detect" the arrival of a singular event: D. Naturally the abstract letters A, B, C, D can indicate musical events as well as sound environments. We thus have the means by a reflexive process of detecting the presence of "a new" contextual environment. Numerical illustration:

Example	Compatible	Compat.	Compat.	Incompatib.
Weight of connection 1	-0,997	-0,995	-0,996	-0,097
Weight of connection 2	-0,771	-0,769	-0,772	0,121

How to make profitable this detection change of environment within our musical automaton? In the general situation of two coupled networks described, the recognition of a new environment makes it possible to load in real-time a particular training. It is besides what seems to occur within the alive world since according to the context and the tasks to be achieved, the organization "instructs" the training instantaneously corresponding enabling him to manage the new situation which occurs at him. However according to the connexionist paradigm, the aptitudes of a network of neurons are related to its general state – that is, its connections.

Taking again these theoretical considerations, the automaton will recover a capacity in adequacy with the new environment met, as soon as connections of its principal network find the weights of connections defined by a previous training corresponding to the type of environment met. Thus the functionalities of the automaton are materialized thanks to a system of charts describing the states appropriate to environments met.

Let us take again the simple example of the previous adaline network. Let us imagine that the letters A, B, C, D correspond to four types of musical events compatible three to three (as in a compositional sequence). All while the automaton perceives (or generates) sequences of events of the type A, B, C, a certain compositional strategy could be implemented to organise them.

When the event D occurs, the detection of this new element will force the automaton to load a new training enabling it to manage correctly the separation of the last three letters, and could trigger the application of a new compositional rule appropriate to the sequences of events of this type. In other words, the detection of a new environment authorises an adaptation by selecting a suitable training, and by initiating a new form of recognition strategy. In that way the system could be adaptive by detecting new situations that occur, and feed them in the learning system.

5. CONCLUSIONS AND PERSPECTIVES

The completion of this elementary project can be viewed as the starting point of a system to aid voice coaching and the teaching of singing, but it could equally be directed towards the production of interactive scenes involving virtual singers.

The analysis of facial expressions and the vocalic formants could lead to extremely realistic expressiveness or to sophisticated artistic effects. A far-reaching project could be based on the fundamental principles of the structure of song in order to develop complex scenography aimed towards interactive operatic creation [21].

Another interesting direction flowing directly from this project concerns the domain of interactivity. We have seen just how tedious it can be using a peripheral such as a keyboard to animate ambitious or complex interactions. It is also interesting to consider the possibility of extended interaction between the user and one or more virtual singers: this situation would undoubtedly find an application in sing class, whether for educational or purely entertainment purposes, but this construction can also be seen from an instrumental point of view. Through the intermediary of sophisticated software the user would be enabled to sing 'virtually' in the manner of a genuine instrumentalist.

---

to reduce the number of data in order to have a rendering in real time. It is the reason why we use the context notion.

Lastly, as we explained earlier, just as this type of virtual performance has helped to experiment with certain artistic ideas in choreography, this interactivity could also provide useful tools in the sphere of operatic creation. The necessary condition for development in this direction remains the development or practicable, easy to use interactive software. It appears that the connectionist orientation may in the medium term provide a seductive solution to this technical difficulty: the user would directly integrate with the performance, either through the use of his voice, or through his facial expressions. One could even envisage a mixed system mixing the two types of approach.

4. REFERENCES

[1] De Bonis M., Nahas M., Chimeric emotional faces : a tool for investigating facial perception of emotions. Smiling mouth and fearful eyes. *8th European Conference, Facial expression of emotion and meaning,* Sarrebruck, Germany. 1999.

[2] Reid C. Bel Canto : Principles and Pratices. NewYork. Coleman-Ross. 1950 ; and Christy (van) A. Expressive Singing. 3 éd. Dubuque IA. wm. C. Brown. 2 Vols. 1974.

[3] Miller R. et Shutte H. The effets of Tongue position on spectra in singing. The NATS Bulletin 37, 3 : 26-27.34.1981

[4] Ladefoged P. Elements of acoustics Phonetics. Chicago : The University Press. 1962.

[5] Barda J., Dusantes O., Notaise J., in, Dictionnaire du multimédia, AFNOR. 1995

[6] Huitric, H., Nahas, M., Rioux M., Domey J., 1990 "Facial Image synthesis using skin texture recordings", The Visual Computer,6, 613-626.

[7] Scotto Di Carlo, N., et Guaïtella, I., Facial Expressions in Singing : A pilot study, Communication au XIII° Congrès International des Sciences Phonétiques. Stockholm, 1995, I.

[8] Peterfalvi J-M., Recherches expérimentales sur le symbolisme phonétique. Paris. Centre national de recherche scientifique. 1970.

[9] Haugland, J., Mind Design. MIT Press. 1981. and alsoVarela F.J., Connaître les sciences cognitives. Trad. P. Lavoie. Paris. Seuil. 1989. p.35-42

[10] Kohonen T., Laine P., Tiits, Torkkola K., A Nonheuristic Automatic Composing method, in, Music and Connectionnism. Massachusetts Institute of Technology. 1992.

[11] Scherer, K.R., & Kappas, A. Primate vocal expression of affective state. Dans D.Todt, P.Goedeking, & D. Symmes (Eds.), Primate vocal communication (pp. 171 - 194). Berlin: Springer-Verlag.1988.

[12] Simon, H.A, Sciences de l'artificiel. 2ème édition 1981. Cambridge Mass. the MIT Press. French traduction Sciences des systèmes, sciences de l'artificiel. Paris. Dunod. 1991.

[13] Angel, E. Interactive Computer Graphics. Addison-Wesley. 2000.

[14] Scotto Di Carlo, N., Analyse sémiologique des gestes et mimiques des chanteurs d'opéra, Semiotica,1973, IX,

[15] Ekman, P., And Friesen, W.V., Manual for the Facial Action Coding System, Palo Alto: Consulting Psychologists Press.1977

[16] Kappas, A., Hess, & Scherer, K.R. Voice and Emotion. in, .R. Feldman & B. Rimé(Eds.), Fundamentals of nonverbal behavior. p. 200-238. New York : Cambridge University Press. 1991

[17] Weede, R. Intelligent care of the singing voice. The Etude December. 65 : 679.

[18] Cohn, M.A., Wertz, J.M, Perrott, M. A., And Parrott, D.J., A Psychometric Evaluation of the Facial Action Coding System for Assessing Spontaneous Expression. Journal of Nonverbal Behavior, 25, p.167-186. University of Pittsburgh

[19] Wyke, B.D. Laryngeal neuromuscular control systems in singing : a review of current concepts. Folia Phoniatrica 26,1.1974

[20] Paquelin, D., Conception d'un environnement d'apprentissage interactif en fonction des attentes des usages, Université d'Avignon et des pays de Vaucluse, Avignon, 1999.

[21] Pecchinenda, A., Kappas, A., & Smith, C.A., Effects of difficulty and ability in a dual-task video game paradigm on attention, physiological responses, performance, and emotion-related appraisal. Présenté au Thirty-Seventh Annual Meeting of the Society for Psychophysiological Research, Cape Cod, Massachusetts. et culturelle. L. 1997

An Experiment in the Perception of Space through Sound in Virtual World and Games

Antoine Gonot[1,2], Stéphane Natkin[1], Marc Emerit[2] and Noël Chateau[2]

[1] CNAM, CEDRIC laboratory, Paris, 75003, France, [2] France Telecom Group, Lannion, 22300, France

Abstract—**This study presents two approaches for representing space through sound, allowing being aware of what is going on out of visible screen. The first one, called *decontextualized beacon*, uses a sound indicating the azimuth of a target. The second one, called *contextualized beacon*, uses a sound indicating the shortest path toward the target. The usability of the two spatial auditory displays has been evaluated during a first-person navigation task in a virtual city. It appeared that *contextualized* beacon was more adapted than the *contextualized* one when navigation was not the major task. However, it was not as relevant as expected for navigation itself. Therefore, the *decontextualized beacons*, seems to be a better compromise between possibility of failure and effectiveness of navigation.**

***Index Terms*— 3D audio, Virtual world, Game, Navigation**

I. Introduction

By using a 3D Audio API, such as Microsoft's DirectSound3D®, and extensions such as Creative Labs's EAX® (see [13] for a review of modern audio technologies in games), one can create a realistic three dimensional audio world, including complex environmental effects (reverberation, reflected sound, muffling, etc.). Those technologies can be used for several purposes. Mostly, three aspects can be considered. First, it is essential to enhance the sensation of presence (related to immersion). Larson *et al.* [12], for example, has shown that "subjects in a bimodal condition experienced significantly higher presence, were more focused on the situation and enjoyed the Virtual Environment more than subjects receiving unimodal information did". Secondly, spatial cues allow increasing intelligibility when multiple sources are presented concurrently. This is typically referred to as the Cocktail Party effect (see [3] for a review). Thirdly, spatial sound can be used to enrich user interface, adding information through another medium. For example, a spatial auditory display can assist navigation in an environment either real or virtual. In this case, spatial audio is used to describe non-speech spatially presented sounds or at least non-linguistically mediated spatial content. Indeed, the works of Klatzky *et al.* [9] on spatial updating has illustrated the fact that speech adds extra cognitive processing load imposed by converting language to spatial content.

Those three aspects could affect navigability and then usability of a virtual environment. Both the perception (at a lower level) of the user and the cognition (at a higher level) can be affected. At the lower level, the study of Larson *et al.* [12] has confirmed that consistent visual and auditory cues can enhance orientation task. In the same way, a study carried out by the present authors [6], has shown that real 3D sound (i.e. using Head Related Transfer Functions over headphone) compared to classical stereo panning improve also the effectiveness of this task. Taking the example of virtual city, it has been observed that users are able to choose a direction faster. However, acquisition of spatial knowledge does not rely simply on perception. At a higher level, learning to navigate a virtual world is referring to the formation of a cognitive map within a person's mind. This *map* "is a structure which is an internal representation of an environment which one uses as a reference when navigating to a destination" [14] (quote in [7]). According to the *image updating model* proposed by Klatsky *et al.* in [10], visual and auditory modalities differ in encoding the target locations into memory. However, the resulting spatial image functions equivalently for spatial updating across modalities. In fact, knowing whether a visual experience is a pre-requisite for image formation is still an issue.

So, the present research is a first attempt to assess what can be expected from a spatial auditory display in terms of navigability in virtual world. Researches seem to show that adding spatial auditory information consistent with visualization rather improves orientation than spatial image and global navigation. Even though Larson *et al.* [12] has observed that bimodal processing significantly improves memory, this effect has shown to be related with auditory content of a sounding object rather than with its spatial property. So, what can be the contribution of spatial auditory cues to spatial knowledge acquisition?

Essentially, two typical acquisition modes can be distinguished in game: "pedestrian mode" and "bird mode". The former is the typical situation in "first-person shooter" and most of adventure-action game in which the world is perceived from the "in-side" (even if third-person view is allowed in some cases). The later refers to the genre of strategic computer simulation, often called "god game", in which the world is perceived from the "out-side". We focus in this study on the "pedestrian mode". The present paper investigates the relative contribution of auditory modality to perceptive and cognitive spatial ability during first-person navigation in a city-like virtual world. An example of a game using auditory navigation

Manuscript received October 13, 2006.

as part of the *gameplay* will be taken to illustrate the details of the problematic. Then two approaches for representing space through sound will be presented. The design of the virtual word used for the experiment will be introduced. Finally, the results of the experiments will be discussed. First conclusions on the contribution of spatial auditory cues to spatial knowledge will be drawn. Future directions for research will be presented.

II. USING SOUND FOR CONTROLING NAVIGATION-BASED CHALENGES IN GAME

A. An example: Eye

The Eye video game (http://eye.maratis3d.com) is a second year project designed by a group of students (Matthew Tomkinson, Olivier Adelh: Game Design, David Elahee, Benoît Vimont: Programming, Johan Spielmann, Anaël Seghezzi: Graphic Design, Timothée Pauleve: Sound Design, Julien Bourbonnais: Usability, Vivien Chazel: Production) from the Graduate School of Games (ENJMIN: www.enjmin.fr). This video game is based on the classical "blind man's buff game". The player character, hero of the game, Vincent Grach, has an extraordinary power: he is able to visit others' people memories. Travelling physically in a lunatic asylum and in the memory of all patients, he tries to save his wife. During this journey, he is confronted to the anguishes of the other characters. To save his mental health, he must close his eyes and progress in an almost dark world where only the circle of the strong lights appears. In this state, he must also protect himself from numerous dangers like falling from a barge or into a fire. His progression relies on his memory of the space and on the location of sound sources.

As a consequence, an original and complex sound world is one of the main features of Eye. It was designed using ISACT™ from Creative Labs©. It relies on a real time 3D localisation of sound sources, using the OpenAL® library which was integrated in the game engine "Maratis". This localisation can be heard trough a 5.1 system using the Sound Blaster® technology. Two other effects are used to help the player when Vincent Grach's eyes are closed. Firstly, the decay of the attenuation curve of sound objects are accentuated (i.e. the "Roll Off" parameter is higher), then The "Eiffel Tower effect"[1] mutes the sounds which are not related to dangers or which do not help for localisation.

B. Auditory navigation in games

Except for audio games for visually impaired (for example, GMA Games's *Shades of Doom®* or Pin Interactive's *Terraformers®*, etc.) or games revolving around a musical experience (Sega's Rez®, Nana On-sha's Vib Ribbon®), only few games use sounds as part of their *gameplay*. However, as point out by Stockburger in [17], although a game can be seen as a larger genre, it sometime uses sound in an innovating way. For example, sound is an important element of *gameplay* in stealth intrusion game like Konami's *Metal Gear Solid 2 Sons of Liberty®* (MSG2), where, most of the time, the player can not see his opponent. Indeed, according to Begault [4], spatial auditory displays are very effective for conveying alarm and warning messages in high-stress environments. One aspect of the *acousmatic*[2] situation of the player in MGS2 is referred to as *sound awareness*, similar to what can be experienced by a pilot in an airline cockpit. In the same game, another type of *acousmatic* situation occurs when the player has to use a directional microphone to locate a specific hostage in the environment. Similar challenge is also encountered in *Eye,* except that, visual cues are only partially available. According to the *image updating model* [10], those two games illustrate two complementary challenges involved by an auditory navigation-based *gameplay*.

The first one is rather based on the initial encoding of target(s). In *Eye*, because visual perception can be frequently interrupted, auditory modality has to be strongly involved in the encoding of the immediate surrounding scene. For example, a fast memorization of the exit's topology of a room in more of the objects it contains turns out to be fundamental. This is part of the *game balance* when considering the navigability of the virtual world the player is exploring. In the case of MSG2, because it is rather visual, the encoding of the surrounding is not a problem *a priori*. The *game balance* mostly relies on another kind of challenge, related to spatial updating. Finding a character by using the directional microphone is similar to find a given street in a town by using a compass. If we assume that the player didn't know the environment, the effectiveness of such task depends mainly on the complexity of the road (or corridor) pattern. For example, the pattern in Figure 1.a can be considered more complex than the pattern in Figure 1.b, referred to as raster pattern by Alexander *et al.* [1] (quote in [19]).

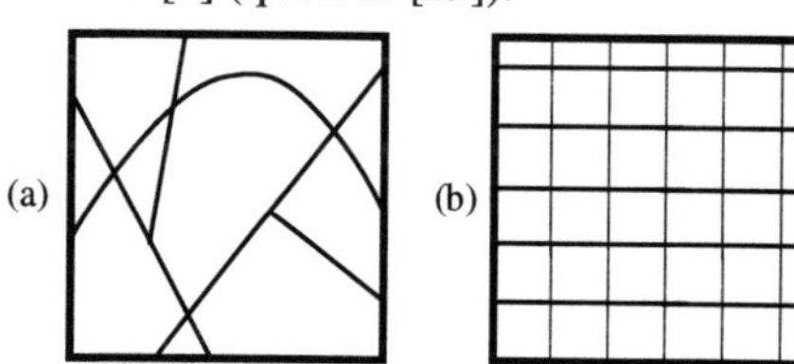

Fig. 1. Example of two different complexities for road-network. (a) is supposed to be more complex than (b)

Thus, controlling the reliance on physical space can be a critical issue for *game balance*. It depends on the relative importance of navigation during the different phases of the game and more generally on the player activity. For example, if the player has to fight an enemy, navigation becomes a secondary task, and should be achieved with the minimum of cognitive load. Indicating the shortest path to the target could then annihilate the complexity of a pattern, removing any

[1] It refers to the study of Roland Barthes on "Eiffel Tower and other mythologies". He believed that the tower was so popular because a person looking out over Paris felt they could master the city's complexity.

[2] According to M. Chion [18], the term "Acousmatic" is used to describe the listening situation of someone hearing a sound without seeing the object which produced it.

challenge in navigating. In the contrary, if the goal is to collect equipments (typically, weapon, armour or ammunition) then, navigation could be more challenging. The following illustrates how to make the most of the potential of 3D audio for this particular balance.

C. *Two approaches for representing space through sound*

In the domain of sonification, the term *beacon* has been introduced by G. Kramer [11] to describe a category of sound used as a reference for auditory exploration and analyse of complex, multivariate data set. *Beacons* do not have intrinsically spatial property, but has been naturally adapted to navigation by Walker and Lindsay [20]. This concept is very close to the concept of landmark used in the domain of urban planning.

As Johnson and Wiles point out in [8] that it is preferable that the interface remains the most *transparent* as possible. They hypothesise that "the focus on, and lack of distraction from, the major task contribute to the facilitation of the flow". For example, Lionhead Studio*'s Black & White®*, have been released with the interface virtually absent during *gameplay*. Such design rule can be transposed to auditory modality, considering its strong ability to facilitate player's selective attention. For example, Andresen [2], creating a blind-accessible game, has installed noisy air conditioning vents into the centre of each hallway to indicate the location of the exits. The importance of this type of *beacons* indicating location in the immediate surrounding has been well illustrated by *Eye*. Then, the previous guideline will be applied to *beacons* which indicate a distant location.

Let's consider the environment shown in Figure 2, presenting many adjacent rooms with opening, communicating each other. The auditory situation the player experiences in *MSG2* and *Eye* involves direct path from the source to the listener. In this case, the use of the information conveyed by sound is similar to the use of a compass. This approach, described as *decontextualized* (a), is common since sound engine only recently support complex environmental effects (*i.e.* take into account the interaction of sound with physical space).

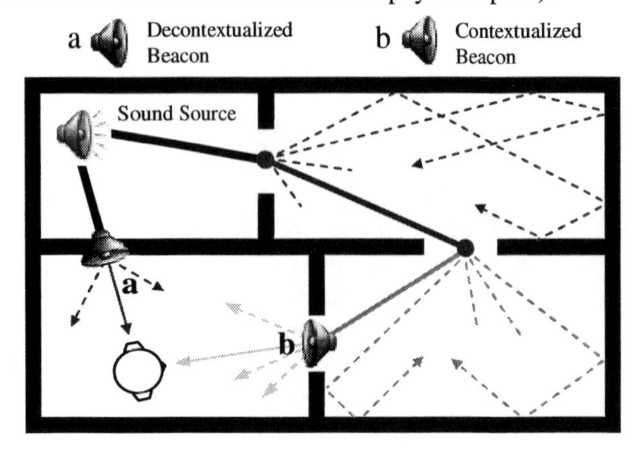

Fig. 2. Two approaches for auditory representation of distant location through sound

Let's now consider a propagation model of acoustic waves from a sound source to a listener. By extrapolating the exclusion phenomenon, the apparent position of the source is the position of the opening. Thus, such approach, described as *contextualized* (b), defines a *beacon* indicating both, exit location in the immediate surrounding and a path to the distant location of an object.

For describing clearly those two *beacons*, two terms have to be defined: the *target* is a location to reach and the *beacon* is a sound, whose spatial cues indicate this location.

The usability of those two types of beacons has been evaluated in a city-like virtual world, enabling one to create complex environment, constraining visual modality to local perception of space.

III. The Experiment: Motivation, Design and Discussion

A. *Presentation of the experiment*

1) *Motivation and hypotheses*

As pointed by Rollings and Adams in [16], "as action games became more complex, the play area began to span multiple screens of action, although the player still needed to be aware of what was going on in the game-world not visible onscreen". There are several common configurations used to achieve this goal. The original one, used in Williams Electronics's *Defender®*, shows the entire game world to the player. Another configuration offers a zoom-out view of the area surrounding the player. At last, a third configuration, rather used in strategy and war game, presents a map building up as the player explore. So, the amount and the quality of the spatial information displayed by this mean can vary, depending on the *gameplay* and the required *challenge*. That way, the *decontextualized* and *contextualized beacons* can be considered as two different approaches of *auditory minimap*. Taking into account the interaction of sound with physical space (*i.e. to use contextualized beacons*) is not just an improvement of sound realism. It offers contrasted, not to say complementary, auditory representations of the virtual world. Thus, the aim of the experiment presented here is to assess the relative contribution of these two *beacons* to spatial knowledge acquisition, even when visual perception is involved. Then, discerning the navigation task (*i.e.* way finding) from the orientation task (*i.e.* choosing a direction when bifurcation occurs), the following hypotheses are ventured for each type of *beacons*.

For *contextualized beacons*, initial encoding of the beacon is facilitated by consistency between visual and auditory cues. This improvement of initial encoding should be reflected in a more effective orientation. Moreover, because the spatial configurations of targets and *beacons* do not fit, auditory modality can not contribute to the formation of the mental map. The later rather relies on local visual perception. However, this also means an effortless navigation that should be reflected by a lower cognitive load. Respectively, using *decontextualized* beacons requires greater focus of auditory attention to the spatial configuration in order to correct bearing (*i.e.* angle between the target and the direction imposed by the road-network). This should involve a higher cognitive load but the formation of a better cognitive map.

2) Task and data

The goal is to find, as quickly as possible, nine “streets” represented by "real"w sound (for example “fireworks”, “fanfare”, etc.). They are equally distributed in three zones (marked on the floor by three different colors), the corresponding sound is always audible, and they are sought one after the other. When the player reaches the target (i.e. enters the right street), the program presents the next one. Interaction log are recorded during the game and subjective evaluation are achieved at the end of a session, including the recall of the street’s location on the map, auto-evaluation of cognitive load (NASA-TLX) and impressions questionnaire. There are two experimental factors: *contextualized* versus *decontextualized* beacons and stereo vs. binaural rendering (using non individualized Head Related Transfer Functions).

B. The design of the Virtual World

Here are presented the design choices that have been made, in order to guarantee *believability* of the virtual world and a control of dependant variables. One can refer to [6] for a complete description of the setup.

1) The foundations of the game

Navigation in a city can be seen as a succession of choices of directions to take. Thus, as shown in Figure 3, the 3D model of the road-network has been simplified drastically, so navigation is like moving from square to square on a chessboard (excepted for corners).

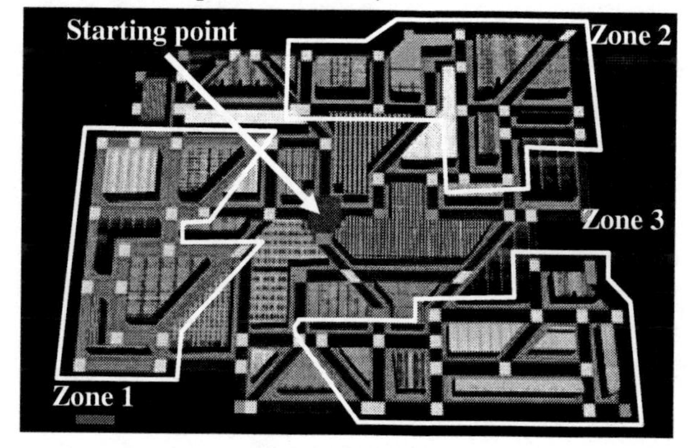

Fig. 3. Road-network of the Virtual City

The game has been designed using Virtools©, and sound sources has been spatialized using algorithms developed at France Telecom Group©.

2) Avoiding cross-modal influence

As pointed by Pellegrini [15], “when assessing psychoacoustic features within an AVE (auditory virtual environment), the auditory test setup needs to be designed with care to minimize unwanted cross-modal influences”. Thus the textures were choosing for their banality, avoiding that a building serves as visual landmark. Moreover, as can be seen in Figure 4.a, the Virtual World is not illuminated. Only few spotlights are used to allow the visualization of the directly reachable nodes. By this way, local visual perception is under control and reduced to desired cues: the direction choices, the distance and the azimuth of next nodes. The Figure 4.b shows a screenshot of the first-person view.

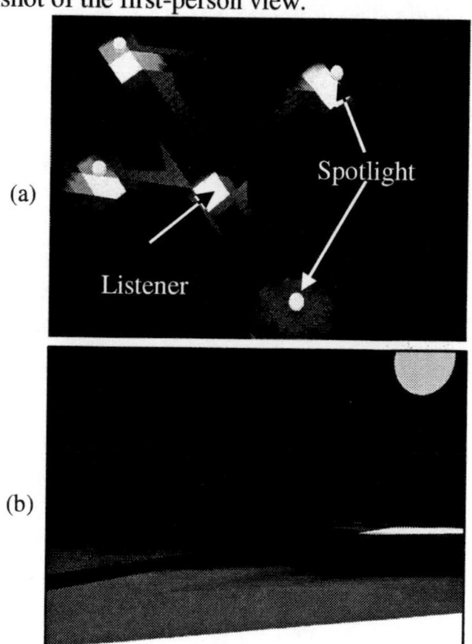

Fig. 4. Lightning (a) and first-person view of the Virtual World (b)

3) The design of contextualized beacons

Researches on usability have shown that "the design goals for Auditory Virtual Environments shift from “reproducing the physical behaviour of a real environment as accurate as possible” to “stimulating the desired perception directly”" [15]. Then, it is recommended to rather reproduce required features for a given specific application. Consequently, implementing *contextualized beacons* does not necessarily require modelling the exclusion phenomenon. However the *beacon* needs to exhibit its main characteristics, that is:

- The sound of the *beacon* is coming from a particular exit. This is implemented by calculating the shortest path toward the location each time a new node is reached. Then, the azimuth of the sound source is given by the first node of the path.
- The sound must reflect the effect of wave's propagation. Only the effect of distance (length of the shortest path) on sound level has been included.

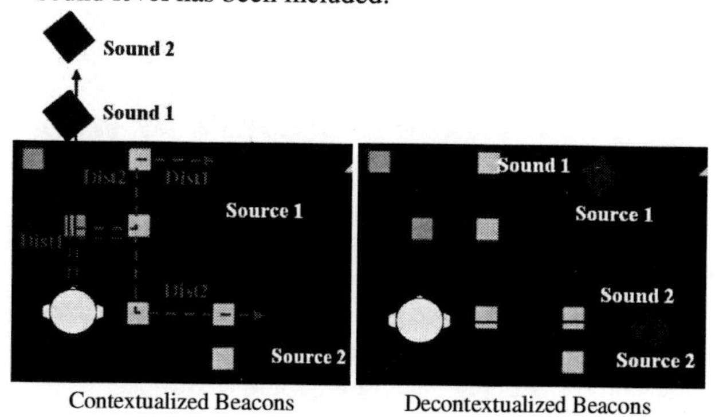

Fig. 5. Implementation of the two approaches for auditory representation of distant location through sound

For smooth changes, the position of the source between two nodes is determined by linear interpolation.

C. *Results and discussion*

As was expected, the *beacon*'s type has significantly affected orientation task. The time for initial encoding and choosing directions was significantly lower for *contextualized* beacons (using binaural or stereo). It was correlated with a lower cognitive load (see [6] for details on the statistical analysis). Those results have confirmed that such *beacon* could be more effective when navigation is not the major task. However, no significant effect has been observed on navigation. Indeed, the two *beacons* have allowed effective navigation. For both, the covered distance to reach the target was close to the shortest path and the perceived performance was high. So, it seems that the reliance on physical space was not as strong as expected for this environment. Even if a comparative measure of complexity with other environments encountered in FPS game should be achieved to rigorously conclude, it shows that *contextualized beacons* were not necessarily relevant for navigation. According to Johnson and Wiles [8], "during *gameplay*, the joy of success is dependant upon the possibility of failure". From this point of view, *decontextualized beacons* could offer a good compromise. Finally, the angular and absolute distance errors when recalling locations on the map did not differ. So the mental map seems not to be better with *decontextualized* beacons. Once again, nothing can be concluded, since the recall task was maybe not a good evaluation of mental map for first-person navigation in virtual city (*i.e.* local visual perception). However, if it was, this result could mean that *decontextualized beacons* could not really improve mental map constructed by visual experience.

IV. CONCLUSION

This study has tried to investigate what could be the relative contribution of auditory modality to spatial ability during navigation with a first-person view. It appears that auditory modality can improve the orientation task. However, the experiment failed to exhibit a real improvement of the mental map constructed by local visual perception. Indeed, it seems that memorizing locations when finding his way as fast as possible is a very difficult task. Memorization could have been better without time pressure. However, pre-test had shown that without this pressure, participant sometimes went all the way trying to better remembering locations. Thus, by achieving a non-effective navigation, no local effect on orientation could have been observed.

Finally, assuming that spatial auditory cues are not predominant in auditory scene analysis, as pointed out by Bregman [5], it has been concluded that spatial auditory display should be reconsidered in a more ecological way. The spatial abilities of the auditory system have been surely overestimated. It seems more relevant to study the player's responsiveness to audio cues more closely related to *diegetic* space (*i.e.* the space figured on screen). Future works will focus on games offering multiple out-side views of the world, as in strategic computer simulation or "god game". This will lead us to the study of audio-visual interactions in a multiresolution interface, introducing the notion of level-of-detail (LOD) for spatial auditory display.

REFERENCES

[1] Alexander, C., Ishikawa, S., Silverstein, M., Jacobson, M., Fiksdahl-King, I. and Angel, S. "A Pattern Language". Oxford University Press, New York, 1977.

[2] Andresen, G., "Playing by Ear: Creating Blind-accessible Game". Gamasutra article, May 20, 2002. URL: http://www.gamasutra.com/resource_guide/20020520/andersen_01.htm

[3] Arons, B.. "A review of the Cocktail Party". Effect. Journal of America Voice I/O Society, 1992.

[4] Begault D. R.,"3-D Sound for Virtual Reality and Multimedia". Cambridge, MA: Academic Press Professional, 2004.

[5] Bregman A.S., "Auditory Scene analysis: The perceptual organization of sound", Cambridge, Mass., MIT Press, 1992

[6] Gonot, A., Chateau, N., Emerit, M., "Usability of 3-D Sound for Navigation in a Constrained Virtual Environment", 120th AES Convention, Paris, France, 2006.

[7] Ingram, R., Benford, S., Bowers, J., "Building Virtual Cities: applying urban planning principles to the design of virtual environments". Proceedings of the ACM Symposium on Virtual Reality Software and Technology (VRST96), pp 83-91, 1996.

[8] Johnson, D., & Wiles, J., "Effective affective user interface design in games". International Conference on Affective Human Factors Design, Singapore, June 27-29, 2001.

[9] Klatzky, R. L., Lippa, Y., Loomis, J. M. and Golledge, R. G., "Learning directions of objects specified by vision, spatial audition, or auditory spatial language". Learning & Memory, 9, 364-367. 2002.

[10] Klatzky, R. L., Lippa, Y., Loomis, J. M. and Golledge, R. G., "Encoding, learning and spatial updating of multiple object locations specified by 3-D sound, spatial language, and vision." Experimental Brain Research, 149, 48-61. 2003.

[11] Kramer, G., "Some Organizing Principle for Representing Data with Sound". Auditory Display: Sonification , Audification and Auditory Interface, SFI Studies in the Sciences of Complexity, Proceedings Volume XVIII, Addison-Wesley Publishing Company, Reading, MA, USA, pp 202-208. 1994.

[12] Larsson, P, Västfjäll, D, & Kleiner, M., "Ecological Acoustics and the multi-modal perception of rooms: Real and unreal experiences of auditory-visual virtual environments". In Proceedings of ICAD, Helsinki, 2001

[13] Menshikov A.,. "Modern Audio Technologies in Games", article based on the presentation given at the Game Developers Conference in Moscow in 2003. URL: http://www.digit-life.com/articles2/sound-technology/index.html

[14] Passini, R., "Wayfinding in Architecture", Van Nostrand Reinhold, 1992

[15] Pellegrini, R. S., Quality Assessment of Auditory Virtual Environments, In Proceedings of ICAD, Espoo, Finland, 2001

[16] Rollings, A., Adams, E., "Andrew Rollings and Ernest Adams on Game Design". New Riders Publishing, May 05, 2003.

[17] Stockburger, A., "The Game Environment from an Auditive Perspective", Level Up (Utrecht Universiteit: DIGRA 2003)

[18] M. Chion, "L'audio-vision, Son et Image au cinéma", 2nd edition, Nathan Cinéma. 1997.

[19] Sun, J., Baciu, G., Xiaobo, Y., Green, M. "Template-Based Generation of Road Networks for Virtual City Modeling". VRST'02, Hong Kong, November 11-13. 2002.

[20] Walker, B. N., Lindsay, J., "Effect of Beacon Sounds on Navigation Performance in a Virtual Reality Environment". Proceedings of the International Conference on Auditory Display, Boston, MA (6-9 July) pp 204-207. 2003

List of Authors